Theatrical Design and Production

Theatrical Design and Production

An Introduction to
Scenic Design and Construction,
Lighting, Sound, Costume, and Makeup

EIGHTH EDITION

J. Michael Gillette

University of Arizona

Rich Dionne

Purdue University

McGraw Hill Education

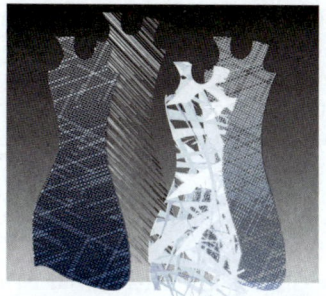

THEATRICAL DESIGN AND PRODUCTION: AN INTRODUCTION TO SCENIC DESIGN AND CONSTRUCTION, LIGHTING, SOUND, COSTUME, AND MAKEUP, EIGHTH EDITION

1 2 3 4 5 6 7 8 9 LWI 21 20 19

ISBN 978-1-259-92230-5 (bound edition)
MHID 1-259-92230-8 (bound edition)
ISBN 978-1-260-68746-0 (loose-leaf edition)
MHID 1-260-68746-5 (loose-leaf edition)

Product Developer: *Alexander Preiss*
Marketing Manager: *Nancy Baudean*
Content Project Managers: *Lisa Bruflodt, Danielle Clement*
Buyer: *Susan K. Culbertson*
Designer: *Egzon Shaqiri*
Content Licensing Specialist: *Ann Marie Janette*
Cover Image: *©numb/Alamy; ©Shutterstock/Anna Jurkovska; ©Pixtal/AGE Fotostock; ©Shutterstock/Niphon Subsri; ©Shutterstock/Nicole S Glass; ©Shutterstock/EBZphotography*
Compositor: *Cenveo® Publisher Services*

Library of Congress Cataloging-in-Publication Data

Names: Gillette, J. Michael, author. | Dionne, Rich, author.
Title: Theatrical design and production : an introduction to scenic design and construction, lighting, sound, costume, and makeup / J. Michael Gillette, Rich Dionne.
Description: Eighth edition. | New York, NY : McGraw-Hill, a business unit of The McGraw-Hill Companies, Inc., [2020] | Includes index.
Identifiers: LCCN 2018042904 (print) | LCCN 2018055338 (ebook) | ISBN 9781260687507 (ebook) | ISBN 9781259922305 | ISBN 9781259922305(alk. paper) | ISBN 1259922308(alk. paper)
Subjects: LCSH: Stage management. | Theater—Production and direction. | Theaters—Stage-setting and scenery.
Classification: LCC PN2085 (ebook) | LCC PN2085 .G5 2020 (print) | DDC 792.02/5—dc23
LC record available at https://lccn.loc.gov/2018042904

mheducation.com/highered

Preface

First courses in the world of theatrical design and production, like the art they introduce, come in a bewildering array of shapes, sizes, textures, and colors. Some students receive their introduction to this subject area in a general overview course that covers the design and production elements of scenery, costumes, lighting, and sound in a single semester. Other students may enjoy the luxury of an entire year in which to discuss the same material. Still others may take individual courses that specialize in the theory and craft of the separate areas that comprise the field of theatrical design and technical production. The course content is very flexible indeed.

To create a text that will serve the needs of all these courses is a distinct challenge. I've tried to rise to that challenge by organizing the material in two ways. The chapters appear in a logical sequence, but each chapter is also an island of information that can stand alone. My hope is that this organization will enable each instructor to pick and choose the type and amount of material that is appropriate for his or her particular course. This type of organization also makes the text a useful reference for students to keep throughout their design and technical production careers.

Organization and Content

Just as a play wouldn't start without the scenery being in place, this book doesn't delve into technical procedures without first setting the stage. Chapters 1 through 4, "Production Organization and Management," "The Design Process," "A Brief History of Theatre Architecture and Stage Technology," and "The Stage and Its Equipment," provide a grounding in real-world issues and are appropriate for use in almost any type of technical production class.

Of special significance is Chapter 2, "The Design Process." It contains material that, prior to the first edition of this book, had not been included in beginning technical theatre texts. It is a problem-solving and conceptual-thinking model created specifically for theatrical practice. Its purpose is to increase each student's creative capacity by reducing the effects of two prime ingredients of creative dysfunction—fear and frustration. The mechanism used to effect this change is a seven-step procedure that enables students to make logical, rational, and considered decisions when making the myriad choices involved in creating a design or solving a technical challenge in any area of theatrical production.

Chapter 3, "A Brief History of Theatre Architecture and Stage Technology," provides a concise chronology, both pictorially and textually, of the history of theatre architecture. I've included this information for two reasons: the functional design of the environment in which a play is produced has always been a major factor in determining the type, style, and design of technical elements used in a production, and all too frequently student designers are not required to take courses in theatre history.

Chapters 7 and 8, "Mechanical Drafting" and "Perspective Drawing," contain specific how-to information on the drafting and mechanical perspective techniques most commonly used in theatrical production. These chapters appear here because it may be helpful for students to learn the grammar of graphic language before they encounter these types of drawings in the scenic and lighting design chapters. Chapter 7, "Mechanical Drafting," provides information about the types of drafting used in the theatre, helpful hints on the process of drafting as well as extensive material on CAD drafting. Chapter 8, "Perspective Drawing," offers a step-by-step procedure, with exercises, for creating accurate scale mechanical perspective drawings.

Chapter 15, "Electrical Theory and Practice," provides a concise explanation of the nature and function of electricity and electronics and the practical use of the power formula, as well as information on wiring practices and standards.

Chapter 22, "Drawing and Rendering," provides an overview of the types of paints, pastels, markers, and papers commonly used in theatrical rendering, as well as information on basic application techniques used with these media.

The remainder of the text provides an overview of the function and responsibilities of the scenic, lighting, costume, and sound designers. It also contains primary information about the tools and basic techniques that are used to bring each designer's concepts to the stage.

As with any art form, the basic element necessary for creating a successful design in theatre is an understanding of design principles and chosen medium. I hope that this text not only provides those basics but also offers encouragement and inspiration to create.

Features

In many ways, *Theatrical Design and Production* is a traditional introductory text for the various design and craft areas of theatrical production. With a number of features, however, I strive to set this text apart.

Philosophy   The underlying spirit of this text is firmly rooted in my belief that learning and creating in the various fields of theatrical design and production can be, and should be, fun. With that thought in mind, I've tried to make this text not only informative and practical but also motivating and inspirational.

Color Analysis   The sixteen-page color analysis section presents a discussion of the practical applications of color theory by analyzing the interactive effects of the color selections for the scenery, costumes, and lighting for two productions — one with a very narrow, muted palette and the other with a full-spectrum, heavily saturated color style.

Safety Tips   Safety tips are discussed throughout the text. They have been placed in special boxes adjacent to the relevant text to help readers integrate learning about a tool, material, or process with its safe use.

Running Glossary   To help students learn and remember the vocabulary of the theatre, new terms are defined in the margin on the page where they first appear.

Production Insights   Placed throughout the text, these boxes identify material that provides further depth and practical information to the discussion.

Design Inspiration   Similar to the "Production Insights" boxes, but located only in design chapters, these include material that will enhance student understanding by providing insights and solutions to real theatrical problems.

Illustration Program   An extensive photo and illustration program provides a very strong adjunct to the textual information. Photos from professional theatre productions are used to provide a model that students can strive to emulate.

New to the Eighth Edition

The eighth edition of *Theatrical Design and Production* has been extensively revised. Every chapter has had minor — and in some cases major — revisions to bring the information it offers in line with current standards and practices.

Chapter 5, "Style, Composition and Design," has been updated with several new pictures and revised text to better explain the concepts involved.

Chapter 7, "Mechanical Drafting," has been extensively revised to reflect current practice. The ubiquity of CAD drafting has almost completely replaced the use of hand-drafting shop plates and light plots. The material on hand drafting has been moved to a separate appendix, and the bulk of the chapter is now devoted to an explanation of CAD drafting.

Chapter 8, "Perspective Drawing," has also been extensively revised to, hopefully, make the guidance for how to mechanically draw in perspective a little more understandable.

Chapter 9, "Scene Design," has been updated with new material on model making and several new photos.

Chapters 10, "Tools and Materials," and 11, "Scenic Production Materials," have both been extensively revised. Technological changes have been myriad since the last edition, many of which have caused revision in both design and production practices. One of the most prominent is the introduction of CNC machining to many phases of both construction and design. The ability of 3-D printers to produce parts has been applied to both scenery and property shops as well as to the construction of the designer's models.

Chapter 16, "Lighting Production," has been revised to reflect that LED lamp sources are now becoming much more common in stage lighting and are demonstrated in the new fixtures illustrated and explained in the chapter.

Chapter 21, "Sound Design and Technology," has been extensively revised to make the material more accessible to the reader. New equipment is also introduced and explained.

It is my pleasure to welcome Rich Dionne as co-author for this eighth edition of *Theatrical Design and Production*. Rich is the Technical Director and Production Manager in the Department of Theatre at the Patti and Rusty Rueff School of Visual and Performing Arts at Purdue University and brings to our book a wealth of knowledge about the tools, techniques, and practices of technical theatre. He's a practicing professional and an educator, and he's well-versed in the art and craft of all areas of theatrical production. He's a welcome addition. His work has been invaluable, and I want to publicly thank him for becoming a member of the team.

The updating for this edition could not have been accomplished without the information, ideas, and counsel provided by the practicing professionals/educators in their respective fields: Rich Dionne (technical theatre), Michael McNamara (lighting), Charlie Calvert (scene design), and Heath Hansum (sound). Their knowledge, information, and assistance have been invaluable in making this edition current in the areas of design, technology, materials, and practice. It's exciting to think about the new developments on the horizon for theatrical design and what the future will bring. The theatre truly is an interesting and fun place to be.

J. Michael Gillette

Being asked to come on board as co-author for this textbook has been incredibly overwhelming and humbling. I can still picture in my mind the cover for the third edition of this book, which came out when I was just starting graduate school (the first time!). This book was my introduction to theatre production as an undergraduate student, and it opened my eyes to the breadth and depth of knowledge, techniques, methods, and materials that make up this craft we call theatre. I remember my excitement at the time, seeing how vast the career — calling — I was entering could be. It's a true honor to be a part of similarly inspiring readers today, some twenty years later.

Theatre somehow has always managed to borrow the best of what other industries do, and as costs go down and technology advances, the way we make theatre continues to change and expand. Theatres and production shops now use CNC machining; CAD dominates the field; computer networks drive communication for lighting, sound, and video systems — all huge leaps forward from what was common in theatre production even ten or fifteen years ago. Keeping up with these advances is a challenge, but one that I'm excited to help this book rise to meet in this and future editions. I'm grateful to Michael for asking me to be a part of it.

Rich Dionne

Finally, we would like to thank those friends and colleagues who have offered suggestions for improving *Theatrical Design and Production*. In particular, we would like to thank the following reviewers for their help in preparing the eighth edition of this text.

Bruce B. Brown, University of the Ozarks

Benjamin Ray Mays, UvaWise

Phoebe Hall, Fayetteville State University

Scott Grabau, Irvine Valley College

Brian Begley, Wayne State College

David M. Makuch, Marietta College

Greg McLarty, Wharton County Junior College

David Lee Cuthbert, University of California Santa Cruz

Students—study more efficiently, retain more and achieve better outcomes. Instructors—focus on what you love—teaching.

SUCCESSFUL SEMESTERS INCLUDE CONNECT

FOR INSTRUCTORS

You're in the driver's seat.

Want to build your own course? No problem. Prefer to use our turnkey, prebuilt course? Easy. Want to make changes throughout the semester? Sure. And you'll save time with Connect's auto-grading too.

65%
Less Time Grading

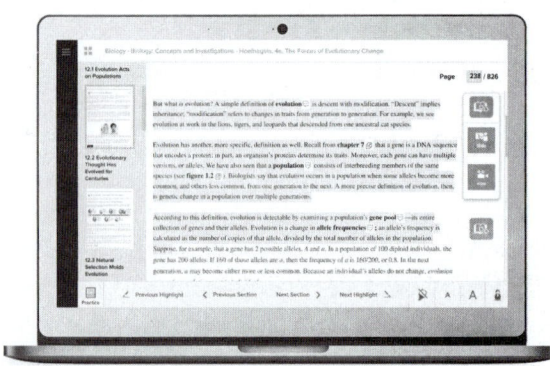

They'll thank you for it.

Adaptive study resources like SmartBook® help your students be better prepared in less time. You can transform your class time from dull definitions to dynamic debates. Hear from your peers about the benefits of Connect at **www.mheducation.com/highered/connect**

Make it simple, make it affordable.

Connect makes it easy with seamless integration using any of the major Learning Management Systems—Blackboard®, Canvas, and D2L, among others—to let you organize your course in one convenient location. Give your students access to digital materials at a discount with our inclusive access program. Ask your McGraw-Hill representative for more information.

©Hill Street Studios/Tobin Rogers/Blend Images LLC

Solutions for your challenges.

A product isn't a solution. Real solutions are affordable, reliable, and come with training and ongoing support when you need it and how you want it. Our Customer Experience Group can also help you troubleshoot tech problems—although Connect's 99% uptime means you might not need to call them. See for yourself at **status.mheducation.com**

Effective, efficient studying.

Connect helps you be more productive with your study time and get better grades using tools like SmartBook, which highlights key concepts and creates a personalized study plan. Connect sets you up for success, so you walk into class with confidence and walk out with better grades.

©Shutterstock/wavebreakmedia

> **"**I really liked this app—it made it easy to study when you don't have your textbook in front of you.**"**
>
> - Jordan Cunningham,
> Eastern Washington University

Study anytime, anywhere.

Download the free ReadAnywhere app and access your online eBook when it's convenient, even if you're offline. And since the app automatically syncs with your eBook in Connect, all of your notes are available every time you open it. Find out more at **www.mheducation.com/readanywhere**

No surprises.

The Connect Calendar and Reports tools keep you on track with the work you need to get done and your assignment scores. Life gets busy; Connect tools help you keep learning through it all.

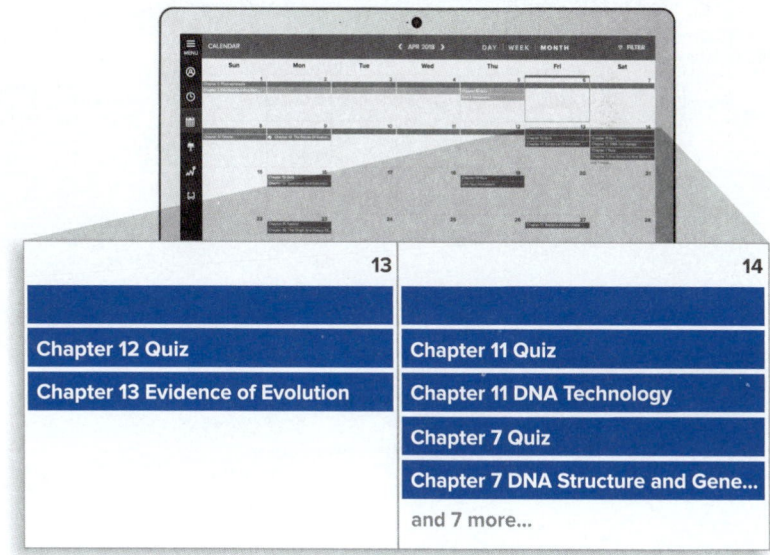

13	14
Chapter 12 Quiz	Chapter 11 Quiz
Chapter 13 Evidence of Evolution	Chapter 11 DNA Technology
	Chapter 7 Quiz
	Chapter 7 DNA Structure and Gene...
	and 7 more...

Learning for everyone.

McGraw-Hill works directly with Accessibility Services Departments and faculty to meet the learning needs of all students. Please contact your Accessibility Services office and ask them to email accessibility@mheducation.com, or visit **www.mheducation.com/about/accessibility.html** for more information.

Brief Contents

Contents

11. Scenic Production Techniques   227

12. Scene Painting   276

Chapter 1

Production Organization and Management

"Great art conceals art." That statement is attributed to Konstantin Stanislavski, founder of the Moscow Art Theatre and developer of Method acting. He was referring to the phenomenon that occurs when actors create brilliantly believable roles. Great actors don't seem to be working. They make us believe that they *are* the characters and that everything they say or do is happening spontaneously, without thought or effort. What Stanislavski meant was that a seemingly effortless job of acting is the end result of years of training, dedication, and just plain hard work.

Great art *does* conceal art, but not just the art of the actor. Imagine an actor, wrapped in a heavy fur cape, standing on a set that resembles a craggy mountain peak. The "mountain top" starts to tip, the actor stumbles, his cape comes off, and the **followspot** reveals the actor standing in his underwear with his cape around his ankles. Horrified, the spotlight operator tries to turn off her light. But, instead of turning it off, she changes its color from deep blue to brilliant white.

This unlikely scenario illustrates the fact that less-than-great art conceals little. It also demonstrates that Stanislavski's injunction is just as true for the design and technical elements of the production as it is for the actors. It is an illusion. Together, they create the illusionary reality we call theatre. The illusion that the spectators see is just that. A theatrical performance doesn't simply happen; it is the product of a great deal of organization, teamwork, talent, and dedication.

Getting a play from the written word to the stage requires a lot of enjoyable, challenging work. The result of all this effort, the **production team** hopes, will be artistic and artful, but the business of making a script come alive on the stage is a process that isn't all that mysterious.

 ## The Production Sequence

What sequence of events must occur for a play to move from the pages of a script to a live performance before an audience? There are several stages of development for every production.

followspot: A lighting instrument with a highintensity, narrow beam, mounted in a stand that allows it to tilt and swivel so the beam can "follow" an actor.

production team: Everyone working, in any capacity, on the production of the play.

1

Script

Most, but not all, theatrical productions begin with a script. Some plays begin with just an idea. That idea may be developed by the performing group in a variety of interesting and creative ways. Some evolve into written scripts, and others remain as conceptual cores that the actors use as guides when they improvise dialogue during the actual performance.

Concept, Design, and Construction

We will assume that our hypothetical production begins with a traditional script. After the script has been selected, the producer options it, which is securing the legal rights to produce it. He or she also hires the director, designers, and actors. The members of the **production design team** read the script and then develop the **production concept,** also referred to as the "production approach."

The production concept or approach is the central creative idea that unifies the artistic vision of the producer, director, and designers. In many ways, any production concept originates with the personal artistic "points of view" of the members of the production design team. The personality, training, and prior experiences of each team member will shape their thoughts about the play. One of the primary jobs of the director is to mold these individual artistic ideas and expressions into a unified vision — the production approach or concept — so that, ideally, each designer's work supports the work of the other designers as well as the central artistic theme of the production. Normally, the production approach evolves during the first few **production meetings** from the combined input of the members of the production design team. The principles of the production concept are best explained by example.

Let's assume that our hypothetical production team is working on a production of Shakespeare's *The Merchant of Venice.* Most productions of this play would probably be traditional: Elizabethan costumes and a set that mimics the appearance of the Globe Theatre, the theatre most scholars think was used by Shakespeare. However, some production groups might choose, for a variety of reasons, to develop a nontraditional production concept. In a production of this play directed by Cosmo Catellano at the University of Iowa, the performance was set inside a World War II Nazi concentration camp. In this production, all of the actors in the play were portrayed as Jewish interns of the camp. **Supernumeraries,** dressed as Nazi officers and their female companions, sat in the auditorium and watched the play alongside the paying audience. Additional extras, in the uniforms of concentration camp guards and carrying weapons, patrolled the stage throughout the performance. While the script wasn't altered, the radical production approach forced the audience to concentrate on the Jewish persecution themes that are very much a part of the script.

After the production concept is agreed on, the sets, props, lights, costumes, and sound are designed. Then the various diagrams, sketches, and other plans are sent to shops for construction, fabrication, or acquisition of the production elements (see Figure 1.1).

While the various visual elements are being built, the director and actors are busy rehearsing (see Figure 1.2). After the rehearsal and construction period, which usually lasts three to seven weeks, the play moves into the theatre, and the technical and dress rehearsals begin.

Rehearsals

Technical rehearsals are devoted to integrating the sets, props, lighting, and sound with the actors into the action of the play. During this period the patterns

production design team: The producer, director, and scenic, costume, lighting, sound, and other designers who develop the visual and aural concept for the production.

production concept: The creative interpretation of the script, which will unify the artistic vision of producer, director, and designers.

production meeting: A conference of appropriate production personnel to share information.

supernumerary: An actor, normally not called for in the script, used in a production; an extra; a walk-on.

technical rehearsals: Run-throughs in which the sets, lights, props, and sound are integrated into the action of the play.

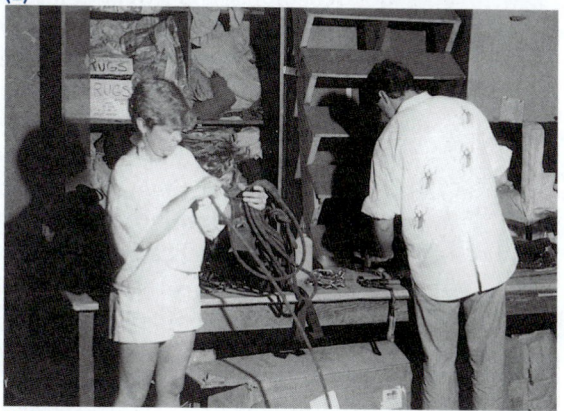

(A)

(B)

(C)

(D)

(E)

(F)

(G)

FIGURE 1.1
A great deal of backstage activity occurs before the production reaches the stage. Photos A, B, Courtesy Erica Von Koerber/Evon Photography. Photos C–G by author.

FIGURE 1.2
The director discusses a scene
with the actors. Courtesy J. Michael
Gillette.

FIGURE 1.3
Scene shifting must be carefully
organized and choreographed.
Courtesy J. Michael Gillette.

blocking: Movement patterns,
usually of actors, on the stage.

shift rehearsal: A run-through
without actors to practice changing
the scenery and props.

cue: A directive for action, for
example, a change in the lighting.

lighting rehearsal: A run-through
without the actors to look at the
intensity, timing, and placement of
the various lighting cues.

and timing for shifting the scenery and props are established. The movements of
any scenic or property elements (see Figure 1.3), regardless of whether those
movements happen in front of the audience or behind a curtain, have to be choreographed, or **blocked,** just as are the movements of the actors. This ensures
that the timing and efficiency of each shift will be consistent for every performance. Scene shifts may be numerous or complex enough to warrant holding a
separate **shift rehearsal,** in which the director, scene designer, technical director, and stage manager work with the scenery and prop crews to perfect the
choreography and timing of all scenic and prop shifts.

The basic timing and intensity of the light **cues** will have been established
during the **lighting rehearsal** (which precedes the first technical rehearsal). But
during tech rehearsals almost all of the light cues have to be adjusted in some
way, because it is the rule rather than the exception that existing cues will be
modified, moved, or deleted and new cues added during this time. The lighting
designer discusses these modifications with the director and stage manager in
the theatre and looks at them on the stage. The intensity, timing, and nature

FIGURE 1.4
Sound is normally run from an in-house position. Purdue Theatre sound mix position. Courtesy of Richard M. Dionne.

of the sound cues are subject to similar changes during the technical rehearsals (see Figure 1.4). Depending on the production schedule and the complexity of the show, there are generally one to three tech rehearsals over the course of a week or so.

Prior to any technical rehearsals, preliminary sound levels will have been roughly set for all prerecorded cues. After **load-in**, those cues will be tweaked for the acoustics of the auditorium. Ideally, separate rehearsals will be held to ensure that all wireless mics are working properly and that the positioning of the orchestra mics, if used, results in a well-balanced mix between the singers and the orchestra.

When producing a musical, there should be a full technical sound rehearsal, often called the sitzprobe, where the actors and orchestra sit (the sitz of sitzprobe), and sing/play through the score. This rehearsal is used to get preliminary balance levels between the orchestra and the performers' wireless mics in the performance space.

Unionized productions normally hold a "10-out-of-12" rehearsal: Ten hours of rehearsal in a twelve-hour period. This is the first opportunity to bring all of the various design/technical elements together into a seamless whole and to practice all shifts and transitions so they will flow smoothly during the ensuing technical and dress rehearsals.

The **dress rehearsals** begin toward the end of "tech week." During these rehearsals, which are a natural extension of the tech rehearsals, any adjustments to costumes and makeup are noted and corrected by the next rehearsal (see Figure 1.5). Adjustments to the various sound, lighting, and shifting cues continue to be made during the dress rehearsals. Depending on the complexity of the production and the number of costumes and costume changes, there may be one to three dress rehearsals.

After the last dress rehearsal, there are sometimes one to ten or more preview performances (with an invited audience and/or reduced ticket prices and no critics) before the production officially opens to the public and critics.

load-in: The moving of scenery and associated equipment into the theatre and their positioning (setup) on the stage.

dress rehearsal: A run-through with all technical elements, including costumes and makeup.

Theatre Organization

More than anything else good theatre requires good organization. Every successful production has a strong "artistic responsibility" organizational structure that follows a fairly standard pattern. Figure 1.6 depicts the organization of a hypothetical, but typical, theatrical production company. Each company's structure is unique to its own needs, and it is doubtful that any two companies would be set up exactly the same. One particular feature of Figure 1.6 should be noted. In this flowchart the director and the designers are symbolized as equals. This equality is essential to the collaborative process that is theatre art and will be discussed at greater length throughout this book. Figure 1.6 delineates the flow of artistic responsibility. It is sometimes called a "make happy" flowchart because the work produced by someone "reporting" to a position higher on the flowchart must artistically satisfy the visual requirements stipulated by that higher position. To illustrate, although they work collaboratively, the visual appearance of the properties must satisfy the scenic designer. It is also important to note what this chart is not: This is not a work responsibility flowchart. A "work responsibility" flowchart would look significantly different. In the real world property masters normally do not "work for" scenic designers. Most property masters work for — are accountable to — the production manager for the on-time, on-budget, as-designed production of properties.

The production meeting is probably the single most important device for ensuring smooth communication among the various production departments. The initial production conferences need to be attended by members of the production design team to develop the production concept. After the designers begin to produce their drawings, sketches, and plans, the production meeting is used as a forum to keep other members of the team informed about the progress in all design areas. At this time, the stage manager normally joins in the discussions.

When the designs are approved and construction begins, the production meeting expands to include the technical director and appropriate crew heads.

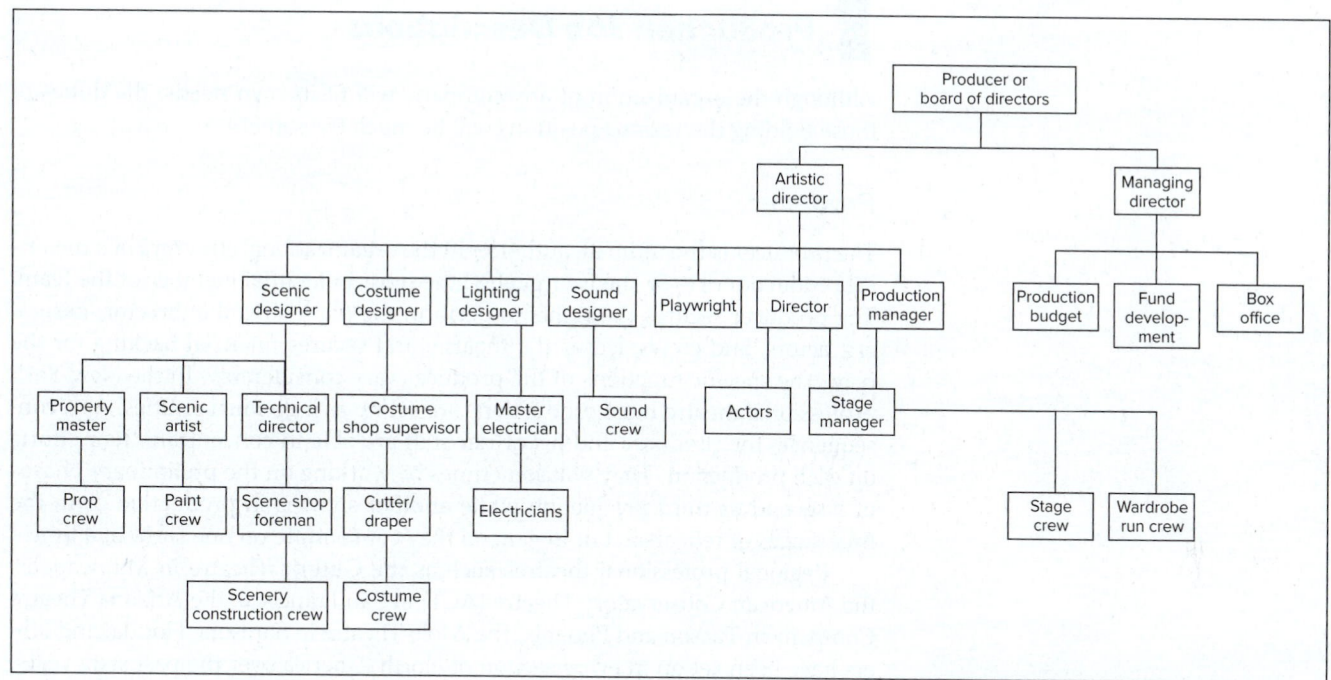

FIGURE 1.6
The organizational structure chart of a typical theatrical production company.

As construction starts, the director becomes heavily involved in rehearsals. At this time, a few adjustments are inevitably necessary in one or more of the design elements. These changes should be discussed and resolved at the production meeting so that all departments are aware of the progress and evolution of the production concept.

While the production concept is being developed, the production meetings are held as often as it is practicable and necessary — daily or less frequently. As the meetings become less developmental and more informational, their frequency decreases to about once a week. The last meeting is usually held just before the opening of the production.

Who participates in production meetings depends, to a great extent, on the nature of the producing organization. A single-run, Broadway-type professional conference usually includes only the members of the production design team and their assistants. A production conference at a regional professional theatre includes the production design team and some of the other members of the permanent production staff, such as the production manager and technical director. For a professionally oriented educational theatre, the staffing of the production meeting is generally the same as for the regional professional production group and ideally will include those faculty supervisors overseeing the work of student designers, technical directors, and crew heads.

The development of advanced communication technologies and the reality that most professional designers are working on more than one project at a time often necessitate that much of the direct communication between members of the production design team take place over great geographical distances. Designs can be sent electronically. Phone, Skype, or video conferences can be used in place of face-to-face meetings. While these developments speed the transfer of data and information, the isolation of the design team members from each other may break down the necessary communication flow within the group. But if everyone is aware of this potential "communication gap," it doesn't have to become a problem.

Production Job Descriptions

Although the organization of any company will fit its own needs, the duties of those holding the various positions will be much the same.

Producer

The producer is the ultimate authority in the organizational structure of a theatrical production. He or she is, arguably, the most influential member of the team. The producer secures the rights to perform the play; hires the director, designers, actors, and crews; leases the theatre; and secures financial backing for the play. The specific functions of the producer vary considerably. In the New York professional theatre most productions are set up as individual entities. As a consequence, the producer and his or her staff are able to concentrate their efforts on each production. They will sometimes be working on the preliminary phases of a second or third production while another show is in production or in the final stages of rehearsal, but in general they concentrate on one show at a time.

Regional professional theatres such as the Guthrie Theatre in Minneapolis, the American Conservatory Theatre (ACT) in San Francisco, the Arizona Theatre Company in Tucson and Phoenix, the Asolo Theatre in Sarasota, Florida, and others have been set up in every section of North America over the past sixty years. Generally, these theatres produce a full seven- or eight-month season of limited-run productions. Some of them have active summer programs. Because of the sweeping responsibilities imposed on the producer within these organizations, the functions of the position are generally divided between two persons, the *managing director* and the *artistic director*. The business functions of the producer — contracts, fund-raising, ticket sales, box-office management — are handled by the managing director, and any artistic decisions — selection of directors, actors, and designers, for example — are made by the artistic director. The managing and artistic directors are hired by the theatre's board of directors, which is responsible for determining the long-range artistic and fiscal goals of the theatre.

In educational theatre, the department chair and administrative staff frequently function in the same capacity as the managing director. The duties of the artistic director are often assigned to a production committee, which selects the plays and is responsible for their artistic quality.

In other nonprofit theatres, such as community or church groups, the functions of the producer are usually carried out by a production committee or board of directors, which functions as previously described.

Playwright

The playwright is obviously a vital and essential link in the production chain. The playwright creates and develops the ideas that ultimately evolve into the written script. In the initial public performance of a play, he or she may be involved in the production process. The playwright frequently helps the director by explaining his or her interpretation of various plot and character developments. During this developmental process, the playwright often needs to rewrite portions of some scenes or even whole scenes or acts. If the playwright is not available for conferences or meetings, the production design team proceeds with the development and interpretation of the script on its own.

Director

The director is the artistic manager and inspirational leader of the production team. He or she coordinates the work of the actors, designers, and crews so that the production accurately expresses the production concept. Any complex activity such as the production of a play must have someone with the vision, energy, and ability to focus everyone else's efforts on the common goal. The director is that leader. He or she works closely with the other members of the production design team to develop the production concept and also works with the actors to develop their roles in a way that is consistent with the production concept. The director is ultimately responsible for the unified creative interpretation of the play as it is expressed in production.

limited run: A production run of predetermined length, for example, two weeks, six weeks, and so forth.

Production Manager

Theatres with heavy annual production programs, such as regional professional theatres and many educational theatre programs, frequently mount several productions or production series simultaneously, often in multiple theatres or venues. In many of these situations the directors and designers are hired or assigned for only one production per year. At the same time the "construction people" — those who actually build the scenery, props, costumes, lights, and sound — are normally hired on an annual basis to work/supervise all of the shows that are produced by that organization. Typically, the technical director runs the scene shop and supervises the production of the scenery for every play in the company's season. Similarly, the property director runs the prop shop and supervises the creation/acquisition of the props used in each production. The same applies for the costume shop supervisor, master electrician, and so forth. Someone on the organization's permanent staff needs to be in control of, and facilitate communication between, the individual design teams and the "permanent" production staff. Enter the production manager.

The production manager is typically responsible for keeping the individual production teams on track, on budget, and on time. He or she oversees the transition from plans to performance for each production and is responsible for managing the producing organization's production budget, personnel, and calendar, and generally keeping everything moving smoothly.

The production manager must be an adept mental gymnast, because this important position has the responsibility for coordinating the complex activities associated with a multishow season. Each production within the theatre's season requires its own logistical structure to bring it from concept to the stage. Figure 1.7 illustrates a typical period needed to develop a play from production concept to reality. Because most regional professional theatres or professionally oriented educational theatres produce eight to twelve **limited-run** plays a season, frequently on several different stages, they must develop rehearsal and performance schedules for all of them simultaneously.

The production calendar shown in Figure 1.8 is used by the production manager to help keep track of the various stages of development for each play in the season. This master calendar contains all pertinent information regarding

FIGURE 1.7
The production calendar shows the time line for each limited-run production from the initial production conference until the closing night.

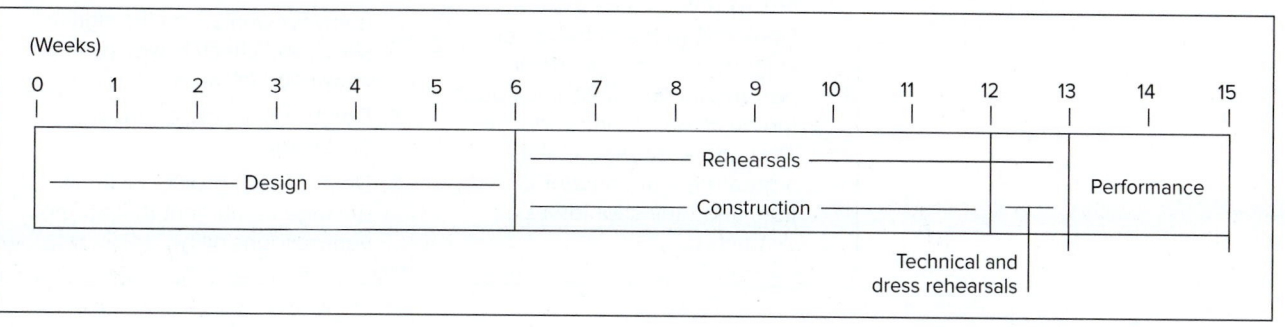

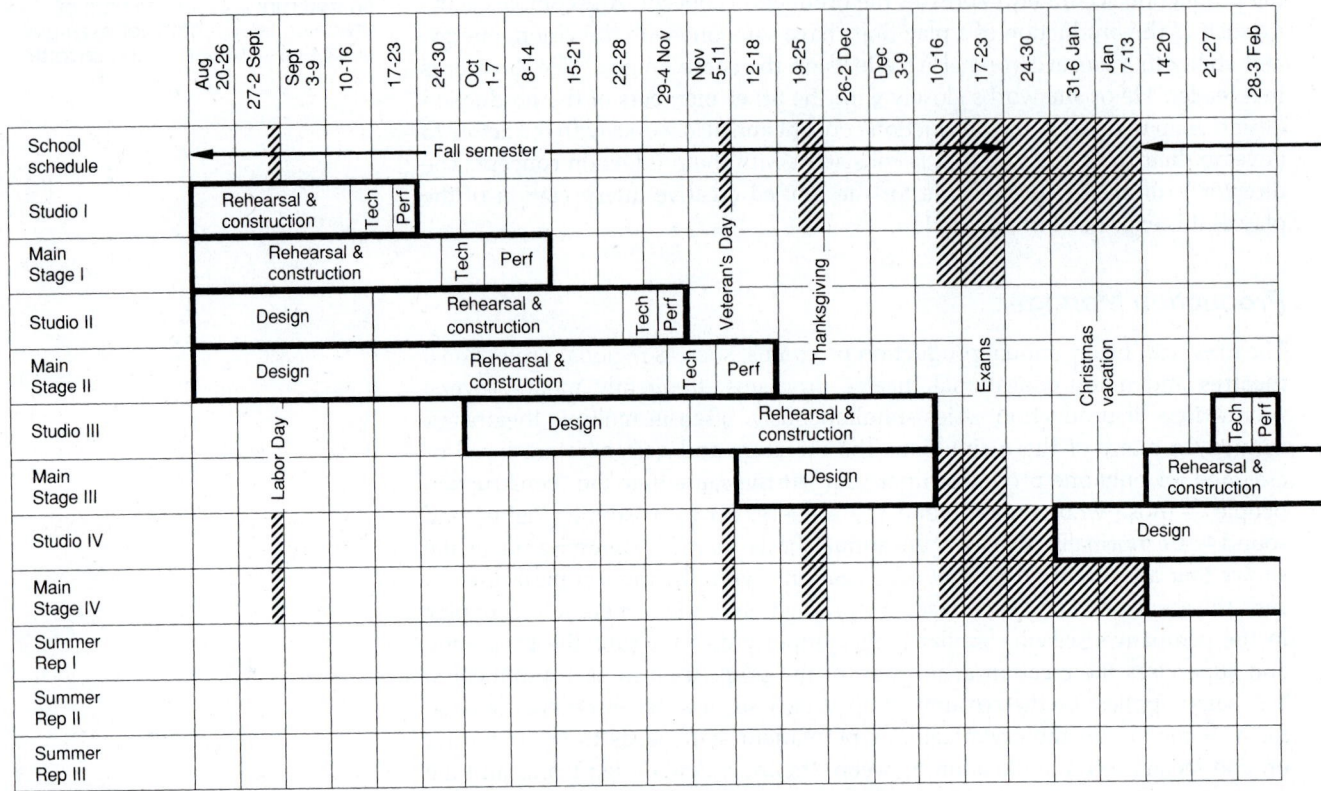

FIGURE 1.8
A sample production calendar.

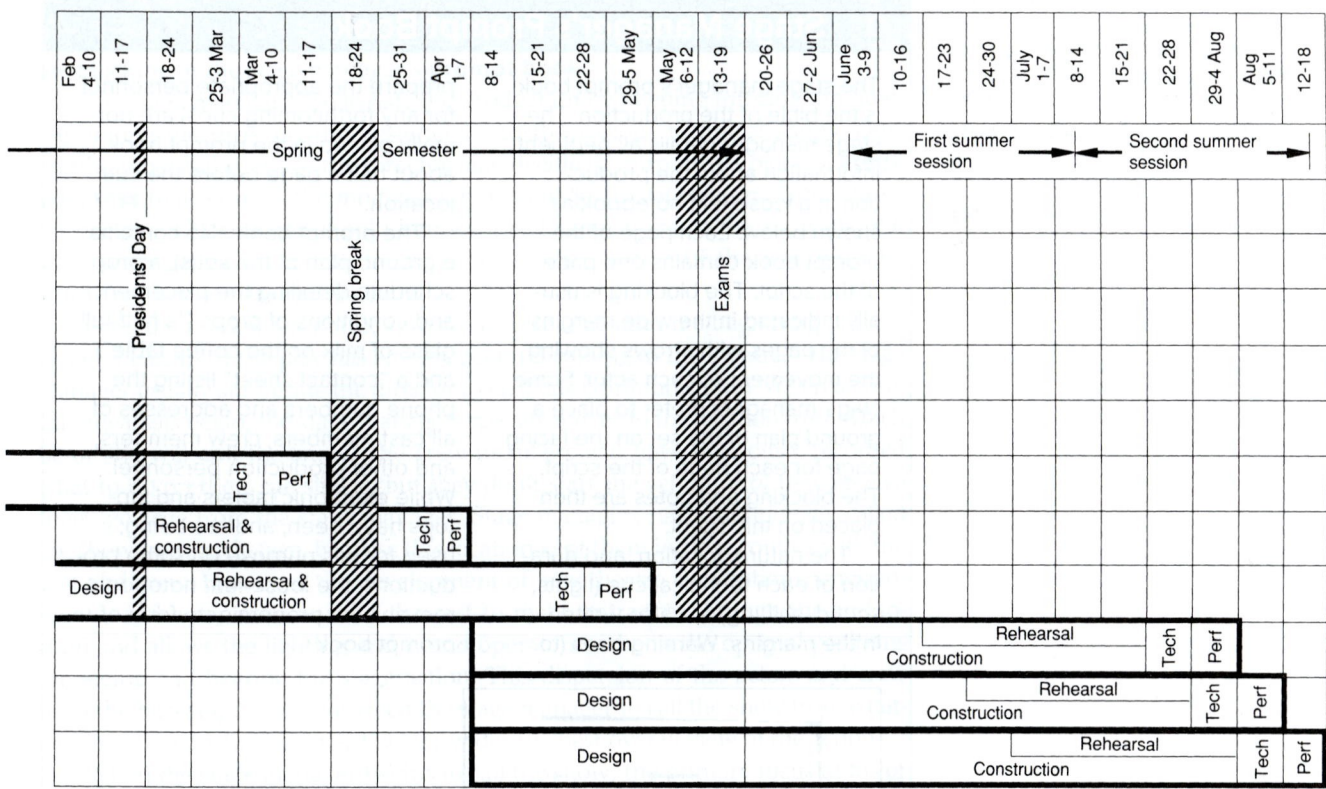

tryouts, rehearsals, design and construction deadlines, technical and dress rehearsals, and performances. From the production calendar, the production manager gleans the information necessary to coordinate the assignment of personnel and rehearsal space as well as the scheduling of the various production meetings and other necessary activities.

Stage Manager

The stage manager can be compared to a gifted, slightly eccentric master mechanic who keeps a cantankerous, highly complex machine running at top efficiency by talking to it, soothing it, and lovingly fixing whatever is broken. The stage manager's overarching function is to serve as the central hub for communications between the director and the various designers and shops. Typically, any communication between those groups is relayed through the stage manager to assure that every note is delivered and "no ball gets dropped." The specific duties of the stage manager can be broken down into two primary categories: (1) Facilitating the director during rehearsals and (2) being responsible for all backstage activity after the show opens.

The stage manager is hired or assigned to the production at about the same time as the director. In the professional theatre, the stage manager must be a member of Actor's Equity, the actors' union. Sometimes the stage manager finds him or herself in an awkward position because he or she not only assists the director but also, if elected the Equity deputy by the union actors, functions as the enforcer of the Equity rules during rehearsals and performances. Because the Equity deputy can be viewed as enforcing the union rules to save money

> **PRODUCTION INSIGHTS**
>
> ## How Did It Look?
>
> Visual references are indispensable when trying to determine what something — a person, locale, or object — looks like. Magazines such as *National Geographic* and numerous online sites contain excellent pictures of costumes, furniture, props, and decoration for plays set in the twentieth century. Visual information about earlier eras can be gleaned from paintings, sculpture, and engravings found either online or in art history books.
>
> The ultimate use of these visual references is up to the individual designer. Some designers faithfully reproduce a costume or furniture piece so they can be sure that the "look" is authentic for the desired period. Others study sources and then design something that reflects the general style of the period.

A great deal of historical research can be accomplished online. For example, if you're designing the scenery for a play set in New York City in the late 1800s, you can conduct a search for interior and exterior photos, paintings, and drawings to help develop a comprehension of the look and feel of the period in that particular locale.

While online research is frequently the fastest way of obtaining information, it may not necessarily be the most detailed. Image clarity can be a little fuzzy. Colors can be off a bit. You may be able to get a better feeling for the *detail* of a particular period by spending a few hours in the library browsing through a stack of books looking at pictures and reading the supporting text. During this kind of general library search, you may also discover interesting information and details that a more targeted online search doesn't provide.

Your research can also involve primary sources. If you are designing costumes for a period play and you're lucky enough to live near a museum with a collection of historical clothing of that period, go look at them. See how they were made, think about how you could adapt the line and silhouette of those garments to the needs of your production design. Make notes. Sketch details that interest you. Ditto for scenic design. If you live in an area similar to the locale of the environment for which you're designing, look at buildings and houses constructed during the period of the play. Look and observe. Make notes and sketches.

Your historical research could also include reading about previous productions of the play and *might* include looking at photos, sketches, and models of those prior productions. But don't think that you *must* look at any visual references of prior productions. If you choose to look at them, simply use them as references for one way that the play was once produced. Don't fall prey to the temptation to copy someone else's work. That stifles your own creativity and, more pragmatically, is illegal in most states. While you shouldn't copy someone else's work, you should also be sure that you don't try to create something so original that it blinds you to the playwright's intention. Remember, the root of any viable design is based in the script.

Conceptual Research

Conceptual research involves devising multiple solutions to specific design challenges. When reading a script, for example, you may discover that the heroine

Historical Relevance for Design

Although each designer (scenic, costume, lighting, projections, properties) must look at visual material relevant to his or her design area, all designers (including sound) should also study the history of the period. As an example, the costume designer needs to know the history and style of dress of the era of the play. This study could begin with a look at a text on costume history to get a general understanding of the style of the time. More detailed study will also be necessary. You can look at paintings, photos, museum displays, catalogs, and any other sources that illustrate the fashion of dress for the period.

An understanding of the socioeconomic background of the play's environment is also useful, because clothing styles are usually a reflection of the morals and economics of the time. Throughout the major periods of fashion, there have been subtle, and sometimes not so subtle, shifts of style based on the socioeconomic status of the individual. Servants have rarely dressed like their employers, and it has usually been fairly easy to differentiate between classes based on the cut and quality of their clothes.

Additional research into the arts (painting, sculpture, literature, music) and history of the playwright's era can provide information on the world that shaped the author's thinking. Essays and critical reviews of the playwright's work are another good source of background information.

leaves the stage at the end of Act I in a beautiful gown and reappears at the start of Act II with the same dress in tatters. Your conceptual research would be to figure out as many ways as possible to solve this challenge.

A snag frequently encountered during conceptual research is our apparently natural inability to conceive of any more than two or three possible solutions to any given challenge. Too often our brains go numb and refuse to dream up new ideas. In psychology this type of nonthinking state is referred to as a perceptual block. If the perceptual block is eliminated, our ability to create additional solutions for any challenge is greatly improved.

Incubation

How many times, having left the room after finishing an exam, have you suddenly remembered the answer to a question that eluded you while you were writing the test? How many times have you come up with the solution to a challenge after having "slept on it"? In both of these cases, the information necessary to answer the questions was locked in your subconscious and only needed time and stress reduction to allow the answer to float into your consciousness.

Incubation provides time to let ideas hatch. During this time, you should basically forget about the project. Your subconscious will use the time to sort through the information you've gathered in the previous steps and may construct a solution to the challenge or point you in a valid direction.

FIGURE 3.6
A typical medieval mansion stage.
©McGraw-Hill Education.

 ## 1500–1650

Theatre became a central part of the cultural reawakening that quickly spread throughout Europe during the Renaissance. Although church-sanctioned pageants continued, secular drama reemerged and became the dominant theatrical form. Theatres, which hadn't been permitted or constructed for over a thousand years, sprang up all over Europe. Because of the strong interest in classical forms and structures, the basic shape of almost all these theatres corresponded in some form with the description of Greek and Roman theatres contained in the architectural writings of Vitruvius. Although the theatres were patterned after the classical forms, their designers made many interesting, and clever, adaptations.

The Teatro Olympico in Vicenza, Italy, was one of these theatres (see Figure 3.7). Built between 1580 and 1585, it was designed in the style of the ancient Roman theatres. Probably the most significant change was that the theatre finally moved indoors, with the entire structure enclosed in a building. The *cavea*, or auditorium, was designed not as an exact semicircle but as an ellipse, and this minor change dramatically improved the sight lines in the theatre. The *scaenae frons* was no longer a single decorated wall but was broken by several arches; elaborate permanent sets of street scenes were built, in **forced perspective**, on a **raked stage** floor in back of the arches. In many Renaissance theatres, the stage floors were raked to improve the visual effects of the scenery. The actors normally performed on a flat playing space in front of the raked stage.

A second minor Renaissance innovation in southern Europe was the introduction of elaborately painted, forced perspective, scenery. The use of **stock sets**—usually painted **drops** of the "comic scene," the "tragic scene," the "satyric scene," and so on—necessitated the evolution of the proscenium, or picture frame, stage. Drops, which greatly enhanced the feeling of depth created by the painted perspective, were usually hung at the upstage edge of the stage.

At this time, and for the next several hundred years, stages were lit like any other indoor location—with varying arrangements of candles, lanterns, and torches. The first recorded use of a stage lighting effect occurred during the

forced perspective: A visual-distortion technique that increases the apparent depth of an object.

raked stage: A stage floor that is higher at the back than the front.

stock set: Scenery designed to visually support a generalized location (garden, city street, palace, interior) rather than a specific one; commonly used from the Renaissance through the early twentieth century and still in use today in some theatres.

drop: A large expanse of cloth, usually muslin or canvas, on which something (a landscape, sky, street, room) is painted.

FIGURE 3.7
The Teatro Olympico.
©McGraw-Hill Education.

Renaissance. In a treatise written in 1545, Sebastiano Serlio recommended "placing candles and torches behind flasks with amber- and blue-colored water."[2]

At approximately the same time, drama in England was being produced in a different type of structure. A number of theatres had been constructed just outside London by 1600. Probably the most famous was the Globe (1599–1632), the home theatre of William Shakespeare (see Figure 3.8). Although these theatres differed in detail, their basic shape was similar.

The stage of a typical Elizabethan theatre was a large, open-air platform generally raised from 4 to 6 feet off the ground (see Figure 3.9). The platform was surrounded by a yard, or *pit*, which served as the space for the lower-class audience — the groundlings — to stand. At the upstage end of the stage platform was the area that formed the *inner below*. There is some dispute about the shape of this structure. One theory maintains that it was a curtained alcove recessed into the upstage wall. Another hypothesis holds that it was a roofed structure, curtained on three sides, that projected a little way onto the stage platform. A final theory contends that there was no inner below at all. Depending on the theory to which you subscribe, the *inner above* was an area above the inner below on the back wall, or the acting area provided by the roof of the structure that projected onto the stage, or an area that didn't exist as a playing space. In any case, separate entrances apparently flanked either side of the inner below to provide access to the stage.

The stage, the pit, and the wall behind the stage were surrounded by the outside of the building, a three-story structure that housed the galleries and private boxes for the wealthier patrons and nobles.

---

[2] "Stage Design." *Encyclopaedia Britannica.* 2003 (http://www.Britannica.com/eb/article?eu=118829).

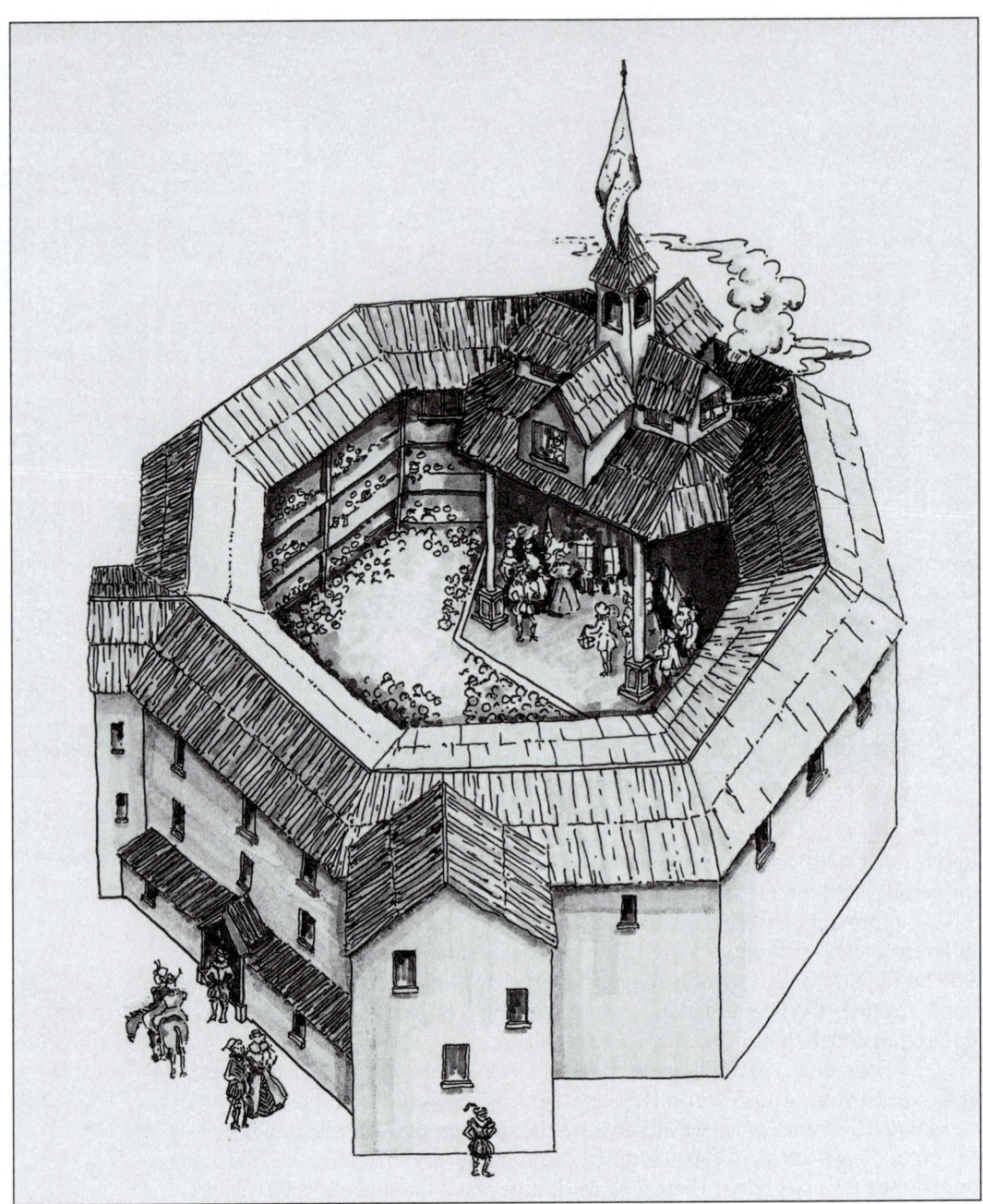

FIGURE 3.8
The Globe Theatre.
©McGraw-Hill Education.

Little scenery seems to have been associated with Elizabethan productions, although contemporary records do indicate that a number of props — rocks, trees, and the like — were associated with the theatres.

In France staging conventions had changed little since medieval times. Mansions were still in common use. Multiple mansions, each representing a specific location, were normally onstage simultaneously. If a play required additional locations, painted coverings were removed from one or more of the mansions, or curtains were opened, to reveal the new locations. Perspective painting and other elements of the creative awakening that was developed in Italy began to be used in France toward the end of this period.

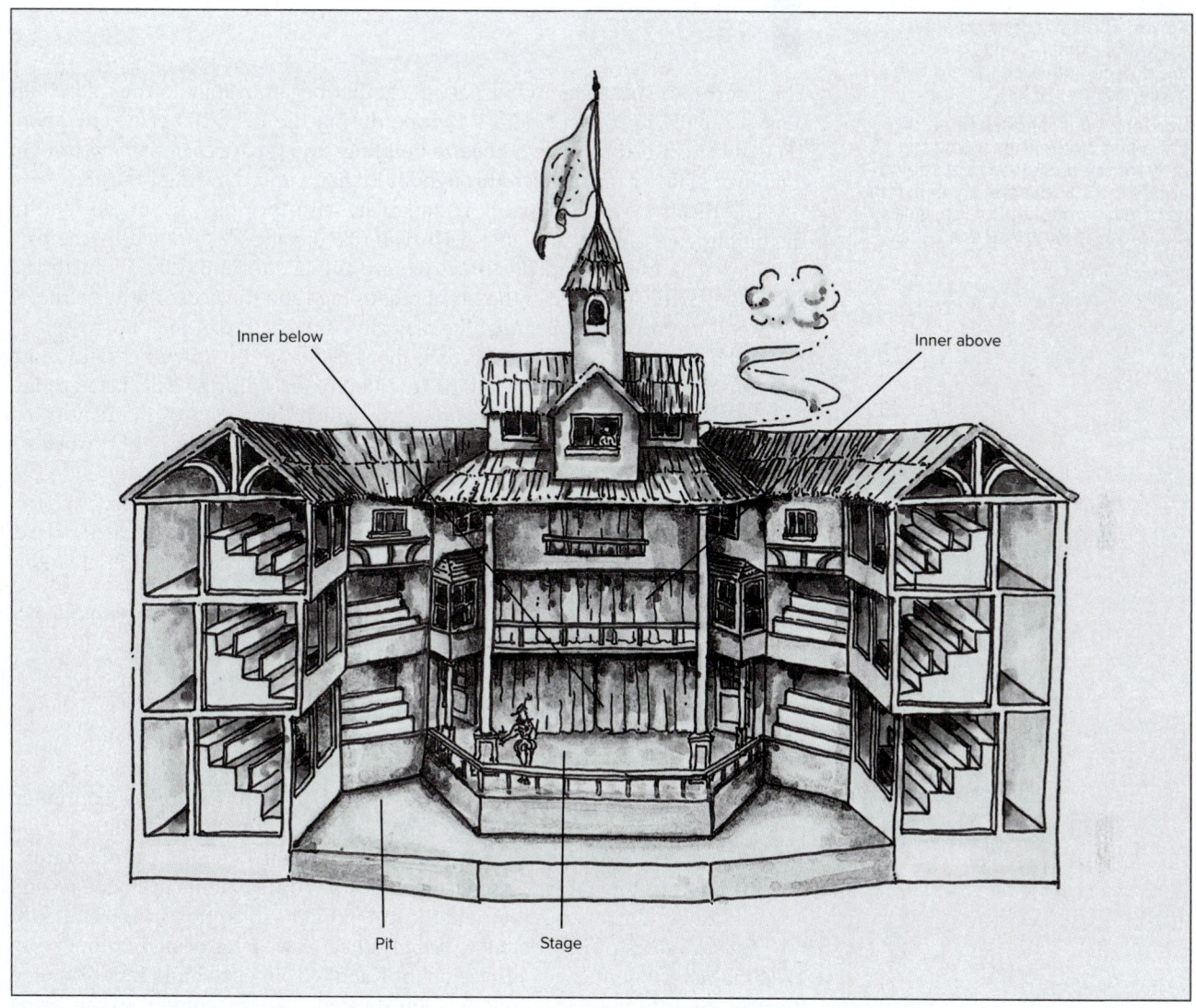

Inner below

Inner above

Pit

Stage

FIGURE 3.9
The stage of the Globe Theatre.
©McGraw-Hill Education.

Stage machinery in Europe also had not evolved much since the 1300s. There are accounts of effects used for flying gods and other supernatural beings above the stage as well as boats with passengers moving across the stage. There are numerous indications that effects — smoke, fire, clouds, and sound — were in fairly common use. These effects had all been in existence for several hundred years. There wouldn't be any significantly new developments in stage machinery in Europe until the late nineteenth century.

Up until this time the primary challenge of lighting stages, and any indoor spaces, was simply providing enough light so people could see. Early efforts usually involved suspending candle-lit chandeliers over both the stage and auditorium. It took considerable effort to make the stage bright enough so the audience could easily see the actors. In the early 1600s reflectors began to be used to intensify the rather meager light output of both candles and oil lamps. About the same time footlights using candles and oil lamps began to be placed along the front edge of the stages. To provide additional light, vertical rows of lamps frequently were hidden behind the **wings** on either side of the stage.

wings: In scenic terms, either tall, cloth-covered frames or narrow, unframed drops placed on either side of the stage, parallel with the proscenium arch, to prevent the audience from seeing backstage; were usually painted to match the scene on the upstage drop.

apron: The flat extension of the stage floor that projects from the proscenium arch toward the audience.

borders: Wide, short, framed or unframed cloth drops suspended to prevent the audience from seeing above the stage; normally match the decorative treatment of the wings and drops in wing and drop sets.

1650–1900

The interest in spectacle and visual effects that began in Italy in the mid-1500s moved rapidly northward across Europe during the next 100 years. By about 1660, the architectural style of theatre buildings and the types of scenery used in them were fairly standardized throughout England and the rest of Europe.

The theatres were primarily rectangular, with the stage set at one end of the building, as shown in Figure 3.10. The raked stage was framed by the proscenium arch, and the **apron** thrust toward the auditorium. Like its historical antecedents, the forestage of the Elizabethan stage and the *platea* of the medieval theatre, the apron was the site of the majority of the action of the play.

Although the scenery had become more elaborate by this time, with more locations depicted, it still followed the tradition of providing a visual background for the play rather than an environment in which the action of the play could happen. It was painted in perspective on movable drops, wings, and **borders** and was placed on the raked stage, where the inclined floor greatly added to the sense of depth created by the perspective painting of the scenery. Most of the plays took place in a generalized location (drawing room, courtyard, palace, garden, and so on), so each theatre owned stock sets that depicted these various scenes. When the action of the play took place in a library, the library set was used. If the theatre didn't happen to have a library set, another stock interior set, such as the drawing room, could be substituted.

The auditoriums of these theatres also followed a traditional arrangement (see Figure 3.11): multitiered boxes (for dignitaries and other notables), galleries (for those who could afford the extra charge), and the pit (for those who wanted to see the play but couldn't afford, or weren't permitted, a better seat). This style of proscenium theatre was essentially modern. Some theatres continued to install raked stages, but more and more new structures were built with flat stages. Theatres were constructed in this style until the late nineteenth century.

During this time period the most significant advancements in stage machinery occurred in the Japanese Kabuki theatre. From its inception in 1603, and for the first 125 years of its existence, Kabuki theatre was performed outdoors. In 1724 the government gave permission for Kabuki troupes to build indoor roofed theatres. Shortly thereafter, highly sophisticated stage machinery began being

FIGURE 3.10
A typical Restoration theatre.
©McGraw-Hill Education.

PRODUCTION INSIGHTS

Function Follows Form

The structure and equipment of theatres has affected theatrical conventions through history. The funeral marches so prominent in Shakespearean tragedies were simply expedient methods to clear bodies from the stage. The Elizabethan theatres didn't have a curtain to hide the stage, and the plays were held in the daytime, so the stage was always lit. This precluded any artful, or semibelievable, method for getting rid of the bodies. Hence the funeral marches.

In the Restoration and eighteenth-century theatres, entrances were made from doors on either side of the apron, because the raked stage was cluttered with scenery and the actors' intrusion there would have distorted the illusion of depth carefully designed into the forced-perspective scenery.

developed. In 1736 **elevator traps** were introduced. This was followed less than twenty years later (1753) by **elevator stages.** Within five years (1758) Kabuki theatres began using **revolving stages** to shift scenery. The stage machinery became even more complex with the introduction of **concentric revolving stages** in 1827.[3]

There were no significant developments in stage lighting between 1630 and approximately the 1780s. Candles and oil lamps continued as the primary illumination source, and they were placed in locations — footlights, wings, overhead chandeliers — where they could get the most light on the stage. With the exceptions of the chandeliers, the sources were normally hidden from the audience's view. In 1783 a new lamp — the Argang oil lamp, was introduced. It had a cylindrical wick enclosed in a glass chimney that produced a brighter, whiter, and cleaner light than its floating wick predecessors.

In 1792 a Scottish engineer, William Murdock, developed a practical method of distilling gas from coal. This was the genesis of gas lighting. Gas lighting was a significant advancement over oil lamps and candles. It was much brighter and

elevator trap: A small elevator used to shift small pieces of scenery, or an actor, from the basement underneath the stage to the stage or vice versa. Usually no larger than 4 × 4 or 4 × 6 feet. Also known as a disappearance trap.

elevator stage: A large elevator used to raise scenic elements or whole sets stored beneath the stage to stage level.

revolving stage: A large, circular disk that pivots on its central axis. Built into the stage floor as part of the theatre's permanent equipment.

concentric revolving stages: A revolving stage with, usually, two sections, one rotating inside the other.

FIGURE 3.11
The auditorium structure of a typical late-seventeenth through late-nineteenth-century theatre. ©McGraw-Hill Education.

[3] Oscar G. Brockett, *History of the Theatre,* 6th ed. (Boston: Allyn and Bacon, 1991), p. 269.

cleaner burning; and, of significant import to theatre practitioners, the intensity of gaslight was easily controlled. Within a relatively short period of time theatres throughout Europe and North America were equipped with gaslight. Distribution of gas throughout the stage and auditorium was accomplished with a maze of pipes and tubing. The gas panel or gas table, a centralized system of valves used to control the intensity of the various onstage gas lamps, was, in effect, the first light board. The group master control systems described in Chapter 16, "Lighting Production," are identical with the control methods utilized on these gas tables or panels. This flexible distribution system was a quantum leap in lighting control. Prior to its development, intensity control had primarily been accomplished by snuffing and relighting candles or lamps. Experiments with various mechanical systems that could control intensity and effect color changes by raising and lowering colored glass cylinders over the oil-lamp flames had not been particularly successful. Although gaslight offered a vast improvement over oil lamps, it was not without its challenges. Even when the flame was enclosed within a glass chimney, the open flame still posed a significant fire hazard.

Thomas Drummond, a British engineer, invented limelight in 1816. Limelight is created when a sharp jet of flame is focused against a block of limestone. As the limestone incandesces, it produces a light that is both very bright and relatively soft. When coupled with a mirrored reflector, the limelight produced a relatively cohesive beam of light that was intense enough to reach the stage from the auditorium and still be significantly brighter than the other areas of the stage. Thus was born the first followspot.

The first electric light used in the theatre was the carbon arc. This light, produced when electricity arcs between two electrodes, is extremely white and bright. By 1860 the Paris Opera had developed a projector, a followspot, and several effects utilizing the carbon arc.

Thomas Edison's development of a practical incandescent lamp in 1879 and the rapid electrification of Europe and North America led to the next great advances in theatrical lighting. By 1900 almost all theatres throughout Europe and North America had converted to electricity. Interestingly, the conversion to electricity did not immediately spawn any significantly new methods or techniques of stage lighting. Stages continued to be lit as they had with gaslight. Conventional footlights, **borderlights**, and **winglights** were simply electrified. Intensity was controlled with resistance dimmers utilizing the group master control methods developed and refined with gas lighting control tables. Resistance dimmers continued to be the standard theatrical dimmer until the late 1940s.

 ## Twentieth Century

A revolution in the style of theatre began in the late 1800s and continued into the early twentieth century. The work of a number of theatre artists was taking a decidedly different turn from the declamatory style of earlier theatre. This new form was devoted to a more realistic and naturalistic type of drama. It stressed the previously unheard-of concepts of unity of style for all elements of the production. The Théâtre Libre, founded by André Antoine in Paris, and the Moscow Art Theatre, founded by Konstantin Stanislavski and Vladimir Nemerovich-Danchenko, were but two of the leading groups in this movement toward a more naturalistic and unified style.

As the productions became more realistic, it was natural for the shape of the theatres to change to support this new form. The new plays required that the settings become environments for the action of the drama rather than backgrounds.

borderlights: Any lights hung above the stage, behind the borders (horizontal masking pieces). In this context the borderlights were striplights — long, narrow, troughlike fixtures usually containing eight to twelve individual lamps.

winglights: Lights hung on either side of the stage, usually concealed by wings (vertical masking pieces). In this context the winglights were striplights — long, narrow, troughlike fixtures usually containing eight to twelve individual lamps.

PRODUCTION INSIGHTS

From the Boxes to the Pits

Throughout history the various shapes of theatre have been determined, to a large extent, by the mores of the sponsoring society. In ancient Greece, everyone (except the slaves) was considered of equal rank, so the seating was similarly democratic and unsegregated. In the southern Renaissance and in Europe for the ensuing 200 years, the majority of theatres were built by the aristocracy for their own amusement. The visual illusions of forced-perspective scenery were best seen from a single point in the center of the auditorium. This ideal location, subsequently known as "the Duke's seat," was usually found in the second-level box at the back of the auditorium.

The theatres of Elizabethan England, such as the Globe, also had elevated boxes surrounding the stage. The aristocracy, and those others who could afford the higher ticket prices, sat in the boxes. The common people stood in the pit. About the time of the French Revolution, seats began to appear in the pit throughout European theatres as the various societies became more democratic.

Consequently, as the action of the play moved onto the stage from the apron, the depth of the apron shrank. When this happened, it became difficult to see all of the action from the boxes and gallery seats adjacent to the proscenium, so the shape of the auditorium began to evolve. The side seats were eliminated, and the remaining seats faced the stage.

Everything speeded up in the twentieth century. Almost as quickly as the realistic movement became the dominant mode of theatre, splinter groups broke off from it to create a number of antirealistic movements. These movements rose, fell, and evolved so rapidly that most of them didn't have a chance to develop distinctive types of theatre structures. Actually, most of these movements didn't need to change the basic shape of the proscenium theatre or its machinery, because the existing theatres provided a workable environment for their divergent styles.

In the United States, the Little Theatre movement of the 1920s and 1930s was an effort to establish quality productions outside of New York City. It also gave new playwrights a chance to improve their craft and have their works produced in an environment that was less critical than the supercharged atmosphere of Broadway. This movement continued and expanded throughout the country. Its crowning glory has been the establishment of a number of excellent contemporary regional professional theatre companies in such cities as San Francisco, Dallas, Denver, Hartford, Washington, San Diego, Minneapolis, Tucson, and Sarasota.

A ripple effect of the Little Theatre movement was that fledgling companies, funded more by inspiration and lofty intentions than money, began to produce theatre in "found" spaces. Existing barns; churches; feed stores; grocery stores; libraries; old movie houses; and other large, relatively open buildings were all candidates for takeover. Many of these groups relished the enforced intimacy between the actors and audience that shoehorning theatres into these cramped spaces provided. Whether by accident or design, many of these converted theatre spaces didn't have the room to erect a proscenium stage and auditorium. For whatever reasons, thrust and arena stages sprang up all over the country.

The form and structure of the physical theatre have gone through a great many developments. Any number of people have attempted to "improve" the spatial relationship between the stage and auditorium. It is doubtful, however, that anyone will ever devise any genuinely new developments in this relationship, simply because the theatrical experience is based on the premise that the actors need a space in which to perform and the audience must be in a position to see and hear them. When the form of the physical theatre is thought of in this context, it becomes apparent that there are no different types of theatre, only variations on a basic theme.

Theatrical lighting began a rapid technological evolution in the early twentieth century with the conversion from gas to incandescent lighting. Since then the speed of that technological evolution has only increased. The conversion from gas to incandescent lamps simply involved refitting extant gas fixtures for electricity.

The first major twentieth-century technological development in stage lighting resulted from refinements to the incandescent lamp that significantly increased the lamps' brightness and longevity. These improvements led to the development of incandescent spotlights. Steady progress in spotlight design continued throughout the twentieth century. Initial designs, such as the plano-convex spotlight, were a vast improvement over gaslight and electric arc technologies. Within a few decades the more efficient Fresnel and ellipsoidal reflector spotlights had largely replaced the plano-convex instruments. The tungsten-halogen (T-H) lamp was introduced in the early 1960s. It produced a whiter light, and its rated lamp life was minimally ten to twenty times longer than that of its predecessor. In the 1970s borosilicate lenses, which produced a much whiter light and were less susceptible to heat fracture than their Pyrex predecessors, became the industry standard. Newer, more efficient fixtures, lenses, and lamp designs were continually introduced in the 1980s and 1990s. In the early twenty-first century, LED lamp technology was used in stage lighting fixtures. This technology has rapidly improved both brightness and color range availability.

The first electronic dimmer was the thyratron tube dimmer, developed by George Izenour in the late 1940s. For the first time the dimmers could be controlled from a remote location. Electronic control allowed development of the preset control system. Preset control was to remain the dominant method of dimmer control until it was supplanted by digital control in the 1980s. The principles of dimmers and control techniques will be discussed in Chapter 16, "Lighting Production."

Sound effects had been a central part of theatre production since the Greeks. Until the development of electrically powered record players and amplified sound in the 1930s, any music used in the theatre was played live. Sound effects were also produced live, utilizing a fascinating array of mechanical devices, many of which had changed little in design or effect in, literally, centuries. The development of the tape recorder in the late 1940s ushered in the beginning of a period of experimentation and development in theatre sound that continues unabated. High-fidelity sound — recorded sound that mimics the full range of human hearing — became commercially available in the early 1950s. Stereo sound followed almost immediately. High-fidelity, stereo, tape-recorded sound had become the standard in effects sound in the theatre by the early 1960s. It continued to be the dominant technology until the introduction of a variety of digital storage, replay, and recording devices began in the early 1980s.

Since computers and digital technology were introduced to the world of technical theatre in the early 1980s, there has been a literal explosion of new developments in all areas of theatre technology. Specific uses of these new technologies will be explored in many of the chapters that follow.

Chapter 4

The Stage and Its Equipment

Theatrical performing spaces have undergone an interesting evolution since about 1960. Influenced by a number of experimental theatre movements as well as economic pressure to make theatres usable for dance groups, symphony concerts, and esoterica such as car, home, and boat shows, companies are changing the shapes of theatres and playing spaces.

One of the more dominant trends in this evolution is the reduction of the physical and psychological barriers that separate the audience from the production, as evidenced in many of the newer production spaces.

Although an ingenious production concept and large budget can radically alter the appearance of almost any stage-auditorium relationship, it is still true that three primary stage configurations — *proscenium, thrust,* and *arena* — dominate the world of theatre.

Proscenium Stage

The proscenium stage is also known as the **picture frame stage** because spectators observe the play's action through the frame of the proscenium arch (Figure 4.1). Although there is debate among theatre practitioners regarding the use of a stage that forcefully separates the audience from the action, the fact remains that the proscenium stage and its machinery have, for more than 350 years, been the dominant mode of presentation. The reason is simple: Things that work don't need to be tinkered with.

Proscenium Arch

The proscenium arch, which gives this type of stage its name, is a direct descendant of the *proskenium* and *skene* of the Greek theatres (see Figure 4.2). This arch, which separates the stage from the auditorium, can vary in both height and width. The average theatre (with 300 to 500 seats) has a proscenium arch that is typically 18 to 22 feet high and 36 to 40 feet wide.

Stage

The playing area behind, or upstage, of the proscenium arch is referred to as the stage (see Figure 4.3). The area of the stage in front of the proscenium arch is called the apron.

picture frame stage: A configuration in which the spectators watch the action of the play through a rectangular opening; synonym for proscenium-arch stage.

The stage floor is a working surface that serves a number of diverse functions. For the actors, it must provide a firm, resilient, nonskid (but not too sticky) surface that facilitates movement. For scenic purposes, a stage floor needs to be paintable. It should be made of wood that is reasonably resistant to the splintering and gouging caused by heavy stage wagons and other scenic pieces. It should also slightly muffle the sound of footfalls and shifting scenery.

Although many directors choose to move the action of their productions onto the apron to bring the play closer to the audience, the primary playing area for many proscenium productions is behind the proscenium arch.

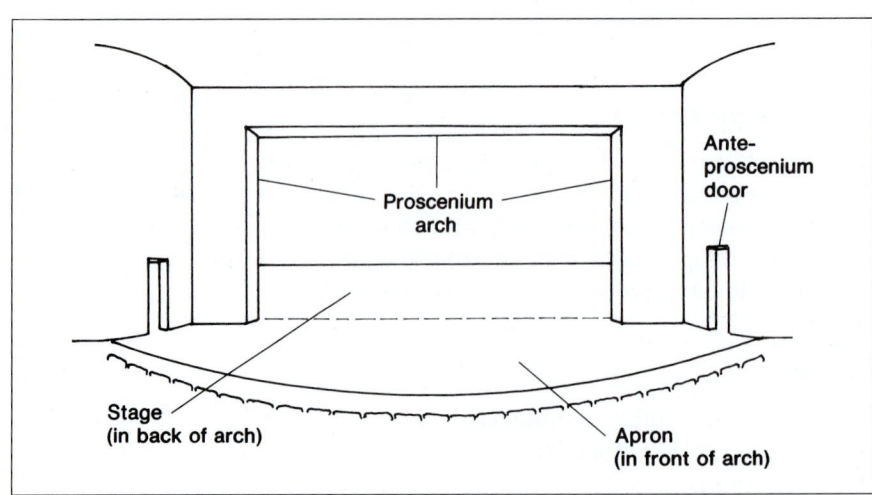

FIGURE 4.2
The parts of a proscenium stage.

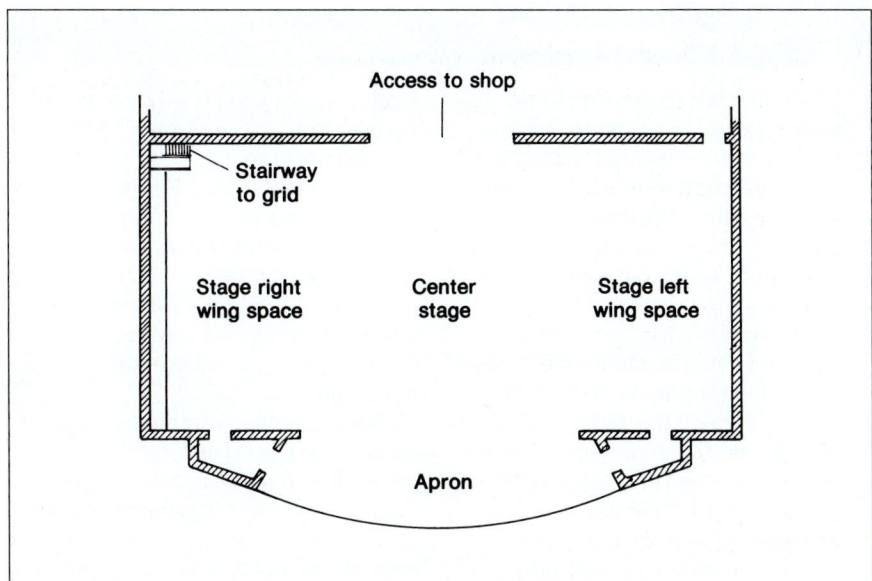

FIGURE 4.3
The proscenium stage and wings.

Wings

The spaces on either side of the stage are called the wings. Wings are primarily used for storage. During a multiscene production, all sorts of scenic elements, props, and other equipment are stored in the wings until needed on stage.

Apron

The apron, or forestage, is an extension of the stage from the proscenium arch toward the audience. It stretches across the proscenium arch to the walls of the auditorium and can vary in depth from a narrow sliver only 3 or 4 feet deep to as much as 10 or 15 feet. It generally extends for 5 to 15 feet beyond either side of the proscenium arch.

Orchestra Pit

Many proscenium theatres have an **orchestra pit**, normally placed between the apron and the audience. It is used to hold the pit band, or orchestra, during performances that have live music. To hold an orchestra, the pit obviously needs to be fairly large. Most pits extend the full width of the proscenium, and their upstage-to-downstage dimensions are roughly 8 to 12 feet. The depth of the pit varies, but a good pit is deep enough so that the orchestra won't interfere with the spectators' view of the stage (see Figure 4.4).

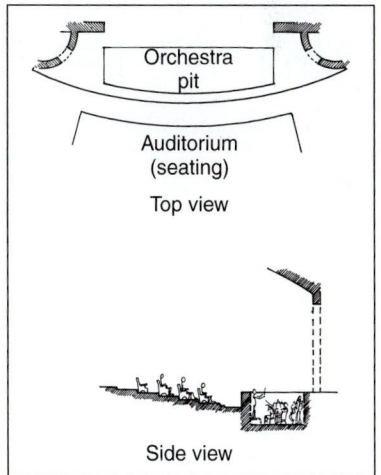

FIGURE 4.4
The orchestra pit usually occupies part of the apron.

Obviously, the size of the orchestra pit imposes a formidable gulf between the audience and stage when it is not in use. Various solutions have been adopted to remedy this situation. In some theatres, the orchestra pit is hidden beneath removable floor panels under the apron; when the pit is needed for a production, the floor panels are removed. In other theatres, the pit is placed beneath the auditorium floor. When not in use it is covered with removable panels, and auditorium seats are placed on top. This method has the obvious advantage that additional tickets can be sold when the pit isn't being used.

In some theatres, the entire forestage area (apron, orchestra pit, front of the auditorium) is built on one or more hydraulic lifts. With their great lifting power, it is possible to raise or lower whole sections of the stage. When more than one

orchestra pit: The space between the stage and the auditorium, usually below stage level, that holds the orchestra.

Stage Directions

It can be frustrating trying to tell an actor what direction to move or telling a technician that "I want the sofa a little further to the left." "My left?" he asks. "No, that way. Over there." Through the years, a system of stage directions has evolved to help clear up these problems.

On the American proscenium and thrust stages, stage directions are understood to mean that you are standing on the stage and looking into the auditorium. Stage left is to your left and stage right is to your right. Upstage is behind you, and downstage is in front of you. The terms *upstage* and *downstage* probably evolved in the sixteenth or seventeenth century during the era of raked stages, when you literally moved up the slope of the stage when moving upstage.

Stage directions in Europe are noted in a slightly different manner. Upstage and downstage are the same, but right and left are reversed from the American system, being given in reference to the auditorium rather than the stage.

Stage directions for arena stages cannot use this system, because the audience surrounds the stage. For arena theatres, it is much easier to describe the stage directions by referring to one direction as north, and then remaining directions are understood to be south, east, and west.

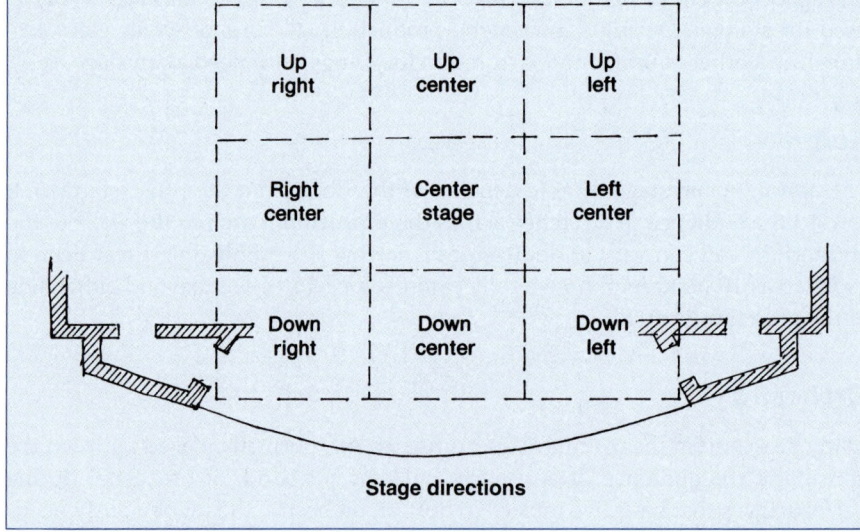

Stage directions

FIGURE 4.5
Hydraulic lifts can provide a variety of interesting auditorium/stage arrangements.

mix: To blend the electronic signals created by several sound sources.

balance: To adjust the loudness levels of individual signals while mixing, to achieve an appropriate blend.

lift is used, they are able to shape the forestage into a variety of configurations, as shown in Figure 4.5.

Bally's Hotel in Las Vegas has created what may be the ultimate answer to the orchestra pit: There isn't any. In the Jubilee Room (a 2,500-seat theatre), the orchestra plays in a room in the basement of the theatre complex while watching the production on closed-circuit television. Microphones are placed as needed in every section of the orchestra, and the sound is **mixed** and **balanced** with that of the singers before it is amplified and sent into the auditorium. Although this solution works well in the high-tech atmosphere of Las Vegas, it is doubtful that every musical director would feel comfortable working in this remote and disconnected manner.

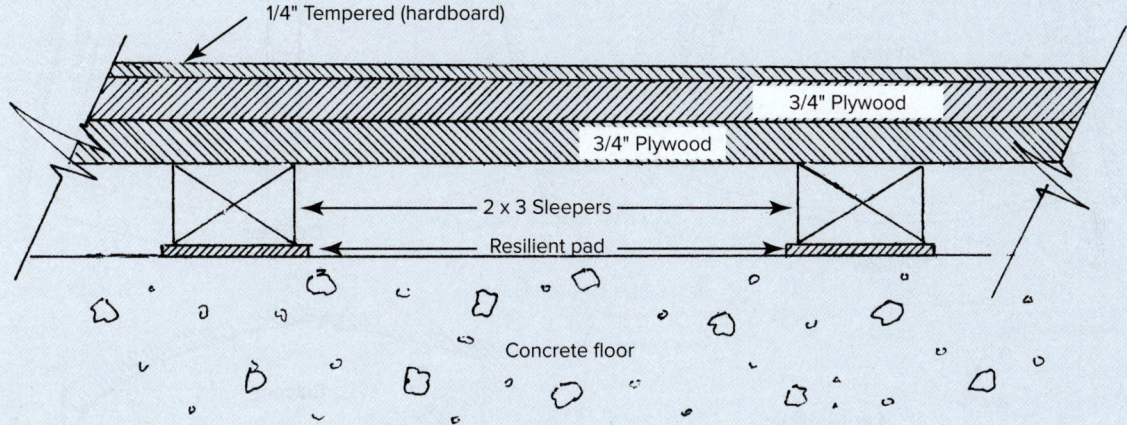

Stage Floors

A good stage floor is actually composed of several layers. The subfloor should be made of soft wood such as pine or plywood. These materials are resilient and tough and will hold nails and other fasteners. Quarter-inch tempered hardboard has all of the qualities needed for a good stage floor surface. It has the added advantage of being fairly inexpensive, and individual sections of the floor can be replaced as needed. The one drawback to this hardboard floor is that it has a tendency to warp when first painted. To alleviate this problem, paint each sheet *on both sides* before nailing it to the subfloor. (Stand the hardboard on edge, and paint both sides simultaneously.)

1/4" Tempered (hardboard)

3/4" Plywood

3/4" Plywood

2 x 3 Sleepers

Resilient pad

Concrete floor

Detail of a typical stage floor. The 2 × 3 sleepers are on 16-inch centers. Sleepers and sleeper pads are not attached to the concrete slab.

Auditorium

The shape of the typical proscenium theatre auditorium, or house, is roughly rectangular, with the proscenium arch located on one of the narrow ends of the rectangle (see Figure 4.6). Normally, each seat is approximately perpendicular to the proscenium arch. Typically, to reduce the reflection of sound waves in an auditorium, none of its finished surfaces (walls, ceiling, floor) are placed parallel with any others. The side walls of most auditoriums angle out from the proscenium arch in the shape of a slightly opened fan. The rear wall of the auditorium is usually curved, and the ceiling generally slopes toward the rear of the house.

The floor of the auditorium is raked, or inclined, from the stage to the rear of the house. Angling of the house floor improves not only the acoustics of the theatre but also the view of the stage by elevating each successive row.

The lighting control booth is generally located at the back of the auditorium. It normally has one or more large windows to provide the light-board operator(s) with an unobstructed view of the stage. Although a sound booth with a large openable window is frequently located in a similar back-of-house location, sound operators typically choose to run the **sound mixer** from a position in the auditorium so that he or she can hear what the audience is hearing and balance all the sound sources accordingly with the focal point of the sound "picture" typically being the voices of the actors or singers.

sound mixer: An electronic device used to adjust the loudness and tone levels of several sources, such as microphones and recorded sources (computer files/tape playback equipment).

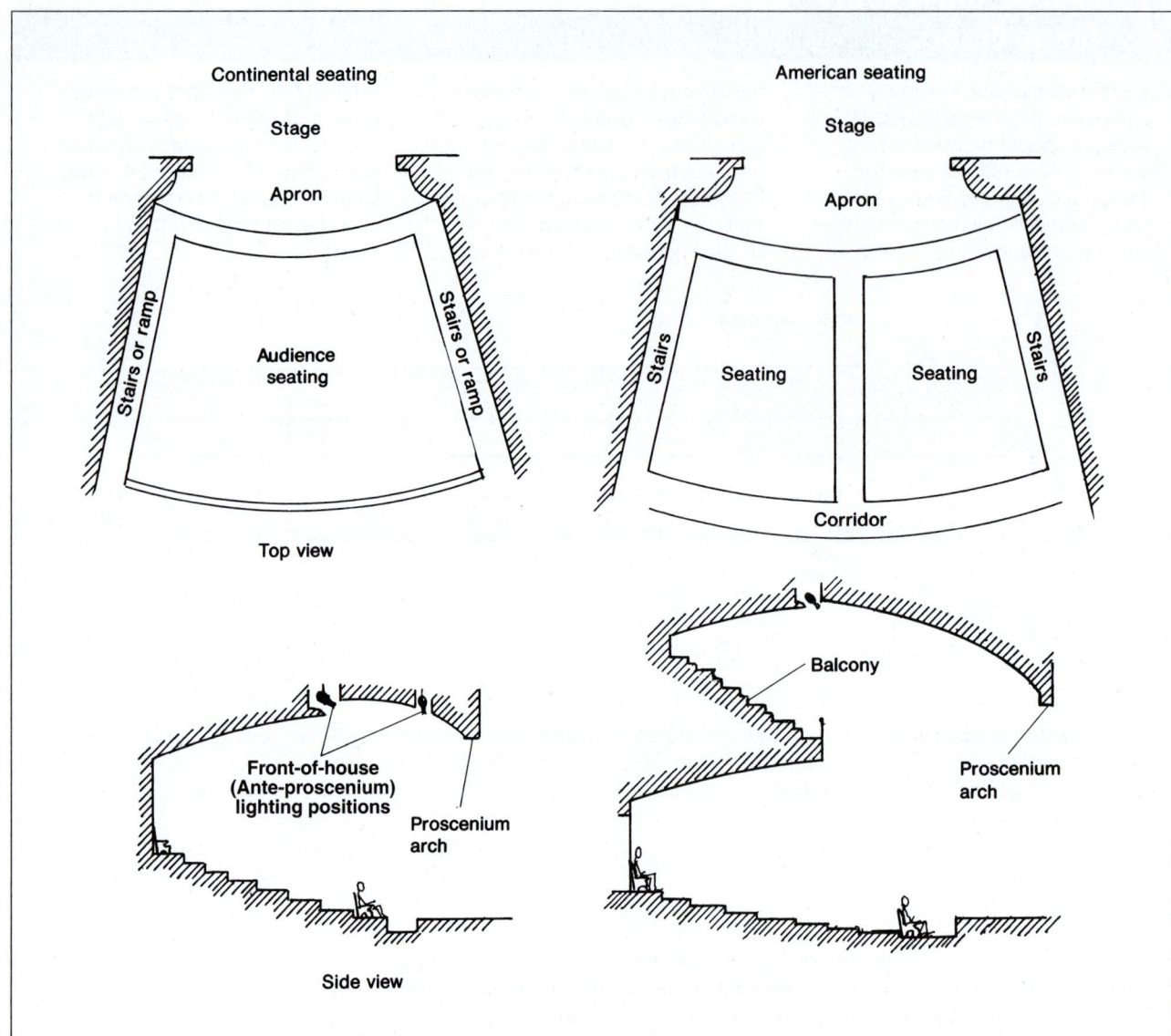

FIGURE 4.6
Types of seating configurations.

Proscenium Stage Equipment

Several interesting pieces of permanent stage equipment are frequently associated with proscenium theatres.

Traps   Many theatres have traps cut into the stage floor. These removable sections provide access to the space beneath the stage (see Figure 4.7). These holes can be filled with stairs, an elevator, a slide, or they can be left open, depending on the desired visual and physical effect. Ideally, the majority of a stage floor will be trapped. If only a few traps have been installed, Murphy's Law indicates that they will almost always be in the wrong place. Although traps are more frequently found in proscenium theatres, there is nothing to prevent this useful piece of equipment from being installed on either thrust or arena stages.

Auditorium Acoustics

Many contemporary performance spaces have been designed to house productions of dramas, musicals, operas, and orchestral music. A significant challenge in the design of these multipurpose theatres is the differing acoustical requirements of their various tenants. Orchestral music requires a long reverberation time (the amount of time it takes a sound to fade to inaudibility). A much shorter reverberation time is needed for spoken words to be heard and understood. To solve this challenge, many theatres designed in the past fifty years have adjustable acoustical panels on the walls and ceilings of the auditoriums. The reverberation time of the auditorium can be changed by adjusting the angle and the reflective quality of these panels.

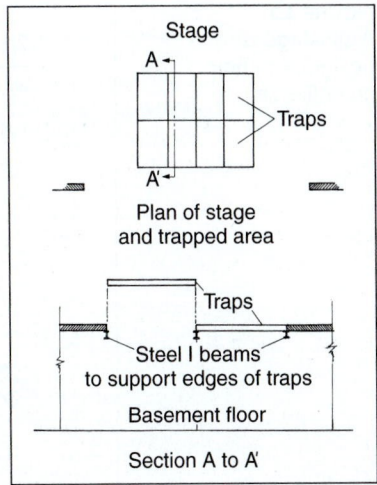

FIGURE 4.7
Stage traps provide access to the area beneath the stage.

Revolve   The revolve, also called a turntable or revolving stage, provides a visually interesting and efficient manner of shifting scenery (see Figure 4.8). Some theatres have revolves built into the stage floor. Depending on the size of the revolve, part or all of a multiset design can be fit onto it and rotated to bring other scenic elements into view.

Slipstage   The slipstage is a huge stage **wagon** large enough to cover the full width of the proscenium arch (see Figure 4.9). When not in use, the slipstage is stored in one of the wings. Entire sets can be mounted on the slipstage. When needed, it is simply rolled onto the stage.

Revolves and slipstages are permanent features of a theatre's stage. Smaller, temporary versions can be constructed to meet the needs of individual productions. Construction techniques for making these smaller versions are discussed in Chapter 11, "Scenic Production Techniques."

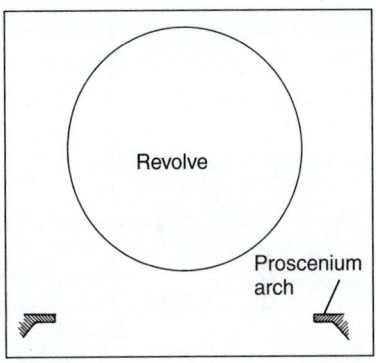

FIGURE 4.8
A revolving stage is sometimes built into the stage floor.

Fly Loft

The area directly over the stage is called the fly loft (see Figure 4.10). The fly loft, also referred to as "the flies," is usually quite tall, minimally two and a half times the height of the proscenium arch, to allow the scenery to be raised out of sight of the audience. The **grid,** or gridiron, is located just below the roof of the fly loft. It serves as a platform to hold some of the equipment used to **fly** scenery, as well as providing the primary support for the weight of the scenery and curtains being flown.

Fly Systems

Several systems are used to fly scenery. The two primary methods, the spot line and counterweight systems, both work on the same operating principle: counterbalancing.

Single (or Spot) Line Hemp Rigging   The oldest and simplest method of flying consists of the object to be flown, rope, two pulleys (or blocks), a place to tie off the rope to, and (optionally) sandbags to counterbalance the weight of the load.

wagon: A rigid platform supported with casters; used to move set pieces on the stage.

grid: A network of steel I beams supporting elements of the system used to raise and lower scenery.

fly: To raise an object or person above the stage floor with ropes or cables.

FIGURE 4.9
A slipstage is designed to hold an entire set.

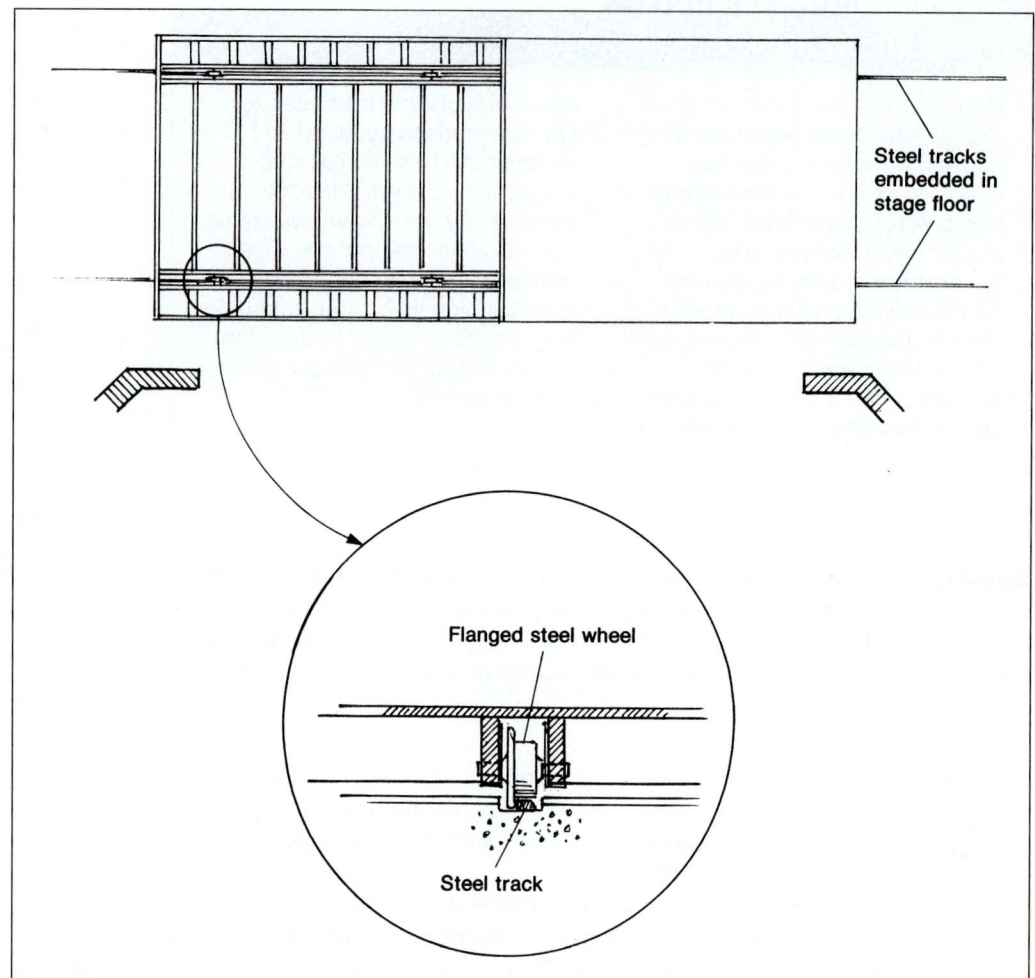

Steel tracks embedded in stage floor

Flanged steel wheel

Steel track

spot lines: Individual rigging lines used to raise/lower scenery. Typically located for a specific purpose. Normally, motorized and computer controlled.

loft blocks: A grooved pulley, mounted on top of the grid, used to change the direction in which a rope or cable travels.

head block: A multisheave block with two or more pulley wheels, used to change the direction of all the ropes or cables that support the batten.

gallery: The elevated walkway where the pin rail is located.

belaying pins: Vertical pipes extending above and below the pin rail. Used to secure the loose ends of spot lines.

pin rail: A horizontal pipe or rail studded with belaying pins; the ropes of the spot line system are wrapped around the belaying pins to hold the batten at a specific height.

cable picks: The attachment point for a bundle of (typically) electrical or sound cables to be suspended above the stage or auditorium.

In a **spot line** system, the rope — traditionally manila, but most theatres now use synthetic rope* — is tied to the load and then run up to the grid and over a **loft block** to the **head block** and down to a **gallery** or the stage floor, at which point it is tied off, as shown in Figure 4.11.

Typically, spot lines are tied off to **belaying pins** on the **pin rail**. For loads that are too heavy for a stage hand to comfortably control, sandbags can be added to the hauling end of the line.

Single-line setups are incredibly flexible. In many venues, loft blocks — also called spot blocks — and head blocks can be placed anywhere they are needed on the grid, making it easy to pick up scenery or **cable picks** for lighting or sound rigs.

Because spot line systems are essentially installed new each time they're needed, each time they're moved extra care must be taken to ensure the new installation is safe. Installation of spot line systems should be undertaken only by those with knowledge and experience in their safe installation.

---

* See Chapter 10, "Tools and Materials," for a discussion of the advantages of synthetic over manilla rope.

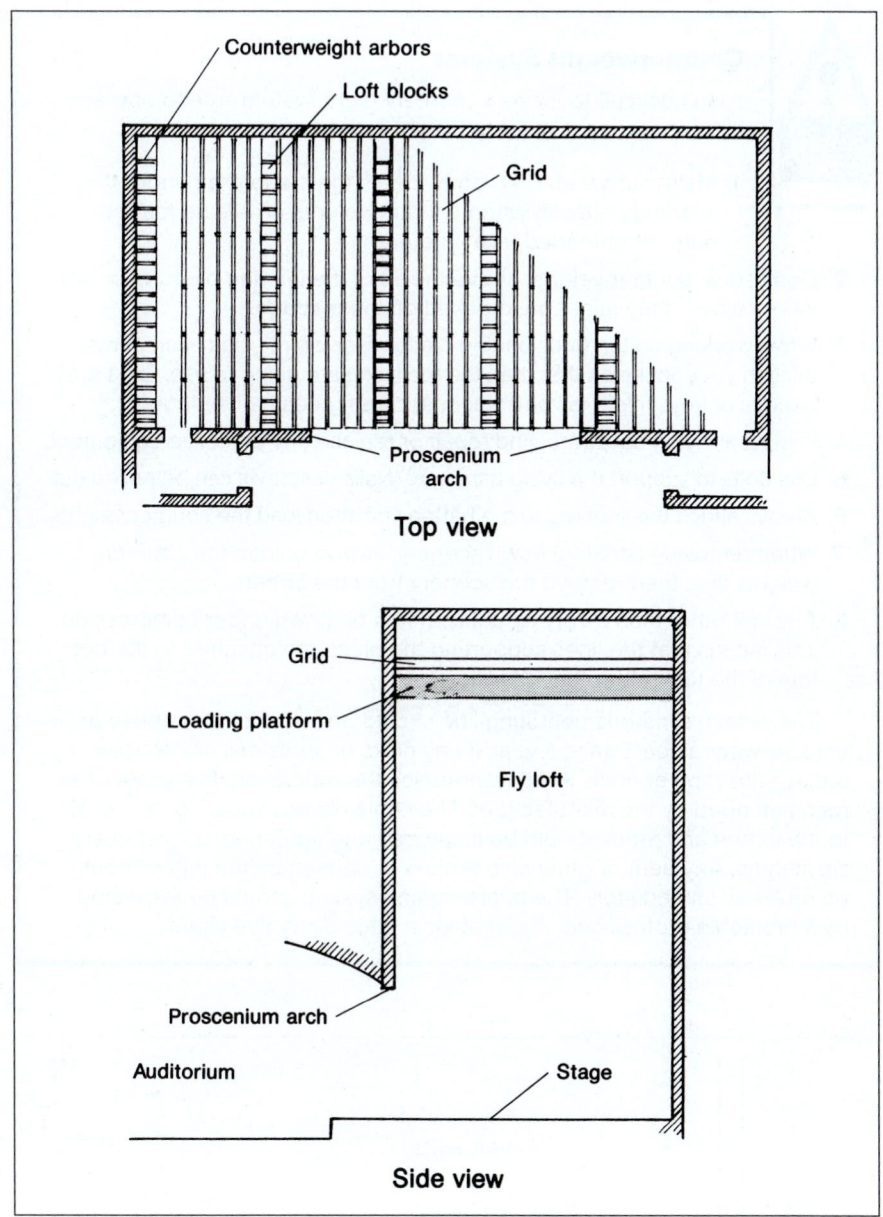

Counterweight arbors

Loft blocks

Grid

Proscenium arch

Top view

Grid

Loading platform

Fly loft

Proscenium arch

Auditorium

Stage

Side view

FIGURE 4.10
The fly loft and grid are integral parts of any flying system. Scenery and equipment can be flown for storage in the fly loft, while the grid supports the loft blocks.

Counterweight System   As shown in Figure 4.12, in a counterweight system, the **battens** are suspended from steel cables. The cables run from the batten up over loft blocks, to the head block, and then down where they are secured to the top of **counterweight arbor**, or carriage.

When the batten is lowered to the stage level, the arbor rises to the level of the **loading platform** just below the grid. This allows counterweights to be safely loaded onto the arbor – to balance the weight of the scenery – while the scenery is still resting safely on the stage.

The system is controlled by an operating line of typically ¾-inch parallel-core polyester rope approved for use as a counterweight system operating line rope. The operating line is attached to the top of the arbor, runs over a head block, down through a rope lock to a tension pulley, and then back to the bottom of the counterweight arbor. To lower the batten, you pull down on the part of the line closest to you. To raise the batten, you pull down on the offstage part

batten: A metal pipe (generally 1¼ to 1½ inches in diameter) from which are suspended scenery and lighting instruments.

counterweight arbor: A metal cradle that holds the counterbalancing weights used in a counterweight flying system.

loading platform: A walkway, suspended just below the grid, where counterweights are loaded onto the arbor.

Counterweight Systems

It isn't difficult to make a counterweight system safe to operate. A few basic rules need to be observed.

1. Make sure that everybody clears the stage area under the loading platform when counterweights are being loaded onto, or unloaded from, the arbor.

2. Don't stack counterweights above the lip of the loading platform or anywhere where they might be knocked off the platform.

3. When working on the grid, loading platform, or pin rail, don't carry anything in your pockets other than the tools you are going to use. Extra tools, pencils, or keys might fall on someone, causing death or serious injury.

4. Inspect all flying hardware, and repair or replace *any* defective equipment.

5. Use bolts to support the flying hardware. Nails or screws can be pulled out.

6. Always attach the scenery to the batten first, then load the counterweights.

7. When removing (striking) flown scenery, always unload the counterweights first, then remove the scenery from the batten.

8. Any unit other than a very light flat should be flown under compression. This means that the lines supporting the piece are attached to the bottom of the unit rather than the top.

The ¾-inch synthetic operating line should be inspected for abuse or unusual wear at least once a year. If any nicks or abrasions are noticed, replace the rope at once. Routinely replace the rope every five years or as recommended by the manufacturer. The cable clamps securing the cable to the batten and arbor should be inspected and tightened at least every six months. Any bent or otherwise broken or abused batten pipes should be replaced immediately. The entire rigging system should be inspected by a reputable professional rigger at least once every five years.

FIGURE 4.11
A single or spot line.

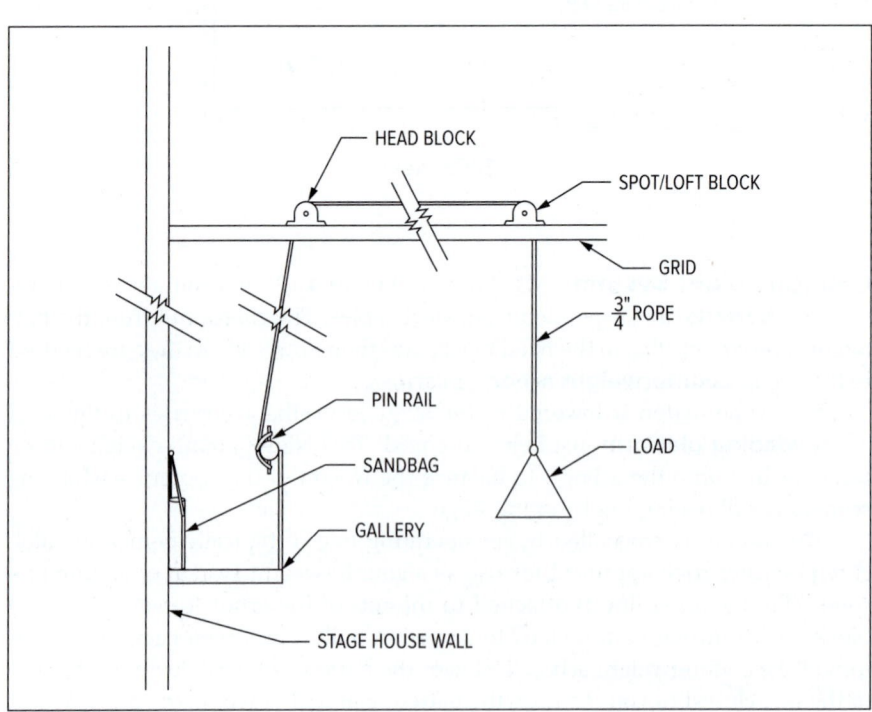

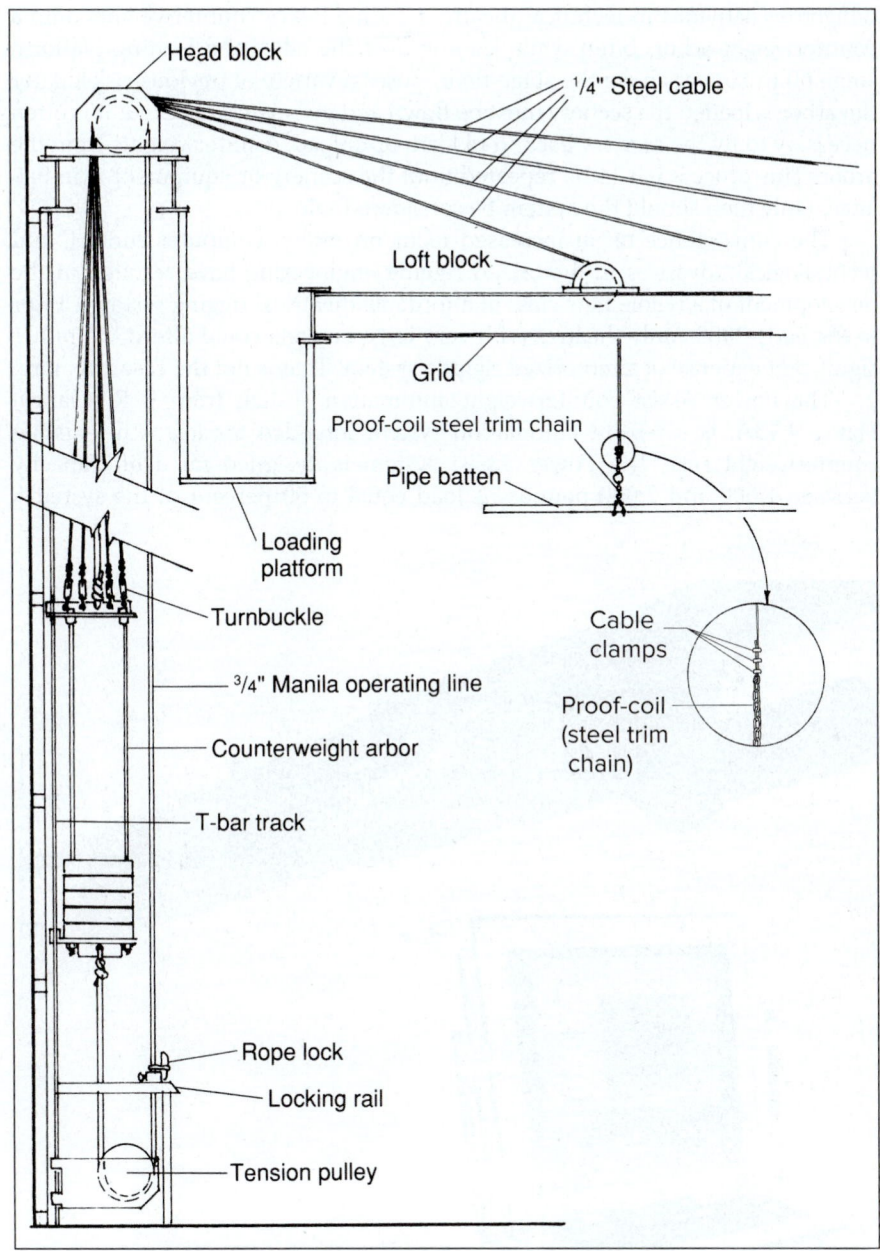

FIGURE 4.12
A counterweight system.

of the line. The **locking rail** is located on the stage floor against the stage-house wall. Although this arrangement is convenient, it does take up floor space that could be used for other purposes.

In theatres with limited offstage space, the use of a multiple-speed counterweight system solves the problem by raising the locking rail off the stage floor. This type of system creates a mechanical advantage (2 to 1) that allows the batten to move twice as far as the counterweight arbor. The drawback to this system is that twice as much weight must be loaded onto the arbor to balance the weight of the scenery.

Motorized Flying Systems   The process of flying and balancing scenery or stage equipment with a counterweight system is one of the more inherently

locking rail: A rail that holds the rope locks for each counterweight set.

dangerous activities in technical theatre. Loading heavy counterweights onto a counterweight arbor, often while leaning over the edge of a loading platform some 60 to 80 feet above the stage floor, poses a variety of obvious risks. After the arbor is loaded the scenery must be flown and its balance checked. It is often necessary to fly the scenery back in to load, or unload, counterweights from the arbor. This process has to be repeated until the scenery or equipment is in balance. Only then should the system be considered safe.

The convergence of an increased focus on safety, computer control, and technological advances in motorized rigging engineering have resulted in the development of a whole new class of affordable theatrical rigging systems. Prior to the early 2000s only theatres with very large budgets could afford the rather significant expense of a motorized rigging system. That is not the case anymore.

The Power Assist counterweight automation system from J. R. Clancy, Figure 4.13A, is a retrofit automation system intended for use with existing counterweight sets. The Power Assist system is designed for a lift capacity between 1,000 and 2,000 pounds. A load equal to 50 percent of the system's

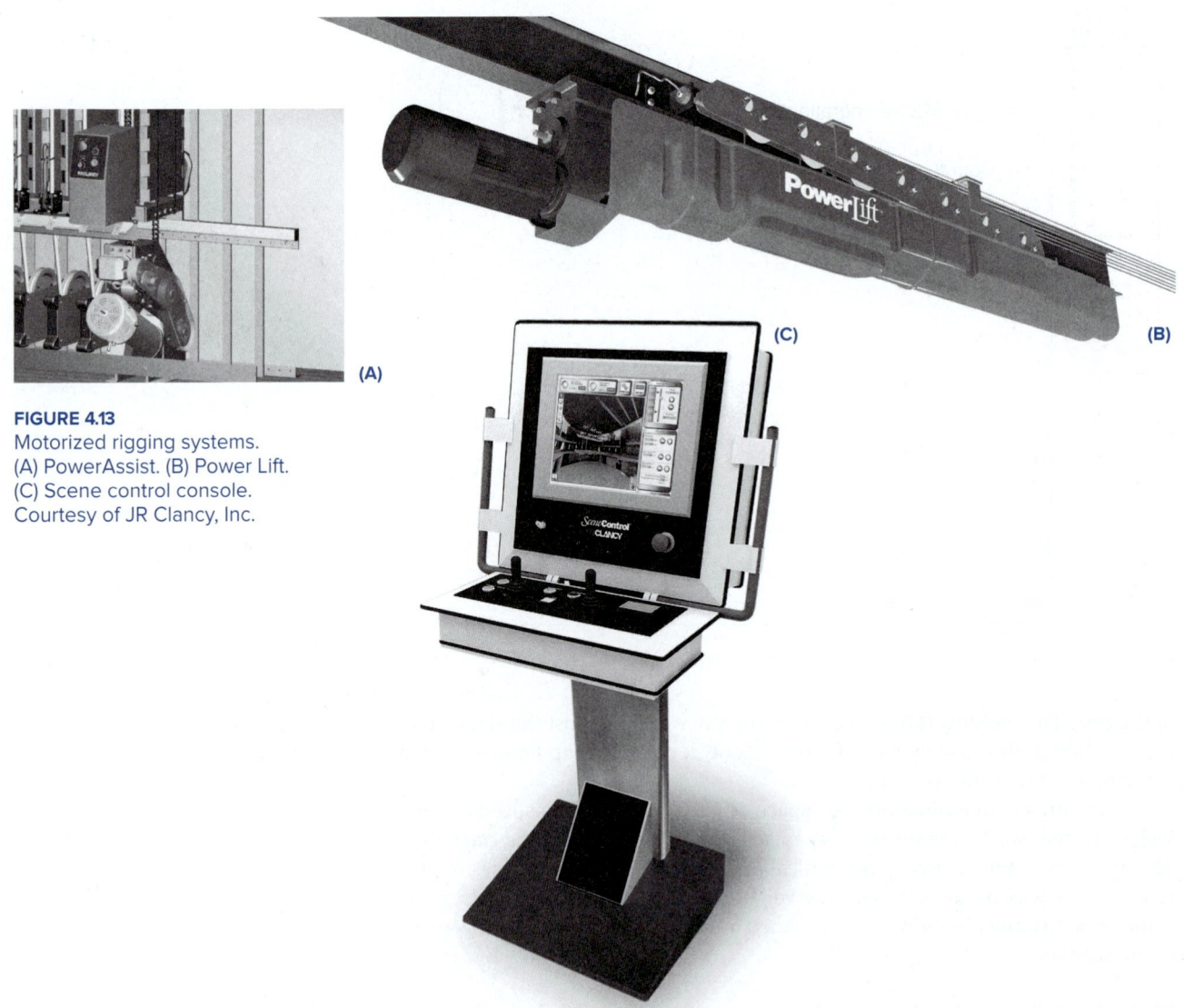

FIGURE 4.13
Motorized rigging systems.
(A) PowerAssist. (B) Power Lift.
(C) Scene control console.
Courtesy of JR Clancy, Inc.

rated capacity is placed on the existing arbor during the installation process. That load is not changed regardless of how much, or how little, weight is placed on the batten. The system's electric winch is strong enough to safely operate the system with any batten weight from 0 to 100 percent of the system's rated capacity. The Power Assist is available in either fixed- or variable-speed configurations.

The Power Lift system, also from J. R. Clancy, Figure 4.13B, is a motorized rigging system designed for new installations or as a replacement for an existing counterweight system. Because the Power Lift system does not use a counterweight arbor, and because the lift unit is relatively compact, it can be hung on a theatre's wall as well as in the traditional "over stage" location. In this system, the steel cables that support the batten are attached to a moving drum. As the drum turns, cable is either taken up or paid out, which raises or lowers the batten. The drum is driven by an electric motor through a transmission/gear box. Interestingly, because the system does not require a counterweight arbor nor its associated wall-mounted steel track and loading platform, the cost of this motorized system is very competitive with the cost of a traditional counterweight system.

Motorized rigging systems are typically controlled in two ways. The retrofit units, which are located at the counterweight locking rail, are readily available to an operator. These units normally have relevant control buttons on the units themselves. The remotely located systems — the ones that hang on the wall or above the grid — have to be remotely controlled. There are a variety of control consoles available. Some are designed to work with a few fixed-speed winches. Others, such as J. R. Clancy's Scene Control console, illustrated in Figure 4.13C, are used to control the variable speed motorized rigging systems typically installed in theatres with active production programs. These consoles record and playback all rigging movements for each motorized set in the system, which facilitates the synchronized movement of multiple battens, each with its own speed as well as its own starting and ending times.

Motorized rigging systems are becoming the new standard for flying scenery and equipment in the theatre. They are a safer alternative to existing counterweight systems and they offer exact, and repeatable, control with their computer control consoles.

Stage Drapes

The proscenium stage uses more types of stage drapery than does either the thrust or arena stage. Although they have specific functions, all stage drapes are designed to **mask** backstage areas from the spectators. Stage drapes are usually made of black, light-absorbing material such as heavyweight velour or similar material (commando cloth, duvetyn, rep). Typical hanging positions for the various types of stage drape are shown in Figure 4.14.

Grand Drape   The purpose of the grand drape (also known as the main curtain, main drape, or grand rag) is to cover the proscenium opening. In theatres that have a fly loft, the grand drape, which is usually made from heavyweight velour, can normally be flown or **traveled.**

Grand Valance   The grand valance is a wide, relatively short drape — typically 8 to 12 feet high — made of the same material as the grand drape. Hung just downstage of the grand drape, it is used to mask the equipment and scenery that are flown immediately upstage of the proscenium.

mask: To block the audience's view — generally, of backstage equipment and space.

travel: To move horizontally relative to the stage floor, as with a drape that opens in the middle and is pulled to the sides.

FIGURE 4.14
Standard hanging positions for
stage draperies.

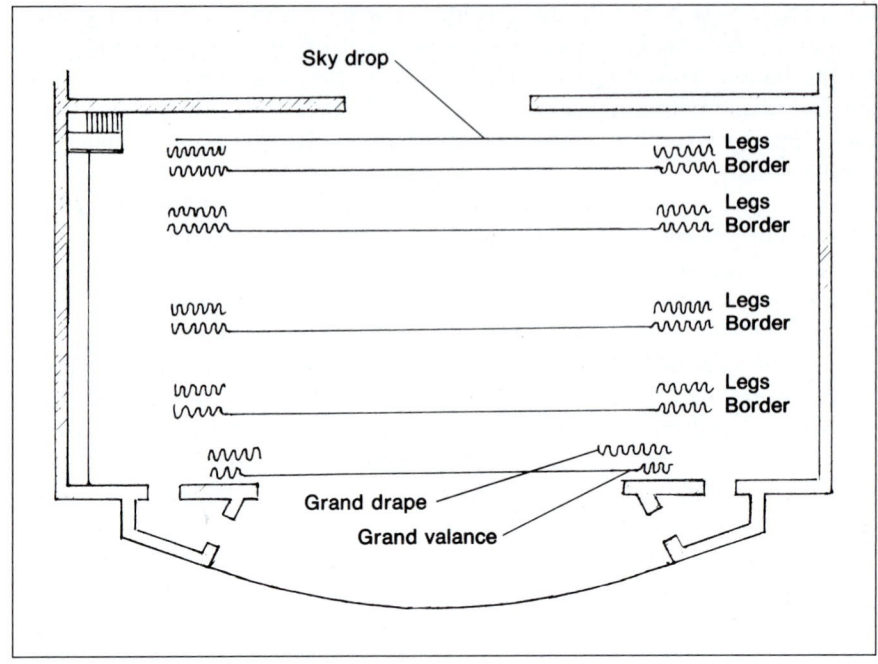

FIGURE 4.14
Standard hanging positions for
stage draperies.

False Proscenium   The false proscenium (Figure 4.15) is located immediately upstage of the grand drape and grand valance. It is normally mounted on a rigid framework. The **flat** structures of both the **hard teaser** and **tormentors** are usually covered with thin (⅛-inch to ³⁄₁₆-inch) plywood, which is then covered with black velour or some similar type of black, light-absorbing material. The primary purpose of the "false pro" is to provide masking. The tormentors mask the sides of the stage, and the hard teaser provides primary masking for the flies. Because both the tormentors and hard teaser are movable, they can also be used to shrink the apparent size of the proscenium opening.

A **show portal** (Figure 4.16) is a false proscenium designed for a specific production. In addition to providing the masking of a false proscenium, a show portal adds a visual element appropriate to that specific production.

Legs and Borders   Legs are narrow, vertical stage drapes used to mask the sides of the stage upstage of the proscenium arch. They are generally made of the same light-absorbing material as other stage drapes.

Borders, also called teasers, are short, wide, horizontal draperies, normally 4 to 10 feet tall, used to mask the flies.

Legs and borders usually have long strings, called ties, either sewn to the jute tape at the top of the drape or slipped through brass **grommets,** which are fixed to the jute tape so that they can be tied to a supporting batten. Ties are usually made from 36-inch pieces of ½-inch-wide cotton tape, although 36-inch shoestrings work very well.

Borders are normally used in conjunction with a set of legs (two legs) to provide a complete framework of masking for the stage, as shown in Figure 4.17. If the theatre is equipped with a counterweight system, borders and legs are rarely hung on the same batten, because the trim height of the borders needs to be variable, whereas the legs should be trimmed so that the lower hem barely brushes the stage floor. Borders are generally hung on the batten immediately downstage of the batten holding the legs. If the theatre doesn't have a counterweight or

flat: A framework, normally made of wood or metal; frequently covered with fabric or thin plywood, although a variety of other covering materials may be used.

hard teaser: The horizontal element of the false proscenium; usually hung from a counterweighted batten so that its height can easily be adjusted.

tormentor: The vertical flats that form the side elements of the false proscenium.

show portal: A false proscenium that visually supports the style and color palette of a particular production.

grommet: A circular metal eyelet used to reinforce holes in fabric.

Mechanical Advantage: Block and Tackle

Certain mechanical systems can provide a power-multiplying effect known as mechanical advantage. A system with a mechanical advantage of 2 to 1 (2:1) allows you to use the same force to move two times the weight compared to a system with no mechanical advantage.

The single whip illustrated in the first figure doesn't create any mechanical advantage, because it is just changing the direction of pull on the operating line. If, however, one end of the rope is attached to a strong beam, as shown in the second figure, and the pulley is attached to the weight, then pulling *up* on the rope would create a 2:1. This system is called a running block.

It is fairly easy to determine the mechanical advantage of any tackle-rigging configuration. Simply count the number of lines that pass through the block. Don't count the operating line if it is hanging down from the last pass through the block (the housing for the pulley wheels). The total number of lines will be equal to the mechanical advantage for that particular block-and-tackle system. Friction reduces the actual efficiency of any block-and-tackle arrangement by 10 percent for each pulley sheave in the system.

With block and tackle you create increased lifting power, but you do so by losing speed. For example, with a double whip (2:1 mechanical advantage), the load moves half the distance that the operating line travels, whereas the watch tackle (3:1 mechanical advantage) moves the load one-third the distance that the operating line travels.

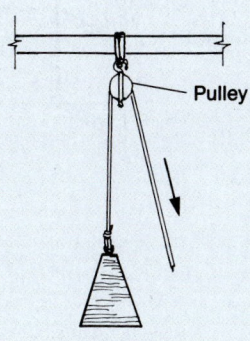

Single whip
(no mechanical advantage)

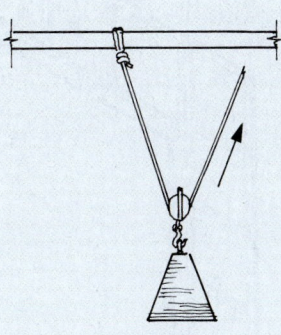

Running block
(2:1 mechanical advantage)

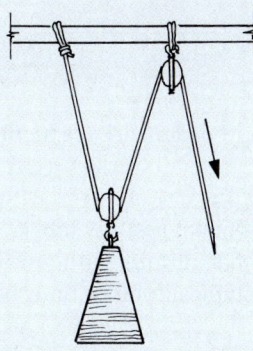

Double whip
(2:1 mechanical advantage)

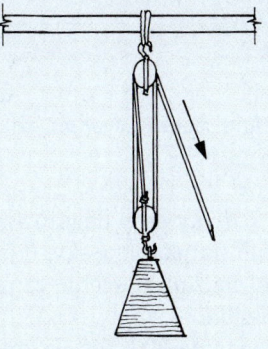

Watch tackle
(3:1 mechanical advantage)

Four common tackle rigs.

FIGURE 4.15
A false proscenium.

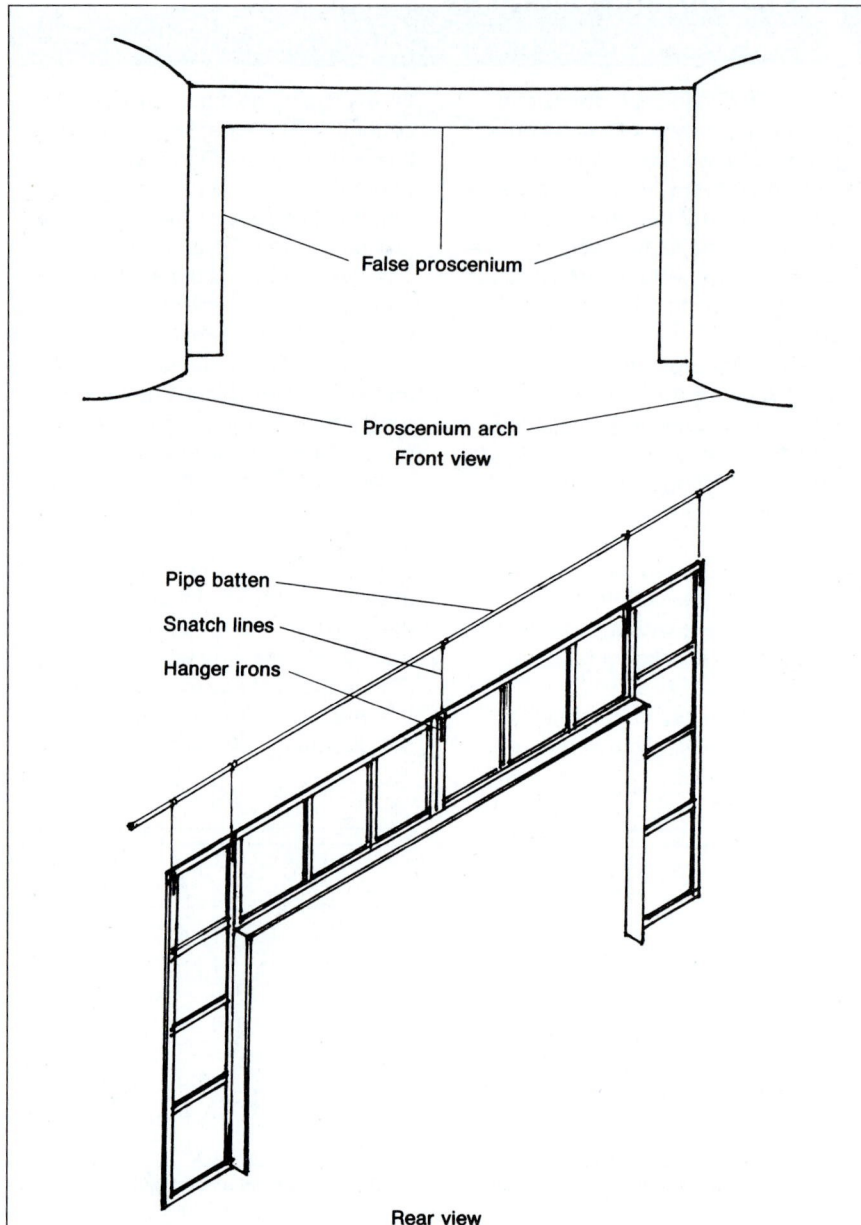

FIGURE 4.16
A show portal.

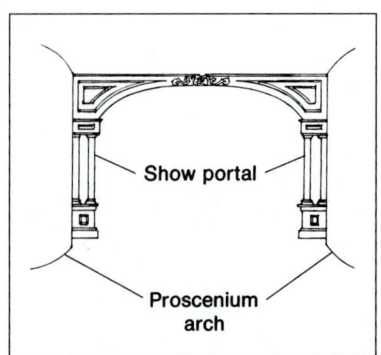

adjustable height rigging system, the legs and borders are frequently hung on the same batten.

Sky Drop   The sky drop (Figure 4.18), also known as a sky tab, is, as its name implies, used to simulate the sky. It is a large, flat curtain, without fullness, normally made of muslin or scenic canvas. It is typically hung on a batten as far upstage as possible.

Prior to the mid-1900s the sky drop was traditionally dyed a uniform blue to help simulate the color of the sky. Contemporary sky drops are normally made from unbleached muslin, which is an off-white color. This neutral color allows the lighting or projection designer to create a sky color that is appropriate to the mood and concept of the production.

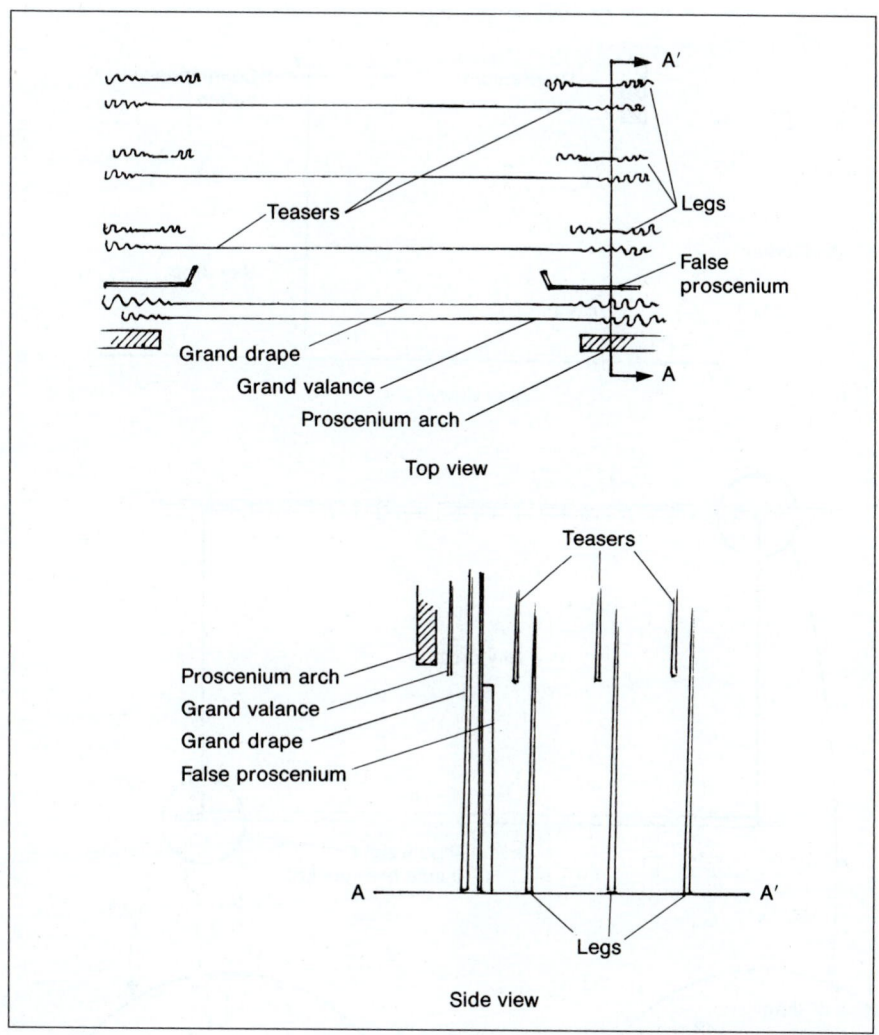

FIGURE 4.17
Hanging positions for legs and teasers.

Cyclorama The cyclorama, or "cyc" (Figure 4.19), is an expansion on the concept of the sky drop. Although the sky drop (Figure 4.19A) works very well for productions that require only a small patch of sky, it doesn't surround the set with the illusion of vast expanses of open sky. Historically, when plays began making this type of scenic demand, technicians responded by hanging two more sky drops, or tabs, at almost right angles to the original curtain to provide a wraparound expanse of sky, as shown in Figure 4.19B. Where the drops met, they were overlapped to prevent gaps in the smooth expanse of simulated sky.

The **fly cyc** (Figure 4.19C) is made from one unbroken expanse of cloth. It is hung on a counterweighted pipe located outside the other counterweighted battens to reduce any possible interference between the two systems.

Sometimes sharkstooth **scrims** are used in conjunction with both sky drops and cycloramas. Sharkstooth scrim is a knit fabric that is actually composed of more open spaces than thread. Because of this structure, the fabric possesses some very interesting properties. When light is projected onto the front of sharkstooth scrim, it is reflected back toward the viewer, and the fabric appears to be opaque. When the front light is turned off and objects behind the scrim are lit, the sharkstooth scrim becomes transparent, and the objects in back of it are clearly visible. When those same objects are lit, and light also strikes the

fly cyc: A single drop, hung on a U-shaped pipe, that surrounds the stage on three sides.

scrim: A drop made from translucent or transparent material.

FIGURE 4.18
A sky drop.

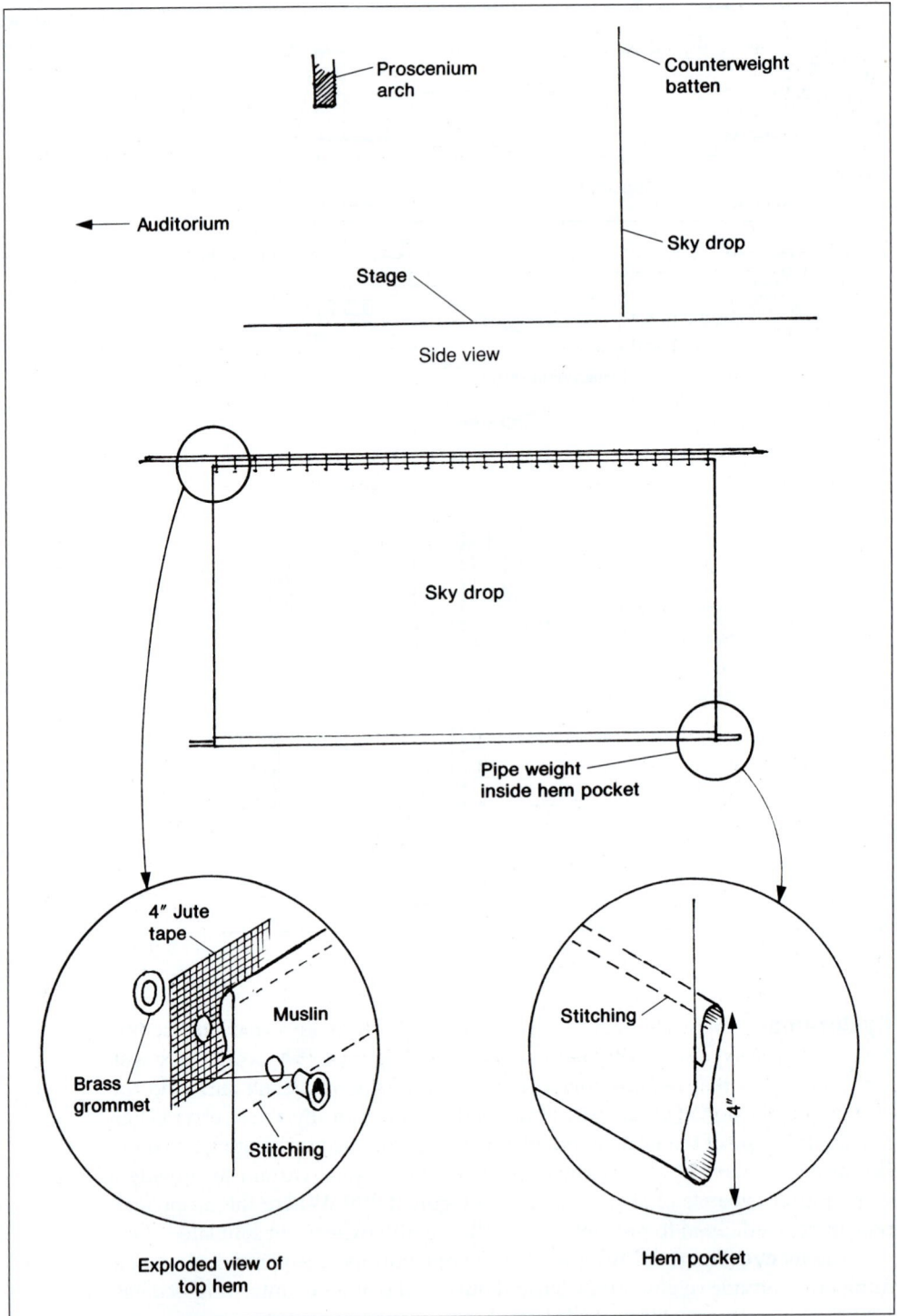

scrim, it becomes translucent, and the objects, while still visible, are hazy and less distinct.

A white scrim hung in front of the cyc helps smooth out any wrinkles, dirty spots, and imperfections on the cyc. If the scrim is hung on a batten a foot or two downstage of the cyc, additional lights can be focused onto the scrim to provide very interesting, and sometimes spectacular, multilayer cyclorama lighting.

Fire Protection

Over the years, fire has destroyed more theatres than any other cause. The traditional mainstay of fire safety for the proscenium stage has been the fireproof curtain. This curtain is located immediately upstage of the proscenium arch. Its purpose is not to put out the fire but to contain it. When a fire starts, the fireproof curtain is lowered, effectively isolating the auditorium from the stage. Although research has shown that inhalation of asbestos fibers is hazardous, most proscenium theatres built before 1965 frequently still have an asbestos curtain as their primary line of fire safety. Some theatre owners have replaced their asbestos curtains with either sprinkler systems or curtains made of fire-retardant synthetic materials.

Nonproscenium-stage theatres, and newer proscenium theatres, are now being protected by sprinkler systems. These systems flood the stage, wings, and auditorium with a heavy mist of water in the event of a fire. They are much more effective than the fireproof curtain.

Regardless of the primary method of fire protection, portable fire extinguishers should be located in easily accessible and clearly identified locations in all shops, on the stage, and in the control booths.

A final suggestion: Always check your local fire codes. Become familiar with them. Know them. Follow them.

A black sharkstooth scrim can also be used to enhance the sky drop or cyc lighting. Used in the same manner as the white scrim, it improves aerial perspective by reducing the intensity and saturation of objects that are lit behind it.

A great deal of stage-lighting equipment could be considered a part of the permanent stage equipment. It will be discussed in Chapter 16, "Lighting Production."

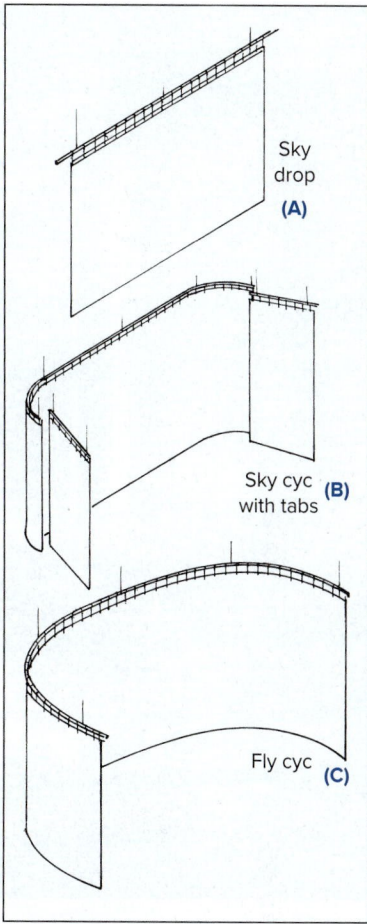

FIGURE 4.19
A sky drop and two types of cycloramas.

Thrust Stage

As we saw in the last chapter, the thrust stage (see Figure 4.20) isn't a new development. Medieval audiences gathered on three sides of the pageant wagons and platform stages to watch passion plays, and research indicates that Shakespeare's Globe Theatre also had a thrust stage. The thrust stage was rediscovered by directors who wanted to move the action of the play out of what they felt were the artificial and limiting confines of the proscenium stage. For a variety of reasons, the mid–twentieth century saw the birth of a large number of thrust-stage theatres in the United States.

The stage of the thrust theatre projects into, and is surrounded on three sides by, the audience, so tall flats, drops, and vertical masking cannot be used where they would interfere with the spectators' view of the stage (see Figure 4.21). But on the fourth, or upstage, side of the stage, drops and flats can be placed to help describe the play's location. Entrances are frequently made through openings in the upstage wall, but the house is also used for this purpose.

The **lighting grid** in a thrust theatre is usually suspended over the entire stage and auditorium space, so instruments can be hung wherever necessary to effectively light the playing area. Lighting grids vary in complexity from designs that hide the lighting instruments from the spectators' view to simple pipe grids from which the lights are hung in full view, as shown in Figure 4.22.

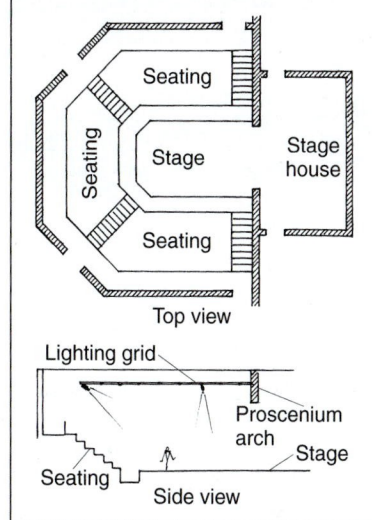

FIGURE 4.20
A typical thrust-stage arrangement.

lighting grid: A network of pipes from which lighting instruments are hung.

FIGURE 4.21
Thrust theatre. The Festival Theatre at the Stratford Festival. Photography by Terry Manzo. Courtesy of the Stratford Festival of Canada.

hanging position: A location where lighting instruments are placed.

dead hang: To suspend without means of raising or lowering.

ratchet winch: A device, used for hoisting, with a crank attached to a drum; one end of a rope or cable is attached to the drum, the other end to the load; turning the crank moves the load; a ratchet gear prevents the drum from spinning backward.

Access to the simpler pipe grids is usually from a rolling ladder or scaffold placed on the stage. More complex grids frequently have access from above to a series of walkways or catwalks suspended adjacent to the pipes to allow the electricians relatively easy access to the lighting instruments.

A number of other creative solutions to grid access have been developed. One of the more ingenious, and effective, is the tension-mesh grid. This can be thought of as a transparent working platform hung underneath the grid. Strung at a convenient working height beneath the grid, the tension-mesh grid is an interwoven series of $1/8$-inch aircraft cables attached, under tension, to the sides of the grid or building. The weave of the cables is small enough so electricians can walk on it without falling through, but the cable diameter is small enough that they don't interfere with the light from the instruments. In addition to the grid, there are usually some additional **hanging positions** above the house, either open pipes or some type of semiconcealed location.

Some thrust theatres retain a vestigial proscenium arch on the upstage wall as well as a small backstage area. Although battens are frequently **dead hung** above this backstage space, some theatres have installed **ratchet winches,** spot lines, or counterweight sets so the battens can be raised and lowered.

The lighting and sound positions are generally located at the back of the house directly facing the stage, although nothing stronger than tradition prevents them from being placed at any location in the auditorium that provides

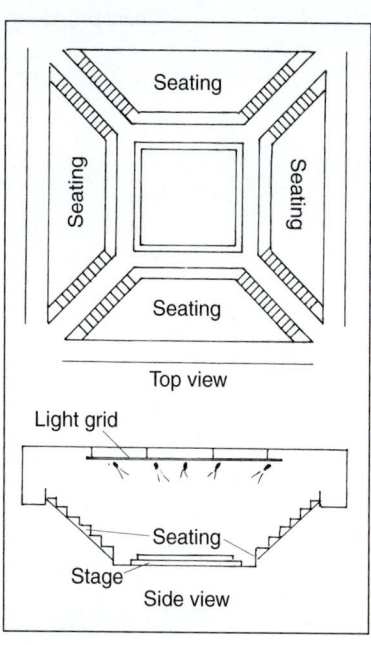

FIGURE 4.22
Lighting grids for thrust theatres are frequently exposed pipe grids. The Tom Patterson Theatre at the Stratford Festival. Courtesy of the Stratford Shakespeare Festival, Canada.

an unobstructed view of the stage. Again, as in the proscenium theatre, and for the same reasons, the sound operator normally runs the mixing console from a position in the house.

 ## Arena Stage

The arena stage (Figure 4.23), also called theatre-in-the-round, is another development in an intimate actor-audience theatre. The audience surrounds the stage and is typically much closer to the action of the play than in either the proscenium or thrust theatres (see Figure 4.24).

The scenery used on an arena stage is extremely minimal. Because the audience surrounds the stage, designing for the arena theatre provides a challenge to all the designers. Anything used on an arena stage — sets, costumes, makeup, props — must be meticulously detailed because the audience sits almost on top of the stage and can see every construction detail.

As in the thrust stage theatre, the space above the arena stage typically has a lighting grid rather than a fly loft. The lighting grid generally covers both the stage and auditorium.

FIGURE 4.23
A typical arena theatre configuration.

FIGURE 4.24
Arena Theatre, the interior of the 827-seat Arena Stage in Washington, D.C. (http://reveryarchitecture.com/ contact). Courtesy Arena Stage at the Mead Center for American Theater.

The stage manager and the lighting and sound operators need to have a clear view of the stage. Many arena theatres have an elevated deck running around the perimeter of the auditorium to provide these people with a variety of potential work locations. Some arena theatres have a traditional lighting booth and sound-control location rather than flexible work stations.

Black Box Theatres

The flexible staging of black box theatres — so named because they are usually painted black and have a simple rectangular shape — encourages, and demands, ingenuity from the production design team. These design-it-yourself performance spaces are a direct result of a number of experimental theatre movements that sought to break down the visual and psychological barriers created by the proscenium stage.

In black box theatres the seating is generally located on movable bleacherlike modules that can be arranged in any number of ways around the playing space. Although the space can be set up in traditional proscenium, thrust, or arena configurations, it can also be aligned into excitingly different staging arrangements that support the production concept for particular productions. This type of theatre is fun to work in, and every production creates a challenge to the ingenuity of the production design team.

The black box theatre was developed partially as a reaction against the artistic confines of more formal types of stage space. Consequently, there isn't a great deal of specific stage equipment associated with it. However, there is normally a grid, similar to that of the arena theatre, located above the stage and auditorium space, and there is usually a variety of additional hanging locations for both lighting and sound equipment, as well as flexible working locations for both the light and sound operators.

"Found" Theatre Spaces

Found theatre spaces lend a great deal of credence to the statement that all theatre needs is "two boards and a passion." These theatres are housed in structures that were originally designed for some other purpose. Almost every conceivable type of space has been, or could be, converted for use as a theatre. In Tucson, Arizona, between 1970 and 1985 a supermarket, movie house, lumberyard, feed store, office building, and restaurant were converted into theatres. The found theatre space conversions experienced in Tucson were not unique. The Lafayette Square Theatre in New York City houses five theatres in what used to be a library. The only criteria for conversion seem to be sufficient square footage to house a stage and its audience and nearby parking or public transportation.

Found theatre spaces are frequently converted into black box theatres, but a number of converting companies have opted for the more traditional arena or thrust stage configurations (see Figure 4.25). For some producing groups, the appeal of the converted space lies in the intimacy of the audience-actor relationship that is inherent in these generally small theatres. For others, the lower production costs of the smaller, more intimate theatre forms are an asset. For all of them, the fact that these spaces were considerably less expensive than building a new structure was a boon.

FIGURE 4.25
Converted theatre space. The stage/auditorium of the Yale Repertory Theatre, housed in a former church. Courtesy of Yale Repertory Theatre/Yale School of Drama.

Chapter 5

Style, Composition, and Design

Designers need to share information and ideas both verbally and visually. Chapter 2 introduced the verbal language of the designer — the questioning process and the dynamics of group discussion, which are vital to the interaction among members of the production design team. This chapter will introduce the other, equally important language of the designer — the visual language.

 ## Style and Stylization in Theatrical Design

What is style? In conversation we frequently refer to a particular "style" of clothing such as blue jeans or military uniforms. When we refer to a "style" of car, we typically use the word to differentiate between models with significantly different appearances, like sports cars and sedans. Narrowly defined, style refers to the compositional characteristics that define the appearance of an object or thing. Style can also be defined as a "reflection of the social and political history of the times, . . . that . . . are eventually reflected in the patterns and shifting artistic trends of the period."[1] Combining both these definitions provides a useful definition of style in theatrical design: a recognizable pattern of compositional elements that provides a distinctive reflection of the social and political history of the time. This definition can be used to identify particular compositional features that are reflective of a moment in history, such as the long, sweeping lines generally characteristic of women's clothing in the Late Gothic period (Figure 5.1) or the mechanistically based repetitive patterns of German expressionism.

 ## Production Style

Production style can be defined as the stylistic theme on which the world of the production is based: a recognizable pattern of visual and intellectual elements used to create the production environment for a particular play.

The identification of a particular production style, which derives in part from a careful and creative interpretation of the script, is the single most important step in the development of a play's production concept.

[1] Douglas A. Russell, *Stage Costume Design,* 2nd ed. (Englewood Cliffs, NJ; Prentice Hall, 1985), p. 170.

Production style: A manner of producing a play in which all production elements (costumes, scenery, lights, acting) adhere to a common set of artistic/philosophical characteristics (e.g., expressionism).

Design Styles and Design Periods

We often refer to specific design styles, such as romanticism or naturalism, and design periods, such as Elizabethan or Late Nineteenth Century. However neither styles nor periods exist within narrowly prescribed time frames. They are simply indicative of major stylistic elements common during a particular period of time. For example, romanticism did not stop on one day and naturalism begin the next. Naturalism began as a reaction against what its practitioners viewed as the stylistic excesses of romanticism. As more artists followed the stylistic leaders of the naturalistic movement, naturalism became the dominant artistic style. Similarly, realism began as a reaction against what some artists viewed as the rigid dictates of the naturalistic style. Again, a new style emerged and became dominant as another declined.

Stylization

It is difficult, and of no particular value, to attempt to create an absolutely accurate historical period or style on stage. The reasons are threefold: (1) expectations of the audience; (2) current stylistic influences; and (3) practical considerations. To illustrate those points, assume we're producing a hypothetical play set in 1820 England. If contemporary fashion, which to a great extent determines audience reaction, dictates that the hair styles of 1820 England were silly or funny looking, any costume designer would be ill-advised to insist on absolute historical accuracy of the hair design for the female romantic lead in the play. Why? Simply because the audience is supposed to like her. If her hair style seems ugly or silly, it will be difficult for the audience to empathize with the character. A modification of the design, based on the historical research, would be more appropriate. Likewise, it is frequently impossible to find historically accurate fabrics from which to make costumes. Similarly, it would be a bit bizarre to think that the walls of the set for the library scene in our play would have to be made with historically accurate materials or that the books on the library shelves would all have to have been published prior to 1820!

Instead of slavishly copying historical designs, designers usually stylize their designs. Stylization refers to the use of specific elements characteristic of a particular style or period to create the essence of that style or period. Designers typically let the degree of stylization communicate the level of reality to the audience. Minimally stylized costume, set, and furniture designs — designs that closely duplicate the line, mass, texture, and color of a particular style or period — are normally interpreted by the audience as historically accurate and realistic. As designs depart further from visual reality — exaggerate or simplify line, shape, mass, texture, and/or color — audience interpretation becomes harder to project. A wide variety of demographic data, such as cultural background and values, as well as the audience's level of theatrical experience, come into play. A theatrically sophisticated audience may think heavily stylized scenic and costume designs reinforce the psychological nature of a play. The same production may seem totally bizarre to a less theatrically experienced audience.

Literary Style and Theatrical Design

Literary style is another type of style that influences theatrical design. The style in which a script is written provides major clues for the designer. Verse drama has a majesty and sweep that simply isn't duplicated in prose. The verse drama's world frequently seems more noble, simply because the story is written in verse.

FIGURE 5.1

Long sweeping lines are a characteristic style of Late Gothic gowns.

FIGURE 5.6
The profile, or cutout line, affects visual meaning. *The Member of the Wedding*, scenic design by J. Michael Gillette. Courtesy J. Michael Gillette.

profile (silhouette): The outline of a form, which determines the form's quality and character.

Harmony

Harmony is the sense of blending and unity that is obtained when all elements of a design fit together to create an orderly, congruous whole. Harmony is achieved when a combination of design elements seem to naturally blend or flow together, avoiding discordant or incompatible contrasts.

Although harmony is primarily concerned with congruity, it doesn't require that all lines, forms, masses, values, and colors within a design be of one particular style, shape, or character. What it does mean is that those elements should be chosen to complement one another. For example, the **profile,** or **silhouette,** for the walls of the set of *The Member of the Wedding* (Figure 5.6) is actually composed of two basic lines. The more apparent is the slightly jagged silhouette of the short, vertical cuts. The second is the long, gentle sweep of the silhouette itself. The jagged line was chosen for two reasons, one aesthetic, the other logical. The jagged line is evocative of the emotional stress that is felt by Frankie, the play's main character. The more mundane reason for selecting this line is that the short, vertical breaks can be thought of as the ends of the clapboards that cover the outside of the house. The long, sweeping line was chosen to reinforce the romantic, nostalgic nature of the play.

Lest you think that harmony is a goal always to be sought, you need to realize that too much harmony can be monotonous, as when a motif, such as the harmony of angle and measure shown in Figure 5.7, is repeated too often. Boring harmony also happens when too many closely related colors are used in the same design.

A design might provide an accurate reflection of the mood and spirit of the play by being deliberately unharmonious.

FIGURE 5.7
Too much harmony can be monotonous.

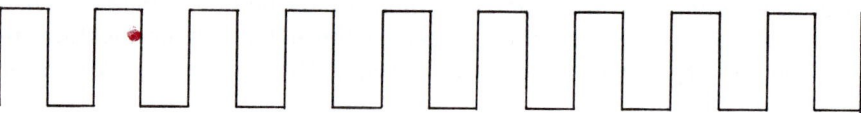

(A)

(B)

FIGURE 5.8
The use of an interesting silhouette can increase visual interest and connotative meaning in a scenic design. The curved lines of (A) create a more relaxed visual personality when compared with the more formal lines of (B). See text for details.

The degree of harmony to be pursued in the design depends on the designer's interpretation of the production concept.

Contrast

Contrast in composition can be defined as the juxtaposition of dissimilar elements. To be effective, contrast must work in opposition to the major, or dominant, visual theme in a composition. Too much contrast can destroy that visual theme just as too little (too much harmony) can be monotonous. The ideal is to create a composition that provides a balance of harmony and contrast reflective of the production style.

In scenic design, visual contrast frequently mirrors the psychological stress levels of the play — tragedies and plays with serious themes frequently have greater visual contrast than comedies do. In costume design, the personality of the character wearing the costume is a prime determinant of the amount of contrast used in an individual costume. As a general guideline, the costumes of flamboyant characters employ greater contrast than do those of their more retiring compatriots.

Manipulation of contrast affects meaning. Note the change in "personality" between the two versions of the scenic design shown in Figure 5.8. The curved cutout lines used in Figure 5.8A create a visual personality for the design by contrasting with the dominant vertical and horizontal lines of the "noncutout" design pictured in Figure 5.8B. The sensuous line makes the entire design seem more relaxed, less formal.

Variation

While too much harmony can create monotony, variation of the monotonous elements can introduce visual interest. A simple pattern repeated many times (Figure 5.9A) can be monotonous, but by varying the shape of every second or third object in the design (Figure 5.9B) visual interest in the whole design is heightened. Similar effects are achieved by varying any of the design elements (line, shape, texture, and so forth) in a repetitive pattern, as shown in Figures 5.9C and 5.9D.

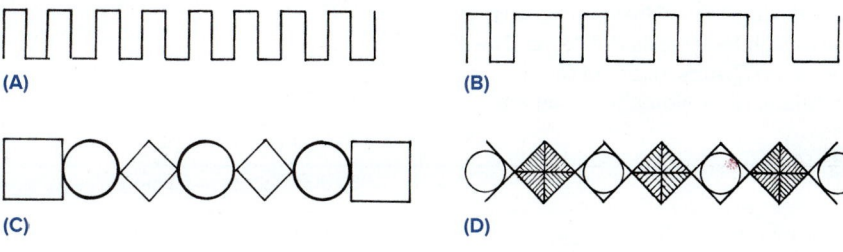
(A)

(B)

(C)

(D)

FIGURE 5.9
Variation creates visual interest. (A) Repetition of a simple pattern can be monotonous. (B) Varying the width of every second shape in the pattern creates visual interest. (C and D) Alternating patterns heighten visual interest.

PRODUCTION INSIGHTS
Terminal Accents

(A)

Carefully selected terminal accents — the lines that define the profile, or silhouette, of a form or mass — can be used to help portray emotional quality. In some productions, the upper parts of the set walls are cut off (Figure A). The quality and character of the line chosen to form this terminal accent on the upper edge of the wall (form) can help shape the audience's understanding of the emotional atmosphere of the play. If the play is a light comedy, a "fun" sort of curlicue line will reinforce the happy nature of the play. If the production is more romantic, a gentle, sensuous line may be more appropriate. If the play is serious and heavy, straight lines with sharp, angular corners are probably more appropriate.

The same effect can be achieved in costume design, where the character of the line chosen to create the silhouette of a costume helps shape the emotional quality of the gown (Figure B).

The emotional quality of the terminal accent can also be used to good advantage in costume design. The hems of the sleeves and skirts of witches' costumes are frequently designed with sharp points (dags) to visually support the menacing nature of the characters wearing those costumes. The unadorned neckline of a collarless smock provides a visual clue to the stiff, unyielding nature of its wearer. But add a soft, frilly, lace collar to that same dress, and our perception of its wearer will similarly be softened.

(B)

(A) *Scenic design for* The Birthday Party *by J. Michael Gillette.* (B) Costume design for the Dancer in *The Rake's Progress* (left); choreographed by Ninette de Valois; book and music by Gordon; designed by Whistler; Vic-Wells Ballet Company at Sadler's Wells Theatre, London, UK; May, 1935. ©Performing Arts Images/ArenaPal/The Image Works Costume design for Priscilla Presley as The Wicked Queen (right) in *Snow White and the Seven Dwarfs*, directed by Ian Talbot at the New Wimbledon Theatre, 6/12/2012. ©Nigel Norrington/Camera Press/Redux.

FIGURE 5.10
Symmetrical balance results when the left side of a design is a mirror image of the right side, as in this scene design for *Lady Precious Stream* by A. S. Gillette. Courtesy J. Michael Gillette.

Balance

Balance is achieved by arranging the design elements to create a sense of restfulness, stability, or equilibrium in the design.

There are two types of balance: symmetrical and asymmetrical. In **symmetrical balance,** if you were to draw a line down the center of a design, the objects on the left side would be the mirror image of the objects on the right, as shown in Figure 5.10. In **asymmetrical balance,** the left side of the design does not mirror the right. Asymmetrical balance is achieved by creating a pattern in which the juxtaposition of the various design elements creates a sense of restfulness, stability, or equilibrium, as shown in Figure 5.11 where the white circle on the left of the design is dynamically balanced by the larger expanse of dark space to its right. This "nonmirrored" balance can be used by the designer to create dynamic balance through the manipulation of the elements of design.

The design of individual costumes is much more likely to involve the use of symmetrical balance (Figure 5.12A), in which the left side of the costume mirrors the right. However, a dynamic visual statement can be made about a character through the use of asymmetrical elements such as diagonal sashes, asymmetrical modular blocks of color, or asymmetrical draping (Figure 5.12B). Additionally, the overall balance of the costume design for the entire production is normally asymmetrical because the ebb and flow of the stage picture will rarely, if ever, contain any moments in which the left side of the stage picture will be a mirror image of the right. The majority of scenic designs employ asymmetrical balance because its dynamic nature presents more opportunities for the personality of the play to be visually described in the scenery, as shown in Figure 5.13.

symmetrical balance: Correspondence in size, form, and relative position of parts on either side of a center dividing line; mirror-image balance.

asymmetrical balance: A sense of equipoise achieved through dynamic tension created by the juxtaposition of dissimilar design elements (line, form, mass, value, color).

FIGURE 5.11
Asymmetrical balance occurs when dissimilar forms appear to be balanced within the framework of the composition.

Proportion

Proportion involves the harmonious relationship of the parts of an object to each other or to the whole. A significant portion of our understanding of beauty is based on proportion. Facial beauty, for example, is predominantly based on

green walls and dark mahogany doors of the up-center hallway diminished the visual importance of that prominent position, again focusing attention further downstage.

The foregoing example employed scenic design to explain the uses of the various principles of composition. An understanding of these tools of the designer will provide you with the basic artistic resources needed to create effective designs in not only scenic design but costumes, lighting, and sound as well.

Chapter 6

Color

Color is easily the most noticeable of the design elements and arguably the most dominant. It is also the least understood. We grow up with color all around us and we see and interact with it every day. It is probably because of our constant contact with color that we accept it without really thinking about it. This chapter attempts to help you understand the complex subject of color.

Defining Color

Unfortunately, color has a variety of definitions and concepts that must be learned and understood. Learning these annoying definitions will actually aid your understanding of this interesting field.

Color can be defined as a perception created in the brain as a result of stimulation of the retina by light waves of a certain length. It can also be defined as the intrinsic physical properties of objects that make those objects reflect and absorb waves of a certain light.

The common denominator for any definition of color is light, because the visual perception of all color is derived from light. The phenomenon that we call light is actually the very narrow portion of the spectrum of electromagnetic radiation that is visible to the human eye. Figure 6.1 shows the position of visible light on this spectrum, as well as that of some of the other types of radiation. The visible spectrum stretches in frequency from approximately 750 to 400 nanometers. (A nanometer is one billionth of a meter.) Figure 6.2 shows the approximate wavelengths for the various colors of the visible spectrum.

Color Terminology

Without a specific set of terms to describe the various properties of color, almost any discussion of it would quickly degenerate into rather meaningless comparisons. For example, if you provide twenty people with one hundred **paint chips**, all yellow, but each slightly different, and asked them to identify canary yellow, they would probably select twenty different chips. This is because the connection between the description of any specific color, such as canary yellow, and the brain's understanding of the physical appearance of that color differs, sometimes significantly, from person to person.

The terms that we will be using in our discussion of color are as follows:

Hue   Hue is the quality that differentiates one color from another, such as blue from green or red from yellow.

paint chip: A small rectangle of paper or thin cardboard painted in a specific hue.

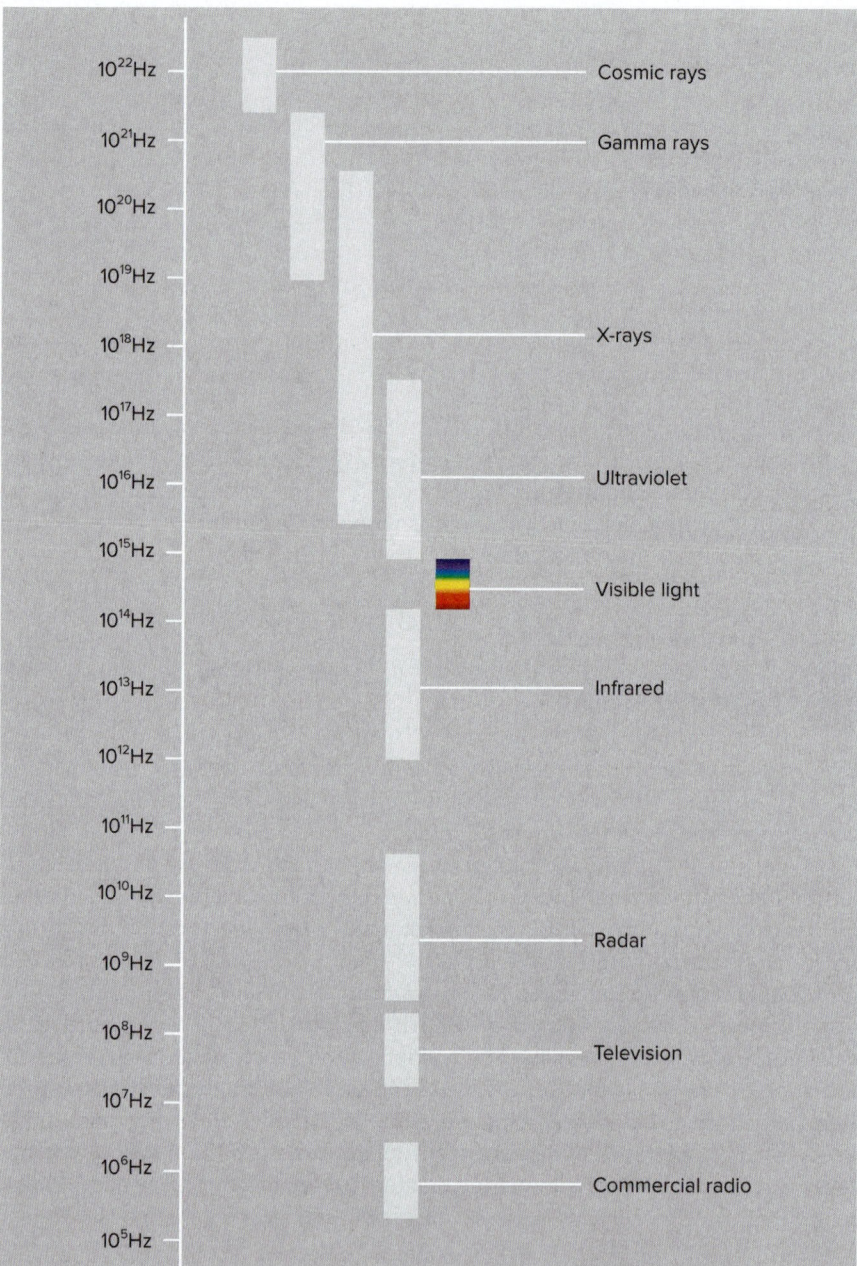

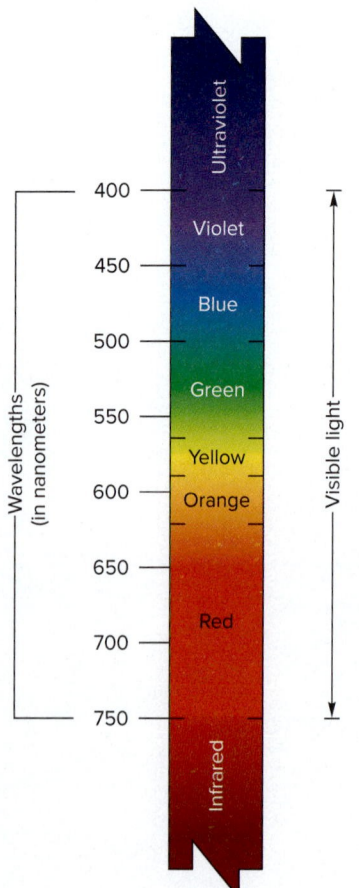

Saturation   Saturation, also known as chroma, refers to the amount, or percentage, of a particular hue in a color mixture. Fire-engine red has a high, or strong, saturation, because there is a lot of fully saturated color in the mixture. Dusty rose, has a low, or weak, saturation, because there isn't a lot of fully saturated color in the mixture; instead, the majority is white or gray.

Value   The relative lightness or darkness of a color is referred to as its value. Pale blue has a high value, and dark brown has a low value.

Tint   A color with a high value is referred to as a tint. It is usually achieved by mixing a hue with either white pigment or white light.

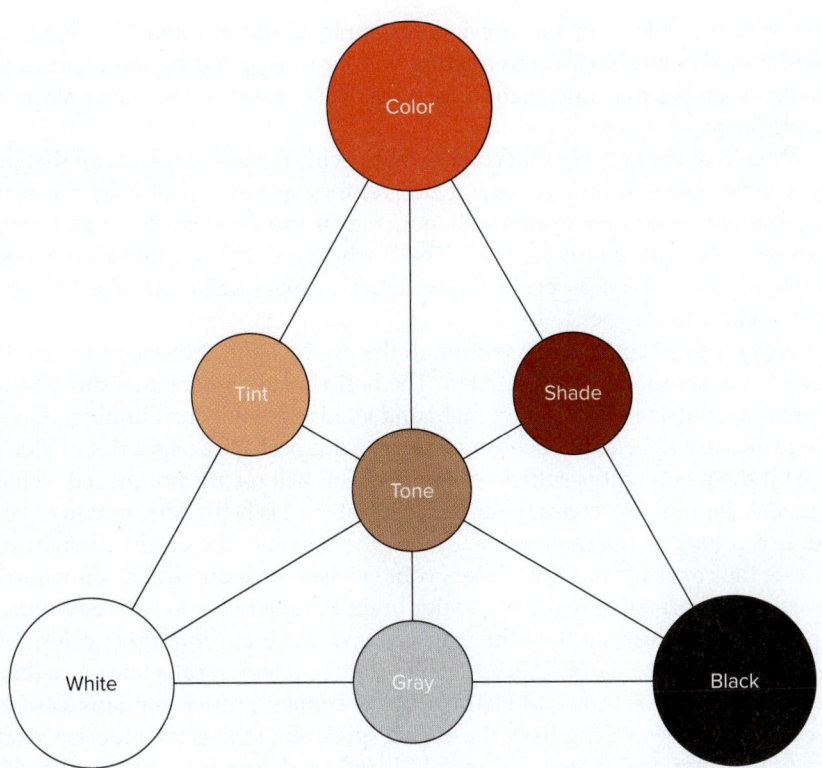

FIGURE 6.3
The color triangle is a visual representation of the relationships that exist among color, shade, tint, and tone.

Shade   A color with a low value is known as a shade. It is usually created by a mixture of one or more hues and black.

Tone   A color of middle value is frequently referred to as a tone. It is a mixture of a hue with black *and* white. The addition of a **complementary** hue tones a color.

The color triangle in Figure 6.3 shows the relationships among hue, white, black, gray (the product of mixing black and white), tint, shade, and tone.

 ## Seeing Color

Before we learn how color works, we need to understand how we see color. Human sight is composed of a complex series of events. When you look at an object, elements within your eye are stimulated by the light being emitted by, or reflected from, the viewed object. Inside the eye an electrochemical reaction occurs in specialized nerve cells in the retina where two distinct types of light-receptor nerves, **rods** and **cones**, emit minute charges of electricity that are relayed to your brain. The brain interprets the received data as a "picture" that you have seen. The cones are divided into three primary groups: those that respond to the wavelengths of light corresponding to hues red, blue, and green, respectively.

When red light enters the eye, the red-responsive cones are stimulated but the others are not. When light that contains both red and blue wavelengths enters the eye, both the red- and blue-responsive cones are stimulated. In this case, the message that is sent to the brain corresponds to the ratio of red and blue light contained in the light mixture that the eye receives.

Notice that the eye only transmits information to the brain corresponding to the input it has received. The brain is the organ that does the interpretative

complementary: Two hues that, when combined, yield white in light or black in pigment; colors that are opposite each other on the color wheel.

rods: Nerve cells in the retina that are sensitive to faint light.

cones: Nerve cells in the retina that are sensitive to bright light; they respond to red, blue, or green light.

mixing of the colors. In the previous example of the red and blue light, the amount of red and blue in the mixture will be interpreted by the brain of the person receiving that information as a particular color in the violet-magenta-purple range.

What that person calls that color — the specific name — depends on that person's experiences. If they've seen it before, they generally call it by the name they learned — lilac, for example. If not, they'll usually describe it as a range of colors — "a light, bluish-purple." (That's why it's seemingly impossible to get people to agree about a specific color: what's canary yellow to one person is lemon yellow to another.)

All perceived color is transmitted to the eye by light. If the light is dim, the cones (color sensors) do not function. The best way to demonstrate this effect is by standing outside on a moonlit night and looking at your surroundings. Everything you see will be a monochromatic gray, with perhaps a slight tint of blue or green if the moonlight is sufficiently bright. You will see no vibrant reds, blues, or greens, because the cones require more light than is being transmitted to your eye. If you look at the same scene during the daytime, the bright sunlight will activate the cones in your eye. Unless your eye has some physical dysfunction or the color-interpretative segment of your brain is impaired, you will see colors.

To further illustrate how the eye sees and the brain interprets color, let's assume that you are standing outside in the sunlight looking at a turquoise (blue-green) color chip, as shown in Figure 6.4. The sunlight, which contains all of the electromagnetic wavelengths of the visible spectrum, strikes the blue-green surface of the color chip. Some of that light is reflected, and some of it is absorbed

FIGURE 6.4

The brain interprets the neurological information it receives from the eye to be a specific hue.

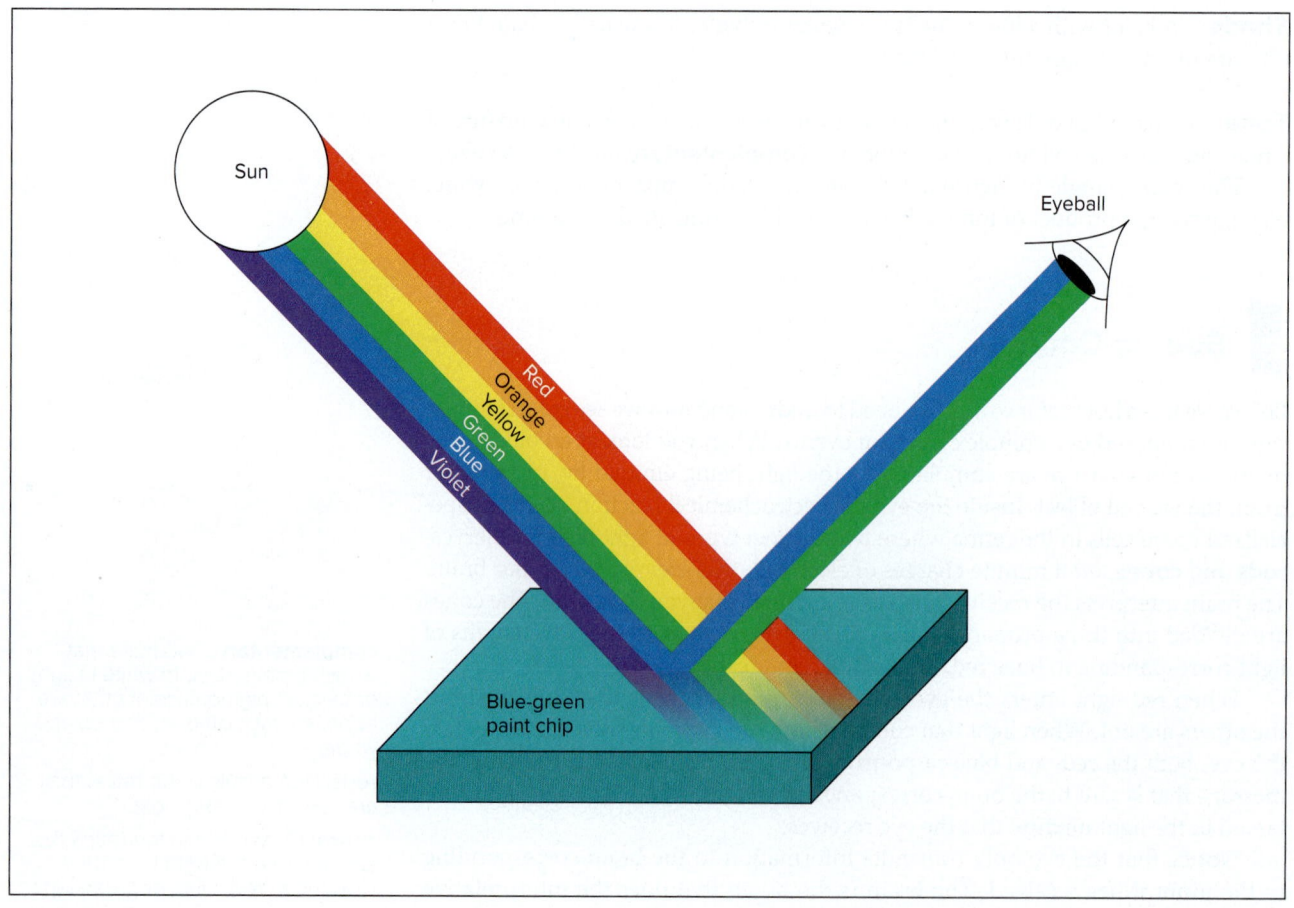

by the pigment on the paint chip. The majority of those wavelengths of light that correspond to the color of the chip (blue and green) are reflected. The majority of all other wavelengths of light are absorbed by the paint chip. The reflected blue and green light is received by the eye. The blue and green cones are stimulated by the light, causing them to send electrical impulses to the brain. The relative strength of these signals from the blue and green cones is proportionate to the specific amount of blue and green in the color mix. When the color-sensitive area of the brain is stimulated by these impulses, it interprets that information as a specific color known to that particular brain as turquoise.

pigment: A material that imparts color to a paint or dye.

Color Mixing

Before examining color mixing, we must unfortunately learn some additional terms. But remember the caveat: learning the terms helps you understand the concepts.

Primary Colors

Primary colors are those hues that cannot be derived or blended from any other hues. In light, the primary colors are closely related to the color sensitivity of the red, blue, and green cones in the eye.

Secondary Colors

Secondary hues are the result of mixing two primary colors. In the color wheel for light (Figure 6.5A), the mixing of adjacent primaries creates the secondary hues yellow, magenta, and cyan (blue-green). The primary colors in **pigment** (Figure 6.5B) are red, blue, and yellow. The secondary colors in pigment are purple, green, and orange.

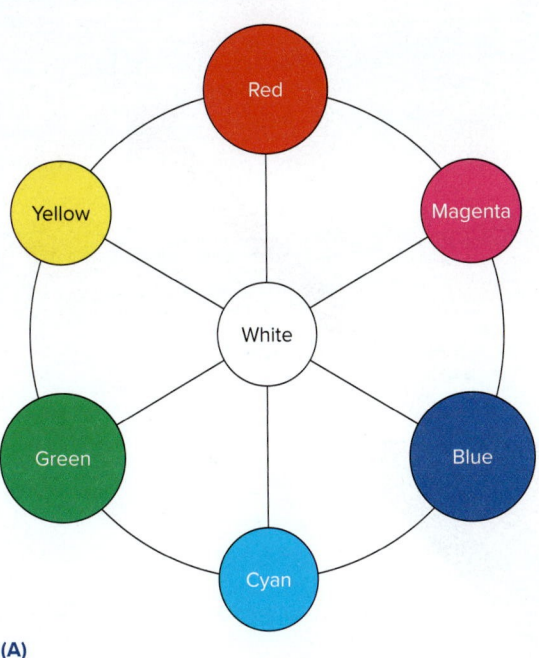

(A)

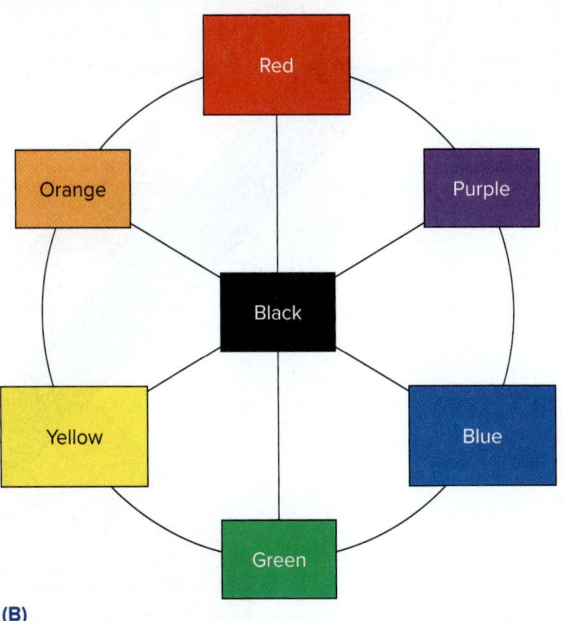

(B)

FIGURE 6.5
Color wheels for (A) light and (B) pigment.

Theoretical Versus Practical Color Mixing

According to color theory, the combination of complementary pigments yields black. The reason is straightforward. Each pigment reflects the wavelengths of light that correspond to its own hue and absorbs all others, as shown in Figure 6.6. Complementary hues are composed of one primary color and a secondary color. The secondary color is created from a mixture of the other two primary hues. The resultant blend of all three primaries should, theoretically, absorb all light that strikes it. This absence of reflected color means no light, which is the same as blackness.

In the practical mixing of pigments, you will be dealing with paints that are not pure colors. There are fillers, extenders, and impure colors in every commercially prepared paint. These impurities and surface diffusion — the scattering of light caused by the texture of the reflecting surface — will result in a deep gray instead of the theoretically correct black when mixing complementary hues.

Complementary Colors

Complementary colors can be described as any two hues that, when combined, yield white in light or black in pigment. For example, when two lights of equal intensity — one yellow, one blue — intersect, the resultant light is white, as illustrated in Figure 6.5A. That resultant white light will accurately reflect the true colors of anything it strikes. Similarly, complementary pure hues in pigment

FIGURE 6.6
Color reflection and absorption are determined by the hue of the pigment. Each hue will reflect its own color and absorb all others.

such as orange and blue (see Figure 6.5B), when mixed together in equal proportion, theoretically yield black.

Complementary colors can also be described as colors opposite each other on a color wheel. The color wheel for light (Figure 6.5A) shows that the complementary hue for red is cyan. When the two are combined, they form white light. In the color wheel for pigment (Figure 6.5B), the complementary of red is green. When the two are mixed, they form black.

Filtered Light

When white light passes through any type of filtering material, such as glass, plastic, or air, a certain portion of the spectrum is absorbed. To fully understand this type of absorption, you need a little background about the nature of light and energy.

Light, as we have seen, is a form of radiant energy (part of the electromagnetic spectrum). According to the laws of physics, energy can be neither created nor destroyed, but its form can be changed or converted. This principle can be demonstrated by touching a window through which the sun is shining. The glass will be warmer than a similar window that isn't in the direct sunlight. This is because the energy being absorbed by the glass is being converted from light into heat.

Subtractive Color Mixing in Light   If the glass in the window mentioned above is colored, another type of filtering takes place. Colored filters allow only their own hue to pass through the filtering medium; they absorb all other wavelengths of light.

Figure 6.7A shows a red filter placed in front of a full-spectrum light source. The white light emitted by the lamp is composed of wavelengths from all portions of the visible spectrum. The red filter allows only the wavelengths of light that correspond to its own color to pass. All other light is stopped by the filter and converted into heat.

When two or more filters, such as the secondary hues magenta and cyan, are placed in front of a single source (Figure 6.7B), each filter removes all but its own segment of the spectrum. The resulting blue light is caused by successive filtration. The magenta filter allows only red and blue light to pass through it. The cyan filter absorbs the red portion of the magenta light but allows the blue portion to pass. In practical application, it is usually preferable to use a single filter, rather than multiple filters. By selectively removing portions of the visible spectrum, subtractive color mixing actually reduces the intensity of the output of the source. A yellow or amber color medium of minimal saturation may reduce intensity by about 5 percent, for example, and a heavily saturated dark blue may reduce it by as much as 95 percent. If more than one filter is used, the output of the source can be significantly reduced.

FIGURE 6.7
Subtractive color mixing in light. A colored filter will allow its own color to pass but will absorb all others.

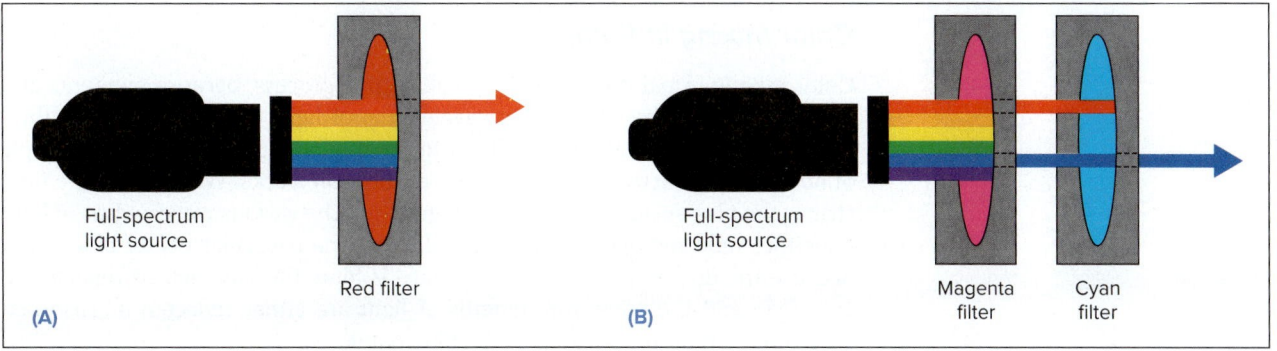

Full-spectrum light source

Red filter

(A)

Full-spectrum light source

Magenta filter

Cyan filter

(B)

FIGURE 6.8
Additive color mixing in light. The eye sees each separate color; the brain interprets the ratio of the color mix to be a specific hue.

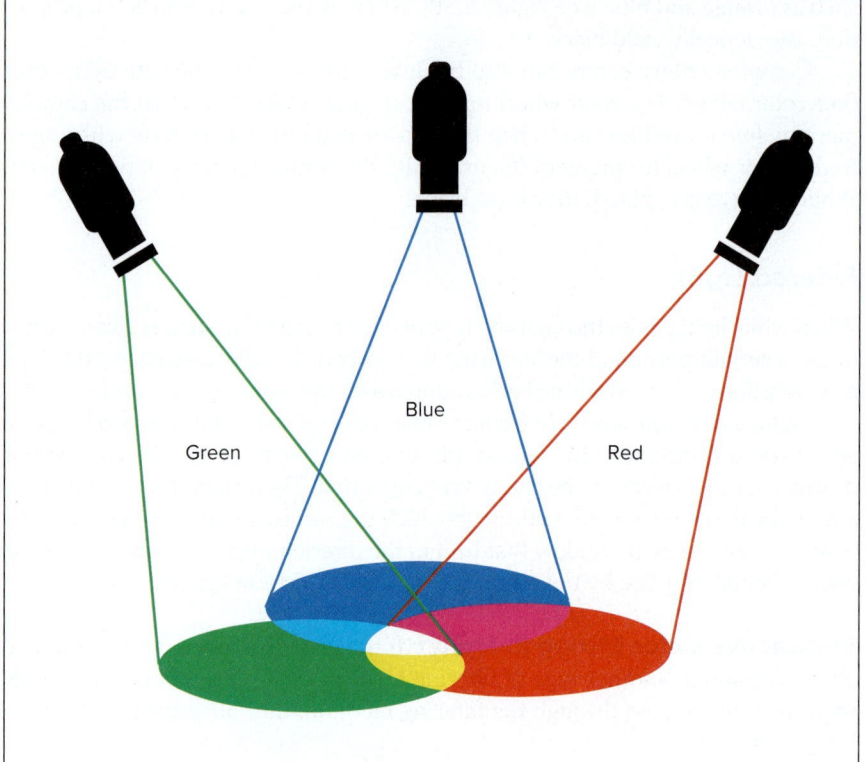

Additive Color Mixing in Light   When several individual hues are transmitted to the eye, added together, and interpreted by the brain, the process is called additive color mixing. Figure 6.8 illustrates additive color mixing in light. The beams of the three lights are being projected onto a neutral or white surface. When a primary hue, such as red, is mixed with an adjacent primary, such as green, a secondary hue, yellow, is created. (It is interesting to realize that this hue is *not* created on the projection surface but is the result of the red and green cones in our eye being stimulated by the red and green light and our brain interpreting this neurological information as the hue yellow.) This same phenomenon occurs when any two or more hues are additively mixed.

All color is perceived in the same way. The subtle tones, tints, and shades of the various hues that you see are all determined by the level of stimulation that the red, blue, and green cones receive from the light reflected to your eye and by your brain's interpretation of that information.

Color Mixing in Paint

Color mixing in paint is primarily a subtractive process, because pigments and dyes of specific hues reflect the wavelengths of light that correspond to their own hue and absorb all others. The primary hue blue provides a good example of how this subtractive process of color absorption works. When the white light strikes the blue surface illustrated in Figure 6.9, the various wavelengths of light are either reflected or absorbed depending on the particular hue of blue paint. Because the dominant color of the surface is blue, the blue light is reflected to your eye, and the other wavelengths of light are either reflected or absorbed according to their proportions in the blue paint.

FIGURE 6.9
Selective reflection and absorption. A pigment will reflect its own color and absorb all others.

The selective absorption characteristics of the individual hues in a paint mix cause a reduction in the saturation, or chroma, of the resultant hue. If yellow and red paint are mixed, for example, the resultant color is orange. But because the yellow pigment absorbs some of the red light and the red pigment absorbs some of the yellow light, the resultant orange hue is not as fully saturated as either of the yellow or red paint.

Integrated Color Wheel

Sir Isaac Newton demonstrated that six principal hues (violet, blue, green, yellow, orange, and red) can be generated when sunlight is passed through a prism. These hues can be placed on a color wheel, as shown in Figure 6.10. Additional hues, which are full chroma equivalents to a mixture of adjacent original hues, can be created and placed between the six principal colors to create a color wheel with twelve specific, fully saturated, hues.

This integrated color wheel can help to clarify the interrelationships between pigment and light. For years a semantic problem has hindered easy understanding of these relationships. The use of the same words to describe some of the primary and secondary hues for pigment and light has tended to create confusion. Although the words red, blue, green, and yellow are used to describe colors in both pigment and light, the specific hues are not identical. The integrated color wheel resolves this problem by renaming the primary colors in light to more accurately reflect the true color relationship that exists between the various hues in pigment and light.

Fully saturated colors don't all have the same value. The twelve principal hues of the integrated color wheel have been arranged in Figure 6.11 in their appropriate relationships to a value scale.

A wide variety of interesting and useful tones can be created by mixing complementary pigments with black and white. Figure 6.12 demonstrates this effect

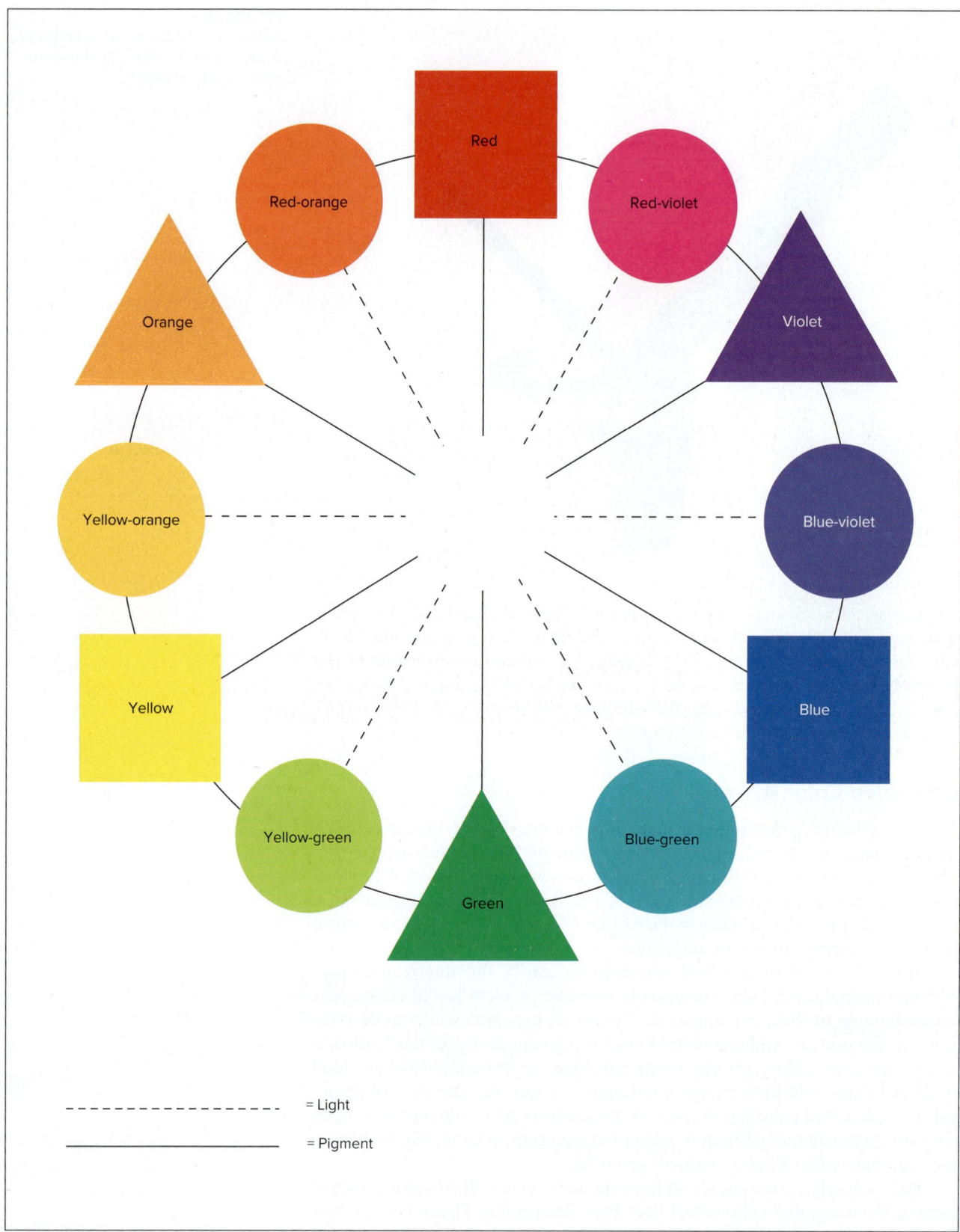

FIGURE 6.10
Integrated color wheel. This device is used to help clarify the relationships that exist between the primary and secondary hues in both pigment and light.

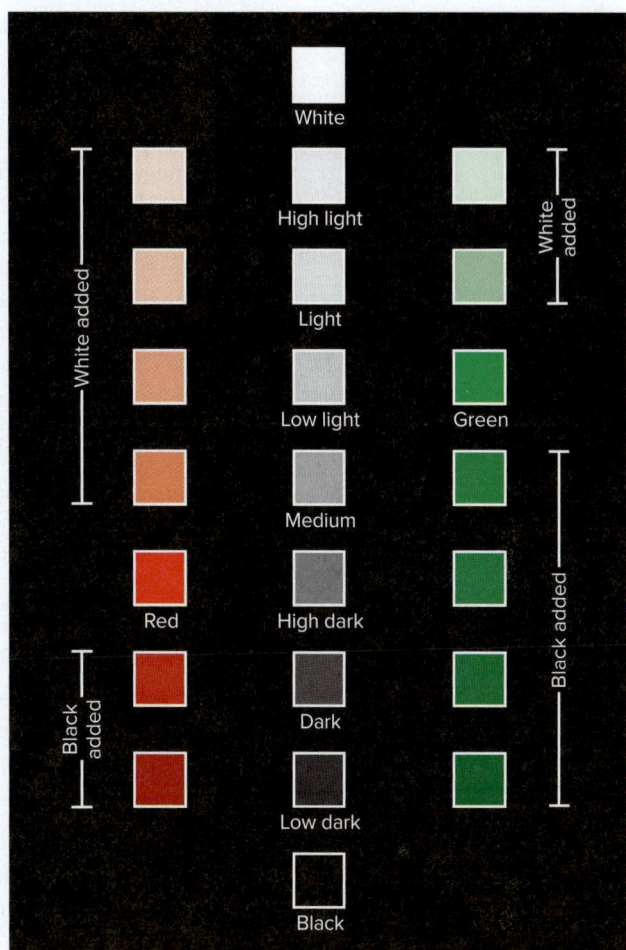

with the complementary hues red and green. The value and saturation (chroma) of the resultant hues change as they are mixed with either black or white. **Neutralization** occurs when mixing complementary hues of the same value.

A Practical Postscript to Color Theory

Any discussion of color theory necessarily revolves around hues of 100 percent purity and saturation. Colors of this strength and value are not used in theatrical work, for two primary reasons: They would be incredibly expensive, and the use of fully saturated colors isn't particularly appropriate in the theatre, simply because the colors would visually dominate anything else on the stage.

Application of Color in the Theatre

In any discussion of color, there is bound to be a disparity between theoretical principles and practical results. Although the principles of color theory are certainly applicable in the practical use of color, the end results of mixing paints, dyes, or lights will be somewhat different from the results projected by the theory. This is because of the impurities and contaminants found in all stage paints, dyes, lamps, and color media.

FIGURE 6.11
A hue-value relationship chart (above left). Because fully saturated colors do not all have the same value, this chart helps explain the relative values of the indicated colors. The values of the colors on the outside columns correspond with the values of the adjacent gray blocks on the center gray-scale column.

FIGURE 6.12
Complementary hue-tone relationships (above right). The value of a specific hue changes as white or black is added to it. The values of the resultant tints and shades on the outside columns correspond with the values of the adjacent gray blocks of the central gray scale.

neutralization: Subtractive color mixing; the selective absorption of light as the result of mixing complementary pigment hues; the creation of gray.

Meaning of Color

People react to color. Sometimes that response is subtle and subconscious, and at other times it is overtly physical. Doctors and drug-rehabilitation counselors have discovered that an extremely violent patient will often become calm and manageable in about fifteen or twenty minutes if placed in an all-pink environment. Many hospitals now have "pink rooms" in which everything — the floor, ceiling, walls, doors — is painted the same hue of pink. Relatedly, the walls and lockers in the visitor's locker room of Kinnick Stadium, the University of Iowa's football stadium, are painted soft pink.

The meanings of color are constantly changing. Color meanings are influenced by many factors: cultural background, age, personality, adjoining colors, and individual mood. The variability of these factors is the primary reason that the following list of affective meanings is necessarily ambiguous. Moreover, these definitions are simply common interpretations of the meaning of specific colors and should not be thought of as being the "correct" ones.

> yellow: stimulating, cheerful, exciting, joyful, serene, unpleasant, aggressive, hostile
>
> orange: warm, happy, merry, exciting, stimulating, hot, disturbed, distressed, unpleasant
>
> red: happy, affectionate, loving, exciting, striking, active, intense, defiant, powerful, masterful, strong, aggressive, hostile
>
> green: youthful, fresh, leisurely, secure, calm, peaceful, emotionally controlled, ill
>
> blue: pleasant, cool, secure, comfortable, tender, soothing, social, dignified, sad, strong, full, great
>
> violet: dignified, stately, vigorous, disagreeable, sad, despondent, melancholy, unhappy, depressing
>
> black: sad, melancholy, vague, unhappy, dignified, stately, strong, powerful, hostile, distressed, fearful, old
>
> white: pure, tender, soothing, solemn, empty
>
> brown: secure, comfortable, full, sad, disagreeable

Practical Color Use

Designers in the theatre normally follow some general color guidelines. The following discussion provides a survey of examples and general practices. Any competent designer will advise you that there are many occasions when it is appropriate, logical, and right to ignore the normal and the conventional if doing so will support the visualization of the production concept.

Pigment   Scenic designers generally use hues of medium saturation and value, because most sets serve as a background environment for the action of the play, and the set needs to recede from the audience's consciousness after it has made its original visual statement. For the same reason, costume designers generally work in a less constricted palette. Colors of full saturation and brilliance will direct the audience's attention to the actors. Generally, the only proviso for their use is that the hue and value be an appropriate reflection of the actor's character.

Color proximity — the placement and relationship of specific hues — has a great impact on the spectators' perception of a scene. Strongly contrasting colors create a greater dynamic tension than do less conflicting hues. A set that had a highly saturated yellow sofa placed in front of a brilliant blue wall would be visually shocking. The startling color contrast would indicate that the owner of that particular apartment was dynamic, eccentric, possibly volatile, and probably wacko. Similarly, a man dressed in an electric blue suit with a brilliant yellow vest would also be thought of in the same basically antisocial way. But if the saturation of those contrasting colors was reduced and modified — a soft-yellow, floral-print sofa against a dusty powder-blue wall of the same or similar value — our perception of the owner of that apartment would be similarly softened.

Accent colors, which are basically small touches of contrasting colors, are continually used by both scenic and costume designers. The color dynamics of an otherwise lifeless set can be enhanced by setting a vase of colorful flowers on a table, hanging a painting on the wall, or accenting a table through the use of a white or color-coordinated tablecloth. Costumers frequently provide accent colors in their designs with accessories such as jewelry, scarves, purses, and shoes. Accent colors generally are interpreted in the same way as other contrasting colors: Greater contrast creates increased dynamic tension.

Light   There are some very pragmatic reasons for using colored light onstage. The light from theatre spotlights is rather bright and harsh. In its uncolored state, and at close to full intensity, it will tend to bleach any color out of the scenery, costumes, and makeup. If colors that are compatible with the scenery and costumes are used to filter the stage lights, however, the scenic designer's and costume designer's color palettes and values will be maintained.

As we have seen, the mixing of complementary hues creates white light. In the discussion on color theory, this principle was demonstrated with fully saturated hues. In practical application, fully saturated hues are rarely used because of their adverse effect on the other designers' palettes and on actors' skin tones. Complementary hues of low chroma are frequently used, however, because pigments lit with additively mixed white light are enhanced rather than bleached. This color enhancement is caused by the brain's interpretation of retinal stimulation, as demonstrated in Figure 6.13. Figure 6.13A shows white light striking a white surface. Because the white light is composed of all wavelengths of light, the white surface simply reflects all the light rather than absorbing or filtering out any specific portion of the spectrum. Figure 6.13B shows two complementary hues of low saturation (light blue and light yellow) striking the same white

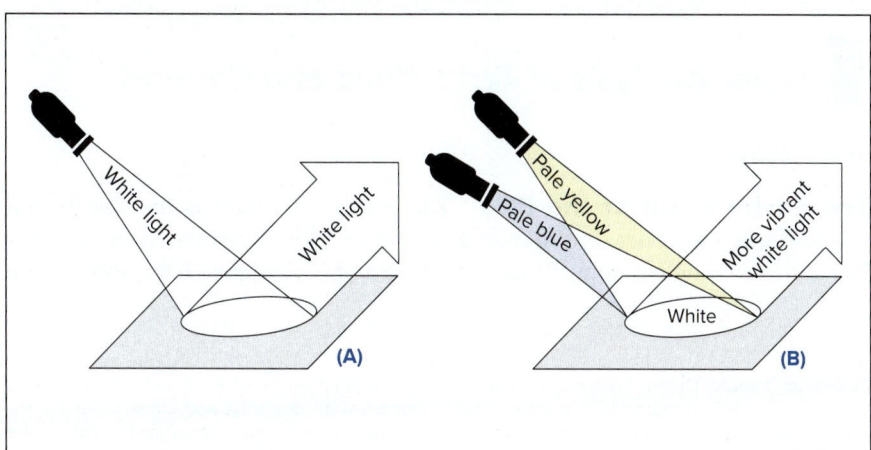

FIGURE 6.13
The use of an additive mix of complementary tints results in a more lively, vibrant light. See text for details of (A) and (B).

surface. These low-saturation hues emphasize a relatively narrow portion of the spectrum (blue and yellow), although there is still a large proportion of the full spectrum (white light) in the mix. The white surface reflects the pale blue and pale yellow, as well as the white light, to your eye. Because blue and yellow are complementary, your brain interprets the mixture of those two lights as white. However, the cones are more strongly stimulated by the blue and yellow light than they would be with plain white light. Interestingly, the brain interprets this stronger color stimulation as a richer, more vibrant color. This phenomenon works for all complementary color mixes. Although the specific color reflectivity and absorption of any colored light from any particular costume or set color will depend on the characteristics of that particular hue, the principles of color vibrancy remain constant.

The palettes used by the scenic and costume designers generally dictate the specific complementary hues that are chosen by a lighting designer. The lighting designer usually selects specific hues that will enhance the primary palettes of the other designers, using the guideline that every hue heightens its own color and suppresses its complementary. If the scenic or costume designer is using a full-spectrum palette, the lighting designer may combine three or more colors to create white light. When more specific hues are used to create the white light mix, the range of hues affected by the color-enrichment characteristics of a complementary mix are similarly broadened.

The lighting designer can also produce a white light mix that is not exactly complementary — either slightly warm or cool — to create a corresponding warming or cooling of the stage environment. This type of not-quite-complementary color mixing is very helpful in establishing an atmospheric feeling of heat or cold on the stage.

An audience can see objects only as a result of those objects reflecting or emitting light. Because the overwhelming majority of objects in a play (actors, costumes, sets, props) reflect rather than emit light, an analysis of the use of color in a design concept would logically stem from an analysis of the effects of the hues used in the lighting design on the various other elements of the total design for the production.

The two sections that follow will analyze the use of color in two distinctly different types of color designs: a muted, predominantly low-saturation, closely coordinated palette in the University of Arizona production of Ted Tally's *Terra Nova* and a vibrant, highly saturated, full-range color design for the University of Arizona production of the Masteroff/Kander/Ebb musical *Cabaret*.

 ## Color Analysis of *Terra Nova* and *Cabaret*

*Terra Nova**

The Environment of the Play   The primary location is the vast frozen whiteness of Antarctica, but numerous vignettes take place in a variety of other locations: an English country garden in spring, a banquet hall, and several

---

* Director: Harold Dixon; scenic and lighting design: J. Michael Gillette; costume design: Jerry D. Allen; property design: Peter Wexler — the properties were designed and constructed for the original production of *Terra Nova* at the Mark Taper Forum in Los Angeles, produced by the Center Theatre Group.

FIGURE 6.14
The color of the set and sail (white) was selected for two reasons: (1) Antarctica is overwhelmingly white; (2) the highly reflective neutral color makes an excellent projection surface for the various colors and images that make up a large segment of the design concept. Courtesy of J. Michael Gillette.

nonspecific memory locations. It is essential for the continuity of the play that scenes flow smoothly from location to location without a break in the action.

The Scenic Design   The color design helped to create the cinematic flow required for the production. To bring to life the vast coldness of Antarctica, the set, which was a jumble of platforms arranged to create an abstraction of the ruptured surface of an ice floe, was painted an off-white (Figure 6.14). On the upstage side of the platforms a large expanse of unpainted, unbleached muslin was suspended from an abstracted ship's spar (Figure 6.15). This sail was used as a projection surface for color washes, visual effects, and photographic images of Scott's ill-fated expedition to the South Pole. The entire set was surrounded by a black cyclorama to help focus the audience's attention on the set and actors.

FIGURE 6.15
The sail was backlit with color washes (left) to provide primary atmospheric and psychological keys about the nature of the individual scenes. It was also used as a projection surface for black-and-white slides of Scott's actual expedition (right). Courtesy of J. Michael Gillette.

FIGURE 6.16
The warm floral-print fabric and diagonal hem of Scott's wife's summer dress provided a strong visual contrast with the vertical and horizontal patterns in the muted gray and brown fabrics of the men's suits. Courtesy of J. Michael Gillette.

The Costume Design The costumes and properties were ultrarealistic. The natural earth tones (primarily shades of browns and grays) of the properties and the men's costumes stood out in strong contrast against the whiteness of the set. Scott's wife, the only woman in the play, was seen only in Scott's memory scenes of home. She was dressed in a floral print (Figure 6.16) to present a stark contrast with the muted patterns and solids that were worn by the men.

Lighting Design The lighting used color as a primary device to create psychological keys in support of the emotional content of the various scenes. Figure 6.17 provides a color key of the lighting used in this production indicating the direction and color of the various light sources. (Note that the numbers indicate Roscolux color numbers.) Figures 6.18–6.21 show how the various design elements (scenic, costume, properties, lighting) blended to create the color impact of the production design.

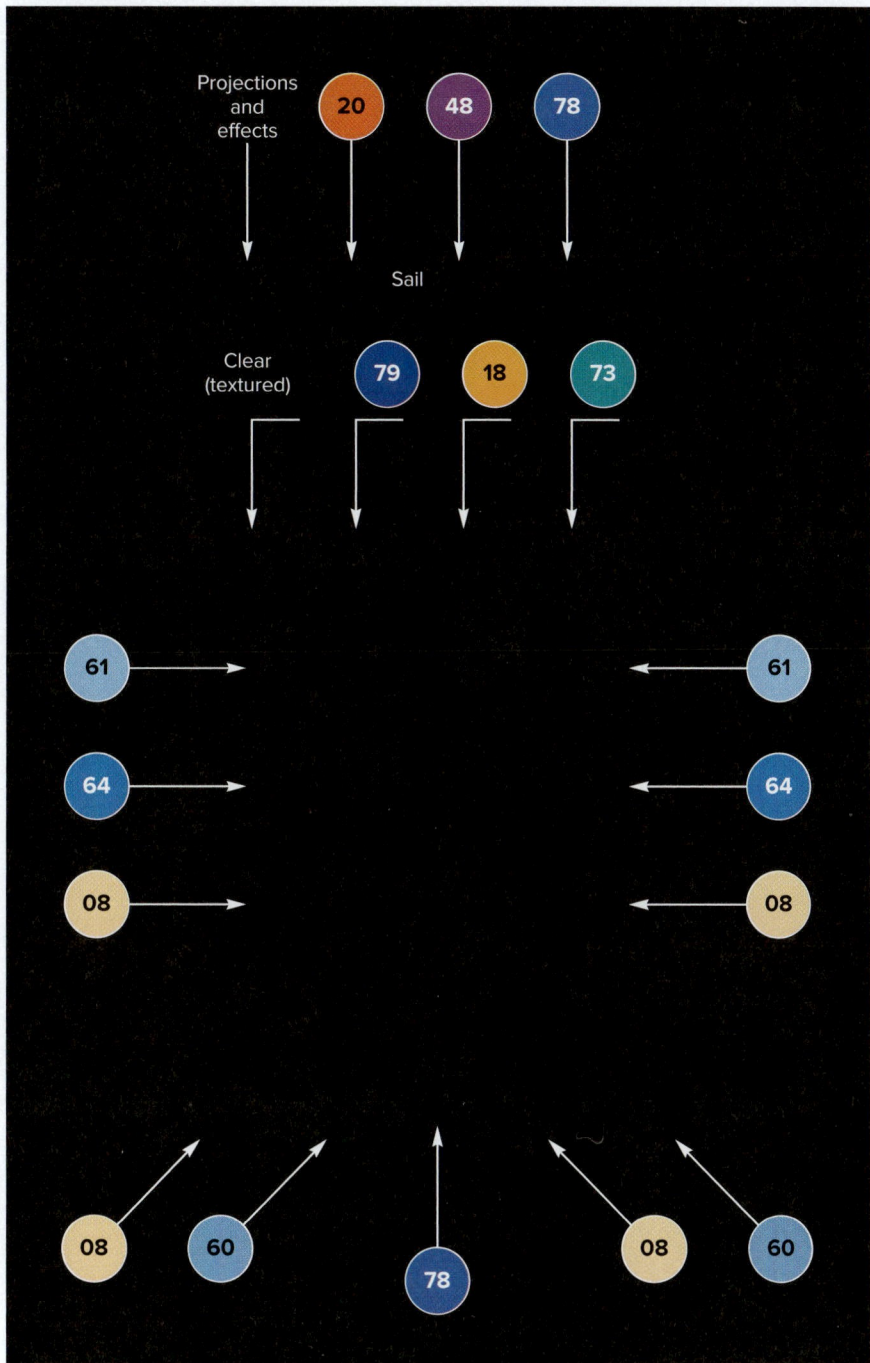

FIGURE 6.17
Color key for the *Terra Nova* lighting design. The arrows indicate the direction from which the light is traveling toward the stage. The horizontal flags on the arrows at the upper part of the illustration indicate that those lights are coming from above, rather than behind, the actors.

The scenes in Antarctica were lit with almost painfully brilliant white light (Figure 6.18), which resulted in the colors of the costumes and properties being portrayed very closely to their true hues.

The memory scenes were lit with textured top lights and color washes selected for their psychological impact: deep blue for Scott's heavier memories (Figure 6.19); soft pastels for the romantic memories of his wife (Figure 6.20); amber candlelight for the banquet scene (Figure 6.21).

FIGURE 6.18
Complementary colors (Roscolux 08 and 60 from the front and 08 and 61 from the sides) were used at high (but equal) intensity to provide a white, very bright, slightly cool color mix. The clear (white) top light helped to edge the actors' heads and shoulders with white as well as wash out any color shadows created by the individual hues in the front and side lights. The rendering of the skin tones as well as costumes and property colors was slightly cooler than if white light (as opposed to the complementary mix) had been used. The "cooler" look was a desired effect. Courtesy of J. Michael Gillette.

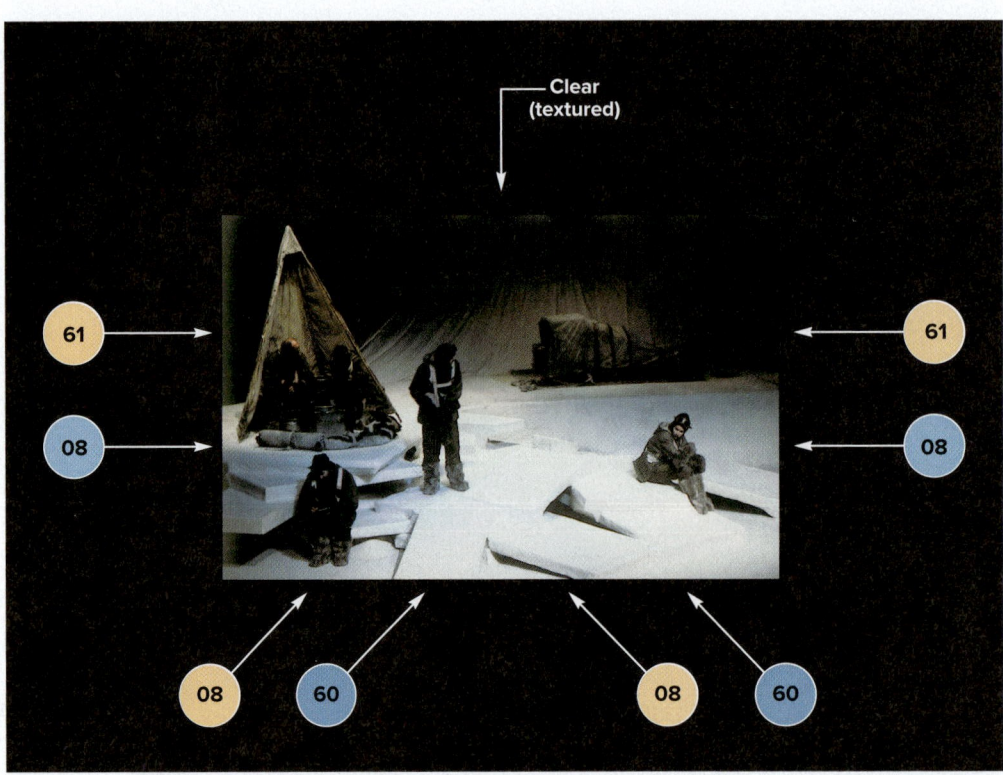

FIGURE 6.19
The textured light was created by bathing the stage with saturated blue (78 and 79) from the front and top. The texture was created by introducing the clear, textured top light at relatively low intensity. Scott's face was framed with a low-intensity followspot whose beam diameter was only shoulder wide. Skin tones and upper-torso costume colors were rendered naturally by the warm followspot (at low intensity the light from the uncolored beam is naturally warm) combining with, and overriding the effects of, the deep blue. Courtesy of J. Michael Gillette.

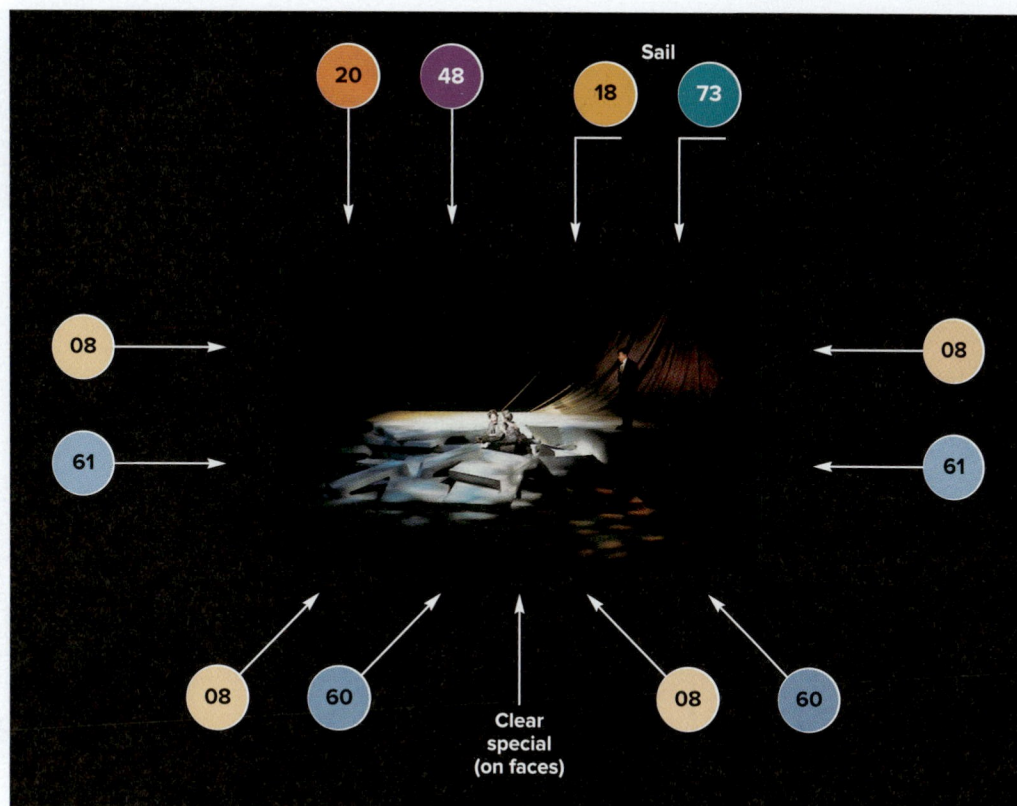

FIGURE 6.20
The atmosphere of England was created by using textured top lights colored in warm, soft hues (18 and 73) and the back lights on the sail (20 and 48) to provide a striking contrast with the blue-white coldness of the lights for Antarctica. Scott and his wife (down stage) were lit with warm-white combinations of 08 and 60 from the front and 08 and 61 from the sides. The figure in the background was side lit with a warm, dim, front/ side light. The warm-white light on Scott and his wife provided accurate color rendering of their costumes. The warm light striking the background figure created a fairly accurate color rendering of his tuxedo. Courtesy of J. Michael Gillette.

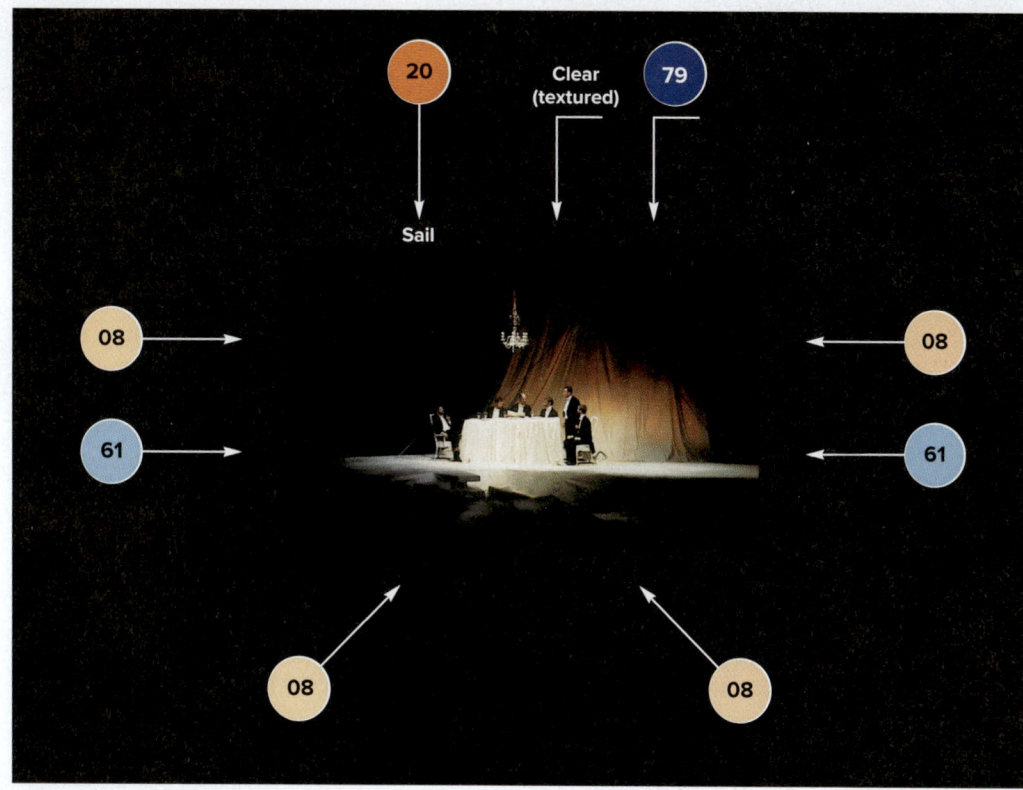

FIGURE 6.21
Primary color for this scene was provided by the warm amber (20) on the sail in the background. The banquet table was lit with a warm-white blend of 08 and 61 from the sides and 08 from the front and un-colored, textured top light. A little blue top light (79) was used to enhance the edging effect of the top light on the black tuxedos. This created a candlelit feeling with warm skin tones, tablecloth and floor, and black tuxedos. Courtesy of J. Michael Gillette.

The use of low-saturation complementary colors to light the acting areas from the front and sides significantly reduced the color-shifting effects of the stage lights on costumes and skin tones. The clear, textured top lights, when used in conjunction with the heavily saturated top washes, created significant changes in the visual appearance of the set. These elements, working together, created a subtly effective color design that worked for the support of the production.

Explanations of how the color palettes of the various design elements (scenic, costume, property, and lighting) interacted are contained in the captions for each illustration.

Cabaret*

The Environment of the Play The primary location of this musical is a seedy, second-rate night club, the Kit Kat Klub, in Berlin, Germany, in the

* Director and choreographer: Richard Hanson; scenic design: Tom Benson; costume design: Peggy Kellner; lighting design: J. Michael Gillette.

FIGURE 6.22
Scenic design for *Cabaret*, by Tom Benson. A number of hues were used on this production, but they were all in a fairly close tonal range. Contrast was achieved primarily by pattern variation and gloss finish coats applied to selected elements of the set. Courtesy of Tom Benson Scenic Design.

years 1929–1930. Additional scenes take place in several other locations: a railroad car, various rooms in a rooming house, and a fruit shop.

The Scenic Design   The scenic design for *Cabaret* created a startling contrast through the juxtaposition of line, color, and finish (Figure 6.22). The strong contrast was appropriate because it helped to heighten the dramatic tension inherent in the script and the production concept. The dominant element of the design was the Kit Kat Klub, which was painted in medium-saturation earth tones. However, the color was applied in an erratically angular pattern on the vertical face of the runway as well as on the floor of the audience portion of the nightclub. The zigzag motif was continued with the busy herringbone pattern on the floor of the runway and the rest of the stage.

The floor and four upstage columns were finished with a high-gloss glaze to heighten the contrast between those elements and the remainder of the set, which was painted with a traditional matte finish. The shimmering aluminized Mylar curtain (Figure 6.23) provided another dazzling type of contrast during one of the production numbers.

FIGURE 6.23
The aluminized Mylar curtain provided a startling contrast with the black background immediately upstage of the curtain and created a spectacular reflective surface for the fully saturated hues in the vertical strip-lights on either side of the stage. Courtesy of J. Michael Gillette.

Small white light bulbs were used to spell CABARET and outline the arches. These little pinpoints of light played against the black void created by the surrounding black cyclorama to create another type of emphatic contrast.

The fully saturated secondary colors (amber, cyan, and magenta) used in the double rows of vertical striplights on either side of the stage, and the 6-inch Fresnel spotlights hung from the upper-level railings of the set, created another jarring note of color contrast.

The color and contrast treatment of the other locations, which slid in on a shuttle stage just upstage of the nightclub runway, were more muted than those of the Kit Kat Klub because, in general, scenes that took place in the other locations were emotionally "softer" and more intimate.

The Costume Design   Contrast was also readily evident in the costume design. The designs for the Kit Kat Girls were based on vibrant, fully saturated colors (Figure 6.24) and high-sheen fabrics. A powerful statement was made by the contrast between the actresses' pale skin and the skimpy, heavily saturated, highly reflective surfaces of the costumes.

The costumes for Sally (the two on the left and the two on the right in Figure 6.25) used a change in saturation and hue as a device to mirror her emotional progression through the play. In the beginning, she was dressed in

FIGURE 6.24
Costume designs by Peggy Kellner.
The full-saturation, high-contrast
"glitzy" materials of the Kit Kat Girls'
costumes were enhanced by the
strongly saturated hues used to light
the cabaret scenes. Courtesy of
Peggy Kellner.

FIGURE 6.25
Costume designs by Peggy Kellner.
The color progression of Sally's
costumes mirrored her emotional
progression through the production.
See text for details. Courtesy of
Peggy Kellner.

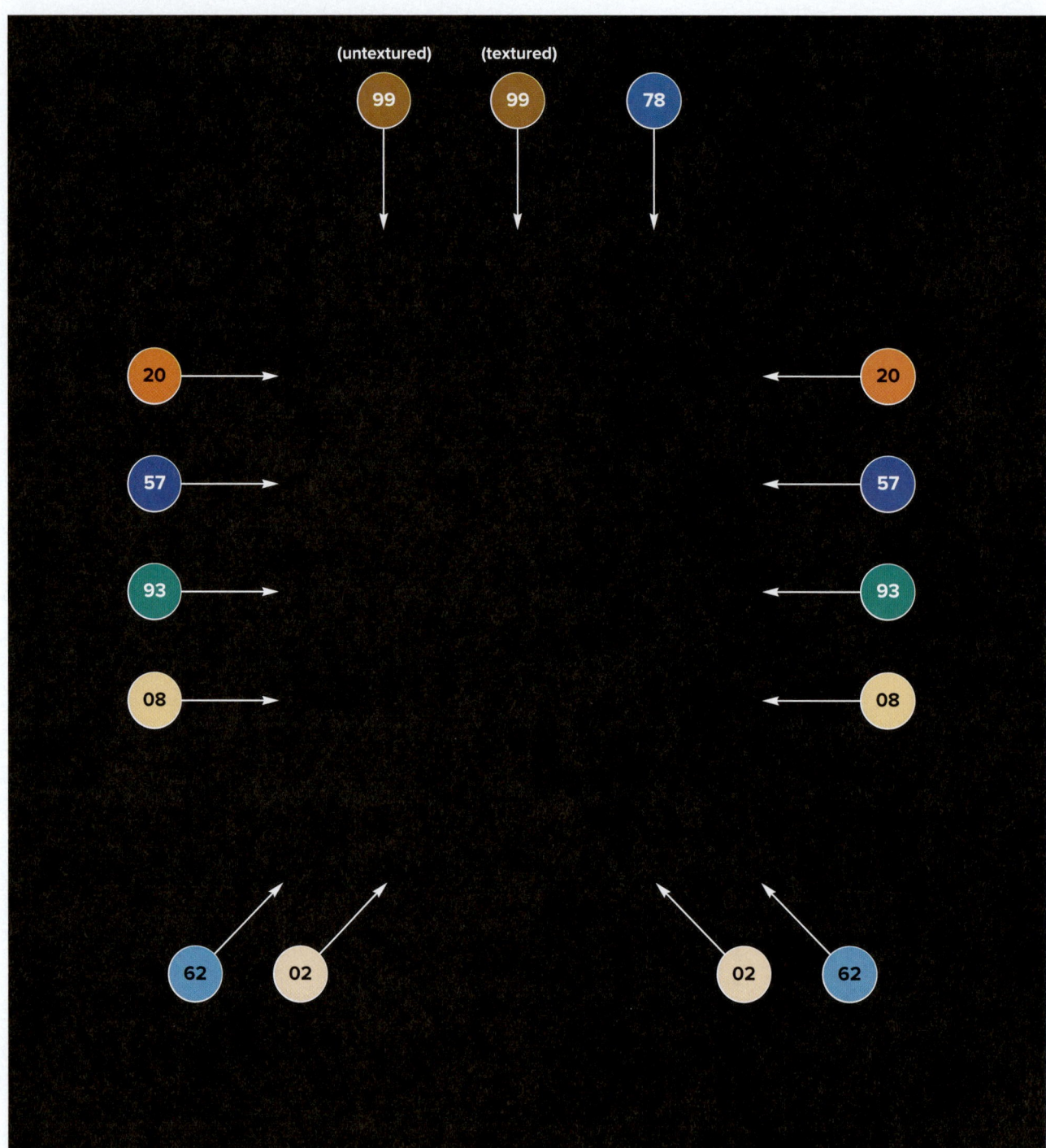

FIGURE 6.26
Color key for the lighting design. Low-saturation colors (02, 62, 08, 99) were used for general acting-area lights, while strong-saturation color washes (20, 57, 93, 78) were added for psychological emphasis. See text for details.

the vibrant, shocking colors and styles of the Kit Kat Girls. As she fell in love with Cliff, she dressed in softer, more muted tones. When Sally chose to stay in Germany as Cliff left, her reimmersion in the world of the cabaret was mirrored in the high contrast of a floor-length black sequin evening dress that she wore in the final scene.

The men's costumes, while being faithful to the period, also mimicked the emotionally based use of high contrast employed for the women's costumes. The Master of Ceremonies and the cabaret ensemble men were costumed in black-and-white evening wear, while Cliff and Herr Schultz were dressed in suits of muted hues selected to mirror their emotional warmth.

Lighting Design   The colors selected for the lighting design were dictated by three primary considerations: (1) the full-spectrum colors of the costumes and set; (2) the heavy, smoke-filled, sensuous atmosphere needed for the cabaret; and (3) the need for a lighter, more realistic atmosphere for those scenes outside the cabaret (Figure 6.26).

Complementary colors of light-to-moderate saturation (Roscolux 62 and 02) were selected for the front lights for the acting areas because they would be appropriately neutral for both the cabaret scenes and those more intimate scenes outside the cabaret. However, those colors had enough saturation to enhance the costume and set colors in both locations. By balancing the color mix between the 02 and 62, the stage could be made neutral, cool, or warm as appropriate. The full saturation necessary for the scenes inside the cabaret was supplied by the Roscolux 20, 57, and 93 used on the vertical striplights and Fresnels on either side of the stage. These saturated color washes, used in conjunction with the acting-area lights, enhanced the full-spectrum, strongly colored palettes of the costumes and scenery used in the cabaret scenes, as well as creating the heavy atmosphere necessary within the cabaret. (Specific hues of strongly saturated light create an impression of more vibrant color than do similar hues of less saturation. If two or more of these relatively saturated hues are additively mixed to create a white light, the resultant white light will create a similar vibrant color reaction from the full color spectrum.)

During production numbers, the set was generally lit with psychologically appropriate color washes, and the six followspots, using white or lightly tinted light, were used to highlight the various leads.

The downstage area of the cabaret audience was lit with a top wash of textured white light to support the concept that the area was lit by the individual table lamps. During the out-of-the-cabaret scenes, the textured top wash was combined with a deep blue wash to reduce the area's apparent visibility. (The deep blue looks like a shadow color but allows the "real" audience to see the shadow detail.)

The difference between the theory and practice of color mixing is only a matter of degree, not principle. Although an understanding of the laws of physics that govern the mixing of color is very helpful in using color in the theatre, the only way that a designer can develop any real understanding of, and facility in, the use of color is through experimentation and experience. Additional information on the practical application of color can be found in Chapters 12 ("Scene Painting"), 14 ("Lighting Design"), and 22 ("Drawing and Rendering"). See the related text about magic or cheat sheets (Figure 6.27) that can also be found in Chapter 6 on page 114.

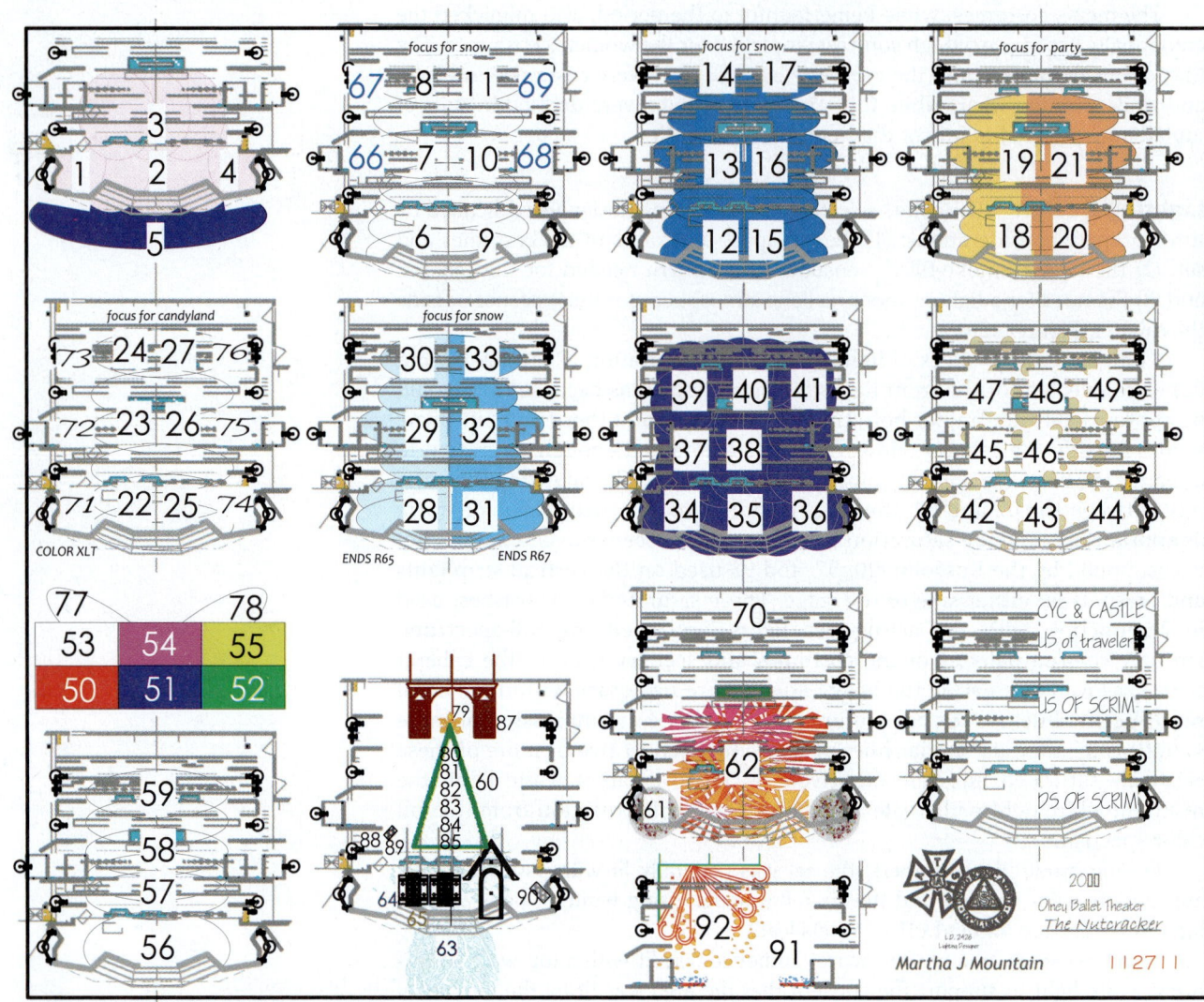

FIGURE 6.27
Magic sheets for the Olney Ballet Theatre's production of *The Nutcracker Ballet*. Lighting design by Martha J. Mountain. Courtesy of Martha J. Mountain.

Selected Reference

Birren, Faber. *Creative Color*. Schiffer, 1987.

Chapter 7

Mechanical Drafting

Diagrams, freehand drawings, and perspective sketches give a clear, general picture of what a proposed design or prop is supposed to look like, but they don't tell you how to build it. Similarly, sketches, notes, and verbal explanations describing the hanging location of the various instruments used to light a production are frequently more confusing than helpful. Fortunately, mechanical drawing, or drafting, provides a convenient, and efficient, solution to these challenges.

Traditionally, mechanical drawings were drawn by hand on vellum (tracing paper). They were **drawn to scale,** and as many views as necessary were created to provide a clear understanding of the shape of the finished object.

Today, most theatrical mechanical drawings are produced digitally using computer-aided drafting (CAD) programs. Both CAD and hand-drawn mechanical drawings, when accompanied by **specifications,** provide a complete visual and verbal description of the object.

Hand drafting for scenic construction is typically done in a scale of ½ inch to 1 foot. This means that each ½-inch measurement on the scale drawing represents 1 foot on the corresponding full-scale object. For example, the width of the flat shown in Figure 7.1 is indicated to be 3 feet, but if you measured its width on the actual scale drawing, you would find that the flat was only 1½ inches wide. Other scales are also used, but the ½ inch to 1 foot scale is traditionally used in most situations.

Mechanical drawings created in the **CAD environment** are usually drawn — **modeled** — full size. When **plates** are **plotted** from that CAD file, they are typically printed in a scale appropriate for the intended use of that drawing.

Mechanical drawings, and the ability to produce them, are extremely important in technical theatre. The scenic designer uses them to accurately describe every element of the setting(s) so those elements can be built as he or she envisioned them. The technical director uses them to show how each object is to be constructed. For the lighting designer, mechanical drafting provides the accurate scale "road map" that the electricians will use as a guide for hanging the lighting instruments. The sound designer and the projection specialist/designer use mechanical drafting to show, in exact scale representation, the location of the sound and projection equipment that will be used in support of the production. The scenic technicians, electricians, and sound and digital projection technicians must be able to read and understand the information contained on the plates.

In previous editions of this textbook, this chapter primarily focused on the tools and methods used to create hand-drafted mechanical drawings. While

draw to scale: To produce a likeness that is a proportional reduction of an object.

specifications: Clarifying notes that explain the building materials, textures, or special effects to be used in a design or other project.

CAD environment: The on-screen digital workspace in which objects are modeled in CAD. Includes the "modeling space" and the tools, menus, and buttons used to control the program.

modeled: In this case, to produce a digital likeness of an object.

plate: A sheet of mechanical drawings, drawn to scale.

plotted: Refers to printing a hardcopy (paper) drawing from a CAD file. The term derived from the historical use of plotters, which have largely been replaced by wide-format conventional printers.

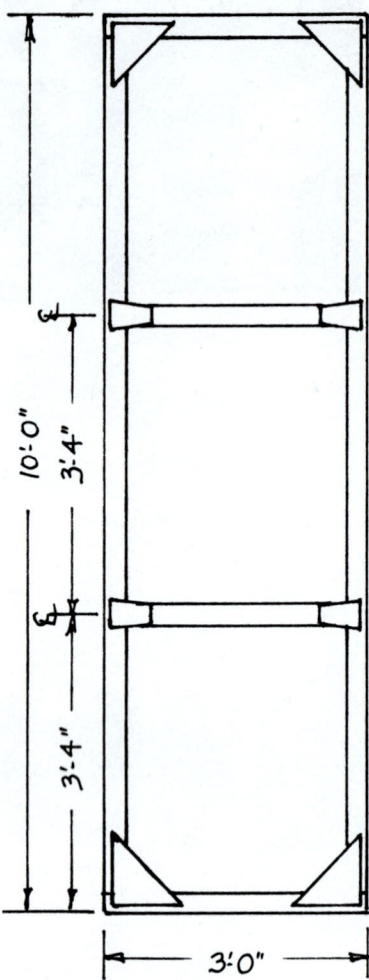

FIGURE 7.1
A flat drawn to scale.

rendering: In CAD, rendering refers to the application of lighting, color, and texture to the digital object.

raster files: Image files composed of pixels of various colors.

vector files: The lines, shapes, and colors of an image stored as mathematical formulae.

geometry: In this case, refers to the lines and shapes that form the object being created.

some theatre practitioners still use these tools — and many think knowing them remains an essential skill — the reality is that the majority of drafting in the contemporary theatre and entertainment industries is created — and often viewed — electronically.

Information about the CAD drafting process will be integrated into the material that follows. Much of the extant information, such as the material on the symbols and conventions used in theatrical drafting, applies equally to hand- and computer-drafting processes and will be discussed as such. However, to reflect current practice, the material on hand-drafting tools and equipment has been moved to Appendix C.

 ## Drawing for Envisioning and Inventing

CAD drawing will probably never entirely replace hand-drawn sketches and the building of functional models. But the ease with which computer models can be edited, adapted, and revised makes the CAD environment an incredibly useful workspace for dreaming up — and drafting — theatrical settings, construction techniques, light plots, and sound plots, or basically anything else that can be visualized.

Once you learn the basic rules of each method, it's relatively easy to create two-dimensional lines and shapes with either method. But the advantages of CAD over hand drafting become quickly apparent when you move beyond two-dimensional drawings. CAD enables you to: (1) create and model three-dimensional objects quickly and combine them to develop more complex shapes such as platforms and multilevel sets; (2) view the results from multiple angles and to zoom in and out for closer inspection of details; and (3) apply a variety of **rendering** techniques to create an accurate picture of what the object will look like when it is actually built. A fourth advantage, as stated previously, is that creating the objects in full scale allows them to be plotted in whatever scale is appropriate for the intended use.

There are two types of digital image files: **raster files** and **vector files**. Digital photographs are good examples of raster files. They are made up of millions of tiny points of color called pixels. The more pixels, the higher is the resolution of the image. A characteristic of raster files is that they contain only the number of pixels with which they are originally created. As a raster picture is enlarged, the original pixels are algorithmically moved apart by the software and new pixels are inserted into the gaps. The nature of these "invented" pixels creates the fuzzy picture seen in enlarged raster images.

CAD drawings are vector drawings. The information about each piece of **geometry** — the object being drawn — is saved as mathematical information instead of pixels. This means no matter how much you zoom in or out on a piece of geometry, no information is lost and the image does not become fuzzy.

The mathematical nature of vector files allows CAD to be both incredibly accurate and incredibly precise. For example, objects can be positioned within extremely narrow tolerances — less than 1/32 of an inch; when a line or object is positioned, it will remain where you put it unless you move it; and, for closer inspection of details, you can zoom in or out on an object without any loss of focus.

Of course, the accuracy and precision of CAD also have drawbacks. CAD doesn't easily lend itself to sketching or freehand drawing. The strength of those techniques lies in their looseness of line and quick execution — almost the complete opposite of the strengths of CAD. Trying to sketch or freehand draw in a CAD environment is frustrating. For those reasons, most CAD programs do not include tools for either sketching or freehand drawing.

The CAD environment is really helpful only when your design idea is to the point where the precision and accuracy of CAD will be helpful. So, gentle reader, sketch first; CAD later.

Drawing for Communication

One of the primary advantages of CAD over hand drafting is that you're creating digital files rather than discrete sheets of vellum. These files can be used in a variety of ways. A primary use is for printing paper plots. But in some shops, CAD files are read on screens and tablets in lieu of paper plates. CAD files are frequently shared electronically between designers, technicians, and the various shops during both design and production phases of a production. CAD files are used to create CAM (computer-assisted manufacturing) files — the files used to run CNC tooling machines. CAD files are also used by designers and technicians to generate models, renderings, and animated simulations.

Mechanical drawings used in technical theatre — whether hand-drawn or computer-generated — have rules and conventions that make the drawings more informative to everyone who reads them. These will be discussed in the next section.

Drafting Symbols and Conventions

The information in this section has been extracted from the United States Institute for Theatre Technology's (USITT) recommendations for standard graphic language in scenic design and technical production.

The concept of a standard must evolve from some logical base. In this case, that base is the only inflexible rule of technical drawing — that any graphic communication must be clear, consistent, and efficient. Although the USITT recommendations do not contain specific guidelines for the spacing of objects on a plate, any graphic presentation needs to adhere to the general recommendation of clarity: Do not crowd or unevenly space individual items on a plate. Equally important, all line weights, line types, symbols, conventions, and lettering should be consistent from plate to plate within a set of drawings. This does not mean that everyone will be expected to letter in the same manner or draw arrowheads in precisely the same way. It means that each drafter should be able to establish his or her style within the guidelines of the recommended standards and conform to that style throughout the drawings for a particular project or production. Finally, the standards and symbols used in any recommended guide should be efficient, both in ease of drawing and in ease of comprehension for the reader.

Line Weights

For hand-drawn plates, line weights show what is important in the drawing. Three line weights are recommended: thick, thin, and extra thick. Thick lines are 0.5 mm wide; thin lines, 0.3 mm; and extra-thick lines, 0.9 mm.

Thick lines are used to draw the object being represented. Thin lines are used to provide supplemental information — dimension lines, annotations, and so forth. Extra-thick lines are reserved for borders and the outlines of cut-through objects. Use of these line weights allows the object being represented with thick lines to visually "pop" from the plate. The supplemental information — drawn with thin lines — recedes in visual importance. The extra-thick lines are used simply for borders. The ground plan in Figure 7.2 provides an illustration of these characteristics.

Most CAD programs do not display line weights well on screen. Instead, color is typically used to represent line weight on screen, even though the line weight is also assigned to the geometry by the software. When working on a drawing with a black background, Figure 7.3, light-colored tints are typically used to represent thick lines, whereas darker tones — generally of the same color — are used to represent thick lines. The opposite is true when using a white or light-colored background: dark-valued hues represent thick lines, and lighter values are used for thin lines.

Line Types

Just as line weight and color are used to indicate the relative importance of the geometry in a drawing, different types of lines — line types — are used to indicate other information. Table 7.1 shows the most common line types used in theatrical production mechanical drawings.

Drafting Conventions

The indication on the ground plan of standard theatrical units such as chandeliers, shelves, fireplaces, and the like should be made using a sectional cutting

FIGURE 7.2
A ground plan for Arizona Summer Arts Festival, production of *K2*, designed by K. Pistor. Courtesy of K. Pistor.

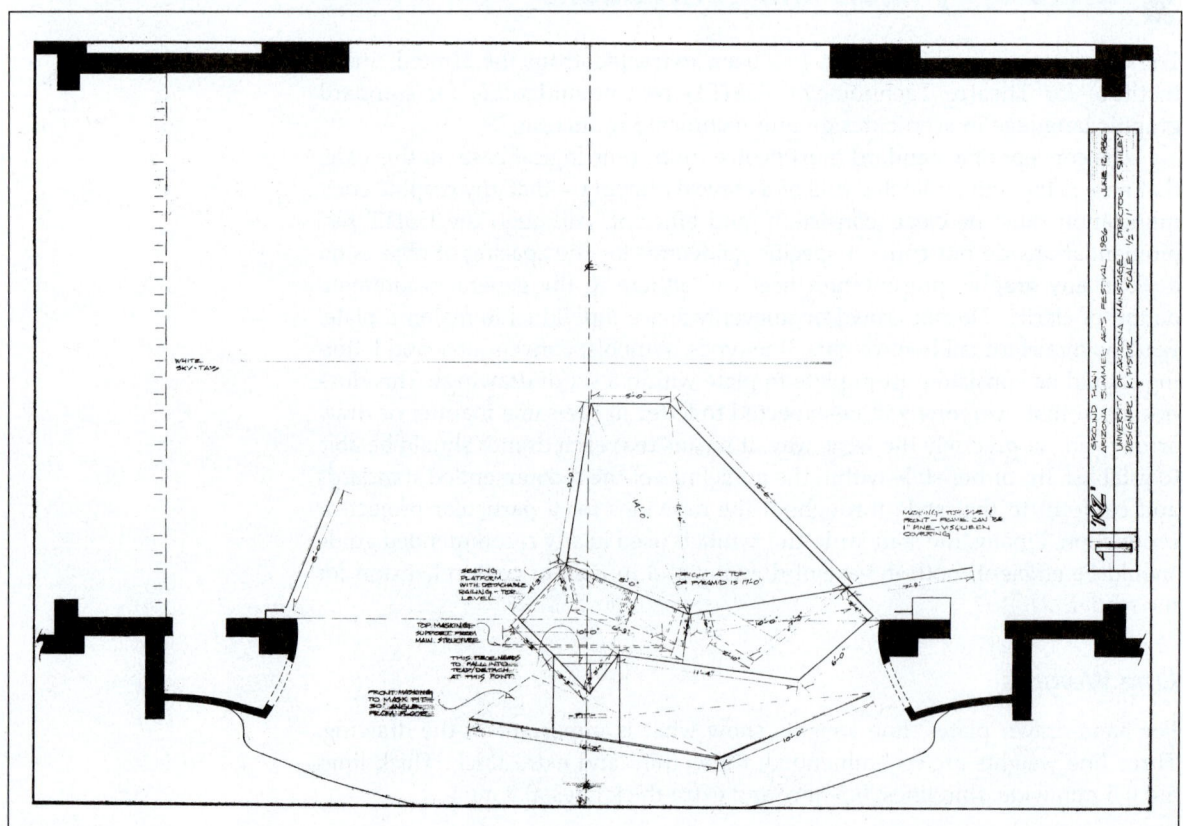

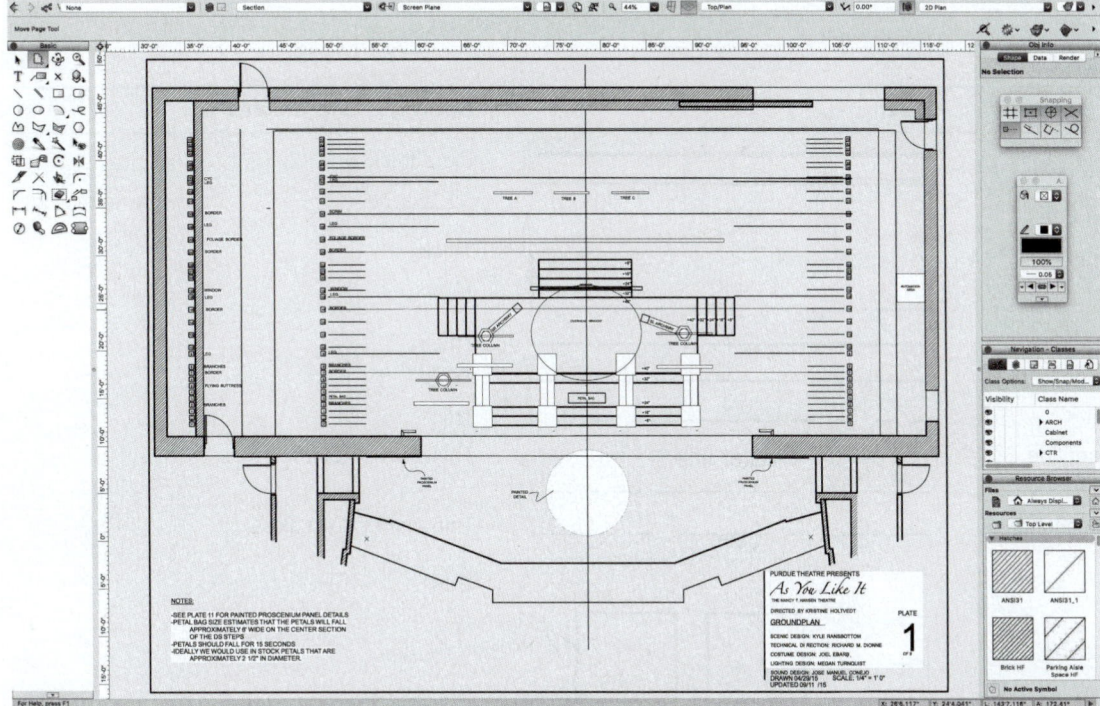

FIGURE 7.3
Screen capture of the ground plan for *As You Like It*. Scenic design by Kyle Ransbottom. Software: AutoCAD by AutoDesk. Courtesy of Kyle Ransbottom.

plan at whatever height is appropriate to provide the most descriptive view of the object. Using this guideline, an item such as a chandelier would be indicated by a circle utilizing a hidden line style (see Table 7.1), because it is not in contact with the stage floor. The circle should be drawn, in scale, the actual diameter of the chandelier at its widest point. This graphic would be placed in its appropriate location on the floor plan.

Other suspended objects such as ceiling beams or drops not in contact with the stage floor (for example, an Act II drop on an Act I floor plan) would be drawn in the appropriate outline using the hidden line type.

Lettering

The rule for hand lettering of mechanical drawings is that all lettering should be legible in a style that allows for rapid execution. That rule holds true for lettering in CAD as well. Characters should conform to the single Gothic style shown in Figure 7.4. Display fonts that are flowery or ornamental are difficult to read and undermine the function of all drafting: to communicate information.

Title Block

The title block on all plates of a single project — whether hand drawn or digital — should be placed in the same location on all drawings. It should be located in either the lower left- or right-hand corner of the drawing or on a strip along the bottom or right-hand side of each drawing. Regardless of location, the title block should include the following information:

1. name of producing organization or theatre

2. name of production, act, and scene, if appropriate

3. drawing title

TABLE 7.1

Drafting Conventions

Type	Style	Notes and Line Weights
Plate border		Extra thick Thick two lines
Cutting plane		Thick
Section outline		Thick
Visible outline		Thick
Hidden construction		Thin
Plaster ceiling and set line	Plaster line	Thin—note indicates type
Center line (all applications)		Thin—label ₵ on axis
Leader line		Thin
Extension and dimension lines		Thin—full arrowhead preferred
Section interior		Thin—evenly spaced at 45° angle to edge of paper or as clarity requires
Break line		Thin—both applications
Phantom line		Thin—used when an object repeats between position line. Also used to designate location of adjacent parts

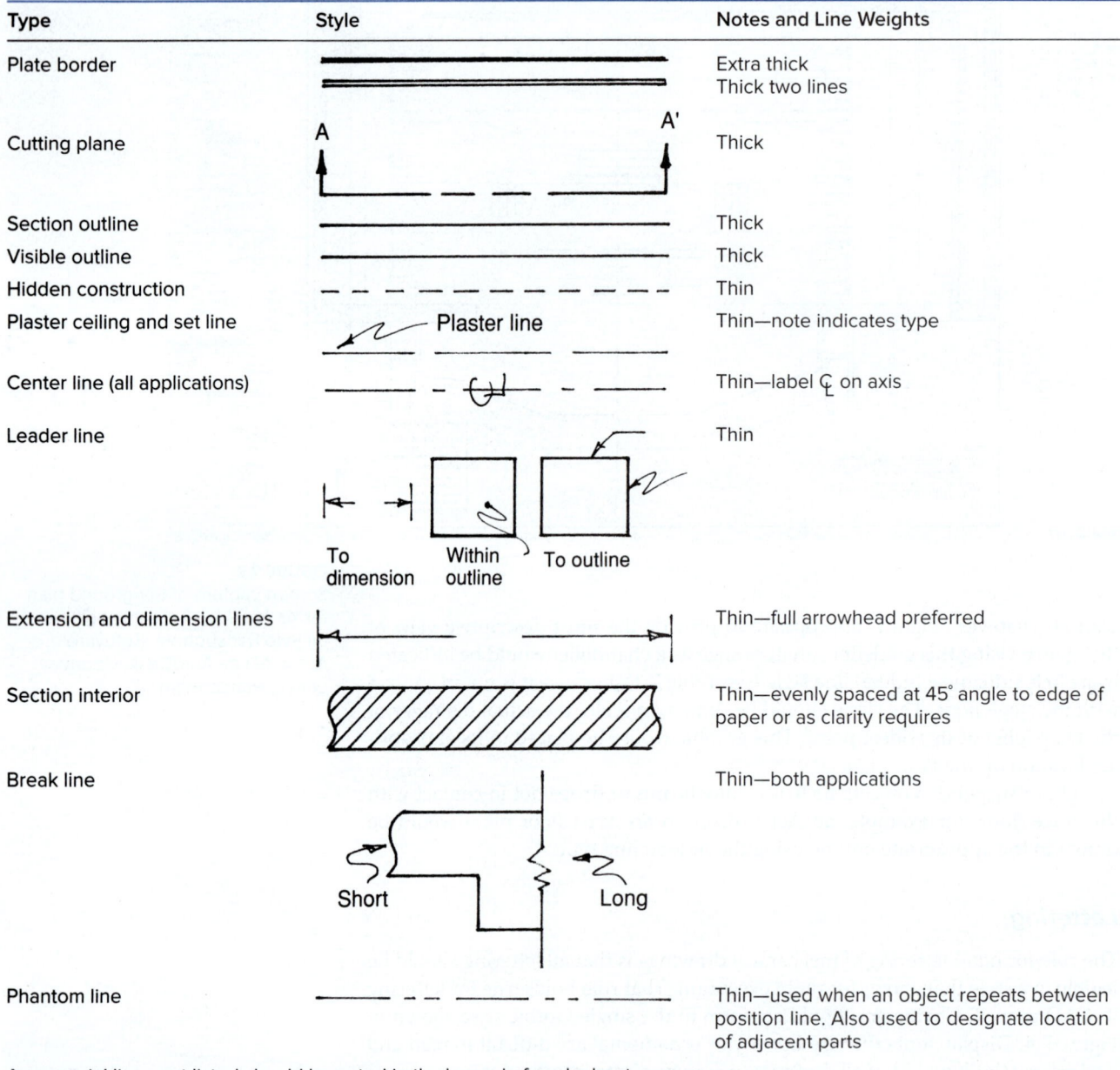

Any special lines not listed should be noted in the legend of each sheet.

FIGURE 7.4
Single-stroke Gothic lettering.

ABCDEFGHIJKLM
NOPQRSTUVWXYZ
1234567890

4. drawing number of drawings in the set: for example, $\frac{2}{10}$

5. predominant scale of the drawing

6. date the drawing was drafted

7. designer of the production

8. drafter, if different from the designer

9. approval of drawing, if applicable

Dimensions

The following guidelines will help ensure that your drawings are easily understood by everyone who reads them. In many cases, CAD software can be set up to apply some or all of these guidelines automatically.

1. Dimensions must be clear, consistent, and easily understood.

2. Dimensions should be oriented to read from the bottom or the right-hand side of the plate.

3. Dimensions less than one foot are given in inches without a foot notation (for example, 6″, 9½″).

4. Dimensions one foot and greater include the whole foot with a single prime mark followed by a dash and then inches followed by a double prime mark (for example, 7′-0½″, 18′-5¼″, 1′-3′).

5. Metric dimensions less than one meter should be noted as zero, decimal point, and portion of meter in numerals (for example, 0.25 m, 0.90 m). All measurements one meter and greater should be given as a whole meter number, decimal point, and portion of meter (for example, 1.5 m, 2.35 m).

6. Dimensions that require more space than available between extension lines are placed in proximity to the area measured, parallel with the bottom edge of the sheet, and directed to the point of reference by means of a leader line (see Table 7.1), as shown in Figure 7.5A.

7. Platform and tread heights are given in inches above the stage floor. Such heights are placed in circles at or near the centers of the platform or tread, as shown in Figure 7.5B.

8. Directions of arrows (when used to indicate elevation change on stairs, ramps, and the like) point away from the primary level of the drawing, as shown in Figure 7.5C.

9. A number of acceptable ways to indicate radii, diameters, centers, and angles are detailed in Figure 7.6.

Symbols

Figure 7.7 shows the standard symbols used in theatrical drafting. Whether hand drawn or drawn using CAD, these symbols should be used as substitutions for drawings of the actual objects.

Objects of nonstandard size, such as doorways, windows, platforms, archways, stairs, and ramps, should be drawn in their actual scale size using the conventions indicated by the symbols for those objects. According to this principle, a 2-foot-wide doorway would use the convention for a doorway, but the width of the doorway would be drawn in scale to 2 feet, as shown in Figure 7.8A. In a similar manner, a 4-foot-wide doorway would use the same convention, as shown in Figure 7.8B, but the scale width of the door would measure 4 feet. In

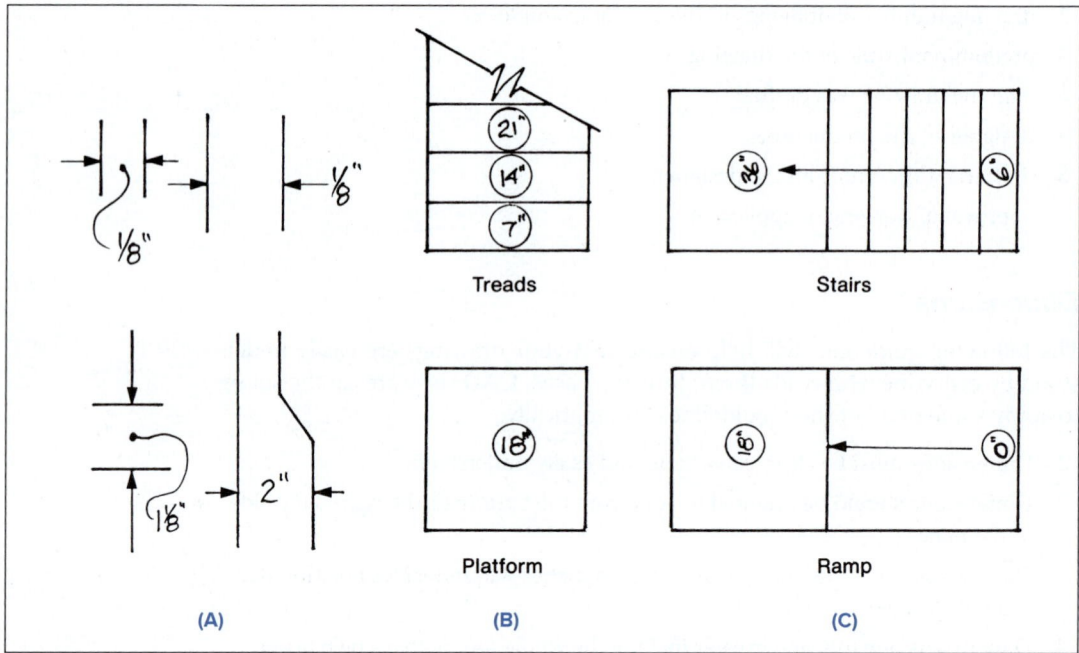

Treads

Stairs

Platform

Ramp

(A)   (B)   (C)

FIGURE 7.5
(A) Methods of indicating dimension. (B) Heights above or below the stage level are placed in circles near the center of the tread or platform. (C) Arrows are used to indicate change of elevation point away from the primary level of the drawing.

both cases, the depth of the door casing would be drawn to its actual scale depth. Decorative detail on either the door or the door casing need not be indicated on the ground plan unless it alters the depth or width of the door or casing.

Layers

Most CAD programs offer the ability to organize geometry in layers. Layers are the digital grandchildren of multiple vellum plates used in hand-drawn projects. The vellum plates — each having additional information —were placed on top of each other. When you looked at the stacked drawings, you could see additional information layered on top of the original — for example, the location of masking in relationship to the ground plan.

FIGURE 7.6
Methods of indicating radii, diameters, centers, and angles.

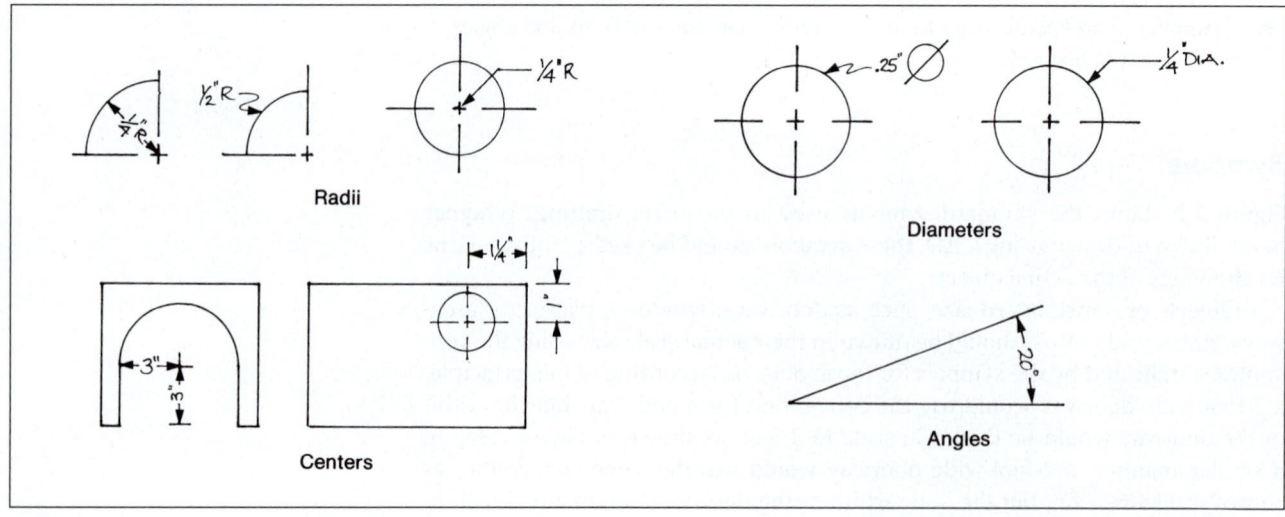

Radii

Diameters

Centers

Angles

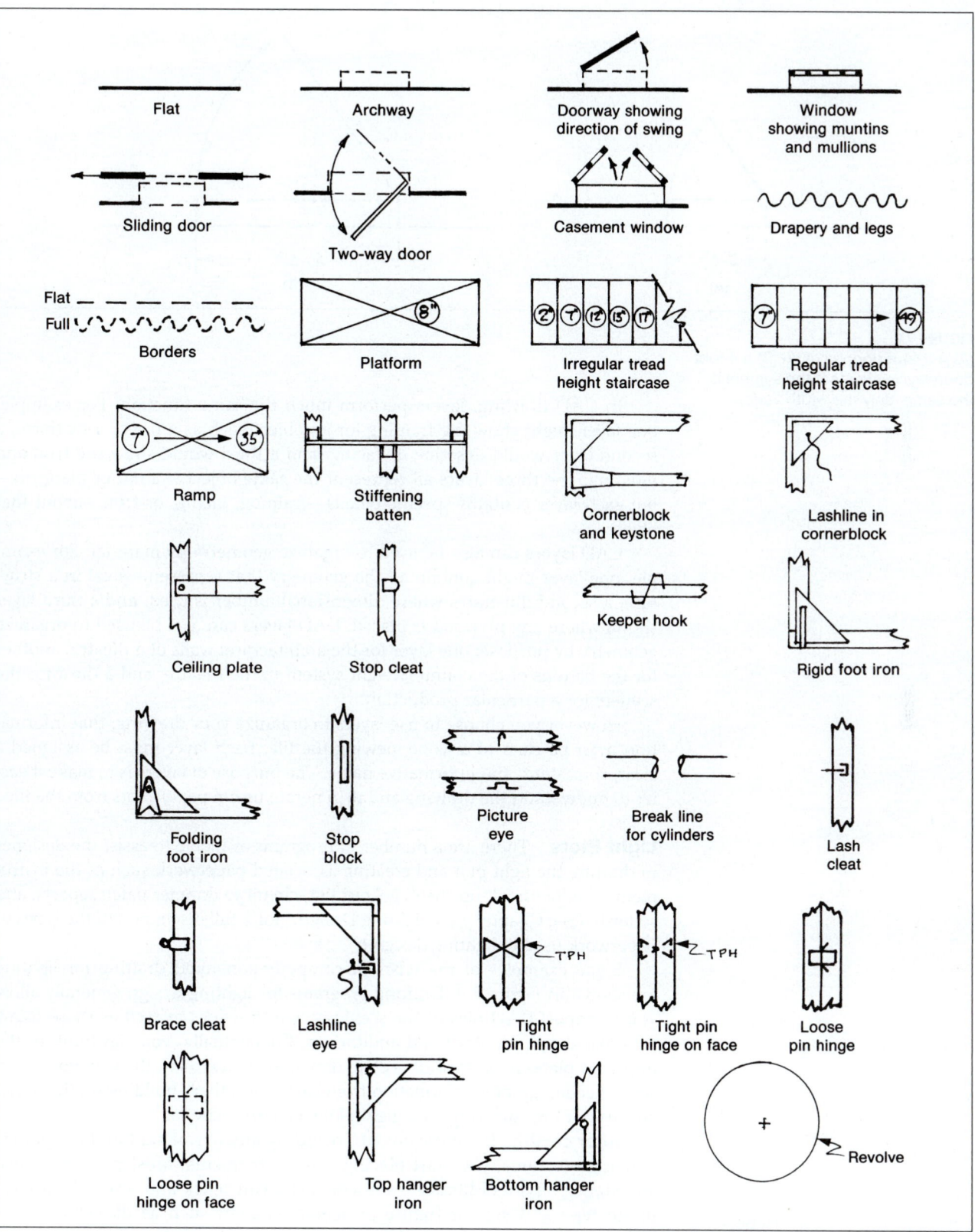

FIGURE 7.7
Technical production symbols.

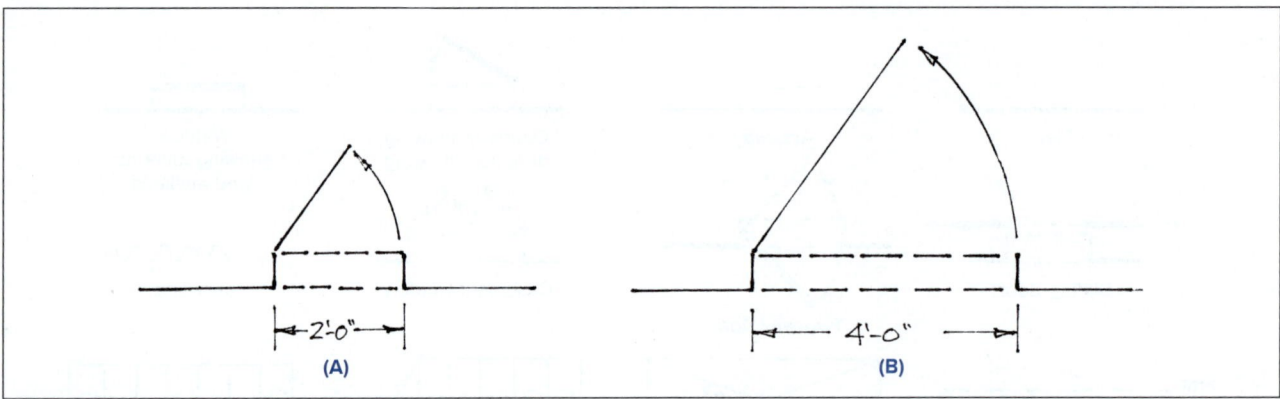

FIGURE 7.8
(A) A 2-foot doorway and (B) a 4-foot doorway. Notice that the symbol is the same, only the width varies.

In CAD drawing, layers perform much the same function. For example, one layer might show the framing for an object such as a flat or a platform, a second layer would describe its facing, and a third would show the trim and molding. The three layers all represent the same object — a flat or platform — but each layer contains specific details —framing, facing, or trim —about that object.

CAD layers can also be used to organize geometry by material. For example, one layer might contain all the geometry that represents steel in a structure, a second illustrates where dimensional lumber is used, and a third layer shows where any plywood is placed. CAD layers can also be used to organize geometry by purpose: one layer for the architectural walls of a theatre, another for the battens of the counterweight system in the theatre, and a third for the scenery for a particular production.

However you choose to use layers to organize your drawing, that information must be clear to anyone viewing the file. Each layer must be assigned a clear, consistent, and informative name. The purpose of layers is to make it easier to understand the drawing and to generate useful paper plots from the file.

Light Plots   There are a number of programs available to assist the designer in drafting the light plot and creating associated paperwork such as the instrument schedule/hook-up sheet, gel **cut list,** circuit to dimmer patch reports, and so forth. (See Chapter 14, "Lighting Design," for a full discussion of the types of paperwork used in lighting design.)

Some examples of the types of computer-generated drafting for lighting are shown in Figure 7.9. Drafting programs for lighting design generally allow you to import CAD files of the scenic design drawings as well as those drawings that detail the stage and auditorium. Conceptually, you can think of the imported plates as a stack of acetate drawings. Stack them the way you want; select needed graphic information from each layer; then, building on that base, create your own drawing – the light plot layout or sectional.

After creating the basic layout, including any permanent and temporary hanging positions, you start placing your instruments. Most programs have an extensive symbol library from which you can "click and drag" the appropriate type and size of fixture or scenic element such as drapes, trusses, and so forth. After placing the instrument symbol on the plot, you assign notational information — instrument number, color, circuiting, focus, and so forth – to each unit. Every time you select/place/edit an instrument or create any of the associated notational information, most programs will list

cut list: A list of the color media required for the lighting design for a particular production categorized by hue and size; used to assist in ordering and cutting the color media for a lighting design.

SoftPlot Report for file: C:\LITDES\USERINFO\SHOWS\GUYS\GUYSPLOT.LDP

Venue: Meadowvale Theatre
Production: Guys & Dolls
Director: Bob Ridell
Lighting Designer: Glen Miller
Date: 06-02-1996

Instrument Inventory Listing

Stock	Used	Hire	Type	Watts	Notes
44	44		STRAND ZOOM Lekolite 2206	1000	
18	18		STRAND 6 x 9 Lekolite 2209	1000	
15	15		STRAND 6 x 9 LEKO 40 - 12240	1000	
8	8		STRAND 6 x 16 LEKO 20 - 12220	1000	
2	2		STRAND 6 x 22 LEKO 15 - 12215	1000	
6	6		STRAND 6 x 12 Lekolite 2212	1000	
4	4		ALTMAN 6 x 12 360Q 6x12	750	
24	25	1	STRAND 8" Fresnel 3480	1000	
15	14		STRAND 6" Fresnel 3380	1000	
6	0		STRAND CODA 500/1 MkII - 5801	500	
6	0		STRAND Iris 1- 5911	1500	
4	2		STRAND 14" 4271	1000	
38	35		PAR-64 Q1000		
2	4	2	STRAND FLOODLIGHT	2000	

End of Report

(A)

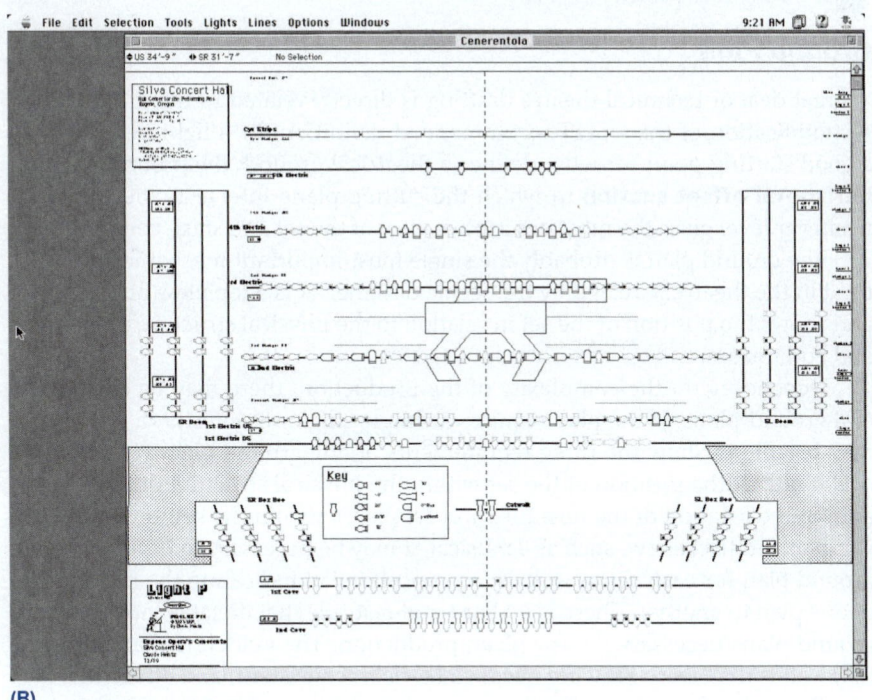

(B)

FIGURE 7.9
(A) Example of paperwork, in this case an Instrument Inventory Listing, produced with Soft Plot by Crescit Software. Lighting design by Glen Miller. (B) On-screen view of a portion of a light plot on the MacLux Pro demo disk. Software: MacLux Pro v. 1.5 by Aladdin Systems, Inc., and Raymond Lau.

it in the embedded database. That information can be selectively extracted from the database to create the various lists needed to organize and track the equipment. Most drafting programs allow you to export data to specialized database programs such as Lightwright for more sophisticated paperwork management. The most widely used lighting design drafting program is Vectorworks' Spotlight.

There are two types of data management programs for lighting design. The first is the sophisticated spreadsheet/database program used to organize the data associated with lighting design — instrument, circuiting, dimmer control, and cueing information — into seemingly endless lists that are a necessary evil in lighting design. The second type is a utility. These programs provide some type of information not normally included in drafting programs.

Lightwright is a popular data management program for lighting design. It provides advanced features not generally available in the data management portion of most drafting programs. "It can find mistakes, compare two sets of paperwork, figure your circuit and dimmer needs, automatically renumber a pipe, renumber or rearrange your channels or dimmers, or even assign dimmers automatically based on your channels."[1] Database information generated by a drafting program such as Vectorworks' Spotlight is imported into Lightwright for manipulation, organization, and printing.

Additional information about currently available software for lighting design can be found online and in articles and advertisements in trade magazines such as *Stage Directions* and *Pro Lights & Staging News.*

Computer drafting for lighting design is clearly the way of the future. What is equally clear is that at the present time, as well as in the foreseeable future, lighting designers will need to know how to do both – draft by hand and draft on a computer.

Types of Drawings

Ground Plan

A great deal of technical theatre drafting is directly related to the ground plan. A modification of the USITT-recommended definition for a light plot provides a good starting point for what defines a theatrical ground: the ground plan is a **horizontal offset section** in which the cutting plane intersects the theatre at whatever level gives the most descriptive view of the set and stage configuration.

The ground plan is probably the single most important mechanical drawing used in the theatre. Created by the scenic designer, it is a top view of the setting and shows the position of the set in relation to the physical structure of the stage and auditorium.

Depending on the complexity of the production, there may be one or several ground plans. If the play requires a simple single-set interior, a single plan may be able to show the three requirements of any ground plan: (1) the shape of the set, (2) the position of the set within the physical structure of the theatre, and (3) the location of the furniture and set pieces within the set. If the play is a complex multiset show, such as a musical, it may be necessary to have a separate ground plan for each set as well as a composite plan indicating the relationship of one plan to another. There is no hard-and-fast rule that dictates the number of ground plans necessary for any given production. The guideline that should be followed is that every drawing needs to be clear, consistent, and efficient.

Ground plans are usually drawn or plotted in a scale of ½ inch to 1 foot. Drawings in this scale are easy to read, and the size of the paper, usually 24 by 30 inches, is convenient for use in the shop. If you are working in a very large, or very small, theatre, it might be appropriate to use a larger or smaller scale for the ground plan. The ground plan shown in Figure 7.10 illustrates all the pertinent data that need to be included for a proscenium production.

The set line is a leader line that extends, parallel with the proscenium arch, across the farthest downstage point(s) of the set. The plaster line is

horizontal offset section: A section drawing with a horizontal cutting plane, which does not remain fixed but varies to provide a view of important details.

[1] John McKernon Software, "What Is Lightwright?"

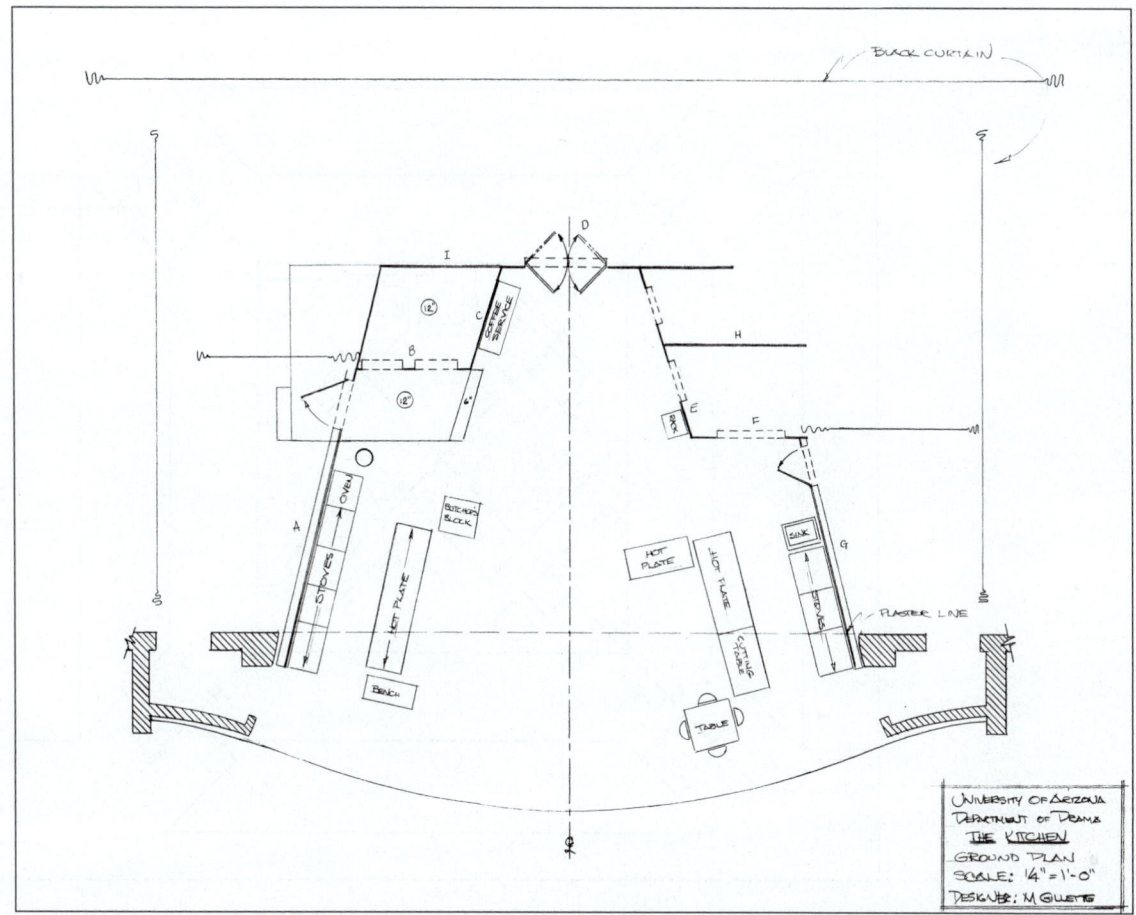

FIGURE 7.10
Ground plan
of *The Kitchen.*
Designed by
J. Michael
Gillette.

a leader line that extends across the opening of the proscenium arch. The fixed point from which this line normally extends is the upstage edge of the proscenium arch, although any other permanent or semipermanent physical element of the stage or its equipment, such as the edge of the false proscenium, could also be used. The center line runs perpendicularly to the set line from the midpoint, or center, of the opening of the proscenium arch. It extends from the apron to the upstage wall of the stage. The margin line is an aesthetically pleasing line that is placed around the border of the plate approximately a ½ inch from the edge of the paper. The margin line can be functionally useful as well. When computer drafting and printing on small paper, you'll know that something isn't missing if the margin line is neatly encircling your entire plate.

Procedurally, it is normally advisable and convenient to draw the structure of the theatre first, then draw the scenery, and finish the plate by drawing the furniture and the margin line. If you are designing for a thrust or arena stage, you will not have a proscenium arch to serve as a reference for your set line and center line. In this case, you still need to establish two reference lines that have an identifiable connection with some permanent element of the stage or auditorium space, as shown in Figure 7.11. Most designers prefer to establish two intersecting lines that cross in the relative center of the set and then extend those lines until they intersect some element of the physical structure of the theatre. It then becomes a relatively simple matter to measure from that point of intersection to an identifiable element of the

FIGURE 7.11
An arena ground plan.

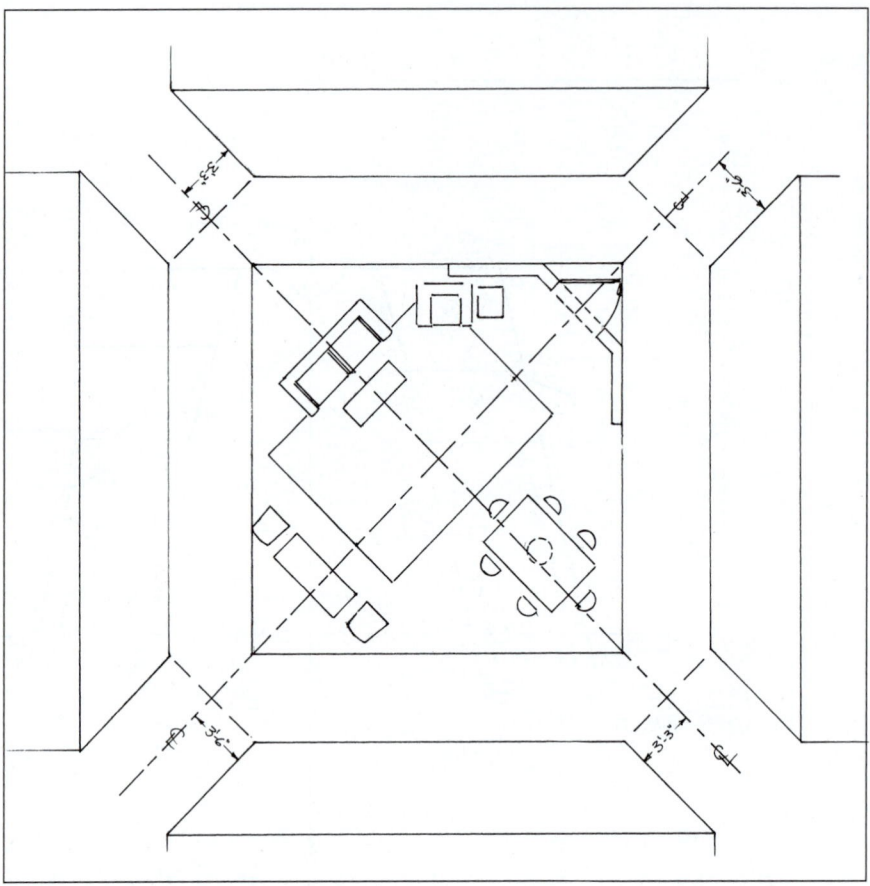

theatre's structure such as a door frame or exposed water pipe. On a proscenium, thrust, or arena stage, these intersecting lines (set and center) are used as the base lines for transferring the scenic designer's ground plan from the drawings to the actual stage floor.

Sectional Drawings

A sectional drawing provides a view of an object as though it had been cut along some imaginary plane. A scenic sectional, also called a hanging plot (Figure 7.12A), shows a sectional view of the stage with the cutting plane of the section being on the center line of the stage. This drawing is used to show the relative position of the set, masking, and various lighting instruments. It is used to help determine trim heights for masking, the heights of various scenic pieces, and similar tasks. A sectional drawing frequently provides the best way of explaining a shape with irregular surfaces, as shown in Figure 7.12B.

Other sectional drawings are used for a variety of purposes. The vertical and horizontal sectional drawings that are used for determining sight-line drawings are discussed in Chapter 8, "Perspective Drawing," and the sectional drawings used in lighting design are discussed in Chapter 14, "Lighting Design."

Front Elevations

A front elevation is a front view of the setting as it would appear if it were flattened out until it was in a single plane and viewed as though the observer were

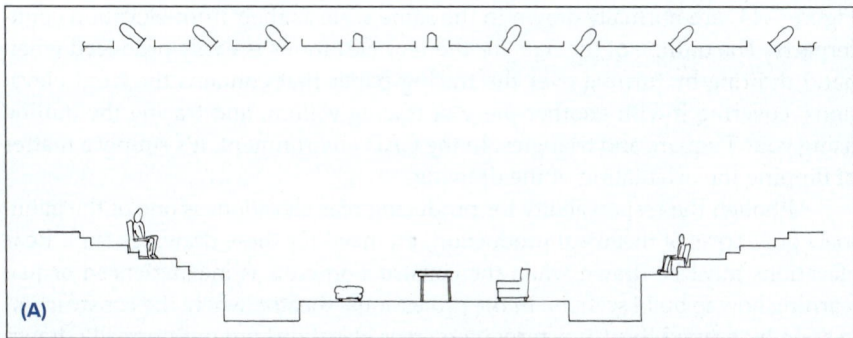

(A)

FIGURE 7.12
(A) Sectional drawing of a stage. (B) An irregularly shaped object can be explained with a sectional drawing.

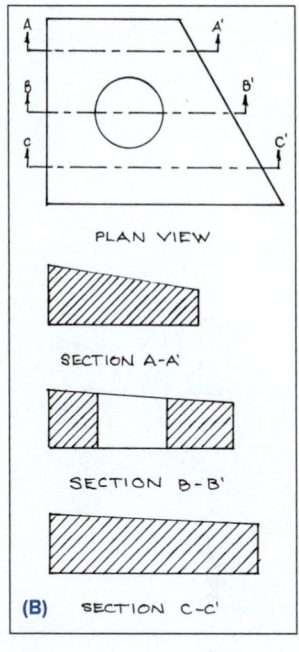

PLAN VIEW

SECTION A-A'

SECTION B-B'

(B)   SECTION C-C'

standing exactly at right angles to it. The purpose of these drawings, usually drafted in a scale of ½ inch to 1 foot when hand drafting, is to show the location and measurements of all objects that cannot be recorded on the ground plan. As shown in Figure 7.13, the position, size, and arrangement of all structural elements such as walls, doors, and windows, as well as the location of any built-in items, are given on the front elevations. Decorative and trim features on the walls, such as pictures, baseboards, chair rails, wainscoting, cornices, and so on, are also indicated on the front elevations.

Rear Elevations

Rear elevations show the reverse side of objects depicted in the front elevations. This rear view allows the construction details — placement and dimensions of stiles, rails, toggles, and so forth — to be shown. Rear elevations, shown in

FIGURE 7.13
Front elevations of *The Kitchen*. Designed by J. Michael Gillette.

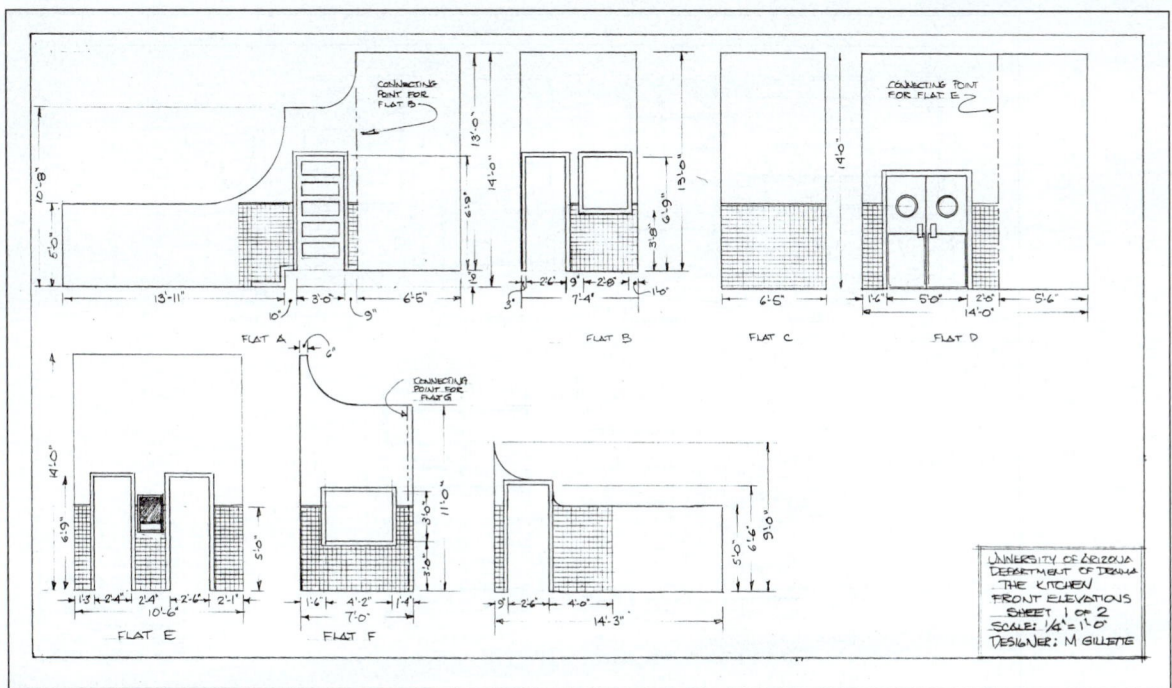

Figure 7.14, are normally drawn in the same scale as their front-elevation counterparts. The outline of the flats for the rear elevations is easily produced when hand drafting by turning over the tracing paper that contains the front elevations, covering it with another piece of tracing vellum, and tracing the outline using your T square and triangles. In the CAD environment, it's simply a matter of flipping the orientation of the drawing.

Although the responsibility for producing rear elevations is one of the genuinely gray areas of theatrical production, the need for these drawings isn't. Rear elevations must be drawn when the construction crew is inexperienced or just learning how to build scenery. In the professional theatre, where the construction is done by trained theatrical carpenters, rear elevations are not normally drawn for ordinary construction items such as flats and platforms. They are made only when the object to be built is unusual enough to warrant the precise explanation that the rear elevation provides. In those instances, the drawings are usually done by the scene-shop foreman in consultation with the scenic designer.

In educational theatre, the responsibility for the production of the rear elevations becomes fuzzier. Generally speaking, the rear elevations are the responsibility of the technical director. Due to a variety of circumstances, however, the drawing may be accomplished by the scenic designer or student assistant designers. Regardless of who actually draws the rear elevations, they are vital, as previously noted, to give student carpenters a precise guide for building every element of the setting. Rewards will be reaped in terms of reduced construction errors, better training techniques, lower costs, better use of time, and less frustrated (therefore happier) students.

Detail Drawings

Many times the scale of ½ inch to 1 foot normally used in drawing or printing front elevations reduces the size of some of the smaller set features to the point that it is difficult, if not impossible, to include all of the dimensions and notes

FIGURE 7.14
Rear elevations of *The Kitchen*.
Designed by J. Michael Gillette.

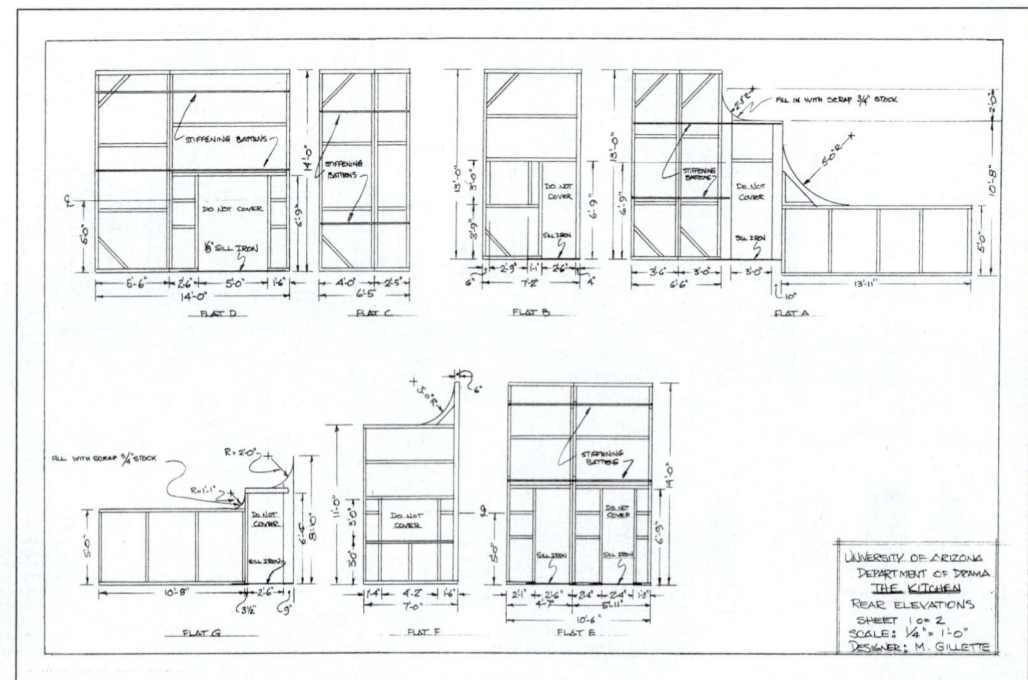

necessary for a complete understanding of the object. In these cases, a larger scale, such as 1 inch or 1½ inches to 1 foot, is frequently used.

If the smaller features of the set are intricately detailed, it is usually both easier and faster to draw them full scale. This would certainly be the case with the design for a turned banister or the pattern for a wallpaper design. It is much easier to construct this type of object from a full-size drawing than from one that has been proportionally reduced to a smaller scale.

Many features of a setting cannot be fully described by drawing them in top and front views alone. Three-dimensional objects normally require a third (usually side) view to supplement the other two. Objects that cannot be fully described with only a front, top, and side view, such as an elaborate fireplace or an intricately designed stained-glass window, can usually be well described through the use of orthographic projection, isometric drawing, oblique drawing, or cabinet drawing. Although this task is somewhat odious when hand drafting, it's a fairly easy process when working in CAD.

Orthographic Projection   Orthographic projection describes an object with a series of scale elevations showing each side of the article, as shown in Figure 7.15.

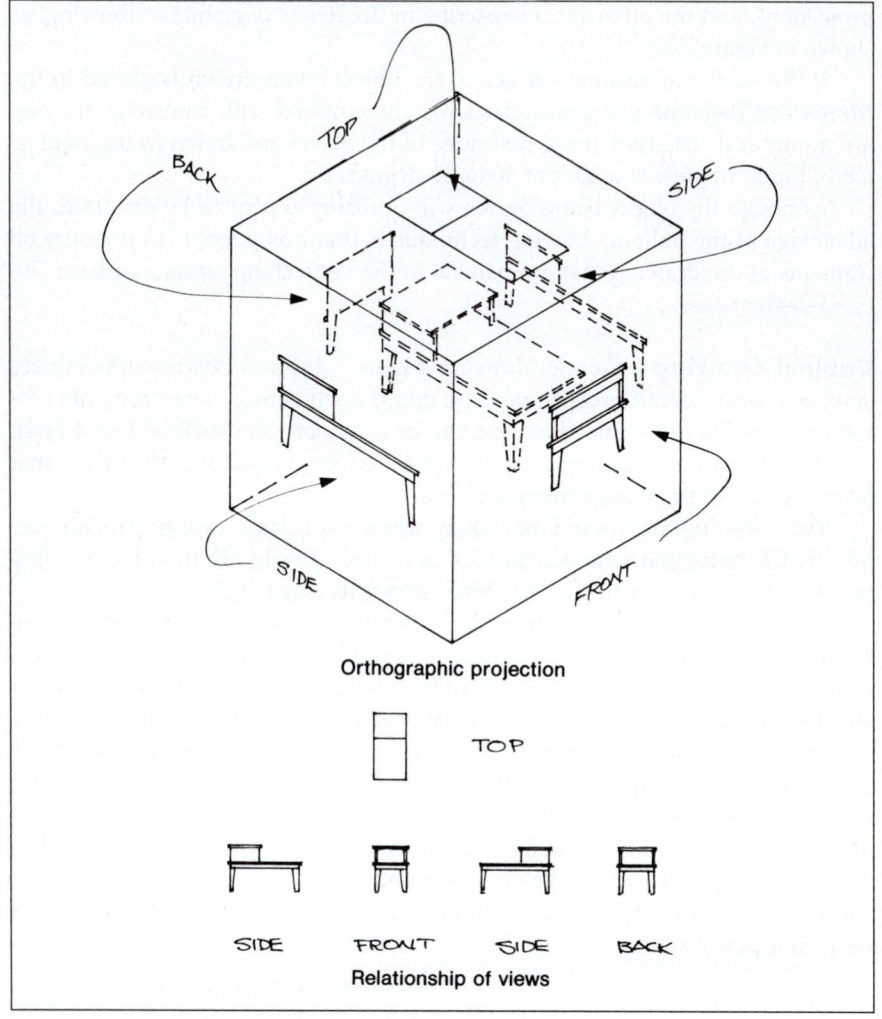

Orthographic projection

Relationship of views

FIGURE 7.15
Orthographic projection.

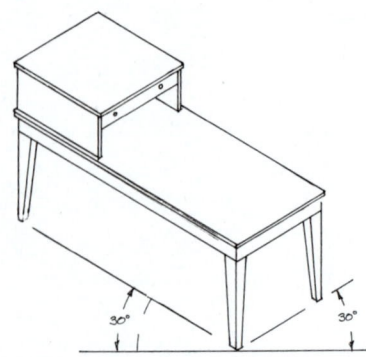

FIGURE 7.16
Isometric drawing.

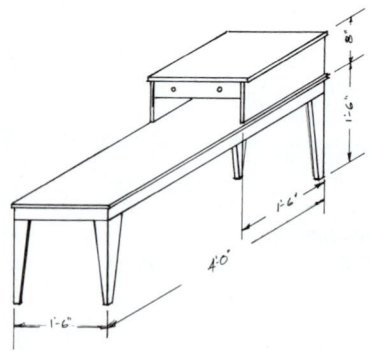

FIGURE 7.17
Oblique drawing.

The different views of the table are each represented by a separate drawing. Notice that each drawing shows the table as if the observer were standing at right angles to that side of the table.

Isometric Drawing   Isometric drawing provides a fast and easy way of representing an object pictorially without becoming involved with perspective. These drawings are based on three lines called the isometric axes. Two of these axes, illustrated in Figure 7.16, are located at 30 degrees above the horizontal plane on either side of the third axis, which is perpendicular to the base line. Dimensions can be measured at their true length along any of the isometric axes or on lines parallel to them. Lines that are not located on or parallel to the isometric axes cannot be measured.

Because isometric drawing does not take into account the effects of foreshortening or the principles of perspective, it is inevitable that some finished drawings will appear to be distorted. This is especially true of large drawings; the larger the drawing, the more obvious the distortion becomes. Irregular shapes (those with non-square bases) are also difficult to draw and, if drawn, may seem to be misshapen. Again, CAD makes this process much easier.

Oblique Drawing   Oblique drawing is a combination of the principles of orthographic and isometric drawing. In oblique drawing, one of the faces of the object is placed at right angles to the observer's line of sight (as in orthographic projection), and the other faces subscribe to the tenets of isometric drawing, as shown in Figure 7.17.

If the most complicated surface of the object being drawn is placed in the front view, then the distortion problems encountered with isometric drawing are minimized. The remaining two sides of the object are drawn to the right or left of the front view at angles of 30 or 45 degrees.

Although the object being drawn will probably appear to be distorted, the advantage of the oblique-drawing technique is that it is possible to measure all elements of the drawing that are parallel to the vertical, horizontal, or base (30- or 45-degree) axes.

Cabinet Drawing   Cabinet drawing (Figure 7.18) and oblique drawing are similar in every detail except one: The depth or thickness measurements of a cabinet drawing are reduced by one-half or a similar ratio such as 1 to 4 (1:4). This foreshortening is done in an attempt to reduce the pictorial distortion that occurs if the depth measurement is excessive.

Two precautions should be taken when using this drafting technique. Be sure the reduction ratio is printed in a conspicuous location on the drawing and specify that the written depth dimension is its true length.

In summary, mechanical drawings — whether hand drawn or drawn using CAD — are created for one purpose — to provide clear, comprehensive visual communication. The standards and guidelines that have been suggested in this chapter are intended to help you reach that goal. But don't follow them blindly simply because they look like rules. Remember that the intended application of each drawing is what dictates the appearance of that specific plate. And for those of you who are still hand drafting, keep your work area and drafting equipment clean; use a "pig" to keep your drawings clean ("pigs" are explained in Appendix C); practice and develop a clear and confident printing style based on single-stroke Gothic; apply consistent pressure to the pencil; and always, always keep your pencil sharp.

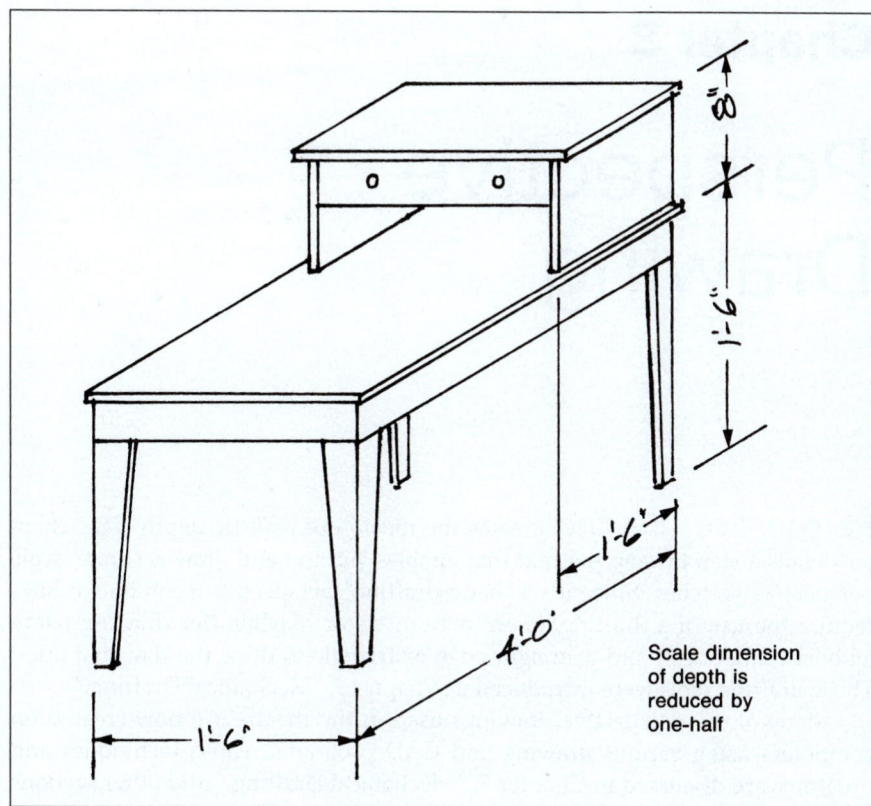

FIGURE 7.18
Cabinet drawing.

Selected References

Dorn, Dennis, and Mark Shanda. *Drafting for the Theatre*. Southern Illinois Press, 1998.
Morgan, Harry. *Perspective Drawing for the Theatre*. Drama Book Specialists, 1979.
Payne, Darwin Reid. *Computer Scenographics*. Southern Illinois University Press, 1994.
Sweet, Harvey, and Deborah M. Dryden. *The Complete Guide to Drawing for the Theatre*. Allyn & Bacon, 2nd ed., 1994.
Warfel, William. *Handbook of Stage Lighting Graphics*. Drama Book Specialists, 1974.

Chapter 8

Perspective Drawing

Perspective drawing creates the illusion of realistic depth. This chapter details a step-by-step method that enables you to hand draw accurate, scale perspective sketches. Since it's a "hand-drafting" perspective technique, it does require the use of a drafting board, a T square or Mayline (for drawing parallel horizontal lines), and a straight edge or triangle to draw the diagonal lines. Those drafting tools were introduced in Chapter 7, "Mechanical Drafting."

Many of the perspective drawings used in the theatre are now created on computers using various drawing and CAD programs. Those techniques and programs are discussed in Chapter 7, "Mechanical Drafting," and other sections of this book.

A pleasant by-product of learning this technique is that once you've mastered this process, you'll probably be surprised that you can "suddenly" freehand draw surprisingly accurate perspective sketches. That's because this technique trains your mind how to draw in perspective.

Principles of Perspective

Drawing three-dimensional objects so they appear to have depth is based on the principle of **foreshortening**, the idea that any set of receding parallel lines apparently converge to a single point. In Figure 8.1, three separate sets of parallel lines are used to create that illusion: the telephone poles, the road, and the fence line.

Part of the perspective illusion is based on the viewer's prior knowledge. We all intuitively understand that telephone poles are relatively uniform in height. When you look at the row of telephone poles depicted in Figure 8.1, it's fairly easy to visualize a straight line connecting the tops of those poles and a separate line connecting the bottoms. Those two lines create a set of parallel lines that, when extended, converge at a single point on the horizon, as shown in Figure 8.1.

A close analysis of Figure 8.1 further explains how foreshortening works. Notice that telephone pole "A" is taller than pole "B." Also notice that each succeeding telephone pole becomes shorter as the center of the drawing is approached. An imaginary straight line could be traced along the tops of those telephone poles and extended to the horizontal line that forms the horizon. A second imaginary straight line could be traced connecting the bottoms of the poles and extended to the horizon. Those two imaginary lines form a set of parallel lines. That's what creates the illusion of depth — those parallel lines receding to the same **vanishing point** on the horizon.

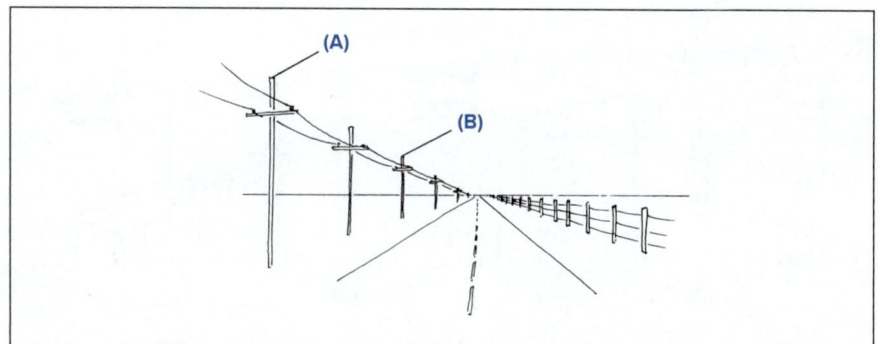

FIGURE 8.1
The principles of foreshortening.
See text for details regarding
(A) and (B).

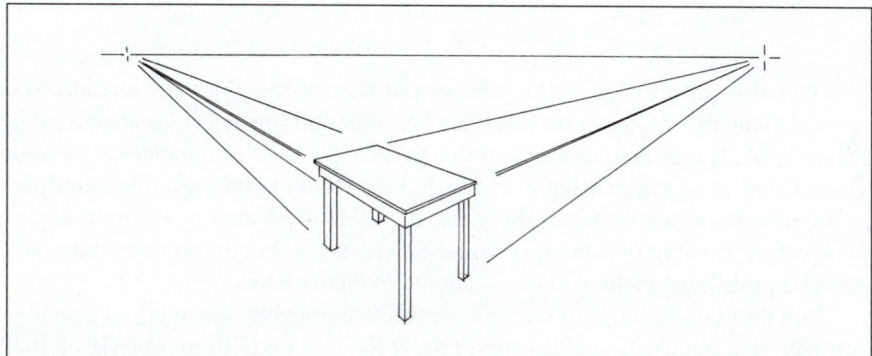

FIGURE 8.2
Parallel sets of lines recede to the
same vanishing point.

The same foreshortening principles are applied to both the road and the fence line. In Figure 8.1, all three sets of parallel lines — telephone poles, road, and fence line — recede to the same vanishing point on the horizon.

Figure 8.2 applies the foreshortening principle — parallel lines receding to a vanishing point on the horizon — to two sets of nonparallel lines. The sides and ends of the table and the feet of the table legs form two separate sets of parallel lines. Each set of parallel lines recedes to its own vanishing point on the **horizon line** (HL).

horizon line: A line in a perspective drawing representing the meeting of the earth and the sky; normally drawn parallel to the top or bottom edge of the paper.

With the above principles in mind, to draw an accurate perspective sketch, you also have to know the following additional information:

1. the distance from the observer to the object being drawn

2. the height of the observer's eye above the object being drawn

3. the size and shape of the object

Figure 8.3 illustrates the interrelationship among these three facts.

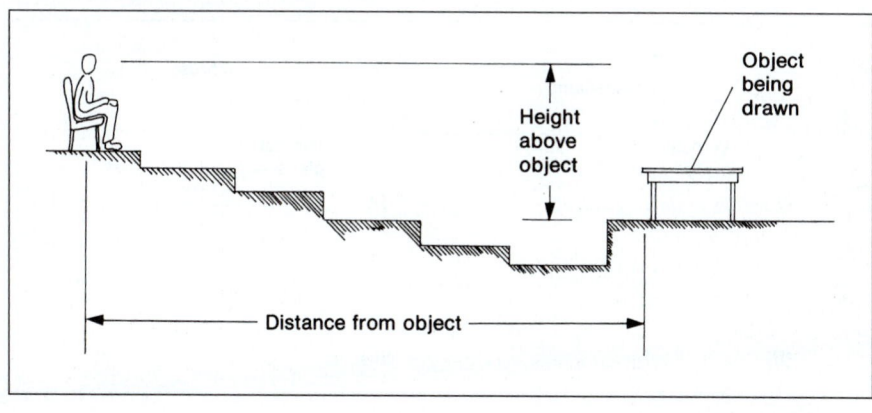

Object
being
drawn

Height
above
object

Distance from object

FIGURE 8.3
To draw in perspective, you need to
know (1) the distance to the object,
(2) your height above the object, and
(3) the size and shape of the object.

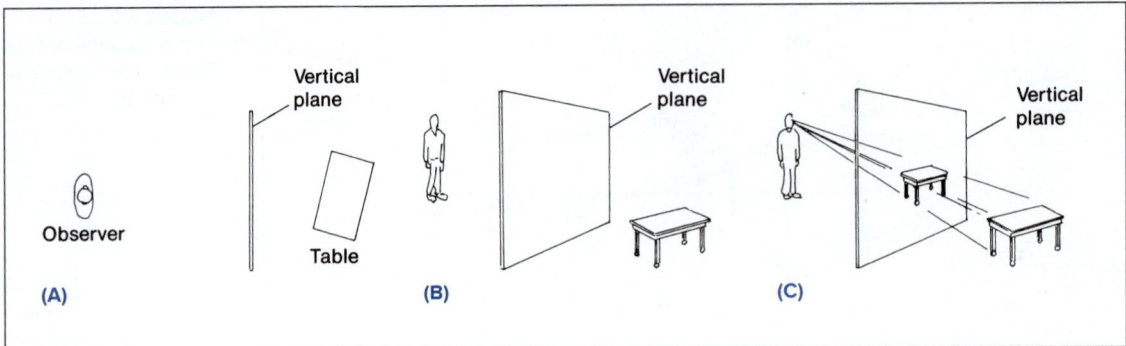

FIGURE 8.4
Perspective drawing is like drawing the outline of the object on a vertical pane of glass erected between you and the object you're observing. See text for explanations of (A), (B) and (C).

You also need to know the relative position of the object in relation to a vertical plane that is placed between the observer and the object, as illustrated in Figure 8.4A. It may help to think of this vertical plane as a transparent piece of glass. Think of yourself sitting in the auditorium looking through this "window" at the objects on the stage (in this case, the table illustrated in Figure 8.4B). A perspective drawing of this table would be created if its outline were magically traced on this huge plate of glass, as shown in Figure 8.4C.

You don't need magic to create a perspective drawing; this method provides you with that ability. It enables you to draw the outline of those objects on that vertical plane. The only significant differences are that the vertical plane is your drawing paper, not glass, and you don't have to be sitting in the auditorium looking at the stage to create the drawing.

The location of this vertical plane is the only adjustment that needs to be made when applying this method of perspective drawing to proscenium, thrust, or arena theatres. As illustrated in Figure 8.5, the vertical plane in a proscenium theatre could be placed to coincide with the proscenium arch. For a thrust theatre, it would be more appropriate to locate the vertical plane just outside the auditorium end of the thrust. For an arena stage, it could be erected in the aisle just beyond the edge of the stage that is closest to the observer.

Experience really *is* the best teacher, so the easiest way for you to develop a full understanding of drawing in perspective is to create a drawing in mechanical perspective. Later in this chapter we'll go step by step through several practice exercises.

FIGURE 8.5
The vertical plane for the three forms of stage configuration is usually located in slightly different places. See text for explanations of (A), (B) and (C).

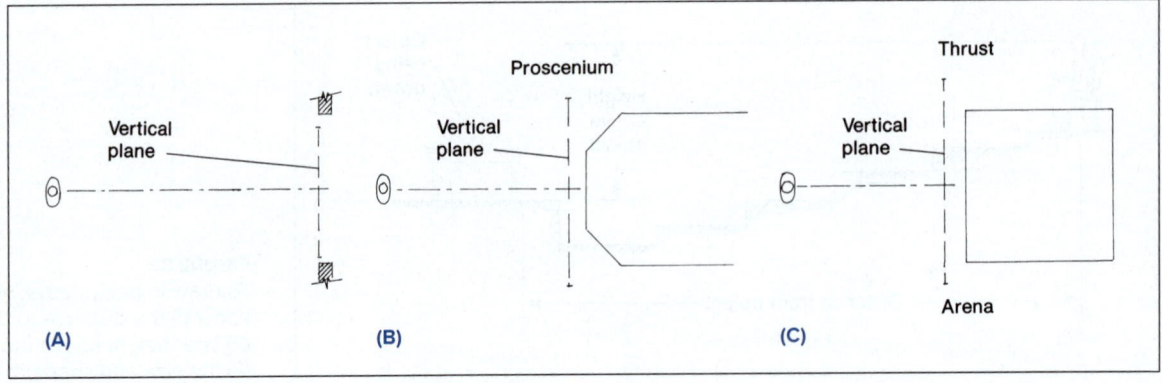

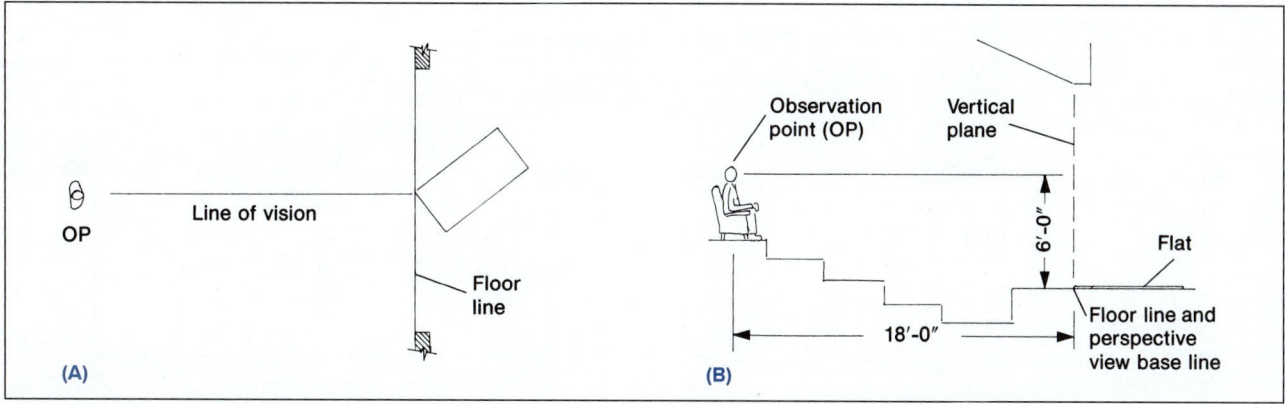

FIGURE 8.6
Plan and section layouts for the practice exercise. See text for explantions of (A) and (B).

Creating a Perspective Drawing

Figure 8.6 illustrates the basic information you need to create a scale perspective drawing using the technique explained in this chapter.

Figure 8.6A is an overhead view of someone seated in the auditorium looking at a flat lying on the stage floor at a 45-degree angle to the **floor line**. Figure 8.6B is a side view of the same scene. The observation point (OP) is 18 feet from the proscenium arch and 6 feet above the stage floor.

Figures 8.7A to 8.7H illustrate how to create a scale mechanical drawing of that scene.

Figure 8.7A shows the basic layout, including the proscenium arch, the 45-degree angled flat lying on the stage, and the basic perspective grid lines — one vertical and three horizontal — used to create the drawing.

After the perspective grid and flat are laid out on a sheet of paper on the drafting board, the vanishing points for the various sets of parallel lines need to be established. (Remember that each set of receding parallel lines converges on a specific vanishing point on the horizon line. The only exception to this rule is lines that are parallel to the floor line — they don't converge; they stay parallel to the floor line.)

The flat in Figure 8.7A is composed of two sets of parallel lines. AB and DC are one set. AD and BC are the other. Each of these systems of lines (AB/DC and AD/BC) has its own vanishing point on the horizon line.

To establish the vanishing point (VP) for lines AB and DC on the perspective grid, draw a very faint guide line, parallel to lines AB/DC, from OP until it intersects the floor line, as shown in Figure 8.7B. From that point — the point of intersection between the guide line for AB/DC and the floor line — drop a vertical line until it intersects the horizon line. This point — the point of intersection between the dropped vertical and the horizon line — establishes the vanishing point for line system AB/DC. The vanishing point for lines AD and BC is found in the same way: draw a very light guide line from OP parallel to lines AD/BC until it intersects the floor line. From this point, drop a vertical to the horizon line. This point will be the vanishing point for lines AD/BC.

A basic rule of this perspective method is that any point in contact with the floor line is unaffected by the laws of perspective. As explained earlier, the reason is that the floor line and the perspective-view base line are simply different views of the same thing. The floor line is a ground plan view of an imaginary line drawn across the stage at some easily identifiable location such as the proscenium arch. The perspective-view base line is the bottom edge of a vertical plane that is erected at the floor line.

floor line: The base of the vertical plane in a perspective drawing; for a proscenium sketch, usually drawn across the stage in contact with the downstage edge of the proscenium arch.

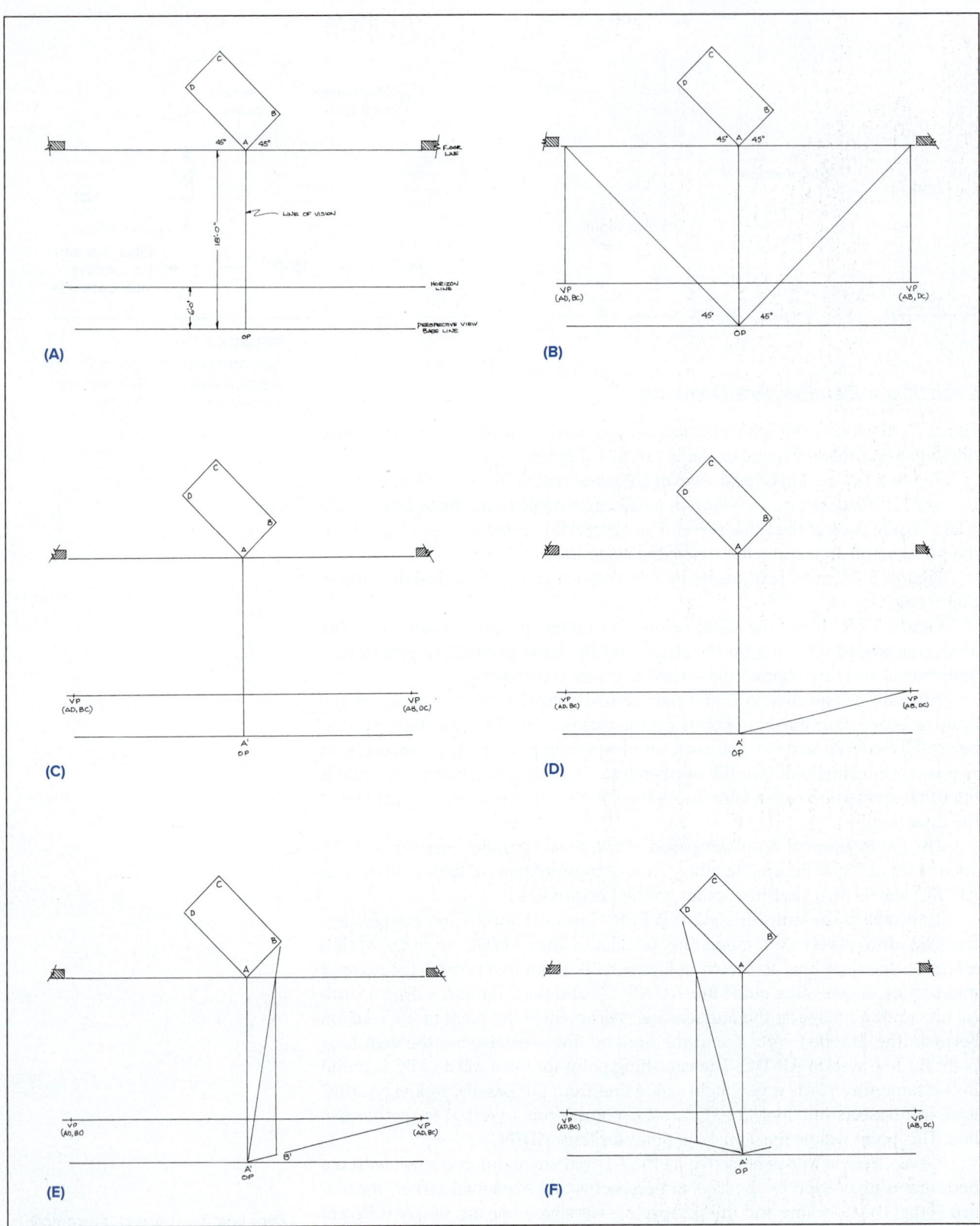

FIGURE 8.7
Sequential layout of the practice
exercise. See text for explanation
of drawings A–H.

(continued)

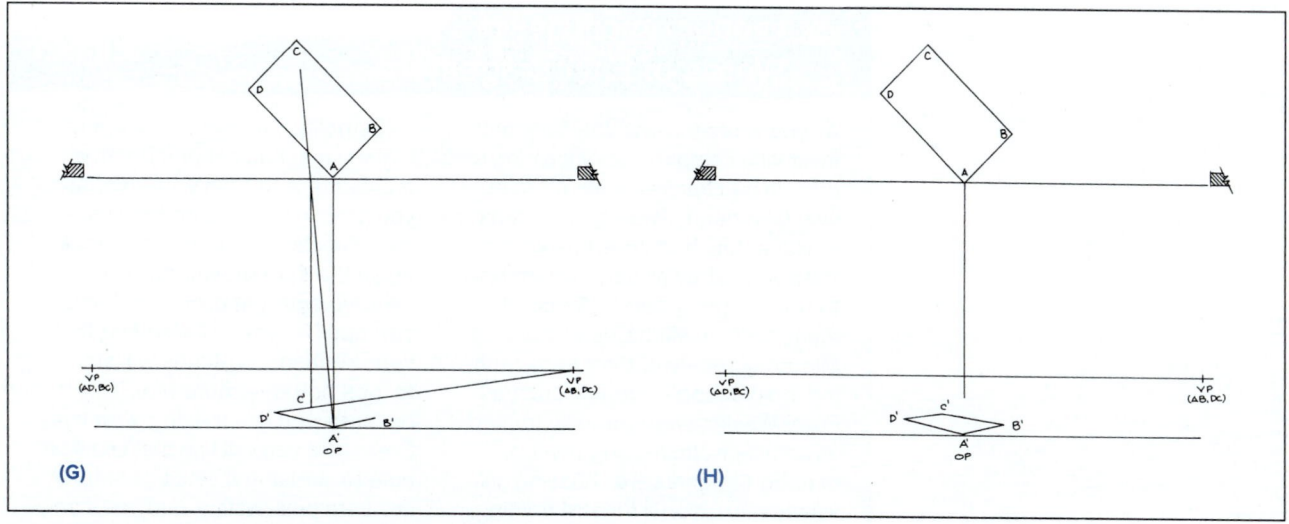

(G)   **(H)**

FIGURE 8.7 *(continued)*

As shown in Figure 8.7C, because point A of the flat is in contact with the floor line, a vertical line can be dropped from that point (A) until it contacts the perspective-view base line at point A′, which coincides with the observation point (OP).

To find the perspective view of line AB, extend a light guide line from A′ to the vanishing point for the line system AB/DC, as shown in Figure 8.7D. This gives you a perspective view of line A′B′ extended.

As shown in Figure 8.7E, to find the location of point B′ on line A′B′ extended, draw a light guide line between OP and corner B on the flat. Where this guide line intersects the floor line, drop a vertical until it intersects line A′B′ extended. This is the location of point B′.

To find the perspective view of line A′D′, repeat the process used to find the perspective view of line A′B′, but this time use the vanishing point for the line system AD/BC. As shown in Figure 8.7F, draw a light guide line from A′ to the vanishing point for line system AD/BC to form line A′D′ extended. Next draw a light guide line between OP and corner D on the flat. Where this line intersects the floor line, drop a vertical until it intersects line A′D′ extended. This will be the location of point D′.

To find the perspective location of the last corner of the flat, point C′, use the same process you used to find the location of B′ and D′. Line D′C′ is parallel to line A′B′, so they have the same vanishing point. To find line D′C′ extended, draw a light guide line from point D′ to the vanishing point for line system AB/DC, as shown in Figure 8.7G. To find the location of C′ on line D′C′ extended, draw a guide line from OP to C. Where that guide line intersects the floor line, drop a vertical until it intersects line D′C′ extended. This point of intersection will be the location of point C′.

To complete the perspective view of the flat, you just need to play connect-the-dots between points B′ and C′, as shown in Figure 8.7H.

In Figure 8.7H, the figure created by connecting A′, B′, C′, and D′ is a scale perspective view of the flat lying on the stage floor as seen by someone 18 feet away from, and 6 feet above, the flat lying on the stage floor.

At this point this process probably seems both arcane and unnecessarily complex. But if you repeat it a number of times, you'll learn the steps and the whole thing will become somewhat second nature. That's the purpose of the exercises in the following section — to help you learn how to hand draw in accurate, scale perspective.

◢◉ PRODUCTION INSIGHTS

Words of Encouragement

As you wade through the frequently frustrating complexities of learning to draw in mechanical scale perspective, take heart. Every major scenic designer has had the same kind of heartburn. They all had to learn how to draw in perspective. Some of them, such as Ming Cho Lee and Jo Mielziner, received their early training in art schools. Others, such as Peter Wexler, were formally trained as architects. Increasing numbers of rising designers are choosing university educational theatre training. All of them have a common bond — learning how to draw in perspective.

Assimilating the principles of any mechanical-perspective technique is difficult. But as with any craft, the more you practice, the easier it becomes.

In reality, the reason for learning any mechanical-perspective technique is to train your eye. As you practice, you learn how various objects are supposed to look when they are drawn. As you become adept at using mechanical perspective, you will also find that your freehand sketches will start to look better — more real. This is because you *are* training your eye. Eventually, you will find that you'll be able to sketch full sets freehand in accurate perspective, and you'll only occasionally need to use the perspective method to monitor or check your work. This kind of proficiency doesn't happen overnight; it comes with practice. But if you have a passion for drawing and designing, the practice won't be work, it'll be fun.

A Review of Perspective Procedure

Before moving on to the perspective exercises, you may want to review the procedure, illustrated in Figure 8.8, that is used to create these drawings.

1. All of the drawings are made on a basic grid composed of four lines, as shown in Figure 8.8A.

2. The object being drawn is a triangular-shaped flat lying on stage with its downstage corner in contact with the floor line.

3. The vanishing point for any line or system of lines is determined by extending, from OP, a line parallel to the ground plan view of that particular line until it intersects the floor line, illustrated in Figure 8.8B. From that point of intersection, a vertical line is dropped until it intersects the horizon line. That point of intersection is the vanishing point for that line system.

4. Any point in contact with the floor line is unaffected by the laws of perspective. Therefore, a line parallel to the line of vision can be dropped from that point to the perspective-view base line, as shown in Figure 8.8C.

5. A perspective view of a line can be established by extending a line from the point of contact with the perspective-view base line to the vanishing point for that particular line, as shown in Figure 8.8D.

6. To find the location of any point on the perspective view of a line, draw a sight line from the observation point (OP) to the ground plan view of that point, as shown in Figure 8.8E. From the point of intersection between that sight line and the floor line, drop a vertical until it intersects the extended line (A′B′ extended and A′C′ extended).

7. After all of the perspective points have been located using the techniques just described, connect those points to provide a perspective view of the object, as shown in Figure 8.8F.

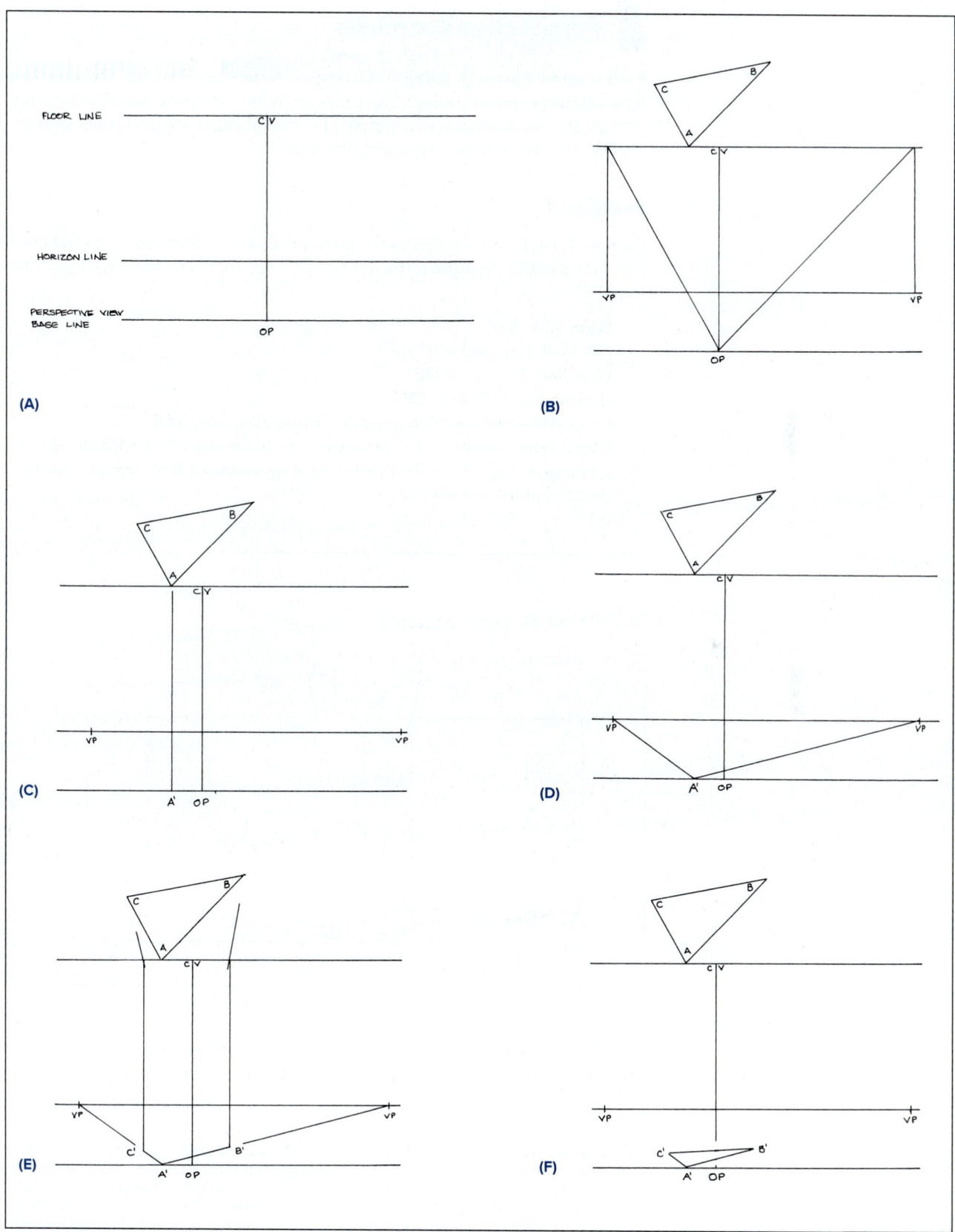

FIGURE 8.8
The perspective procedure. See the text for explanations of steps A–F.

Perspective Exercises

Craft is learned through doing. This perspective method is a craft. The following nine practice exercises, which are arranged in an ascending order of difficulty, provide specific examples of a variety of common situations and challenges frequently encountered in perspective drawing.

Exercise 1

Exercise 1, Figure 8.9, illustrates the principle that the closer your eye level (horizon line) is to the stage floor, the less you actually see of an object resting on the stage.

> **Scale:** ¼″ = 1′-0″
> **OP:** 36′-0″ right and 8′-0″ up[1]
> **Floor line:** 20′-0″ from **OP**
> **Horizon line:** 3′-0″ from **OP**
> **Perspective-view base line:** extends horizontally through **OP**
> **Object being drawn:** an 8′-0″ square resting on the stage floor with its sides at a 45-degree angle to the floor line and the near corner **(A)** in contact with the floor line at the line of vision.

FIGURE 8.9
Exercise 1.

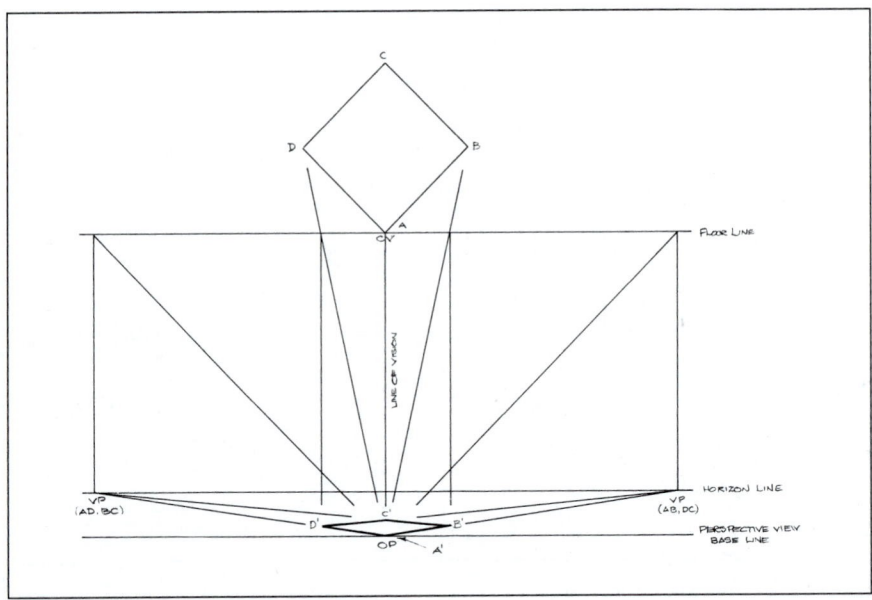

Procedure No new challenges have been introduced in Exercise 1, so you can follow the procedure summarized in the previous section to do this exercise.

---

[1] These dimensions are intended to help you center your drawing in the middle of a 12 × 18 sheet of paper. By measuring, in ¼-inch scale, 36′-0″ to the right of the lower left-hand corner and 8′-0″ up from the bottom edge of the sheet of paper, the observation point **(OP)** will be placed in a position that will center the perspective exercise in the middle of the paper. These dimensions don't have a thing to do with drawing in perspective; they just help to make the whole sheet look attractive and balanced. These exercises won't fit on a sheet smaller than 10 × 14, but if you are using paper larger than 12 × 18, just center the **OP** about one-quarter or one-third of the way up from the bottom of the sheet.

Exercise 2

This exercise shows what to do if an object contacts the floor line in some location other than the point of intersection between the floor line and the line of vision.

Scale: ¼″ = 1′-0″
OP: 36′-0″ right and 8′-0″ up
Floor line: 22′-0″ from **OP**
Horizon line: 7′-0″ from **OP**
Perspective-view base line: extends horizontally through **OP**
Object being drawn: a flat 6′-0″ by 10′-0″ with its sides at a 45-degree angle to the floor line. The near corner **(A)** is in contact with the floor line and 7′-0″ to the left of the intersection between the line of vision and the floor line.

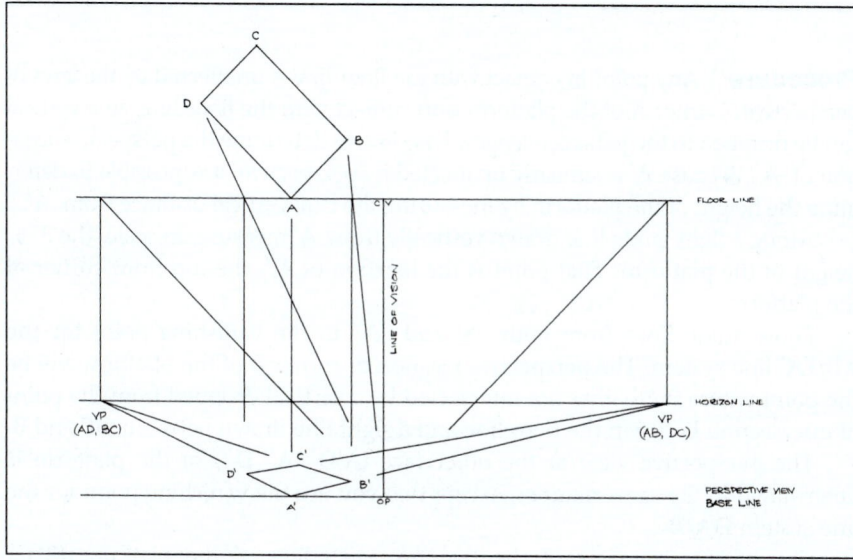

FIGURE 8.10
Exercise 2.

Procedure   Because the corner of the flat **(A)** is in contact with the floor line, it is unaffected by the laws of perspective. A vertical can be dropped from point **A** until it intersects the perspective-view base line, as shown in Figure 8.10. This point will be the perspective location of point **A′**.

After determining the location of **A′**, you can do the rest of the exercise using the procedure summarized in the previous section.

Exercise 3

Finding the perspective of an object that has height, as well as width and length, requires an additional step in the perspective procedure as illustrated in Figure 8.11.

Scale: ¼″ = 1′-0″
OP: 50′-0″ right and 8′-0″ up
Floor line: 23′-0″ from **OP**
Horizon line: 8′-0″ from **OP**
Perspective-view base line: extends horizontally through **OP**
Object being drawn: a platform 8′-0″ square by 3′-6″ high is placed on the stage with its sides forming 30- and 60-degree angles with the floor line. Corner **A** is in contact with the floor line and 12′-0″ to the left of the intersection of the floor line and the line of vision.

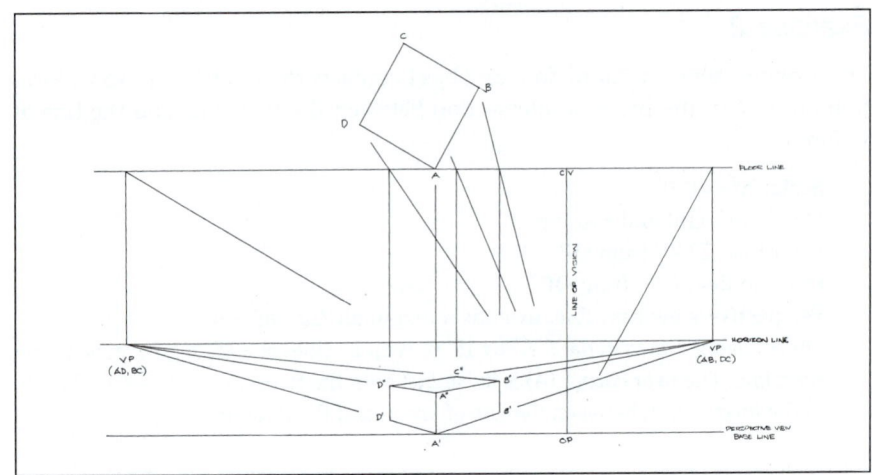

Procedure Any point in contact with the floor line is unaffected by the laws of perspective. Corner **A** of the platform is in contact with the floor line, so a vertical can be dropped to the perspective-view base line to determine the perspective location of **A′**. Because **A′** is similarly unaffected by perspective, it is possible to determine the height of the platform by measuring the true vertical distance from **A′**.

Along a light guide line drawn vertically from **A′** measure, in scale, the 3′-6″ height of the platform. That point is the location of **A″**, the top front corner of the platform.

Draw guide lines from both **A′** and **A″** to the vanishing point for the **AB/DC** line system. The perspective location of corner **B** of the platform will be the point where these lines are intersected by a vertical dropped from the point of intersection between the floor line and a sight line drawn between **OP** and **B**.

The perspective view of the other face (**A′D′/A″ D″**) of the platform is determined in the same manner, except that you use the vanishing point for the line system **DA/BC**.

The perspective view of the two upstage edges of the platform (**B″C″** and **D″C″**) is determined by drawing lines between **D″** and the vanishing point for the **AB/DC** line system and between **B″** and the vanishing point for the **AD/BC** line system. Where these two lines intersect will be the location of **C″**.

Point **C″** can also be located in the conventional manner by drawing a sight line from **OP** to **C**. Where the sight line crosses the floor line, a vertical can be dropped until it intersects line **B″C″** extended or **D″C″** extended. This will be the location of **C″**.

Exercise 4

Drawing a perspective view of an object that is not in contact with the floor line adds one more step to the procedure but uses the same principles.

> **Scale:** ¼″ = 1′-0″
> **OP:** 40′-0″ right and 10′-0″ up
> **Floor line:** 20′-0″ from **OP**
> **Horizon line:** 8′-0″ from **OP**
> **Perspective-view base line:** extends horizontally through **OP**
> **Object being drawn:** a small flat, 6′-0″ by 10′-0″, lying on the stage floor with its sides at a 45-degree angle to the floor line. The near corner **A** is 4′-6″ to the left of the intersection between the floor line and the line of vision and 2′-6″ upstage of it (Figure 8.12).

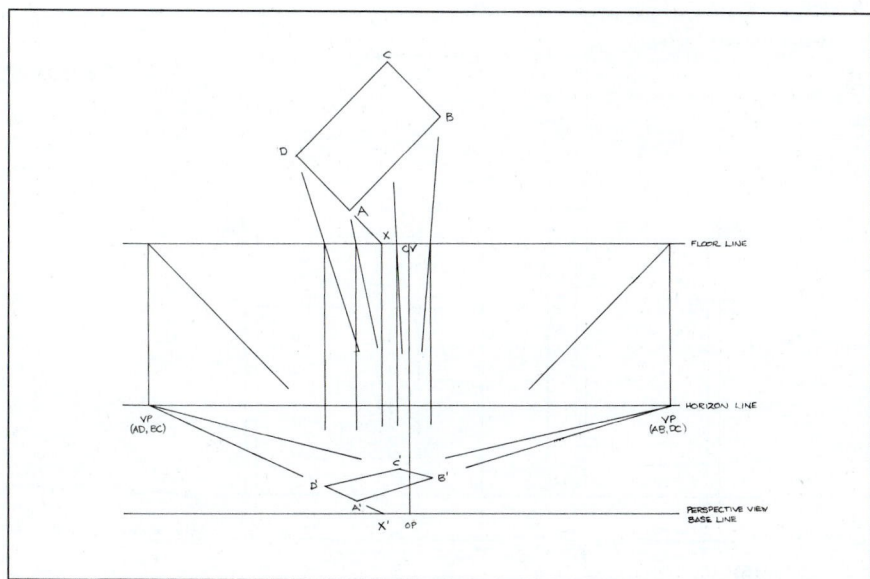

FIGURE 8.12
Exercise 4.

Procedure Extend the line that forms one side of the flat **(DA)** until it intersects the floor line **(X)**. Drop a vertical to the perspective-view base line to determine the perspective location of point **X'**. Draw a light guide line between **X'** and the vanishing point for line system **AD/BC**. The locations of points **A'** and **D'** are determined in the usual manner — sight lines are drawn between **OP** and points **A** and **D**. Where those sight lines cross the floor line, verticals are dropped until they intersect the guide line drawn between **X'** and the vanishing point for line system **AD/BC**.

The perspective view of the rest of the flat is determined using the same principles used in the previous exercises. Guide lines are drawn between **A'** and **D'** and the vanishing point for line system **AB/DC**. Sight lines are drawn between **OP** and points **B** and **C**. Where those sight lines cross the floor line, verticals are dropped until they intersect the guide lines drawn between **AD** and the vanishing point for line system **AB/DC**. These points of intersection will be the location of **B'** and **C'**.

Exercise 5

Drawing a perspective view of an object whose sides are either parallel with or perpendicular to the floor line doesn't differ in principle from the procedures that have been previously established.

Scale: ¼" = 1'-0"
OP: 36'-0" right and 8'-0" up
Floor line: 20'-0" from **OP**
Horizon line: 3'-0" from **OP**
Perspective-view base line: extends horizontally through **OP**
Object being drawn: a large rectangular ceiling flat, 10'-10" by 14'-0", lying on the stage floor with its longer side parallel with, and 2'-0" upstage from, the floor line. Notice that the floor line has been placed at the outer face of the proscenium arch to facilitate your creating a perspective drawing of the arch. The proscenium arch is 32'-0" wide, 16'-0" high, and 1'-0" thick, as shown in Figure 8.13.

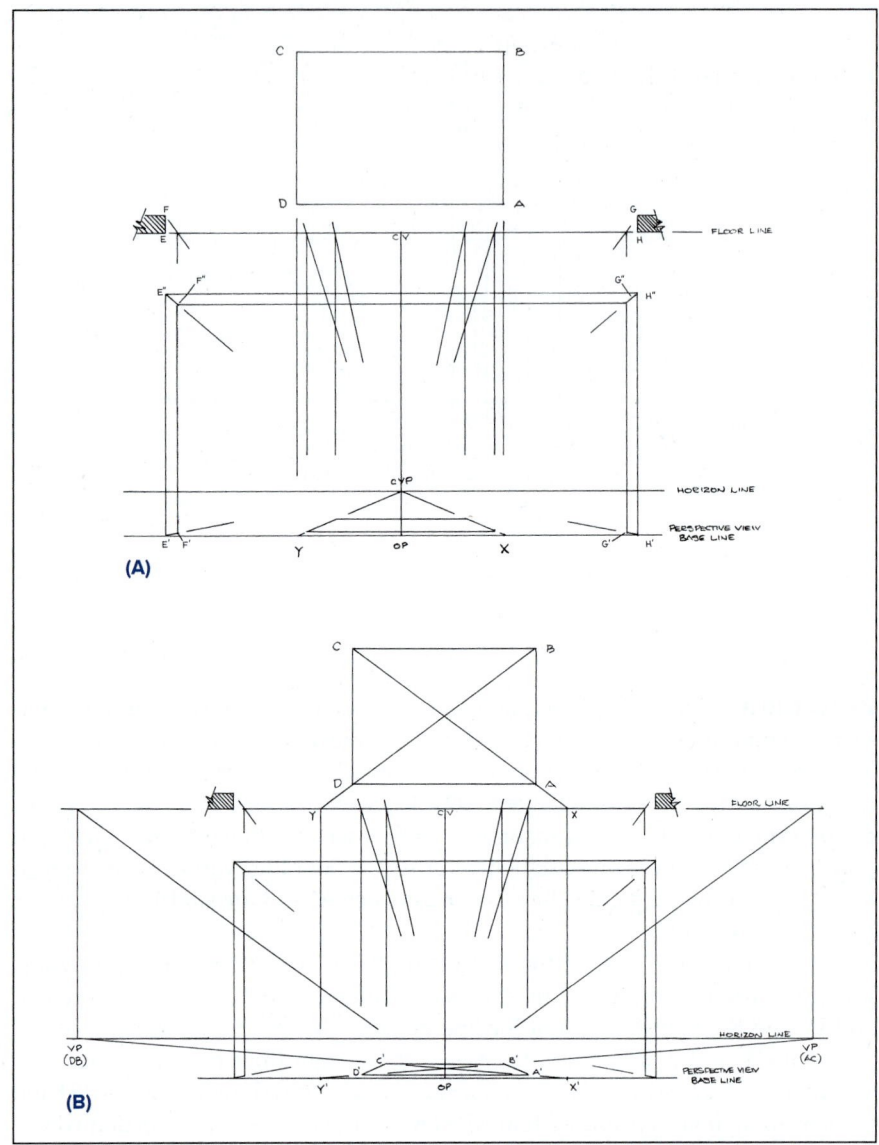

Procedure Creating a perspective drawing of objects whose sides are parallel with or perpendicular to the proscenium arch follows exactly the same procedure used in the previous perspective exercises. First, you have to find the vanishing point for the line system **AB/DC,** as shown in Figure 8.13A. To do that, from **OP** draw a line parallel to **AB** and **DC** until it intersects the floor line. From that point, drop a vertical until it intersects the horizon line. This point of intersection (between the horizon line and the line of vision) creates a center vanishing point (CVP) and introduces another principle: any line perpendicular to the floor line will always have a center vanishing point (CVP).

To find the perspective location of the lines that form the sides of the ceiling piece (**AB** and **DC**), extend those lines until they intersect the floor line. From those points, drop verticals until they intersect the perspective-view base line (points **X** and **Y**). From **X** and **Y,** draw light guide lines to the CVP (vanishing point for line system **AB/DC**). You can determine the perspective location of points **A** and **B** or **D** and **C** in the usual manner and connect the dots to form a perspective view of the ceiling flat lying on the stage floor.

An alternative method: Instead of using the CVP, you can draw diagonal lines between **CA** and **BD,** as shown in Figure 8.13B. Extend those diagonals until they intersect the floor line, and then locate the vanishing point for those lines in the usual manner. The rest of the exercise can be done using the procedure previously outlined.

Determining the perspective location of the proscenium arch is fairly easy, because the downstage edge of the arch is in contact with the floor line. From points **E** and **H,** drop verticals to the perspective-view base line. The vertical height of the proscenium arch can be measured from **E′** and **H′,** because those points are in contact with the perspective-view base line and are consequently unaffected by the laws of perspective. Locating the top of the perspective view of the proscenium arch is done by connecting the dots between **E′** and **H′.**

The perspective view of the depth of the proscenium arch can be determined by using the methods previously described. To locate the base of the stage-right side of the arch, draw a light guide line from **E′** (the downstage edge of the proscenium arch) to the CVP. To locate **F′,** draw a sight line from **OP** to **F.** Where that sight line crosses the floor line, drop a vertical until it intersects the guide line drawn from **F′** to the CVP. This will be the location of **F′.**

The top of the stage-right side of the proscenium arch is found by drawing a guide line from **E″** to the CVP. Where this line intersects the vertical erected from **F′** will be the location of **F″.**

The other side of the proscenium arch is determined in the same manner. The top of the proscenium arch can be determined by connecting **E″** and **H″** as well as **F″** and **G″.**

Exercise 6

This exercise synthesizes all of the previous material and allows you to draw a perspective view of a full stage set.

Scale: ¼″ = 1′-0″
OP: 36′-0″ right and 6′-0″ up
Floor line: 22′-0″ from **OP**
Horizon line: 6′-0″ from **OP**
Perspective-view base line: extends horizontally through **OP**
Proscenium arch: 16′-0″ high, 36′-0″ wide, 1′-0″ thick
Object being drawn: a full stage setting, as illustrated in Figure 8.14

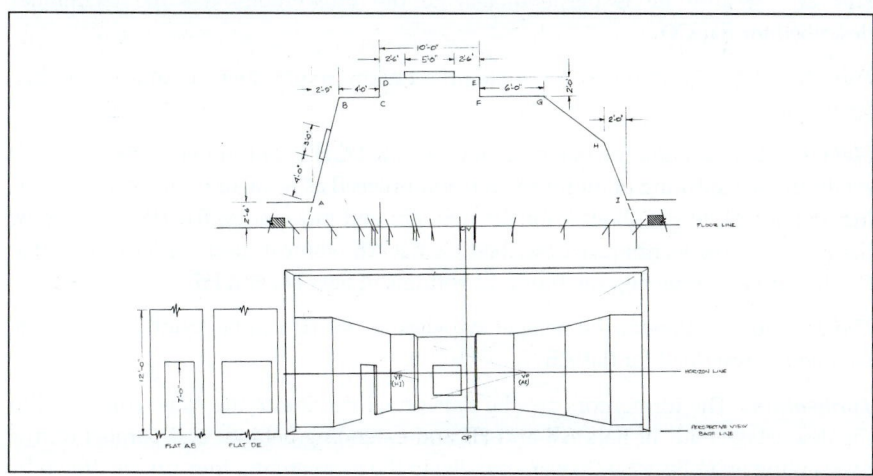

FIGURE 8.14
Exercise 6.

Procedure Although the concept of drawing a full setting may, at first glance, be somewhat overwhelming, you can accomplish it by using the techniques described in this chapter. You might wonder, "Where do I begin?" You can start with either the set or the proscenium arch. But drawing the proscenium arch first provides a visual framework and reference that makes most designers feel fairly comfortable. After you've drawn the proscenium (refer to Exercise 5 for detailed instructions, if you need them), start on the set. It is easiest to begin by drawing the set at one corner of the ground plan. Point **A,** the downstage end of the bottom of flat **AB,** provides a convenient beginning place.

Flat AB To find the location of point **A,** you will need to set up the vanishing point for flat **AB.** This can be done by measuring, with a protractor, the angle of intersection between **AB** extended and the floor line, and duplicating that angle from **OP,** to lay out the vanishing point. The full perspective view of flat **AB** can then be drawn using the techniques previously described. The sides and top of the door opening can be drawn by using the same techniques that are used to locate the sides and tops of the flat.

Flat BC Because flat **BC** is parallel to the proscenium (and the floor line), horizontal lines can be extended from the top and bottom of the upstage end of flat **AB** to create a perspective view of the top and bottom of flat **BC.** The onstage **(C)** end of flat **BC** is determined by drawing a sight line between **OP** and **C.** Where that sight line crosses the floor line, a vertical is dropped toward the perspective-view base line. Where that dropped vertical intersects the horizontal lines extending from the upstage end of the top and bottom of flat **AB** determines the location of the onstage edge of flat **BC.**

Flat CD Because flat **CD** is perpendicular to the floor line, it will have a CVP. Draw guide lines from the top and bottom edges of the onstage **(C)** end of flat **BC** to the CVP to determine the perspective view of the top and bottom edges of flat **CD.** To find the upstage end of the flat, draw a light sight line from **OP** to **D.** Where it crosses the floor line, drop a vertical until it intersects the guide lines that define the top and bottom edges of flat **CD.**

Flat DE Flat **DE** is parallel to the proscenium, so you use the techniques described for flat **BC.** To create a perspective view of the window, determine the height of the top and bottom edges of the window on either edge **(D** or **E)** of the flat, using the techniques described in Exercise 3. From those points, extend horizontal lines across the flat. Draw light sight lines from **OP** to the edges of the ground plan view of the window. Where those sight lines cross the floor line, drop verticals until they intersect the horizontal lines that describe the top and bottom height of the window. These lines will denote the sides of the window.

Flat EF Because **EF** is perpendicular to the proscenium, use the techniques described for flat **CD.**

Flat FG Flat **FG** is also parallel to the proscenium, so use the techniques described for flat **BC.**

Flat GH You can find the perspective view of flat **GH** in one of two ways: Either (1) establish the vanishing point for the flat and proceed as usual or (2) instead of working on flat **GH,** forget about it for the moment and move on to flat **HI.** If you draw flat **HI,** using the techniques described for flat **AB,** you can find the location of flat **GH** by simply connecting the tops and bottoms of flats **FG** and **HI.**

Flat HI As mentioned, the perspective view of flat **HI** can be found by using the techniques described for flat **AB.**

Tormentors The tormentors are the flats on either side of the stage connected to the downstage ends of flats **AB** and **HI** and extending behind, and parallel to, the proscenium arch. Because they are parallel to the proscenium, they can be drawn by extending horizontal lines from the tops and bottoms of the downstage ends of flats **AB** and **HI** until they intersect the sides of the proscenium arch.

Exercise 7

Drawing furniture presents a significant challenge to many beginning scenic designers. This technique helps visually anchor the furniture to the floor. Almost all furniture can be placed in a box, as shown in Figure 8.15. If these "furniture boxes" are placed on the ground plan, it becomes fairly simple to draw them, in perspective, on the scenic sketch, as shown in Figure 8.16.

Scale: ¼″ = 1′-0″
OP: 36′-0″ right and 4′-0″ up
Floor line: 20′-0″ from **OP**
Horizon line: 6′-0″ from **OP**
Perspective-view base line: extends horizontally through **OP**
Proscenium arch: 32′-0″ wide, 16′-0″ high, 1′-0″ thick
Objects being drawn: a very simple set with 14′-0″ walls, a 7′-0″ door, a sofa, a chair, a table, and a rug. The sofa is 6′-0″ long, 2′-6″ deep, and 3′-0″ high. The wingback chair is 3′-0″ wide, 3′-0″ deep, and 4′-0″ high. The table is 2′-0″ square and 3′-0″ high.

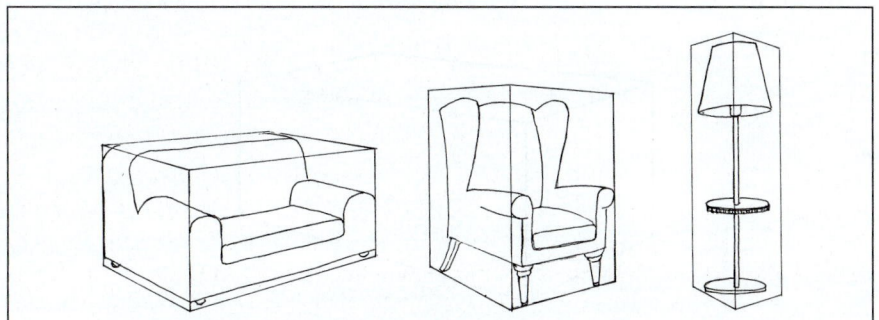

FIGURE 8.15
Furniture can be sketched fairly easily if it is placed inside boxes.

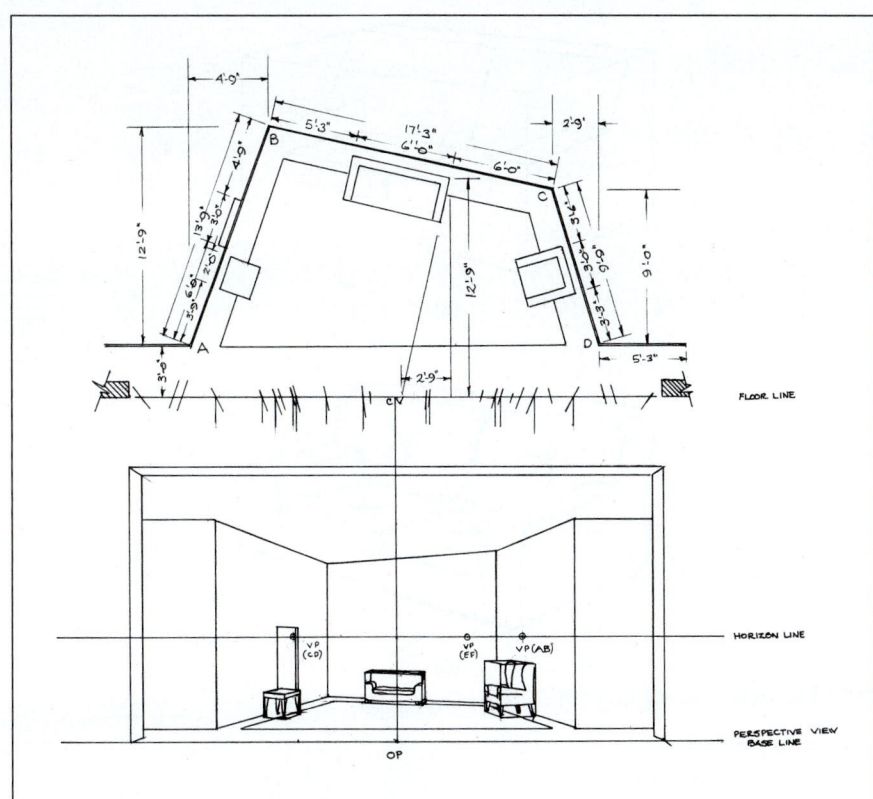

FIGURE 8.16
Exercise 7.

Procedure As in Exercises 5 and 6, drawing the proscenium arch first provides a good visual reference. If you are a little hazy on the procedure for drawing the arch, refer to Exercise 5 for specific instructions.

Second, draw the walls of the set. It will probably be easiest to draw a perspective view of flat **AB** first and then flat **CD.** After these two flats have been laid out, you can connect the dots between their tops and bottoms, respectively, to create flat **BC.** Exercise 6 reviews the procedure for drawing the walls of a set.

Finally, put the "furniture boxes" on the set. The corners of the boxes coincide with the corners of the furniture that you are trying to draw. All of the furniture boxes are located on the set according to the instructions detailed in Exercises 3 and 4.

After you have drawn the furniture boxes (use light lines) on the perspective sketch, you can sketch the appropriate view of the furniture piece on each exposed face of the box, as illustrated in Figure 8.17, and then erase the "box lines."

FIGURE 8.17
How to draw furniture in a box:
(A) Draw a box the height, width, and depth of the overall dimensions of the furniture item. (B) Sketch the furniture on the faces of the box. (C) "Uncrate" the furniture by erasing the box.

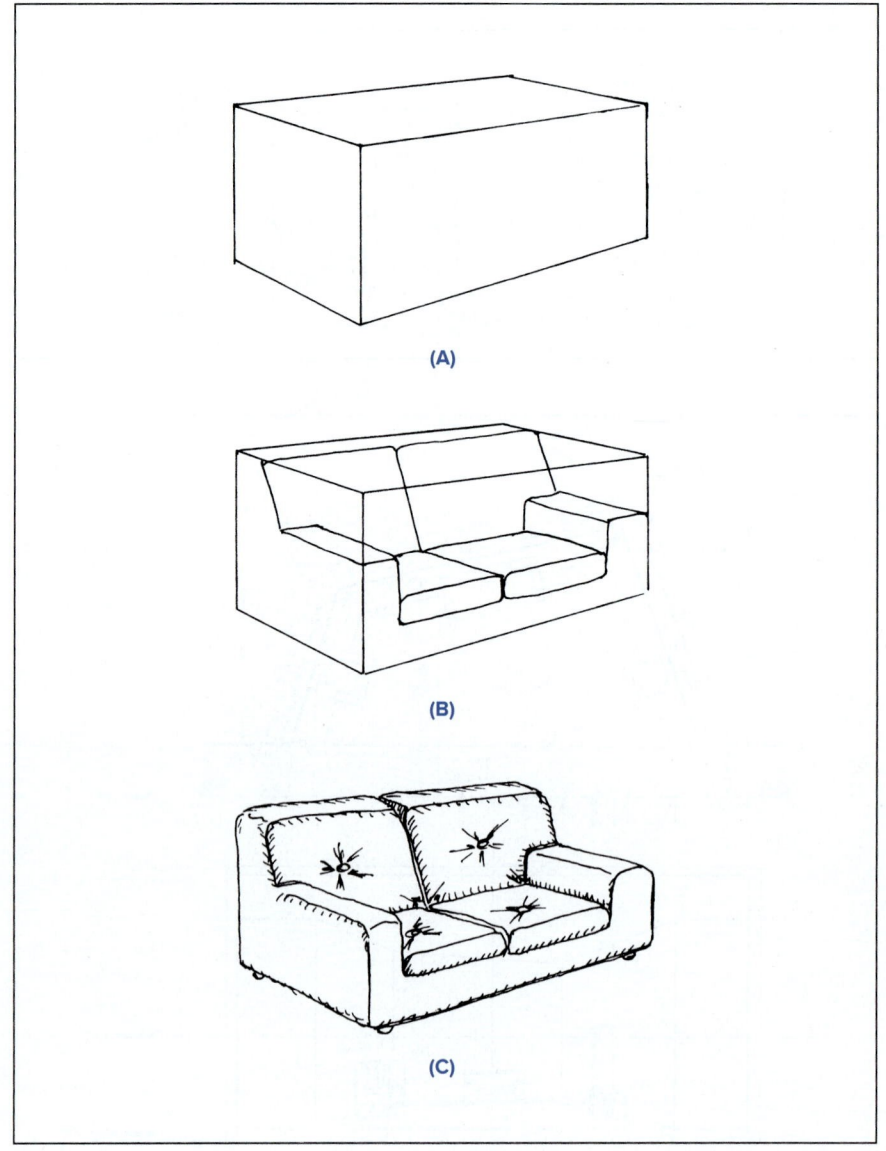

(A)

(B)

(C)

Exercise 8

The technique explained in this chapter can also be used to create perspective sketches for arena and thrust productions. This exercise shows the procedure for creating a perspective sketch of an arena production and is illustrated in Figure 8.18.

> **Scale:** ¼″ = 1′-0″
> **OP:** 36′-0″ right and 6′-0″ above
> **Floor line:** 15′-0″ from **OP** (Note that the floor line is placed 2′-0″ toward the audience from the edge of the stage. This placement allows you to create a drawing of the full stage.)
> **Horizon line:** 8′-0″ from **OP**
> **Perspective-view base line:** extends horizontally through **OP**
> **Object being drawn:** a scenic design for an arena production

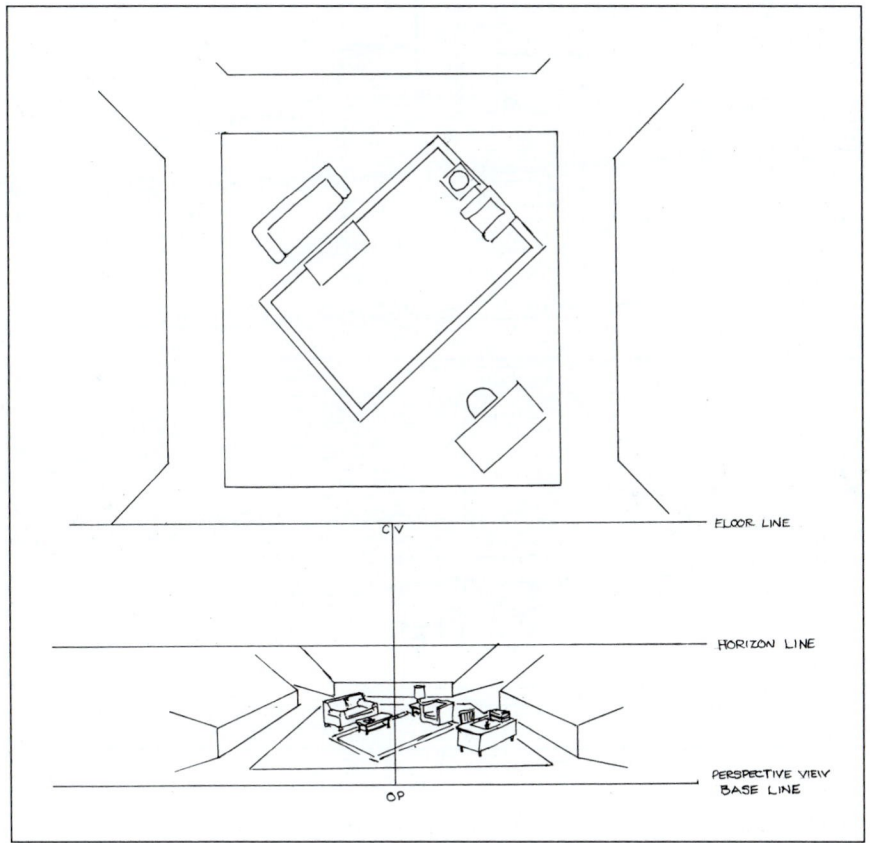

FIGURE 8.18
Exercise 8.

Procedure   The procedure for drawing an arena design is exactly the same as for any other production. Although most scenic designs for arena stages are noticeably devoid of any tall vertical elements such as walls and doorways, the design may contain some low walls or cutaway doors. If these elements are present, they will provide the visual framework for the design and will consequently be an appropriate beginning point for drawing the sketch. After the visual framework has been established, the furniture and other set pieces can be drawn using the furniture-box technique described in Exercise 7.

Exercise 9

This exercise shows how this perspective technique can be used for a play produced on a thrust stage. The exercise is illustrated in Figure 8.19.

Scale: ¼″ = 1′-0″
OP: 24′-0″ right and 14′-0″ up
Floor line: 25′-0″ from **OP** (Note that the paper has been turned 90 degrees and the floor line is located just in front of the front edge of the thrust stage. This placement allows you to achieve a full view of the stage and the set.)
Horizon line: 7′-0″ from **OP**
Perspective-view base line: extends horizontally through **OP**
Object being drawn: a scenic design for a thrust production. The flats are 14′-0″ tall and the doors are 6′-9″.

FIGURE 8.19
Exercise 9.

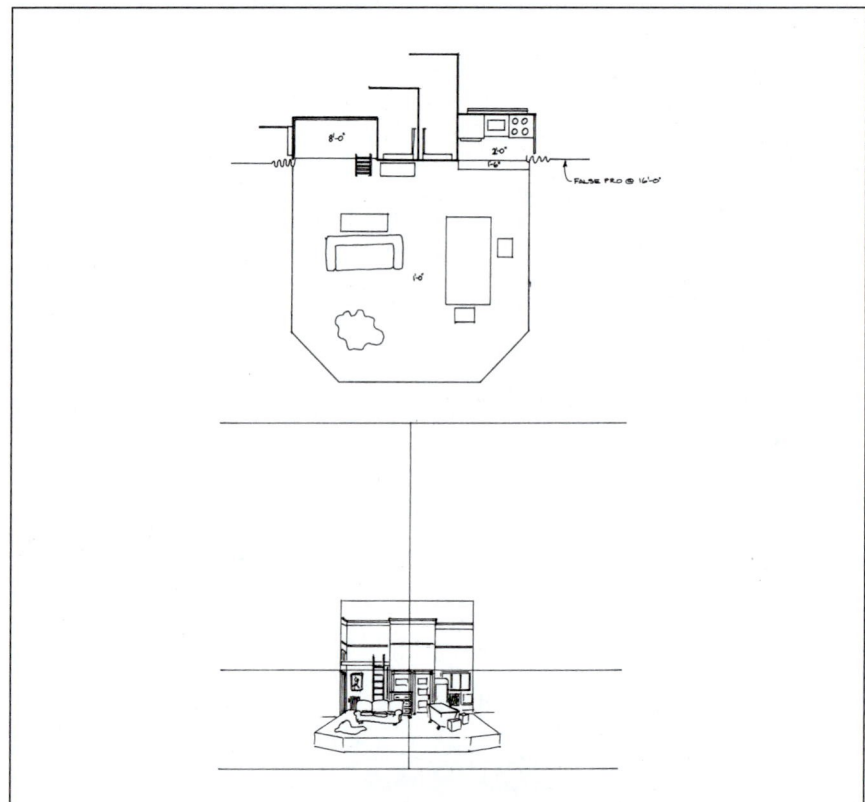

Procedure The procedure for creating a perspective sketch of a thrust stage design is exactly the same as that for the other stages.

The understanding and use of the perspective method presented in this chapter should enable you to create accurate scale perspective drawings of scenic designs for proscenium, thrust, and arena productions. However, this mechanical method is just a tool to show you *how* to draw in perspective. Once you become confident in your ability to use this technique, you should wean yourself from it. Learn to sketch in reasonably accurate perspective. If you encounter a problem or if some element of your design doesn't look right, you can check its accuracy with this perspective method. But once you've learned how to use the method, try to work without it so that its necessarily mechanical processes won't inhibit the free flow of your design ideas.

Chapter 9
Scenic Design

(This chapter has been updated thanks to significant input from Charlie Calvert, professional scene designer and educator. The author wishes to publicly thank him for his extensive knowledge and expertise on this subject and for his contributions to this chapter.)

Scenery helps the audience understand and enjoy a play by providing a visual reinforcement of the production concept. However, the scenery hasn't always been designed with a production concept in mind.

Before about 1875, no one paid any great attention to specifying the elements (period, country, locale, socioeconomic status, and mood) that most contemporary designers believe make up a well-conceived stage setting. Greek and Roman productions were performed out of doors with little or no scenery. Medieval drama used standardized scenic elements (heaven, hell, the courtyard, and so on) that represented the various locations needed for almost all productions. The Renaissance was a period of evolutionary development in scenery. Some theatres had permanent sets built as part of the theatre architecture (Teatro Olympico). Other theatres (the Globe) had bare, open stages with no scenic elements. From the Restoration (1660) until the mid–nineteenth century, plays were performed in front of stock sets. Only in the past 150 years has scenery evolved into its present form.

Considerations for the Scenic Designer

Before we look at the various elements that must be considered to create a quality scenic design, a cautionary digression seems appropriate. Beware of any so-called rules of design. There aren't any. What works in one design situation may not work in another. If every design choice we make is a rational, considered decision, there is no need for rules such as, "Never paint a set white," "Don't use green light," "Never wear taffeta on stage," and so forth. In terms of creativity, these rules are debilitating, because they arbitrarily limit our ability to select from the full breadth of our knowledge and experience. Having said that, I'm now going to contradict myself. There is one guideline that *does* apply to all scenic designs: The design should create an environment for the play that is supportive of the production concept.

Although we should be wary of arbitrary rules, most good scenic designs do comply with a majority of the principles discussed in this section.

In addition to the scenery, the scenic designer has traditionally been responsible for the design of the properties. He or she may have the luxury of working with a properties master — variously known as the property director or property designer. The prop master collaborates with the scenic designer and other members of the production staff to design and fabricate any necessary stage properties. In situations where a separate prop master hasn't been hired, this responsibility still belongs to the scenic designer, or an assistant working under the supervision of the scenic designer. Current practice is for many scenic and property designers to be hired to design only one show in a company's full season. They're frequently not "in residence" during the construction/early rehearsal period.

It is a truism that the design of many props evolves during the rehearsal period as the director and actors figure out how a particular prop is going to be used and handled. It's essential that the prop master be either "onsite" to keep up with the changes or available by phone/email/Skype/Internet. The prop master receives notes from the director/stage manager — while either onsite or via electronic communication — about any business that requires changes to the prop design and/or construction. Depending on the exact nature of the previously agreed-upon working relationship between the two designers, the property designer will either discuss the proposed adjustments with the scenic designer, and they'll make a mutually agreed-upon change, or the property designer will simply make the necessary changes while keeping them within the spirit of the original design.

Props are an important element of the stage picture, and they subscribe to all of the qualities discussed in this section. In black box and arena theatres, furniture props take on added significance as the primary visual elements of the scenic design, because flats, drops, and other vertical elements of scenery generally aren't used. Additional information on stage properties appears in Chapter 13, "Stage Properties."

Mood and Spirit of the Play

One guideline works for all plays: the design should be expressive of the **mood** and **spirit** of the play. Within this context, mood usually refers to the dominant emotional quality of the production. Spirit is generally interpreted to refer to the production concept — the way in which the production design team (producer, director, and scenic, costume, lighting, and sound designers) decide that the play is going to be presented. Some directors prefer the term "approach" instead of "concept" — perhaps because some people have a tendency to overthink ideas when trying to devise a "meaningful concept." A simple approach often provides the best solution for the production. Either term is acceptable. Use whatever works for you.

For the design to effectively express mood and spirit, the designer needs to incorporate some elements that suggest the emotional characteristics of the play, as shown in Figure 9.1. If the play is a gentle romance, it might be appropriate to use soft curves to define the outline of the set, and the scenery could be painted with delicate pastel to reinforce the romantic qualities of the play. If the play is an intense tragedy, hard lines, sharp angles, and a palette of dark colors would express the heavy mood that the production concept seeks to project.

Assume that an old melodrama is being considered for production. The play has many situations that are essentially serious (the heroine, her widowed mother, and her seriously ill little brother are being thrown out of their house for nonpayment of rent), and most of the characters are likable people who just happen to be down on their luck. Unhappiness, sadness, and despair seem to be the general emotional qualities of the play. Instead of emphasizing these depressing qualities, however, the director decides to change the emotional tone of the play. He or she chooses to concentrate on the comic aspects. The serious and dramatic

mood: The feeling of a play — comic, tragic, happy, and so forth.

spirit: The manner and style in which a play is presented to the audience.

(A)

(B)

FIGURE 9.1

Scenic designs can provide reinforcement of the mood and spirit of the play. (A) *Ragtime* by Stephen Flaherty, Lynn Ahrens and Terrence McNally; L-R, top level: Valerie Cutko as Emma Goldman, Simon Anthony as Willie Conklin, Anthony Cable as Grandfather, Jonathan Stewart as Younger Brother; L-R, bottom level: Gary Tushaw as Tateh, Alana Hinge as The Little Girl, Sufia Manya (ensemble), Tom Giles as Henry Ford, Nolan Frederick as Booker T. Washington, Ako Mitchell as Coalhouse Walker, Jr. (seated at piano), James Mack as Harry K. Thaw (immediately behind Mitchell), Joanna Hickman as Evelyn Nesbit (seated, in front of Mitchell), Jennifer Saayeng as Sarah Brown (at piano behind Mitchell), Bernadette Bangura as Brigit, Ethan Quinn as Edgar/The Little Boy (standing on piano), Jordan Li-Smith (onstage musical director), Lemuel Knights (ensemble), Kate Robson-Stuart as Kathleen, Christopher Dickins as Harry Houdini, Martin Ludenbach (ensemble); Earl Carpenter as Father, Anita Louise Combe as Mother. Directed by Thom Southerland; set designers: Tom Rogers and Toots Butcher; costumes designed by Jonathan Lipman; lighting designed by Howard Hudson; choreography by Ewan Jones; at the Charing Cross Theatre, London, United Kingdom; October 8, 2016. ©Scott Rylander/ArenaPal/ The Image Works. (B) John Bottom and Ben Halley, Jr., in *Endgame*, produced by the American Repertory Theatre (Cambridge, Massachusetts); scene design by Douglas Stein, costume design by Kurt Wilhelm, lighting by Jennifer Tipton. Courtesy of American Repertory Theatre. Richard Feldman, photographer.

situations are exaggerated to the point that they no longer seem believable, and the whole spirit of the production changes.

The design work should mirror this change in the mood and spirit of the production. For the original mood, the settings could appropriately have been realistic and depressing, and the color palette would logically have been muted and somber. For the reinterpretation, the settings can be simplified and exaggerated in a cartoon style that supports the same spirit of overemphasis and artificiality that is evident in the acting and business of the play.

Historical Period of the Play

A caveat: The following discussions of period, locale, socioeconomic status, and season all assume that the design style chosen by the production team is based in realism. If your production concept is nonrealistic, then the primary visual clues probably will be much more sharply guided by the evocative/emotional content of the script and production concept. Even when using a nonrealistic design concept, some period research may be useful to help clarify the chosen approach.

If the design style for the production is going to be based in realism, the scenic designer will probably want to provide historically accurate visual clues that will help the audience identify the period of the play. To provide these clues, the designer needs to do historical research.

Historical research may mean that the set designer looks at furniture, rooms, knickknacks, and buildings from the period of the play. Or the designer may search the library for pictures of furniture, room design and decoration, architecture, landscape photos, paintings, and so forth, in books and periodicals. Such background research is extremely important, because the style of the trim, furniture, and furnishings, as well as their arrangement within the room or building, varies tremendously from generation to generation and from one geographic area to another. It is this change of appearance that helps the audience identify the period, country, and locale of the play, as shown in Figure 9.2.

Although it is vital that you do historical research, your design doesn't have to adhere to every stylistic quirk of the period in which you are working. It isn't necessary to make exact copies of furniture pieces and trim styles. You will need to understand the general motifs and idiosyncracies of the period and use them in a way that creates a faithful visual representation. But you don't have to duplicate every variation and nuance. A scenic design is not a reproduction; it should be a creation that mirrors the essence of a period to provide a physical environment that will enhance the mood and spirit of the play.

Locale of the Play

Geography has a significant impact on the design of buildings and their furnishings. In the days before air conditioning and central heat, climate shaped the buildings. For example, steeply pitched gables helped the snow slide off the roofs of houses built in the northern climes like Minnesota and Sweden. Homes in the warmer climates had lower-pitched roofs and large overhanging eaves to keep the summer sun off the walls and out of the windows. By using these and similar visual keys, the scenic designer can help the audience identify the play's location.

Styles in the design of houses and business structures change rapidly. These changes stem more often from socioeconomic circumstances than from architects' aesthetic yearnings. Thus, the oil crisis of the 1970s strongly influenced American architecture. As the cost of heating oil, natural gas, and electricity rose, the size of the average residential dwelling decreased accordingly. The all-glass designs for commercial buildings of the 1960s and early 1970s were replaced by structures that could be heated and cooled more economically. Subsequent changes in the cost and availability of energy have similarly affected commercial and housing design in the decades since the 1970s.

Even more noticeable than the differences in the exterior design of houses and buildings are the differences in interiors. Depending on the historical period and the socioeconomic status of the occupants, ceilings may be high or low. Walls may be plain, painted, or covered with wallpaper. They may contain window arrangements, recessed bookcases, or ornamental niches. The only

(A)

(B)

FIGURE 9.2
Historical detail helps provide visual keys to the period of the play. (A) Everyman Theater (Baltimore, Maryland) production of *Crimes of the Heart*, 2014, by Beth Henley. Directed by Susanna Gellert; scenic design by Debra Booth; lighting design by Jay A. Herzog; costume design by LeVonne Lindsay. Photo ©Stan Barouh Photography. (B) Asolo Theatre (Sarasota, Florida) production of *Misalliance;* scenic design by Jack Doepp; photo courtesy of Gary W. Sweetman.

guideline for their inclusion in a design is that they be appropriate for the period of the play and the social status of the characters.

The walls of the room in which the action of the play takes place may be made from rough logs, finished boards, or broken lath and plaster. They may also have a variety of decorative trim — for example, baseboards, wainscoting, chair rails, plate rails, picture rails, or cornices (see Figure 9.3). Depending on the type of room and the period of the play, there may be a fireplace. The fireplace may be built into the wall, or it may project into the room and be surrounded by a plain or decorative hearth.

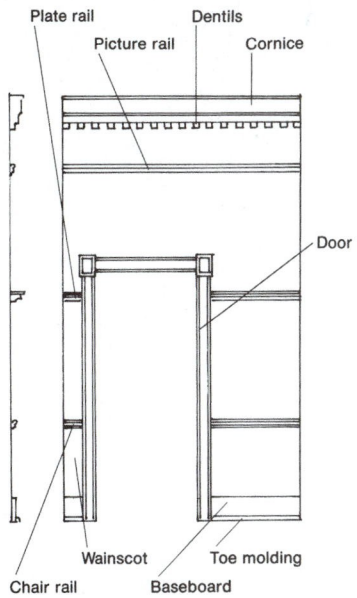

FIGURE 9.3
Various types of wall trim.

In addition to the shape, arrangement, and details of the walls, the furnishings also provide the scenic designer with an excellent opportunity to help create an appropriate environment for the play. In selecting furniture, the designer should study the types of arrangement appropriate for the period and adapt them to the blocking needs of the play. In selecting the appropriate number of chairs, sofas, or other seats to be used on a set, for example, a good rule of thumb is to have enough places for everyone to sit if all the principal actors are on stage at the same time.

Decorative properties can also aid in creating a believable environment. Decorative props, also called stage dressing, are generally considered to be those furnishings that aren't used by the actors and serve no specific purpose in the business of the play but that help project atmosphere and feeling. Small pieces of furniture and stage dressing, such as occasional chairs and end tables, pictures, wall hangings, rugs, knickknacks, lamps, lighting fixtures, and similar decorative articles, all fall into the category of decorative properties.

The floor needs to be considered when doing historical research. It provides a unifying visual element that ties the whole set together and can provide the foundation for the color scheme for the entire design. In many arena and thrust stages, the audience is seated above the stage floor. In these theatres the floor treatment becomes even more important because of the visual dominance that it has over other elements of the design. The stage floor can be covered with ¼-inch Masonite fairly inexpensively, and it can be painted in whatever treatment (boards, earth, stone) is appropriate for the design. Rugs or some similarly individualized, movable treatment can be used for the individual scenes of a multiset production.

Socioeconomic Level and Personality of the Characters

Most realistic sets give some indication of what sort of characters will inhabit the environment of the play. The designer normally uses set and decorative props as tools to achieve this effect. A living room that is decorated with inexpensive but reasonably tasteful furnishings suggests one type of occupant, and the same room furnished with expensive but incredibly gaudy things indicates that a completely different sort of person inhabits the space. If either of the preceding rooms were littered with a month's accumulation of dirty dishes, clothes, and other junk, it would seem likely that a completely different type of character was living there.

Selecting furniture can be a bit complex, simply because so many factors can influence what furniture should be used. The status of the "owners" of the furniture greatly affects not only the style but also the amount of furniture. If the principal character is a "pack rat" type, it is usually appropriate to have more furniture on the set than if the lead is a more fastidious type.

There are, of course, many production situations that prevent a scenic designer from giving any indication of the socioeconomic level or personalities of the characters. Examples of this type of situation would include "studio productions," in which a series of neutrally painted blocks are used for the furniture, as well as those low-budget productions that depend on borrowed furniture and props. But when the circumstances permit, furniture selection is another means by which the designer can enhance the audience's understanding and enjoyment of the play.

Season of the Year

Normally, it is difficult for the scenic designer to provide anything other than a cursory indication of the season in which the play is happening. If the play takes place in summer, the designer can suggest heat by having the doors and windows open and using screen doors and windows. The selection of light colors and fabrics for any upholstery and curtains can help create a feeling of summer, but by and large the projection of seasonal atmosphere is usually left to the lighting, media, and costume designers.

Elements of Composition

Full discussions of composition and color were presented in Chapters 5 ("Style, Composition, and Design") and 6 ("Color"), respectively. However, this is an appropriate time to remind you that scenic, property, and costume designers will be able to communicate more effectively if they are able to draw freely and easily. This is a skill that can be learned, and instructions for basic perspective drawing and sketching are included in Chapter 8, "Perspective Drawing," and Chapter 22, "Drawing and Rendering." Although these instructions will provide you with a beginning point, the best way to become adept at drawing and painting is to take art classes and practice, practice, practice.

Manipulation of the compositional elements (line, form, mass, value, and color), as we have seen in Chapters 5 ("Style, Composition, and Design") and 6 ("Color"), is the root of any design. We will now explore the applicability of this principle to scenic design.

Line   Line defines form. The characteristics of any line are defined by its physical properties (dimension, quality, and character). These properties, especially character, give any particular line its emotional content.

Cartooning is almost always based on the principle of line simplification. Walt Disney's cartoon characters Mickey Mouse and Donald Duck are simplified outlines of a mouse and a duck. There is no mistaking the objects for anything else, yet their simplicity gives them distinctive personalities that are uniquely their own.

Simplifying or altering the line of a natural form within a scenic design creates the same type of unique character definition as does line simplification in cartooning. The personality of the object created by this process is directly related to the emotional quality of the line style chosen by the designer. Generally, an object drawn with strong (heavy, sharply angular, bold) lines creates an emotional response that the object is more powerful, dominant, and purposeful than if it were drawn with weak (soft, curvilinear, lightweight) lines.

Form   In compositional terms, form refers to a space enclosed by a line. The evocative characteristics of the line defining any form will dictate the emotional qualities of that form. The character of the chosen line (heavy, light, straight, squiggly, softly curving, sharply angled) will create a perceptual key that helps explain the psychological nature of the object being depicted (Figure 9.4).

Mass   Within the context of composition, mass is defined as the three-dimensional manifestation of an enclosed form, and the perceived meanings of mass are closely related to those of form. The exaggeration of either form or mass can be used to stylize a design. By exaggerating the height, width, or depth of the natural dimensions of an object, we can change the character of that object. The illustrations from almost any book or cartoon version of *Alice's Adventures in Wonderland* illustrate this point. Once Alice encounters the March Hare and enters the strange land ruled by the Queen of Hearts, hardly anything is seen in its normal size or shape.

Value   Value refers to the relative lightness or darkness of a line, form, or mass. The emotional reaction to the value or reflectance of an object has become

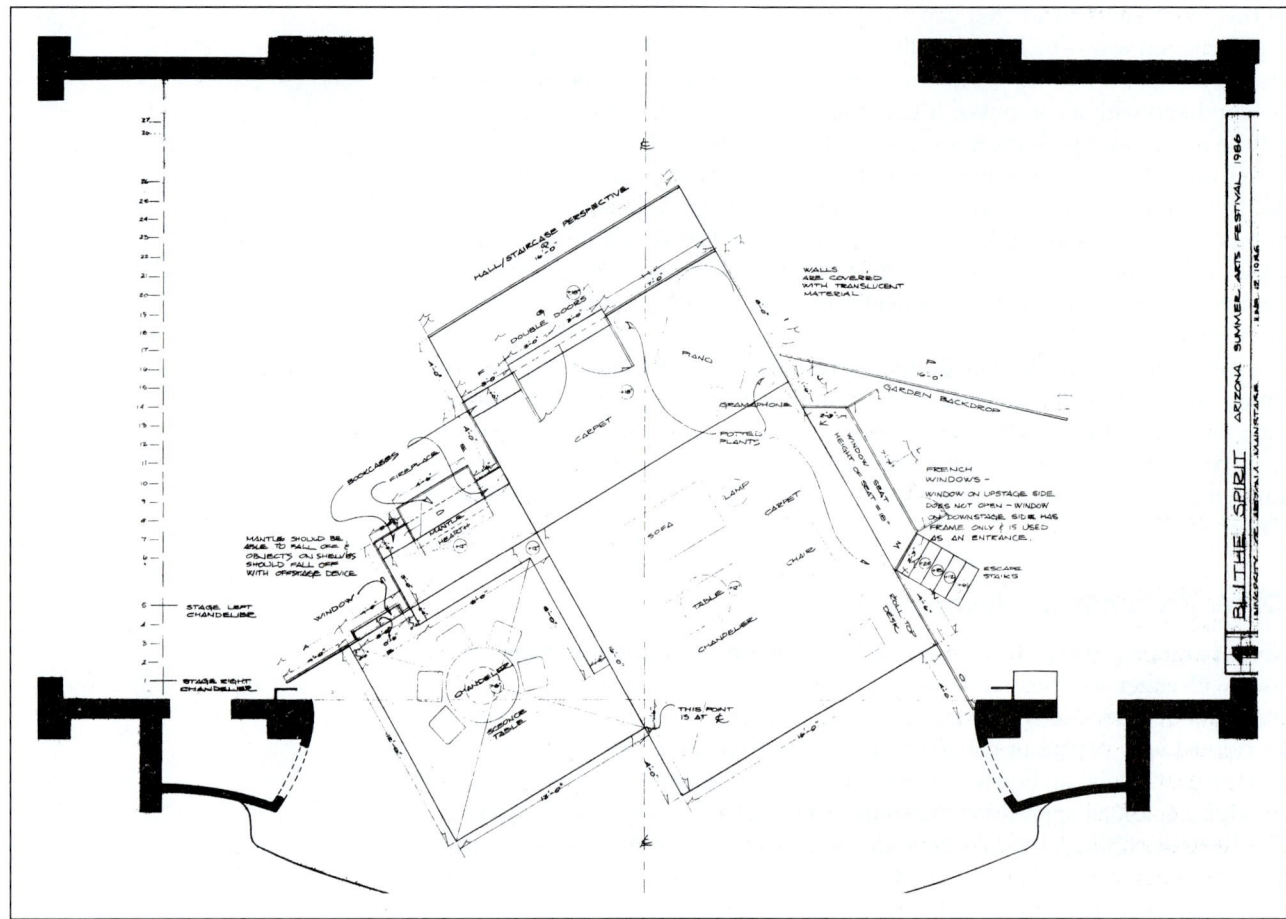

FIGURE 9.9
Ground plan for *Blithe Spirit*, produced at the University of Arizona; scenic design by K. Pistor. Courtesy of Kitty Culbert Pistor.

The primary ground plan normally shows only the architectural information about the set as described earlier. Frequently a second ground plan is created. This one shows how the set "functions." It shows the placement of furniture, rugs, hanging chandeliers, window dressings, and other relevant information. This ground plan is quite useful to the stage manager so he or she will know where the various functional and decorative props will be placed in relationship to the physical structure of the set. Frequently the location/placement of these pieces will be adjusted during the rehearsal process, but this "functional" ground plan provides a good beginning point.

A majority of the work done in planning a production depends on the information provided by the ground plan. During the rehearsal period, the director has the stage manager, using the ground plan as a guide, tape or chalk the outline of the design onto the rehearsal room floor. Then the actors can rehearse and perfect their blocking in a space that corresponds to the actual set.

The lighting designer, when drawing the light plot, uses the ground plan to provide information about the shape and placement of the set within the theatre. This type of information is needed when making decisions about the hanging positions for the various instruments that will light the production.

The technical director uses the ground plan for a wide variety of functions. Together with the **center-line sectional,** it tells the technical director where the set will sit on the stage and where to place the masking. It also indicates a great deal of information about the amount of materials that will be needed to construct the set(s).

center-line sectional: A sectional drawing whose cutting plane is the center line of the stage and auditorium; used to show the height of the various elements of the theatre, stage and any pertinent set pieces, lighting, sound and other equipment.

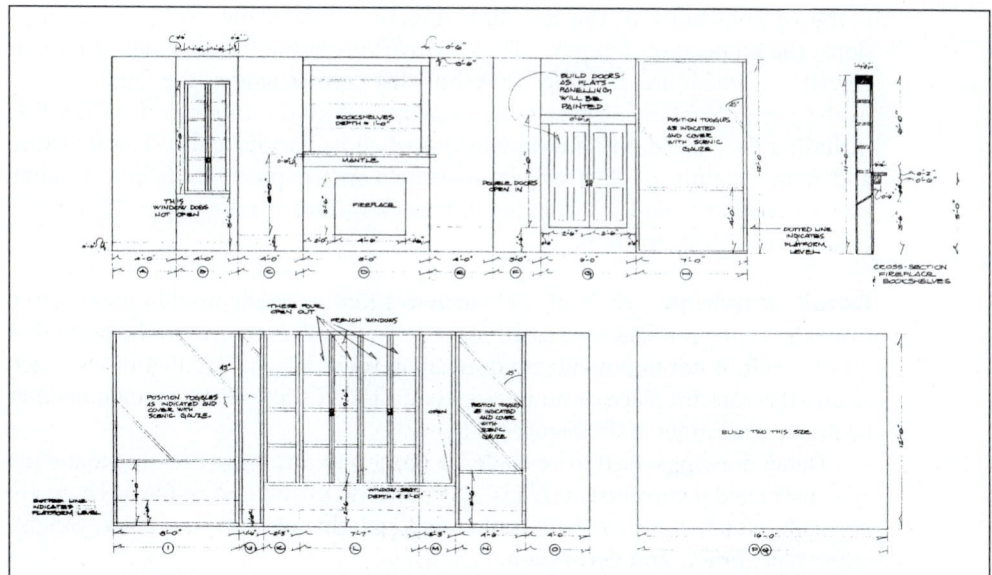

FIGURE 9.10
Front elevations for *Blithe Spirit*, produced at the University of Arizona; scenic design by K. Pistor. Courtesy of K. Pistor.

Information on how to draw a ground plan, as well as the other drawings that make up the designer's plans, is contained in Chapter 7, "Mechanical Drafting."

Front Elevations   Front elevations (Figure 9.10) show a front view of the set as if it were flattened into a single plane. The main purpose of these scale drawings (normally ½ inch to 1 foot) is to indicate all of the vertical measurements that cannot be shown on the ground plan. These dimensions include the height of walls, doors, and windows as well as the location of any features on the walls such as baseboards, wainscoting, chair rails, cornices, paintings, or other decorative features.

Frequently a second set of front elevations will be drawn to show the location of decorative items such as style of window dressings, shelf/fireplace dressing, pictures, mirrors, and so forth. These details can range from relatively complete pencil drawings that show the style, fabric, and fullness of a window treatment to simple outlines with notes such as a rectangle with a note "landscape painting with moose — gold frame." These detail elevations suggest what the scenic designer envisions for the set dressing and are of great benefit in communicating those ideas to the property designer.

Even if the scenic designer has constructed a functional model of the set, he or she will actually be designing as much when drafting the elevations as when producing the thumbnail sketches, renderings, or models, because what appears on the elevations is actually a proportional reduction of the appearance of the finished set. If the designer wants to change or adjust any element, with CAD it is fairly easy to redraw the elevations. Most CAD programs automatically make corresponding changes to the ground plan whenever changes are made on the elevations, such as widening or moving a flat. If hand-drawing these plans, adjustments will have to be made manually to the ground plans whenever changes are made to the elevations and vice versa.

The primary purpose of the front elevations is to describe the appearance of the set; they don't tell how to build it. For this reason, no attempt is made to indicate the width of the individual flats that will be used to construct the various wall units. This breakdown of the wall segments into manageable units is the responsibility of the technical director or, in some professional situations, the scene shop foreman. The construction of the flats is made from rear elevations, which are drawings that show the reverse side of the flats depicted in the front elevations. These scale drawings show the framework of the flat, including the placement and dimensions of all its various parts. The structure and nomenclature of flats will be discussed in Chapter 11, "Scenic Production Techniques," and the drawing of rear elevations is taken up in Chapter 7, "Mechanical Drafting."

Detail Drawings   The scale of ½ inch to 1 foot normally used in drawing the front elevations reduces the size of some of the smaller features to the point that it is difficult, if not impossible, to draw all of their details. Detailed pieces, such as an elaborate fireplace or an intricately designed stained-glass panel, need to be drawn in a larger scale (Figure 9.11).

Detail drawings need to be made for properties and stage dressing that must be constructed — furniture, torches, specific hand props, and so forth. These are normally sketched rather than drafted and include notes on size, color, weight, fabric type, finish, and decoration.

Many features of a setting cannot be fully described by drawing them in top and front (or rear) views only. Three-dimensional objects often require a third view to supplement the other two. There are several methods of drafting (orthographic projection, isometric drawing, oblique drawing, and cabinet drawing) that show more than two sides of an object. The techniques of these methods of drafting are discussed in Chapter 7, "Mechanical Drafting."

Full-Scale Drawings   A few of the smallest features of a set should be drawn in full scale, or actual size. If the design is unusually intricate or the object rather small, such as the pattern for a turned bannister or a wallpaper pattern, it is usually both easier and faster to draw it in full scale. It is also easier to construct something from a full-scale drawing than one that has been proportionally reduced.

Sight-Line Drawings   An improperly or inadequately masked set is a sign of a second-rate production. Most people come to the theatre to be entertained, to escape into the world of the play. When they can see backstage and watch actors waiting for their cues, stagehands lounging around, or any of the backstage paraphernalia, their concentration on the substance of the play is broken. All of these unnecessary distractions can be avoided if the scenic designer takes the time to draft some **sight-line drawings.**

The sight lines of any set can be checked through the use of two drawings, a ground plan and a vertical section of the stage and auditorium, with the set in its proper position on the stage (Figure 9.12). The horizontal section, or plan view, shows the view of the stage, or sight line, of the people sitting in the extreme side seats of the first and last rows of the auditorium. The vertical section shows a side view of the sight line for the same seats.

The little time required to draft sight-line drawings is time well spent. Too often the scenery is built, painted, and assembled on stage before the sight lines are checked. The sight lines may be perfectly satisfactory, but occasionally some area of the set is out of sight of the audience, the backing flats are too small, or the masking drapes have been hung in the wrong position. Sight-line drawings can reveal any potential problems with masking in sufficient time to correct them.

sight-line drawings: A scale drawing (plan and section views) of sightings that extend from the extreme seats (usually the outside seats on the front and last rows of the auditorium) to any position on the stage; used to determine how much of the stage and backstage will be visible from specific auditorium seats.

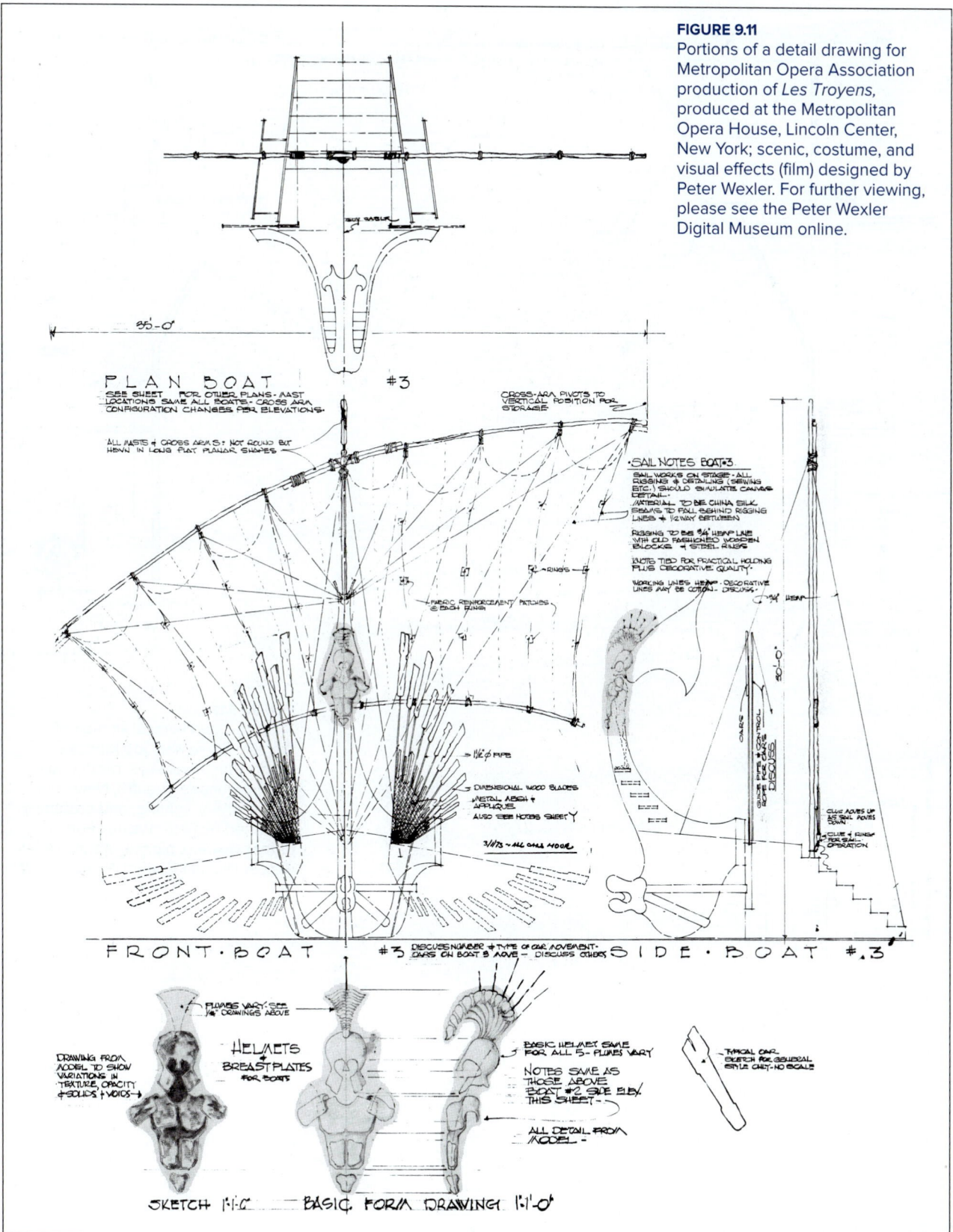

FIGURE 9.11
Portions of a detail drawing for Metropolitan Opera Association production of *Les Troyens,* produced at the Metropolitan Opera House, Lincoln Center, New York; scenic, costume, and visual effects (film) designed by Peter Wexler. For further viewing, please see the Peter Wexler Digital Museum online.

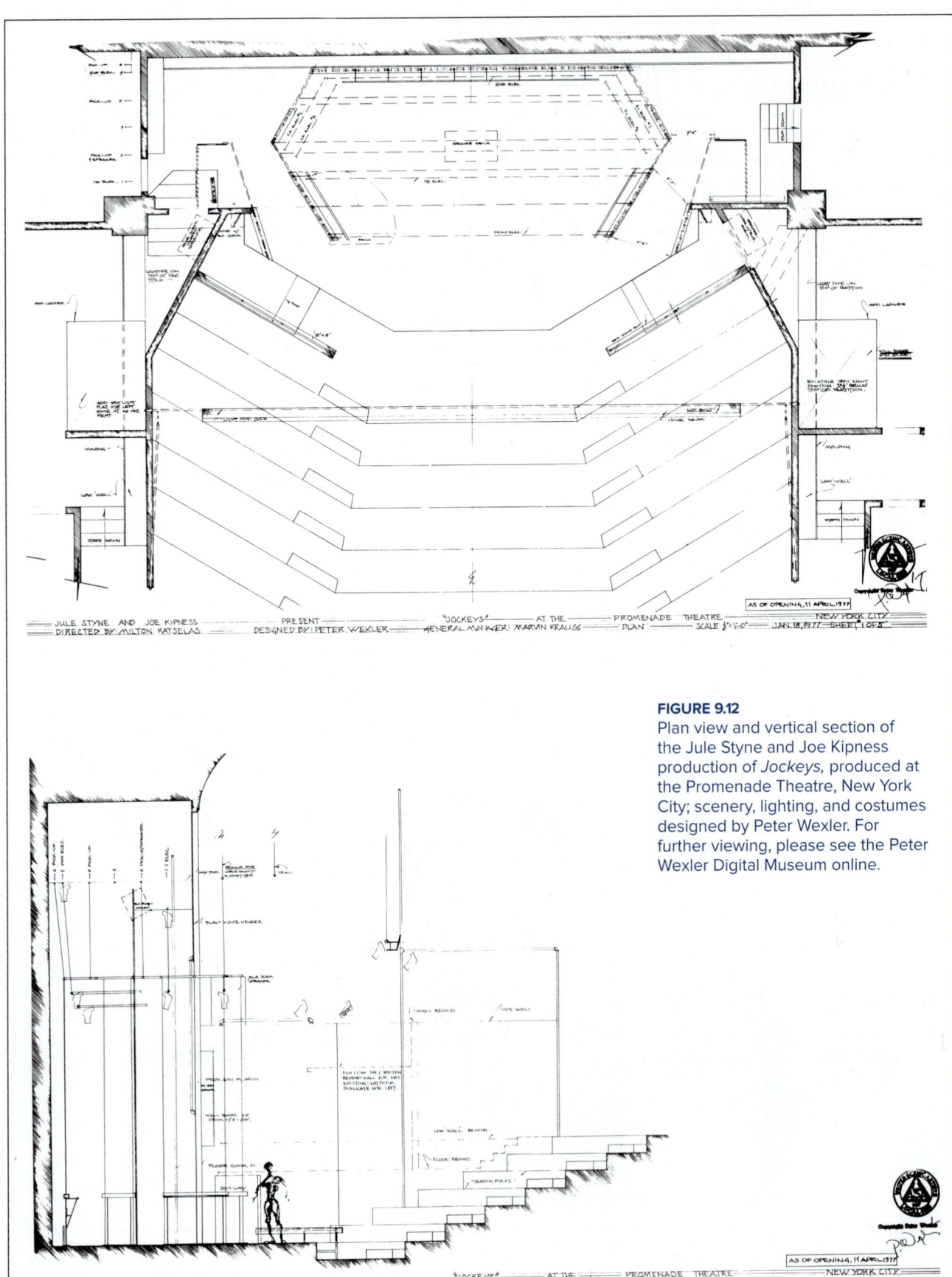

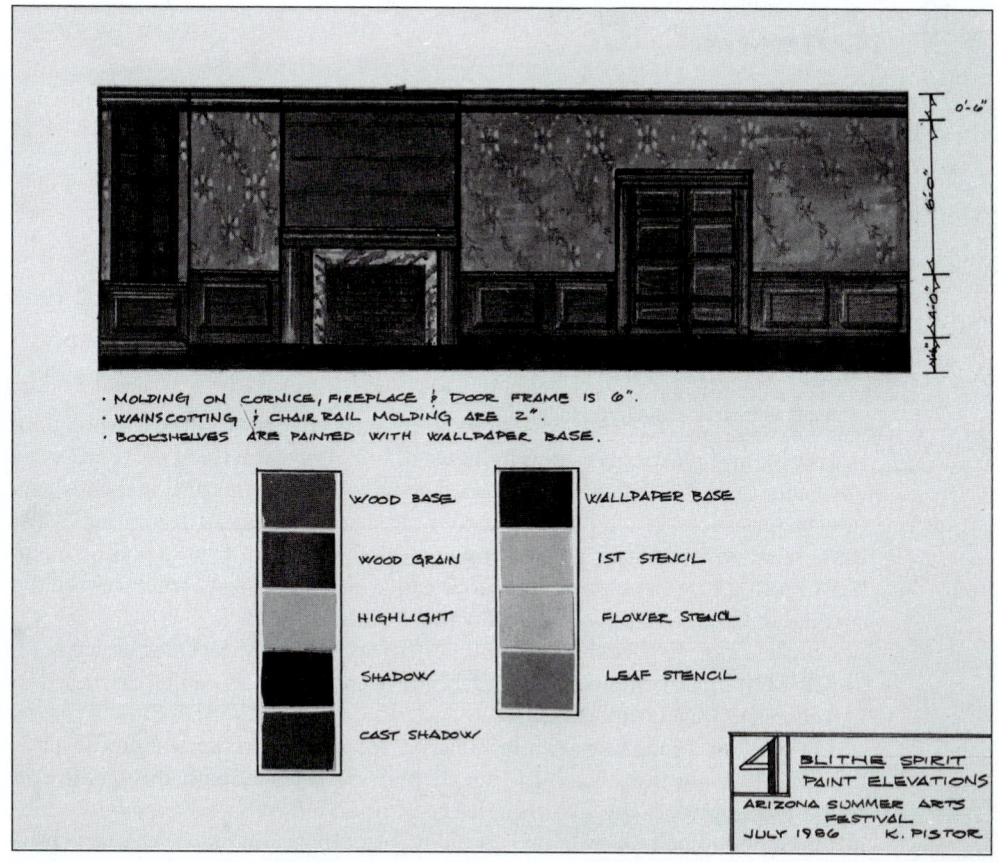

FIGURE 9.13
Painter's elevations for *Blithe Spirit*, produced at the University of Arizona; scenic design by K. Pistor. Courtesy K. Pistor.

Painter's Elevations   Painter's elevations are front elevations of the set, but they are either computer rendered or drawn on watercolor board and painted to show not only the colors but also the painting techniques that will be used in finishing the set. The painter's elevations (Figure 9.13) are the renderings that the scenic artist and paint crew use when painting the set. The scenic artist mixes the colors to match the palette used on the painter's elevations, and the crew applies the paint using techniques that will duplicate the style illustrated in the painter's elevations. Information on the materials and techniques of scene painting is contained in Chapter 12, "Scene Painting."

Scenic design is both a demanding and a rewarding practical craft. In order to create a quality scenic design you have to use your imagination, sketch, paint, construct scale models, and produce accurate mechanical drawings. Although this process may seem to be an almost overwhelming task, seeing your design standing on the stage as tangible proof of a viable production concept is an extremely rewarding experience.

Chapter 10

Tools and Materials

Almost any material can be used to make scenery or props. Wood, fabric, metal, and plastics are commonly used, but almost anything else can be, or has been, used in scenic construction. The majority of nontraditional construction materials are generally applied to a basic scenic form as decoration. Most basic scenery is made by constructing a supporting form from wood or metal and covering that structure with wood, fabric, or both. These structures will be covered in Chapter 11, "Scenic Production Techniques."

Stage properties are made in a number of fascinating ways using an amazing variety of materials. Some of those techniques and materials will be discussed in Chapter 13, "Stage Properties."

Regardless of whether you're building scenery or properties almost all of the tools that are introduced in this chapter are used by both the scenic and property personnel. The following list isn't intended to be exhaustive. Rather, it is intended to be representative of the types of tools and materials that can be found in a typical scenic or property shop.

Hand Tools

Almost any type of scenery or prop can be built with just a few hand tools; after all, people were building scenery and props long before the discovery of electricity and the development of power tools. The only advantages that power tools provide are speed and reduced effort.

Measuring Tools

Measuring tools are used to measure dimensions and angles.

Tape Measure   A metal tape (Figure 10.1A) housed in plastic or metal case; has a lock to hold tape in position and a self-return spring to retract tape into case. Lengths range from 6 to 35 feet; 50- to 100-foot lengths (Figure 10.1B) are manually wound and usually made of fabric or thin steel.

Tri Square   A small, rigid hand square (Figure 10.1C). A steel blade; wood, steel, or composite handle. Used as a guide for 90-degree angles.

Combination Square   A 12-inch steel rule (Figure 10.1D) with a movable handle angled at 45 and 90 degrees; used for marking 45- and 90-degree angles; rule used for measuring.

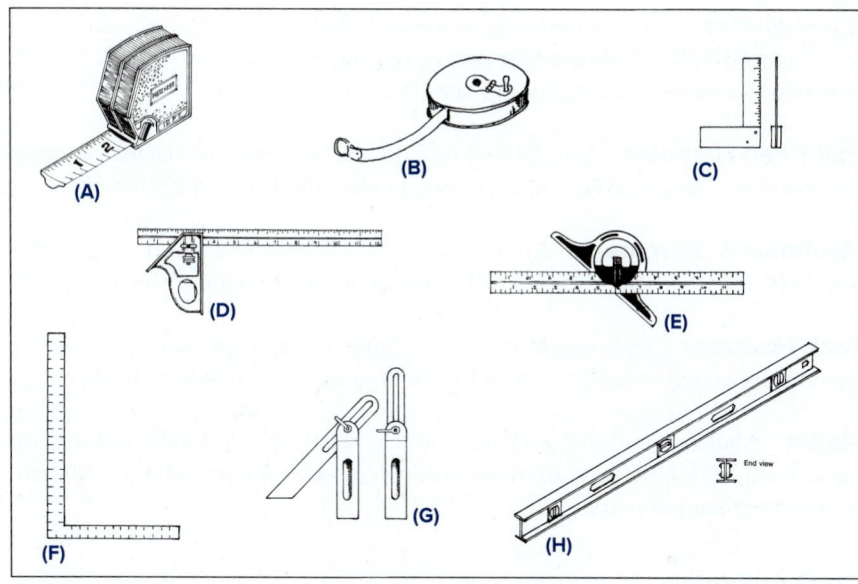

FIGURE 10.1
Measuring tools.
(A) Tape measure
(B) 50-foot length steel tape
(C) Tri square
(D) Combination square
(E) Bevel protractor
(F) Framing square
(G) Bevel set
(H) Carpenter's level

Bevel Protractor   A combination square whose angle is adjustable (Figure 10.1E).

Framing Square   A steel L with 16- and 24-inch legs (Figure 10.1F). Used for making 90-degree corner joints in flat construction.

Bevel Set   A handle with a movable metal blade lockable in any position (Figure 10.1G); used for transferring angles.

Carpenter's Level   Used to determine true horizontal and vertical angles; 6-foot-long levels (Figure 10.1H) are typical for theatre shop and stage use.

Marking Tools

Marking tools are used to mark dimensions and angles. Mark wood with carpenter's pencils or #2 yellow pencils. Don't use pens — ink stains wood and bleeds through paint. Mark metal with wax pencils, Sharpies, soapstone, and scribes.

starter hole: A small hole bored into a piece of wood or metal to hold the tip of a screw or drill bit; also called a pilot hole.

Scribe   The scribe, also called a scratch awl (Figure 10.2A), has a sharp metal point; used for marking wood, metal, plastic and making screw **starter holes** in wood.

Chalk Line   A chalk-covered string in a metal or plastic housing (Figure 10.2B) filled with chalk or dry scenic pigment; the twine is stretched and snapped to leave a straight line.

Hammers

Hammers are used for nailing and starting screws, as well as shaping and forming metal.

Claw Hammer   Has a hammering face and two sharply curved claws (Figure 10.3A) for removing nails; available in a variety of weights and handle/grip compositions.

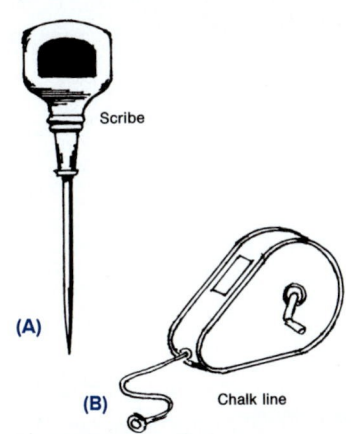

FIGURE 10.2
Marking tools.

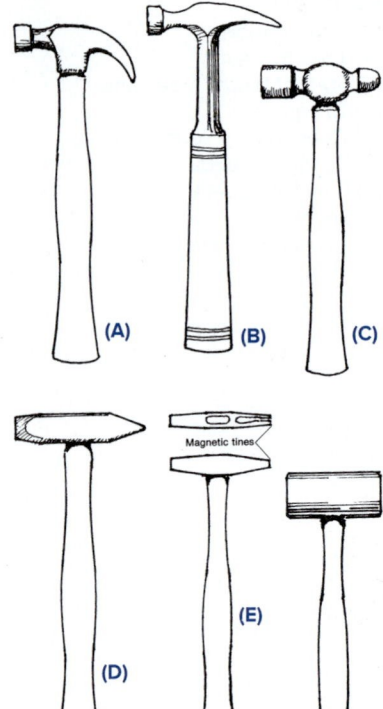

FIGURE 10.3
Hammers.
(A) Claw hammer
(B) Rip hammer
(C) Ball peen hammer
(D) Mechanic's hammer
(E) Tack hammer
(F) Mallet

Rip Hammer   Has a hammering face and straighter claws than the claw hammer (Figure 10.3B); claws used for prying/ripping apart previously nailed wood; available in a variety of weights and handle/grip compositions.

Ball Peen Hammer   Has flat and rounded faces (Figure 10.3C) for bending/shaping metal/seating rivets; made of harder steel than claw or rip hammers.

Mechanic's Hammer   Also known as blacksmith's/heavy duty hammer (Figure10.3D); has heavy head (1 to 3 pounds); used for shaping metal.

Tack Hammer   Lightweight hammer (Figure 10.3E) with two faces; smaller face is magnetized to hold/insert tacks, the larger face used to seat them.

Mallet   Mallets (Figure 10.3F) have wooden, plastic, or hard rubber heads and wood/composition handles; used for striking chisels or shaping thin metal without leaving hammer marks.

Cutting Tools

Saws   Saws are used to cut wood, metal, or plastic. The number of teeth roughly indicates the material a blade will cut; the harder the material, the smaller the number of teeth, referred to as "tooth count."

Crosscut Saw   Used to cut across wood grain (Figure 10.4A); to prevent binding, alternate teeth are bent outward so the **kerf** is wider than blade width; normally has 10 to 12 teeth per inch; higher tooth count gives smoother cut.

Rip Saw   Used to cut parallel with wood grain (Figure 10.4B); normally has 6 teeth per inch; teeth filed straight across to give chisel cut.

Backsaw and Miter Box   A fine-toothed (12 to 14 teeth per inch) crosscut saw with a rigid blade-stiffening spine (Figure 10.4C); the spine fits in a guide in the **miter** box; used to make accurate angle cuts in wood.

Keyhole Saw   Used for making curved cuts in wood (Figure 10.4D); 10 to 12 teeth per inch.

Coping Saw   Used for making intricate curved cuts in thin plywood (Figure 10.4E); interior cuts made by drilling hole in wood, removing blade, inserting it through hole, reattaching blade to frame; 16 to 18 teeth per inch.

Hacksaw   Used for cutting mild steel, copper, and aluminum (Figure 10.4F); 20 to 25 teeth per inch.

Utility Knife   Used for light-duty cutting/carving (Figure 10.5A); has replaceable blades; safer models have retractable blades; also called matte knife.

kerf: The width of the cut made by a saw blade.

miter: An angle that is cut in a piece of wood or metal, usually in pairs, to form a corner.

Using Hammers

Claw hammers and rip hammers should be used only for nailing, because their face may chip if they are used for pounding metals harder than nails. These chips can cut your hands or cause serious eye damage. The ball peen hammer has a hardened face that won't chip when used for beating metal.

Safety Tip

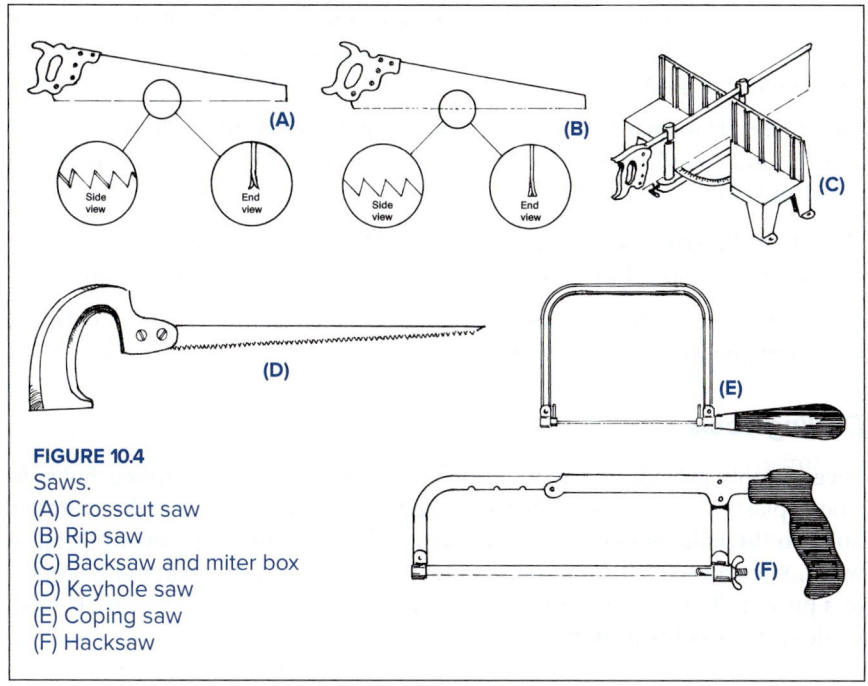

FIGURE 10.4
Saws.
(A) Crosscut saw
(B) Rip saw
(C) Backsaw and miter box
(D) Keyhole saw
(E) Coping saw
(F) Hacksaw

Scissors   Used for cutting paper and fabrics (Figure 10.5B).

Tin Snips   Used for cutting thin (under 18 gauge) metal (Figure 10.5C); different models cut straight, left- or right-hand curves; compound-leverage snips multiply cutting force; do not use to cut nails or wire.

Wood Chisel   Used for gouging, carving, or smoothing wood (Figure 10.5D); the wood or plastic handle is lightly struck with mallet or heel of the hand; ½-, ¾-, and 1-inch blade widths most useful in theatre shop; other widths available.

Cold Chisel   Used on mild steel and nonferrous metals (Figure 10.5E); made of very hard steel; struck with ball peen or mechanic's hammer.

Planes   Knife-bladed tools used to smooth or round edges or corners of wood.

Block Plane   Used to smooth across the grain of board ends (Figure 10.6A); blade can be raised or lowered to adjust depth of cut.

Smoothing Plane   Used parallel with wood grain (Figure 10.6B); adjustable blade depth.

Spoke Shave   Used to soften/round sharp edges (Figure 10.6C); pulled rather than pushed across the wood.

Surform Tools   Trademarked tools (Figure 10.6D) that use thin, disposable spring steel blades honeycombed with sharpened protrusions; used cross or parallel with grain for general shaping; finished surface is not smooth.

Files   Files are used to rasp or grind wood, metal, plastic, other materials. The teeth of a file are formed in diagonal ridges across its face. Coarse teeth are used for working wood; medium teeth for wood and plastic; fine teeth for metal.

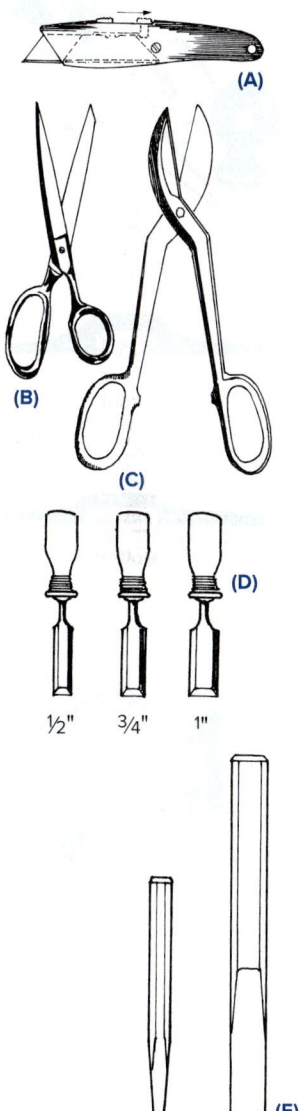

FIGURE 10.5
Miscellaneous cutting tools.
(A) Utility knife
(B) Scissors
(C) Tin snips
(D) Wood chisels
(E) Cold chisels

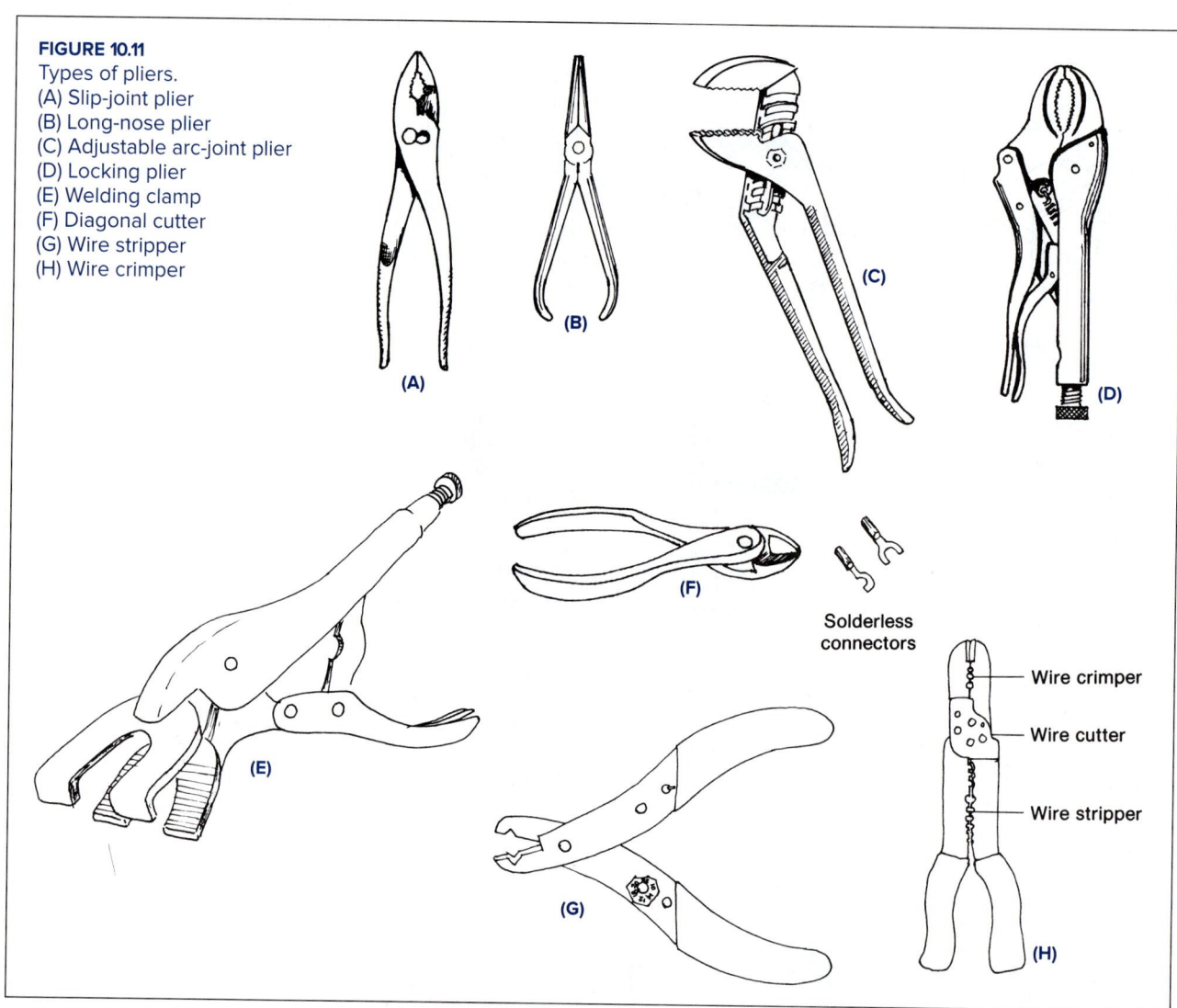

FIGURE 10.11
Types of pliers.
(A) Slip-joint plier
(B) Long-nose plier
(C) Adjustable arc-joint plier
(D) Locking plier
(E) Welding clamp
(F) Diagonal cutter
(G) Wire stripper
(H) Wire crimper

Locking Pliers   Known by trade name Vise Grip (Figure 10.11D); used to grasp, hold, and lock just about anything; locking pressure adjustable; numerous configurations including welding clamp (Figure 10.11E).

Diagonal Cutters   Used for cutting soft electrical wire (Figure 10.11F).

Wire Strippers   Used for stripping insulation from electrical wire without cutting the wire (Figure 10.11G).

Wire-Crimping Tool   For pressure-clamping solderless connectors to electrical wire (Figure 10.11H).

Wrenches   Wrenches are used to hold and/or tighten bolts and nuts.

Open-End Wrench   Non-adjustable, open-end, smooth-jawed wrenches for standard- or metric-sized nuts (Figure 10.12A).

Box-End Wrench   Non-adjustable, closed-end, toothed socket, frequently offset (Figure 10.12B); for standard- and metric-sized nuts.

Adjustable-End Wrench Adjustable, smooth jawed; known by trade name Crescent Wrench (Figure 10.12C); 6- and 8-inch sizes most common in theatre shops.

Monkey Wrench Heavyweight, smooth-jawed, adjustable wrench (Figure10.12D); for use on large nuts.

Pipe Wrench Has serrated jaws to bite and grip metal pipe (Figure 10.12E); used to hold/twist pipes and couplings.

Socket Set and Ratchet Handle Sockets are cylindrical wrenches; used with a reversible ratchet handle (Figure 10.12F); nuts can be tightened or loosened without removing wrench from nut.

Screwdrivers

Screwdrivers are used for inserting and removing screws. They are available in a variety of configurations and sizes.

Standard or Slotted Screwdriver A metal shank, tapering to a flattened tip with plastic/composite handle (Figure 10.13A); a wide variety of bit sizes (000, 00, 0, 1, 2, 3) are available; bit sizes 1 and 2 with 6- to 8-inch shanks are most common in theatre shops.

Phillips Screwdriver Screwdriver with a four-flanged tip to fit the crossed slots of a Phillips head screw (Figure 10.13B); in bit sizes 000, 00, 0, 1, 2, 3; bit sizes 1 and 2 with 6- to 8-inch shafts are common in theatre shops.

FIGURE 10.12
Types of wrenches.
(A) Open-end wrench
(B) Box-end wrench
(C) Adjustable-end wrench
(D) Monkey wrench
(E) Pipe wrench
(F) Ratchet and socket

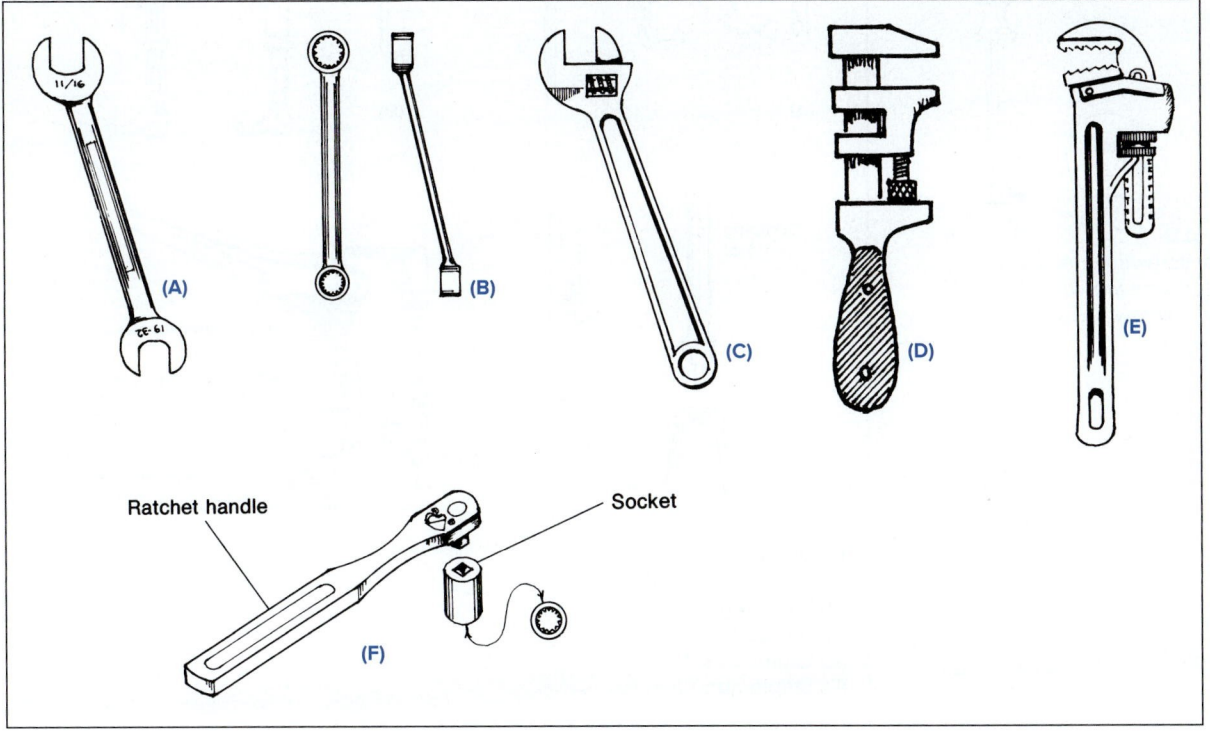

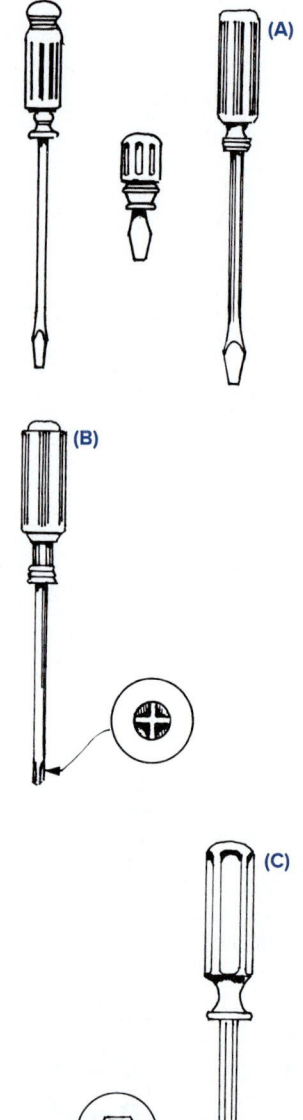

FIGURE 10.13
Types of screwdrivers.
(A) Slotted screwdrivers
(B) Phillips screwdriver
(C) Nut driver

Nut Driver A screwdriver with a socket tip (Figure 10.13C); socket sizes generally range from ⅛- to ⅜-inch.

Miscellaneous Hand Tools

Several useful hand tools don't fit conveniently into any particular category.

Sandpaper Used to smooth materials before finishing; fine (220), medium (120), and coarse (80) grits are typical in most shops.

Wrecking Bars Used to pry previously nailed wood apart and remove nails (Figure 10.14A).

Nail Puller For extracting nails (Figure 10.14B); sliding handle drives the jaws into wood to grasp the nail and lever it out.

Grommet Set Consists of a hole punch, a small anvil, and a crimping tool (Figure 10.14D); used to attach brass reinforcing rings (grommets) to drops and stage draperies.

Staple Gun A spring-powered tool for driving staples (Figure 10.14D); ³⁄₁₆- to ⅝-inch leg lengths; used for attaching fabric to wood and similar jobs.

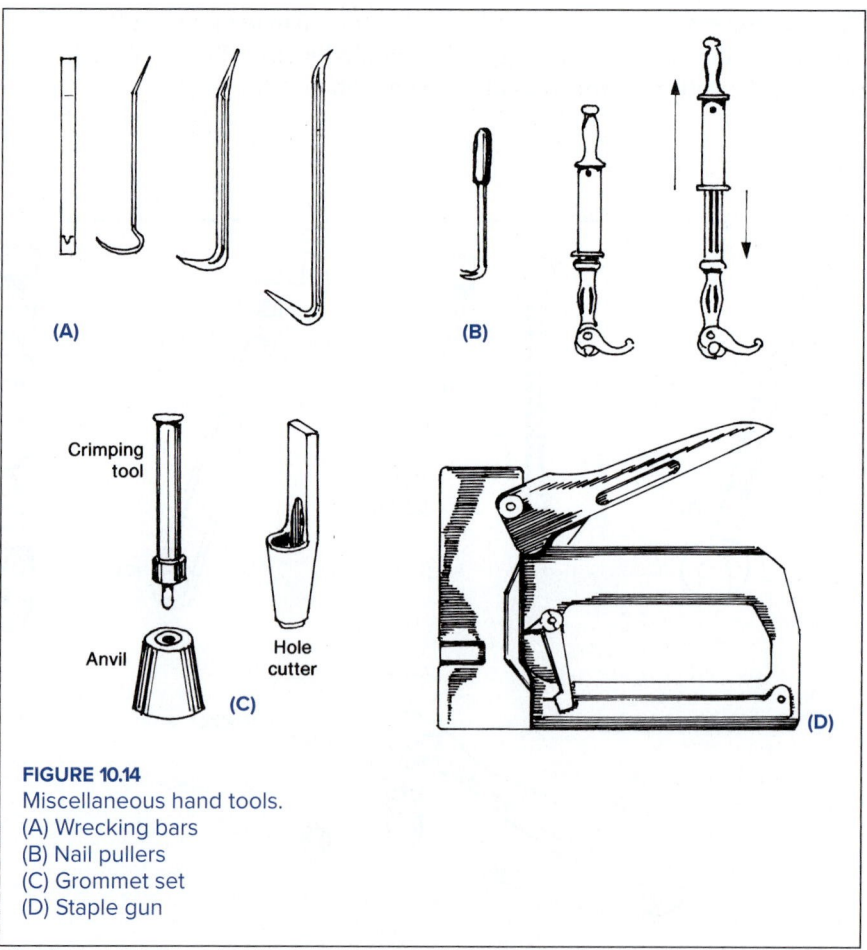

FIGURE 10.14
Miscellaneous hand tools.
(A) Wrecking bars
(B) Nail pullers
(C) Grommet set
(D) Staple gun

Metalworking Hand Tools

Although many of the basic woodworking tools are equally useful when working with metal, there are a few additional tools designed specifically for metalwork.

Anvil Heavyweight anvil (Figure 10.15A); used when bending metal rod and strap.

Conduit Bender Used to bend thin wall conduit (Figure 10.15B).

Center Punch Used to make starter holes for drill bits in both metal and wood (Figure 10.15C); the spring-driven center punch works faster and easier.

Bolt Cutter Heavy-duty metal shears (Figure 10.15D); cuts mild steel round stock up to ½ inch in diameter.

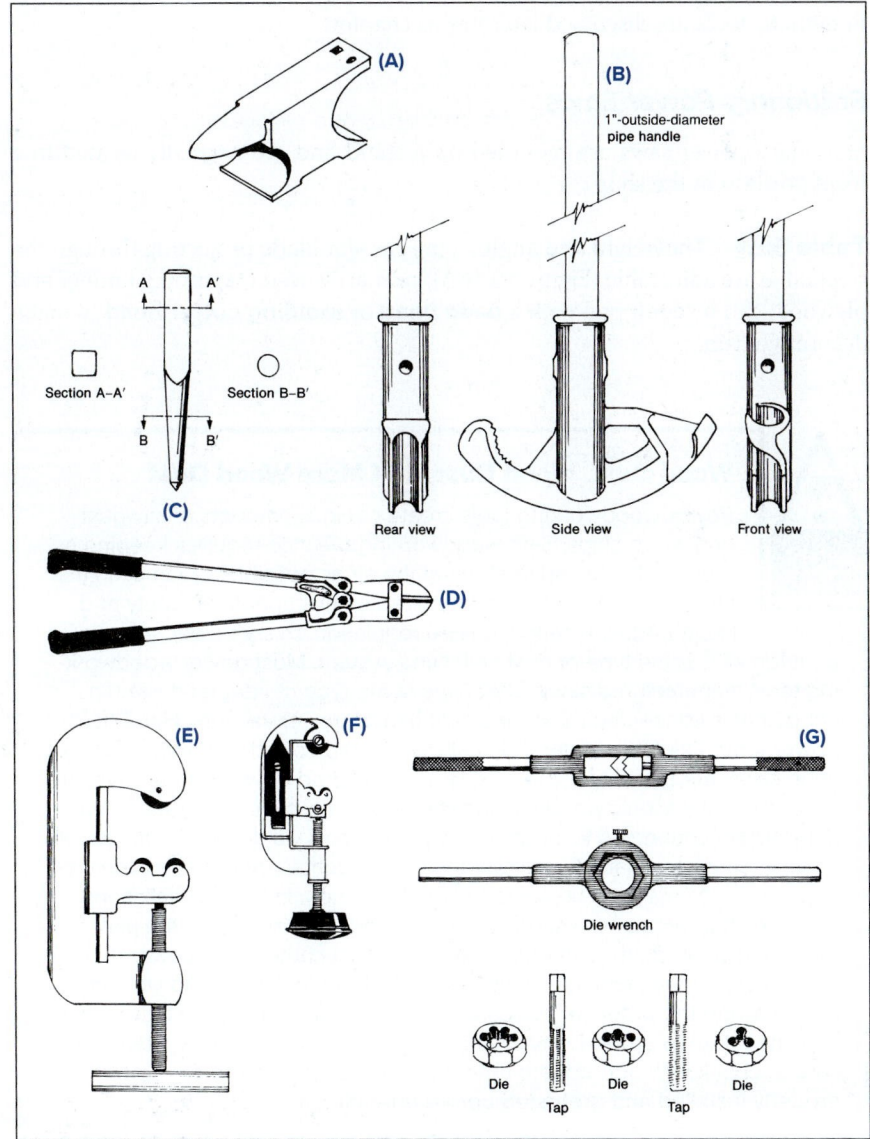

FIGURE 10.15
Metalworking hand tools.
(A) Anvil
(B) Conduit bender
(C) Center punch
(D) Bolt cutter
(E) Pipe cutter
(F) Tube cutter
(G) Tap and die set

Pipe Cutter   Used to make right angle cuts in ½-inch and larger steel pipe (Figure 10.15E); tube cutter (Figure 10.15F) is used on non-ferrous (copper, aluminum) tubing ½ inch or less in diameter.

Tap and Dies   Tap and dies (Figure 10.15G); tap cuts threads on the inside of pipes (internal threads); die cuts threads on the outside of pipes and rod stock (external threads).

 ## Power Tools

Power tools perform the same tasks as hand tools. They just do it faster and with less effort. The use of power tools does increase safety hazards in the shop. Be sure that you receive adequate instruction — and follow it — before operating any power tool.

Power hand tools are commonly available with 120-volt (corded) power and/or rechargeable batteries. Some are also available with pneumatic drives. Pneumatic tools are discussed later in this chapter.

Stationary Power Saws

Stationary power saws are mounted on a stand and are normally located in a fixed position in the shop.

Table Saw   The height and angle of the circular blade projecting through the steel table are adjustable (Figure 10.16A); primarily used for ripping lumber and plywood; can be equipped with a **dado head** or **molding cutter head** to make decorative trim.

dado head: A saw accessory consisting of a set of toothed blades that sandwich a chisel-like chipper; the blades smooth-cut the outside edges of the kerf while the chipper gouges out the wood between the blades; the distance between the blades is variable.

molding cutter head: A heavy cylindrical arbor in which a variety of matched cutter blades or knives can be fit.

Wood Dust, Wood Dust, and More Wood Dust

Power woodworking tools create copious amounts of sawdust and wood chips. Safe woodworking practice requires keeping as much of this wood dust out of the air as possible. Clean air in the shop environment is also required by Occupational Safety and Health Administration (OSHA) regulation. Every power saw should be fitted with some type of dust-collecting system. Most power woodworking tools manufactured since 1990 have some type of integral dust/chip chute that is connected to either a dust bag or power vacuum. Hand-held power tools, like belt sanders, typically use a bag collector. Larger tools, like table saws, are typically connected to a whole-shop power vacuum system.

Professional scenic woodworking shops typically have a centralized vacuum system connected to all stationary power tools via ductwork and flexible hoses. Sometimes stationary power tools are mounted on castered benches or platforms so they can be moved around the shop. In these installations, portable shop vacuums — shop vacs — are typically attached to the platforms and connected via flexible hose to the dust chute of the power tool.

Because of the static electricity generated within these shop vacuum systems, and the potential explosiveness of airborne wood dust, great care must be taken to properly install and ground all shop vacuum systems. Be sure to check with appropriate authorities to determine that the system is properly installed and grounded before operating it.

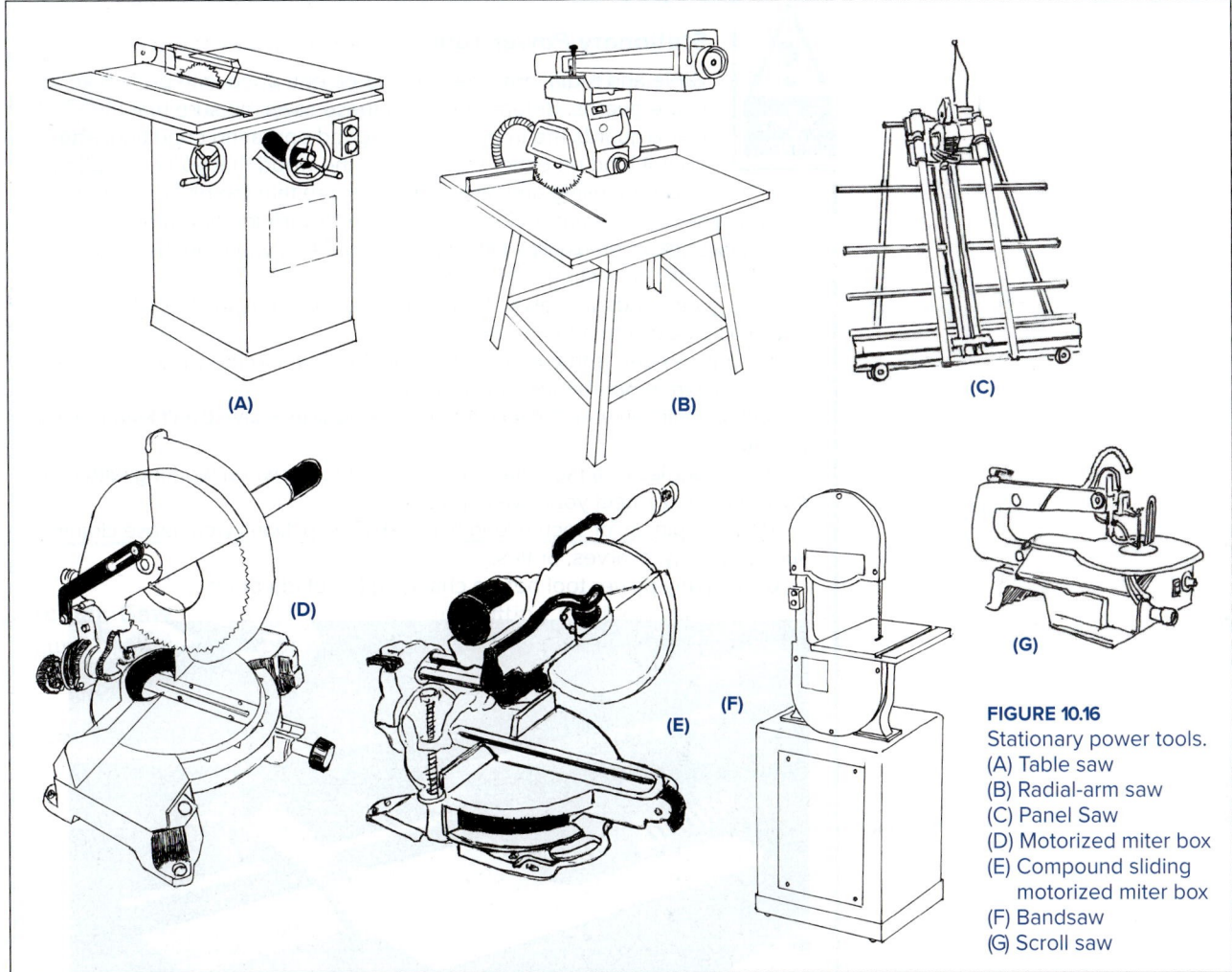

FIGURE 10.16
Stationary power tools.
(A) Table saw
(B) Radial-arm saw
(C) Panel Saw
(D) Motorized miter box
(E) Compound sliding
    motorized miter box
(F) Bandsaw
(G) Scroll saw

Radial-Arm Saw   The motor/blade housing is suspended beneath an arm that adjusts up/down and pivots side-to-side (Figure 10.16B); also called a pull-over saw; primarily used for cross- and angle-cutting.

Panel Saw   Used to make straight cuts in panel materials like plywood or Medium-density fiberboard (MDF); the vertical rack holds the sheet goods; cuts are made with a moveable, track-mounted circular saw (Figure 10.16C); safely operated by one person; horizontal model also available.

Motorized Miter Box   Also called a chop saw (Figure 10.16D); the motor/blade housing pivots (chops) down onto the work; makes straight and angled cuts; frequently stand- or bench-mounted.

Compound Sliding Motorized Miter Box   Combines sliding action of pullover saw with chopping action of chop saw (Figure 10.16E); cuts wider stock than chop saw; makes angled and/or bevel cuts; normally stand- or bench-mounted.

Bandsaw   Used for curvilinear cuts (Figure 10.16F); the narrow loop (or band) blade passes through a table that supports the work; equipped with mechanical

saw; speed control and appropriate blade selection enables use on wood, plastic or metal; also called jig saw.

Cut Awl Combines reciprocal action with a swiveling blade (Figure 10.17C); the saw sits on, and is pulled across, the work; makes very intricate, smooth-edged cuts in stock, plywood, composition board, plastic, paper, and cloth.

Dremel Tool Trade (and common) name for a high-speed, rotary action, hand-held power tool (Figure 10.17D); used for a wide variety of drilling, cutting, polishing actions; models in fixed and variable speeds; has many available specialized bits.

Rotozip Tool A high-speed, rotary-action cutting tool (Figure 10.17E); uses specialized bits to cut interior holes in plywood, drywall, metal, and ceramic tile.

Reciprocating Saw Known by its trade name Sawzall[1] (Figure 10.17F); normally used in demolition, not theatre construction; bare blade uses reciprocal action to cut through wood/plastic/metal; useful for trimming/carving Styrofoam and during **strike.**

Biscuit Cutter Used to cut narrow grooves in wood (Figure 10.17G) when making **biscuit** joints; biscuit joints reinforce/strengthen edge-to-edge or edge-to-face, miter and similar glued wood joints.

Power Drilling Tools

Power drills speed the process of drilling holes.

Drill Press A variable speed, very accurate, stand or bench mounted power drill (Figure 10.18A); takes bit shanks up to ½ inch diameter; accessories enable cutting mortise joints, sanding, and polishing.

Electric Hand Drill A lightweight, hand-held drill (Figure 10.18B); most models accept bit shanks up to ⅜ inch in diameter; available in 120-volt and battery-powered models.

Heavy-Duty Hand Drill A heavier, more powerful, 120-volt hand-held drill (Figure 10.18C); accepts bit shanks to ½ inch in diameter; used for drilling wood thicker than 1½ inches, mild steel thicker than ¼ inch, and concrete.

Hammer Drill A drill that combines rotary drilling with up-and-down hammering action (Figure 10.18D); drills holes faster than "rotary-only" drills; 120-volt AC or battery-powered; most models can be switched between straight-drilling and hammer-drilling operation.

Battery-Powered Tools

Every type of electrically powered hand tool is now available with rechargeable batteries. New technologies such as lithium-ion batteries have increased battery life and power while reducing recharge time and negating **battery memory** issues. For these reasons, battery-powered drills have replaced "corded" versions in many shops, although circular saws and most heavy-duty applications still use 120-volt power.

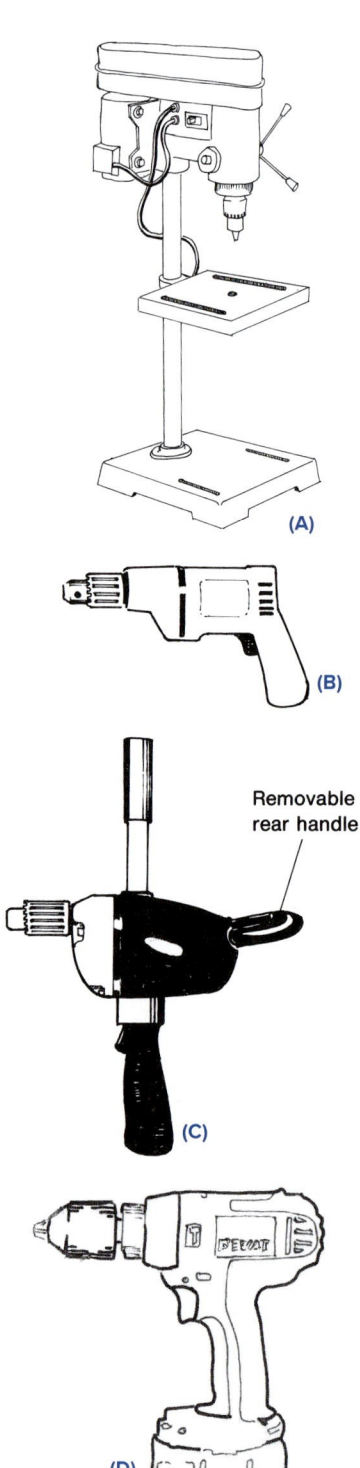

Removable rear handle

FIGURE 10.18
Power drilling tools.
(A) Drill press
(B) Electric hand drill
(C) Heavy-duty electric drill
(D) Hammer drill (battery powered)

[1] Trade name of Milwaukee Power Tools.

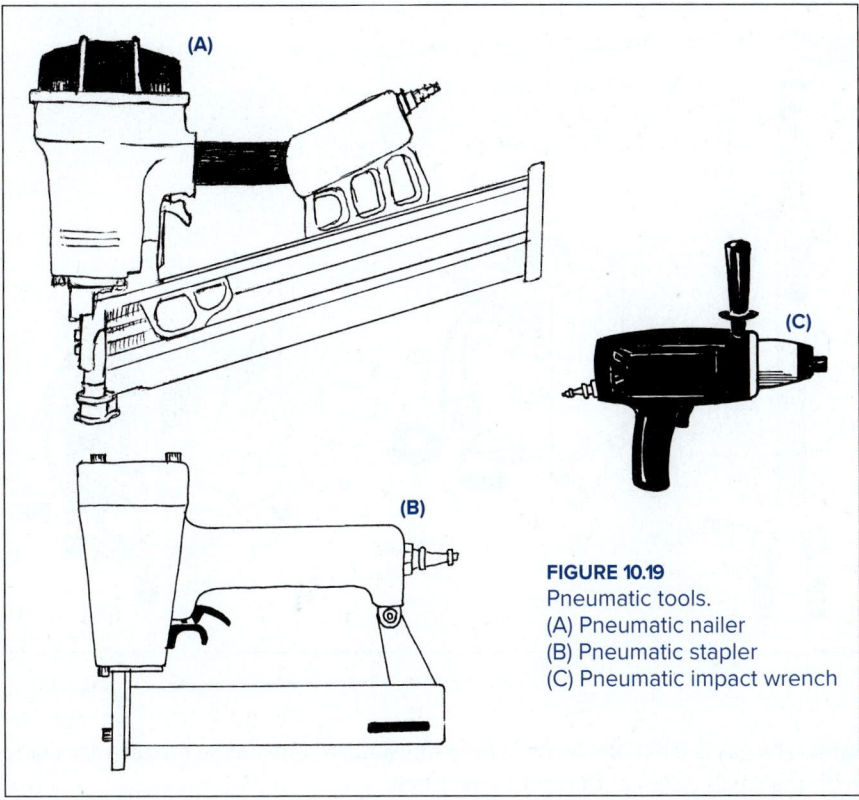

FIGURE 10.19
Pneumatic tools.
(A) Pneumatic nailer
(B) Pneumatic stapler
(C) Pneumatic impact wrench

strike: Taking down and/or destruction of the set following the conclusion of a play's production run.

biscuit: Thin, oval-shaped; made of compressed wood shavings; expands when wet with glue.

battery memory: Recharging batteries with nickel-cadmium (NiCd) technologies shortens the life of the batteries unless they were fully depleted prior to recharging. Nickel-metal-hydride (NiMH) batteries have the same memory loss issue, just not as severe.

Pneumatic Tools

Pneumatic tools are driven by air pressure. Almost every type of electric hand tool is available in pneumatic form. To effectively use pneumatic tools, a shop needs a large-capacity compressor and air tank as well as an efficiently designed system for distributing the compressed air to convenient locations around the shop and stage.

Pneumatic Stapler   Uses air pressure to drive staples; staple lengths vary from about ¼ to 2 inches; available with friction-activated adhesive; replaces nails in some wooden construction projects (Figure 10.19A).

Pneumatic Nailer   Drives clips of adhesive-coated nails with air pressure (Figure 10.19B); used for rapid assembly of platforms and similar structures.

Impact Wrench   Uses a staccato rotary motion to tighten or loosen nuts (Figure 10.19C); electric version also available.

Other pneumatically driven tools, such as sanders, grinders, and drills, work exactly as their electrically powered counterparts do.

Metalworking Power Tools

Welders   Several types of welders are used for fusing metal in the scene shop.

Oxyacetylene Welder   The oxyacetylene welder (Figure 10.20A) combines oxygen and acetylene to produce a 6000°F flame capable of melting most metals. The oxygen and acetylene are stored under pressure in steel tanks. The amount of each gas in the mixture is controlled by pressure regulators on top of each

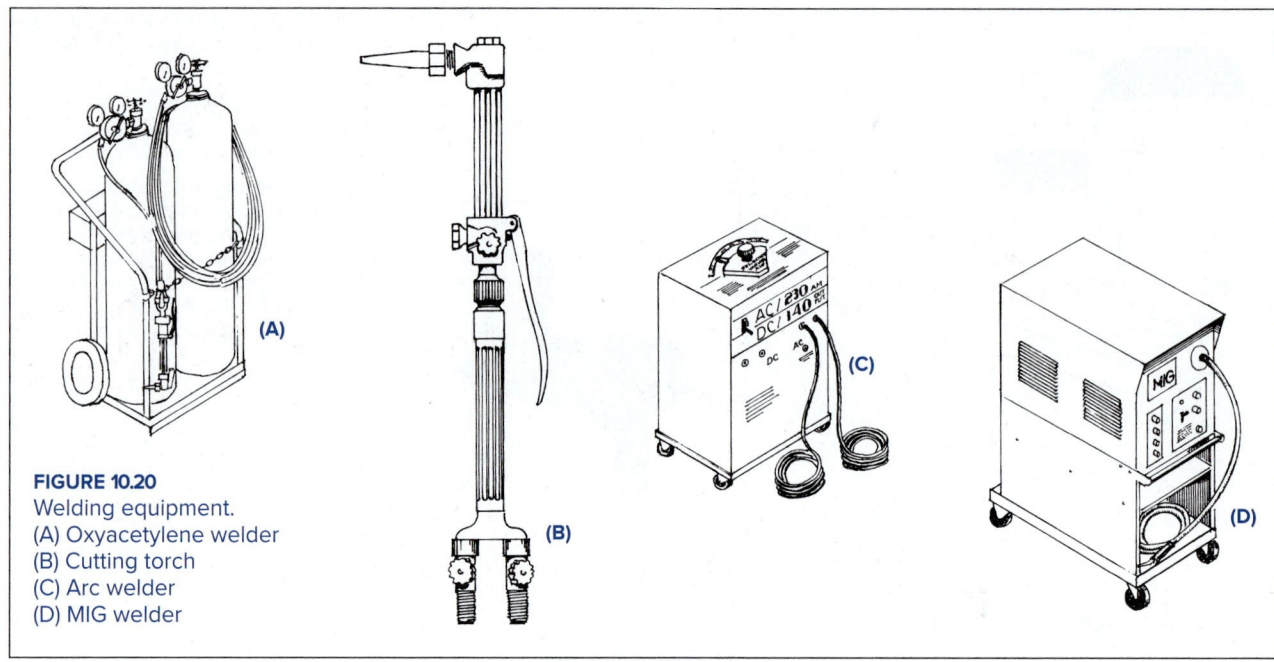

FIGURE 10.20
Welding equipment.
(A) Oxyacetylene welder
(B) Cutting torch
(C) Arc welder
(D) MIG welder

tank. The gas is fed to the torch, where fine adjustments to the mixture are made with the small valves at the end of the torch.

A cutting torch (Figure 10.20B) has an extra lever that introduces more oxygen to the mix, enabling the flame to burn through the metal. (See Chapter 11, "Scenic Production Techniques," for a discussion of using welding equipment.)

Arc Welder   The arc welder (Figure 10.20C) consists of a power housing unit, cables, and a welding handle. It creates an electrical arc to melt the metals being welded. Power settings can be adjusted for the heat range appropriate for the metal being welded.

MIG Welder   The MIG (metal insert gas) welder (Figure 10.20D) is an arc welder that focuses a flow of inert gas (usually argon) on the welding zone as the weld is being made. The electrode of the MIG welder is a thin piece of wire automatically fed through the welding handle from a spool stored in the housing of the power unit. The MIG welder can be used without the inert gas if flux-coated electrode wire is used. The **flux** provides the same "clean" welding environment as the inert gas.

Soldering Equipment   Soldering creates a low-strength bond between most common metals such as steel, copper, and brass. Aluminum can be soldered, but it requires high heat and a special flux.

Various soldering pencils, guns, and irons are used to heat solder to its melting point. Soldering pencils (25 to 40 watts) are used for lightweight projects such as working on the circuitry of electronic equipment (Figure 10.21A). Soldering guns (50 to 200 watts) are trigger-operated, rapid-heating, medium-to-heavy-usage devices (Figure 10.21B). Soldering irons (Figure 10.21C) are larger versions of soldering pencils with proportionally higher wattages (80 to 500). They are used for heavy-duty soldering projects in which the iron is required to heat a relatively large mass of metal.

flux: A chemical that reduces surface oxidation, which would prevent the solder or filler rod (welding) and the metal being soldered or welded from melding.

Propane Torch   The propane torch (Figure 10.21D) has a number of fittings that produce different flame shapes. Used for heavy-duty soldering and heating metal while bending and/or forming.

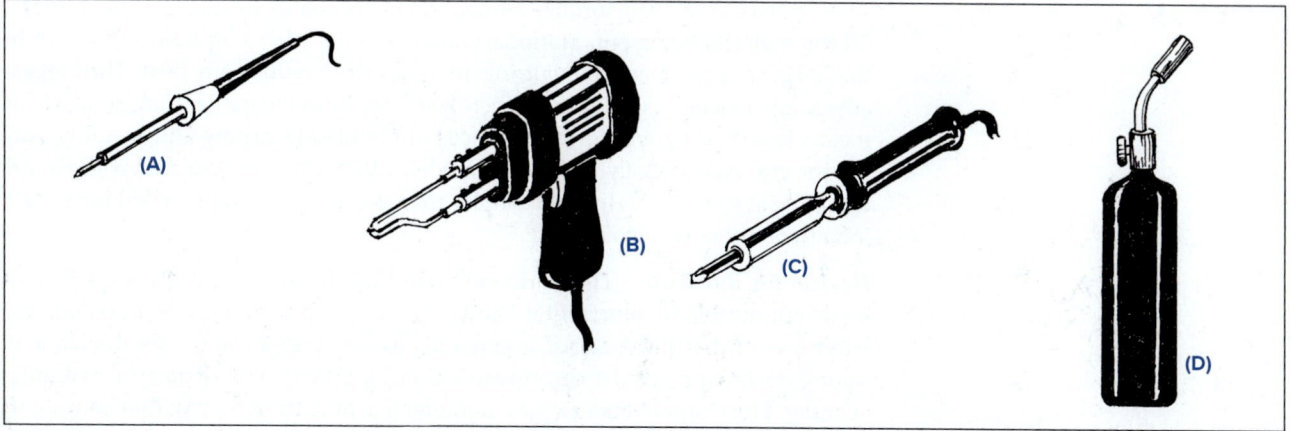

FIGURE 10.21
Soldering equipment.
(A) Soldering pencil
(B) Soldering gun
(C) Soldering iron
(D) Propane torch

Metal Cutting Tools A variety of tools are used in the scene shop for cutting metals.

Abrasive Cutoff Saw The abrasive cutoff saw (Figure 10.22A) uses an abrasive wheel to grind (rather than cut) through hard materials including many metals. Abrasive saws are reasonably accurate when making straight 90-degree cuts but quickly grow less accurate when making angled or miter cuts. The abrasive disc can bend when cutting thick or very hard materials. This increases inaccuracy even when making straight cuts. Finally, abrasive saws generate heat through friction, which can cause both disc and metal to expand, increasing both the risk of binding and the energy required to make a cut.

Cold Saw Cold saws (Figure 10.22B) use toothed blades specifically designed to transfer heat from the cutting operation to the chips created by the cutting action. Cold saws, available in hand-held and stationary varieties, operate at

FIGURE 10.22
Metal-cutting power tools.
(A) Abrasive cutoff saw
(B) Cold saw
(C) Horizontal bandsaw
(D) Portable bandsaw
(E) Plasma cutter
(F) Power pipe cutter
(G) Pipe bender/roller
(H) Hydraulic metal punch
(I) Hossfeld bender

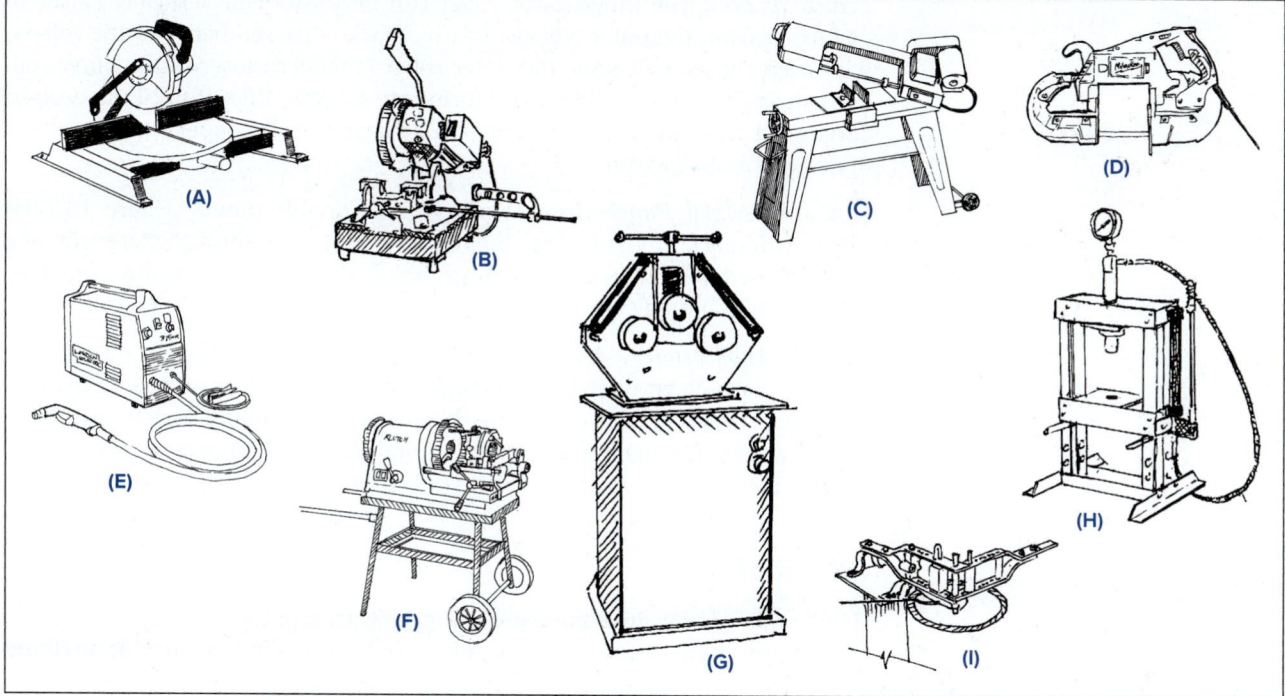

slow speeds with high torque, which allows the teeth to shear chips of metal off the material being cut. Stationary models come with a liquid-cooling system that lubricates the blade and cutting area to further reduce any heat. The biggest advantage of cold saws is their accuracy: less heat means less friction, which means less binding and fewer instances of the blade warping and bending during the cut. Additionally, stationary models often are manufactured with robust clamping systems, which enables them to make more accurate angled miter cuts than their abrasive cousins.

Horizontal Bandsaw   The horizontal bandsaw (Figure 10.22C) uses a looped metal-cutting blade. Horizontal bandsaws differ from traditional wood-cutting bandsaws in that the material is generally locked into a clamp and the blade is swung down through the cut, driven either by gravity, coil spring, or hydraulic cylinder. Horizontal bandsaws are not effective at cutting curves: they're used to cut bar or pipe stock to length.

Portable Bandsaw (Porta-band)   The portable bandsaw (Figure 10.22D) is a smaller, handheld version of the horizontal bandsaw.

Plasma Cutter   Plasma cutters are used to cut electrically conductive materials (like steel). Plasma cutters (Figure 10.22E) create a superheated electrical channel of plasma through the material, effectively making the cut by melting through the material. Plasma cutters are often seen in shops in handheld varieties for cutting through both thin and thick materials. Higher end shops may employ CNC-controlled versions, which are described in a following section.

Power Pipe Cutter   The power pipe cutter (Figure 10.22F) performs the same functions as the manual pipe-cutting tools: cutting and threading metal pipes.

Metal Shaping and Bending Tools   Many shops employ a variety of power tools for shaping and bending metal stock.

Pipe Bender/Roll Bender   Roll benders are used to roll metal bar or tube into constant-radius shapes. A roll bender consists of three rollers: one inner roller and two outer rollers, oriented in a triangular pattern as show in Figure 10.22G. The inner/lower roller can be positioned vertically closer to or further from the outer wheels. In use, stock is passed between the rollers; with each subsequent pass, the inner roller is moved closer to the outer rollers, causing the stock to bend and form into a curve. Repeat until the desired curve — all the way to a full circle — is achieved. Roll benders can be either manual or motor-driven.

Hydraulic Metal Punch (Iron Worker)   A hydraulic punch (Figure 10.22H) uses a hydraulic cylinder to drive dies of different shapes through plate and tube stock. These tools can be used to punch holes, shear, and notch various materials accurately and quickly.

Hossfeld Tube Bender   A Hossfeld tube bender (Figure 10.22I) is a rotary-draw bending machine for tube, bar, and angle stock. Using either manual or hydraulic power, a tube bender can be used to bend tubing into a variety of curves, including irregular curves (for example, spirals) that roll benders are not capable of making.

CNC Tooling

"CNC tooling" refers to equipment using CNC (computer numerical control) to control a machine's operation. In scene shops CNC tooling can include anything from three-dimensional (3-D) printers to computer-controlled cutters using router, water jet, plasma, or laser cutter heads.

CNC tooling involves using a CAD (computer-aided drafting) drawing to determine the tool-path program in CAM (computer-aided manufacturing) software. The CAM software is used to control the machine during the manufacturing process.

The CNC cutting machines described below typically cost many thousands of dollars. For that reason, they are generally out of reach for most scene and property shops. They are included here because high-end shops do have some of these machines and, as the costs come down, they will become part of the inventory in more shops.

CNC Router   A CNC router is one of a number of **subtractive manufacturing** tools. It consists of a router or **tool spindle** mounted on a **gantry**. Stepper motors move the gantry in the X and Y axes (along and across) of the machine table with a high level of precision. Additional stepper motors move the cutter in the Z axis (up or down). Sophisticated units can allow for automated tool/bit changes during a manufacturing job.

3-D Printer   **Additive manufacturing** involves creating a manufactured part by adding material instead of cutting or carving it away. 3-D printers are additive manufacturing tools. The two most common types of 3-D printers found in scene or prop shops are fused filament and stereolithography printers. Fused filament printers use a heated nozzle (an extruder) to melt and deposit successive layers of soft materials (often thermoplastics) onto a tool bed. Stereolithography printers use focused light to harden successive layers of a liquid material. In either case, and like other CNC machines, stepper motors controlled by the printer's computer move the extruder or light emitter on the printer's gantry in the X and Y axes and the bed in the Z axis.

Laser Cutter   Laser cutters and engravers use high-intensity laser-light beams to cut and/or engrave various materials from wood to plastics and some metals. A laser cutter works like other CNC machines. It uses an optics module (a laser and focusing lens and mirrors) to perform the cutting functions. Like other CNC machines, the optics module head travels in the X and Y axes on the gantry and the work bed travels up and down in the Z axis. The power of the laser, the speed of the gantry, the vertical position of the table relative to the focus point of the laser, and the frequency of laser pulses work together to determine the engraving depth and/or cutting power of the laser cutter.

Water Jet   CNC water jets work in almost the same fashion as a laser cutter, except that instead of highly focused light, a stream of highly pressurized water (between 60,000 and 90,000 **psi**) is used to cut through materials from cement to metals to glass and stone. For some materials (like glass and metals) abrasive particles are added to the water jet. Water jets can be used to cut materials up to 10 inches thick while generating very little heat. Like other CNC machines, the jet stream travels on a gantry in the X and Y axes, with tables that can be moved up and down in the Z axis.

Plasma Cutter   CNC plasma cutters use a superheated channel of plasma to cut through electrically conductive materials. Two-dimensional plasma cutters have an X-Y gantry like the other CNC machines discussed earlier. Some plasma cutters (as well as some water jets and laser cutters) have cutting heads that can be tilted to allow for beveled cutting.

subtractive manufacturing: Cutting away or removing material during the manufacturing process.

tool spindle: The rapidly spinning shaft of a machine tool. Includes anything attached to the spindle; e.g., a chuck used to hold cutters and bits.

gantry: A bridge-like structure. In this case, a device mounted above the CNC machine's working surface that is used to support the cutting equipment.

additive manufacturing: Creating a manufactured part by adding material instead of cutting it away; applies to 3-D printing.

psi: Pounds per square inch. A measurement of pressure used in the United States.

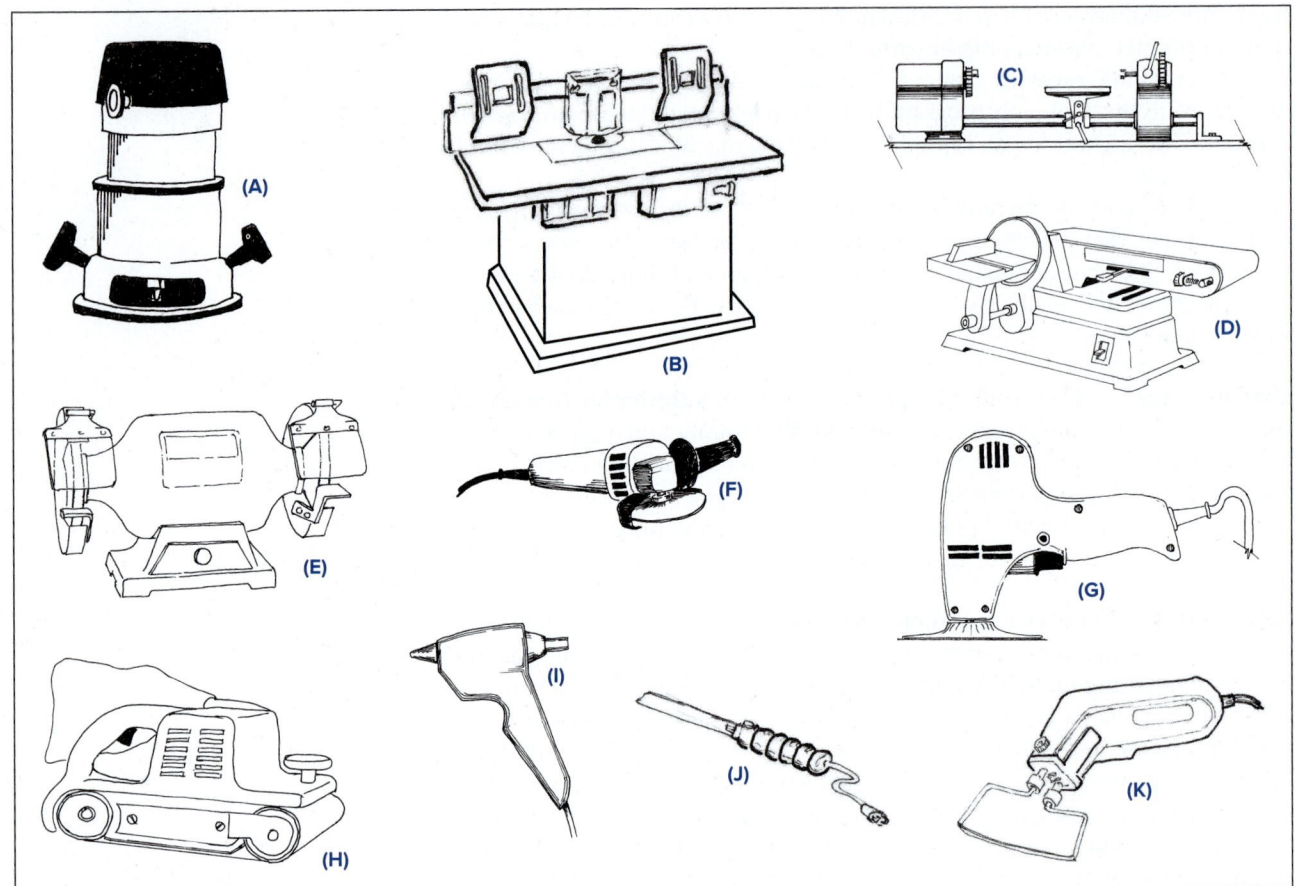

FIGURE 10.23
Miscellaneous power tools.
(A) Router
(B) Router table
(C) Wood lathe
(D) Bench sander
(E) Bench grinder
(F) Hand power grinder
(G) Hand power sander
(H) Belt sander
(I) Hot-melt glue gun
(J) Hot wire knife
(K) Hot wire cutter

Miscellaneous Power Tools

Some additional power tools cannot be neatly placed into any particular category.

Router A router (Figure 10.23A) is a hand-held, motor-driven tool used for shaping wood. The chisel-like rotating bit is driven at extremely high speed (generally 25,000 revolutions per minute) to shape or carve designs from the surface or edge of the piece of wood. It is primarily used for shaping decorative moldings and trim pieces.

Router Table The router is attached to the underside of a smooth (typically) metal table (Figure 10.23B). The bit projects through a hole in the table. Used to shape wooden trim.

Wood Lathe A bench- or stand-mounted tool that rapidly spins wood for carving (Figure 10.23C). Wood-turning chisels used for carving; turning speed is variable; can be modified to turn Styrofoam.

Bench Sander A bench- or stand-mounted belt and disk sander used to smooth or bevel wood or plastic (Figure 10.23D).

Bench Grinder Used for grinding/polishing metal (Figure 10.23E).

Hand Power Grinder A portable version of the bench grinder (Figure 10.23F); used for cutting/grinding/smoothing metal, or with different blade, concrete.

Hand Power Sander   Spins a replaceable sandpaper disk to sand/smooth wood, plastic, and metal (Figure 10.23G).

Hand Belt Sander   The powerful belt sander (Figure 10.23H) uses belts of sandpaper for rapid sanding of (primarily) wood.

Hot-Melt Glue Gun   One of the most versatile tools in the shop, the hot-melt glue gun (Figure 10.23I) uses sticks of heat-activated adhesive for making rapid-hold glue bonds on and between just about any type of material.

Hot Knife Cutter   A hand-held tool for cutting foam products. The electrically heated knife melts the foam (Figure 10.23J). Heat cutting foam products releases potentially dangerous gases. Be sure to read the Safety Tips, "Urethane Foams," (page 208) and "Foam Carving," (page 275).

Hot Wire Cutter   Hot wire cutters use thin, electrically heated, nichrome or stainless steel wire to cut polystyrene foams (Figure 10.23K). Hot wire cutters are available in numerous hand-held, stand-mounted, and CNC versions. Heat cutting foam products releases potentially dangerous gases. Be sure to read the Safety Tips, "Urethane Foams," (page 208) and "Foam Carving," (page 275).

 ## Wood

Three categories of wood are used in scenic construction: stock lumber, moldings, and sheet goods.

Stock Lumber

To be appropriate for use in scenic construction, stock lumber must be strong, lightweight, free of knots, splinter resistant, easily worked, and fairly inexpensive. White pine, a generic name applicable to a number of separate species of pine grown in the western United States, generally satisfies these requirements. White pine is used to build wooden flat frames and other lightweight projects.

White pine isn't always called white pine. The name varies considerably depending on the locale. Because of these regional name variations, it isn't possible to simply call up your friendly lumber store and order "white pine." First, visit the lumberyard or home center and look for the wood with the required characteristics. Then, find out what it's called.

Another commonly used wood in scenic construction is Douglas fir. This wood is heavier than white pine, is stronger, and generally sells for one-half to one-third the cost of white pine. It is normally used for heavier construction projects such as weight-bearing structures and platform legs.

Lumber Classification   Lumber is subdivided into three general categories.

Boards   Boards are defined as **rough-cut** wood 1 to 1½ inches thick and 2 inches wide or wider. Boards such as 1×2s through 1×12s are classified as "boards."

Dimensional Lumber   Dimensional lumber is defined as rough-cut wood 2 to 4 inches thick and 2 inches wide or wider. Lumber such as 2×4s through 2×12s fall in this category.

Timber   Any rough-cut wood minimally 5 inches thick or thicker and 5 inches wide or wider.

rough cut: Wood, roughly cut, not smooth. A piece of wood's rough-cut dimensions are used to identify its size. For example, a 1 by 3 is initially cut 1 inch thick and 3 inches wide. The finishing process reduces the overall dimensions of the piece.

Lumber Grading All lumber is visually graded at the mill after it is cut. Graders inspect each board to determine its grade classification.

Appearance-Graded Boards The grade a board receives is based on its appearance — the straightness of the grain, imperfections, and so forth. There are two primary grades for boards: select and common. Each of these categories is further subdivided.

A Select "A select" wood is free of all knots, blemishes, erratic graining, and warps.

B Select Also known as "B or Better," "B select" wood is primarily the same as A select except that the grain can be less uniform and the wood can contain more pitch, which increases its weight.

C Select "C select" wood can have a few tight knots (that will not fall out) of less than ½ inch in diameter, slightly less uniform graining, and still more pitch.

D Select "D select" wood can have more tight knots (still only ½ inch in diameter), an occasional pitch pocket, and some warping.

No. 1 Common No. 1 common lumber can have knots up to 1½ inches in diameter. The knots do not have to be tight; in other words, they may fall out, leaving a knothole in the plank. Warping and twisting are more prevalent in this grade of lumber.

No. 2 Common The knots in No. 2 common lumber can be greater than 1½ inches in diameter, and the edges can show an occasional strip of bark. The wood will probably be warped and twisted.

The cost of appearance-graded lumber goes down as you move from A select to No. 2 common. It is difficult to find A select in most lumberyards. When it is available, it is very expensive. Most stage construction can be accomplished by using C select or D select. The occasional knot, split end, or slight warp that will be found in these grades can usually be trimmed to prevent it from interfering with the construction project. The common grades of lumber are not particularly suitable for stage purposes, although they can be used for applications where their appearance and structural weakness would not adversely affect the appearance or safety of the set.

Structurally Graded Lumber Structurally graded lumber is divided into the following categories.

Select Structural May contain sound, firm, tight, well-spaced knots no more than ⅞ inch in diameter. Loose knots or holes up to ¾ inch, spaced no closer than one every 4 feet, are permitted.

Number 1 May contain sound, firm, tight, well-spaced knots no more than 1½ inches in diameter. Loose knots or holes up to 1 inch, spaced no closer than one every three feet, are permitted. **Wane** is allowed.

Number 2 May contain well-spaced knots of any quality up to 2 inches in diameter. One hole up to 1¼ inches every 2 feet is permitted. Wane is allowed.

Number 3 May contain knots of any quality up to 2½ inches. One hole up to 1¾ inches in diameter every 1 foot is permitted. Wane is allowed.

wane: Missing wood, and/or untrimmed bark on the edge or end of the piece of lumber.

blemish (in wood): Refers to any defect that weakens the wood by breaking its continuous parallel graining. Examples include knots, missing wood, wane, and so forth.

Studs The grade of "Construction" or "Standard" is determined by the vertical (wall-bearing) strength of each individual piece of lumber.

Construction Grade At least 57 percent of the lumber must be clear of **blemishes.**

Standard Grade At least 43 percent of the lumber must be clear of blemishes.

Utility Grade At least 29 percent of the lumber must be clear of blemishes.

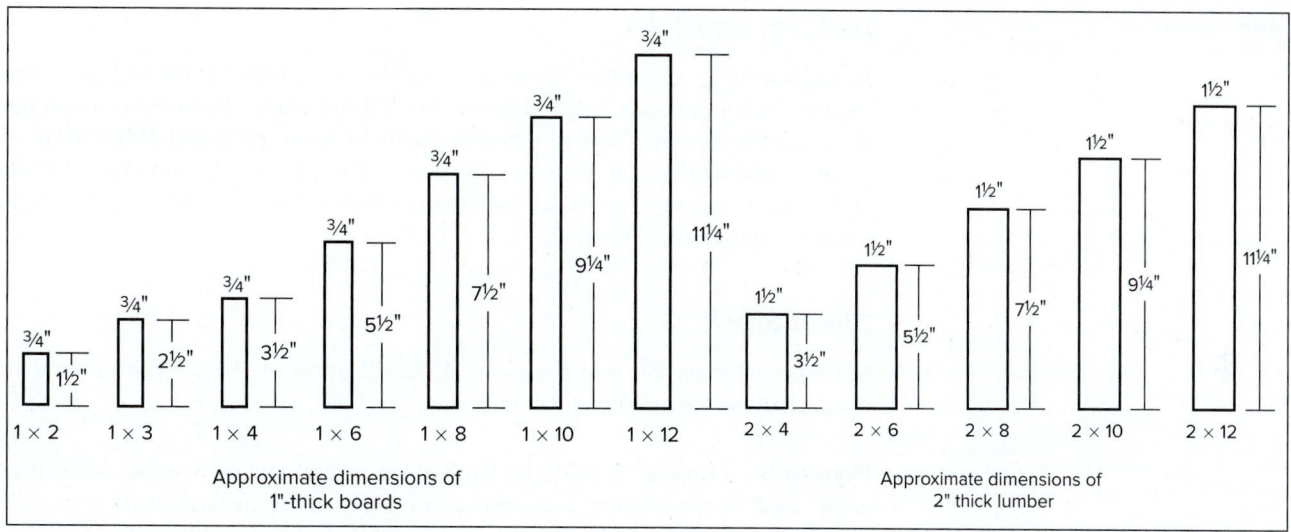

Approximate dimensions of
1"-thick boards

Approximate dimensions of
2" thick lumber

FIGURE 10.24
Standard lumber dimensions.

The cost of structurally graded lumber goes down as you move from Select Structural to Utility grade. Number 1 and 2 and construction grade studs are suitable for most stage construction projects.

Dimensions of Stock Lumber The Department of Agriculture determines the standards for the thickness, width, and length of all stock lumber sold in the United States. Since the sizing of lumber is done before the boards are milled to a smooth surface, the actual dimensions of the lumber that we buy are smaller than the indicated size, as shown in Figure 10.24. Slight variations in the actual dimensions of the lumber can be measured on almost any piece of stock because of milling variations and shrinkage. Because of these discrepancies, it is a good practice to measure the width of every piece of lumber before you use it. The typical scenic uses of the various sizes of lumber are described in Table 10.1.

TABLE 10.1

Standard Uses of Lumber in Scenic Construction

Indicated Size (cross section)	Actual Size	Typical Stage Uses
1 × 2	¾ inch × 1½ inches	small flats; lightweight corner bracing of flats
1 × 3	¾ inch × 2½ inches	standard flat framing (6–14 feet); diagonal bracing of platform legs
1 × 4	¾ inch × 3½ inches	large flat framing (over 14 feet)
1 × 6	¾ inch × 5½ inches	door and window frames and similar architectural trim work; narrow sweeps
1 × 8	¾ inch × 7½ inches	
1 × 10	¾ × 9¼ inches	stair treads, sweeps, profile cutouts, furniture
1 × 12	¾ inch × 11¼ inches	
2 × 4	1½ inches × 3½ inches	platform framing, platform legs, and similar weight-bearing structures
2 × 6	1½ inches × 5½ inches	
2 × 8	1½ inches × 7½ inches	
2 × 10	1½ inches × 9¼ inches	temporary scaffolding; some stair carriages
2 × 12	1½ inches × 11¼ inches	not normally used for stage scenery

MDF: Medium-density fiberboard. A fine-grained particle board.

Molding and Trim

In addition to stock lumber, there are a number of standard trims and moldings (Figure 10.25) that can be used in theatrical production. Decorative moldings are normally available in most lumber yards in white pine and **MDF.** MDF is cheaper and works well for scenic purposes. Trim is used on and around door and window casings as well as to provide visual interest on baseboards, chair rails, cornices, and wall panels.

Sheet Stock

Various materials fall into the general classification of sheet stock or lumber products manufactured in sheet form.

Plywood Plywood is made by laminating several layers of wood. Most plywood used in the theatre is composed of either three or five layers of wood. The direction of the grain of each successive layer lies at a 90-degree angle to the layers immediately above and below it, as shown in Figure 10.26. Because

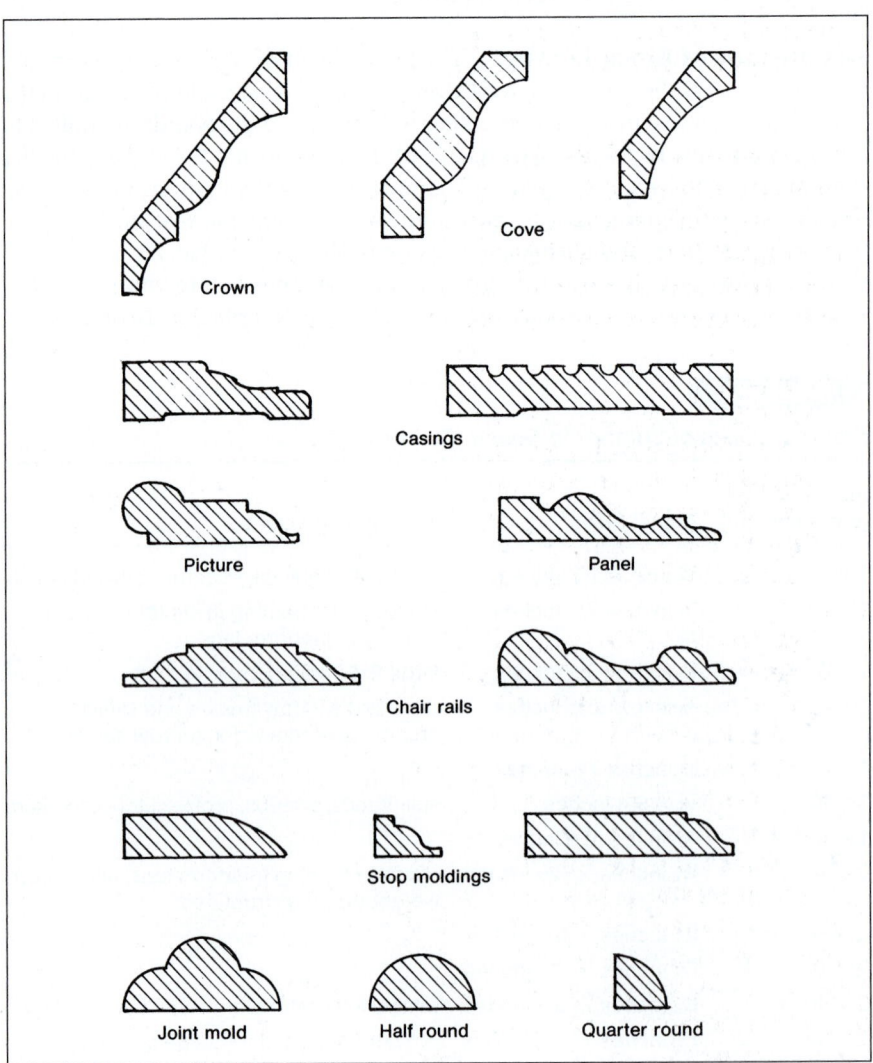

FIGURE 10.25
Specialty-cut lumber and moldings.

the strength of wood lies across its grain, plywood is much stronger than solid wood of a similar thickness.

Plywood is manufactured in interior and exterior grades. The only difference between them is that the exterior grade is laminated with a waterproof glue, whereas the interior grade uses a glue that is water soluble.

Plywood is available in most lumberyards in thicknesses of ⅛, ³⁄₁₆, ¼, ⅜, ½, ⅝, and ¾ inch. Almost all plywood, unless precut by the lumberyard, is sold in 4-by-8-foot sheets. Generally, the only exception to this 4×8 foot rule involves ⅛-inch **lauan** (also spelled luan), or Philippine mahogany, plywood. While lauan plywood is available in 4×8 foot and 4×10 foot **paper clad** sheets, in both ⅛-inch and ¼-inch thicknesses, it is also sold as "door skin" in which the ⅛-inch-thick sheets are typically 3 feet wide and either 6'-9" or 7'-0" long.

Plywood is graded according to its surface finish, as shown in Table 10.2. Although there are other grades of plywood, those listed in the table are the most common and are readily available.

AD plywood, despite the fact that it has **plugs,** small knotholes, and grain irregularities on one face, is the standard grade for almost all theatrical construction purposes. BC plywood is available in some areas of the country, is generally less expensive than AD, and can be used in applications like platform decking. The AA grade is rarely used because of its high cost. **Keystones** and **cornerblocks** are made from ¼-inch AD plywood. Sweeps, profile pieces, and other curvilinear forms can be cut from any appropriate thickness of AD plywood. Three-quarter-inch AD plywood (A side up) is often used for platform tops. CD plywood costs less than AD, and its inherent strength is not reduced by its surface imperfections. As the price of AD plywood has risen, more and more technicians are opting to use ACX as their plywood of choice. ACX plywood has almost the same characteristics as AD. The D face is upgraded to C, it is made with exterior glue, and it is frequently easier to find than AD. CD or CDX plywood can be used instead of AD or ADX for platform tops if the rough surface is going to be covered with some other material or if it is not going to be seen by the audience.

Furniture-grade plywood is manufactured with higher-quality filler layers. The outer surfaces are usually AA or AD and are made from hardwoods such as mahogany, birch, oak, or walnut. There is also a wide variety of plywoods, usually ³⁄₁₆- or ¼-inch thickness, that have prefinished, painted, or hardwood veneer surfaces. These prefinished panels can be used to cover flats as well as in other applications.

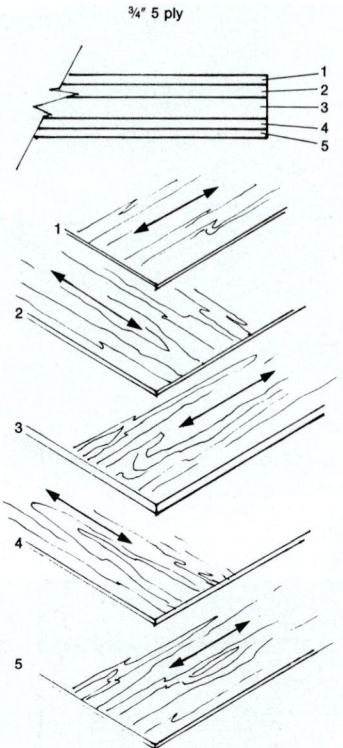

FIGURE 10.26
Plywood laminations.

TABLE 10.2

Plywood Grading System

Grade	Surface Appearance
AA	smooth sanded on both sides; both faces free from knots, plugs, or grain irregularities
AD	smooth sanded on both sides; one face (A) is free from imperfections, and the other (D) is not
BC	rough sanded on both sides; one face (B) may have plugged surface imperfections, the other side (C) may have plugs, some open knotholes, and slight grain irregularities. Whole sheet may have slight warp.
CD	rough sanded on both sides; each face may have many surface imperfections, some open knotholes, and grain irregularities; whole sheet may be slightly warped

lauan: Also known as Philippine mahogany. This ⅛-inch lauan plywood is strong and quite flexible. Commonly used as a flat-covering material and for covering curved-surface forms. Also spelled luan.

paper clad: Both sides covered with paper.

plug: A wooden insert used to replace a knothole or other imperfection in the surface layer of a sheet of plywood.

keystones and cornerblocks: Pieces of ¼-inch AD plywood used to reinforce joints in the construction of stage flats.

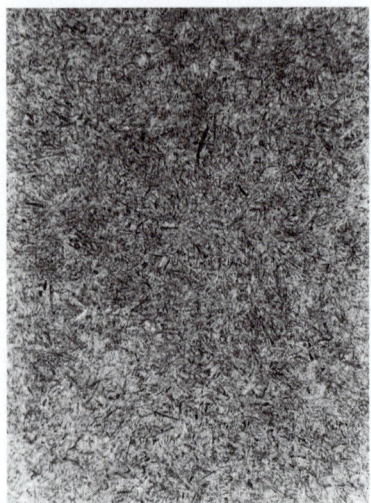

(A)

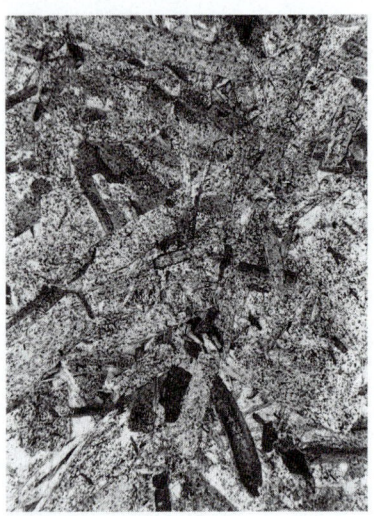

(B)

FIGURE 10.27
Closeup views of (A) particle board and (B) oriented strand board (OSB). Courtesy of J. Michael Gillette.

Particle Board   Particle board (Figure 10.27A) is composed of wood chips and sawdust mixed with a glue binder and compressed into 4-by-8-foot sheets. Particle board is usually available in ⅜-, ½-, ⅝-, and ¾-inch thicknesses. It is much heavier than plywood of similar thickness and isn't nearly as strong, but it can be used for subflooring, cabinet shelves, and similar structures.

MDF is a finer-grained version of particle board. It is widely used in the furniture and cabinet industries. Like particle board, it isn't as strong as either stock lumber or plywood. In scenic construction it can be used for a variety of non-load-bearing functions — cabinets, shelves, trim — where its finer grain and lower cost make it an acceptable substitute for stock lumber or sheet goods. Because of these qualities the use of MDF has increased in professional scene shops. Most MDF is made using urea-formaldehyde resins. Just sitting uncut in the shop, it emits small amounts of formaldehyde. When cut, the dust particles likewise contain formaldehyde. It can irritate the eyes and respiratory system and can cause severe reactions in people with an extreme sensitivity to formaldehyde. Be sure to wear an appropriately rated particulate screening respirator when working with this material. Two brands of "alternative MDF" are manufactured with resins that emit extremely low levels of formaldehyde. They are Medex and Medite II from the Medite Corporation (www.sierrapine.com).[2]

Oriented Strand Board (OSB)   Similar to particle board but composed of much larger chips, OSB (Figure 10.27B) is actually as strong as plywood and is lighter and cheaper. OSB (also called wafer board) is finished with one smooth face and one that has a slight texture. Because it is more "springy" than plywood of similar thickness, if used for platform-topping the number of cross supports in the platform structure needs to be increased. Its other construction uses, such as the web material for manufactured wooden I beams used as joists and rafters, are continually being discovered. Its use in professional scenic studios has increased in the past decade.

Hardboard   Hardboard, sometimes referred to as Masonite, a registered trade name, is manufactured from wood pulp that is compressed into 4-by-8 sheets of ⅛-, ¼-, and ⅜-inch thickness. It is available in two degrees of hardness, untempered and tempered. Untempered hardboard, which is light brown, has a soft, easily gouged surface. Tempered hardboard is dark brown and has an extremely hard surface.

Although hardboard is brittle and can be broken easily with a sharp blow, the ⅛-inch board can be used as a facing surface for counters, stair risers, and other vertical surfaces that may receive moderate physical abuse during the production. It is flexible enough to be bent around slightly curved forms. Either ¼- or ⅜-inch tempered hardboard can be used to cover the permanent wooden stage floor, because the hard surface resists the abuse caused by heavy stage equipment and can easily be painted with casein, latex, or acrylic paint.

Upson Board   Upson board is basically paper pulp and binder that have been mixed and compressed into 4-by-8 sheets. It is available in thicknesses of ⅛, ³⁄₁₆, and ¼ inch. The material is fairly flexible and has little inherent strength. Unless the edge of a piece of Upson board is supported by a wooden framework, it can be easily bent, broken, or frayed.

Upson board ⅛-inch thick, also known by the trade name of Easy Curve, is used to cover fairly sharply curved surfaces such as columns or curved walls.

[2] Duckworth, William, "Is MDF Hazardous?" *Fine Woodworking,* Taunton Press, November/December 2006, p. 98.

The ³⁄₁₆- and ¼-inch Upson board can be used as a hard cover for flats or profile cutouts if they won't be subject to too much physical abuse.

Sonotube

Sonotube is a paper tube used for forming concrete. In the world of theatre it also makes a great column. Sonotube is available in a variety of diameters ranging from 8 to 56 inches, and in lengths up to 18 feet. The wall of the tube is about ¼ inch thick, but since it is strong enough to hold concrete, it should be strong enough for almost any decorative stage use.

Manufactured Wood

An ever-increasing number of woodlike construction materials made from wood by-products (chips, strands, sawdust, and so forth) are finding their way into scenic construction. One significant advantage to these products is their dimensional stability. They are milled to much closer tolerances than stock lumber and generally don't swell or shrink as much as stock lumber. In larger sizes they are also cheaper than stock lumber. Lumberlam (a trade name) is a laminated, engineered material used as a replacement/substitute for stock lumber. Glue-lam beams are laminated beams made from relatively short pieces of stock lumber. They can be used to span openings of up to 18 to 20 feet and still have sufficient load capacity to support platforming on top. Other stock lumber substitutes are molded by subjecting a slurry of sawdust and high-tech adhesives to heat and high pressure.

Theatrical uses for these products will undoubtedly expand as more types and variations are introduced and more technicians try them.

Metal

Metal is being used with increasing frequency in scenic construction. This popularity can be attributed to three specific factors: (1) The increasing cost of wood has eliminated what was once a significant cost difference between wood and steel; (2) metal is inherently stronger than wood; and (3) with proper tools, metal can be worked as easily as wood.

The greater strength of metal allows the construction of frameworks for platforms and large flats that are as strong as or stronger than, but weigh less than, similarly sized wooden units. Additionally, metal's strength encourages its use in the fabrication of delicate or irregular shapes that would be impossible to duplicate in wood.

Although there are literally hundreds of metals and alloys, only two types — mild steel and aluminum — are used extensively in scenic construction. Other metals, most notably bronze, brass, and copper, are occasionally used in prop construction, but their relatively high cost and working characteristics argue against their being used for other than decorative purposes.

Mild Steel

Mild steel, officially known as AISI (American Iron and Steel Institute) C-1020, is the most commonly used type of steel in theatrical construction. It is malleable and is fairly easy to cut, bend, drill, and weld, and its strength is sufficient for most general scenic uses such as flat and platform frameworks.

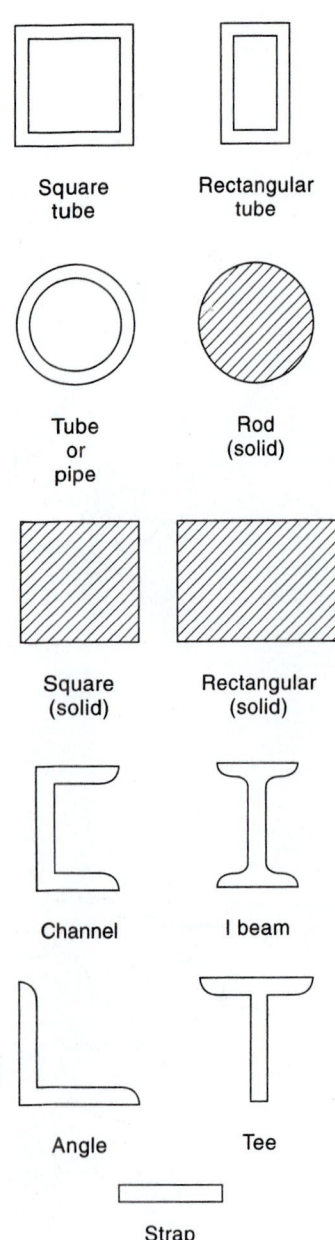

Square tube

Rectangular tube

Tube or pipe

Rod (solid)

Square (solid)

Rectangular (solid)

Channel

I beam

Angle

Tee

Strap

FIGURE 10.28
Basic forms of metal.

AISI C-1020 is manufactured in two primary forms: *structural* and *merchant bar*. Structural steel has a uniform chemical composition throughout, complete internal soundness (no air pockets, cracks, nonuniform crystallization formations, or other weaknesses that would affect its strength), and no significant surface flaws. Merchant bar may have internal defects that would affect the material's strength and more apparent surface flaws. Because of its questionable strength, merchant bar shouldn't be used for critical weight-bearing structures. Mild steel is finished at the mill with several different surfaces. The two most common finishes are *plain oxide* and a treatment called *oiled and pickled*. Plain oxide is the most common and least expensive finish. The steel is covered with a gray oxide that naturally forms as the steel cools and has some **scale** and a light coating of rust. For welding, brazing, or painting, the contaminants (oxide, scale, and rust) must be removed, usually by wire-brushing or grinding. An oiled and pickled finish creates a clean surface on the steel. At the mill, the steel receives an acid bath and a neutralizing rinse while it is still hot. It is then coated with oil to prevent the natural formation of oxide as it cools. The oil coat also prevents the formation of rust. Steel that has been *plated* or *painted* is also available from many suppliers. Generally, it isn't used in scenic construction because of its higher cost. But a galvanized finish has a bright silvery finish that is difficult to duplicate with paint and may be appropriate for some applications. See the Safety Tip, "Heating Galvanized Coatings", the bottom of page 206, before cutting or welding galvanized steel.

Mild steel is readily available from steel suppliers in the shapes illustrated in Figure 10.28 as well as in sheets of varying sizes and **gauge** or thickness.

Typical scenic-construction uses of the various shapes of steel are listed here.

Square and Rectangular Tubing   Square and rectangular tubing are arguably the most used and useful shapes of steel for theatrical construction. Rectangular tubing is typically used for platform framing and similar weight-bearing structures, while square tubing is normally used for flat framing and similar lightweight forms to be covered with thin hard coverings (plywood, Upson board, hardboard, and so forth).

Rectangular tubing is available in sizes ranging from slightly under 1 by 2 inches up to 6 by 12 inches with a variety of wall thicknesses ranging from 0.0359 inch (20 gauge) up to ½ inch. The cross-sectional dimensions of square tubing range from ⅜ inch to more than 4 inches, with wall thicknesses ranging from 0.0359 inch (20 gauge) to 0.1196 inch (11 gauge). For small- to medium-sized platforms and flats, 1-inch-by-2-inch rectangular and 1-inch square tubing with wall thicknesses of 20 and 15 gauge (0.0673 inch) are typical.

Tubing or Pipe   One of the most common uses of metal pipe is electrical conduit. There are two types of conduit, rigid and EMT (electrical metallic tubing). Rigid conduit is sold with internal diameters ranging from ½ inch to 6 inches. EMT, commonly known as thin-wall conduit, is available in sizes ranging from

scale: A black scaly coat that forms on iron when it is heated for processing.

gauge: A method of describing metal thickness by its weight. Steel, copper, and aluminum all have different gauge numbers. Gauge charts are available online. The rule of thumb for gauge numbers is as follows: The higher the number, the thinner the metal.

Heating Galvanized Coatings

Galvanized finishes — the mottled, silvery finish frequently found on steel water pipes, rigid and thin wall conduit, water/paint buckets, and thin steel sheet colloquially known as "galvanized tin" — emit noxious fumes when the galvanized finish is drilled, welded, or flame-cut. Be sure to work with these materials in well-ventilated areas or outdoors, and wear a proper respirator.

Safety Tip

⅜ inch to 2 inches. Thin-wall conduit can be bent in fairly intricate shapes with a pipe or conduit bender and is primarily used for decorative elements. Before bending thin-wall conduit, fill the pipe with sand to prevent the walls of the pipe from collapsing. Neither type of conduit is strong enough to be used for weight-bearing structures.

Thicker-walled pipe, such as galvanized pipe or the "black pipe" used for gas lines, is more typically used in the theatre for structural purposes such as platform legs and battens.

Channel   Channel is most typically used in structures requiring significant strength, such as the framework for large platforms or wagons.

Angle   Angle, or angle iron, is frequently used in those situations requiring less strength than rectangular or square tubing provides — lightweight frames, braces, and stiffeners.

Strap   Strap is used to strengthen or brace existing wooden structures. Its most apparent use is as the sill iron that spans the bottom of door openings in wooden framed flats.

Proprietary Structural Systems

Several companies manufacture steel structural systems that can be used like giant Erector sets to construct a wide variety of structural and scenic items ranging from lighting grids to stairways, platforms, scaffolds, flat frames, and open frameworks. The advantage of these systems is the speed with which structures can be assembled and the reusability of the materials. The disadvantage lies primarily in the cost of the materials and specialized fastening hardware.

Unistrut   This system consists of U-shaped channels of differing sizes, as shown in Figure 10.29A. The Unistrut system requires only that the channels be cut to length and bolted together with the specialized hardware (Figure 10.29B).

Telespar   Also manufactured by the Unistrut Company, Telespar (Figure 10.30) is a system of telescoping square steel tubing. Tubing with ⅜-inch holes on **1-inch centers** punched into all four faces of each section of tubing is available in sizes ranging between 1½ and 2½ inches. Telescoping plain-tube sizes range between 1 inch and 2½ inches. The telescoping feature allows its length to be adjusted without cutting.

Slotted Angle   Slotted angle (Figure 10.31) is manufactured with a variety of holes and slots punched into both faces of the stock. These holes permit the slotted angle stock to be bolted together without additional drilling. The slotted angle is cut to length and fastened together using standard bolts, washers, and nuts.

This listing of the shapes and uses of steel materials is far from exhaustive, but it does provide an introduction to the use of mild steel in theatrical construction. A trip to your local steel distributor can show you the materials available in your area. A trip to your metal scrap junkyard can be equally illuminating.

Aluminum

Aluminum is manufactured in the same shapes as mild steel. Additionally, decorative panels made of aluminum can be purchased in many hardware or lumber stores.

(A)

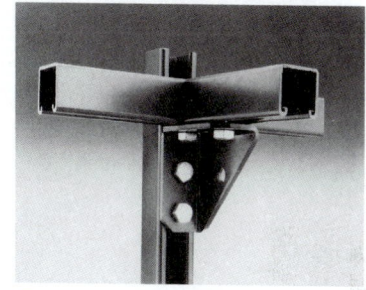

(B)

FIGURE 10.29
(A) Unistrut metal framing. (B) Joining requires special hardware. Courtesy of Unistrut International Corporation. Unistrut® is a registered trademark of Unistrut International Corporation or its affiliates.

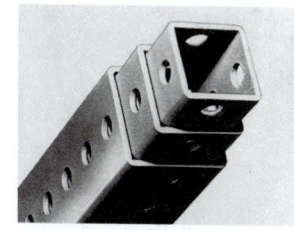

FIGURE 10.30
Manufactured by Allied Tube & Conduit Corporation, Telespar is square telescoping tubing. Courtesy of Unistrut International Corporation. Telespar® is a registered trademark of Allied Tube & Conduit International Corporation or its affiliates.

1-inch centers: The centers of adjacent elements, such as holes, are spaced 1 inch apart.

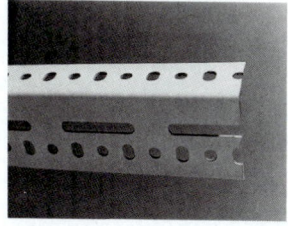

FIGURE 10.31
Slotted angle. Courtesy of J. Michael Gillette.

Aluminum is not used as extensively as mild steel, primarily because it is more expensive and is more difficult to weld than steel. It is used mainly for decorative purposes in scenic construction.

Plastics

Various plastics are useful in technical production, but more substantial safety hazards are involved in forming and processing plastics than in dealing with any other common construction material.

Friction between a saw or knife blade and plastic creates heat. This heat liberates gases from the plastic. Some of these fumes simply smell bad; some are noxious, or unhealthy; others are toxic, or poisonous; and still others can be lethal.

Because it is frequently difficult to determine the level of toxicity of these various fumes, it is vital that you work with plastics only in a well-ventilated area. If your workshop isn't equipped with a good fresh-air circulation system, create your own. Set up a cross-ventilation pattern, illustrated in Figure 10.32, between outside windows and doors. Use box fans or similar large-bladed fans set on high speed to move a large volume of air. When you first open the windows or doors, check the natural direction of the airflow and reinforce it with your fans. However, be sure that you ventilate the fumes to the outdoors rather than simply blowing them into another part of the building. If your shop doesn't have direct access to outside fresh air, don't work on plastics in the shop. Work on them outdoors, or if that isn't possible, appropriate a room that can be properly ventilated. The necessity for a high volume of air movement cannot be stressed too much. Your physical health, and the health of everyone else in the shop, depends on it.

Be sure to wear a respirator specifically designed for use with the plastic with which you are working. Respirators filter the air through appropriate materials to remove the harmful elements. The use of a respirator and an effective fresh-air ventilation system, when combined with the commonsense rules of shop safety, can make working with plastics safe.

Acrylic

Frequently identified by one of its trade names, Plexiglas, acrylic is available in rigid sheets of varying sizes and thicknesses in clear, translucent, textured, and colored finishes. It is also available in rods, tubes, and bars and in a liquid form for use as a **casting resin.** It is commonly used as a glass substitute, and the casting resin can be used to make decorative baubles for costumes, props, and

Urethane Plastics

If at all possible, completely avoid using urethane foams. When the formed foam is heated, either with a saw blade or an open flame, it emits a toxic gas. The same gas is emitted as the pour-in-place foams set up and cure. If you must use this material, be absolutely sure to wear an appropriate respirator and have a high volume of fresh-air ventilation in the workplace. Additionally, all personnel in the area should also wear appropriately rated respirators.

casting resin: Liquid plastics used for creating forms in molds.

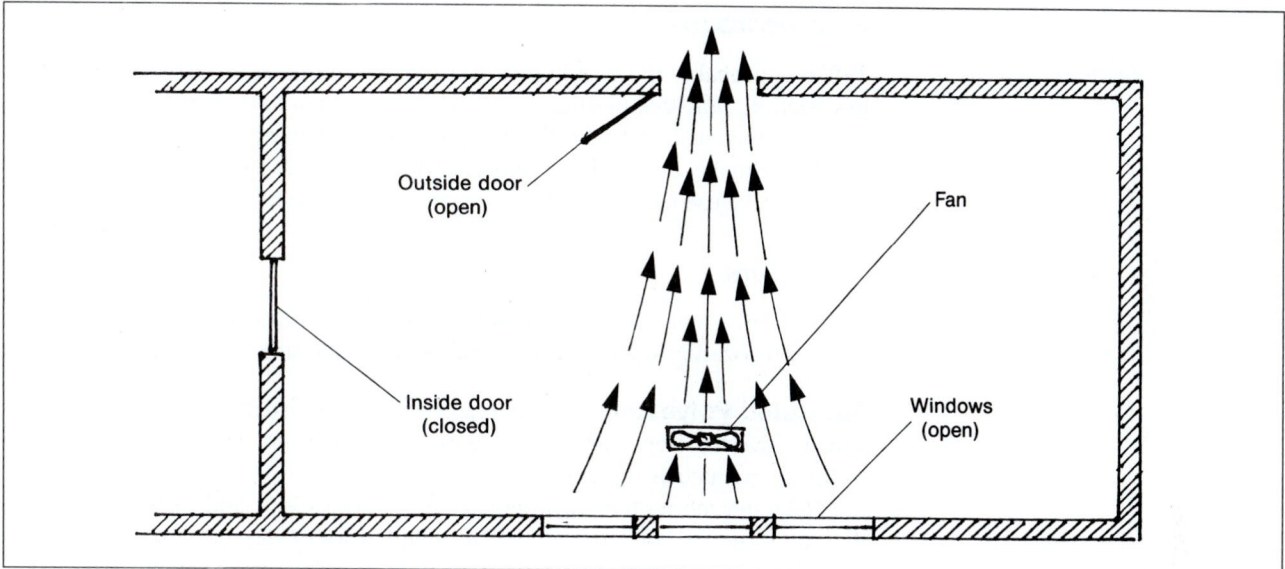

FIGURE 10.32
Cross-ventilation airflow pattern for a shop.

stained glass. The sheets, rods, and tubes can be formed by heating and bending the material to the desired shape.

Epoxy

Epoxies are available in a variety of formulations to suit a number of purposes. In theatrical construction the most commonly used types are adhesives and casting resins. All epoxies are extremely durable and moisture resistant. Depending on the particular formulation, epoxies can be worked with either wood- or metal-cutting tools.

Epoxy adhesive is useful for scenic and property construction projects that require strength or water resistance. Epoxy auto-body putty is useful for molding and sculpting decorative detail on sets and props. The casting resin can be used to make objects that are much stronger than those cast with either acrylic or polyester casting resins.

Safety Tip

As of June 2015, OSHA adopted Safety Data Sheets (SDSs) as a replacement for Material Safety Data Sheets (MSDSs). More than simply shortening the name, this shift put OSHA requirements for reporting material safety information in line with the internationally standardized Globally Harmonized System. Unlike MSDSs, which could have a variety of formats containing different (and different amounts of) information, SDSs all must adhere to a single format and list of reporting requirements.

SDSs in the United States must include data on the following: identification of the material; identification of specific hazards the material may present; the composition of the material and/or list of ingredients; specific first-aid measures; fire-fighting measures; accidental release measures; handling and storage instructions; exposure controls/information on required PPE; physical and chemical properties; stability and reactivity; and regulatory information.

As with MSDSs, everyone working in any shop should be familiar with the SDSs for the materials to which they will be exposed. All shops should have SDSs readily available for anyone who wishes to see them, for any materials that may be used in the shop.

Fluorocarbons

Teflon is probably the best-known trade name in this family of tough, durable, low-friction, nonstick plastics. Although it is commercially available in a variety of forms, the most useful for theatrical purposes are the sheets and tapes.

Teflon makes an excellent bearing surface because of its extremely slippery qualities. It can be used for turntables or for covering the tracks and runners of **skids.**

Polyesters

There are two types of polyester, saturated and unsaturated. All polyesters have a characteristically smooth surface and great tensile strength.

Saturated Polyesters   Saturated polyesters are used to form the fiber from which polyester fabrics are woven. Saturated polyesters are also used to manufacture films such as Mylar.

Polyester fabrics have a variety of uses in both scenic and costume construction, and they can be worked with normal fabric-cutting tools. The film, which is available in a variety of textures, treatments, and colors, has many uses in the scene shop. Aluminized Mylar film is frequently used as a lightweight, unbreakable stage mirror, and Mylar film is used as the base material for several lines of lighting-instrument color media.

Unsaturated Polyesters   Unsaturated polyesters can be used in casting or to create the multipurpose material known as fiberglass.

The unsaturated polyester casting resin can be used for the same purposes as the acrylic and epoxy casting resins. Fiberglass, also called glass-fiber plastic, is used in situations where its great strength and flexibility of form are an advantage. Water-based resin, such as Aqua Resin, manufactured by Sculptural Arts Coatings, is a safer alternative casting resin when working with fiberglass. It has the same general working characteristics as unsaturated polyester resin.

Unsaturated polyesters can be worked with both woodworking and metalworking tools. A basic introduction to working with glass-fiber plastics can be found in Chapter 13, "Stage Properties."

Polyethylene

Polyethylene plastics are available in a variety of formulations, but the forms most commonly used in the theatre are film and foam. All polyethylenes have a characteristically slick, waxy surface.

Polyethylene film, generally available in black, white, and clear, can be used for such things as drop cloths and projection screens. Polyethylene foam, generally known by the trade name Ethafoam, is very flexible and is generally available in sheets and rods. It is frequently used for architectural trim and similar non-structural functions. It rejects every type of paint except acrylic, and even acrylic will chip off if the surface of the foam is flexed. Ethafoam can be painted after it is applied to the scenery, if it is first covered with Sculptural Arts Coating' Sculp or Coat or Rosco's Flexcoat, or covered with several layers of glue-coated cheesecloth, or simply coated with latex contact adhesive before painting. Sheets of polyethylene foam, sold under the trade name of Bubble Board, make excellent rear-screen projection surfaces.

Polystyrene

As with other plastics, the strength of polystyrene is directly dependent on the density of its molecular structure. High-impact polystyrene has a fairly dense

skid: A low-profile substitute for a wagon; usually a piece of ¾-inch plywood on which some small scenic element is placed.

molecular structure; has a hard surface; and is moderately flexible, fairly strong, and somewhat brittle. It becomes very limp when heated, and it is the primary plastic used in vacuum forming (to be discussed in Chapter 13).

Polystyrene foam, commonly known by the trade name Styrofoam, does not have a dense molecular structure, yet it retains the basic characteristics of all polystyrenes — a hard surface, moderate flexibility, strength, and brittleness. It is frequently used for making decorative trim such as cornices and statuary. Techniques for carving Styrofoam will be discussed in Chapter 13.

Polyvinyl Chloride

Although there are probably more formulations of vinyls than any other family of plastics, arguably the most useful formulations for stage purposes are those members of the polyvinyl chloride group. Characteristically, polyvinyl chlorides (PVCs) are strong, lightweight, and rigid.

PVC pipe has those characteristics. Normally used in lawn sprinkler systems, it can also be used for a variety of decorative scenic purposes. PVC is available in a variety of other forms (sheet, rod, and so forth) that are useful for the theatre artisan.

PVC pipe, and its other forms, can be formed using heat. Heat forming will be discussed in Chapter 13.

Urethanes

Urethane plastics have a number of uses in technical production. Flexible urethane foam is commonly used for cushions and padding in furniture. The rigid foam, which has a tighter cell structure than polystyrene foam, is used as the modeling block in floral displays and has also been used as an insulation material in building construction. Urethane is also available as a casting resin.

Kits for hand-mixing rigid or flexible foams can be purchased from building-insulation companies and scenic or plastics supply houses. Two types of kits are generally available. The hand-mix, or pour-in-place forms are two-part compounds that are mixed together and poured into molds. Spray-pack foams, such as the Insta-Foam Froth Pak, are also two-part formulations, but they are automatically mixed as they are sprayed. Both molds and casting techniques are discussed in Chapter 13.

Be sure that you don't use any kind of heat — friction-generated heat from saw blades, open flames, or otherwise — when working with urethane foams. Heating the urethane releases a toxic gas. That same gas is emitted during the curing process when using foam-packs or pour-in-place urethane. If at all possible, entirely avoid working with urethane foam. If you must, be sure to adhere to the safety procedures outlined on the SDS for the specific material with which you are working.

 ## Fasteners

Fasteners in a variety of forms are used in scenic and property construction.

Nails

Nails are the most commonly used mechanical fasteners. They are driven into two or more pieces of wood with a hammer to hold them together. The strength of the fastening depends on the gripping pressure that the wood exerts on the shaft of the nail.

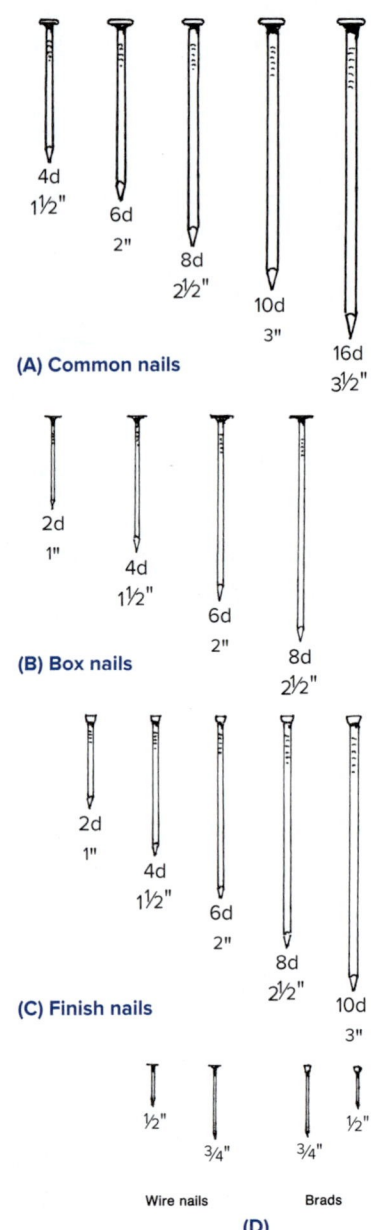

(A) Common nails

(B) Box nails

(C) Finish nails

Wire nails   Brads

(D)

FIGURE 10.33
Standard nails.

The size of nails is designated by the term *penny*, which is symbolized by the letter *d*. There is a rough equivalency between the length of the shaft, or shank, of a nail and the penny designation: the higher the number, the longer the shaft.

All of the nails, screws, and bolts listed in this section are commonly used in nontheatrical construction and are readily available at lumberyards and home centers.

Common Nail   The common nail (Figure 10.33A) has a large head and thick shank. It is used for heavier general construction — platforms, bracing, and the like.

Box Nail   Similar in shape to the common nail, the box nail (Figure 10.33B) has a narrower shaft that reduces the chance of splitting the lumber.

Coated Box Nail   Similar to the box nail but with a slightly narrower shaft, the coated box nail has an adhesive applied to the shaft. The friction generated when the nail is driven activates the adhesive to tightly bond the nail to the wood.

Finish Nail   The finish nail (Figure 10.33C) has a slender shaft and a very narrow, almost nonexistent head. It is designed so that the head can be driven below the surface of the wood and the resultant hole filled with putty or filler. The finish nail is not normally used in general scenic construction but is employed in the building of props or furniture and at any time that it is desirable to hide the nail head.

Wire Nail and Brad   Wire nails and brads (Figure 10.33D) are small (under one inch length) finish or box nails with very slender shafts. They are used in property construction or for attaching delicate decorative moldings or panels to larger scenic elements.

Double-Headed Nail   Double-headed nails (Figure 10.34A) are also known as scaffolding nails. They are driven into the wood until the lower head is flush with the surface, leaving the upper head exposed so that it can be pulled out easily. As the secondary name implies, these nails are used for scaffolding or any temporary structure that you may want to dismantle quickly.

Screw Nail   The screw nail (Figure 10.34B) has a threaded shank that rotates as it is driven into the wood. It has more holding power than a common nail and is used for attaching platform tops and for similar jobs where the greater holding power would be useful.

T-Nail   Nails with thick, strong shafts. The head forms a T (Figure 10.34C). Manufactured in clips for use with pneumatic nailers in wood, metal, and concrete. Used for attaching platform tops to steel-framed platforms and similar uses.

FIGURE 10.34
Specialty nails.
(A) Double-headed nail
(B) Screw nail
(C) T-nail

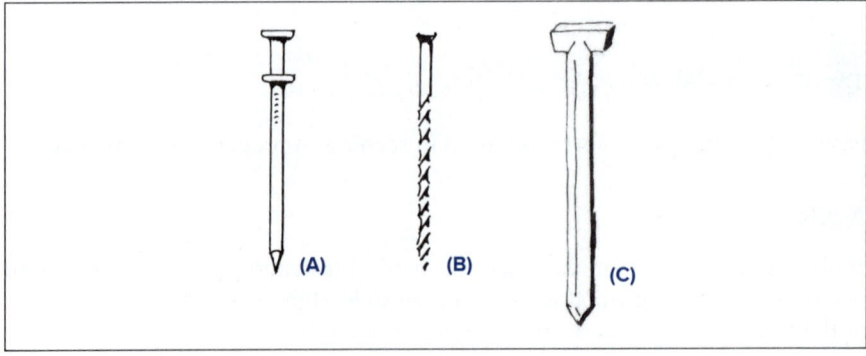

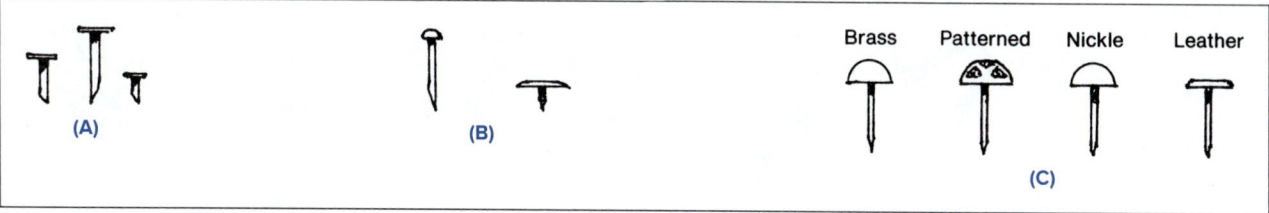

Tack Various tacks are used in scenic construction. Carpet tacks (Figure 10.35A) have very wide heads and tapered shafts varying from approximately ⅜ to ¾ inch in length. Carpet, gimp, and thumbtacks (Figure 10.35B) are generally used for attaching fabric to some type of wooden backing — for example, tacking carpeting to the floor, upholstery fabric to furniture frames, and so forth. Decorative tacks have rounded heads and straight shanks, as shown in Figure 10.35C. Although they do hold upholstery fabric to its wooden frame, their primary purpose is simply decoration. They are also very useful to the property master in the decoration, or "glitzing," of various stage props.

Corrugated Fastener Corrugated strips of metal about ⅜ inch tall and 1⅛ inches wide, shown in Figure 10.36, are primarily used to hold lightweight frames together.

Staple Staples are U-shaped fasteners sharpened at both ends. Fence, screen, and poultry staples (Figure 10.37) are driven with a hammer and can be used to attach wire, rope, cording, chicken wire, screening, and similar materials to supporting wooden frameworks.

Spring, and electric/battery-powered staple guns use short-legged staples (¼ to ½ inch) to attach fabric to wooden frames. Relatively long-legged staples (¾ to 1½ inch), when driven by a pneumatic stapler, are used to fasten various types of wooden structures together.

Screws

Screws provide a stronger method of joining than nails, because their auger-like thread digs into the material on the sides of the screw hole to mechanically bind them to the material. Various screws are used in scenic construction. The type of screw appropriate for an individual job depends on the type and thickness of the material being worked and the strength needed in that particular joint. Most screws are designed with either a standard or slotted or a Phillips head (Figure 10.38A and B), although some are manufactured for use with an **Allen wrench** (Figure 10.38C) or have a combination slotted hex head or square head (Figure 10.38D and E). Robertson-head screws (Figure 10.38F) are becoming more popular probably because the square, slightly tapered drive hole seems to hold the screwdriver bit more securely than slotted or Phillips-head screws, particularly important when driving the screws with a powered screwdriver.

Flat-Head Wood Screw The flat-head wood screw (FHWS), with the possible exception of the drywall screw, is probably the most common type of screw used in the scene shop (Figure 10.39A). It has a flat head that is beveled on the under-side to easily dig into the wood. This countersinking action allows the upper face of the head to be flush with the surface of the work. Common uses for the FHWS are attaching hardware (hinges, doorknobs) and joining various wooden elements together. FHWS's range in length from about ½ inch to

FIGURE 10.35
Tacks.
(A) Carpet tacks
(B) Gimp tack (left) and thumbtack (right)
(C) Upholstery tacks

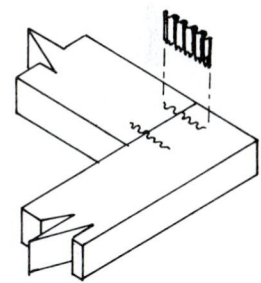

FIGURE 10.36
Corrugated fastener.

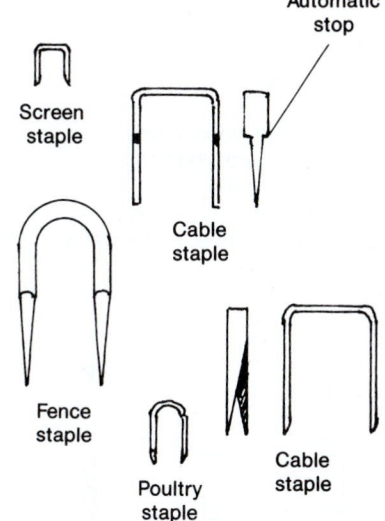

FIGURE 10.37
Staples.

Allen wrench: An L-shaped piece of steel rod with a hexagonal cross-sectional shape; used for working with Allen-head screws and bolts.

FIGURE 10.38
Types of screw heads.
(A) Standard or slotted
(B) Phillips
(C) Allen
(D) Slotted hex
(E) Hex
(F) Robertson (square)

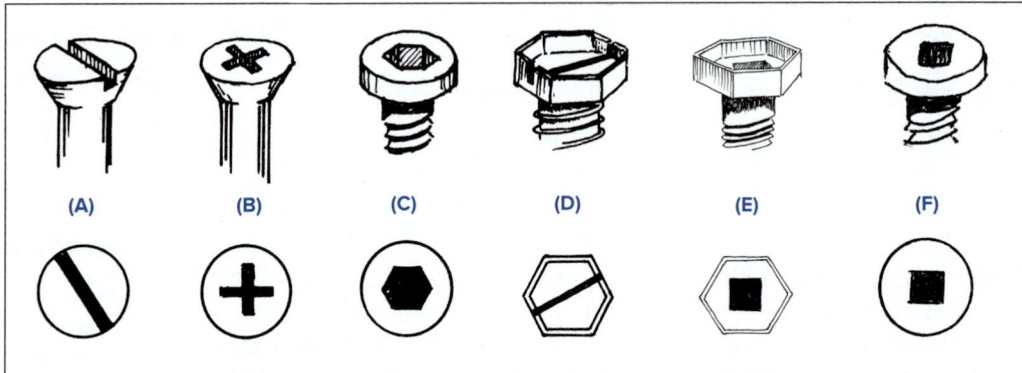

3 inches, although the most common sizes used in the shop vary from ¾ to about 1¼ or 1½ inches, with a screw shank diameter of No. 8 or No. 9. (The numerical rating of screw shank sizes is roughly dependent on their diameter: the higher the number, the larger the diameter.)

Round-Head Wood Screw   Identical in most respects with the FHWS, the head of the round-head wood screw (RHWS) is flat on the underside and rounded on the top (Figure 10.39B). The RHWS is used in those situations in which you do not want to have the top of the screw flush with the surface of the work, such as when you are attaching thin metal or fabric to a wooden frame.

Drywall Screws   Drywall screws are used in general construction to attach gypsum board or drywall to wooden wall and ceiling studs (Figure 10.39C).

The screws are coarse-threaded, Phillips-head, self-starting (which means they don't require a pilot hole) and are designed to be driven with a power screwdriver. Drywall screws have excellent gripping power and can be quickly attached and easily removed. They do, however, have a disconcerting habit of shearing or breaking when being driven into thick or particularly dense wood. The yellow/gold drywall screw has the same shape and characteristics as the dark grey drywall screw, but seems stronger than the regular drywall screw and better resists shearing.

When paired with the latest generation of battery-powered power screwdrivers, the yellow-gold colored drywall screws are the fastener of choice for many types of wooden scenic construction. One note of caution: The points of drywall screws are extremely sharp. Use caution when picking them up.

FIGURE 10.39
Screws.
(A) Flat-head wood screw
(B) Round-head wood screw
(C) Drywall screw
(D) Pan-head sheet-metal screw
(E) Hex-head sheet-metal screw
(F) Lag screws
(G) TEK screw

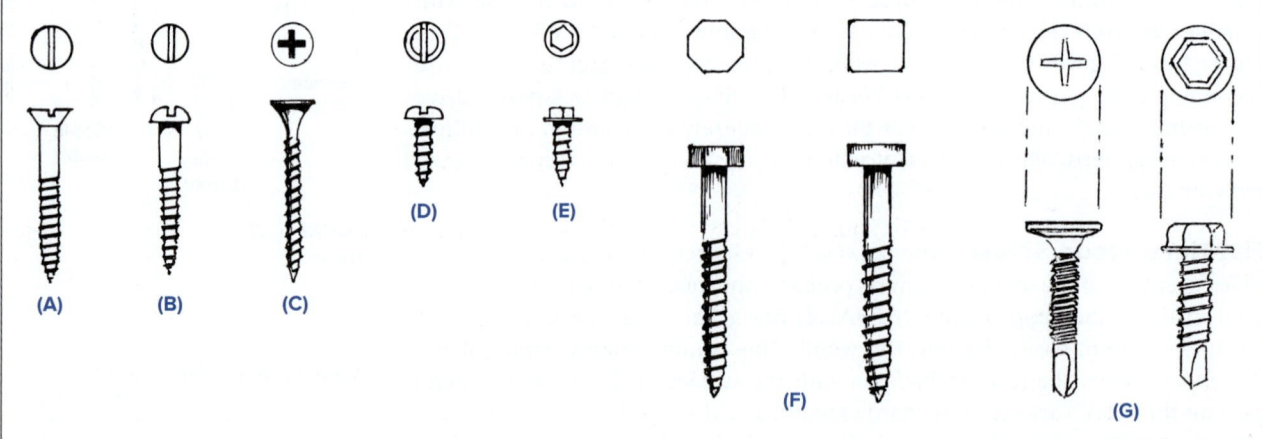

PRODUCTION INSIGHTS

Starter, or Pilot, Holes

Unless you are using a power screwdriver, a screw is much easier to use if you drill a starter, or pilot, hole. Ideally this hole should be the same diameter as the solid shaft of the threaded portion of the screw (not counting the flange of the screw thread).

Specialty drill bits called screw starters, designed for use with power screwdrivers, can drill starter and countersink holes in the same action. They are available for most common sizes of screws.

The starter hole for a bolt should be the same diameter as the full diameter of the bolt (including the screw flange).

Sheet-Metal Screw   As the name implies, sheet-metal screws are used for joining sheets of metal. They are commonly available with either a pan head (Figure 10.39D) or a hex head (Figure 10.39E). Most jobs using sheet-metal screws in the scenic or property shop require shank lengths between ¼ and ¾ inch.

Lag Screw   Lag screws, also called lag bolts, are very large wood screws with hexagonal or square heads (Figure 10.39F). They are used where the lack of access to both sides of the work prevents the use of bolts, such as when attaching something to a wall or the floor. Shaft diameters generally range from ¼ to ⅝ inch with shaft lengths commonly varying from 1 to 6 inches. A washer should be used under the head of the lag screw to increase the bearing area and prevent the head from biting into the surface of the wood.

TEK Screws   In scenic construction TEK, or self-tapping, case-hardened, screws primarily are used to attach plywood coverings to metal frames. Figure 10.39G illustrates two of the more common configurations — a pan, or flat, head and a hex head. A round head is also available. The pan or flat head is more commonly used in scenic construction because the top of the head can be driven **flush** with the face of the covering material. The tip of the screw is hardened and sharpened so, when driven with a power screwdriver, it drills a hole and screws itself into the work in one operation.

flush: Smooth, level, even.

Bolts

Bolts are used when you want the strongest type of mechanical fastening. When using a bolt, a hole is drilled in both members of the work, the appropriate type and size of bolt is inserted into the hole, a washer is slipped onto the bolt shaft, and a nut is threaded onto the bolt shaft and tightened (Figure 10.40).

Carriage Bolt   The upper face of a carriage-bolt head has a rounded surface, and the underside has a slightly tapered square collar a little wider than the diameter of the bolt shaft, as shown in Figure 10.41A. The carriage bolt is used to join either wood to wood or wood to metal. After the bolt has been inserted into the hole, the head is struck with a hammer to make the square collar seat, or bite into, the surface of the wood to prevent it from turning. This type of bolt is commonly used to fasten legs to platform frames and in similar types of work. Carriage bolts range in diameter from ¼ to ¾ inch and in length from 1 to 24 inches.

Machine Bolt   Machine bolts are designed to join metal to metal, although they can be used to join wood to wood if a washer is used under the head of the

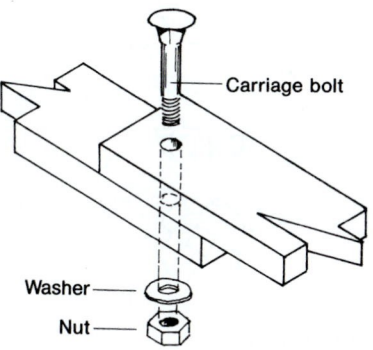

FIGURE 10.40
Bolts are the strongest form of mechanical fastener.

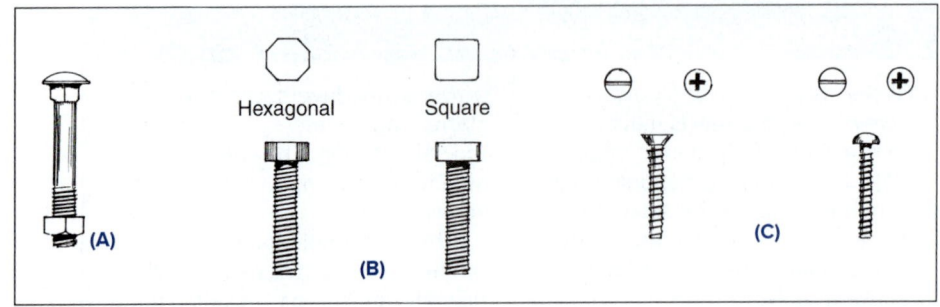

bolt as well as under the nut. Machine bolts are manufactured with both square and hexagonal heads (Figure 10.41B). The bolt shaft diameters range from ¼ to 1 inch and the lengths from 1 to 6 inches.

Stove Bolt   Stove bolts (Figure 10.41C) are smaller than carriage or machine bolts and have threads on the entire length of the shaft. They have head shapes identical to flat- and round-head wood screws to serve similar purposes. Shaft diameters appropriate for general scenic purposes range from ⅛ to ⁵⁄₁₆ inch, with shaft lengths ranging between 1 and 6 inches. Much smaller stove bolts (shaft diameters less than ⅛ inch and lengths under 1 inch) are available from hobby or electronic stores.

Stove bolts are generally used for attaching stage hardware, hinges, and similar items in situations that might require the extra fastening strength available with the use of bolts instead of screws.

Washers

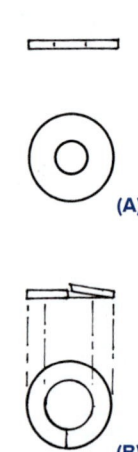

Washers are flat steel disks with a center hole cut for the bolt shaft. When placed between either the nut or the head of the bolt and the material being joined, a washer (Figure 10.42A) increases the bearing surface of the nut or bolt head and prevents the head from cutting into the surface of the work. Lock washers (Figure 10.42B) are made from spring steel and are cut and slightly spread apart to form a compression tension when the nut is tightened. The purpose of the lock washer is to prevent the nut from turning after it has been tightened.

Torque washers (Figure 10.42C) are designed to prevent carriage bolts from twisting once they have been seated. The torque washer is slipped onto the shaft of the carriage bolt before it is inserted into the predrilled bolt hole. The square collar on the underside of the bolt head fits into the square hole on the face of the torque washer. When the bolt is seated, the four prongs bite into the surface of the wood. By firmly seating the head of the carriage bolt in the wood, the torque washer allows more torque, or pressure, to be applied when tightening the nut.

Nuts

Nuts are applied to the threaded ends of bolts to close and tighten this type of fastener. Nuts designed to be tightened with wrenches are generally either square (Figure 10.43A) or hexagonally shaped (Figure 10.43B). The wing nut (Figure 10.43C) is designed to be tightened with your fingers. Nuts are available in sizes and metallic compositions identical to the shaft diameters and composition or coating of their corresponding bolts.

The T-nut (Figure 10.43D) is a slightly different kettle of fish. It is basically an internally threaded tube surrounded by a pronged washer. A hole, the same diameter as the tube portion of the T-nut, is drilled into the wood in the proper location. The T-nut is then driven into the hole. Similarly to the torque washer, the prongs prevent the T-nut from turning when the bolt is tightened.

The thread insert (Figure 10.43E) is similar in function to the T-nut, but rather than being held in place with prongs, the outside of the tube is threaded. Basically, it is a tube that is threaded on both the inside and outside. It can be used in wood, plastic, or metal. The top of the insert is slotted so a screwdriver can be used to twist it into the supporting wood, plastic, or metal.

Glues and Adhesives

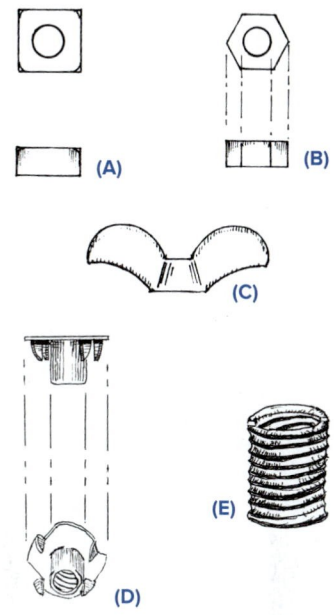

FIGURE 10.43
Nuts.
(A) Square nut
(B) Hex nut
(C) Wing nut
(D) T-nut
(E) Thread insert

Myriad glues and adhesives are currently manufactured, and many of them have applications in theatrical work, particularly in the area of property construction. Although the following list is far from exhaustive, it does introduce you to the glues and adhesives commonly used in scenic and property construction.

There are general guidelines for using all glues and adhesives. Be sure that the faces being glued are clean, dry, and free from oil and dust. Most glues, except contact cement, require some type of clamping. The amount of pressure and the time that it must be maintained depend on heat and humidity as well as the type of glue being used. The working characteristics of each glue and adhesive are discussed in the following sections.

Glues

Glue is made of, or primarily derived from, natural substances. Animal and flexible glues (by-products of the meat-packing industry) used to be commonly used in scenic construction and painting. They have almost entirely been replaced by synthetic adhesives. The only glue still occasionally used is wheat paste.

Wheat paste is made from a mixture of unrefined wheat flour, preservatives, and water. Some wheat pastes also include insecticides and/or poisons to prevent critters from eating it while it is in storage. It is used for hanging wallpaper, as the glue in papier-mâché, and as one of the ingredients in the glue used for attaching **dutchmen** to wall units. After wheat paste has dried, it is reasonably flexible and has a dull, or matte, surface finish. It can be purchased at paint and wallpaper stores, hardware stores, lumberyards, and home centers.

Adhesives

Adhesives perform the same functions as glues but are primarily composed of synthetic materials. They have a distinct advantage over natural glues in that they will not spoil, rot, or turn sour, and they generally come in ready-to-use formulations.

Drying and curing times for adhesives vary considerably depending on type and manufacturer. Read the label of the specific product to determine its particular characteristics.

White Glue   White glue (widely known by the trade name of Elmer's Glue-All™) is a synthetic glue that is used extensively in scenic construction. It is reasonably fast drying, is slightly flexible, and adheres to wood, paper, cloth, Styrofoam, and some other plastics as well. When dry, it leaves a slightly glossy surface. It can be purchased from almost any lumber, paint, hardware store, or home center. White glue dries in about 1 or 2 hours depending on heat, humidity, and air circulation around the glue joint, but for the joint to develop strength, the glue must be allowed to cure for about 24 hours.

dutchman: A 5- to 6-inch-wide strip of cloth of the same material as the flat covering; applied over joints between flats to give the appearance of a smooth, unbroken wall unit.

Carpenter's Glue Carpenter's glue is another readily available synthetic glue extensively used in woodworking. Similar in many respects to white glue, carpenter's glue is yellow when liquid but dries almost clear. It is stronger and generally dries more quickly than white glue.

Latex Cement A milky-white, flexible cement commercially used in laying carpet, latex cement can be used whenever a very flexible glue joint is required. It adheres to cloth, paper, wood, and many other materials and can be purchased from many carpet shops, some furniture stores, scenic supply houses, and home centers.

Contact Cement Contact cement is an adhesive for bonding nonporous surfaces together. As the name implies, the surfaces being joined are bonded as soon as they come in contact with each other. Each surface is spread with a light coating of the contact cement and allowed to dry for a few minutes; then the pieces are brought together and are immediately bonded. There are two types of contact cement: One has a highly volatile, extremely flammable base, and the other has a water-soluble latex base. Most scenic construction projects can be accomplished with the much safer, non-volatile latex base.

Polyvinyl Glue A white liquid adhesive that resembles white glue in appearance, polyvinyl glue is a synthetic with excellent adhesion to porous surfaces and good flexibility. It can be used for a number of jobs, ranging from furniture repair and construction to use as the binder for scene paint.

Cyanoacrylate Cement Cyanoacrylate cements are very powerful adhesives that will bond almost any porous or nonporous surface to almost anything else. Therein lie their strengths and dangers. Sold under trade names such as Super Glue™, Krazy Glue™, and so on, these powerful adhesives are too expensive for scenic construction but are excellent for use in property construction. Because they bond to anything, including skin, almost immediately be sure to follow the instructions very carefully.

Epoxy Resin Adhesive Two-part epoxy resin adhesive is available in a number of formulations that enable the user to do gluing, filling, and painting. The epoxy adhesive bond is extremely strong and waterproof. It is used in the shop in situations where its strength can be an advantage, such as furniture construction and property work.

Almost all of the above-described adhesives can be purchased at any well-stocked hardware store or home center.

 ## Hardware

A great deal of hardware is used in the construction of stage scenery. Most of this hardware is also used in building construction and can be purchased at a lumberyard or hardware store. The specialized hardware designed for specific stage applications is usually not available locally and must be purchased from a scenic supply house.

Construction Hardware

Eye Bolt Eye bolts (Figure 10.44A) can be used for almost any situation that requires attaching lines or ropes to an object, such as the pull rope for a stage wagon or a guide for the piano wire or cable on a piece of flying scenery. The diameter of the steel rod used to manufacture the eye bolt varies from approximately ⅛ to ⅜ inch. The shaft length varies from about 1 to 6 inches.

Screw Eye   Screw eyes (Figure 10.44B) are similar to eye bolts but are used when the additional strength of the bolt fastener isn't necessary or when the back of the surface to which the screw eye is being attached cannot be reached. Screw eyes are available in a wide range of sizes: Shaft diameters vary from about 1/16 to ⅜ inch and lengths from ½ inch to 4 inches.

Screw Hook   Screw hooks (Figure 10.44C) are similar to screw eyes but have a hook instead of an eye so that items hung from the hook can be removed quickly. Size variations are similar to those of screw eyes.

U Bolt   U bolts (Figure 10.44D) are made from metal rod that has been bent in a U shape and threaded on both ends. They are typically used to secure or fasten pipe, tube, or rod to a flat surface.

Cable Clamp   Another type of U bolt, the cable clamp (Figure 10.44E), also known as a cable clip, has a grooved metal clamp that fits over the bolt shafts. The diameter of the clamp's U-shaped opening corresponds to the diameter of the wire rope or cable that is used to hang scenery and battens. For safety reasons, cable clamps should always be used in pairs. When attaching wire rope clips always place the saddle — as opposed to the U-bolt portion of the clip — on the live, or free, end of the cable. Doing this will ensure that the saddle bites into the free end of the cable, which makes for a safer and more secure attachment.

Nicopress Tool   Another cable fastener, the Nicopress tool (Figure 10.44F), provides a permanent, nonremovable friction clamp for wire rope or cable. Nicopress sleeves, which are thin, soft metal tubes approximately ½ to ¾ inch long, are designed for specific diameters of cable and must be crimped or tightened with the Nicopress tool. Like the sleeves, Nicopress tools are designed to work with only one diameter of cable. Each Nicopress tool is packaged with a gauge — generically referred to as a "go/no go" tool — that is used to check sleeve compression. When making any Nicopress connection be sure to use these gauges to determine whether the sleeve has been adequately and safely attached to the cable.

Thimble   The cable thimble (Figure 10.44G) is a narrow, grooved, teardrop-shaped piece of sheet metal used to protect wire rope or cable from sharp bends or kinks when the cable is attached to a ring or similar device.

Turnbuckle   A turnbuckle (Figure 10.44H) has a long, oval body with a threaded eye bolt protruding from either end. When attached as a link in a cable, it can be used to lengthen or shorten that line system. This property makes it an excellent device to place between a flying line and a flown piece of scenery to adjust the trim of the flown unit. When using these in a flying system, be sure to securely twist 12-gauge wire around the threaded ends of both eye bolts so they cannot become uncoupled from the turnbuckle body.

Snaps   There are various types of snaps — some with swivel bases (Figure 10.44I); some designed for use with rope; and others intended for use with cable, chain, and curtains (Figure 10.44J). But they all have the same purpose — they provide a quick means of attaching a line to its associated load.

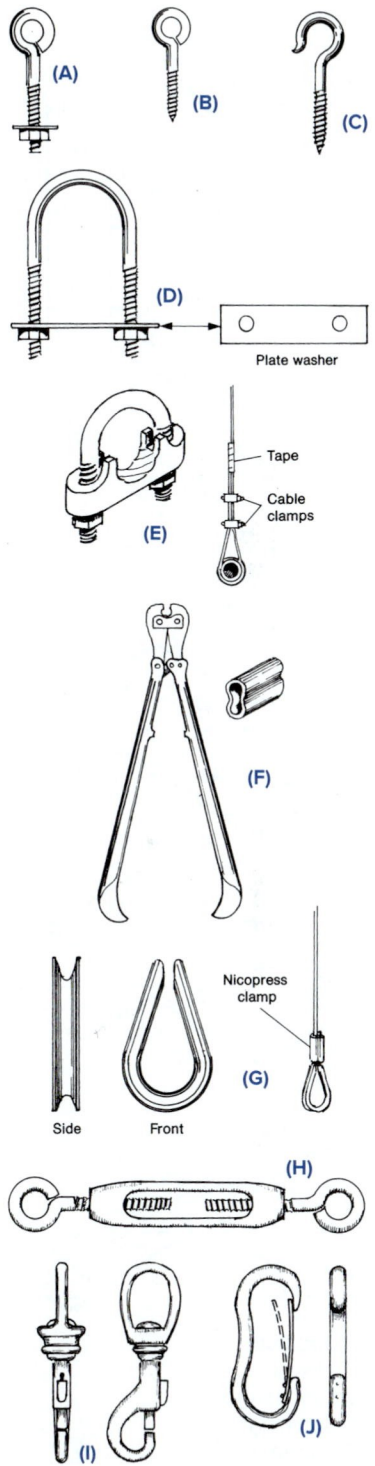

FIGURE 10.44
Common construction hardware.
(A) Eye bolt   (G) Cable thimble
(B) Screw eye   (H) Turnbuckle
(C) Screw hook   (I) Swivel snap
(D) U bolt   (J) Spring snap
(E) Cable clamp
(F) Nicopress and sleeve

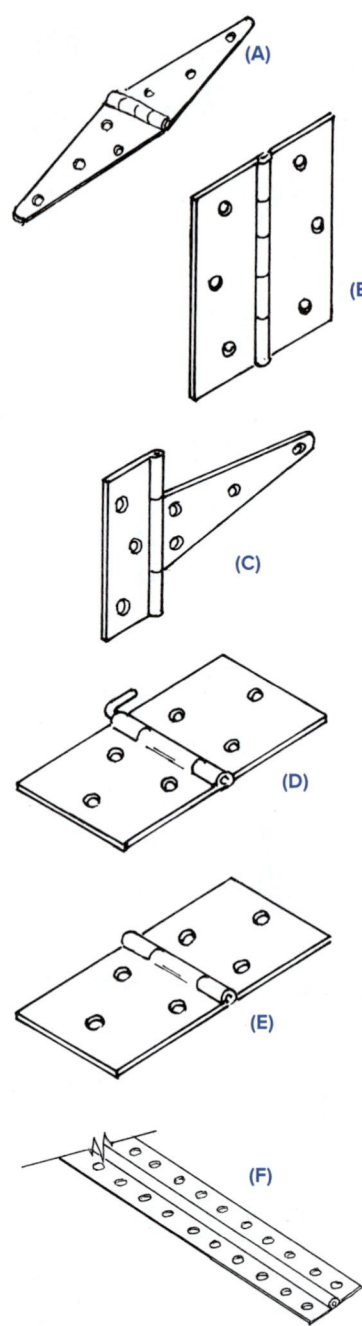

FIGURE 10.45
Hinges.
(A) Strap hinge
(B) Butt hinge
(C) T-strap hinge
(D) Loose-pin back-flap hinge
(E) Tight-pin back-flap hinge
(F) Piano hinge

Leaves: The moveable flaps on hinges.

Hinges   A hinge is composed of two joined metal plates that swing around a pivot point. Several types of hinges have applications in scenic construction.

Strap Hinge   Strap hinges (Figure 10.45A) are composed of two tapering leaves that are joined by either a loose or a fixed pin. Strap hinge **leaves** vary in length from 2½ to 8 inches. Each leaf is drilled and countersunk to accept flat-head wood screws or stove bolts. They are commonly used to hinge stage doors by bending one leaf, attaching it to the depth piece of the casing, and attaching the straight leaf to the back of the door.

Butt Hinge   Butt hinges (Figure 10.45B) are available in a wide variety of sizes and finishes, but they are all used for the same general purpose — hanging doors. They are composed of rectangular leaves joined by either a fixed or a loose pin. The holes are countersunk to accept flat-head wood screws or stove bolts.

T-Strap Hinge   A combination of one leaf from a strap hinge and an elongated leaf from a butt hinge, the T-strap hinge (Figure 10.45C) is used for hanging doors, gates, and box lids.

Loose-Pin Back-Flap Hinge   Loose-pin back-flap hinges (Figure 10.45D) have square leaves in sizes ranging from approximately 1¼ to 2½ inches in width. The 1½- and 2-inch sizes are the most commonly used in scenic construction. These hinges can be used as "regular" hinges, but in scenic construction they are primarily used for joining scenery. The individual hinge leaves are attached to the separate pieces of scenery, and the pin is inserted to hold the unit together. The pin can be removed whenever it is necessary to break the unit into its component elements for shifting or storage.

Tight-Pin Back-Flap Hinge   The tight-pin back-flap hinge (Figure 10.45E) is primarily used for the same purposes as its loose-pin companion whenever a permanent joining is desired. It is frequently used when two or more flats are joined to form an unbroken expanse of wall. Details of this type of wall construction are covered in Chapter 11, "Scenic Production Techniques."

Piano Hinge   The piano hinge is a narrow-leaved, very long, tight-pin hinge made of thinner metal than the other hinges described in this section. It gets its name from its original use — attaching piano lids. If only three or four "regular" hinges were used to attach the lid, its weight would quickly tear the screws out of the wood. Enter the piano hinge; the screw holes are typically spaced an inch or less apart for the entire length of the hinge. These numerous attachment points allow the leaves to be quite narrow — typically less than an inch. Piano hinges are generally 6 feet long but can easily be cut to fit the needed length.

Stage Hardware

Flying Hardware   Several pieces of stage hardware aid in flying scenery and stabilizing flown scenery. For reasons of safety, all flying hardware should be attached with bolts. A minimum of one bolt and screws can be used if the piece is quite light. Never suspend or fly anything using only screws.

Hanger Iron   The hanger iron (Figure 10.46A) is a metal strap with a D ring at the top. It is attached to the stile at the top of the flat in a position that keeps the D ring hidden behind the top of the flat. The hanger iron, also called a top hanger iron, is used in conjunction with a bottom hanger iron for flying heavy scenery, but it can be used by itself for flying lightweight pieces.

Bottom Hanger Iron   The bottom hanger iron (Figure 10.46B) is a metal strap with a hooked foot at the bottom and a D ring at the top. The bottom hanger iron, also called the hook hanger iron, is attached so the bottom of the flat rests on the hooked foot. The flying line is attached to the D ring so that the flat will, in effect, be picked up from the bottom or lifted under compression.

When rigging a heavy or tall flat for flying, use the bottom hanger iron in conjunction with a hanger iron. The hanger iron is attached to the top of the flat in a line directly above the bottom hanger iron. The flying line is fed through the D ring of the hanger iron and attached to the D ring of the bottom hanger iron. If the flat is very small and light, a screw eye can be substituted for the top hanger iron.

Ceiling Plate   The ceiling plate (Figure 10.46C) is bolted to primary structural members of the ceiling to provide a means of attaching the flying lines to the ceiling.

D Ring and Plate   The D ring and plate (Figure 10.46D) is another piece of hanging hardware. It is normally used on vertical pieces that are to be flown such as flats.

Bracing Hardware   Most flats need some type of external support to be able to stand up. If the flats don't need support to stand, they will probably need some type of bracing to prevent them from wiggling.

Stage Brace   The stage brace is the mainstay of scenic bracing. It is an adjustable wooden (Figure 10.47A) or aluminum (Figure 10.47B) pole that can be quickly attached to a brace cleat (Figure 10.47C) on the back of a flat. The other end of the stage brace is secured to the stage floor by one of the several methods to be described.

Brace Cleat   Attached to the stile of a flat with the end projecting past the inside edge of the stile, a brace cleat (Figure 10.47C) provides a point of attachment between the scenery and the stage brace.

Rigid Foot Iron   The rigid foot iron (Figure 10.47D) is an L-shaped piece of metal. The long leg is attached to the bottom of the scenery with screws or bolts. The horizontal foot sticks out and is secured to the stage floor with a stage screw inserted through the ring at the end of the foot.

Hinged Foot Iron   The hinged foot iron is similar to the rigid foot iron. Its horizontal foot (Figure 10.47E) is hinged to fold out of the way when the scenic unit is being shifted or flown.

Stage Screw   The stage screw is a large, coarse-threaded, hand-driven screw used to anchor a foot iron or the foot of a stage brace to the wooden stage floor. Although stage screws (Figure 10.47F) provide an effective means of anchoring stage braces, they leave ragged holes and splinters wherever they are used.

Improved Stage Screw   The improved stage screw (Figure 10.47G) doesn't tear up the stage floor nearly so much as its unrefined cousin does. A steel plug, threaded on the outside and inside, is inserted into an appropriately sized hole that has been drilled into the stage floor. The improved stage screw screws into the plug. When the production is over, the plug can be removed from the floor, and the hole patched by gluing a small piece of hardwood **dowel** into the hole.

Floor Plate   It is rather difficult to use either a stage screw or an improved stage screw if your stage floor is concrete or if the building owner or administrator has said, "Thou shalt not put any holes in the stage floor." Fortunately, the floor plate (Figure 10.47H) can come to the rescue.

The lower end of the stage brace is secured to the floor plate, a block of wood with nonskid material (foam, rubber) attached to the bottom. Sandbags or counterweights are piled on the plate to anchor it to the floor.

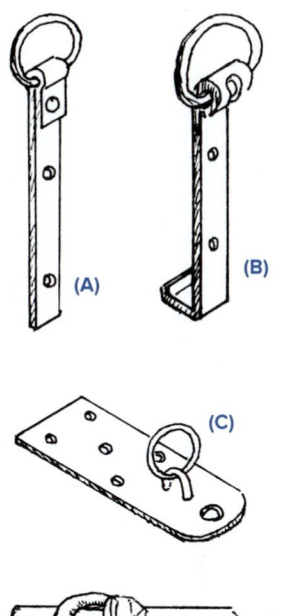

FIGURE 10.46
Flying hardware.
(A) Hanger iron
(B) Bottom hanger iron
(C) Ceiling plate
(D) D ring and plate

dowel: A short cylinder of hardwood (usually birch).

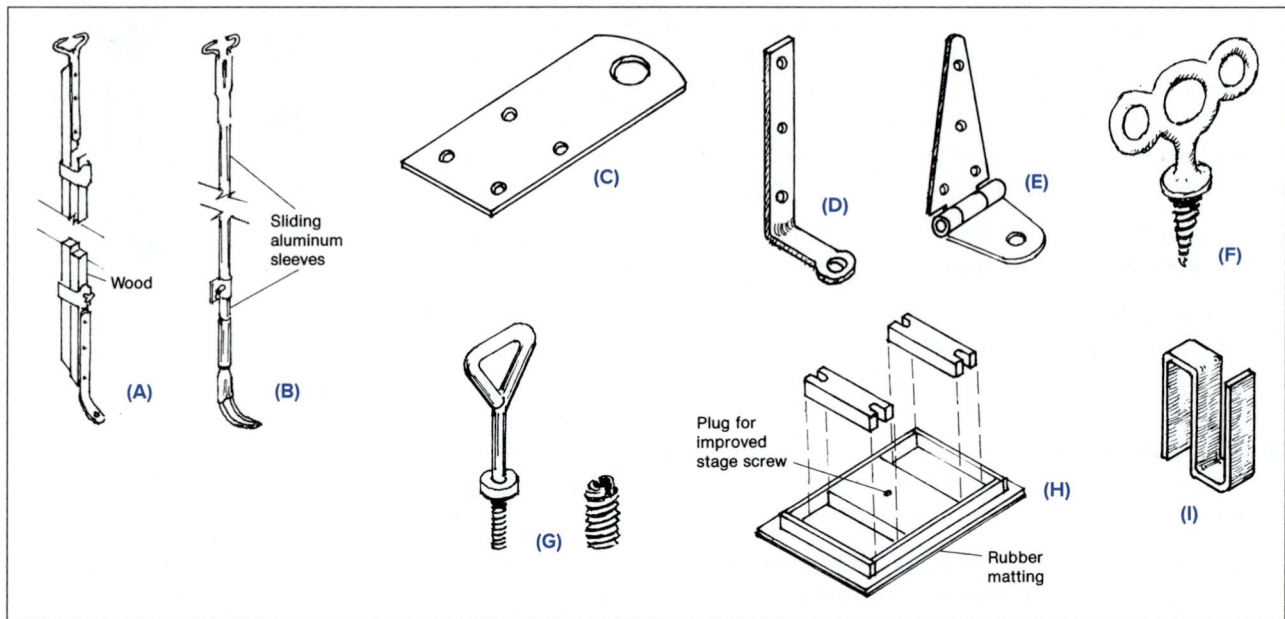

FIGURE 10.47
Bracing hardware.
(A) Extension stage brace
(B) Lightweight stage brace
(C) Brace cleat
(D) Rigid foot iron
(E) Hinged foot iron
(F) Stage screw
(G) Improved stage screw
(H) Floor plate
(I) S hook

S Hook   Also known as a latch keeper, the S hook (Figure 10.47I) is used to hold stiffening battens on the back of wall units that are made up of two or more flats. Normally used on flats that must have the stiffening battens removed for shifting, S hooks can be purchased or made in the shop from ⅛- or ³⁄₃₂-by 1 inch mild-steel strap.

Miscellaneous Hardware   There are several additional pieces of stage hardware that cannot be neatly categorized because their use is not necessarily limited to a single purpose.

Corner Plate   The corner plate (Figure 10.48A) is an L-shaped piece of ¹⁄₁₆-inch galvanized steel, available in a variety of sizes. Each leg is predrilled, or tapped, for use with No. 8 or No. 9 flat-head wood screws. Corner plates are used to reinforce the corners of doors, windows, door or window casings, and picture frames and in similar applications.

Tee Plate   Made of the same galvanized steel as the corner plate, the tee plate (Figure 10.48B) can be used as a substitute for keystones or in similar applications.

Picture Hook and Eye   Picture hooks and eyes (Figure 10.48C) are shop-made pieces (³⁄₃₂-by-¾-inch or 1-inch mild-steel strap) that facilitate the rapid hanging and removal of decorative draperies on a set. They are used in sets of two or more. The sockets are attached to the face of the flat with screws or bolts, and the hooks are similarly attached to the drapery rod.

Casket Lock   The casket lock (Figure 10.48D) is a heavy-duty hidden lock that is used to hold platforms together or in similar applications. Its use as a platform lock is detailed in Chapter 11, "Scenic Production Techniques."

Casters   Casters come in a bewildering array of sizes, styles, and load ratings. To be useful for stage purposes, casters should meet a few specific requirements. They should have hard rubber tires, should have a load rating of at least 300 pounds, and should be sturdily constructed. Although stage casters can be purchased from theatrical-equipment supply houses, it is sometimes advantageous to buy your casters at a local building-equipment supply firm.

Swivel casters (Figure 10.49A) are mounted on a bearing plate that allows the wheel to pivot around a vertical axis. To turn easily under a load, the pivot should be supported by ball bearings. For use with stage wagons, the overall height of the caster should be 4 to 5 inches. The tires on a swivel caster should be made of rubber to reduce the rumble that inevitably accompanies the movement of a stage platform. The wheel of the caster should be metal, and it should have some type of bearing (ball, tube) to decrease the friction between the axle and the wheel. The axle should be removable so that a metal strap can be attached to the axle and the platform to lock the swivel caster in a stationary position. Some swivel casters are equipped with built-in pins that can be used to hold the caster stationary.

Triple-swivel (or "tri-swivel") casters (Figure 10.49B) are specialty units consisting of three swivel casters mounted on the corners of a triangular plate that also swivels about its center. This setup allows for instant changes in direction without the "swinging around" of the caster due to the offset between the wheel's axis and the vertical axis of the swiveling action. Although expensive, triple-swivel casters allow for effortless direction changes and curving movement onstage.

Rigid casters (Figure 10.49C) are permanently locked in position so that they cannot pivot. The specifications for the swivel caster regarding the structure of the tire, wheel, axle, height, and load rating are applicable to the stationary caster.

Furniture casters do not have the same rigorous specifications as stage casters. They should be sturdily constructed, but because they are often seen by the audience, they need to look as if they belong to the period being depicted in the production. Furniture casters can be purchased at furniture and hardware stores and home centers.

The compressed-air lifter literally floats heavy objects on a thin cushion of air. The *air caster* or *air bearing* (Figure 10.49D) is an inflatable saucer-shaped disk

FIGURE 10.48
Miscellaneous stage hardware.
(A) Corner plate
(B) Tee plate
(C) Picture hook and eye
(D) Casket lock

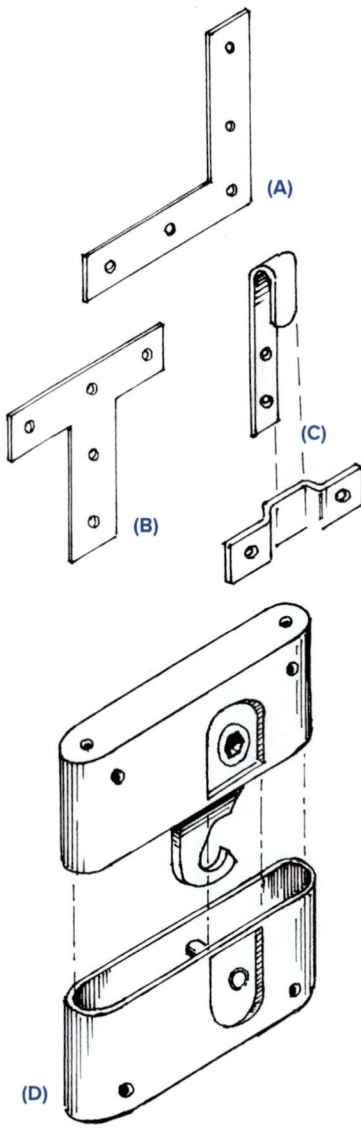

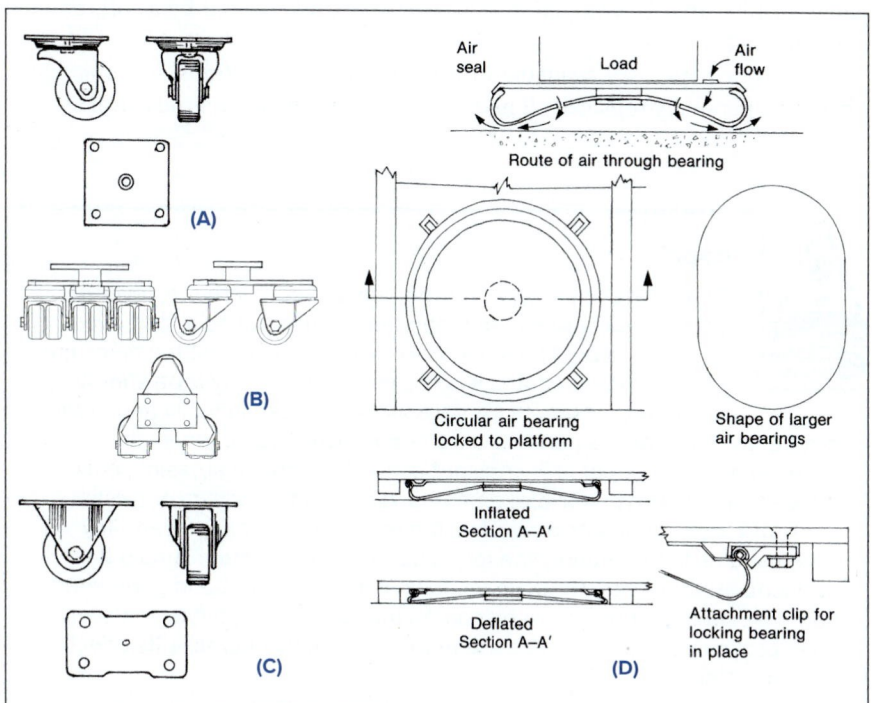

FIGURE 10.49
Types of casters.
(A) Swivel caster
(B) Tri-swivel caster
(C) Rigid caster
(D) Air caster

of rubberized fabric. The air caster works as follows: Compressed air inflates the doughnut-shaped bearing to raise the load; the compressed air continues to flow, creating an air cushion under the bearing. Three or four air casters are needed to raise most objects. Although they are available in a variety of diameters ranging from 1 to 4 feet, the 1-foot size, which is load rated at approximately 2,000 pounds, is adequate for almost any theatrical use. Air casters don't work well if the stage floor isn't perfectly smooth. Another drawback to the air caster is the noise of the compressor needed to supply the low-compression, high-volume air. The noise problem can be solved, however, if the compressor (a shop vacuum cleaner works well) is located in an adjacent, sound-deadened space and air hoses are run to the casters.

 Rope, Cable, and Wire

Several types of ropes are used for a variety of purposes in the theatre.

Synthetic Rope

Manila rope used to be the primary type of rope used for raising and suspending loads (scenery, equipment) in the theatre. That is no longer the case. Synthetic ropes such as Multiline II and Stage-Set X, offered by the stage rigging company J. R. Clancy, have replaced manila. The Multiline II handles like manila but weighs less, is stronger, and has better durability. Unlike manila it does not change length with temperature/humidity variations. Because of their superior characteristics synthetic ropes of this type have replaced manila as the operating line in counterweight systems.

It is a common characteristic of most natural-fiber ropes that, when stretched out, they have a tendency to twist. This is because of the way that they are made. Stage-Set X however, has a nonrotating construction. It has a parallel core of polyester fiber that is wrapped in polyester tape and covered by a soft, braided polyester jacket.

Synthetic ropes are available in a variety of compositions and diameters. They have generally replaced all natural-fiber ropes in general theatrical use.

Safety Tip

Rope

Regardless of the type of rope being used, there are several general safety rules. Any rope that is suspending a load over the stage should have a breaking strength at least ten times the weight of the load that it is required to bear. Any rope should be carefully inspected before use — at least annually and more frequently if the rope is part of a permanent system (counterweight, rope set and the like) or is in constant use — for signs of abrasion, cuts, gouges, seriously worn or broken fibers, discoloration, kinks, or twists. If any of these conditions is evident, the rope should be replaced. Any rope used as the operating line for a counterweight system should be replaced at least every three years, even if it appears to be in good condition. The strain that has been placed on the rope during those years will have broken down the fibers enough to significantly decrease its effective working strength.

Monofilament Line

Commonly sold as fishing line, monofilament line is basically a single-strand plastic string. It is transparent, comes in a variety of breaking strengths ranging from 2 to more than 100 pounds, and is used whenever an "invisible" or "trick" line is needed.

Aircraft Cable

Aircraft cable is frequently used in the theatre, because it is very flexible and very strong. One-eighth-inch aircraft cable is often used for flying heavy stage scenery because its breaking strength is approximately one ton.

Wire

Wire is used for a variety of purposes in both scenic and property construction.

Stovepipe Wire Soft-iron stovepipe wire is approximately $\frac{1}{16}$ of an inch in diameter and is generally colored black. It is quite flexible but has very little tensile strength. It is normally used for tying or binding things together. It shouldn't be used for flying scenery, because it isn't strong enough to support a load. Stovepipe wire of slightly greater diameter is known as baling wire. Soft-iron, or stovepipe, wire is also manufactured with a galvanized finish to prevent rust.

Piano Wire Piano wire is made from spring steel and is frequently used to fly scenery because of its remarkable tensile strength in comparison with its diameter. Care should be taken to avoid making sharp bends in piano wire, because kinking greatly reduces its strength.

Block and Tackle

The term *block and tackle* refers generically to arrangements of pulleys and ropes that provide a mechanical advantage. A pulley has one specific job: It changes the direction of travel of the rope passing through it. An ideal pulley accomplishes this task with no friction and little noise. Unfortunately, all pulleys create friction and make noise. But some pulleys are better than others. The small galvanized pulleys found in a hardware store can be used for lightweight applications such as the curtain pull for some decorative set drapes, but they are rather noisy. A better solution can be found in the marine-hardware section of a boat supply shop. These stores usually stock high-quality pulleys that are very quiet and have relatively little friction loss.

For heavy-duty use, the best pulleys are available from scenic supply houses or, sometimes, from well-stocked hardware stores or home centers. These pulleys have wooden bodies, have well-matched sheaves (wheels) and axles, and are fairly quiet in operation. Three common tackle rigs are illustrated and explained in Chapter 4, "The Stage and Its Equipment."

Safety Equipment

The types and specifications of personal protective equipment (PPE) and shop safety equipment are determined by the materials with which you will be working.

Clear-lensed goggles, safety glasses, and face shields will protect your eyes from flying wood and metal chips as well as from chemical splashes. Specially tinted eye shields such as welding goggles or (preferably) welding masks need to be worn when welding.

A **dust mask** should be worn when working with any material that produces dust. A **respirator,** equipped with an appropriate type of filter, should be worn any time that you are working with materials which produce fumes or vapors.

Proper hand protection is necessary to prevent possible injury: chemically resistant rubberized gloves for working with chemicals; heavy leather gloves for welding; heat-resistant gloves (not asbestos) for handling heated objects; and regular light leather or cotton work gloves for handling the operating lines of the counterweight system.

When working with noise-producing objects, wear hearing protectors such as noise-abatement earmuffs or earplugs. When working with heavy objects such as metal pipe, tubing, or sheet or when moving or building large stage platforms, you should wear steel-toed shoes or steel shoe caps. When there is any danger of something being dropped from above the stage floor, all personnel should wear protective headgear, such as a plastic helmet that meets or exceeds the minimum federal standards. (American National Standards Institute [ANSI] Type 1 hard hats protect against blows to the top of the head. ANSI Type 2 hats protect against both top of the head and off-center blows. Class E hats are proof-tested to provide electrical protection up to 20,000 volts; Class C hats offer no electrical protection.)

There are a variety of other safety-related issues that need to be addressed in the shop. Most of the following have specific OSHA guidelines that dictate minimum levels of acceptability. Check with appropriate school or city/county authorities to determine if your shop is in compliance. The air in the shop should be run through some type of recirculating filtering system to meet OSHA guidelines for clean air. As mentioned earlier, every power tool that generates wood dust or chips should have some type of collection system, either a vacuum draw or collector bag. There should be an OSHA-approved eye wash station in the shop area. Fire extinguishers should be placed in strategic locations around both the shop and stage. Make sure that they are *always* accessible and fully charged. First-aid kits should be clearly visible in the shop and stage areas. Their contents should be kept up-to-date and fully stocked. Do not place or lean anything in front of, or on, either fire extinguishers or first-aid kits.

Use common sense in the shop. It is filled with equipment and materials that can injure or kill. But if you are careful and abide by commonsense safety practices and OSHA-prescribed safety regulations, it can be a safe and enjoyable work environment.

This chapter has outlined the tools and materials used in the construction of scenery and properties. Chapter 11, "Scenic Production Techniques," will discuss basic techniques of scenic construction, and Chapter 13, "Stage Properties," will take up some of the more specialized techniques and materials — foams, thermoplastics, and fiberglass — used to make stage properties.

Selected References

A.C.T.S. *Arts, Crafts, and Theatre Safety.* http://www.artcraftstheatersafety.org

Bryson, Nicholas L. *Thermoplastic Scenery for the Theatre, Vol. 1: Vacuum Forming.* Drama Book Specialists, 1972.

Rossol, Monona. *Stage Fright: Health and Safety in the Theatre.* Allworth Press: New York, New York, 1991.

Rossol, Monona. *Health and Safety Guide for Film, TV and Theatre.* Allworth Press: New York, New York, 2000.

Rossol, Monona. *The Artist's Complete Health and Safety Guide.* Allworth Press: New York, New York, 3rd ed., 2001.

dust mask: A device covering the nose and mouth that filters particulate matter from the air.

respirator: A mask covering the nose and mouth that filters out gases as well as particulate matter.

Chapter 11

Scenic Production Techniques

Playwrights have set their plays in almost every imaginable environment. Thousands of plays have been set in ordinary living rooms. Thousands more have been set in representational settings like caves, mountain-tops, wheat fields, war zones, and even the gondolas of hot air balloons. Nonrepresentational scenery is often highly imaginative and beautifully evocative of the emotional content of the play. Whether wheat field or moonscape, representational or nonrepresentational, the setting must work as conceived by the scenic designer and director — and it's the technical director's job to see that it does.

Technical production refers to the broad field concerned with taking the design from conception to reality. Specifically, the field encompasses the construction and painting of the scenery and properties, the assembly of the set(s) onstage, the shifting of those sets and props during the production, and the tools that are used to accomplish those tasks. The specific organization and assigned responsibilities vary considerably depending on the type of producing unit.

In the Broadway theatre, personnel are generally hired for a single production. After the producer has approved the construction bids, the designs are constructed and finished by independent professional scenic and property studios. During construction and painting, the scenic designer is in frequent contact with the scene-shop foreman to answer artistic and practical questions about the scenery. When the scenery is completed, it is moved from the studio to the theatre and set up on the stage. This load-in is carried out by union stagehands under the supervision of the production's stage manager. The scenic designer and the stage manager work together to choreograph any scene shifts, and the stage manager is responsible for supervising the work of the union crews that will be shifting the scenery.

The Broadway theatre's single-production concept is the exception rather than the rule in the American theatre. Most theatre in the United States is produced on a limited-run, multiple-production basis by colleges, universities, community theatres, and regional professional theatre groups. Almost all of these theatres produce three or more productions a year. They are almost always working on more than one production at any given time. This situation creates a definite need for some very specific organization to keep all of the production activity flowing smoothly. The primary organizer of the scenery construction is the technical director. If the organization does not have a property master, then the tech director is also in charge of property construction and acquisition. The tech director must be able to effectively organize and manage time, resources, and people to get the scenery and props built on time and within budget.

The technical director's work on scenic and property construction cannot begin until the designer provides plans (ground plan, front elevations, detail

technical production: All organizational and procedural aspects of the construction, painting, and operation of scenery and properties.

FIGURE 11.1
Standard wood joints.
(A) Four types of butt joints
(B) Lap joint
(C) Battened butt joint
(D) Butt joint reinforced with
    a cornerblock
(E) Butt joint reinforced with
    a keystone
(F) Miter joint

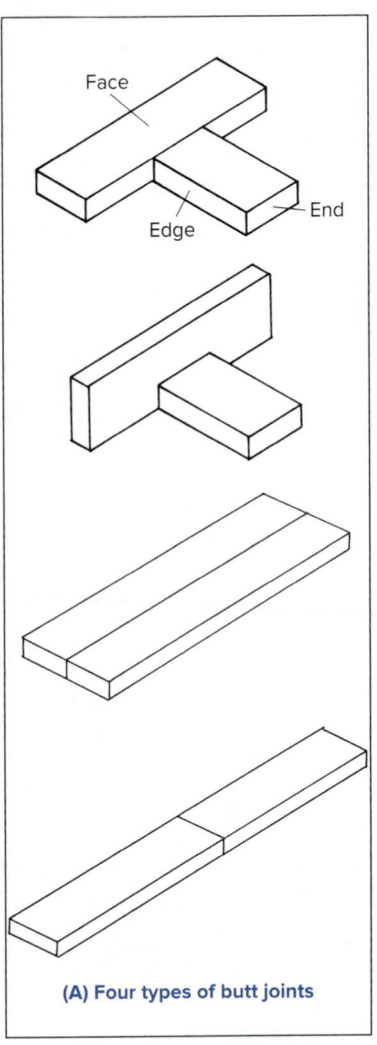

Face

Edge

End

(A) Four types of butt joints

PRODUCTION INSIGHTS
The Production Calendar

The production calendar (see Figure 1.8) helps the technical director and/or production manager keep track of progress on the various productions. It specifies pertinent information (try-outs, design due dates, construction and painting schedules, rehearsals, and performances) for every play being produced by the theatre during the season. It also provides a visual reference that shows at a glance the status of each production. The production manager normally develops the production calendar. If the theatre does not have a production manager, other staff members must absorb that duty. The production calendar is developed in conjunction with the organization's managing/artistic/producing directors with input from any resident technicians, directors, and designers.

sheets, functional models, painter's elevations) for the production. After studying the plans, the technical director or an assistant draws any necessary rear elevations or construction drawings that will facilitate the building of the scenery and props, then orders the construction materials. At this same time, he or she also creates a construction calendar. This calendar specifies the amount of time scheduled for the construction, painting, and assembling of the individual elements of the sets.

Scenic Construction Techniques

Although the overall construction plan, as well as the specific methods used to build each piece of scenery, should be guided by the basic tenets of the design process (see Chapter 2, "The Design Process"), some fairly standardized construction techniques are used to fabricate stage scenery.

Woodworking

Wood is used extensively for building two- and three-dimensional scenery. It is relatively inexpensive and can be worked easily with a variety of the tools described in Chapter 10, "Tools and Materials." Wood joints commonly used in theatre construction are illustrated in Figures 11.1, 11.2, and 11.3.

Three additional types of joints—the open dowel joint, the pocket hole joint, and the biscuit joint—are discussed in Chapter 13, "Stage Properties," because these joints are more commonly used in furniture-making and other property-related construction projects than in typical scenic construction.

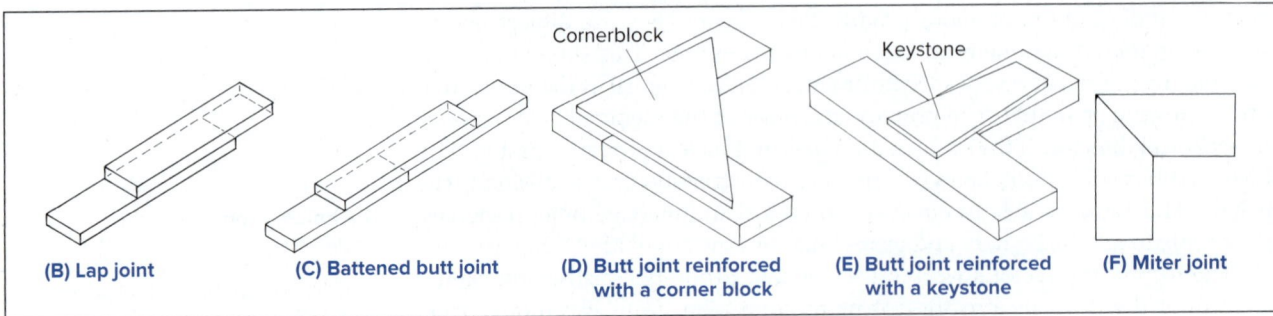

(B) Lap joint   **(C) Battened butt joint**   Cornerblock **(D) Butt joint reinforced with a corner block**   Keystone **(E) Butt joint reinforced with a keystone**   **(F) Miter joint**

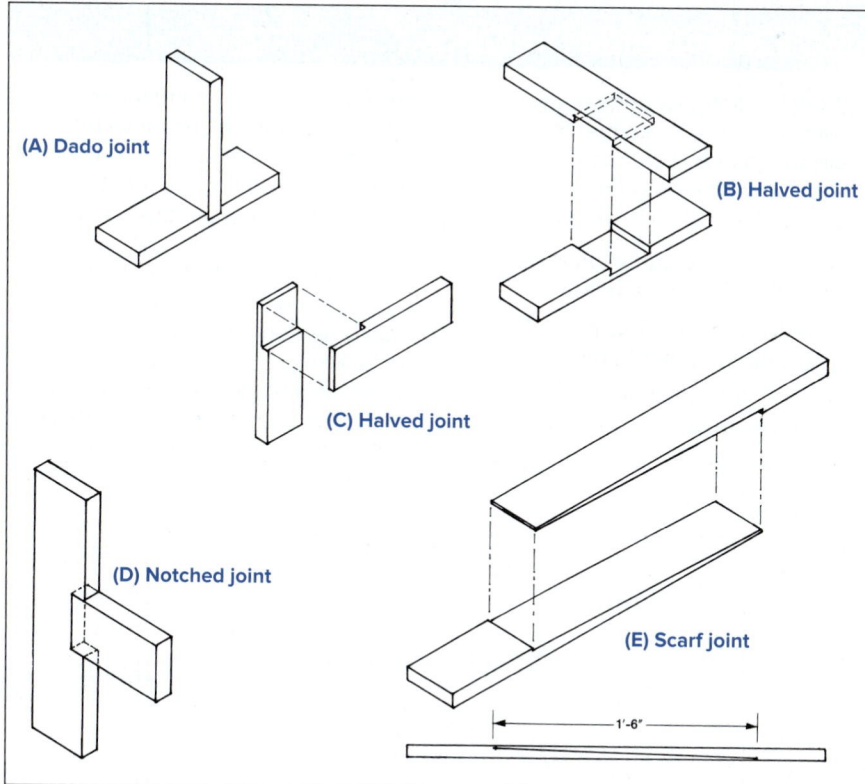

(A) Dado joint

(B) Halved joint

(C) Halved joint

(D) Notched joint

(E) Scarf joint

1'-6"

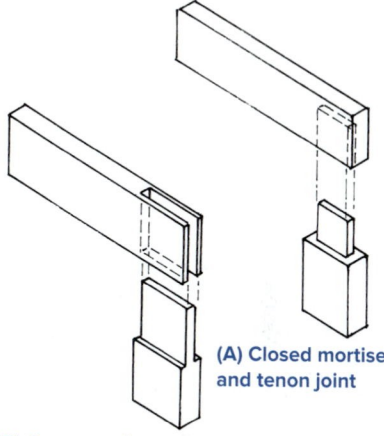

(A) Closed mortise and tenon joint

(B) Open mortise and tenon joint

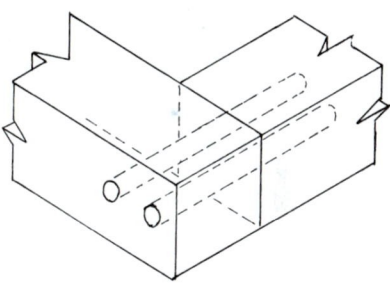

(C) Open doweled joint

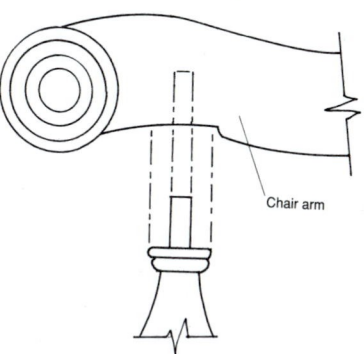

Chair arm

(D) Closed doweled joint

FIGURE 11.2
Specialty wood joints.
(A) Dado joint
(B) Halved joint
(C) Halved joint
(D) Notched joint
(E) Scarf joint

FIGURE 11.3
Internally supported wood joints.
(A) Closed mortise and tenon joint
(B) Open mortise and tenon joint
(C) Open doweled joint
(D) Closed doweled joint

filler rod: Metal piece, of the same composition as material being welded, used to replace the metal lost during the welding process or to fill a hole or groove in the work.

Welding

Welding is the process of fusing metal by heating the pieces being joined to their melting temperature and inducing the metal to flow together before it cools. The **filler rod** is used to replace the lost metal.

Surface Preparation   Before welding, the surface of the metal must be cleaned of any oil, grease, paint, rust, and other contaminants. This is done by

---

PRODUCTION INSIGHTS
Scenic Construction Priorities

It takes a tremendous number of hours to construct the scenery for even a simple production. The following list provides a construction sequence that makes very efficient use of available construction time.

1. Build practical elements of the set that will be needed by the actors in the early rehearsals.

2. Build and hang flying units, including any masking, that either will be flown over the set or will use counterweighted battens hanging above the set.

3. Build anything that will have a complicated or time-consuming paint job.

4. Base the construction schedule for any remaining scenic elements on the complexity of the item. The least complex scenic elements, such as flats, should be built last.

5. Allow some time at the end of the construction sequence for adjustments, repairs, and the inevitable changes that will be made to the set.

PRODUCTION INSIGHTS

Construction Drawings

Construction drawings or rear elevations are scale mechanical drawings that show the back of the flats depicted on the front elevations. These drawings:

1. show the construction details of the framework of the flats.

2. indicate which flats are to be joined to form wall units.

3. show the unusual construction challenges.

In professional scene shops, the foreman is responsible for drawing any rear elevations. In practice very few are drawn, because the carpenters working in these scenic studios are very knowledgeable about construction methods and techniques.

In educational theatres, however, the construction crews are usually students who are just learning how to build scenery. Rear elevations should be drawn to provide the student carpenters with all of the information needed to build the scenery.

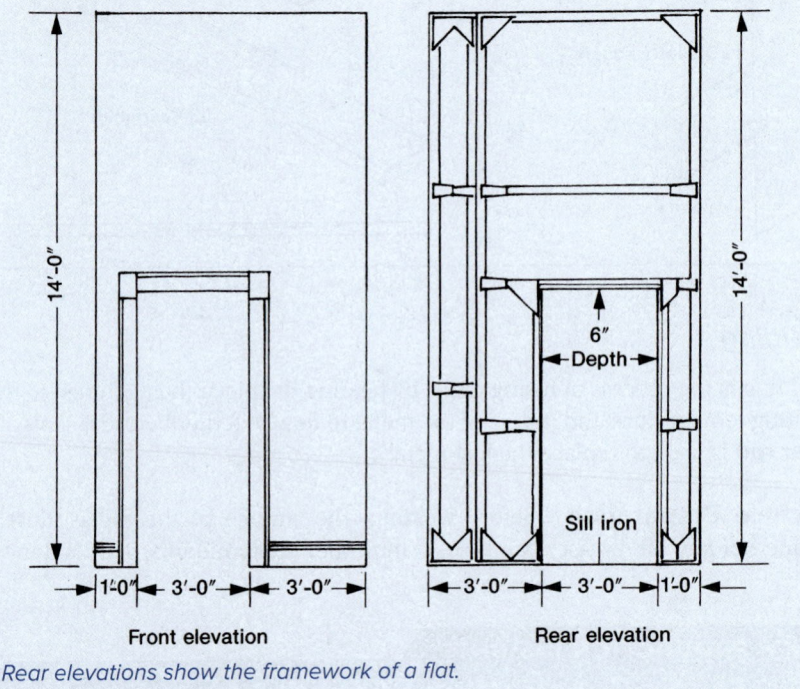

Front elevation   Rear elevation

Rear elevations show the framework of a flat.

polishing the welding zone with a wire brush, sanding, grinding, or cleaning the area with commercial chemical removers.

Welding Techniques   Several welding techniques have been developed to use with the various types of welders.

Oxyacetylene Welding   Oxyacetylene welding employs the **two-handed welding** technique. The welder holds the torch in one hand and the copper-clad filler rod in the other. As the flame melts the pieces being joined, the operator feeds the filler rod into the welding zone. The rod melts, flows into the joint, and replaces the lost metal.

In oxyacetylene welding (Figure 11.4), the strength of the weld depends on a chemically neutral flame. This neutral flame is achieved through a proper mix of the oxygen and acetylene gas. After the torch flame has been lit (using acetylene

two-handed welding: A technique in which the torch or welding handle is held in one hand and the filler rod in the other.

(A)

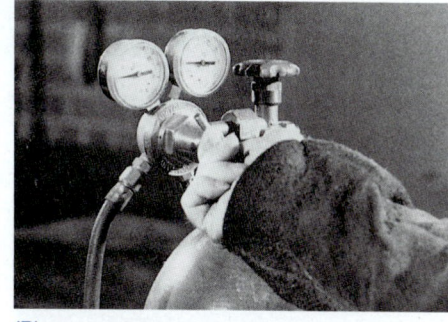

(B)

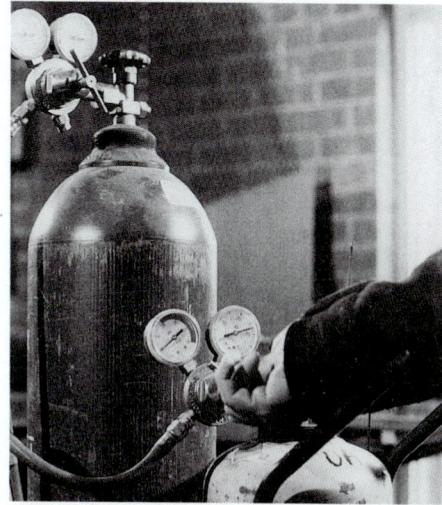

(C)

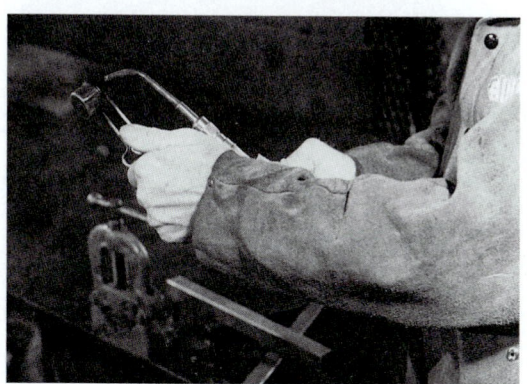

(D)

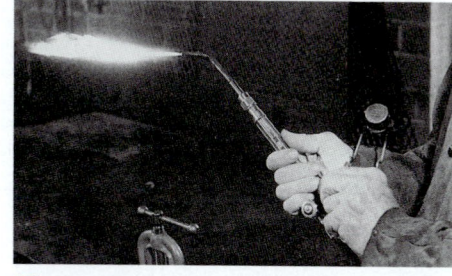

(E)

(F)

(G)

FIGURE 11.4
Oxyacetylene welding technique. For portability the oxygen (tall) and acetylene tanks are normally secured to a rolling cart (A). To light the welding torch, close the valves on the handle of the torch, then turn on the oxygen (B) to approximately 30–35 pounds and the acetylene (C) to 5–7 pounds. (The pressure settings will vary with the composition and thickness of metals.) Open the acetylene valve on the torch handle and light the torch (D). Adjust the acetylene flame until the base of the flame just touches the tip of the torch (E), then slowly open the oxygen valve on the torch and adjust the flame until the small inner cone at the base of the flame is approximately ¼ long (F). Be sure to wear protective clothing and use welding goggles (G) or a welding mask. A–G Courtesy of J. Michael Gillette.

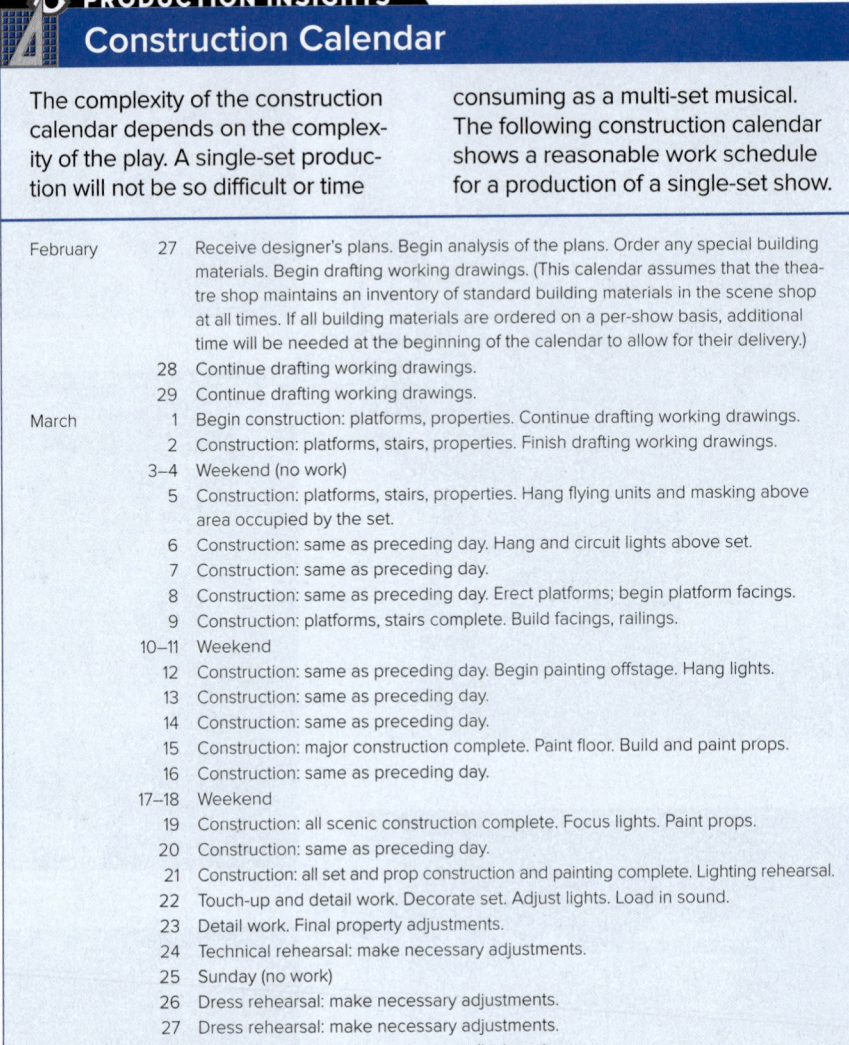

PRODUCTION INSIGHTS
Construction Calendar

The complexity of the construction calendar depends on the complexity of the play. A single-set production will not be so difficult or time consuming as a multi-set musical. The following construction calendar shows a reasonable work schedule for a production of a single-set show.

February	27	Receive designer's plans. Begin analysis of the plans. Order any special building materials. Begin drafting working drawings. (This calendar assumes that the theatre shop maintains an inventory of standard building materials in the scene shop at all times. If all building materials are ordered on a per-show basis, additional time will be needed at the beginning of the calendar to allow for their delivery.)
	28	Continue drafting working drawings.
	29	Continue drafting working drawings.
March	1	Begin construction: platforms, properties. Continue drafting working drawings.
	2	Construction: platforms, stairs, properties. Finish drafting working drawings.
	3–4	Weekend (no work)
	5	Construction: platforms, stairs, properties. Hang flying units and masking above area occupied by the set.
	6	Construction: same as preceding day. Hang and circuit lights above set.
	7	Construction: same as preceding day.
	8	Construction: same as preceding day. Erect platforms; begin platform facings.
	9	Construction: platforms, stairs complete. Build facings, railings.
	10–11	Weekend
	12	Construction: same as preceding day. Begin painting offstage. Hang lights.
	13	Construction: same as preceding day.
	14	Construction: same as preceding day.
	15	Construction: major construction complete. Paint floor. Build and paint props.
	16	Construction: same as preceding day.
	17–18	Weekend
	19	Construction: all scenic construction complete. Focus lights. Paint props.
	20	Construction: same as preceding day.
	21	Construction: all set and prop construction and painting complete. Lighting rehearsal.
	22	Touch-up and detail work. Decorate set. Adjust lights. Load in sound.
	23	Detail work. Final property adjustments.
	24	Technical rehearsal: make necessary adjustments.
	25	Sunday (no work)
	26	Dress rehearsal: make necessary adjustments.
	27	Dress rehearsal: make necessary adjustments.
	28	Dress rehearsal: make necessary adjustments.
	29	Opening of play.

gas only), oxygen is introduced to the mix. When the oxygen is first introduced, a small white cone appears at the base of, and inside, the flame. At first this cone is rather long. Sometimes it is a double cone. As more oxygen is added, the cone gets smaller. A neutral flame is produced when this white cone is short and slightly rounded. An oxidizing flame, which will burn the molten metal, is produced when more oxygen is added to a neutral flame.

A cutting torch (see Chapter 10, "Tools and Materials") is equipped with a lever-actuated valve that introduces additional oxygen to the flame, creating an oxidizing flame. The flame burns the metal, producing the cut.

Arc Welding   The arc welder utilizes electricity to generate an **arc** that has a temperature of approximately 13,000°F. This extremely high heat almost instantaneously melts most common metals.

To use an arc welder, first attach the ground cable from the welder to the work. This effectively turns the work into a ground for the electrode. When a flux-coated **welding rod,** which is connected to the power side of the welding machine, comes into close proximity with the work, an arc is formed across the

arc: An electric current that leaps the gap between two closely placed electrodes.

welding rod: A rod, usually covered with flux, that serves as the positive electrode in arc welding.

Safety Tip

The Scene Shop

Any workplace that uses electricity, flammable and toxic materials, and tools capable of cutting, gouging, and sawing is an inherently dangerous environment. With a healthy dose of common sense and a few safety rules, however, working in the scene shop can be safe, efficient, and enjoyable.

1. Wear clothing suited to the work: long pants, short- or long-sleeve shirt, and hard-toe, hard-sole shoes (not sandals or sneakers). Clothing should be reasonably close fitting. Don't wear flowing robes — they might get caught in power equipment.

2. Tie back, put under a cap, or otherwise contain long hair so that it won't get caught in a power tool. For the same reasons, don't wear jewelry.

3. Always get instructions before operating any power or hand tool. Be sure you know what you're doing before you do it.

4. Pay attention to what you are doing. Don't operate any tool unless you are giving it your undivided attention. Watch your work area for potential hazards such as wood with protruding nails and potential fire or electrical hazards. Either correct the hazard (if you know how) or report it to your supervisor.

5. Keep your work space clean. If the shop is kept neat, clean, and organized, accidents are reduced and you can find the tools and supplies you need.

6. Know where the first-aid materials are kept. Disinfect all cuts and splinters, and bandage even minor cuts. Report all accidents to your supervisor.

7. When working with materials that emit dust or fumes, make sure that the work area is well ventilated and that you wear an appropriate mask.

Safety Tip

Guidelines for Welding

According to OSHA guidelines, welders shall be required to wear (1) non-flammable gloves with gauntlets, (2) shoes, boots, or leggings, (3) leather aprons, (4) shirts with sleeves and collars, (5) face shields or helmets suitable for head protection, (6) suitable eye protection, and (7) respiratory protection.

The necessity to protect your body from the sparks of molten metal is obvious. What isn't so obvious is the necessity to protect your eyes and respiratory system.

Gas and arc welding generate differing levels of visible and ultraviolet light. Ultraviolet (UV) light can cause temporary and/or permanent diminution or loss of sight. Be sure to wear the type of protective lens appropriate to the type of welding in which you're engaged. If you aren't sure whether your eye protection is correct for the type of welding you're doing, don't weld.

Various metal compositions and/or finishes, such as the silvery coating used to galvanize steel, emit noxious or toxic gases when heated or burned. High-volume ventilation and the use of an appropriate respirator will eliminate this health risk. OSHA regulations state that there must be a 100-CFM (cubic feet per minute) airflow in a welder's breathing zone or that an appropriate respirator must be worn. Whenever you weld, be sure you have adequate ventilation.

single-hand welding: A technique in which one hand holds the welding handle and the other hand is not used.

oxidation: A chemical reaction between the metal and air that forms a very thin, discolored "skin" over the metal; this skin effectively prevents heat transfer and reduces the strength and conductivity of the joint.

gap. The arc melts the metal, and the weld is made. The electrode, which also acts as a filler rod, is consumed in the welding process. Because the welding handle is held with only one hand, the process is referred to as **single-hand welding.**

The MIG (metal inert gas) welder (discussed in Chapter 10, "Tools and Materials") is another singlehand arc welder. It differs from the arc welder in that a thin, flexible wire electrode is automatically fed through the handle to the welding zone from a spool stored in the power unit. The welding handle also focuses a flow of inert gas — normally carbon dioxide or argon — on the welding zone as the weld is being made (Figure 11.5). The inert gas reduces **oxidation,** which can

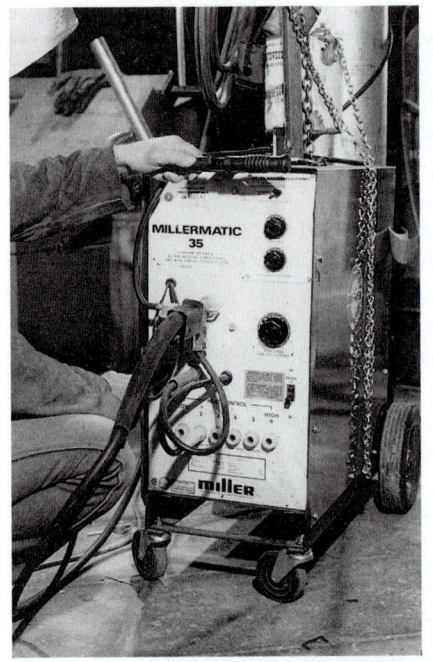

(A)

(B)

FIGURE 11.5
MIG (metal inert gas) welding technique. (A) Adjust the power setting of the welder to suit the composition and thickness of the metal being welded (consult the welding machine's instruction book). (B) Attach the ground cable to the welding table or the work. (C) Turn on the gas (carbon dioxide or argon) to 5–9 pounds (consult the welder's instruction book for appropriate setting for your specific equipment). (D) Bring the welding wire close to the welding zone, press the trigger, and weld. Be sure to wear appropriate safety equipment and clothing. A–D Courtesy of J. Michael Gillette.

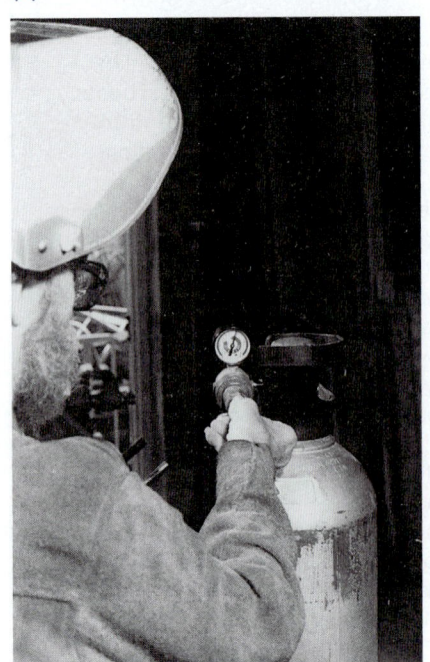

(C)

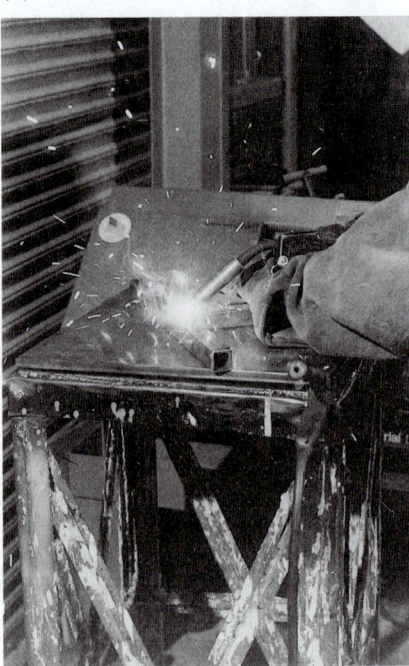

(D)

substantially weaken the weld. A flux coating for the wired electrode isn't necessary as the inert gas performs the same oxygen-reducing function as the flux. The MIG welder can also be used without the inert gas if you use substitute a flux-cored welding wire for the solid wire electrode. However, you'll always get a cleaner, better quality weld when using solid welding wire and inert shielding gas.

Whether equipped with either the flux-cored or solid welding wire and inert gas, the MIG welder does an excellent job of welding steel. It can be used for welding aluminum if aluminum wire and argon gas are used.

In practice, the MIG welder is generally acknowledged to be easier to use than an arc welder. It is probably the easiest welder on which to learn how to weld, because the electrode is automatically fed to the welding zone and, if shielding gas is used, the MIG yields a substantially better weld than either the arc or oxyacetylene welders.

The TIG (tungsten inert gas) welder uses a nonconsumable tungsten rod as the electrode and requires a two-handed welding technique. A filler rod of the same composition as the materials being welded is held in the other hand and fed into the welding zone as the weld is being made.

Types of Welds   Common welding joints are described next and illustrated in Figure 11.6.

Butt Weld   The butt weld (Figure 11.6A) is probably the most common, and strongest, type.

Flange Weld   A flange weld is similar to a butt weld, except the edges of the material being joined are bent up, as shown in Figure 11.6B.

Lap Weld   A lap weld is made when two pieces are overlapped, as shown in Figure 11.6C.

Fillet Weld   A fillet weld (Figure 11.6D) is made when the edge of one piece is joined to the face of another.

Soldering

Soldering is the process of heating metal (usually lightweight steel, copper, or brass) until it is hot enough to melt **solder.** The solder flows over the surface of the metal and bonds the pieces together. For an effective soldering bond to be made, there must be a good mechanical connection between the parts being soldered. The parts must be clean and free of grease, oxidation, and other contaminants.

Soldering flux is applied to further clean the metal and prevent oxidation when the joint is heated. Flux is manufactured in solid, powder, paste, and liquid forms. The type of flux used depends on the project. Rosin flux is noncorrosive and should be used on all electrical work. Soldering wire with a rosin-flux core can be purchased at almost any hardware store. Acid fluxes are very effective,

solder: A metal alloy of lead and tin.

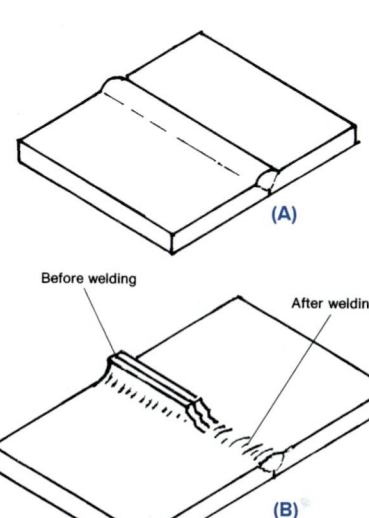

Before welding

After welding

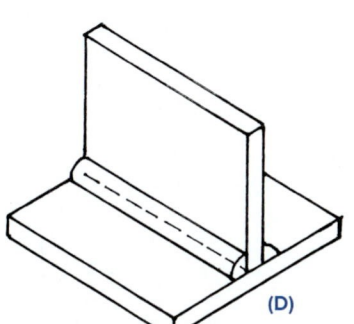

Strength of Welds

The strength of any weight-bearing welded structure depends on the strength of its welds. Before attempting to construct any metal platforming or other structures on which actors are going to stand, be sure to practice enough so that you are sure you are producing high-quality welds. Have your work checked by an instructor so that you know your welds will be strong.

FIGURE 11.6
Types of welded joints.
(A) Butt weld
(B) Flange weld
(C) Lap weld
(D) Fillet weld

PRODUCTION INSIGHTS

Making a Good Solder Joint

A good solder joint can be made only if you heat the work to the melting point of the solder. If the work is not heated sufficiently and the solder is melted by touching it to the soldering iron, the solder will just sit on top of the work rather than bonding with its surface. This produces what is known as a "cold" solder joint. A cold solder joint isn't very strong, and it doesn't conduct electricity very well. Cold solder joints can be identified by their appearance. The solder looks dull, whereas a good solder joint will be shiny. A cold solder joint can generally be fixed by adding a little flux to the joint and reheating the work until it is sufficiently hot to make the solder flow freely.

but the acid is corrosive, so the work must be washed with warm water to prevent corrosion. Be sure to wait for the solder joint to cool before you wash it.

If you aren't using a soldering wire with a flux core, it will be necessary to apply flux to the joint before it is heated. After the joint has been fluxed, heat is applied to the work. The solder should be melted by touching it to the work, not the iron. The melted solder should freely flow over and through the joint where the hot solder bonds with the surface of the metal and fuses the joint together.

CNC Manufacturing

As the cost of CNC machining, rapid prototyping, and other computer-controlled manufacturing tools has dropped, these tools have become more common in theatrical scenery shops, from academic institutions to large commercial shops. Laser cutters, CNC routers, millers, lathes, and 3-D printers are becoming more ubiquitous. These tools were described in Chapter 10, "Tools and Materials."

In CNC manufacturing, a model or representation of an object is made in CAD software. That CAD drawing is imported into CAM (computer-aided manufacturing) software, which determines the machine's tool paths — how the tools and material move around the workspace. Some CAM software does this transparently, with little or no need for the user/programmer to worry about specifics; other software requires the user to determine factors such as tool speed, movement speed, depth, and so forth. Once this work is completed, the tool paths CAM file is exported to control the machine and create the object.

It is easy to see how access to CNC manufacturing can be a game changer for theatrical production. Consider how easy it would be to build a scale model of a stage and set if you had a laser cutter that would cut all of the model pieces. Many theatres currently use CNC routers to cut sheet goods — plywood, MDF, and so forth — into furniture or scenic units (in the "flat-pack" style of inexpensive furniture) or to carve intricate designs into materials like polystyrene foam. In some prop shops, 3-D printing is now used to create masters for molds. The possibilities — both in the present and the future — are exciting and extensive.

 ## Two-Dimensional Scenery

Two-dimensional scenery can be divided into two basic subgroups: hard scenery and soft scenery. Hard scenery generally refers to flats, and soft scenery to unframed units such as drops and draperies.

Flats

Nothing stays the same forever. Flats provide a prime example of this phenomenon. For more than two hundred years fabric-covered wooden-framed flats were the standard construction technique for making scenic walls. In recent years several trends have converged to reduce the dominance, and usefulness, of this type of flat.

Perhaps the most important reason that soft flats have fallen into semi-disfavor is that contemporary scene designs tend to be more sculptural than pictorial. Soft flats worked well when designs attempted to re-create the look of a drawing room interior with its large expanse of walls. When there aren't large expanses of wall on a set, the need for soft flats is reduced. The walls that remain in a sculptural scenic design are frequently treated with some type of 3-D coating to simulate stone, brick, or whatever. If applied to fabric-covered flats these coatings, if they adhere at all, will frequently flake off if the scenery is moved or cause the fabric to sag and pull out of shape. Either of these situations generally ruins the desired effect. Sculpturally applied coatings need the base support of a hard, solid surface — hard-covered flats.

The increased use of **scenery automation** and other methods to shift scenery in front of the audience have also added to the fading away of soft-covered flats. If the scenery, which is supposed to be the stone wall of a castle, glides onto the stage and twirls around, the illusion would be totally destroyed if the "stone walls" flap and wiggle as they are moving. Those walls need to be hard-covered simply so they will be firm and solid — so they'll look like what they're supposed to be.

For these and several other reasons, most contemporary flats are made for specific applications, are not reused, and are generally hard- rather than fabric-covered. These techniques, as well as wooden-framed construction, will be discussed next.

There are three types or styles of flats: soft, or soft-covered; hard, or hard-covered; and studio, also called Hollywood or face-on-edge flats. Each type has its own general characteristics and will be discussed in the following section.

Regardless of the type or style of flat, the various pieces that make up the framework of a flat have specific names, as shown in Figure 11.7. The top and bottom horizontal members are called **rails,** the outside vertical elements are called **stiles,** and the interior horizontal members are referred to as **toggle bars. Corner braces** are located in the upper and lower corners of the same side of any flat over 3 feet wide.

The toggle bars are used to keep the stiles parallel on a soft-covered flat and to provide support and attaching points for the facing material on a hardcover flat. On fabric-covered flats if toggle bars were not used, fabric shrinkage (caused when the flat is painted) would cause the stiles to twist and bow in toward each other. Toggles should be spaced approximately 3 to 4 feet from the nearest toggle bar or rail.

Individual flats normally are not constructed wider than 6 feet because anything wider is awkward to handle. Flats less than 2 feet wide are generally referred to as **jogs,** and jogs less than 1 foot wide are normally made from solid stock rather than fabric-covered framework. The solid jog is covered with the same fabric so that when it is included in a wall, which is normally made up of several flats and jogs, all elements of the wall will look the same when they are painted.

Soft Flats   Soft, or soft-covered, flats generally refer to wooden-framed flats covered with some type of fabric. Soft flats can be designed to be almost any size or shape, but the vast majority resemble tall rectangles from 1 to 6 feet wide and

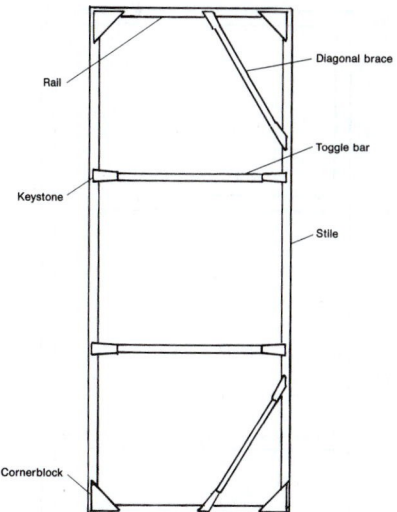

FIGURE 11.7
The parts of a flat.

scenery automation: The use of computer-controlled, motorized devices to shift scenery, almost always in view of the audience.

rail: A top or bottom framing member of a flat.

stile: A vertical side member of a flat.

toggle bar: An interior horizontal framing member of a flat.

corner brace: A diagonal internal framing member that helps keep a flat square.

jog: A flat less than 2 feet wide.

FIGURE 11.8
Positioning of butt joints on a flat.

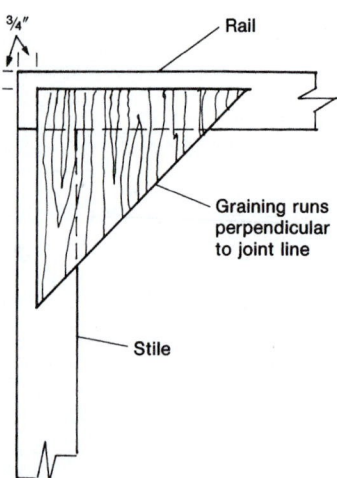

FIGURE 11.9
The placement of cornerblocks on a flat.

rip: To saw parallel with the grain. Ripping is generally done with a table saw.

PRODUCTION INSIGHTS
Keystones and Cornerblocks

Keystones and cornerblocks are used as reinforcement for the butt joints commonly used in flat construction.

The *cornerblock* is a triangle of ¼-inch AD plywood with 8- to 10-inch legs. To provide effective reinforcement, position the cornerblock so that its grain runs perpendicular to the joint between the rail and the stile.

Also made of ¼-inch AD plywood, the *keystone* is 6 inches long and shaped like a keystone of an arch. The small end is slightly narrower (½ inch) than the width of the toggle bar that it is covering; the wide end is approximately ½ inch wider than the toggle bar.

Some technicians prefer rectangular strips of plywood, called straps, to keystones. These straps should be cut approximately ½ inch narrower than the width of the toggle bar. Both keystones and rectangular straps provide about the same amount of bracing for the joint, but many technicians think that keystones are prettier, so they continue to use them in preference to the plywood straps.

8 to 16 feet high. The wooden framework for a flat up to 14 feet tall is usually made of 1 × 3 white pine ("B or better" or "C select"). Because of the cost, and frequent nonavailability, of "B or better" or "C select" 1 × 3 white pine, many scene shops now use 1 × 4 pine, or its locally available equivalent, even if it has a few tight knots. The significant factor of whether to use 1 × 3 or 1 × 4 is the quality of the wood. Lumber used to build wooden flats needs to be straight, free from warps or twists, relatively lightweight, and it should have few knots. If it has knots, they need to be small enough so that they don't interfere with the strength of the wood. Many shops will buy higher quality 1 × 6s or 1 × 12s and **rip** them into 1 × 3s or 1 × 4s. This is generally less expensive than purchasing individual 1 × 3s or 1 × 4s. Generally, flat frames over 14 feet tall are built from welded metal tubing rather than wood.

The general structure of a wood-framed flat is illustrated in Figure 11.8. The rails extend the full width of the flat. The stiles are inset inside the rails so their total length equals the full height of the flat minus the combined width of both rails. The toggle bars — which are normally evenly spaced 3 to 5 feet from adjacent toggle bars or rails — are placed inside the stiles so their overall length equals the width of the flat minus the combined widths of both stiles.

The butt joints of a wooden-framed flat are reinforced with cornerblocks and keystones. On fabric-covered flats the cornerblocks — used to reinforce the outside corners of the frame — are inset ¾ inch from the outside edge of the frame as illustrated in Figure 11.9. The keystones, Figure 11.10, are similarly inset from the outside edge of the frame by ¾ inch. The reason that they are inset ¾ inch is so that the ¼-inch thickness of the cornerblock, or keystone, won't interfere with a smooth, or flush, joint between the edges of the flat when they are placed at 90 degrees to each other when forming a wall unit.

Both keystones and cornerblocks are typically attached using pneumatic glue-coated staples or power-driven screws.

When the flat is wider than 3 feet, diagonal corner braces made of 1 × 2 are placed in the upper and lower corners of the same side of the flat. These are secured with plywood straps ripped in half and angle cut so they can be inset ¾ inch from the outside of the flat as illustrated in Figure 11.11.

Detailed information on how to build, and cover, a standard soft flat with muslin is contained in Appendix B.

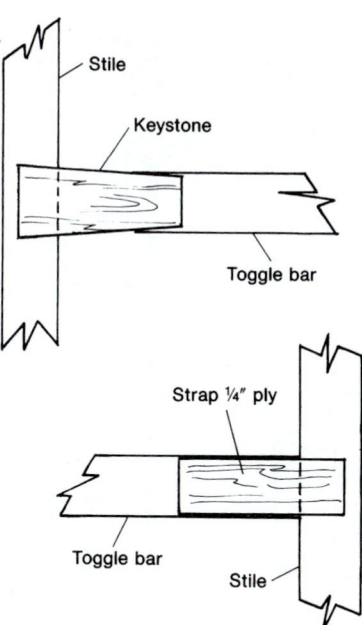

FIGURE 11.10
The placement of keystones on a flat.

Hard-covered Flats   Hard-covered flats are simply traditional wooden flat frames covered with a hard material such as plywood, hardboard, or other hard covering material.

Generally the "hard cover" material is ¼ inch thick although other thicknesses can be used as necessity, budget, or availability dictates. Many technicians have discovered that ¼-inch lauan plywood seems to warp less than the more common AD plywood. The wooden structure of a hard flat is the same as its fabric-covered cousin. The only significant difference is that the keystones and cornerblocks are inset 1 inch to account for the increased thickness of the covering material.

The covering material is generally attached to the frame using pneumatic glue-coated staples or power-driven screws spaced around the outside edge of the frame, and across each toggle bar, on 12- to **18-inch centers.** If the flat cannot be covered with one sheet of material, a toggle bar needs to be centered behind any joints in the covering material so both edges of the covering sheets can be secured to the flat. To ensure a smooth surface for finishing – either paint, fabric, wallpaper, or sculptural coating – many technicians like to fill any joints between covering sheets or indentions caused by the staples or screws with some form of **spackle or spackling.**

Metal-frame Flats   Many production companies now routinely make their flat frames from metal rather than wood. There are two linked reasons for this: quality and cost. As previously discussed, the quality of wood needed to make traditional flats has become increasingly expensive. In most locations it now simply costs less to make a metal-framed flat than a similarly sized wooden one. Case closed.

Metal-frame flats employ the same structural design as traditional wooden flats. The rails extend to the full width of the flat, the stiles are the full height minus the combined width of the rails, and the toggle bars are inset inside the rails. The use of diagonal braces follows the same general guidelines as wooden flats – any flat wider than 3 feet requires the use of diagonal braces.

Typically metal-frame flats will be made from 1×1 metal tubing, although the structural needs of the individual flat may dictate the use of some other dimension of tubing or angle iron.

Each tubing butt joint – rails to stiles, stiles to toggle bars, and so forth – should be welded on at least two or three sides. Normally the face of the flat frame is not welded. If, however, a weld is made on the face of the flat, it should be ground flat so the covering material will smoothly mate with the metal surface of the frame.

It is almost impossible to "soft-cover" a metal-frame flat with fabric. Typically metal-frame flats are covered with lauan plywood or "regular" AD plywood (see the previous discussion of hard-covering materials). The covering material is normally

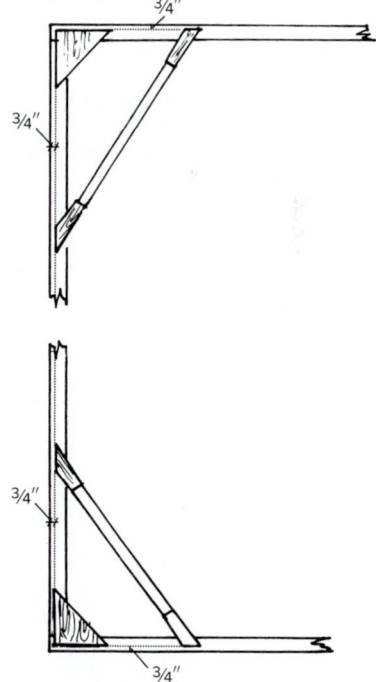

FIGURE 11.11
The placement of reinforcement for diagonal braces on a flat. Be sure that all cornerblocks, keystones, and straps are placed with their outside edges ¾" from the outside edge of the flat.

18-inch centers: Spaced 18 inches apart.

spackle: A plaster-like paste used to fill holes and cracks in walls.

spackling: A paste used to fill small holes in walls.

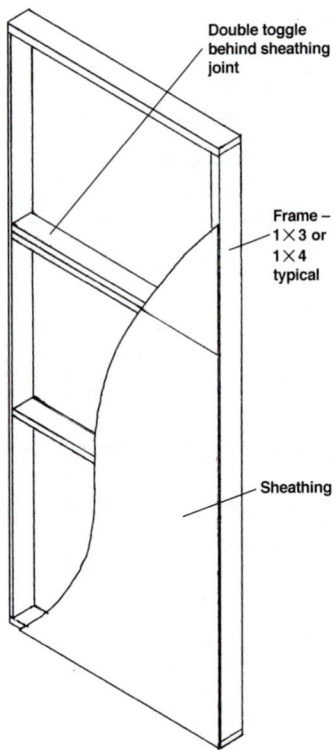

Double toggle behind sheathing joint

Frame – 1×3 or 1×4 typical

Sheathing

FIGURE 11.12
Studio flat. Constructed of 1 × 4 placed on edge and covered with hard material such as plywood. See text for details.

Flat-Covering Fabrics

A variety of fabrics can be used to cover flats. Remember that they need to be certified flame retardant.

Unbleached Muslin

Heavyweight unbleached muslin is an excellent, low-cost flat-covering material. It is available in a variety of widths — 72, 81, 90, and 108 inches and 33 feet. The narrower widths are used for flat covering, and the 33-foot material is usually used for making seamless drops and cycloramas.

This type of muslin, which is available from scenic supply houses, has a high-thread count — 128 or 140 threads to the inch — which gives sufficient strength for flat covering and most other scenic uses. Muslin accepts all scenic paints well and has a uniform shrinkage rate.

Although bleached muslin is available in fabric stores, it isn't particularly useful for scenic purposes, because the bleaching process weakens its fibers, it normally isn't available in sizes wider than 48 inches, and it is more expensive.

Linen Canvas

Linen canvas is an excellent flat-covering material, because it is extremely durable and has a coarse weave similar to artist's canvas. The fabric is 69 to 72 inches wide and weighs 12 to 16 ounces per square yard. It accepts paint well and doesn't shrink much. Unfortunately, it is also the most expensive of the flat-covering materials, is not always available, and can be purchased only from scenic or fabric supply houses.

Cotton Canvas

Cotton canvas is an excellent substitute for linen canvas, because it has many of the same properties, is approximately the same weight (9 to 16 ounces), is readily available, and is much less expensive. It is the preferred type of canvas for making platform covers and ground cloths.

Cotton canvas is available in widths up to 72 inches, is sometimes available from tent and awning suppliers, and can also be purchased from scenic or fabric supply houses.

Cotton Duck

Cotton duck is a lighter weight — 5- to 8-ounce — cotton canvas. It has the same properties as cotton canvas and is generally available locally, although it may be difficult to find in sizes wide enough for stage purposes (generally 69 inches or wider). It is available from local fabric stores, tent and awning suppliers, and scenic-fabric supply houses.

---

attached using **construction adhesive** and/or power-driven flat-head TEK screws or T-nails driven by a pneumatically powered T-nail gun. The screws or nails are typically spaced 12 to 18 inches apart. They are normally driven into the covering material so the top of the screw head or nail is flush with the surface of the covering material. The resulting "ding" is then patched with spackling to create a uniformly smooth surface. The finish covering for metal-framed hard flats follows the guidelines outlined for wood-framed hard flats, which is provide earlier.

Studio Flats Studio flats, also called Hollywood- or Broadway-style, or "on edge" flats, are wood-framed flats similar in structure to hard flats with one major exception: the framing material, usually 1 × 3 or 1 × 4, is placed "on edge" rather than flat, as illustrated in Figure 11.12. The studio flat is then covered with hard material such as ¼-inch lauan plywood and attached using pneumatically driven, narrow-crown staples on 12- to 18-inch centers. Lauan

construction adhesive: Also called panel adhesive, an adhesive contained in a caulking tube; dispensed with a caulking gun. Available in a number of formulations for use in gluing wall panels to studs (wood to wood), Styrofoam to wood, wood to metal, and so forth.

There are several effective methods of gluing covering fabric to flats.

Paint

Probably the easiest method of gluing muslin to a flat frame is with casein, acrylic, or latex paint. When using paint, either select white paint (which is close to the color of muslin) or mix a color that closely approximates the prime coat that you will be using to paint the set. Simply paint the stiles and rails with the paint, apply a very light coat of paint to the underside of the fabric flap, flop the fabric back onto the wood, and smooth it out. The binders in the paint will glue the fabric to the wood. This method works well if the flat is going to be used for a single production, as the binders in the paint are not strong enough to permanently bond the fabric to the flat. If the flat is going to be reused, one of the following glues would be more appropriate.

White Glue and Water

A mixture of two parts of white glue thinned with one part of water makes a good muslin glue. Take care to use a light coat of glue, because if the white glue bleeds through to the surface of the fabric, it can leave a glaze coat that may discolor any subsequent coats of paint.

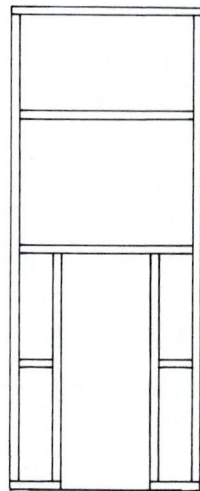

FIGURE 11.13
Standard door flats.

FIGURE 11.14
Standard window flats.

plywood is lightweight, relatively rigid, and takes paint reasonably well. Alternative covering materials such as plywood, **drywall,** or hardboard can be used for special needs and attached with narrow-crown staples or drywall screws driven flush with the surface. Any surface imperfections are normally covered with spackling. If the flat cannot be covered with one sheet of material, a doubled toggle bar or stile — two toggles/stiles, placed on edge and nailed/screwed together — needs to be centered behind any joints in the covering material so both edges of the covering sheets can be secured to the flat.

In a studio flat the wood is placed "on edge" rather than flat for one simple reason: strength. To illustrate: If you pick up the end of a 10- or 12-foot 1 × 4, you'll notice that the board flexes and bounces up and down quite freely because the movement is being countered only by the ¾ inch thickness of the plank. But if you turn the board on edge and wiggle it again it barely flexes up and down. This is because the wood countering the up-and-down movement is now 3½ inches, rather than ¾ inch, thick. For this reason the wooden frame of a soft flat is designed so the 3½-inch width of the lumber counters the inward pull created by the shrinkage of the covering fabric. But the covering material of hard-covered flats doesn't flex in that direction. They only flex perpendicular to the material's thickness. Therefore, the wood in a studio flat frame is placed on edge to counter any flexing of the covering material.

When several studio flats are used to form a wall unit, bolts and nuts normally are used to join them. Holes are drilled approximately one-quarter of the distance down from the top and up from the bottom of the stiles of adjacent flats, then bolts are inserted and nuts are used to snug the units together. Alternatively, the individual studio flats can be clamped together with C-clamps.

Door and Window Flats All wooden and metal-framed flats can be constructed and covered using the general principles previously listed. The stiles of all flats (regular, irregular, door, window) are always placed inside their respective rails to prevent splintering of the stiles (if wood is used). The sizes of any interior openings in the flats (doors, windows, and so forth) are determined by the position of the toggle bars and door or window stiles, as shown in Figures 11.13 and 11.14.

drywall: Gypsum board typically used to cover interior walls in home construction. Normally ½ inch thick although other thicknesses are available.

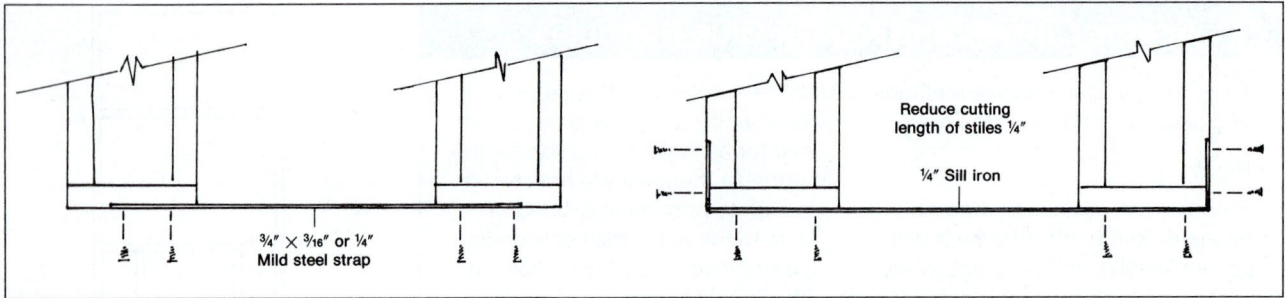

FIGURE 11.15
A sill iron is used to replace the bottom rail that is cut out when constructing a door flat.

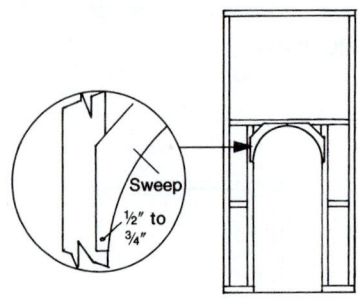

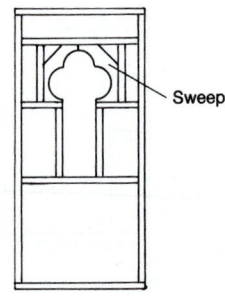

FIGURE 11.16
Sweeps are used to create irregularly shaped openings in door and window flats.

sill iron: A strap of mild steel attached to the bottom of a door flat to brace it where the rail has been cut out.

sweep: A wooden curvilinear form, generally used to outline an arch or irregular form in door- and window-flat openings.

Door flats have one construction variation. The bottom rail across the door opening of a wooden framed flat is removed and replaced with a **sill iron,** which is a mild-steel strap ³⁄₁₆ or ¼ inch thick and ¾ inch wide, as shown in Figure 11.15. The sill iron should extend at least 1 foot beyond either side of the doorway. For maximum strength, the sill iron should run to the outer edges of the door flat, bend at right angles, and run up the outside edge of the stiles a minimum of 6 to 8 inches. With either method, a thin strip of wood the thickness of the sill iron needs to be removed from the bottom of the rail and/or the outside edge of the stile to maintain the overall height and width of the flat. The sill iron is attached with 1- or 1¼-inch No. 8 or 9 flat-head screws or yellow zinc drywall screws. On metal-framed door flats, unless the door opening is quite wide, the sill iron isn't needed.

Arches and irregular openings in flats are made by insetting **sweeps** in regular door and window openings, as shown in Figure 11.16. Sweeps can be made from ¾-inch stock or plywood. Stock is preferable, because it will better hold the nails driven into its edge to support the depth pieces, also known as reveals. Sweeps that are used to create arches in either doors or windows should be notched into the door or window stiles approximately ½ to ¾ inch. If they aren't, the end of the sweep will have to be cut to a feather edge, and the chances of breaking that slivered end will be very good.

Trim enhances the realistic appearance of a door or window flat. Depth pieces create the illusion that the flat has actual thickness. Straight-line depth pieces can be made from lauan plywood, 1 × 6 stock, ¼-inch hardboard, or similarly rigid material, as shown in Figure 11.17; curved depth pieces can be made

---

PRODUCTION INSIGHTS

Standard Door Dimensions

Although the appearance of any door is the province of the scenic designer, certain dimensions and characteristics of doors are fairly standard.

1. Doors that people will pass through need to be at least 2 feet 6 inches wide. Set doors normally vary in width from 2½ to 3½ feet, depending on the height and style of the door. Closet doors are often narrower. Double doors are usually 5 to 7 feet wide.

2. "Normal" standard door heights vary between 6 feet 9 inches and 7 feet 6 inches.

3. Doorknobs are generally placed about 3 feet above the floor, although certain European styles place the doorknob closer to 4 feet.

4. Doors normally swing offstage. They are usually hinged on the upstage side of the doorway unless other needs (stage business, architectural faithfulness) dictate that the door be hung in some other manner.

from ⅛-inch Easy Curve, ³⁄₁₆-inch Upson board, or ⅛-inch hardboard. The actual depth of the door or window depends entirely on the style and architectural period chosen by the scenic designer. The appearance of the window or door is similarly dependent on its architectural model.

There are two types of stage windows and doors: dependent and independent. The basic difference between the two is that the dependent unit is fixed to the flat, whereas the independent unit is largely self-contained and can easily be attached to or removed from the flat. Figure 11.18 shows exploded views of dependent doors and windows, and Figure 11.19 shows similar illustrations of independent doors and windows.

There isn't really a single, "correct" way to build either stage doors or windows. The appearance and function of doors and windows are determined by the scenic designer, and their appearance largely determines how they need to be built.

It is fairly standard practice to design doors to pivot on their upstage side and swing offstage (Figure 11.20), because, with this arrangement, they are self-masking. Self-masking doors block the spectators' view of the backstage area, they don't mask the actors' entrances, and they don't cut off the spectators' view of any part of the set. Because doors usually swing offstage, the spectators normally see only one side of them. Doors have to be hard-covered so they look and sound "real." They are frequently constructed as **double-sided,** lauan-covered, hard flats with a 1 × 4 stile (laying flat) on the side with the knob, and 1 × 2s — also laying flat — for the other stile and the rails and togglebars. Decorative trim can be added to the on-stage face of the door (Figure 11.21). If both sides will be seen, trim should be added to the off-stage side as well.

Joining Flats   Up to this point, the discussion has been confined to constructing individual flats no more than 6 feet wide. But most designs call for walls that are considerably wider. Individual flats are joined to construct larger

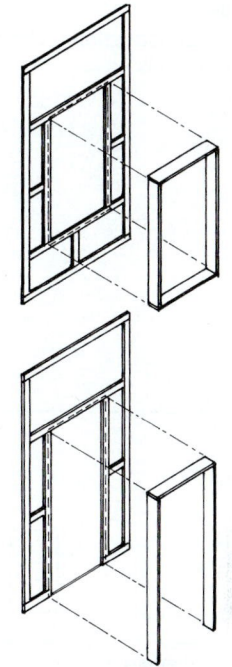

FIGURE 11.17
Depth pieces, or reveals, help create the illusion of wall thickness.

double-sided: Covered on both sides.

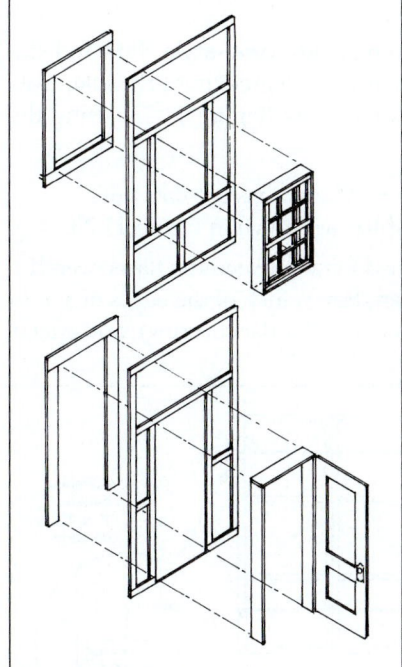

FIGURE 11.18
Dependent doors and windows.

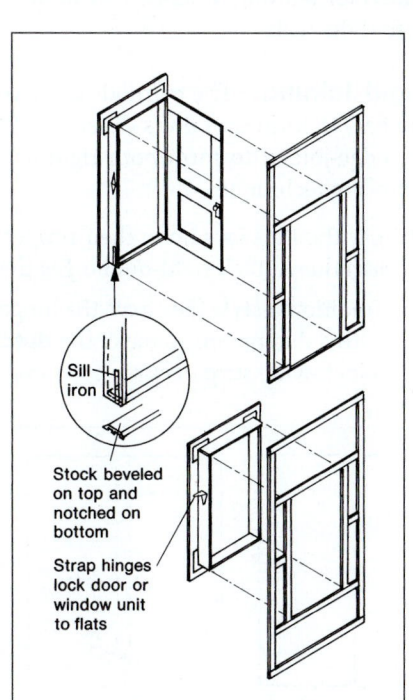

Sill iron

Stock beveled on top and notched on bottom

Strap hinges lock door or window unit to flats

FIGURE 11.19
Independent doors and windows.

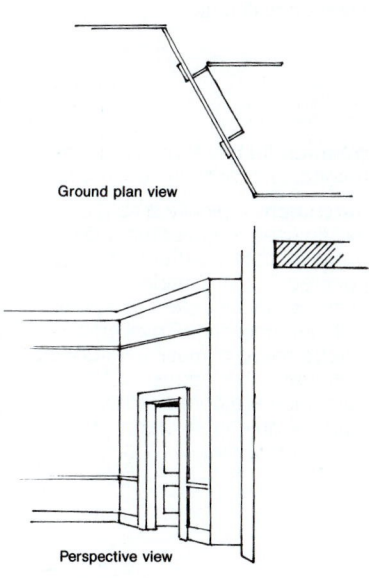

Ground plan view

Perspective view

FIGURE 11.20
Stage doors are usually hinged to swing offstage.

FIGURE 11.21
Typical door construction technique.
See text for details.

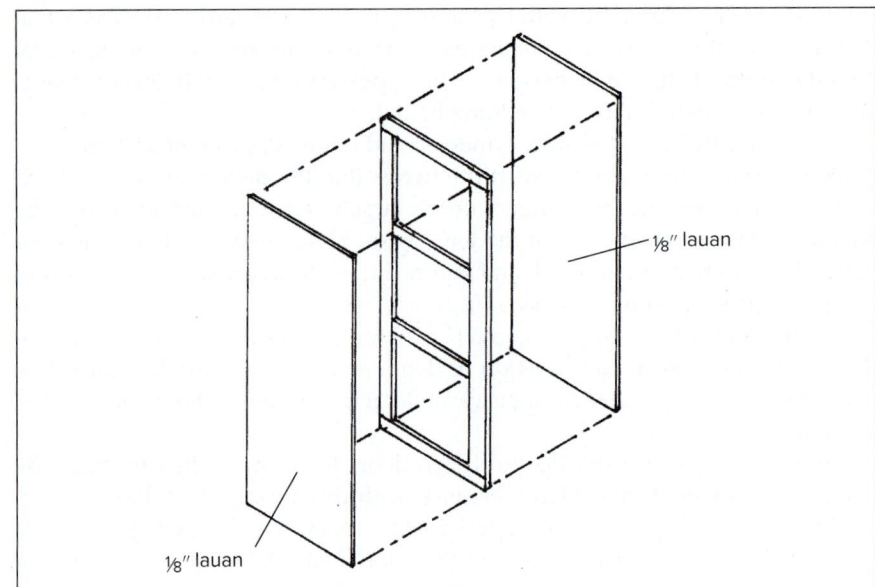

⅛″ lauan

⅛″ lauan

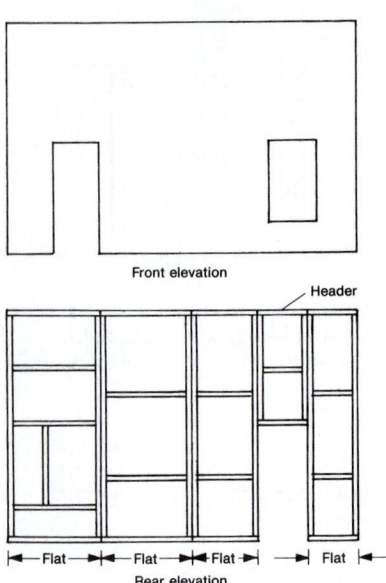

Front elevation

Header

Flat — Flat — Flat — Flat

Rear elevation

FIGURE 11.22
Flats can be joined together to create a wall unit.

traditional-style flats: Wooden-framed, soft- or hard-covered flats.

dutchman: Typically, a strip of muslin used to cover the seams between flats. Dutchmen for soft-covered flats are made of the same cloth as the flat-covering material. Dutchmen for hard-covered flats can be made of muslin or masking/cloth tape. The edges of cloth dutchmen are normally frayed to help the dutchman blend into the flat-covering material.

wall units. As shown in Figure 11.22, varying styles of door, window, and plain flats can be joined to form a wall unit.

Wall units of wider than 8 to 10 feet are rarely made with studio flats because the weight of those units makes them difficult to move. Designers normally create natural breaks in the wall — corners, setbacks, and so forth — that hide the seams where the units will be joined once they are placed onstage.

There are two primary methods of joining flats to form wall units: rigid and flexible. The rigid joining method is used when the wall unit doesn't have to be folded for shifting or storage. The flexible method is used when it is necessary to fold the wall.

Rigid Joining   The methods used for joining **traditional-style flats** and studio flats to form wall units differ only in a matter of degree, not principle. Flats are edge-joined to form both rigid and flexible units (Figure 11.23) using the following techniques.

1. Lay the flats face up in their proper order. Where adjacent flats butt together, attach tight-pin hinges to the stiles, as shown in Figure 11.23.

2. Traditional-style flats have the hinge-joined joint between the flats covered with a dutchman. To make the **dutchman,** fray ¼ inch of the edges of a 5- to 6-inch-wide strip of cloth (the same material as the flat covering), and attach

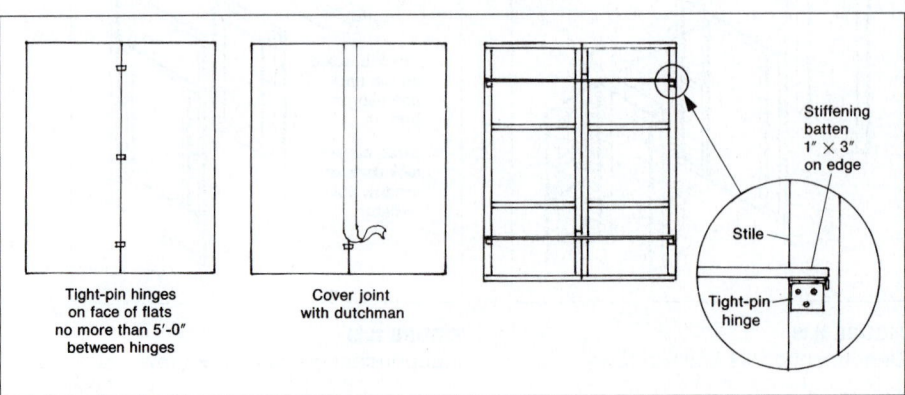

Tight-pin hinges
on face of flats
no more than 5′-0″
between hinges

Cover joint
with dutchman

Stiffening
batten
1″ × 3″
on edge

Stile

Tight-pin
hinge

FIGURE 11.23
Rigid flat-joining techniques.

it to the flat by coating one side of it and the stiles with latex, acrylic, or vinyl paint the same color as the **prime coat.** Apply the dutchman to the joint, smooth out any wrinkles, and allow to dry. (Note: The dutchman doesn't have to be applied until you're ready to begin painting the set.) The joints between studio flats are normally filled with **joint compound** or spackle and sanded level when dry. Alternatively, a dutchman made of masking or gaffer's tape can be applied, particularly if the unit will not be moved.

3. Turn the wall unit onto its back and attach **stiffening battens.** Stiffening battens are 1 × 3s, on edge, that are attached to the back of a multiflat wall as stabilizers. If the wall does not need to fold, the stiffening battens are held in place with tight-pin hinges. One flap of the hinge is attached to the batten and the other to a stile or toggle bar of the flat. To keep the stiffening batten standing perpendicular to the flat, the hinges are attached alternately to opposite sides of the batten. If the stiffening batten needs to be removed for shifting or folding, the tight-pin hinges should be replaced with loose-pin hinges. To remove the batten simply pull out the pins.

Some technicians prefer to lay the stiffening battens on their sides and attach them to the flats with screws. Although this method holds the flats together, it does not provide nearly the stiffening effect that is supplied by the 1 × 3 standing perpendicular to the flat. The stiffening effect will be regained if another 1 × 3 is screwed to the edge of the stiffening batten, as shown in Figure 11.24.

S-hooks provide another method of attaching removable battens, as shown in Figure 11.25.

A **tumbler** is used when two flats need to be **booked.** Tumblers are made from 1-inch boards that are the full height of the flats. Tumblers act as spacers between adjoining flats that allow the flats to be closed face to face, as shown in Figure 11.26. The width of tumblers for traditional flats is 1 inch.

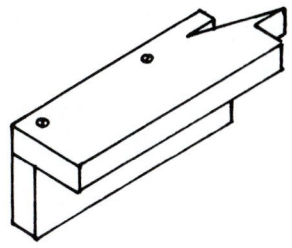

FIGURE 11.24
An effective stiffening batten can be made from two 1 × 3s.

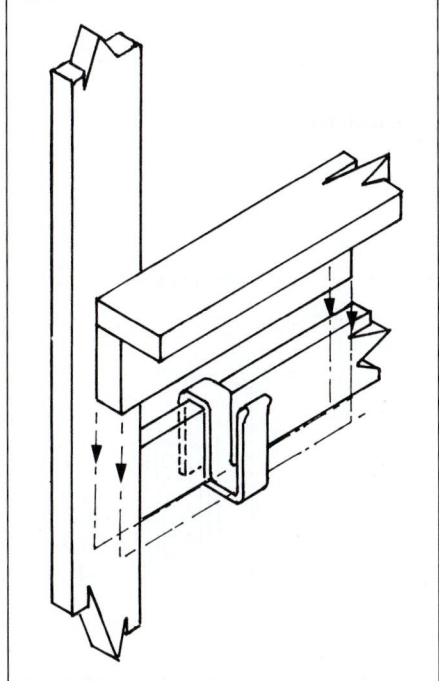

FIGURE 11.25
S-hooks can be used to hold removable stiffening battens.

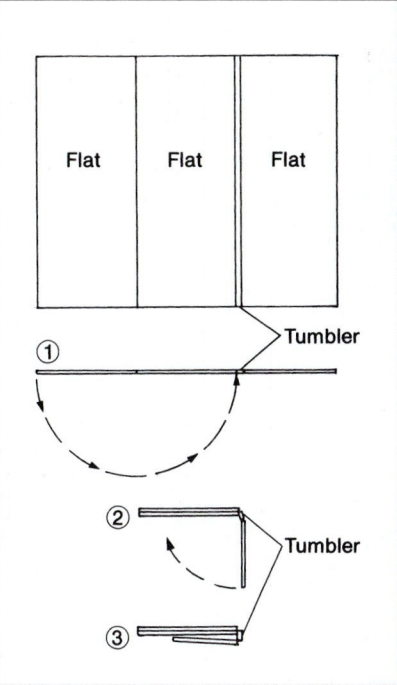

Flat   Flat   Flat

① Tumbler

② Tumbler

③

FIGURE 11.26
A tumbler permits the flats being booked to fold completely. See text for details.

prime coat: The first layer of paint; applied to all elements of the scenery to provide a uniform base for the rest of the paint job.

joint compound: A finishing material the consistency of pudding. Normally used to cover drywall seams.

stiffening batten: A length of 1 × 3 attached to a multiflat wall unit to keep it from wiggling.

tumbler: A ¾-inch-thick-by-1-inch-wide (or 1 × 3) piece of stock used as a spacer when three or more flats are going to be booked.

book: To fold hinged flats together (so that they resemble a book).

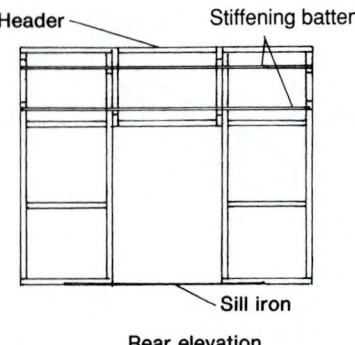

FIGURE 11.27
A header can be used to create a doorway.

header: A small flat that can be placed between two standard-sized flats to create a doorway or window.

book ceiling: Two large flats about the same width as the proscenium arch, stored in a booked position in the flies; when needed to create a ceiling, they are opened and lowered onto the walls of the set.

Studio flats are rarely booked. If they are, the tumbler needs to match the width of the flat's framing plus the thickness of its covering material. Tumblers for both styles of flats are attached with tight-pin hinges and covered with dutchmen.

Headers can be used to create door openings or archways by placing them between to regular-sized flats as shown in Figure 11.27.

Ceilings   Ceilings for sets are primarily used on proscenium stages. They are really large, horizontal flats, but they do provide some special challenges simply because of their size. The **book ceiling** (Figure 11.28) is a permanent piece of stage equipment in many proscenium theatres. It is composed of two large flats approximately the same width as the proscenium arch. The depth of the opened book ceiling is normally about 16 to 20 feet. It can be stored on a single counter-weight line.

Irregular ceiling pieces (Figure 11.29) that do not completely cover the set can be built just as any other flat is. They are normally built of 1×4 stock for additional strength. Spot lines of $1/16$-inch aircraft cable dropped from the grid or a batten to support the downstage edge of the ceiling.

Soft Scenery

Soft scenery refers to unframed fabric units such as drops and draperies, which are usually suspended from the grid, a batten, or some type of structure capable of supporting their weight.

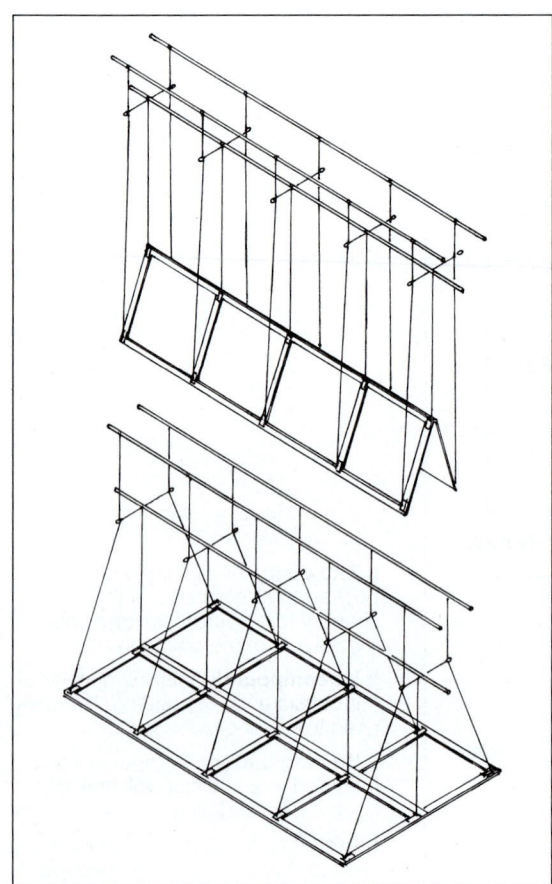

FIGURE 11.28
A book ceiling.

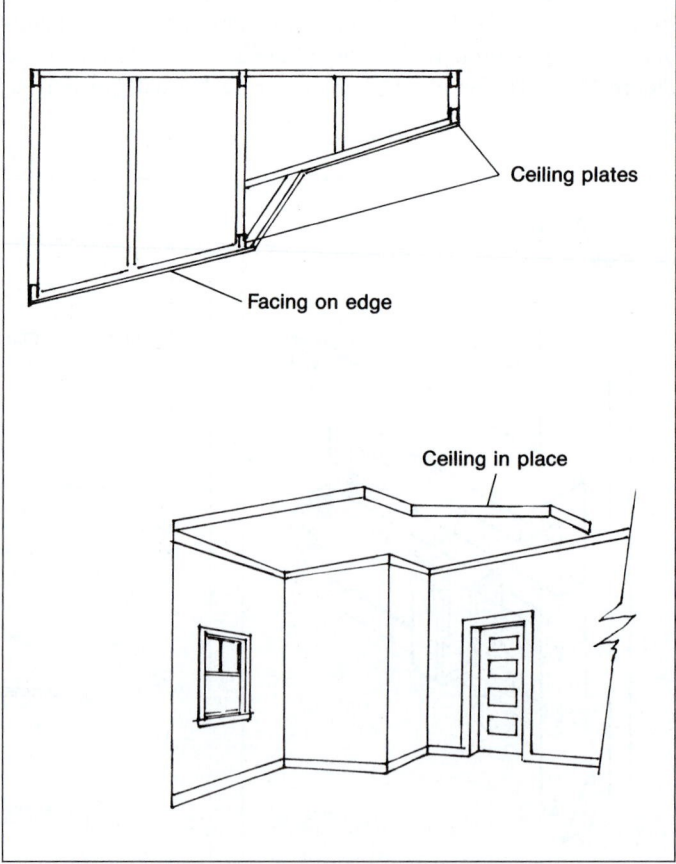

FIGURE 11.29
An irregular ceiling.

Drops Drops are large, flat curtains with no fullness. There are two primary methods of attaching drops to their respective supporting battens: ties and batten clamps.

Tie-Supported Drops The easiest way of hanging a drop is to tie it to the batten. Ties made from strips of scrap muslin, ½-inch heavy cotton tape, 36-inch shoelaces, or similar materials are attached to the top of the drop, then tied to the batten. Cotton-tape ties can be sewn to the 4-inch jute backing tape at the top hem of the drop, as shown in Figure 11.30. The other kinds of ties are used in conjunction with grommets in the jute-tape backing of the drop. The grommet-reinforced holes are usually spaced on 1-foot centers across the width of the drop. The ties (ideally 36 to 40 inches long) are looped through the grommet holes and tied to the batten.

Batten-Clamp Drops Drops are sometimes attached to a counterweight batten with batten clamps. The batten clamp facilitates rapid hanging or removal of a drop from the batten. The top of the drop is sandwiched between two 1 × 3s, as shown in Figure 11.31. The batten clamp is designed to hold the wooden batten "sandwich" without touching the drop.

A variety of effects can be achieved with drops. Drops are generally hung on an upstage batten and provide a background such as a forest, street scene, or the upstage wall of a ballroom. To an extent, the effects the drops create are dependent on the type of material from which the drop is made and the manner in which it is painted and lit.

Opaque Drops Commonly made of heavyweight muslin, opaque drops are painted with opaque paints (scene paint, casein, latex, acrylic, and so on) and are lit from the front. The audience cannot see through them.

Translucent Drops Made of heavyweight muslin, translucent drops are painted with dyes or a combination of dye and opaque paint and are lit from both front and back. This makes the areas that have been dyed translucent, increasing the apparent depth of the scene. Because any seams would show when such drops were back-lit, they are frequently made from large pieces of seamless muslin.

Scrim Drops Made from sharkstooth scrim or theatrical gauze, scrim drops have the unique ability to become transparent when the scene behind the drop is lit. The material can be painted with dyes or thinned paint. Be sure that the paint does not fill the large holes in the fabric.

Cutout Drops Cutout drops have sections or pieces of the drop actually cut out of the material. The sense of depth in a design can be greatly enhanced by the use of a series of cutout drops placed in back of one another. The drops are painted before they are cut to keep the cut edges from curling. Bobbinet or similar loose-weave netting can be glued to the back of the drop to support the cutout areas if necessary.

Draperies The two types of draperies used in the theatre are discussed elsewhere in this book. Stage draperies are covered in Chapter 4, "The Stage and Its Equipment," and the drapes and curtains used to decorate sets will be discussed in Chapter 13, "Stage Properties."

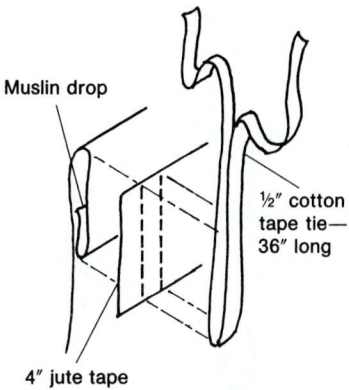

Muslin drop

½" cotton tape tie— 36" long

4" jute tape

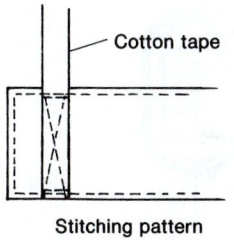

Cotton tape

Stitching pattern

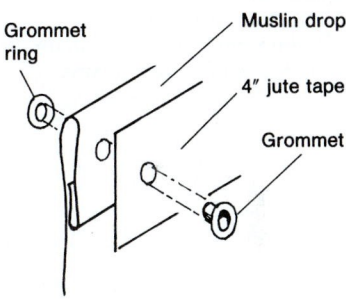

Grommet ring

Muslin drop

4" jute tape

Grommet

FIGURE 11.30
Methods of attaching drops to battens.

Three-Dimensional Scenery

Although flats and architectural trim actually have three dimensions, the term *three-dimensional scenery* generally refers to platforms, stairs, and similar objects.

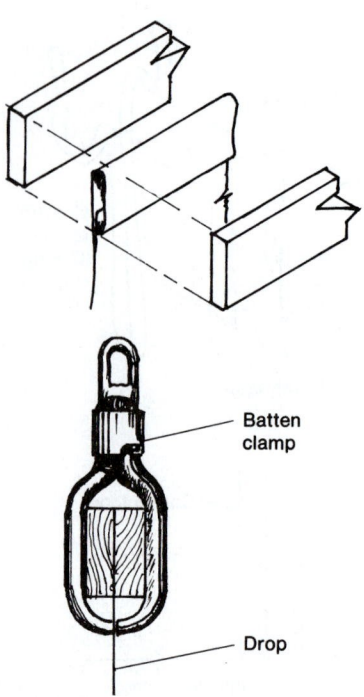

Batten clamp

Drop

FIGURE 11.31
A drop that has to be quickly removed from the batten can be supported with batten clamps.

PRODUCTION INSIGHTS
Scenic Specialty Fabrics

A variety of fabrics can be used for special scenic-construction purposes. These fabrics are not normally available in local fabric stores and must be purchased from scenic supply houses.

Sharkstooth Scrim

The 30-foot-wide, seamless cotton material called sharkstooth scrim has a unique property. When lit from the front, the material is opaque. When light is taken off the fabric and objects behind it are lit, the scrim becomes transparent because the material has a very open weave that creates rectangles of open space about $\frac{3}{16}$ inch wide by $\frac{3}{16}$ inch high.

A close-up view of sharkstooth scrim.
Courtesy of J. Michael Gillette.

It is available from scenic-fabric supply houses in natural (a creamy white), white, and black. It can be painted with dye or paint, although if paint is used, care must be taken to avoid filling the open spaces.

Sharkstooth scrim is used for transparent drops, in illusion effects, and in similar applications. It can also be used as a diffusion drop (a drop that softens light) for cyc lighting. If sharkstooth scrim is hung in front of a muslin cyc, it diffuses and softens the effects of the cyc lighting and creates a greater illusion of depth.

Bobbinet

Another 30-foot-wide, open-weave cotton material is bobbinet. It is lighter in weight than sharkstooth scrim, is more transparent, and has a hexagonal weave. It is also available from scenic supply houses in natural, white, or black. It can be used as a substitute for glass in windows, as a diffusion drop for cyc lighting, as net backing for cutout drops, and in similar applications.

A close-up view of bobbinet.
Courtesy of J. Michael Gillette.

Theatrical Gauze

Theatrical gauze is a cotton fabric with a fine-mesh weave similar to cheesecloth, but its threads are thicker and the weave is slightly tighter. It is 72 inches wide and can be purchased from scenic-fabric supply houses in natural, black, and a limited range of colors. Its applications are similar to those of sharkstooth scrim with the exception of those situations where the seams every 6 feet would prove objectionable.

A close-up view of theatrical gauze.
Courtesy of J. Michael Gillette.

Stage Platforming

Directors love multilevel stage floors, because they make it easy to create interesting blocking pictures. Platforms are used to create these levels. There are several types of platforming and a number of techniques for joining them.

Rigid Platforms   Rigid platforms are arguably the most common platform used in the theatre. They are the easiest to build, and they're relatively inexpensive.

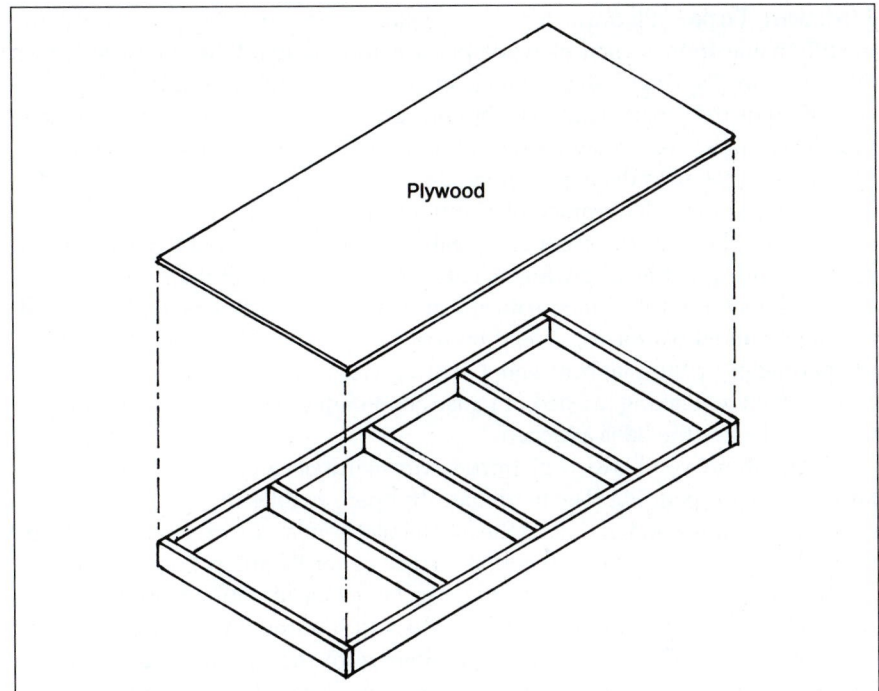

FIGURE 11.32
A rigid wooden platform consists of a top and a ladderlike supporting structure. See text for details.

An added bonus is that the legs are detachable, so the finished height of a legged platform is easily adjusted.

Rigid platforms come in two basic varieties: those with frames made of lumber and those with frames made of steel tube. In either case, the frame is a ladder-like construction with the rungs, or joists, usually spaced about two feet apart, as shown in Figure 11.32. The spacing of the joists is primarily dependent on the strength of both the framing material and the top. Rigid platforms can be easily constructed in almost any irregular shape, but the standard rigid platforms kept in a theatre's stock inventory are normally 4 feet wide by 8 feet long. They can be supported using various styles of removable legs as well as stud wall systems, both of which will be discussed later in the chapter.

Wood-Framed Platforms   Wooden-framed rigid platforms are typically constructed of 2 × 4, 2 × 6, or 1 × 6 lumber. Strength limitations dictate joist spacing required in building the platform frames. Frames made of 2 × 4 or 1 × 6 need the joists to be spaced 2 feet apart **on center.** Frames made of 2 × 6s can have the on-center joist spacing increased to 32 inches if the decking will be ¾-inch AC or BC plywood. Note that 32-inch joist spacing with a ¾-inch CDX top gives the platforms a spongy feel — not a good thing. When using CDX, keep the joist spacing at 24 inches on center regardless of the dimensions of the framing lumber.

Typically, joists are secured to the frame using wood glue and screws, nails, or staples. Nails and staples are sometimes preferred because of speed of installation. A carpenter using pneumatic nailers or staplers can construct the framing for a wooden-framed platform in a very short length of time.

Steel-Framed Platforms   Steel-framed rigid platforms are normally constructed from 16 gauge 1½-inch square tubing or 16-gauge 1 × 2 tubing (with the 2-inch dimension placed vertically) or from ⅛-inch by 2-inch by 2-inch angle iron. The shape of the steel-tubing framework mirrors that of the wooden platform; the intended covering material determines the number of joists required and their spacing; and all joints are welded.

on center: The distance from the center of one object to the center of the next.

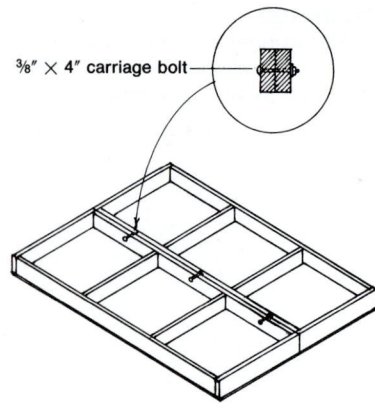

FIGURE 11.33
Platform modules can be bolted together to create a larger platform.

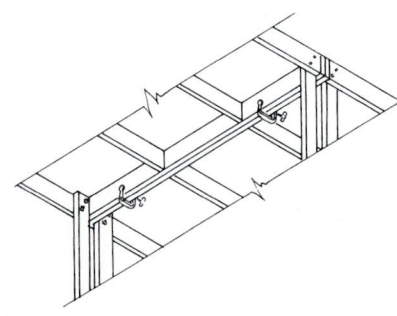

FIGURE 11.34
Platforms can be temporarily joined together with C-clamps.

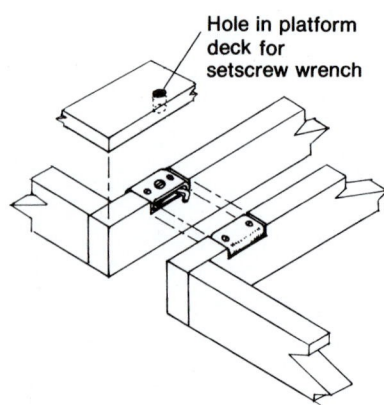

FIGURE 11.35
Casket locks can be used for permanent or temporary platform locking.

Platform Tops Platform tops, also called "decks" or "lids," are most frequently made from ¾-inch plywood or ⅝-inch or ¾-inch OSB. Because ⅝-inch OSB is more "springy" than ¾-inch materials, a platform's joists should be spaced no further apart than 16 inches on center when using this decking material. When using ¾-inch plywood or OSB, joists can be on 2-foot centers unless special circumstances dictate otherwise.

The tops of wooden-framed platforms can be attached with nails, but screws are preferred because they reduce squeaking. Lids are attached to metal-framed platforms using flat-head ply-metal TEK screws (which drill their own holes in deck and steel tubing) or pneumatically driven T-nails. Fasteners, for both wood- and steel-framed platforms, should be spaced about 9 inches on center around the perimeter of the platform and 1 foot on center on the cross members. To help prevent squeaking, a bead of construction adhesive is often run on top of the frame before the lid is attached.

Topping plywood-lidded platforms with hardboard creates a smooth, uniform surface for painting. The hardboard "topper" enables the use of less expensive CD-grade plywood, reducing the overall platform's cost. (See the box, "Stage Floors," on page 55 for a discussion of the use of hardboard as floor covering.)

Soundproofing for rigid platforms can be achieved with a variety of ways. A ⅛-inch thick strip of Ethafoam that is the width of the framing members can be stapled or glued with construction adhesive to the top of the entire frame before the lid is attached; a sheet of ½-inch sound board (Celotex or equivalent) can be nailed or glued to the frame before the lid is attached; fiberglass batting insulation – without the paper backing – can be installed between the framing members on the underside of the platform.

Connecting Rigid-Framed Platforms When several rigid-framed platforms are used together to create a new floor level, the platforms must be connected to improve the lateral stability of the unit. Fastening them together can be accomplished a number of ways.

Bolting Wooden platforms can be bolted together by drilling through the framing members of adjacent units and using ⅜-inch × 4-inch bolts, as shown in Figure 11.33. Two or three bolts per long side and one at each end are usually sufficient.

Steel platforms have shallow framing members. For this reason, the bolt holes or slots are normally drilled prior to attaching the top to the frame. Two or three ⅜-inch × 3-inch or ⅜ × 4-inch bolts on the sides and one at each end are used to bolt the platforms together.

Clamping If the platforms need to be shifted during the production, C-clamps can be substituted for the bolts just described, as illustrated in Figure 11.34.

Casket Locks Casket locks can be used to tied platforms together by inseting them into the framing members of rigid wooden platforms as shown in Figure 11.35 or by welding them to the bottom of steel-framed platforms.

If casket locks are attached to every stock platform in a standard pattern (Figure 11.36), it will be easy to lock any platform to an adjacent unit of the same height. Because platforms equipped with casket locks can be locked or unlocked quickly, they can be used for either permanent or temporary staging.

Stressed-Skin and Sandwich-Core Platforms

Two developments in the construction industry have led to the use of stressed-skin and sandwich-core panels as platforming in scenic construction. Although they cost more and take longer to build, these panel designs offer a number of advantages over traditional rigid framing. Both stressed-skin and sandwich-core

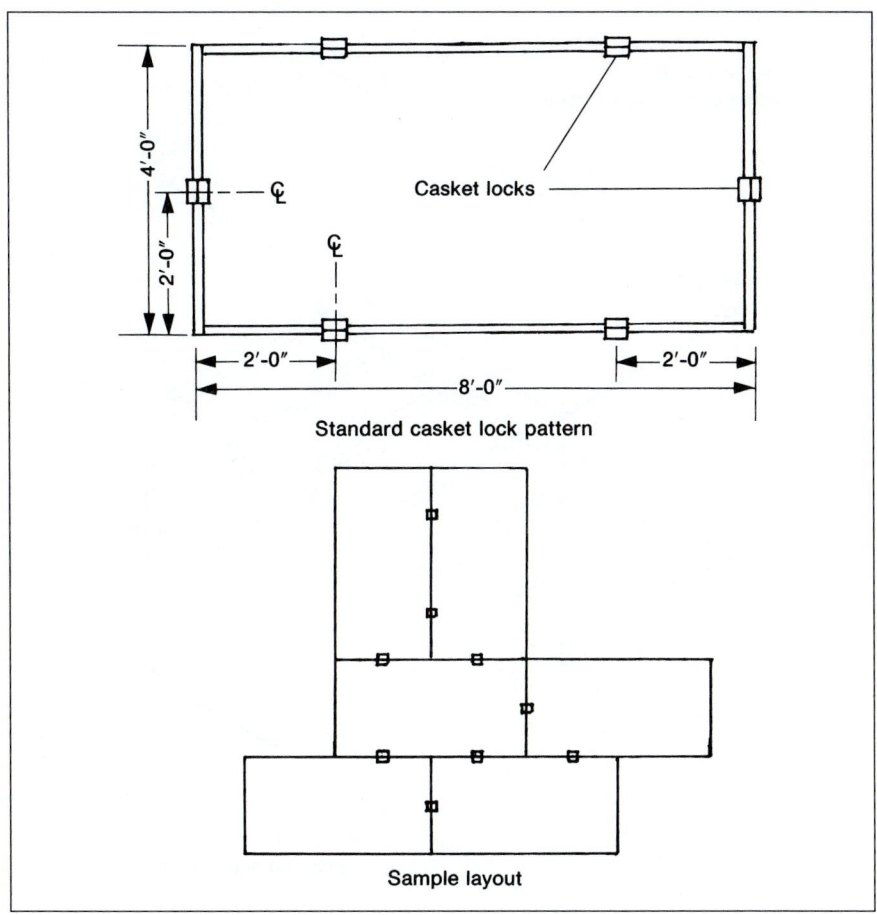

FIGURE 11.36
A standard casket lock pattern.

platforms are supported using stud walls or trusses. Stud wall supports and trusses both will be discussed later in this chapter.

Stressed-Skin Platforms   The concept of stressed-skin construction is illustrated in Figure 11.37. A wooden support frame is normally covered on both the top and bottom with plywood. The advantages of this deceptively simple structure are many. They are lighter and have less give/sag/bounce than similarly sized rigid platforms. They take less storage space. They have a high strength-to-weight ratio. They can carry a heavier load than the typical ¾-inch plywood-covered rigid platform.

The primary disadvantage of stressed-skin platforms? They require precise construction techniques that take more time than traditional wooden-framed platforms. Additionally, depending on the choice of materials, they can cost more than rigid platforms. In many situations, the advantages of stressed-skin construction clearly outweigh their disadvantages. (Additional information about stressed-skin panels can be found by conducting an online search for "APA Supplement 3 to PDS, Design and Fabrication of Stressed Skin Panels.")

Probably the most common type of stressed-skin platform used in theatre is the triscuit — so-called because the platforms look like giant versions of the little crackers — a design developed at the Yale School of Drama in 1990.[1] The

[1] Triscuit information source: http://www.hstech.org/how-to-s/how-to-tech/carpentry/platforming-stage-decks-things-to-stand-on/165-platforming-article-3

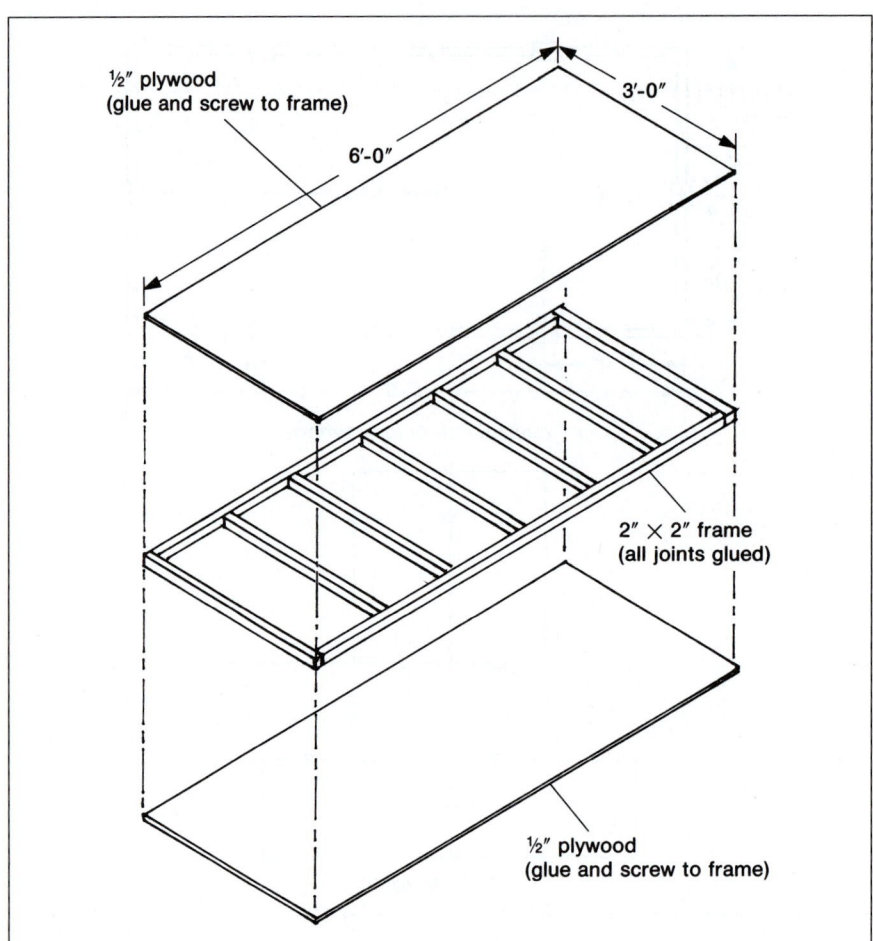

stringers: Structural pieces inside a
framework; e.g., the pieces spanning
the width of a stressed-skin panel's
framework.

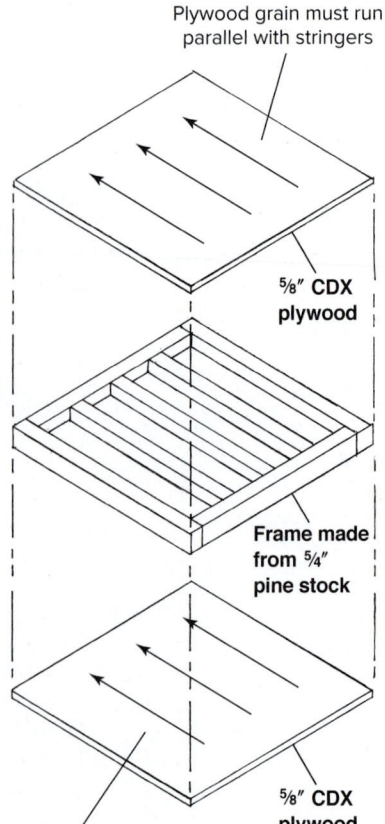

triscuit is a 4-foot by 4-foot stressed-skin platform 2½ inches thick, illustrated in Figure 11.38. The frame must be built of specifically dimensioned, knot-free lumber. The top and bottom skins — placed so the grain runs parallel to the **stringers** — must be glued to the frame, with no gaps or dry spots, and both skins must be screwed to the frame on 6-inch centers around the perimeter and along each cross member. Specific plans and construction information for building triscuits can be found by searching online for "Triscuit stressed-skin platforms."

The Texas Triscuit[2] was developed at Trinity University. Like the triscuit, it is a 4-foot by 4-foot platform, but the frame is constructed of 1½-inch square-steel tubing, and the bottom isn't covered with a second skin. The top is made of ⅝-inch OSB. Complete design and construction details can be found by conducting an online search for "Texas Triscuit" or at the footnoted website.

Sandwich-Core Panels   Like their stressed-skin cousins, sandwich-core panels have plywood top and bottom skins. However, the core is a sheet of rigid material instead of wood or steel framing — hence the name "sandwich core."

The characteristics of sandwich-core panels are similar to those of stressed-skin panels: They have a high strength-to-weight ratio; they tend to be lighter than similarly sized wooden-framed platforms; they take less storage space; they are stiffer than their rigid-framed counterparts. They also have one distinct advantage: They are acoustically quieter than any other form of platforming.

[2] Ibid., p. 4.

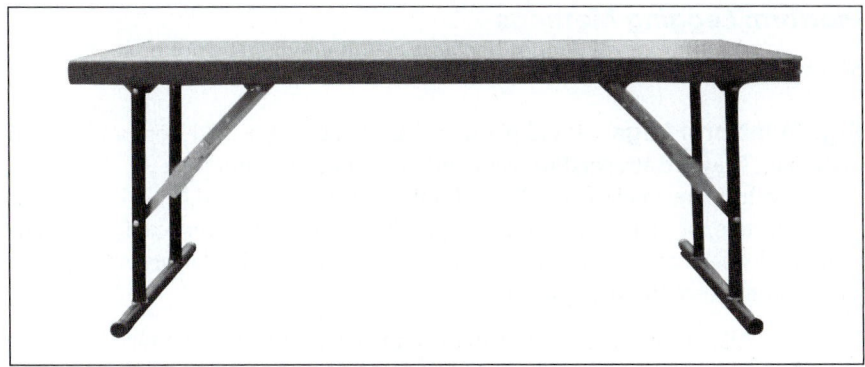

FIGURE 11.39
A portable table top made of a foam core panel. Courtesy of Rich Dionne, Technical Director, the Patti and Rusty Rueff School of Visual and Performing Arts, Purdue University.

vacuum clamping: Using vacuum pressure to exert force.

Gaffer's tape: Cloth tape, similar in appearance to duct tape. Used for a variety of scenery and lighting shop applications. It is less sticky and easier to tear than duct tape.

The technical difference between stressed-skin and sandwich-core construction is that the structure of a sandwich-core panel is consistent throughout its width. This allows them to easily be fabricated or cut into organic profiles.

The disadvantages of sandwich-core panels are the same as stressed-skin panels: They require precise construction techniques; they take longer to build; they tend to be more expensive than rigid-framed platforms.

Styrofoam insulation panels are a commonly used core material for making sandwich-core panels. At Pennsylvania State University, a 1-inch foam panel has been sandwiched between OSB skins, which results in a platform only 2 inches thick. At Purdue University, lightweight rehearsal benches and worktables (Figure 11.39) have been manufactured using ¼-inch plywood skins and 2-inch foam panels. Conducting an online search for "Sandwich-Core Panels" will provide additional information.

Borrowing from aircraft construction practices, the use of honeycomb paper (Figure 11.40) as a core material results in exceptionally lightweight and strong panels.[3]

Sandwich core platforms are constructed as follows:[4] The inside face of one skin is covered with a strong adhesive (polyvinyl/white glue or other strong-bonding glue appropriate to the core material); the core material is placed on that face; the inside face of the other skin is covered with glue, aligned, and gently lowered onto the core material. Application of the glue with a brush, short-nap roller, or sprayer assures a quick and even coating.

The sandwich-core panel needs to be clamped while the glue cures. Pieces of ¼-inch steel plate or counterweights can be used. **Vacuum clamping** can be used instead of weights.

Vacuum clamping a sandwich-core panel is accomplished as follows: Sweep and damp mop the floor thoroughly to remove all particles and dust; cover the assembled platform with heavyweight plastic sheeting; tape the plastic to the shop floor with **gaffer's tape.** The hose of a shop vacuum is inserted under the plastic and securely gaffer-taped in place. The "vacuum" vent will quickly exhaust most of the air under the plastic, but a genuine vacuum pump may be needed to remove the remainder. Clamping pressure needs to be maintained for the length of time it takes for the adhesive to set — generally 3 to 4 hours. It's better to maintain the clamping pressure overnight. The adhesive should be fully cured in roughly 24 hours. No weight or stress should be placed on the units for a day or two longer. The edges of the platform are then filled in with ½-inch stock or MDF to protect the integrity of the core material.

[3] Tom Corbett, "Laminating Stage Platforms Using Honeycomb Paper," *Theatre Design and Technology* (Winter 1980): 24–25, 57–58.

[4] This construction technique is equally applicable to sandwich-core panels fabricated with other core materials such as rigid sheets of Styrofoam insulation.

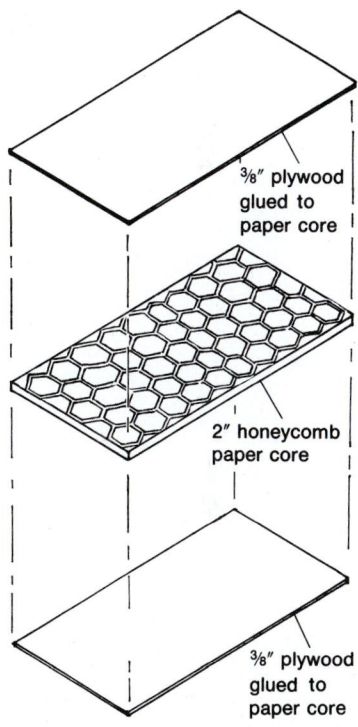

⅜" plywood glued to paper core

2" honeycomb paper core

⅜" plywood glued to paper core

Enlarged view of honeycomb paper

FIGURE 11.40
Honeycomb-laminate platform construction principles. See text for details.

shear force: Side-to-side movement.

Platform Legging Methods

Several methods are used to "leg" the different types of platforms.

Rigid Platform Legs   Rigid platform legs can be fabricated from a variety of materials. They are attached to platforms with several techniques.

Most legs are made from 2 × 4 lumber, ¾-inch plywood, or 1-inch stock, steel box tube, or Schedule 40 black pipe. The strength and vertical flex of both wood and steel framing materials requires that legs for rigid platforms be spaced a maximum on-center distance of 4 feet apart.

Bracing   All platform legs greater than 18 inches tall need to be braced, regardless of whether they are wood or steel, because the sideways forces exerted on the platform by actor movements can easily break the joint between the leg and the platform or possibly the leg itself. Braces should be placed so they form a triangle between the leg and the platform to take advantage of the structural strength of the triangular form, as shown in Figure 11.41A. Braces will be effective if placed at any angle between 30 and 60 degrees, as shown in Figure 11.41B, although 45 degrees provides the maximum strength. There should be no more than 4 feet between bracing support points, as shown in Figure 11.41C.

Leg Attachment Methods   There are several methods used for attaching legs to rigid platforms.

Traditional Legging Technique   As shown in Figure 11.42A, 2 × 4 legs for wood-framed platforms are traditionally placed inside the frame and bolted to it using carriage or hex bolts. Legs less than 1 foot tall can made from ¾-inch plywood or 1 × 3 or 1 × 4 stock and attached to the inside of the frame with dry wall screws as shown in Figure 11.42B.

For steel-framed platforming, the steel legs are also placed on the inside of the steel frame and typically welded into place. With this method, the **shear forces** exerted by the actor's movements on the platform legs are largely borne by the welds, which makes it vital that those welds be of high quality and carefully inspected.

It is important that a small gap (¹⁄₁₆ inch) is left between the top of the leg and the underside of the lid because, if the leg is in contact with the lid, actor

FIGURE 11.41
Platform-leg bracing techniques. See text for details.

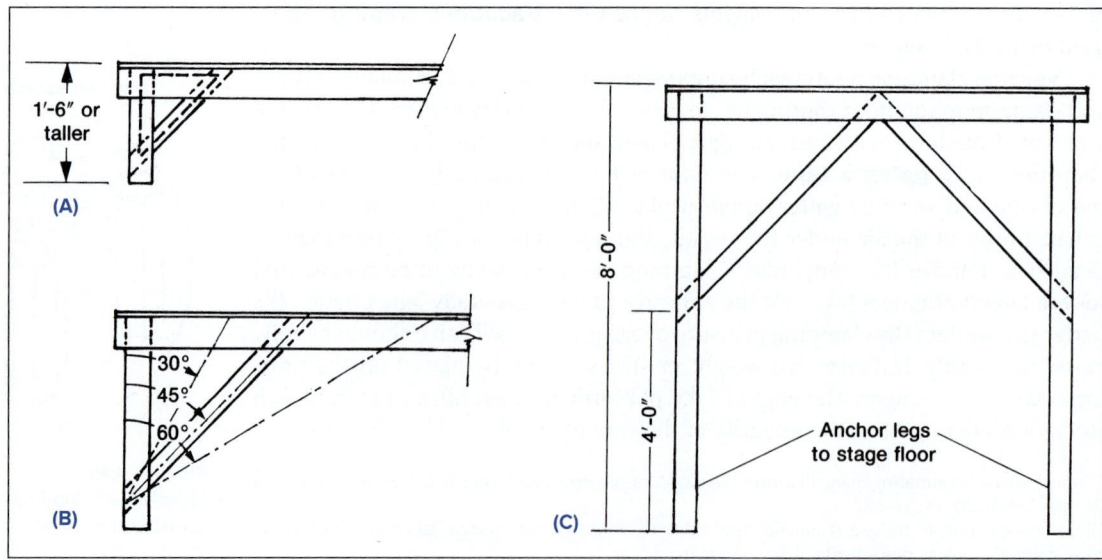

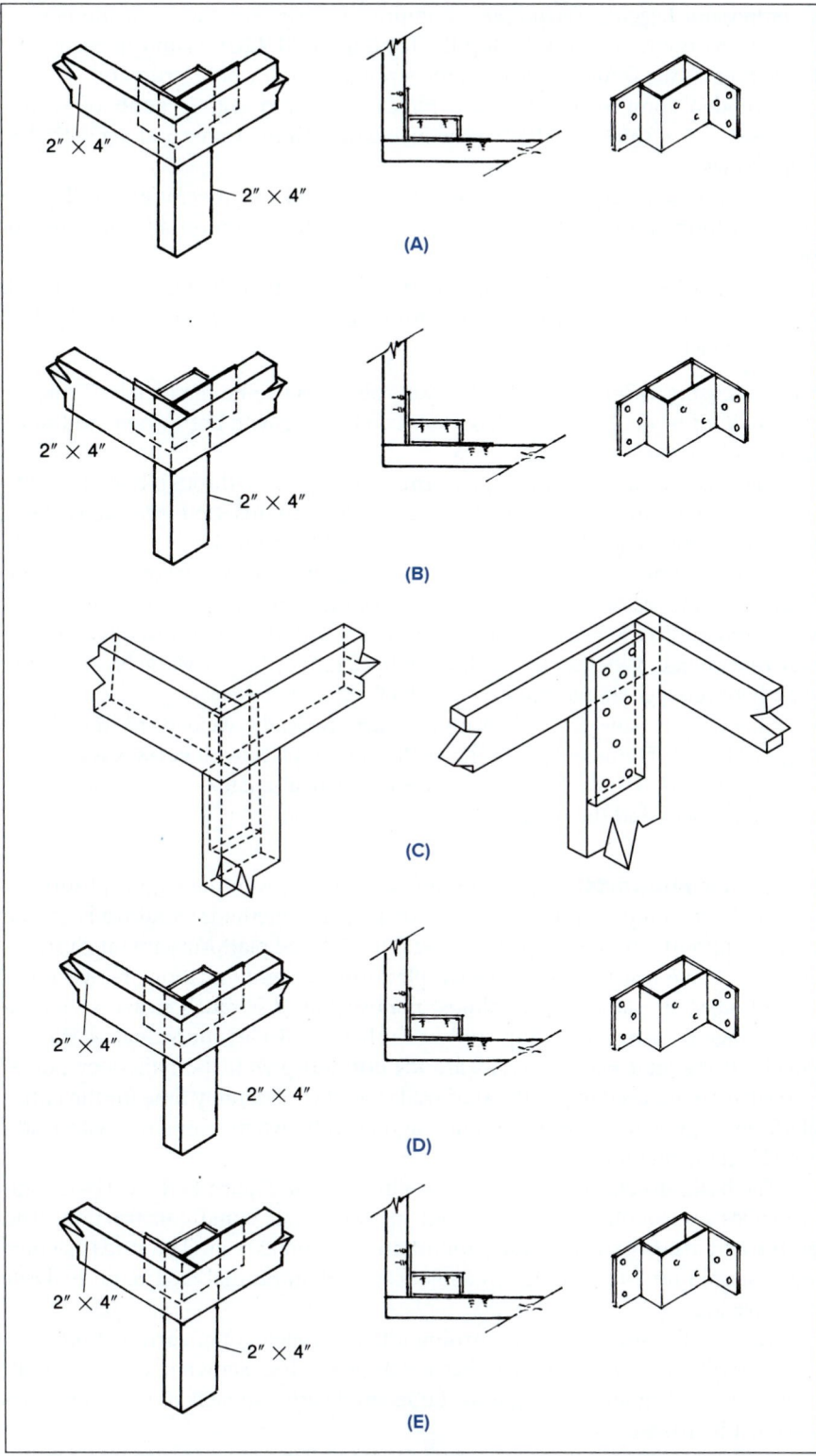

FIGURE 11.42
Types of platform legs and methods of attachment. (A) Traditional 2 × 4 leg. (B) Traditional method with ¾-inch plywood. (C) Compression legs. (D) Sockets with 2 × 4 legs and sockets with steel legs. (E) Steel legs are typically welded to the frame.

(A)

(B)

(C)

(D)

(E)

movements can force the lid to separate from the frame, significantly weakening the whole structure.

If **facing** is to be applied to the platforms, spacers the same thickness as the frame need to be attached to the bottoms of the legs to ensure that the facing will be vertical when installed.

facing: Thin hardboard, MDF, or plywood attached to the face of a platform.

scab: A small piece of scrap material.

setscrew: Typically, a short hex-head machine bolt with the other end cupped or pointed. Screwed through one part of a machine or device — such as socket on a steel-framed platform — to hold another part — the leg — in place.

kit cut: To pre-cut all the materials necessary to build something.

plate: The horizontal pieces at the top and bottom of stud walls.

stud: The vertical elements in a stud wall.

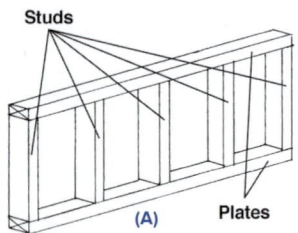

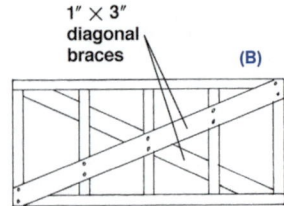

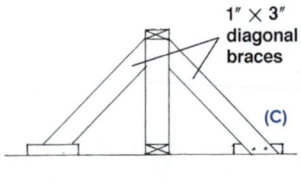

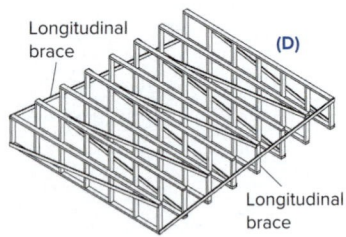

FIGURE 11.43
A stud wall legging system. (A) Stud walls are constructed with 2 × 4s. (B) Each wall section must be diagonally braced in both directions along its long (longitudinal) axis. Stud wall bracing is typically 1 × 3 or 1 × 4 stock. (C) Diagonal bracing *perpendicular* to the wall's long (longitudinal) axis keeps the wall from tipping over. (D) Longitudinal bracing is used to help stabilize multiple stud wall structures.

Compression Legging Technique   Compression legs are placed so the bottom edge of the frame rests on the top the leg (Figure 11.42C). With this technique the legs carry the frame, increasing the strength of the whole structure.

Wooden compression legs are typically secured with a **scab** of ¾-inch plywood or 1 × stock attached to the inside of both the frame and leg with drywall screws.

Compression legging is the preferred method for attaching steel legs to steel platform frames. The legs are welded to the frame on all four sides of the leg.

A distinct advantage of compression legging is that the legs are flush with the edge of the platform frame so additional spacers are not required when attaching facing.

Socket Legging Technique   Metal sockets allow legs to be removable. Typically shop-built of ⅛- or 3⁄16-inch steel, sockets can be used with both wood- and steel-framed platforms.

Sockets for wood-framed platforms are typically through-bolted to the frame as shown in Figure 11.42D and 2 × 4 legs are inserted into the sockets. Drywall screws hold the legs in place. Leg-O-Matic brackets, a commercially available aluminum product, perform the same function as sockets. The Leg-O-Matic brackets are mounted in the corners of the frame, and 2 × 4 or metal legs are inserted into the bracket and held in place with drywall screws (wood) or a setscrew (metal). Whether using shop-built sockets or Leg-O-Matic brackets, the span between legs should not exceed 4 feet.

Sockets for steel-framed platforms are typically welded to the frame (Figure11.42E). The steel legs are normally held in place with **setscrews.**

Again, care should be taken to ensure that a small (1⁄16-inch) gap is left between all legs and the platform lid.

Stud Wall Supports   There are several advantages to the stud wall support system when comparing it with traditional legging methods. Stud walls can be used to support any style of platforming. The finished platforms are much stronger and "shake resistant" than legged platforms. Height variations between the tops of adjacent platforms are almost nonexistent. It is much easier to build a raked stage by using raked-top stud walls than it is to leg individual platforms. Finally, if the stud wall materials are **kit cut** and pneumatic nailers or power screwdrivers are used to put the stud walls together, assembly time for the entire platform stage is reduced, sometimes significantly, when compared with traditional legging methods.

The basic structure of a stud wall is illustrated in Figure 11.43A. The design principles are identical to those used in frame-wall home construction. The **plates** and **studs** of a stud wall support are cut from 2 × 4s. The studs are normally spaced on 2-foot centers. Loads heavier than normal may require closer stud spacing.

To keep the stud wall from turning into a parallelogram, each section must be diagonally cross braced with either 1 × 3s or 1 × 4s as shown in Figure 11.43B. Each piece of diagonal bracing must be secured with two nails or screws to each stud that it crosses.

To secure a stud wall in position, the bottom plate is nailed or screwed to the stage floor or supporting wagon.

To keep the stud wall vertical, it must be braced diagonally, perpendicular to its longitudinal axis, as shown in Figure 11.43C. Longer braces (Figure 11.43D) can replace much of the diagonal bracing needed to stabilize the individual walls in multiple stud walls systems.

Stud walls can be built to any length, although they are generally made in 8- to 12-foot lengths for economy and ease of handling. If a longer run is necessary, several shorter sections can be **butted** end-to-end and bolted or screwed together.

Stud walls can be built to any reasonable height, although 12 to 14 feet is the generally accepted maximum height.

Spacing of Stud Wall Supports The spacing between stud walls, and their orientation with respect to the platforms they support, depends on the load being carried.

Rigid-Framed Platforms Typical wood- and steel-framed platforms minimally need to be supported every 4 feet to carry a **typical stage load.** This requires the stud walls to be spaced 4 feet on center. To make the most efficient use of materials, 4 × 8 platforms are usually supported under their 8-foot sides. Four-foot-wide stud walls, located at both ends and the middle of the platform, will also provide effective support.

Platforms are secured to the top plates of the stud walls with either drywall screws or bolts. Drywall screws are inserted into the wooden platform frame from the underside of the top plate. Bolts need to have their heads inset into the platform's lid so their tops are flush with the deck's surface. The bolt shaft passes through the top plate of the stud wall and is secured on the underside of the plate with a washer and nut.

Stressed Skin and Sandwich Core The load-bearing strength of both stressed-skin and sandwich-core panels is dependent on the direction of the grain of their plywood skins and, for stressed-skin panels, the orientation of the internal stringers. Both types of panels should be placed on the stud walls so the grain of their skins is perpendicular to the stud walls, as shown in Figure 11.44A. Not following this guideline severely weakens the load-bearing capacity of both stressed-skin and sandwich-core panels.

The spacing to be used between stud walls supporting stressed-skin and sandwich-core panels is dependent on the strength of the panel design. The triscuit, which is 4-foot square, only requires support beneath the outside edges of the panel, as shown in Figure 11.44B. Other panels may be designed to span distances as large as 6 or 8 feet. Still others may need to be supported on 2-foot centers. It is important to understand the strength of the specific panels with which you're working to understand the spacing requirements for their stud wall support locations.

butted: To push two or more items together; in this case, placing them end to end.

typical stage load: Fifty pounds per square foot is the load-carrying standard to which stage platforming is normally built. Depending on the platform's use, the required load rating may be higher or lower.

FIGURE 11.44
Stud wall legs are used to support platforms. (A) Stud walls placed on opposite ends of the triscuit provide its support. The grain on the plywood skin must be placed perpendicular to the supporting stud walls. (B) Two triscuits can share the top of one stud wall.

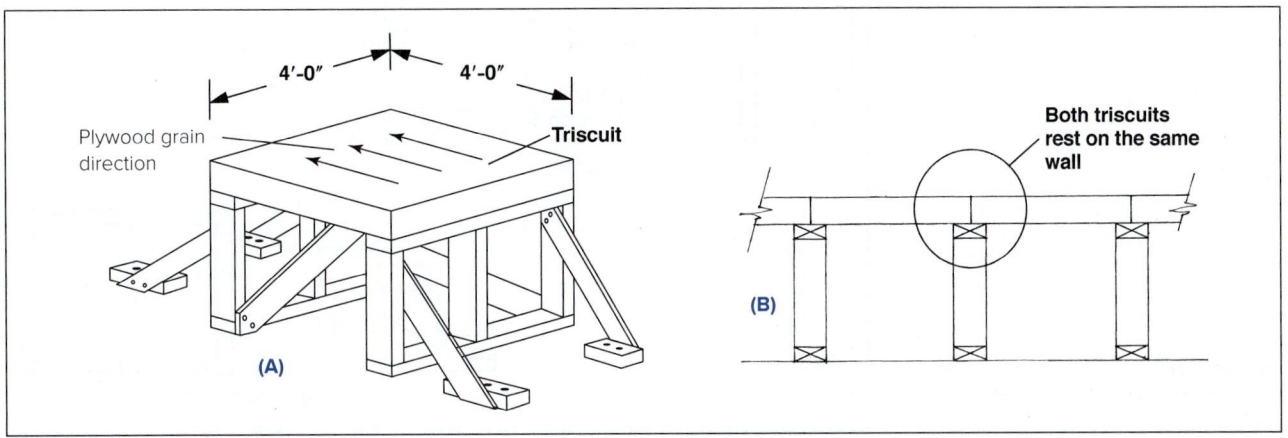

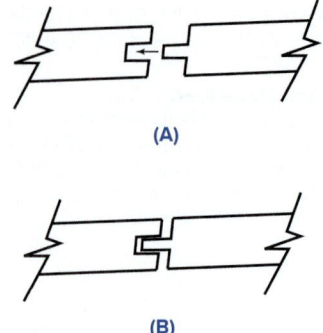

FIGURE 11.45
Tongue and groove joining increases joint strength. (A) The tongue and groove edges of Sturd-I-Floor sheets. (B) The edges of adjoining sheets are interlocked to prevent sagging or movement.

Sturd-I-Floor: The tradename of a plywood subflooring used beneath carpet, vinyl flooring, and tile in home construction.

nailer: A piece of plywood or stock used to join adjacent pieces. When used to prevent movement between adjoining pieces of flooring, the nailers should be attached with screws.

carriage: The part of a stair unit that supports the tread and risers.

tread: The horizontal surface of a stair.

riser: The vertical face of a stair unit.

Once all the stud walls are constructed, placed, and braced in their proper positions onstage, the triscuits, platforms, or sheathing can be quickly loaded onto the top of the walls and secured in place using the platform-securing techniques described on page 257.

Plywood Decking   Stud walls allow decking made from sheets of ¾-inch ply wood such as **Sturd-I-Floor** to be used as platforming *without* the use of any underlying framework. The thickness of the sheathing and the load being carried determines the spacing required between the stud walls. Typically, the stud walls are spaced on 24- to 32-inch centers. Sheathing with tongue-and-groove edges is preferred so adjoining sheets can be interlocked, as shown in Figures 11.45A and B. If sheathing with straight edges is used, additional bracing, **nailers,** or stud walls must be placed under any seams to prevent sagging or movement. The sheathing is attached to the tops of the stud walls with screws, and the screws must be countersunk so their tops are flush with the top of the deck.

Using plywood decking instead of rigid platforms can also resolve the storage-room challenges encountered in many theatres.

Stairs

Two basic types of stairs are used in scenic construction: dependent and independent. The dependent units require support from some other element, usually a platform, for support; the independent units are self-supporting, as shown in Figure 11.46. Although the primary difference between independent and dependent staircases is in their method of support, the actual units are built in much the same manner.

The **carriage** can be built in a variety of ways, as shown in Figure 11.47. Carriages can be cut from 1 × 12 for stair runs of less than 6 feet. For runs over 6 feet or in those instances where the stairs must support an unusual amount of weight, 2 × 12 should be used.

The **treads** can be made from ¾-inch stock or plywood. They should be cut with the grain running parallel with the long side of the tread (Figure 11.48A) to take advantage of the strength of the wood. For safety reasons, the unsupported span of a tread should never exceed 2 feet 6 inches. **Risers** are usually

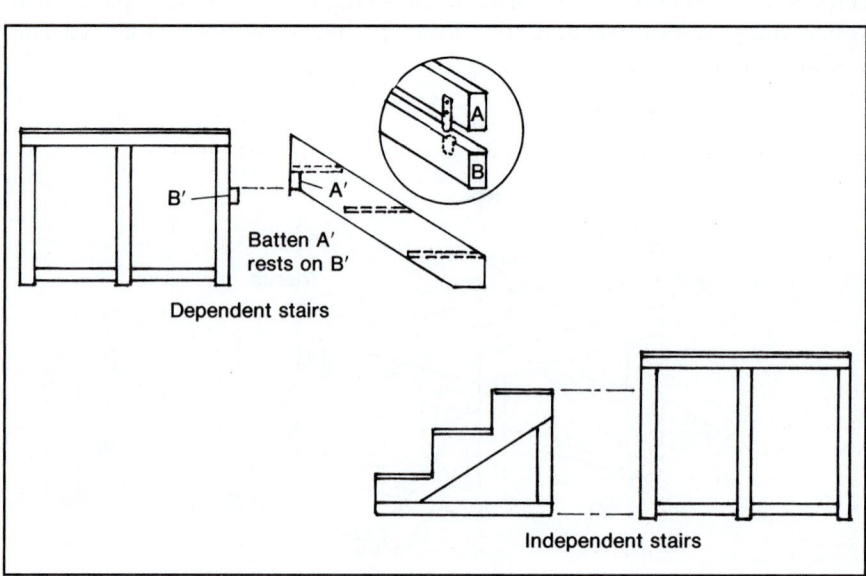

Batten A'
rests on B'

Dependent stairs

Independent stairs

FIGURE 11.46
Dependent and independent stair units.

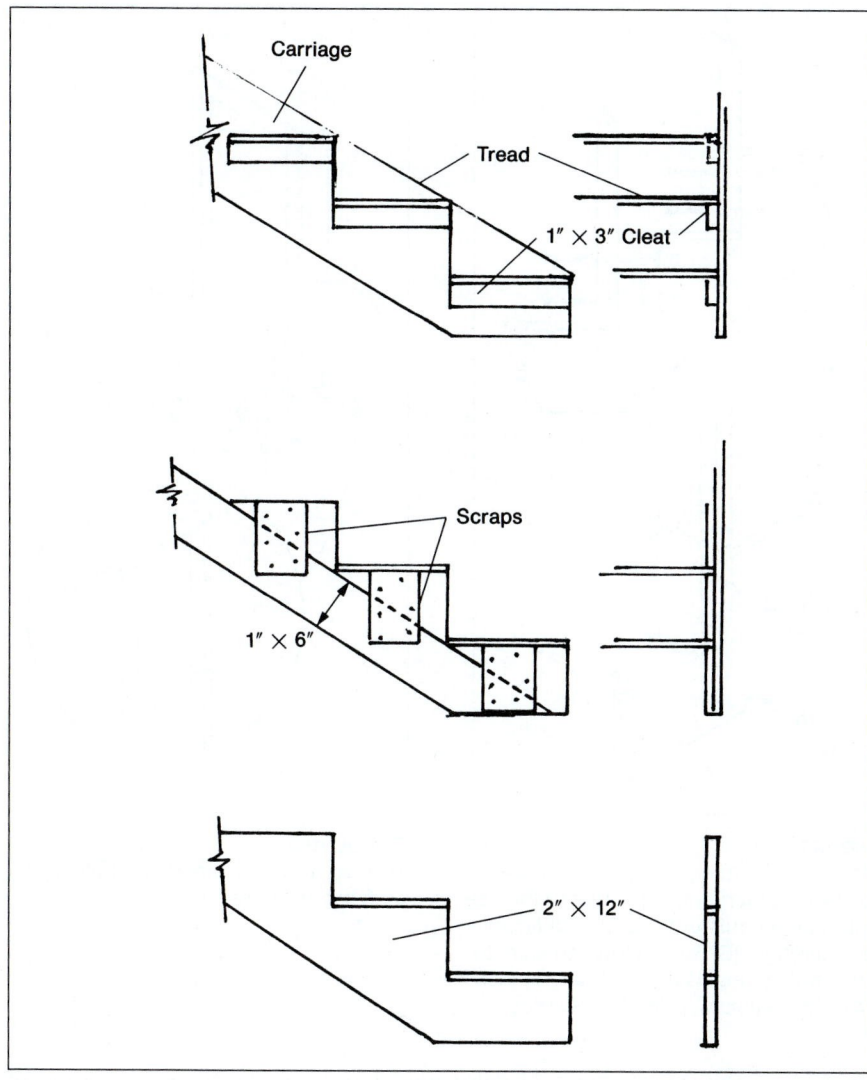

FIGURE 11.47
Carriages can be built in a variety of ways.

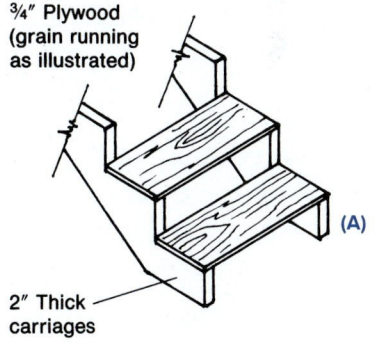

¾" Plywood (grain running as illustrated)

2" Thick carriages

(A)

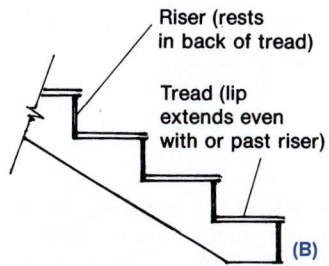

Riser (rests in back of tread)

Tread (lip extends even with or past riser)

(B)

FIGURE 11.48
Tread construction. See text for details.

made from ¼-inch tempered hardboard or plywood. If the riser has to curve, ⅛-inch hardboard or plywood can be used, and the back of the ¼-inch sheet stock can be **scored** so that the wood can be bent more easily. Scoring can be done by adjusting the blade height of the radial-arm saw so that it cuts about halfway through the wood. Depending on the arc of the anticipated bend, cuts are spaced between ⅜ and 1 inch apart.

Although the size of treads and risers varies considerably, 10 to 12 inches could be considered a fairly normal tread depth, and a riser of 6 to 7 inches would be typical and appropriate.

Another way of thinking about riser height and tread width is known as "the rule of 18." The design of a staircase is considered comfortable and easy to use for most people if the total of the riser height plus the tread width equals 18 inches. For example, a 12-inch tread with a 6-inch riser subscribes to "the rule of 18," as would a 10-inch tread with an 8-inch riser. While useful, it is important to remember that "the rule of 18" is a guideline and not an absolute. Ultimately, the scenic designer determines the riser height and tread width for any design. The important point is that the stairs work within the context of the scenic design and that the actors need to be comfortable and secure when

score: To cut partially through.

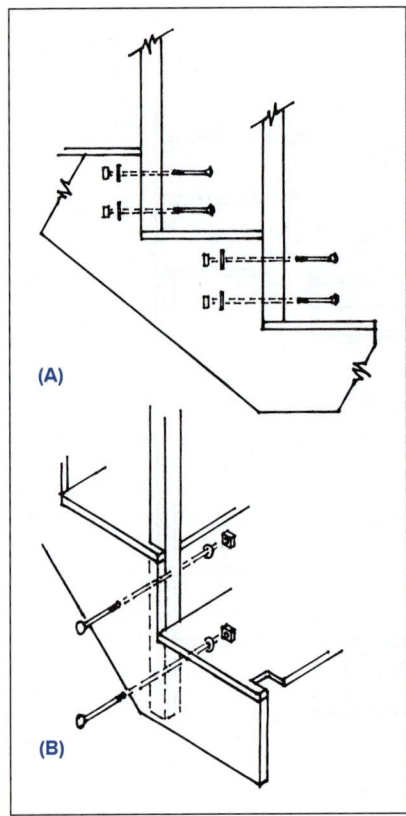

(A)

(B)

FIGURE 11.49
Methods of attaching banisters to stair units. (A) Bolting the banisters to the riser allows the banister to be placed flush to the carriage. (B) Bolting the banisters to the carriage insets the banister 1½-inch from the outside edge of the carriage.

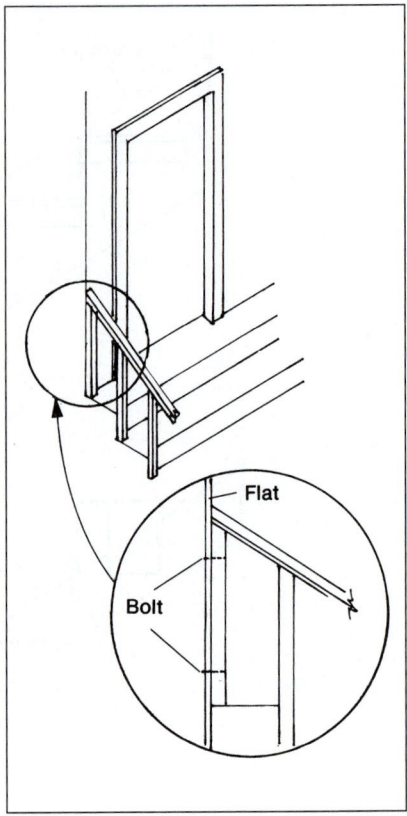

Flat

Bolt

FIGURE 11.50
The top newel post and handrail must be firmly anchored.

moving on the stairs. Figure 11.48B shows the usual construction method of butting the treads into the bottom of the risers.

Staircase Railings

Although the design of any staircase railing is the province of the scenic designer, some seemingly universal challenges are encountered in the construction of these units. Unless **handrails, banister,** and **newel posts** are firmly anchored to the stair unit, they will wiggle and detract from the action of the play. For this reason, it is generally preferable to securely attach at least every other banister post to the stair riser with screws or bolts, as shown in Figure 11.49A. If the design indicates that the banisters and lower newel post cannot be butted against the risers, the base of the banister posts should be extended through the tread and screwed or bolted to the carriage, as shown in Figure 11.49B.

The lower newel post should be firmly anchored to the bottom tread, and the top newel post and handrail should be solidly attached to the flat at the top of the stairs, as shown in Figure 11.50.

Wagons

Wagons are usually rigid platforms that rest on casters instead of legs (Figure 11.51). They can vary in size from very small (1 foot square or less) to very large. (The

handrail: The part of the stair railing that is grabbed with the hand; supported by the banister and newel post.

banister: The vertical member that supports the handrail of a staircase railing.

newel post: The post at the bottom or top of a flight of stairs that terminates the handrail.

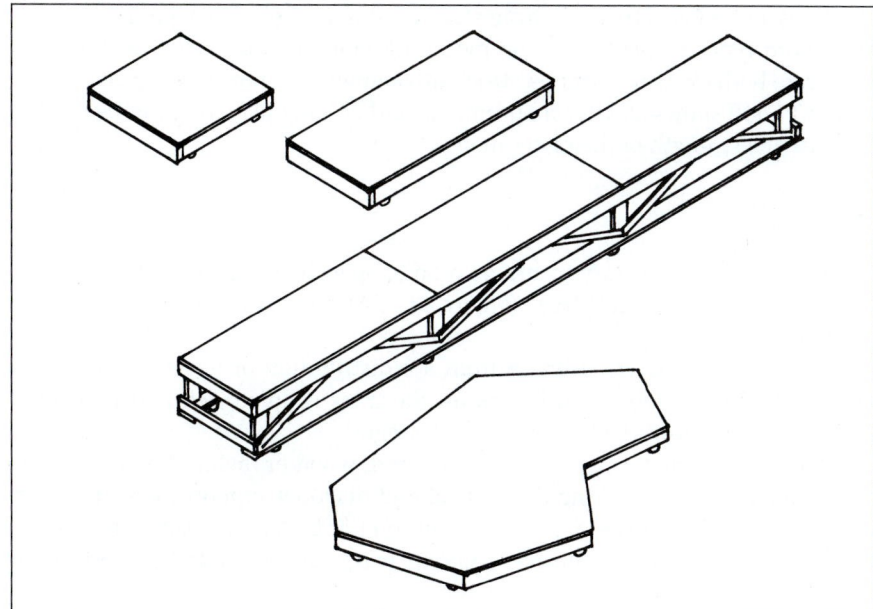

FIGURE 11.51
Wagons.

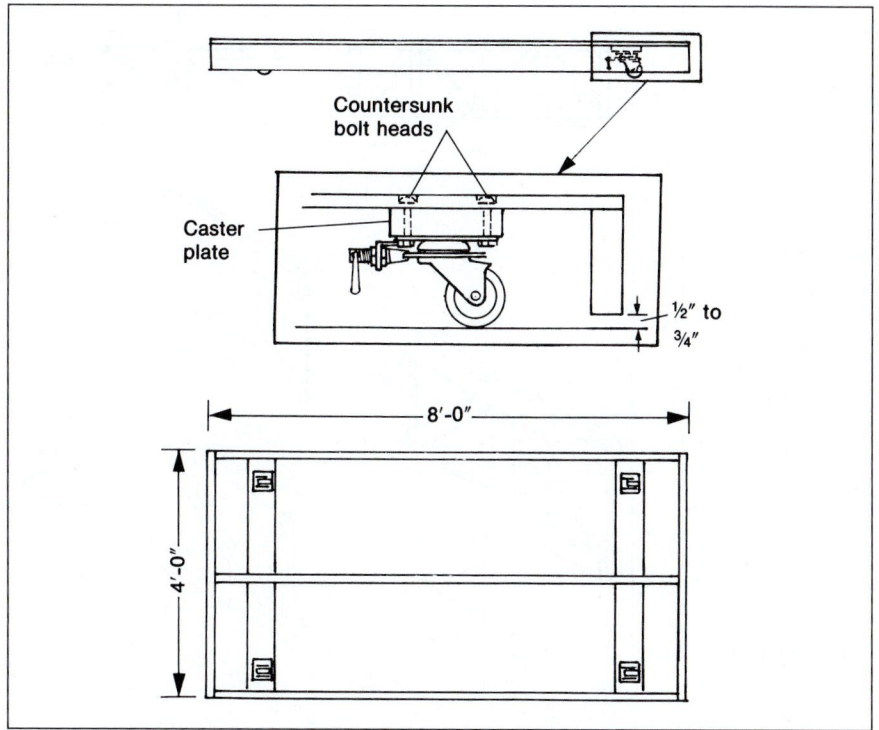

FIGURE 11.52
Caster mounting techniques for rigid platforms.

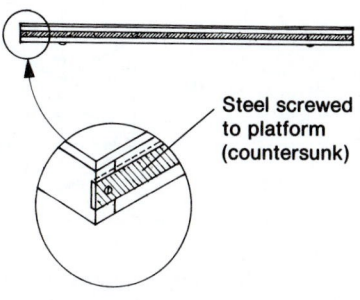

FIGURE 11.53
Reinforcing a 2 × 4 frame with strap steel decreases the springiness of a wagon.

slipstage is a huge wagon slightly larger than the normal playing area of the stage. It can hold an entire set.)

Casters, either rigid or swivel, are usually bolted onto caster plates attached to the underside of the platform (Figure 11.52). The caster plates should be sufficiently tall to create a clearance of ½ to ¾ inch between the bottom edge of the platform and the stage floor. Unless the platform framing is very stiff (2 × 6 or 2 × 4 reinforced with 1½- to 2-inch by ³⁄₁₆-inch or ¼-inch mild-steel strap — see Figure 11.53), the casters should be spaced no more than 48 inches apart to prevent the platform from bouncing when it is walked on.

Wagons can also be made from stressed-skin and sandwich-core platforms. With both types of platforms, the mounting bolts for the casters will have to penetrate both skins to ensure a strong attachment, as shown in Figure 11.54A. Figure 11.54B shows a caster-mounting jig and bearing plate that can be used to increase the strength of the caster mount.

Trusses

Many times it is necessary to bridge a large span between supporting points. A wooden or welded-steel truss (Figure 11.55A) offers another solution to this challenge.

The truss derives its strength from a redistribution of forces, as shown in Figure 11.55B. The downward force on the truss is channeled and redirected into a horizontal force by the legs of the triangle.

Trusses, as noted, can be made from either wood or metal. Wooden trusses can be made by sandwiching the vertical and diagonal support pieces between the two longitudinal joists, as shown in Figure 11.55C. A more easily constructed, but heavier and more expensive, wooden truss can be made by substituting

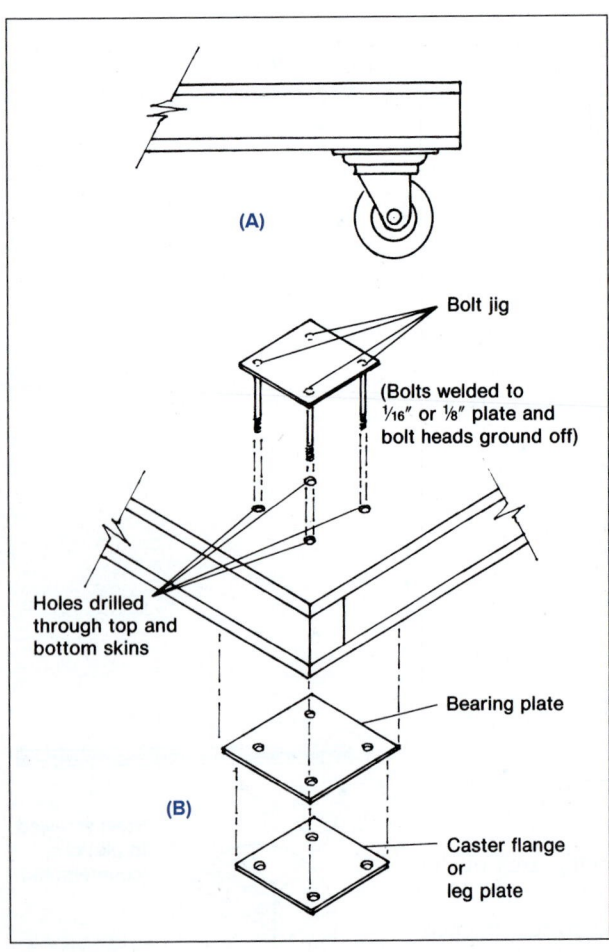

FIGURE 11.54
Caster mounting techniques for stressed-skin and honeycomb-laminate platforms. (A) Side view of a stressed-skin or sandwich-core platform with caster. (B) Exploded view showing method of attachment of caster to a stressed-skin or sandwich-core platform.

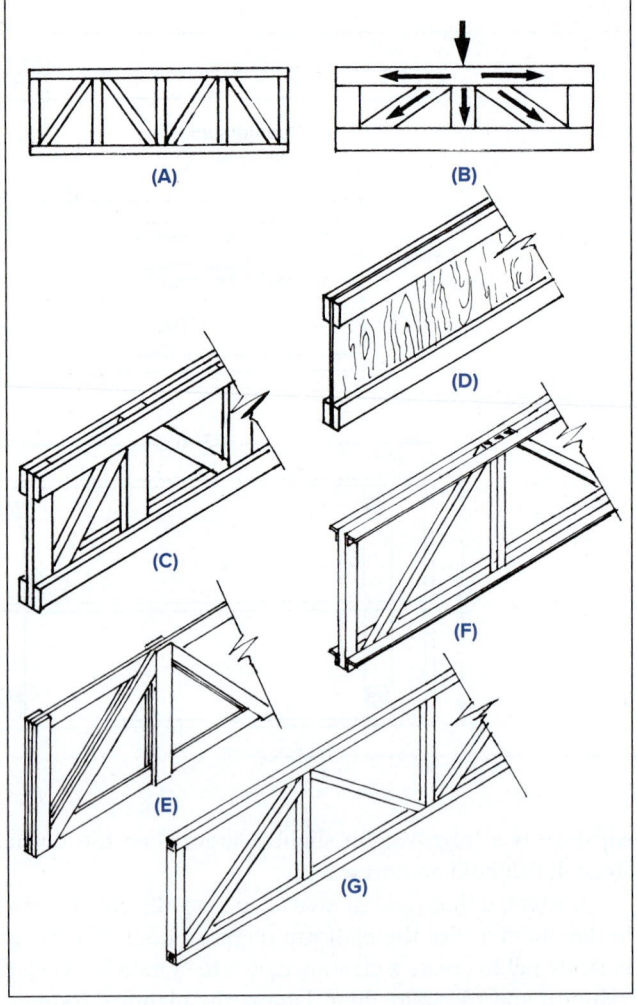

FIGURE 11.55
Principles of truss bracing and types of trusses. See text for detailed explanation.

⅜-inch plywood for the diagonal bracing. Be sure that the grain of the plywood runs vertically, as shown in Figure 11.55D. The top and bottom rails of the truss can also be made by sandwiching 2 × 4 rails with the diagonal and vertical elements, as shown in Figure 11.55E. All joints in any type of wooden truss should be fastened with a high-quality synthetic adhesive (polyvinyl or epoxy glue) and nails, screws, bolts, or staples.

Metal trusses can be made by using bar stock for the diagonal supports and angle stock for longitudinal rails, as shown in Figure 11.55F. Again, to keep the truss from twisting, the rails should sandwich the diagonal bar stock. Metal trusses can also be made from square tubing, as illustrated in Figure 11.55G. In the interests of making strong and safe welds, use an arc welder (preferably MIG), rather than oxyacetylene for this type of weight-bearing, welded structure.

Trusses should be spaced no farther than 2 feet apart if the **decking** attached to the top of the truss is ¾-inch plywood. If the truss is to be decked with rigid, stressed-skin, or honeycomb-laminate platforms, the spacing between the trusses can be varied accordingly. The design of any weight-bearing truss should be checked with a structural engineer to ensure that it will be safe to use and will perform as intended.

Movable Scenery

Nothing is more spectacular than scenery that seemingly moves by itself. The various techniques, methods, and machines used to mechanically move scenery are the subject of this section.

Revolves

Revolves, also called turntables, are large, circular platforms that pivot on their central axis. Revolves are used in a variety of ways to shift scenery. The primary challenges in constructing a smooth-turning revolve are (1) attaching the casters so that the wheels are absolutely perpendicular to the radii of the turntable and (2) placing the pivot in the exact center of the revolve.

Revolves can be built using any of the standard platform-construction techniques, although the rigid platform method, shown in Figure 11.56, seems to work best, particularly if the scenery that will be placed on the revolve requires that you cut through its surface for support points. Revolves can be turned by hand but are more frequently rotated with some type of powered system. Methods of power-rotating revolves will be discussed a little later in this chapter.

Skids

Skids (Figure 11.57) are low-profile, casterless substitutes for wagons. They are generally pieces of ½- or ¾-inch plywood that are "skidded" across the stage. Skids are normally used to shift lightweight scenic elements such as chairs, tables, and small scenic pieces. Although skids can be pushed across the stage with a pole or pulled with a monofilament fishing line, they are frequently propelled by friction-cable or drive wheel systems, which will be discussed in the next section.

Winch-Drive Systems

Almost every machine that moves scenery employs the basic operating principle of the **winch,** which is a machine that converts rotational motion into linear

decking: The covering surface of a structure on which people will walk.

winch: A machine having a drum around which one end of a cable is wound and the other end attached to the load. Used for hoisting or hauling.

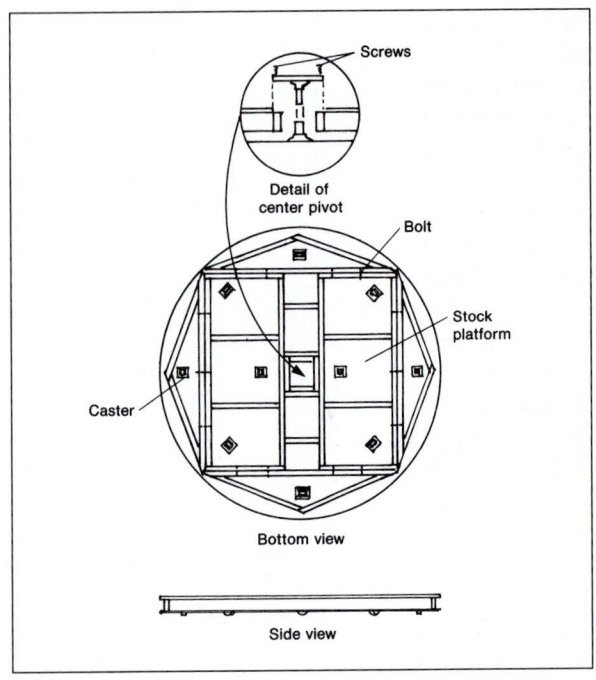

FIGURE 11.56
Revolve construction principles.

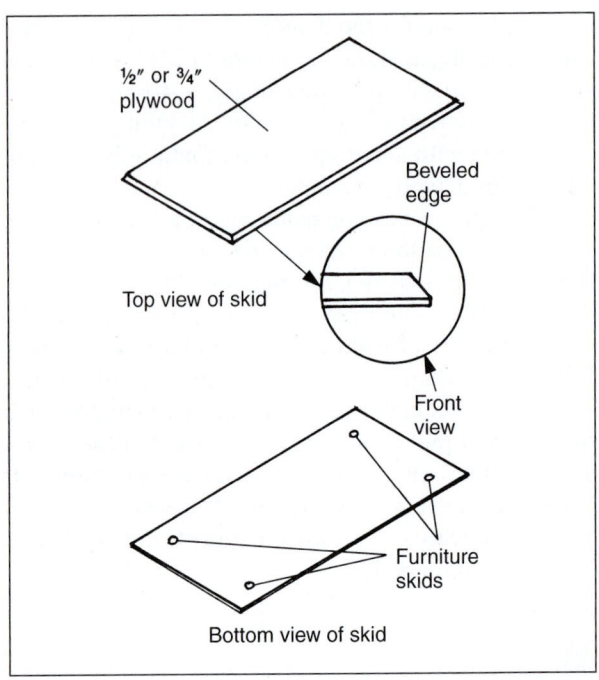

FIGURE 11.57
Skids.

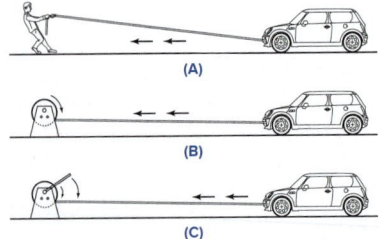

FIGURE 11.58
The principles of mechanical advantage. No mechanical advantage is created when:
(A) Pulling a car with a rope; or
(B) winding the rope around a winch drum. (C) Mechanical advantage *is* created when a level is used to turn the drum.

mechanical advantage: A measure of force amplification. A ratio comparing "force produced" to "force applied" for a tool or machine.

pulley: A grooved wheel. Used to change the direction of travel of ropes, cables, or belts. Encased in a wooden or metal sheath for use in block and tackle systems. Attached to the motor and drum shafts in belt-drive systems.

movement. Winches increase power through **mechanical advantage.** This enables heavy loads to be moved with relatively little effort.

Mechanical Advantage   When an object such as a car is pulled with a rope (Figure 11.58A) no mechanical advantage is created because the force required to pull the car must equal the weight of the object being moved. For example, if a stage wagon weighs 100 pounds, then a force of 100 pounds needs to be applied to move it.[5] Wrapping the "pulling" end of the rope around a drum (Figure 11.58B) doesn't provide any mechanical advantage because the force required to turn the drum still must equal the weight of the wagon. But a mechanical advantage is created when the length of the crank turning the drum is longer than the radius of the drum (Figure 11.58C.)

The amount of mechanical advantage created is determined by comparing the length of the crank handle with the radius of the winch drum: the greater ratio, the greater the mechanical advantage. For example, if the crank handle is twice as long as the radius of the drum, a 2 to 1 mechanical advantage is created. Only 50 pounds of force will be needed to move a 100-pound load. The trade-off is that the handle will have to turn twice as fast to move the wagon at the same speed.

Power-driven winches use the same principles. They just substitute motors and (typically) belt-drive systems to turn the drum. The mechanical advantage of belt-drive systems is determined by comparing the radius of the **pulley** on the drum to the radius of the drive-shaft pulley. If the drum pulley is twice the radius of the drive-shaft pulley a 2 to 1 mechanical advantage is created. A 4 to

---

[5] Technically, to overcome inertia and begin moving the object, the force applied must be greater than the weight of the object. But the required "overcoming force" is so small as to be negligible for purposes of this discussion. Additional force will also be needed to overcome friction within the system, but that is also tangential to a discussion of the operating principles of mechanical advantage.

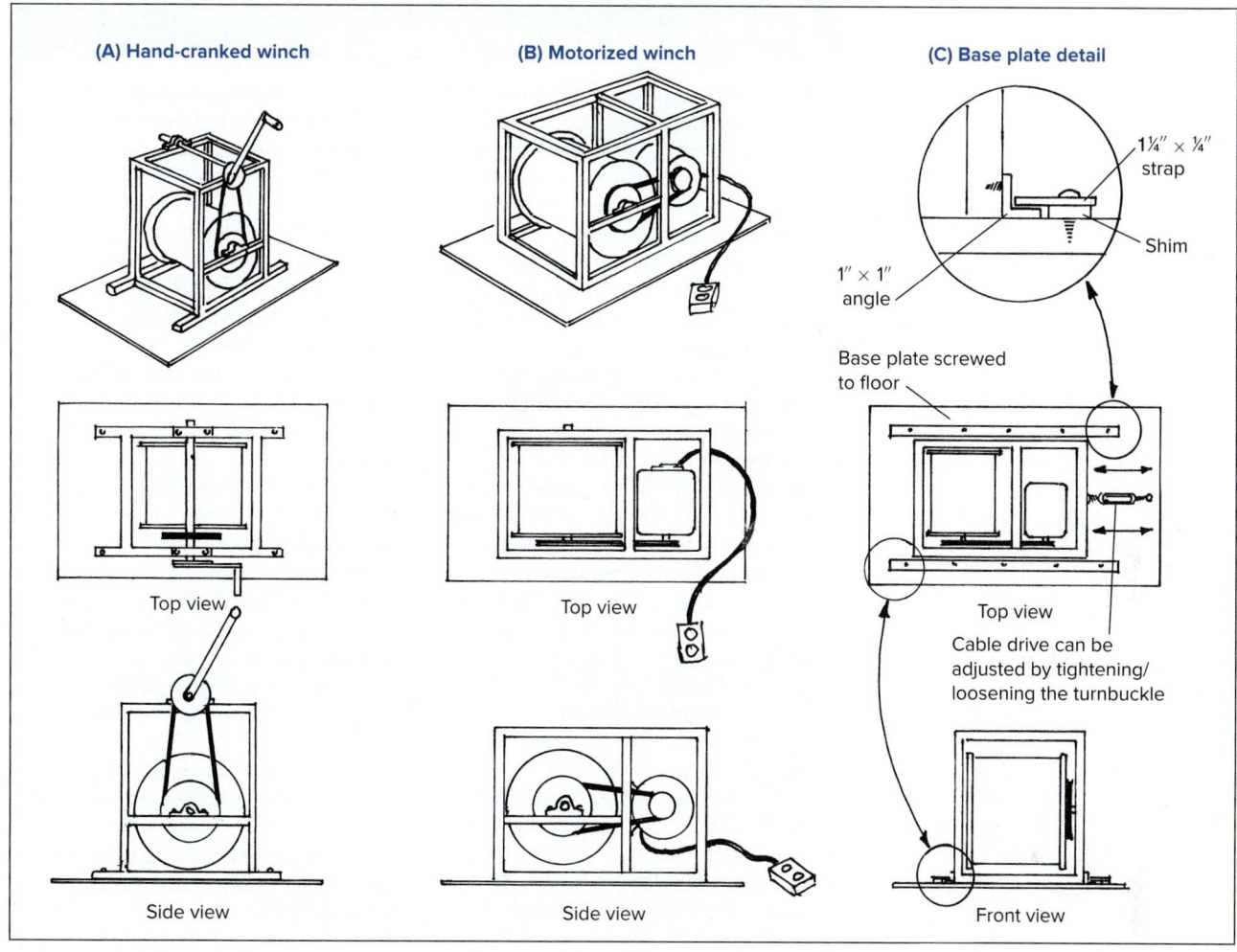

(A) Hand-cranked winch

Top view

Side view

(B) Motorized winch

Top view

Side view

(C) Base plate detail

1¼″ × ¼″ strap

Shim

1″ × 1″ angle

Base plate screwed to floor

Top view

Cable drive can be adjusted by tightening/ loosening the turnbuckle

Front view

FIGURE 11.59
Hand-cranked and motorized winches.

1 mechanical advantage will be created if the radius of drum pulley is four times the radius of the drive-shaft pulley.[6]

Figures 11.59A and B illustrate shop-built examples of both hand-cranked and motorized winches. Figure 11.59C illustrates a method of adjusting cable tension. Every winch system needs some means of adjusting cable tension to keep the cable snug because a loose cable can easily become tangled and/or stuck.

Motorized Winches Variable-speed electric motors have replaced hand-cranked winches in almost all theatrical applications. Because the average electric motor typically has less power and more speed than is useful for stage purposes almost all theatrical drive systems have motors with integrated gear-boxes (devices using mechanical advantage) to increase the unit's **torque.**

Two types of motors — named for their power sources — are used with theatrical drive systems. DC motors are powered by direct current. AC motors are powered by alternating current electricity. (Information about AC and DC power can be found in Chapter 15, "Electrical Theory and Practice.")

DC Motors DC motors were for a long time the standard for theatrical drive systems because their speed is more easily and precisely controlled than AC

---

[6] Additional information on mechanical advantage can be found on the Web.

torque: Rotational force.

PRODUCTION INSIGHTS
DC Motor Speed Control

The speed at which a DC motor runs is directly proportion to its input voltage. It will spin twice as fast if supplied with twice the voltage and half as fast with half the voltage. But adjusting the supply voltage isn't efficient. Fortunately, the same effect — apparent voltage variation — can be achieved another way.

A process known as the "gating principle" controls DC motor speed. Visualize a light bulb connected to a switch. If, in a given period of time, you repeatedly turn the light on then off, you effectively control the total amount of light emitted for that given period of time. For example, if a light bulb is turned on for 1 second, it glows at full intensity for that 1-second period. If it is turned on for half a second and off for half a second, it effectively emits half the light (burns at half intensity) for that 1-second period. Turning the light on for a ¼ second and off for ¾ second results in ¼ of the light being emitted for the 1-second period (one-quarter intensity).

In each of these examples, you would obviously see the lamp being turned on and off. But if the time span of the on–off cycle were reduced to 1/120 of a second, you would perceive the on–off sequence as providing a continuous level of illumination at the average ratio of the on-off cycle. (This is the same gating principle used by SCR [silicon-controlled rectifier] dimmers. Those dimmers will be discussed in Chapter 16, "Lighting Production.")

DC speed controllers use the gating principle to vary the ratio of the on–off cycle for the full-voltage DC power being supplied to the motor. A **MOSFET chip** does the rapid power switching. The **inertia** of the motor's relatively heavy rotor keeps the motor spinning during the MOSFET's momentary "off" cycles.

The extreme speed of the MOSFET's on–off cycle, when combined with the rotor's inertia, creates an effective tool for precisely controlling the running speed of DC motors.

---

motors. The speed of a DC motor is directly proportional to the amount of voltage applied to it. For example, a DC motor turns half as fast with a 6-volt supply as it does with a 12-volt supply. DC speed controllers employ this principle — altering speed by varying the applied voltage — to control the speed of DC motors. (See the box, "DC Motor Speed Control," for a more detailed discussion of this process.)

AC Motors   As technologies for controlling the speed of AC motors have improved and prices for AC motor controls have dropped, the use of AC motors for moving scenery has become more common.

Like DC motors, the speed at which an AC motor runs is directly proportional to its **input voltage:** As the voltage decreases, the motor slows down; as the voltage increases, the motor speeds up. Unfortunately, it's not efficient to directly manipulate AC voltage. But the voltage can be effectively changed by altering its frequency.

AC speed controllers use a **variable-frequency drive** (VFD) to manipulate the frequency of the AC power delivered to the motor. Any frequency change makes a proportional change to AC voltage: When the frequency decreases, the voltage drops, and the motor slows down. The reverse is also true: As the frequency increases, the voltage increases and the motor spins faster. (See the box, "AC Motor Speed Control," for more detailed information.)

MOSFET chip: MOSFET (metal-oxide-semiconductor field effect transistor) chips use a low-voltage control circuit to rapidly switch a higher voltage current flow on and off.

inertia: The tendency of a body in motion to remain in motion, or a body at rest to stay at rest.

input voltage: The voltage being fed to a device.

variable-frequency drive: A solid-state device used to change the frequency of electrical power.

PRODUCTION INSIGHTS

AC Motor Speed Control

AC motor speed control is achieved by using a variable-frequency driver (VFD) to change the frequency of the 60-Hz, three-phase AC electricity powering the motor. Single-phase motors can be used with VFDs but three-phase motors are more efficient.

A full understanding of how the variable-frequency driver works isn't needed to understand how the VFD controls the speed of an AC motor. As its name implies the VFD is used to *variably* alter the frequency of its output power. The voltage of any power AC power source is proportional to its frequency. For example, electrical power is delivered at a frequency of 60 Hz[a] in the United States. If the 60-Hz frequency of a power source is reduced, its voltage proportionally decreases. The speed of both AC and DC motors proportionally changes when their supply voltage is altered. Lower the supply voltage of an AC motor, and its speed will decrease proportionally. For example, when the frequency of electricity supplying an AC motor is cut from 60 Hz to 30 Hz, the voltage is cut in half, which causes the motor's speed to be cut in half. Increase the frequency, the voltage increases, and the motor speeds up.

You may have noticed that the speed of both AC and DC motors is controlled in the same way — by manipulating their supply voltage. The difference between the two is that the AC units need an extra electronic step (frequency variation) to manipulate the voltage. This "extra step" costs more, which is one of the reasons variable-speed AC motors haven't been used as often in the theatre as DC counterparts. The price of these units is dropping, which has made their use more viable.

Technically advanced information about VFDs and how they work can be found online at a number of sources.

[a]Frequency is measured in cycles per second. The unit of measurement for cycles per second is the hertz, abbreviated as Hz.

Step (or Stepper) Motors   A step motor is an electric motor whose rotational movement consists of discrete angular steps rather than continuous rotation. More expensive than either AC or DC motors, precise movement is achieved by programming the motor to run, in either direction, for a specific number of steps. Stepper motors, particularly when run at high speed, are often noisier than either of the other motors.

Motorized Scenery

There are several methods and techniques used to move scenery with variable-speed drive systems.

Motorized Revolves   Revolves can be rotated using cable-friction winch drives or drive wheel units.

Cable-Friction Winch Drives   A cable-friction winch drive is illustrated in Figure11.60. Although the illustration shows a hand-cranked winch, these units are frequently powered with variable speed drives. If a **continuous-loop cable** is used, the revolve can be rotated continuously in either direction.

The outer edge of a revolve using a cable-friction drive needs to have a relatively smooth gripping surface for the cable. Figure 11.61 shows 2 × 8 curved-face sweeps attached to the underside of the ¾-inch plywood deck to create the

continuous-loop cable: A cable whose ends have been spliced or joined to form the cable into a loop.

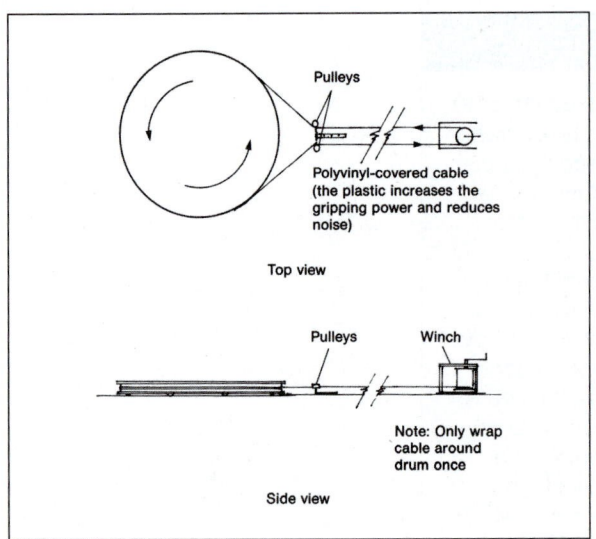

FIGURE 11.60
Cable drive for a small revolve.

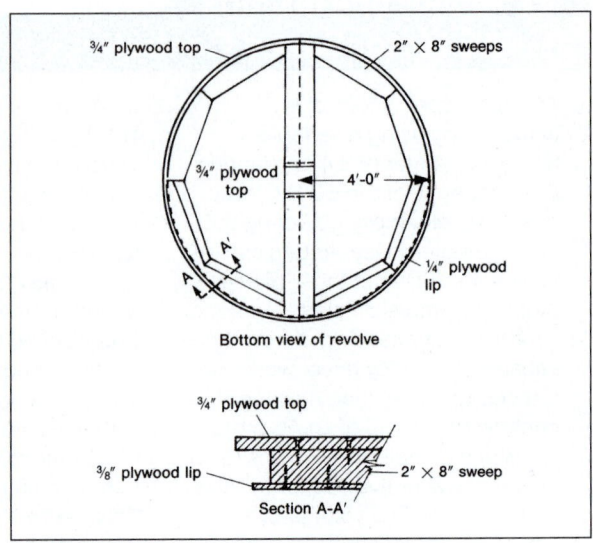

FIGURE 11.61
Revolve edge-finishing techniques.

track for the drive cable. Additional sweeps of ⅜-inch-plywood are fastened to the underside of track to prevent the cable from falling off. Plastic-coated cable is normally used on friction-cable systems because the plastic increases the cable's grip on both the revolve and drum.

Drive Wheel Units   Revolves can also be turned with motor-driven, variable speed, rubber-tired, **drive wheel** units. These units can be mounted on the revolve itself or secured to the stage floor beneath the revolve.

Revolve-mounted units (Figure 11.62A) are bolted to the revolve with the drive wheel in contact with the stage floor. When activated, the drive wheel accelerates along the stage floor, turning the revolve.

Floor-mounted drive wheel units (Figure 11.62B) are fastened to the stage floor with the drive wheel firmly in contact with the edge of the revolve. When the power is switched on the drive wheel rotates, spinning the revolve.

Motorized Wagons and Skids   With the help of a concealed winch system, wagons and skids can appear to magically glide across the stage. Figure 11.63 shows a wagon or skid running on top of a slightly raised deck. The wagon is fitted with steel knives (also called dogs) that stick through a slot in the floor called the knife track. The ends of the winch-system cable are attached to the knives. The system can be operated with either hand-cranked or motorized winches.

Motion Control

Imagine a bare stage, blackness everywhere. From upstage, an old two-story building glides downstage, slowly turns and the walls swing open revealing both floors of the grungy house. From the other side of the stage a whaling ship slowly glides into place as a gangplank descends from its side. Simultaneously, a cluster of ship's sails flies in upstage, and a dock emerges from the floor. When this slow-motion ballet ends, we find ourselves looking at the dockside of a nineteenth-century New England whaling village.

This highly choreographed dance would have taken 10 to 12 seconds to complete. And it would have been repeated, exactly, in precisely the same order and rhythm, performance after performance. That is the beauty of motion control.

drive wheel: A motorized rubber-tired wheel driven by a variable-speed electric motor.

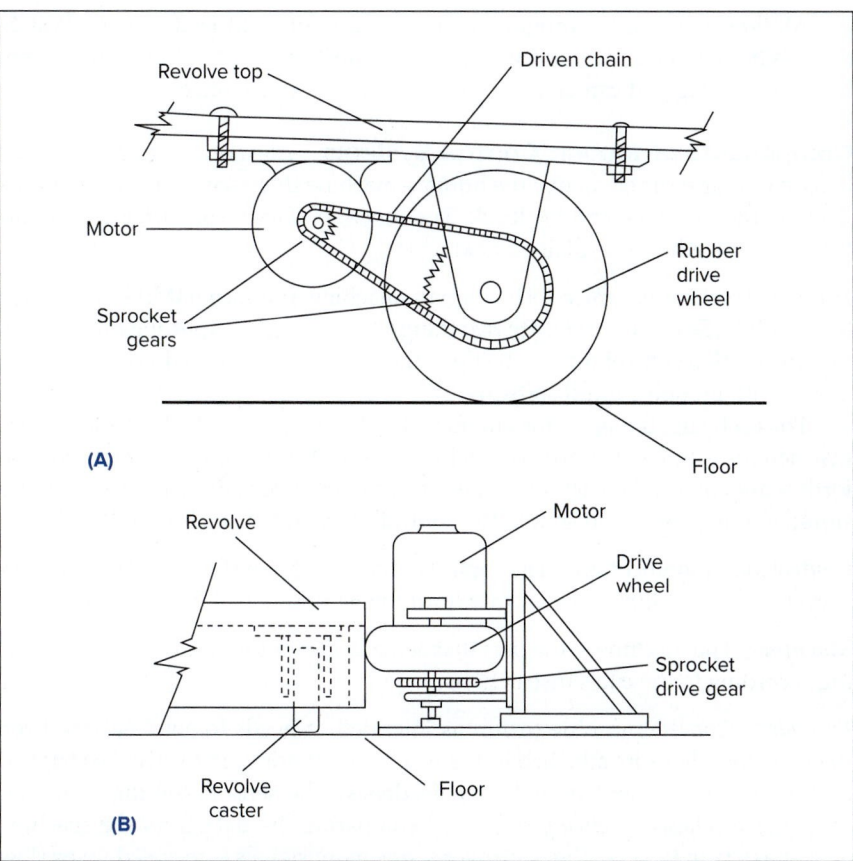

(A)

(B)

FIGURE 11.62
Revolve-mounted and floor-mounted drive wheel units.

PRODUCTION INSIGHTS

Motors Are Basically Stupid

Electric motors are basically stupid. They can't think. They just "do." Turn them on and they run. Turn them off and they stop. And that's the problem.

Most people don't think about how a motor works. They just assume when they turn it on *it will work as they think it should.* But the exact speed at which an electric motor runs is dependent on a number of factors with input voltage — the applied voltage that makes the motor run — being the most important.

The power in both residential and commercial buildings is rarely constant at 120 volts AC. It varies a few volts up or down depending on a number of factors. In most instances (running a dishwasher, turning on kitchen lights, and so forth), those

minor voltage fluctuations don't matter because their effects aren't really noticeable. But motors used in motion control systems must run at *exactly* the speed they were programmed to run.

If any motor is fed its rated voltage, it will run at its rated speed. For example, a 120-volt AC motor with a rated speed of 1750 revolutions per minute (RPM) will run at 1750 RPM *only* if it is supplied with exactly 120 volts AC. If the voltage is lower, the motor runs slower. If the voltage is higher, the motor speeds up.

That's why **feedback** loops in motion control systems are important. They instantly respond to any changes in the motor's speed and make equally fast adjustments to keep the motor running at the intended speeds.

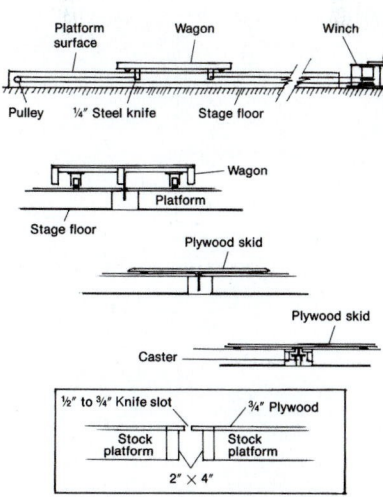

FIGURE 11.63
Winch-driven wagons and skids.

feedback: The return of information about the result of an activity.

Motion control is the programmed movement of motorized scenery. Watching it is both entertaining and very theatrical. Just about any kind of movement that can be imagined can be realized — if your budget is large enough.

Components of Motion Control Systems All motion control systems consist of four basic elements: the human–machine interface, control and amplification, the machine, and feedback. The function of each component, and how they work together, is explained next.

Human–Machine Interface The human–machine interface (HMI) — also called the user interface (UI) — refers to two things: the process of inputting information into the motion control console by the operator and the console itself — usually a laptop with motion control software.[7]

For each cue, the operator enters instructions into the HMI console. Those instructions — move forward, go backward, speed, rate of acceleration, and so forth — are entered for each movement the scenery needs to make. The cues are stored in the console and sent to the controller when the cue is called.

Control and Amplification The controller receives the cue from the HMI and forward those instructions — usually via an amplifier of some kind — to the machine.

Machine The machine — the part that actually moves the scenery — starts moving according to the cue's instructions.

Feedback For the machine to run as intended, it needs to get feedback from the machine.[8] Sensors attached to the machine's motor (and to switches tripped by the moving scenery) provide that feedback. The sensors tell the controller what the machine is *actually* doing. By comparing the data from the machine with the data in the cue, the controller sends more signals — to speed up or slow down — to the machine so it will ultimately do what the cue intended it to do. This machine–controller–machine **feedback loop** is continuous (many times per second) as long as the scenery is in motion. It is the feedback loop that ensures the machine will do what was planned when the cue was originally written.

As additional cues are sent from the HMI, the controller compares the new data with the data it is receiving from the feedback sensors and adjusts the machine's movements accordingly.

The cruise control on a car provides a perfect analogy of the interaction between the components of a motion control system. The driver, cruise control buttons, and speedometer all working together are the HMI of the cruise control system. Once the driver gets the car up to speed and sets the car's cruise control, the work of the HMI is done. The computer under the hood (the controller) constantly monitors the rate of revolution of the wheels and adjusts the throttle (the amplifier) to increase or decrease the power sent to the wheels to maintain the car's speed at the programmed rate.

Safety An essential part of every motion control HMI is an emergency stop switch that immediately cuts off power to the machines. Its importance cannot be overstressed. Swiftly moving computer-controlled machinery can involve significant weights and rates of speed — more than enough to seriously injure or kill. *Never*[9] operate a motion control system that does not have an emergency stop switch.

feedback loop: The flow of information within a control system that allows for self-correction based on differences between the actual output and the desired output.

---

[7] Spikemark (www.creativeconners.com) is a motion control program that provides animated views of both proposed and "in action" scenic movements.

[8] To understand why a machine needs feedback to run according to a cue's instructions, see the box, "Motors Are Basically Stupid."

[9] This is the *only* time the order to "Never" do something has been used in this book. That's how important it is to *never* operate a motion control system without an emergency kill button.

acrylic concentrates
for use as an interior
latex or any type of
that the scenery has

Vinyl Acrylic Pai
has excellent adhesi
fabric, and most met
24 hours, it becomes
The paint is mix
with either a clear o
is mixed with the cle
of concentrated pigr
mixed with the base
mixed paint (pigme
can be used to prov
finish is needed, wa

Aniline Dye And
sion of **aniline** dye
priate safety equip
handling or mixing
which you are worl
issues, and the ava
anymore.
Aniline powde
water. A very stror
spoon of dye with
stored in sealable
trated dye solution

The **limit switch** is another safety-related feedback device. Limit switches are used to stop the movement of a piece of scenery in a specific location. When the limit switch is contacted by the moving scenery, it sends a signal to the controller that kills the power to the machine, effectively stopping the scenery's movement.

The safety issues involved in having multiple scenic elements pirouetting about the stage cannot be stressed enough. But those concerns can be addressed and solved.

The advantages of a motion control system are fairly obvious: Complex movement can be precisely and consistently controlled. The downside is that the equipment can be highly sophisticated, expensive, and requires rigorous maintenance and constant inspection by highly qualified personnel.

With the costs of motion control equipment continuing to come down, these types of systems are no longer out of reach for many theatres and producing organizations. And there's no question that motion control is a highly entertaining addition to the bag of magic tricks that are used to amaze the audience.

Platform-Anchoring Techniques

Large, three-dimensional scenic elements are frequently mounted on wagons to facilitate shifting by hand or motion control systems. Once the wagon is in place, however, the casters will still wiggle or roll unless the wagon is anchored. Figure 11.64 illustrates a number of methods that can be used to anchor platforms.

Lift Jack The lift jack (Figure 11.65) is another platform-anchoring technique typically used when the scenery is shifted manually. The casters are placed in contact with the stage floor when the platform needs to be moved, but the

limit switch: A switch that opens or closes when contacted by a moving object. Used to limit the travel of that object.

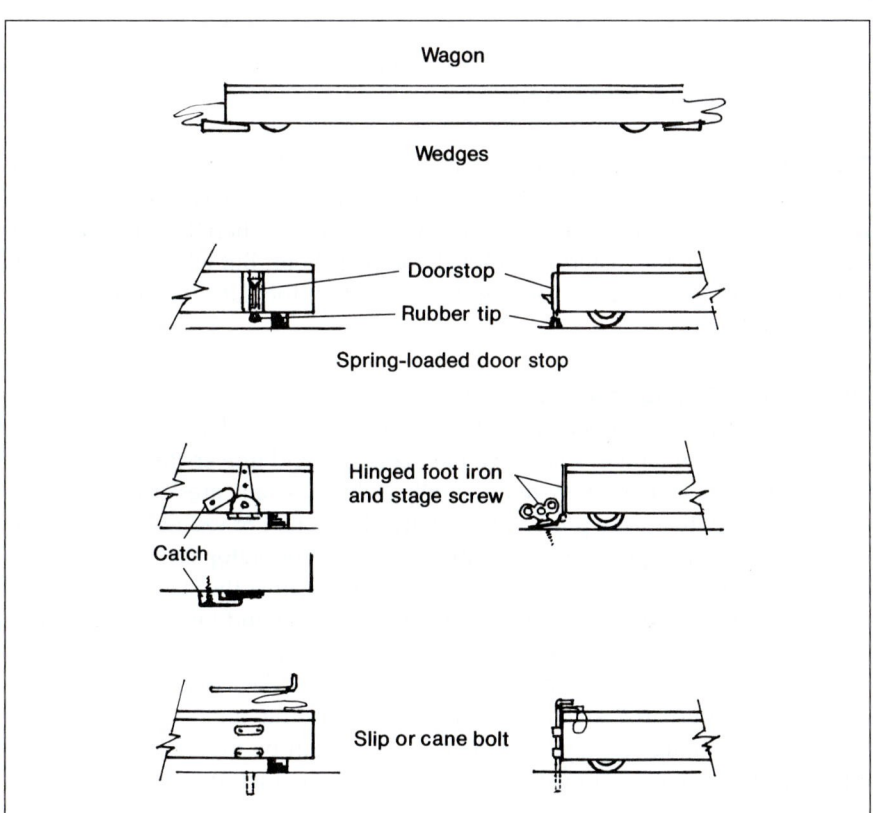

FIGURE 11.64
Platform anchoring techniques.

TABLE 12.1

A Representa

Whites

Black
Yellows

Oranges
Reds

Violets
Blues

Greens

Earth colors

Other

vinyl acryli
saturated p
binder; mixe
(for tints) or
fully saturat
working pa

compressor: A pump, typically electric-or gasoline-powered, that drives air into a tank; output pressure from the tank is controlled by a valve called a regulator.

PRODUCTION INSIGHTS

Spray-Painting Tips

If these general guidelines are followed, you should find that your spray-painting experiences will be productive and relatively trouble free.

1. Always rinse the spray gun before using it to make sure that there is no dust or grit which could clog the nozzle in the gun or paint container.

2. Be sure to strain the paint with a commercial strainer or small-mesh nylon, such as the material in pantyhose. Straining the paint will remove any little globs of paint that might clog the nozzle.

3. Run a momentary blast of compressed air through the hoses before attaching them to the gun to remove any dust or grit from the hoses.

4. Keep the gun a uniform distance from the work, and move it parallel with the surface to deposit a uniform coat of paint.

5. Be sure to wear an appropriate respirator to filter out the atomized paint from the air you breathe; wear goggles to keep the airborne paint out of your eyes. Consult the SDSs for the materials with which you are working for specific information about required safety equipment and other safety considerations.

6. Be sure to keep the compressor pressure within the recommended levels for the gun and type of paint you're using.

An air gun spraying system is composed of three separate parts: the spray gun, the paint container, and the compressor. The normal spray gun has a 1-quart paint reservoir and is designed for continuous-duty applications — painting flats, floors, houses, and so forth. Touch-up guns have much smaller containers (2 to 6 ounces) and are designed for light-duty jobs such as painting chairs and picture frames and for situations in which the color may need to be changed frequently. Air brushes are equipped with small paint containers (½ to 2 ounces) and are used for fine detail and lining work. Most air brushes can be varied to spray a hard- or soft-edged line as well as a typical misty cone.

Compressors provide the motive power for most spray guns. The smallest serviceable compressor for general theatrical spraying would have an electric motor of approximately one horsepower with (minimally) a 10-gallon air tank. The larger, permanent compressor systems found in many shops provide an excellent air source for spray painting. Much smaller ⅛-horsepower compressors, as well as disposable compressed-air cans, are frequently used to power air brushes. Small electrically powered airless spray guns such as the Wagner Power Painter can be used in many theatrical applications as an effective substitute for the more expensive compressed-air systems.

Cartooning

Some scenic designs, particularly those that include backdrops, have a great deal of detail that must be transferred from the painter's elevation to the scenery. Cartooning refers to the process of drawing large-scale details on the scenery after the prime and base coats have been applied. Large, simple designs can usually be applied simply by taking scale measurements of the object on the painter's elevation and transferring them to the scenery. Any further details can

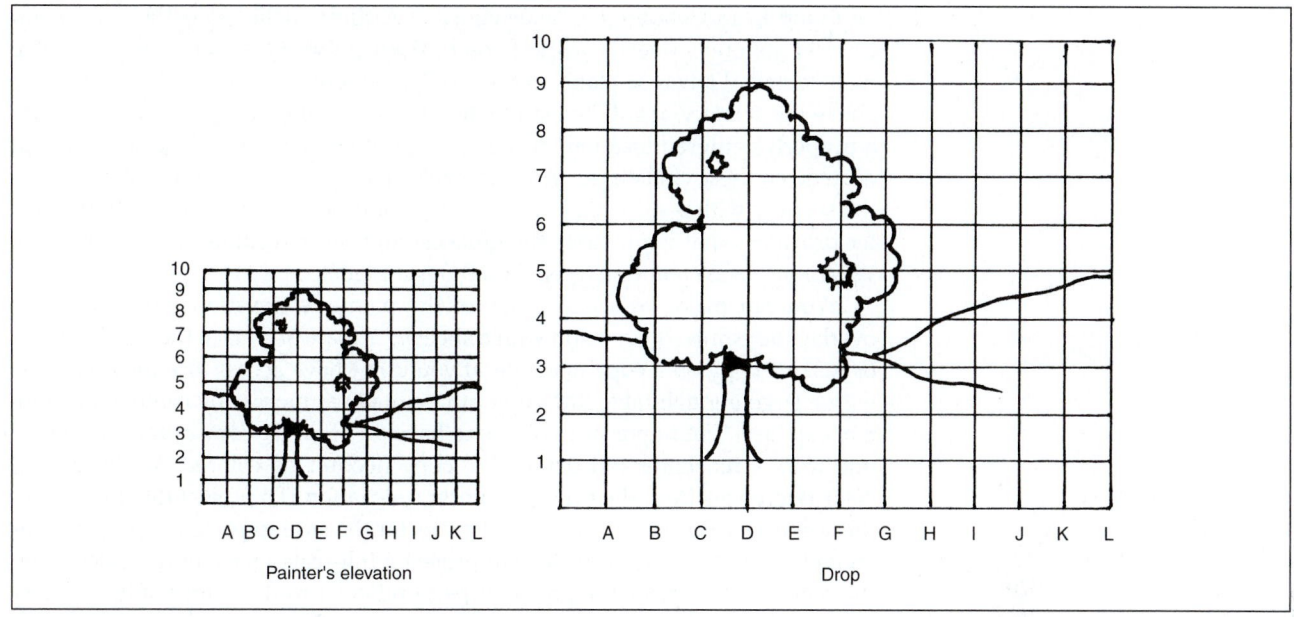

FIGURE 12.8
Grid-transfer technique.

usually be duplicated by freehand sketching with frequent references back to the painter's elevation. If the object is quite detailed, one of the following methods can be used to duplicate it accurately on the scenery.

Grid Transfer

In the appropriate scale, draw a 1-foot-square grid on the painter's elevation. (To preserve the elevation, cover it with a sheet of acetate, and use a fine-point acetate marker or well-sharpened grease pencil to draw the grid.) Also draw a full-scale 1-foot-square grid on the scenery, as shown in Figure 12.8. If the scenery is small, this grid can be drawn using a snap or chalk line, a straightedge, and charcoal or chalk. If the scenery is large, such as a drop, the grid can be created by tacking four-penny box nails, 1 foot apart, around the edge of the drop. String is laced back and forth between the nails to create the grid. Be sure to use the same beginning point for both grids, such as the lower left corner or some other readily identifiable point, on both the painter's elevation and the scenery.

If the horizontal grid lines on both the painter's elevation and the drop grid are designated with letters and the vertical lines with numbers, as shown in Figure 12.8, it becomes a fairly rapid process to accurately transfer the points of intersection between the drawing on the elevation and the elevation's grid to the full-scale grid on the scenery. When those points have been located, connect the dots using a piece of charcoal or chalk to complete the transfer of the design to the scenery.

Projection Transfer   The idea behind projection transfer is that an image of the painter's elevation can be projected, full scale, onto the scenery, and the details can then be traced onto the scenery or drop using charcoal or chalk. There are a couple of challenges to projection transfer. The first is that the projector has to be bright enough, and/or the shop dark enough, for the projected image to be sufficiently visible for it's outlines to be traced onto the scenery. A second consideration is that unless the projector is placed perpendicular to the center point of the drop or flat **keystoning** will occur. (A discussion of keystoning can

keystoning: The distortion that occurs in a projected image when the projector is placed at some angle other than perpendicular to the center of the projection surface.

be found in in Chapter 17, "Projections.") A third challenge is that projection transfer generally doesn't work if you're **floor painting** because, unless you've made detailed advance plans on how to fly, maneuver, and adjust the projector above the scenery, it will be extremely time-consuming to rig the projector into a properly centered location, at the appropriate height, above the scenery. But even given these challenges, if you can get the painter's elevation projected onto the scenery with a sufficiently bright image and no distortion, projection transfer provides what is probably the quickest and most accurate transfer method. What follows are some suggested methods and ideas.

You can make an acetate copy of the painter's elevation. You can either overlay the painter's elevation with a sheet of acetate and trace the detail outline or make a copy on a copy machine. If you don't have access to a copy machine with a large enough table, the copy can be made at most copy centers for minimal expense. The important point is to have an accurate copy of the elevation's line work — its shape and detail. The copy needn't be colored. You'll take all color references from the original painter's elevation. To project the image onto the scenery or drop use an overhead projector. Be sure to place the projector far enough from the scenery or drop to project a full-scale image of the object onto the scenery. Also place the projector perpendicular to the center of the scenery to minimize any keystoning.

Projection transfer is commonly used to copy the gross outlines of shapes onto the scenery and drops. Specific small details are normally transferred simply by sketching them, using the painter's elevation as a guide, and "painting inside the lines" that were created with the projection transfer.

The computer has opened up worlds of new transfer methods based on video projection of computer files. Images can be scanned in or created in the computer, manipulated as desired, then projected onto the scenery for copying by the scenic artist or paint crew. While exciting, there is the very real issue of bringing this high-tech, high-priced equipment into the rather dirty environment of the shop. It would be a rather expensive "oops" if a bucket of paint were inadvertently dumped on either a video projector or computer. However, instead of direct video projection of the files, the files can be printed on either paper or acetate, and these prints can be projected with an overhead projector.

The computer can also be used to create full-scale layout patterns such as wallpaper patterns or drop details. Generally, these pieces need to be printed on a plotter as they are normally too large to be printed on the paper used in an ordinary desktop printer. For a really large piece, or if a plotter isn't available, the original drawing can be broken into segments, the segments can be printed, then the various pieces taped together to create the full pattern. These patterns can then be transferred to the scenery.

Standard Texture Coats

The following techniques are normally applied on top of the base coat to provide visual interest, variety, depth, and patina to the scenery.

Spattering   As mentioned earlier spattering is the process of applying small drops of paint to a surface. Spattering is done over the base coat to help age the paint job, slightly alter the hue, or smooth out any apparent irregularities in an unevenly applied base coat. Spattering can be done either by hand or with a garden sprayer (the Hudson and Chapin brands are preferred) and with the scenery in either a vertical or a horizontal position. It is a very effective painting technique that can be mastered with a little practice.

floor painting: Painting scenery — flats, drops, and so forth — on the floor rather than standing up or attached to a paint frame.

Hand spattering is done by lightly loading a lay-in brush with paint the consistency of 2 percent milk. Dip only about one-third of the bristles into the paint and tap (don't scrape) the brush against the side of the bucket to remove any excess paint. Using a gentle forward flick of the brush, stop it when the brush is parallel to the surface you're spattering. Stand about 3 to 5 feet from the surface being painted and as the bristles snap forward they throw tiny paint droplets at the scenery. The amount of paint on the brush and the distance that you stand from the object being spattered will determine the size and density of the individual droplets. Having too much paint on the brush may result in large drops that run, particularly if the scenery being spattered is vertical. In most circumstances that's a no-no. If you have trouble controlling the spatter using the technique described earlier, you might try the following. Rather than simply flicking the brush toward the work, use less paint, bring the brush forward, and slap the ferrule of the brush against the heel of your other hand. This forcibly stops the brush's forward movement and more energetically flings the paint drops at the work. But it can also bruise the heel of your hand. Either way, if you constantly change the relative position of the brush, you will make a cross-hatch design that creates an appropriately neutral spatter pattern, as shown in Figure 12.9.

A garden sprayer can also be used to spatter. The nozzle of the sprayer can be adjusted to spray a pattern that varies in density from a fine mist to medium-sized droplets. The sprayer handle should be moved in a circular pattern as you spatter to avoid any tendency to create a linear pattern. To avoid clogging the nozzle, strain the paint through several layers of cheesecloth, window screening, or commercially available paint strainers before putting it into the sprayer. Be sure to thoroughly clean the sprayer after each use.

Stippling   Although similar to spattering, stippling applies a heavier texture to the scenery. As shown in Figure 12.10, stippling can be done with the tip of a brush (Figure 12.10A), a sponge (Figure 12.10B), or a feather duster (Figure 12.10C). It can also be done with the frayed end of a rope or the edge of a piece of burlap.

Stippling is accomplished by loading one of these applicators with paint and touching it to the scenery. To avoid making an obvious pattern, you need to

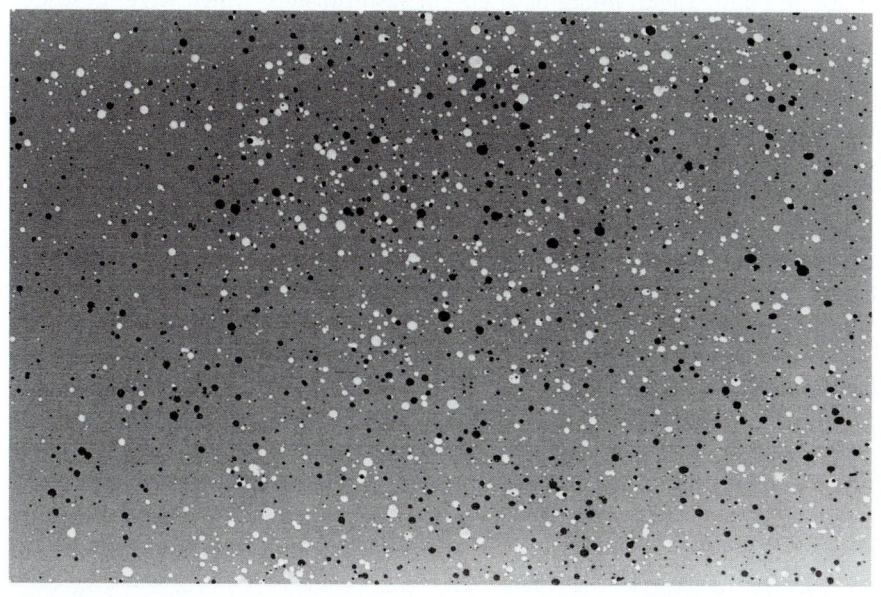

FIGURE 12.9
Spattering is created when drops of paint are applied to a surface. This is an example of a two-tone spatter. Courtesy of J. Michael Gillette.

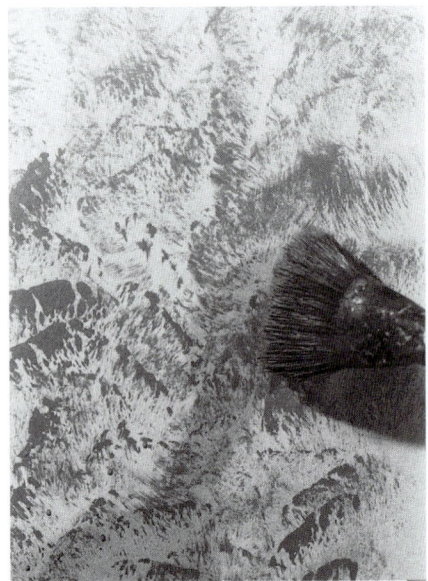

(A)

(B)

(C)

FIGURE 12.10
Stippling with a brush (A), with a sponge (B), and with a feather duster (C). Stippling is frequently used to create the appearance of surface texture. Courtesy of J. Michael Gillette.

FIGURE 12.11
Dry brushing is often used to create the appearance of wood grain. The tip of the brush is dipped in paint, scraped across the lip of the bucket (to remove excess paint), and lightly dragged across the surface of the work to create the appearance of wood grain. Courtesy of J. Michael Gillette.

source light: The apparent source of light that is illuminating a scene or an object.

constantly change the position of the applicator and the pressure with which you apply it to the scenery.

Dry Brushing   Dry brushing is painting with a brush that holds very little paint. Just the tip of the brush is dipped in the paint. Any paint that has been picked up by the bristles is scraped off on the lip of the bucket. The brush is then lightly drawn across the surface to deposit a linear, irregular pattern of paint (see Figure 12.11).

Dry brushing is very effective in creating the appearance of wood. If the dry-brushing paint(s) is fairly close in hue and value to the color of the base coat, the result will look like smooth wood. If the contrast between the hue and value of the base and dry-brush paints is greater, the result will look more rough-hewn.

Lining   Lining involves painting narrow, straight lines of varying width. The lines are painted with lining or angle-cut sash brushes, which were illustrated in Figure 12.1, with larger brushes used to create wider lines. A straightedge is used in conjunction with the lining brush, as shown in Figure 12.12A.

Lining can be used to create the appearance of depth. The illusion is primarily achieved through the use of highlight, shade, and shadow lines. The effect of the **source light** on an object will determine where the highlight and shadow lines need to be positioned. For the bricks shown in Figure 12.12B, see how the highlight is a thin whitish line along the top edge of each brick and the dark lines beneath each brick realistically represents their shadows. On the paneling, Figure 12.12C, notice that the placement of the highlight, shade, and shadow lines creates the illusion of depth. Both of these examples are effective because the highlights and shadows look as if they were created by some specific source light. The location of the source light should appear to be some specific source within the design — either a practical onstage lamp or a specific position and angle (agreed on by the scenic and lighting designers) for an offstage, unseen source such as the sun. It is important that you do not put a gloss or shiny top-coat or glaze over these carefully created highlight/shadow illusions. To do so destroys the effect. Figure 12.12D demonstrates the technique of lining while painting "down" or on the floor.

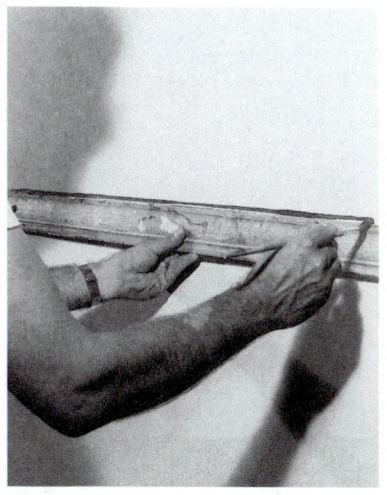

(A)

(B)

(C)

(D)

FIGURE 12.12
Lining is accomplished with a straightedge and a lining brush (A). It is frequently used to create the illusion of highlight and shadow, as shown in B and C. D shows how lining is done when "painting down" (continental style) with a brush extension — painting on the floor. A, Courtesy of J. Michael Gillette. B, C, and D, Courtesy of Kimb Williamson.

Applications of Painting Techniques

Figure 12.13 shows a potpourri of the various painting techniques that have been discussed in this section. Careful study of the individual pictures can be helpful in understanding how the images were created.

Specialized Finishing Techniques

The following techniques are not used so frequently as the previously discussed methods of painting, but when the design opportunity presents itself, they can provide dazzling and effective results.

Texturing   Texturing refers to the use of materials that create a three-dimensional relief on an otherwise flat surface. With the ready availability of manufactured texturing products, as well as a number of recipes for shop-mixed coatings, many illusions can be created that range from rough wood to brick, stone to tree bark, as well as stucco, ice, and snow. The number of textures that can be created is only limited by the scene painter's imagination.

FIGURE 12.13
Scene-painting techniques can be combined to create a variety of realistic forms. Wood grain (A) is primarily accomplished with successive layers of dry brushing in (generally) two or three tones of paint and an overcoat of glaze(s) in one or more tints. Stone (B) is usually created by scumbling two or three tones of a similar hue with a light, uneven overlay of stippled or spattered highlight and shadow to provide a slightly rougher texture. Marble (C) is created by wet-blending (scumbling with a lot of paint) several tones or related hues in a loose, vaguely linear pattern and over-spattering with large drops of the same paint. Painted foliage (D) uses a combination of all techniques; the tree trunk and branches are created by scumbling and dry-brushing, the foliage and grass with scumbling, stippling, and spattering, and the distant bushes with stippling and a light spatter. A, Courtesy of J. Michael Gillette. Scene painting and photos for B, C, and D, courtesy of Kimb Williamson.

(A)

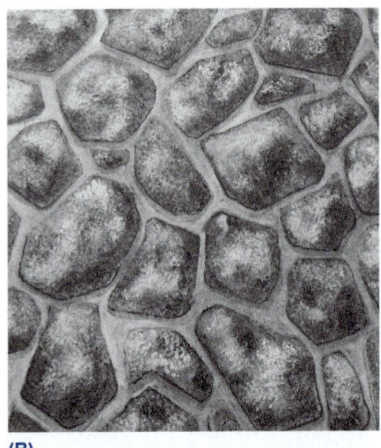

(B)

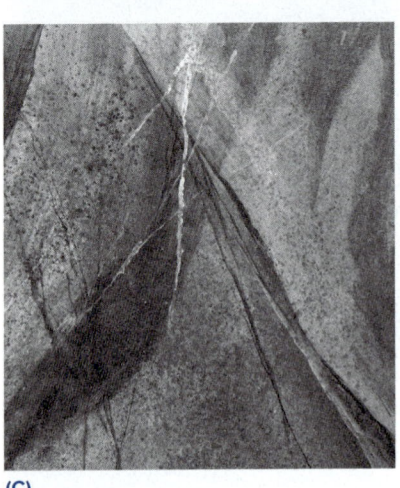

(C)

(D)

These texturing products generally need to be applied to a solid surface so they won't crack or flake off if the scenery is moved. There are several products available that can be used as a coating over flexible foams such as polystyrene (Styrofoam) or ethafoam. General practice is that if a texture coating is going to be applied to flats those flats are hard-covered, usually with minimally ³⁄₁₆-inch plywood or hardboard. Because texture coats are heavier than paint and because each particular mixture or recipe has its own working characteristics it is highly advisable to make a test patch. Apply some of the texturing mix to a sample piece of the actual material that's covering the scenery to determine if it will adhere and how it's going to behave after you've applied it.

There are many commercial texturing products available from scenic or builder's suppliers that can be applied directly from the can and troweled, rolled, brushed, and or otherwise annoyed onto the scenery, until they create the desired effect. Sculpt or Coat from Sculptural Arts Coatings (http://www.sculpturalarts.com) is an excellent smooth water-based plastic texture coating that will stick to just about anything — wood, metal, and most plastics. It is not particularly flexible when cured. It will stick to polystyrene (Styrofoam) but if the foam is flexed the Sculpt or Coat may crack. It is sufficiently thick to be built up into three-dimensional shapes such as stucco, bricks, bark, adobe, and so forth. FoamCoat, CrystalGel, and FlexCoat are several coating products offered by Rosco (www.rosco.com). FoamCoat is a water-based hard protective coating for use on foam plastics such as polystyrene. CrystalGel is a water-based material used to create a clear coating on just about any surface. FlexCoat is a water-based coating designed to preserve and protect the flexible surface of most foam plastics — polyurethane, polystyrene, ethafoam, among others. Jaxsan 600 (by Plastic Coatings, Inc.) is a water-based roofing product that dries to a flexible, rubbery finish. It is good for coating polystyrene and other foam plastics as well as wood and metal. Joint compound — the pre-mixed plaster used with drywall in home construction — is a good, if heavy, coating that is quite brittle when dry. In thin coats it will adhere to just about anything. Paint and/or commercial colorants can be added to any of these products to color the basic texturing coat. They can also be supplemented with a wide variety of what are euphemistically referred to as additives — common materials such as sand, sawdust, *clean* kitty litter, newspaper, tissue — that can be added to texturing base to create a variety of useful textures.

Texturing coats with additives and colorants that are mixed in the shop are appropriately referred to as "goop." There is no limit to the variety of texturing coats that can be created as long as attention is paid to the compatibility of the products. Because most texturing products are water-based, compatibility usually won't be an issue, but it is important to check the labels and read the SDS sheets for the products you'll be using before mixing them together. When creating your own batch of goop, consider not only the texture that you're trying to create but the surface upon which it's going to be applied. Is it going to be walked on? Are the actors wearing costumes that might be snagged by a highly textured surface? Is it going to be handled repeatedly? All of these considerations are used to determine the type of mixture that you should use.

A semi-universal general recipe for an effective non-commercial, non-flexible texture coating would be a base of joint compound, thinned and supplemented with either Flexbond, white glue, or flexible glue until it is a good working thickness. Mix in any appropriate additives, paint, or colorants to create the desired look, then apply.

There are a delightfully wide variety of tools that can be used to apply texture coats. Basically the only rule about which applicator to use is that you want to use something that will get the material on the object being textured with as little mess as possible, while creating the desired texture. If an old piece of 1 × 3 works, that's great. Trowels, spackle knives, brooms, and large synthetic sponges can be used to quickly apply almost any mixture of goop. Rollers are generally more useful than brushes for smoothing it out. The ultimate texturing treatment depends entirely on the effect desired. The secret to creating a realistic texture is to carefully study an example of the actual thing that you're trying to copy and then duplicate its general shape, surface quality, and color.

Stenciling Stencils are large cut patterns that facilitate the creation of repetitive, intricate designs such as wallpaper patterns. The stencil can be cut from **stencil paper,** a commercial product made of heavy, stiff paper impregnated or coated with oils that make the paper water-resistant. Stencil paper can be made in the shop by painting thin illustration board with a water-resisting coating such as shellac, lacquer, or spray varnish. Be sure to coat the paper *after* you have cut the design. The high-impact polystyrene plastic used for **vacuforming** is completely waterproof and is excellent for use as stencil material.

After the stencil is cut, it is normally framed with 1 × 2 stock to hold it flat and make it easier to handle. The paint can be applied with a brush, **stencil brush,** roller, paint sprayer, or sponge, as shown in Figure 12.14. Generally,

stencil paper: Stiff, water-resistant paper used for making stencils.

vacuforming: The process of shaping heated plastic, usually high-impact polystyrene, around a mold through the use of vacuum pressure.

stencil brush: A short, squat brush with a circular pattern of short, stiff bristles; the bristles are pressed onto, rather than stroked across, the work, to prevent the paint from bleeding under the edges of the stencil.

FIGURE 12.14
Stencils are often used to apply repetitive patterns, such as for wallpaper. Courtesy of J. Michael Gillette.

spraying works best, simply because it is gentler on the stencil. Regardless of the application tool used, the stencil will have to be cleaned frequently to remove any excess paint that could be accidentally transferred to the scenery.

Translucency   An incredible depth can be created when you paint, and light, both the front and back of muslin-covered scenery. Although this technique, also called translucent painting, is normally used with drops, equally effective results can be achieved on flats and other framed scenery.

Imagine you are painting a landscape on a small drop that will be hung upstage of a window of an interior set. The normal tendency is to paint the entire scene with paint and light in from the front. However, if you paint the solid objects (ground and trees) with paint and the translucent or transparent items (sky and clouds) with dye, you can light the drop from both the front and the back. The apparent depth that is created with this technique is really amazing.

The technique is particularly effective if the scene involves a sunset effect. If the front lights are dimmed and the back lights are up, the painted areas will appear in silhouette. If, after looking at the drop with the back lights turned on, the silhouetted areas still allow light to bleed through, the challenge can be solved by **backpainting.** On the back, or reverse, side of the scenery or drop simply paint the silhouetted area — only the silhouetted area — with a light coat of opaque paint, preferably black or dark brown to reduce reflection. Apply a relatively light coat — but thick enough to be opaque — when backpainting to prevent any paint from bleeding through the material and ruining the finished paint job on the front of the drop or scenery. The hue of the backlights, and projections, can be used to create spectacular sunset or night-sky effects.

Translucent painting can also be used to create stained-glass windows and similar effects. Be sure to work with the paint before the dye, because the paint will act as a "dam" to prevent the dye from bleeding into other areas of the fabric.

Glazing and Glossing   The difference between glaze and gloss coats is simple. A glaze has a matte finish while a gloss coat is shiny — generally either satin or gloss. Both are applied over existing dried paint jobs. A glaze is a thin, translucent layer of very thin paint made by adding water to acrylic, vinyl, or casein paint. The one caveat is that the glaze must be translucent, not opaque. Its purpose is to tone the underlying paint job, not cover it. The purposes of glaze coats are varied: they can be tinted to tone down the brilliance or slightly change the hue of the paint job over which they are being applied; they are frequently used to add shadow details to the set. Glaze coats are normally applied by spattering or by applying a uniform coat with a brush or sea sponge or synthetic sponge. However, there aren't any laws that dictate the particular uses of glaze coats. Use the type of glaze that is appropriate to the specific design need.

Gloss coats, which impart a shine to whatever they're painted on, are generally used on furniture and natural woods. Thinned white glue, clear vinyl acrylic paint, lacquer, shellac, and polyurethane varnish are all frequently used to create gloss coats. The choice of which material to use is predicated on the use that the particular piece will receive. Finishes that are more water- and scratch-resistant (shellac, clear vinyl acrylic, polyurethane varnish) should be used for those objects that may be subjected to water or abrasive physical treatment.

Metallic Finishes   The types of material that can be used to create metallic finishes have been discussed in various other sections of this chapter. Briefly, bronzing powders, which are powdered metal (available from scenic supply

backpainting: Literally to paint on the back. You paint the back, or reverse, side of the scenery or drop.

houses or well-stocked art stores), are mixed with a vehicle and applied to the work. High-gloss materials such as shellac, clear vinyl acrylic, varnish, and polyester resin all work very well as vehicles for the bronzing powders. Bronzing powders are highly toxic. The standard safety caveat applies: Read, and follow, the information contained in the SDSs for the products with which you are working.

The secret to a good metallic finish is the undercoat. The wood, plastic, or fabric to which you are applying your alchemy must be filled until there is absolutely no evidence of any wood grain or other texture. The best undercoat is a water-based polyester resin such as Aqua resin. Generally, one coat of resin will create the desired glassy-smooth surface on any but the roughest material.

After the undercoat has dried or cured, the bronzing powders or colorants are mixed with vehicle and applied to the work. For small areas, metallic spray paints create a nice metallic appearance when used on top of a smooth undercoat.

There are healthier alternatives to bronzing powders. Mica powders, which come in a wide variety of colors, when mixed with **polyvinyl alcohol** (PVA) or clear vinyl acrylic base produce a highly reflective, metallic-like surface. An aluminum finish can be created by mixing silver mica powder with PVA and applying it over a matte gray-blue base color. Gold-tone mica powder applied over a muted dark yellow base coat produces a similarly convincing gold finish. The secret to this technique is that the colored base coat must have a matte finish. Experimenting with different colored mica powders and base coats will produce an amazing array of metallic finishes. A number of sources for mica powders can be found by doing an online search for "mica powders." Additionally, many scenic and art paint manufacturers, such as Nova Color, Rosco, and Sculptural Arts Coatings, now sell a wide variety of water-based metallic paints that produce very convincing results when correctly applied over a base coat of similar color. Visit their websites for more information.

Wallpapering

As an alternative to painting, particularly in theatres where the audience is sitting very close to the stage, real wallpaper can be used. For the best appearance wallpaper should be applied to flats covered with some type of hard surface — ⅛-inch lauan plywood, Masonite, or ³⁄₁₆- or ¼-inch plywood. The wallpaper is applied with vinyl acrylic wallpaper paste, which is available in wallpaper stores as well as paint stores and home improvement centers. When using wallpaper on the stage particular attention needs to be paid to the size of any images in the wallpaper. The scale of the image on many manufactured wallpapers is too small for use on stage. The distances at which the audience sits from the set will, in many cases, make the use of small, delicate patterns impractical and hard to discern. The small pattern that you think is absolutely perfect will, many times, simply be a blur when viewed from 25 to 50 feet. It's best to take a sample roll from the store and view it as the audience will see it. Unroll it vertically — drape it down the side of a step-ladder placed on the stage or in the shop — and look at it at a "typical audience distance." If the pattern "works" from that distance — if it is clearly visible and supports the designer's intent — then you have a winner.

Drop Painting Techniques

Drops need to be stretched and framed in some manner before they can be painted. The stretching not only produces a smooth surface on which to paint

polyvinyl alcohol (PVA): A water-soluble synthetic thickener/adhesive.

bogus paper: A heavy, soft, absorbent paper. Similar to blotter paper.

but also minimizes shrinkage. The drop can be stretched on a vertical paint frame by:

1. Nailing a framework of boards the same width and height as the drop to the paint frame. It is imperative that these boards be squared — all corners at 90 degrees — so that the drop will remain square.

2. Attaching the drop to the framework. Staples with ½-inch legs, spaced 3 to 4 inches apart, normally secure any muslin drop to the framework. If the drop is going to be saturated with dyes or paint (which causes it to shrink a great deal), it will be better to secure it with staples spaced 1 to 2 inches apart.

Some painting techniques are more easily executed with the drop in a horizontal position. In these cases, the drop will need to be stretched and secured on a wooden floor with staples spaced on 3- to 4-inch centers. (Partially seating the staples will make them easier to remove.) Again, if the drop is going to be heavily saturated, space the staples 1 to 2 inches apart to prevent scalloped edges on the drop. Be sure to put a layer of **bogus paper** under the drop to absorb the dye or paint. Place a layer of Kraft or butcher paper underneath the bogus paper. (If the bogus/butcher paper backing isn't used, the paints or dyes may stain the floor or the drop may pick up some staining from dirt, old paint, or dye already on the floor.)

If you do not have a wooden floor large enough to accommodate the size of the drop, you will need to build a temporary frame large enough to stretch the drop. The frame can be made of notched 2 × 4 or 1 × 6 so that it will hold its shape against the strong force created when the fabric shrinks. As shown in Figure 12.15, the toggle bars of this oversized frame are made of 1 × 4s. Be certain that the drop frame is square. After painting, the drop will shrink to the shape of the frame. If the frame is out of square, the drop will also be out

FIGURE 12.15
Temporary drop stretcher.

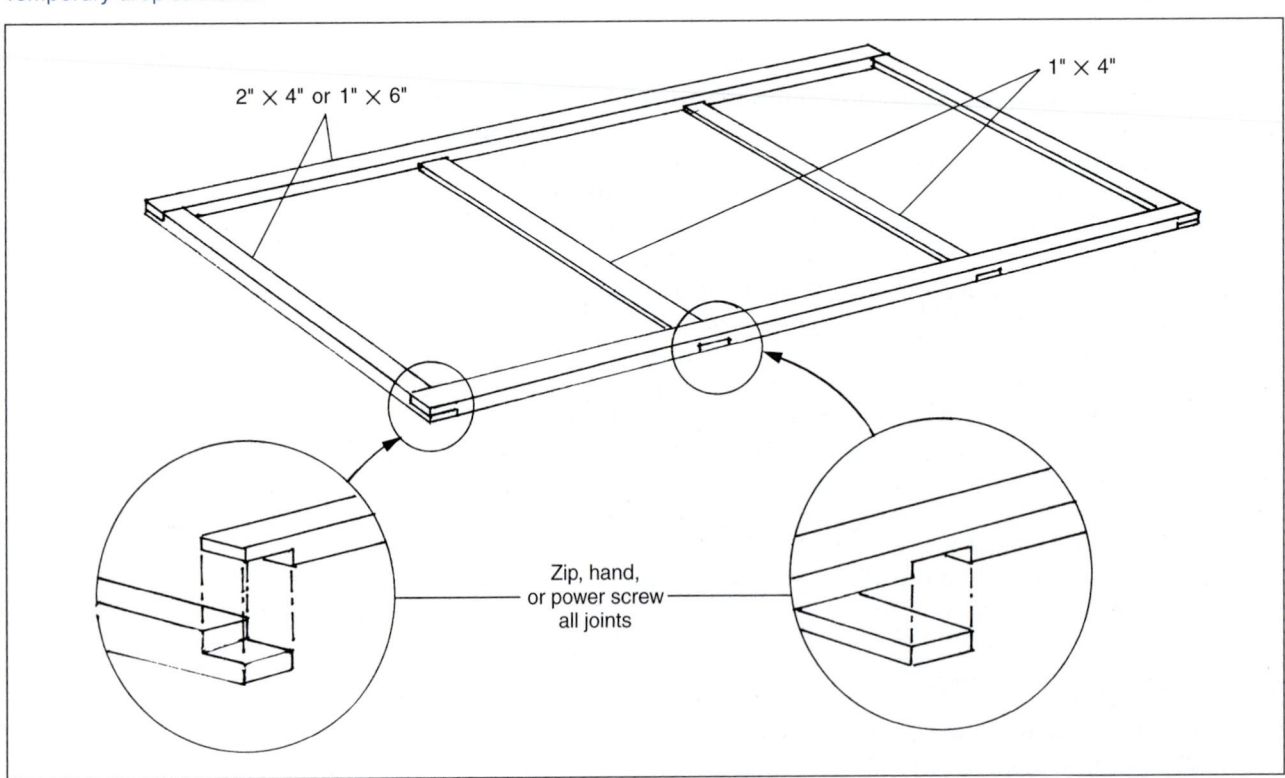

of square and may be impossible to hang or trim properly. Finally, before you stretch the drop and staple it to the framework, don't forget to cover the area under the drop with the aforementioned layers of bogus and butcher paper.

In the final analysis, the quality of any scenic paint job depends on the talent and ingenuity of the scenic artist. The materials and techniques suggested in this chapter provide only a beginning point for the scene-painting artist. Although each of the materials has specific properties, there aren't any artistic "rules" to which the painter must adhere. Experimentation, trial and error, and learning from your happy accidents are the only guidelines that need to be followed as you work to develop your skill in the challenging field of scene painting.

Selected References

Crabtree, Susan, and Peter Bendart. *Scenic Art of the Theatre: History, Tools and Techniques*, Focus Press, 2nd ed., 1998.

The Painter's Journal: A Forum and Resource for Scenic Artists in Theatre. www.paintersjournal .com

The Scenic Artist's Forum. Scenic_Artists_Forum@Yahoogroups.com

Chapter 13

Stage Properties

(This chapter has been extensively updated thanks to the input of Sandra J. Strawn, professional property director and educator. The author wishes to publicly thank her for her extensive knowledge and expertize on this subject and contributions to this chapter.)

In the proscenium theatre, the stage properties are the icing on the scenic designer's cake. Although the set usually creates the dominant visual motif, the properties are coequal design elements. They can be considered the primary design tool used to provide clues about the personality and socioeconomic status of the inhabitants of the set. Figure 13.1 demonstrates these principles by depicting a rather nondescript living room furnished in three different ways. In Figure 13.1A, the room is furnished with utilitarian props that don't say much about the nature and character of the inhabitants or the period of the play. Figure 13.1B illustrates how changing the style of the properties from nondescript to late Victorian changes our perception of the social class of the room's inhabitants and suggests a fairly clear idea of the period of the play. These visual clues are again demonstrated in Figure 13.1C, where the absence of any furnishings other than the cardboard boxes, broom, and crumpled newspaper suggests that the room's inhabitants are either moving in or out and that the period could be anywhere within the last 100 years. That "guessitmate" of the period is based on the shapes and sizes of the cardboard boxes. Specific information about the period *could* be gleaned from any words and font style printed on the sides of the boxes.

The visual importance of stage properties increases significantly when the play is produced in either a thrust or arena theatre or any of the other configurations that precludes or restricts the use of vertical scenic elements such as flats and drops. In these intimate theatre spaces where the audience is usually sitting close to the stage, the furniture and decorative props are frequently the major visual elements of the scenic design.

Although the duties and responsibilities of the members of the prop department were covered in Chapter 1, "Production Organization and Management," it bears repeating that the property master needs to have a detailed working knowledge of every craft area in theatre. Woodworking metalworking, electrical wiring and electronics, mold making, ceramics, sewing, upholstery, furniture construction, weaponry, special effects, and scene painting are but a few of the craft areas in which a true property master will be competent. A good props person also has a solid knowledge of a variety of computer programs ranging from word processing to spread sheets to drawing, drafting, and CNC machine programing skills.

When you understand the impact of properties on the appearance of a design and the scope of knowledge that a prop master or director must possess, it becomes obvious that a full discussion of how to construct stage properties cannot be contained in this chapter. Probably more than in any other single craft area in theatre production, someone who is interested in property design and construction needs to know it all — the history of fashion, architecture, furniture, and decoration; design theory and practice; and craft construction techniques.

FIGURE 13.1
Stage properties can be used to provide information about the character and period of the set. See text for details.

What Is a Prop?

Stage properties have traditionally been divided into three categories: (1) set props, (2) hand props, and (3) decorative props or set dressing.

Set Props

Set props are generally defined as larger movable items, not built into the set, that are used in some way by the actors. This group would include such things as furniture, floor lamps, rugs, stoves, tree stumps, swings, and so forth.

Hand Props

Hand props refer to small items that are handled or carried by the actors. This group includes plates, cups, letters, books, fans, lanterns, and similar items.

Decorative Props

Decorative props, also known as set dressing, include all the things used to enhance the setting visually but are not specifically touched by the actors. Such items as window curtains, pictures, doilies, table lamps, bric-a-brac, and the books in a bookcase are typical of decorative, or dress, props.

Property Design

As discussed in Chapter 1, "Production Organization and Management," the credit for property design is evolving into a collaborative effort between the scenic and property directors/designers in both commercial and educational theatres. In the design illustrated in Figure 13.2 the initial property sketches were made by the scenic designer. Not all prop sketches are that ideal or precise. Some harried scenic designers will simply give the property director a collection of printed or photocopied material from online sources, books, and/or magazines that show pictures of items close to the look of what they want with clarifying notes jotted in the margins. But these lists work. In whatever form the initial visual information is received from the scenic designer, in current practice the property designer, who is frequently the property director, takes those images

FIGURE 13.2
Property designs for the Metropolitan Opera Association's production of *Les Troyens*, produced at the Metropolitan Opera House, Lincoln Center, New York. Scenery, costumes, and visual effects (film) designed by Peter Wexler. Courtesy of Peter Wexler. For further viewing, please see the Peter Wexler Digital Museum online.

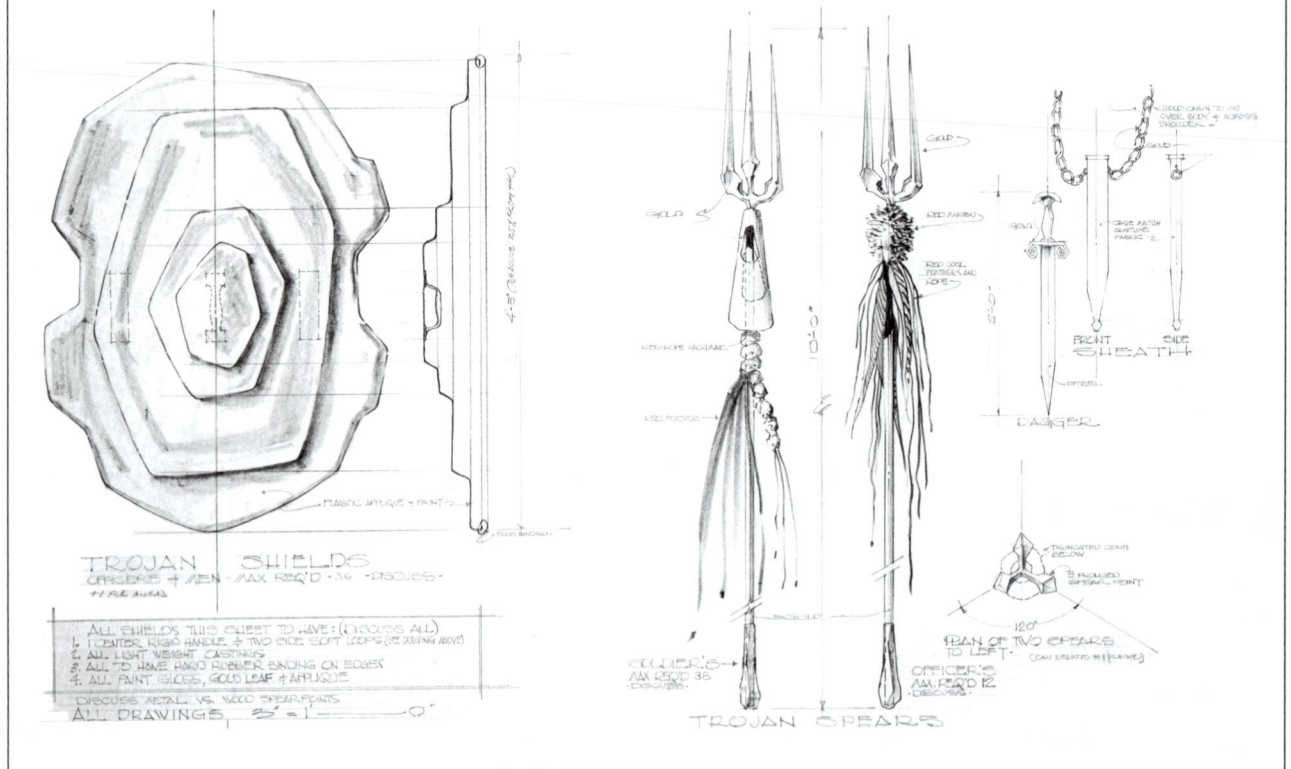

and, after doing appropriate period and style research, makes sketches, working drawings, detail drawings, and construction/acquisition decisions. During this phase the scenic and property designers are normally in frequent communication, face-to-face, electronically, or by e-mail (with attachments), as the designs evolve from the original material. When all parties — designers, director, and production manager (the person usually in charge of budgetary decisions) — are satisfied with the designs, the property director gets down to the actual work of making and collecting all the props for the production.

Real or Fake?

If an actor is going to touch or pick up a prop, it should feel real. For example, assuming that you are trying to project a realistic or naturalistic appearance, a book should look and feel like a real book and, if it is going to be opened, it should have pages. The scenic designer and the property master may want to alter the appearance of the book by painting or staining the cover, covering it with cloth or leather, or hot-gluing jewels or appliqués to it.

Props can be faked if they aren't going to be used by the actors. If the decorated prop book just discussed isn't going to be touched by an actor, and if you were adverse to the idea of "defacing" a real book, it could simply be a box or piece of wood painted and decorated to look like a book. Frequently, the books in a bookshelf are the spines of actual books that have been attached to a frame. Other types of props can be treated in the same way.

Property Organization

What does the property designer/director really do? And how are the props for a production actually acquired? This section explains the duties of the property director and the organization of a prop shop. Obviously, not every producing organization has the funding available to have a property director and/or a separate prop shop with its own staff of artisans and equipment. But the duties and procedures outlined in this section provide a good understanding of the practices and procedures used in a typical regional professional theatre organization to build, collect, and run the stage props for a production and, as such, provides an excellent how-to guide. If a producing organization has only one faculty/staff member/graduate student/volunteer assigned as property director and a few students and/or volunteers to make, assemble, and run the props for a show, it should be obvious that the property design cannot be as complex as for a theatre with a complete, fully staffed prop shop. But the procedures and processes outlined should work for any type of non-union producing organization.

Property Director   The property director is ultimately responsible for all props used during the production. His or her number one job is to assure the timely production of appropriately designed props for each play produced by the organization. Property directors assign the prop shop artisans to specific buying/building/collecting projects and then supervise the actual work. The property director determines which props will be pulled from the theatre's property storage and which will be built, bought, rented, and/or borrowed. She or he is responsible for managing both the time and fiscal construction-phase budgets. Property directors need to determine how many hours it will take to build/buy/acquire all the props so they can plan for an adequately sized crew. To determine the budget needed to cover a show, they need to know the cost of buying/renting any props as well as the cost of the materials needed for prop construction.

It is a standard practice when estimating a prop budget to build in a contingency of 10 to 20 percent of the total prop budget to cover the inevitable changes that will occur during the rehearsal process. This seems to be an appropriate time in this discussion to offer another axiom/caveat: In theatre production there's never enough time or money. (Sort of like life, eh?) Striking a happy balance between what the budgets — time and fiscal — will allow you to do, and what is wanted, is a constant battle not only for props, but in the scenic, costume, lighting, and sound departments as well. However, it can be done with patience, energy, collaboration, compromise, and integrity. Maybe that's one of the things that makes this business so interesting.

Like other members of the production design team, the properties director attends all necessary production meetings and technical rehearsals. If the property director has not already done period and style research as the property designer, he or she familiarizes him- or herself with the period and style of the production. This information is used to keep all relevant personnel "on track" regarding the appearance and function of the props. The property director must be aware of the status and progress of all projects and must keep all the property artisans on schedule so the props can be completed on time. He or she is also the conduit through which notes about any prop changes reach the property artisans. The property director also oversees the maintenance of the prop shop's tool, equipment, and supplies inventories. She or he also needs to be computer savvy and minimally be conversant with word processing, spreadsheets, graphics, and drawing/drafting/painting software.

Property Acquisition

To create an aura of authenticity, property masters frequently try to find actual objects appropriate to the period of the play to use as props. For a contemporary production, props can usually be purchased, rented, or borrowed from local stores. For a play set twenty or thirty years ago, it is fairly easy to find most props in junk shops or used-furniture stores. However, when producing a period play such as *Amadeus,* which moves in time between 1780 and 1820 and is set in Vienna, it is often very difficult to find actual furniture or decorative props of that period. Even if you could find them, you wouldn't want to put them on the stage for fear that they might be damaged. In these situations, the property director frequently builds the props or acquires reproductions. When acquiring props for a show, property directors are frequently guided by an aphorism some of them refer to as "The 3Bs and a P" — Build, Buy, Borrow, and Pull.

Building Props   Every production has some props that must be built or altered. It might be a nonstock item like the warrior's shield shown in Figure 13.2 that is stipulated by the designer. It might be a piece of period furniture or a 1920s-era gramophone that won't be played. It might be a period newspaper or magazine, or a food-stained tablecloth, 1940s-era Venetian blinds, or a colorful vase that sits on the mantle. It is the property artisan's job to build or acquire whatever it is.

Let's look at that gramophone. While doing research the designer finds a picture of the gramophone and indications of its general size. The prop artisan's challenge is to find it or build it. With specifications and dimensions provided by the property designer, the box and lid could be fabricated from oak-faced plywood, then stained a mahogany hue, (the most common color of 1920s gramophones), and varnished or shellacked to a suitable satin or gloss finish. A plywood disk topped with dark felt and edged with metal tape could be used for the record platen, while a bent metal rod with a wooden bead glued to the end could serve as the winding crank. The gramophone's signature playing arm and horn could be fashioned from tin, aluminum, or plastic sheet goods and finished with a mica-powder metallic silver treatment and black paint to match the look of the period piece.

Furniture frequently requires special attention. If an actor is supposed to dance on a sofa while it twirls about the stage, the prop artisan will probably start with a stock sofa and build a complete metal undercarriage with heavy-duty castors to guarantee its strength and ease of movement, and underpin the stock upholstery on the seat and arms with plywood supports and extra-firm padding so the sofa will provide a firm, nonwiggly base for the actor.

Many props require "toning" or "distressing" to fit the look of the scenic design. The clever use of spray paint/dyes on the fabric and tinted shellac, bronzing/mica powders, and paints on woodwork can frequently make a new piece seem appropriately ancient and decrepit.

If a newspaper from the 1930s is required it is frequently possible to download an actual front page from an online source, import it into Photoshop, add or change the required headline, then print it on newsprint or similar thin paper with either a plotter or large-format printer. Paper goods of all types can be similarly created. Because the audience is frequently only a few feet from the stage it is essential that paper items such as menus, newspapers, matchbooks, and the like be period are accurate. This level of accuracy also helps the actors stay in the moment. Besides, doing this sort of thing is fun.

As you can see, the range of construction work that the prop artisans do is amazing and endless. A prop item can be found, built, or purchased. It can be altered, aged, strengthened, painted, or re-covered to fit the look of the show. A solid understanding of the materials and processes used to construct props from wood, metal, fabric, plastic, and so forth, provides the prop artisan an arsenal of problem-solving and innovative techniques with which to build props.

Buying Props   Buying props that cannot be built, borrowed, or pulled from stock often falls to the props director and/or the artisan designated as the props buyer.

Any show will have a given amount of shopping to be done if only for consumables — food that will be eaten onstage or materials (lumber, fabric, paper, and so forth). Having good money management skills and a willingness to bargain makes a good props shopper.

The Internet has revolutionized the props shopper's job. It used to be that he or she had a thick Rolodex of numbers, numerous catalogues, and a keenly honed sense of where-to-buy-what. Those skills are still helpful, but now online auction sites such as eBay allow props shoppers to find the frequently arcane items that props people need to get quickly and cheaply. With express mail, purchases can be delivered to the theatre in relatively short order. Traditional sources and supply houses, with online catalogues, are still equally useful.

One of the specific challenges that props people face is the need to find an item that has a very specific look but must be altered — either to survive or have the appropriately worn look — to work on stage. Furniture pieces with the "correct" look are frequently purchased from retail stores, stripped back to the frame, the understructure rebuilt to make the pieces more **stage worthy,** and covered in a different fabric and trim — frequently aged or distressed — that more accurately matches the look of the production.

Many props that are purchased are retained after the show closes and are added to the theatre's prop stock. Items that are inexpensive and/or can be easily replaced are usually not stored if storage space is at a premium.

Borrowing or Renting Props   Some special challenges need to be considered when borrowing props. Any type of prop used in the theatre is subject to

stage worthy: Strong enough to withstand the use inflicted on them when used on the stage. Examples would include sofas/chairs that are stood and/or danced on; tables that break apart during fights, and so forth.

unusual stresses and wear. Furniture, which is designed to sit in one location in a room in someone's house and occasionally be moved for cleaning, when used in the theatre will be moved around the stage as the scenery is shifted. Even if it isn't moved, the director may block someone to stand on it, flop on it, run across it, or spill a drink on it. It should be obvious that if any of these things are going to take place, the furniture involved shouldn't be borrowed or rented.

It should also be obvious that borrowed items should not be altered in any way without the express written permission of the owners. Even then it's an "iffy" proposition. Some theatre organizations form alliances with other theatre groups to facilitate a borrowing/sharing system between members of the group. Generally, other theatre organizations are more amenable to allowing some modifications to the borrowed pieces than are most stores and production rental houses. But even if you've borrowed something from another theatre be sure to get permission, in writing, before performing any modifications to the piece.

Many retail rental companies stock a variety of items used for weddings and parties that can be rented for the length of a production run. Some retail furniture companies also rent furniture. But you'll frequently find that the rental costs are equal to, if not more than, the cost of buying the item. Cultivating the relationships that allow for prop rental or borrowing generally take a long time to establish and are maintained only through taking diligent care of the borrower's goods. Just one careless "oops" has doomed many of these relationships.

If you are borrowing furniture from a person or company, you should be able to assure the lending party that whatever you've borrowed will be returned intact. Lenders are frequently more at ease if a lending agreement (Figure 13.3A) is executed. This agreement stipulates the use of the item, that the object will be returned in good condition, and that the borrower will be responsible for any necessary repairs resulting from accidental damage. If the borrowed prop is expensive or rare, the borrowing organization should investigate the cost of insurance to cover any possible repairs or replacement. Finally, if the producing organization cannot afford to replace the prop, it should not be borrowed in the first place.

Many producing organizations loan or rent properties. Figure 13.3B shows a sample form typical of a prop lending agreement used when organizations/individuals borrow props from another theatre organization. Unfortunately, all too frequently borrowed props are damaged or "modified" in some manner. That is why much of what is contained in this form relates to costs associated with repair/replacement if a prop is damaged or lost. It lets the borrower know the potential costs associated with the act of borrowing.

Pulling Props Almost every theatre organization has a "prop room." This is a storage space in which props that were built or bought for previous productions are stored. This reservoir of often fascinating furniture and knick-knacks forms the basis of most theatres' property production work and offers valuable savings as pieces can be altered, reupholstered, used for parts, or "freshened up" for use in a current production.

Furniture pieces with classic designs that have been in vogue for decades can be easily altered by changing the upholstery, adding different pillows or cushions, or trimming with ruffles, new braid, or decorative nails. A stock piece can be altered by using different legs to better match a particular period or stained darker to match a newly acquired piece to make a nicely matching set of furniture. Designers often use existing prop furniture as a pattern or guide for designing/building new pieces of furniture.

Hand props such as kitchen dressing — pots, pans, silverware, plates, glasses, and so forth — can be used without alteration on a variety of shows. Paper props, such as the previously mentioned 1930 newspaper, can be saved and reused as set dressing for every subsequent 1930s-era show.

LENDING AGREEMENT FORM

1. Old Time Productions agrees to return the below listed borrowed items in the same condition in which they were borrowed.

2. If any item is damaged while in the possession of the theatre, Old Time Productions will be responsible for its repair.

3. The items will be borrowed on _____ and returned no later than _____ .

4. The prop will be used in the following manner: _____
_____ .

ITEMS

_____

For Old Time Productions: _____   Date: _____

Lender: _____   Date: _____

(A)

Stock items can also be used during rehearsal until the actual prop is built. Obviously, the wear and tear on the stock item must be balanced against having the rehearsal needs met. Sometimes it is more appropriate for the prop artisans to simply rough out an approximation of the finished prop for rehearsal use rather than using something from stock.

Many theatres now have the furniture stock — note that this refers to *furniture* stock, not *all* props — on a computerized inventory system. Data management files can be created for each piece. Each file typically includes photo(s) of the item, its dimensions, as well as alteration information — dates for upholstery/trim changes, and so forth — and other pertinent data such as shows/dates in which the piece was used and so forth. These programs can be used to search all stock items by category — "Victorian," "settee," and so forth — which can significantly speed up the design/communication process between the prop director and the scenic/property designers. Obviously, maintaining the currency of the computerized inventory by updating the material on each item every time it is used/altered is absolutely essential.

Organizing Props for a Production

The process used when assembling the props for a production is similar to the design/construction process used for the scenery, costumes, lighting, and sound. There is preproduction planning and organization followed by the construction and adjustments, then running of the props during the technical/dress rehearsals and performance, and finally the strike or taking-down-and-putting-away phase.

Theatre Prop Borrowing Form

LOANED TO: _____ ADDRESS: _____

PHONE: _____ PICKED UP: ___/___/___ TO BE RETURNED: ___/___/___

CONTACT: _____ PRODUCTION: _____

The Theatre Properties Department is loaning the following items for use in your production/workshop/class as listed above. You *personally,* and for your organization (when applicable), by accepting these items and signing this loan form, agree to the following conditions:

1. Appointments must be made with the Prop Manager to: (1) look thru props storage; (2) for PICK-UP and RETURN of props. If an appointment is missed by more than 15 minutes, it must be rescheduled at the convenience of the prop shop.

2. All borrowed items will be kept in a safe and secure location at all times.

3. All items will be returned in the same condition as they left prop storage, excluding **normal** wear and tear.

4. If modifications are desired, permission must be obtained from the Prop Manager in advance. Any "modifications" made without prior permission will be viewed as damage to the specific item, and repair charges will be accessed.

5. All repairs to damaged items must be completed by the Theatre prop shop (based on an hourly fee plus materials) unless other arrangements are made with the Properties Manager *in advance* of any actual repairs being started. REPEAT: Repairs done without permission will be considered "damage."

6. The borrowing organization is responsible for the stated value of any item that is lost, stolen, or damaged beyond reasonable repairs. Damaged items remain the property of Theatre Company even when total replacement cost is accessed.

7. The Theatre Properties Manager must be notified A.S.A.P. after any item is damaged. Please do not wait until the end of your rental to let us know.

8. All items are to be returned *on or before the date specified* on this form. Props must be checked in by the Properties Manager at the time of their return. REPEAT: If an appointment is missed by more than 15 minutes, it must be rescheduled at the discretion of the prop shop.

9. Renter is responsible for all shipping fees, moving and pick up arrangements. Items must be insured for stated value if returned by shipment

THEATRE: _____
Prop Master, phone number, e-mail

CONTACT _____

Returned: Donation due: ☐

Notes: paid: ☐

Item	Description	Value	Fee

RENTAL CHARGE: _____

CHECKS SHOULD BE MADE OUT TO: THEATRE COMPANY

FIGURE 13.3 (B)

Preproduction Planning

The first thing that the property director does when working on a new show is create the prop list. The prop list, illustrated in Figure 13.4, is a complete listing of all the props needed for the show including set props, hand props, decorative props, consumables, special effects, weaponry, and any "crossover" props such as wallet dressing or flying electrical units such as chandeliers. Normally the process of making the prop list begins when the property director reads the script and studies the scenic design. He or she will make note of any props specifically called for in the script or design as well as any props that she or he feels might

Gem of the Ocean

Prop List

McCarter Theatre ✱ 91 University Place ✱ Princeton, NJ 08540
Prop Shop ✱ 609-258-6580 ✱ props@mccarter.org

#	Pg	Prop	Description/ Movement	Character/ Placement	Status/ Questions
F00			**Furniture**		
F10		Kitchen Table	6' x 2'6", splayed leg, country table	DSL	Built by McCarter
F14		4 Kitchen chairs	Simple, country, some turning, not necessarily matching	Around table	McCarter Stock
F18		Aunt Ester's Chair	Large arm chair with heart carving on top	DSR	McCarter Stock
F19		Aunt Ester's Side table	Short, square table w/ shelf & drawer, scalloped skirt; has a strike pad on it; has doily bottom shelf	SR of AE's chair	McCarter Stock
F20		Side Chair	Windsor back chair w/ rush seat	SL of AE's chair	Empire Antiques
F22		Tall side table	Round table w/barley twist pedestal & pom poms; has round doily on top	DS of stiars	McCarter Stock
F26		Square side table	Fluted legs, bottom shelf & a drawer; green; has embroidered runner on top.	US of stairs	Wal-Mart
F30		Counter		US	Built by McCarter
F34		Long Side table	Black w/ drawer & bottom shelf; has embroidered runner on top	SR of counter	American Country
F38		Sink	Metal basin, big blue legs	SL or counter	Built by McCarter
F42		Stove	2.5' - 3.5' wide, wood burning, black cast iron	Against back wall	Anything But Costumes
F46		Coat rack	Turned post, Victorian hooks	SL of front door	McCarter Stock
F50		Cupboard	Painted green milk paint	In SR corner	Built by McCarter
F54		Half Moon Table	Dark brown, turned legs; has oblong doily on top	US of Ester's door	E-bay
F58		Half Moon Table	Orangy finish, swirly detail	In Ester's room	E-bay
D00			**Dressing**		
D10		2 Sconces	Antique copper, amber shade	SL & SR sides of column	Rejuvenation
D14		Shelf dressing	Bowls, crocks containers, cracked blue glaze		Bought/McCarter Stock
D18		Large Rug	9' x 5'-6", braided, browns, reds	DSR	E-bay
D26		Pantry Door Curtain	Dark red calico, on rings, never moves	Pantry Door	Built by McCarter
D34		Door Shade	Hempish looking roll shade	On porch door	Lowe's
D38		Cupboard Dressing	Dishes, pans, pitchers, bowls, etc	In Cupboard	Bought/McCarter Stock
D42		Kitchen Dressing	Utensils, pans, garlic, peppers		Bought/McCarter Stock
D46		Coal Shuttle	Galvanized metal w/ red handle; has logs inside	SL of stove	McCarter Stock
D48		Large Stoneware Jar	Off white, tall	SR of Stove	Bought
D50		Little Shelf	Wooden, green, cups hung underneath, bottles on top	On wall SL of Stove	Built by McCarter
D51		Curio Shelf	Dark brown, 3 shelves	US of Ester's door	Built by McCarter
D52		Oil Lamp	Large, brass, frosted chimney, electrified	On half moon table #F54	McCarter Stock
D53		Round box	Small, bronze colored, decorative	On shelf on Aunt Ester's Table #F19	McCarter Stock
D54		Reed Basket	Dark brown, side handles, red & of f white fabric inside	On shelf on square side table #f26	McCarter Stock
D56		2 African Baskets	Round, woven, red fabric in one	On shelf on long side table #F34	Bought
D58		Vegetable basket	Small woven basket filled w/ fake vegetables	On DS end of counter	McCarter Stock

Director: Ruben Santiago-Hudson   Set Designer: Michael Carnahan

FIGURE 13.4
A prop list from McCarter Theatre production of *Gem of the Ocean.* This is the first page of a four-page list. Courtesy of Michele E. Sammarco

help establish the mood and flavor of the play. It is important to understand that this is just a beginning, and this preliminary props list will be added to and adjusted, probably many times, as the process continues.

After the prop list has been started the prop director normally will make the preproduction budget estimate from that list. This is an estimate of the cost and time that it will take to assemble and/or build the props for the production.

The preliminary prop list is distributed to the scenic and property designers, the director, and the stage manager for their study and input. A prop meeting is held, usually during one of the regular production staff meetings, to discuss the preliminary designs, color, fabric choices, research, and so forth. It is normal for the original prop list to be modified at this time as new props are discussed and added by the director and other members of the production design team.

During one of the preliminary production meetings there is frequently a "renegotiating" of the production budget — taking a little from here, giving a little there — so that the various departments can stay within the overall budget for the production. If the props department needs more money for an essential prop, then it normally has to come from somewhere else within the overall production budget — scenery, costume, lights, and sound. This type of negotiation is normal for all areas of production and should be expected. Remember, theatre production is a collaborative process.

Properties Production The property director and/or the prop shopper, fabric swatches in hand, will go shopping for any needed furniture and/or upholstery materials when property production begins. He or she will also start pulling props from storage and acquiring needed supplies.

Digital technology has been a boon to the prop master. Cell phones allow the prop shopper to communicate with the designer, regardless of their respective locations. Cell phone photos let the designer see what the shopper has found and voice, e-mails, and Tweets can be used to discuss design issues — color, scale, finish, patterns, and so forth — that previously took much more time to resolve.

Digital photography can also be used to speed up prop design. For example, if the designer intends to change the leg style on a table, rather than drawing the new design the designer can take photos of the table and the new leg style, import them into a photo-editing program such as Adobe Photoshop, and "attach" the new legs to the table. The modified design can be e-mailed to the director and other members of the design team for feedback. When the design is finalized, the photo can be attached to the prop list.

Photo-editing programs can also be used to modify photos of actors by adding a beard or mustache, changing hair color, or aging the photo to make it look very old. As indicated earlier, photos of pages from period newspapers can be imported and new head lines or photos can be added with cut-and-paste editing. Many plotters and large-format printers allow the printing of newsprint so a whole newspaper can be effectively created in-house.

Online purchasing can also speed the acquisition process. An online search for a specific prop normally reveals multiple sources. Photos of the options can be sent to the show designers for their feedback. When a decision is reached, the item can be purchased and shipped directly to the prop shop.

Properties production requires clear and constant communication between the director/stage managers and the property department during the rehearsal process. During rehearsals it is normal for props to be added or cut or the use of a specific prop to be changed. Remember: this is normal. Getting information about those changes from the rehearsal hall to the prop shop on a daily basis is vital and essential. The stage manager normally generates that information in the daily rehearsal report. That report is delivered, frequently by e-mail, to all technical production departments on, surprise(!), a daily basis. Of importance to the prop department are the notes about any changes to the props: additions, cuts, changes in use, maintenance issues, and general information/questions affecting props. The property director updates the prop list from the rehearsal report then goes through the collaborative communication/design process with the scenic and property designer for any new props, and discusses any changes with the artisans working on the affected props. This constant back-and-forth communication, both e-mail and verbal, goes on daily as well as during the weekly production meetings.

As the communication flows and props are added, deleted, and changed it is absolutely essential that the prop list be updated by the property director every time a change is made. Without this level of organization it is very easy to forget to make or buy some essential prop.

It is very common for there to be overlap between technical departments in relation to stage props. For example, table lamps theoretically could belong to both the props and lighting departments. The prop department will normally design, fabricate, and wire the lamp, but there must be coordination with the lighting department regarding the circuit into which the lamp will be plugged, as well as who is going to plug/unplug it and who is going to move it during a scene shift. Similarly, many "costume properties" fall into both camps. While there is a general rule that, "If you wear it, it's a costume. If you carry it, it's a prop," every producing organization works out its own guidelines in this area. Irrespective of whether it's a costume or a prop, there needs to be strong coordination/ communication between the prop and costume departments regarding the design and function of items such as parasols, umbrellas, purses, flower bouquets, and so forth. Similarly, there needs to be strong coordination between the prop and scenic departments. In many small theatre operations the props are painted by the scenic artists. But even if the prop shop is lucky enough to have its own painters, there still needs to be strong consultation between the departments when it comes to the selection of upholstery fabric, as well as the painting and finishing of furniture, picture frames, and so forth, so that the finished props work well with the look and palette of the scenic design.

Rehearsal Props Every prop that will be handled by an actor should be duplicated in some fashion during rehearsals. Because of the potential for loss or damage "performance props" are generally not used during the rehearsal period, although they may be rotated into the rehearsal period for a few days so the actors can adjust to the real item. The only exception to that general rule regards specialty items. If there is a sword or pistol fight the weapons that will be used during the performances may be used during rehearsals so the actors will feel comfortable and confident in their use. For props such as paper goods and books, items of similar size and weight can be substituted until technical rehearsals begin. Furniture of similar size and shape is normally used during rehearsals instead of the performance furniture. The key to all these substitutions is that they provide a reasonable match in terms of size, weight, and design to the items that are going to be used during the production. Perishable props, which include items like cigarettes, matches, letters that will be written, food that will be eaten on stage, and so forth, are often requested early in the rehearsal process to allow the use of the props to be integrated with the dialogue and other stage action. A sufficient supply of these items for the rehearsal period is usually supplied by either the prop department or stage management. For almost every non-union production the question of "who supplies what and when" is typically decided by the members of the production team on an as-needed basis.

Load-in and Technical Rehearsals Property directors generally try to attend one rehearsal prior to the load-in to the theatre to work out running crew concerns and finalize the prop set-up and load-in logistics with the stage manager.

Prior to the first technical rehearsal it is helpful if the furniture props, and ideally any window dressings, can be placed on the set(s) for at least some of the sessions when the lighting designer is initially setting the light levels, simply because those props — their colors, textures, and shadows — will affect, sometimes significantly, the appearance of the stage picture.

Food and drink props require special consideration. If food is to be consumed onstage, stage management needs to ask the actors about food allergies or preferences they may have. Obviously, any food that would trigger an allergic response must be avoided and an acceptable substitute is found. If an actor is gluten intolerant and the script requires them to eat a meat sandwich, gluten-free bread must be used. If that actor doesn't eat meat, then a visually acceptable substitute must also be found. For obvious reasons, it's also preferable to avoid food props that are hard to chew or swallow and foods that are crumbly or messy.

Food and beverage props require sanitary handling and storage to ensure the safety and health of the actors. A "prop food only" refrigerator should be used to store food. Prop food should not be pre-set until just before going onstage.

The running of props during the technical and dress rehearsals as well as during performances is under the supervision of the stage manager. During the technical and dress rehearsals either the property director, or a designated assistant, should be in attendance to go over all the props, show the actors and, if the props are particularly complex, the director and stage manager as well, how the props work. They will also discuss any special needs with the appropriate personnel and take notes on any changes. The furniture props are placed onstage in collaboration with stage management. Set dressing is often placed in coordination with the scenic designer. Hand props are turned over to the run crew who place them in the prop storage cabinets.

The run crew, under the supervision of the stage manager, is responsible for placing the hand props on the props tables as well as monitoring their whereabouts during all technical/dress rehearsals and performances.

The property director advises the stage manager and scenic designer regarding any special treatment that the props might need during any scene shifts.

All set dressing, hand props, and furniture will need to be onstage for the first technical rehearsal. Set dressing can usually start as soon as the finished set is in place.

Because there are many notes generated during a technical rehearsal there is frequently a mini-production meeting following each tech rehearsal. These meetings are normally attended by the director, stage manager, designers, and department heads. The meeting is used to go over those notes and discuss/resolve changes and challenges. The prop director, and other department heads, then prioritize that information and work the next day to resolve as many of the challenges as possible. This process normally continues throughout the technical and dress rehearsal period and may even extend through previews to the actual opening of the show.

Running Props

If properties are going to be an effective addition to a production, they must be consistently placed in their proper locations on or around the set. If a floor lamp that is supposed to be placed next to a specific chair is misplaced, the concentration of the actor who is supposed to turn it on at a crucial moment in the play will undoubtedly be broken. Similarly, if an actor is supposed to pick up a book from a stack of books on an end table, the specific book must always be placed in the same location and position in or on the stack so that the actor can pick it up without having to look for it. A little thought, preparation, and organization will smoothly integrate the use of properties into the flow of the production.

The property director together with the property running crew head, and in coordination with the stage manager, will carefully organize and orchestrate the storage, placement, and use of all properties.

Hand props and small set props, such as lamps, pictures, radios, and so forth, should be locked in storage cabinets adjacent to the stage area between rehearsals and performances. Many theatres have lockable storage bins in the wings for this purpose. Other organizations use small lockable storage rooms. Valuable and borrowed props should always be stored in a secure area. Ideally, all props will be stored under lock and key. However, some pieces may be too large and/or cumbersome to move into a locked storage area. These items should be moved off the set, if possible, and covered with muslin dust covers and marked with a sign stating: "Theatrical Property. Do Not Use or Remove."

A written list, including a ground plan or location indicator, detailing the on-stage placement of all set props *must* be created by the person in charge of running the properties while the show is being performed. That person is the prop running crew head. This list should also indicate where each item is stored between rehearsals and performances. The exact placement of the set props will be determined by the scenic designer, and any electrical connections will be coordinated with the master electrician. During rehearsals and performances the property running crew, under the guidance of the crew head and the stage manager, will place the set props in their appropriate locations. Depending on the union rules, if any, affecting the producing organization, any electrical connections will be made by either electricians or members of the prop running crew.

The organization of hand props must be equally exact. The prop running crew head and the stage manager create a precise, written master list of what props are handled by which actors during each scene. This list includes the secure location where these items will be stored between rehearsals and performances. If the show is complex or multiscene, a separate list should be compiled for each scene in the play.

A hand-prop list normally includes the identity of all handled props; the location of each prop at the beginning of the scene, and whether that location is different from the preceding scene (thus necessitating replacement by the prop crew); the condition of the prop if it is functional (wine glasses full or empty, book opened or closed, and so forth); where the prop is to be left by the actor (on- or offstage location); and any other pertinent information.

A **prop table,** on which all hand props are placed, is normally set up in the wings adjacent to the stage. To aid in organizing the props, this large table is frequently covered with brown butcher paper and "mapped" with names of specific props, such as "Act I, Scene 2, tray/4 glasses" for the silver tray and four stemmed glasses that the butler carries onto the set during Act I, Scene 2. The tray and glasses are placed just above or below the caption. If there are a lot of props, or if the actors make entrances and exits from a variety of directions, it may be helpful to have more than one prop table.

Because it is so easy to misplace small hand props such as eyeglasses, snuff boxes, and the like, it is essential that the location of all props be carefully tracked and that prop running crew members be responsible for placing all props in their appropriate locations and for retrieving them from the actors when they leave the stage if the actor does not have time to return the item to the prop table.

Sometimes, as during productions that do not use an act curtain, the prop running crew will move the props as the audience watches. At other times, the crew may be required to shift the props during a **blackout.** Frequently, the prop running crew accomplishes its work with the act curtain down and the stage worklights on. Regardless of the circumstances under which the crew works, it is essential that the prop running crew head hold specific rehearsals to train the crew in the coordinated, speedy, and accurate placement of all props (both set and hand) in their appropriate locations about the stage.

Opening   From opening night onward the actual running of the props during the show is in the hands of the stage manager. Daily performance reports, similar to daily rehearsal reports, are sent to all departments. Sometimes during the course of the production a prop may be damaged or consumable supplies run low. The prop artisans fix those challenges that can't be resolved by the prop running crew.

Strike   All props and set dressing need to be removed from the set immediately following the final performance to facilitate other departments' strikes and

prop table: A table, normally located in the wings, on which hand props are stored when not in use onstage.

blackout: When the stage is completely dark. The stage lights are out and no other lights are on.

to guarantee the safety of the props. Following strike all rentals and borrowed items need to be returned and all stock items cleaned and/or laundered and returned to their proper storage location. If a prop inventory list is maintained, it should be updated to reflect the most recent additions and alterations to those props that are part of the theatre's permanent collection.

 ## Craft Techniques

Properties construction utilizes a wide variety of skills and processes that overlap with many other areas of production. Many props can be built using the tools and techniques discussed in the various chapters covering scenery, lighting, and costuming. A number of additional construction techniques primarily used in building stage properties are discussed in the rest of this chapter.

Furniture

Prop furniture is always seemingly in need of restoration, alteration, or change. Stock and newly purchased furniture — frequently acquired from second-hand stores — is subject to an abnormal amount of wear and stress just in the course of being moved from props storage to the shop, shop to stage, and then the normal shifting/movement that occurs in almost every play. This abuse is in addition to anything that is inflicted upon it during the action of the play. So it is not at all unusual for furniture props to be in need of repair — glue joints tightened/reglued, broken parts mended/remade/replaced, or strengthened — to withstand the sometimes amazingly physical action of the play. It is also normal for the appearance of stock furniture to be altered — the style of leg changed, wood trim replaced with a different style, the whole piece reupholstered, and so forth. To handle all of this, prop people need to know how to disassemble, clean, repair, replace, and generally resurrect and reconstruct all types of wooden and upholstered furniture.

The ability of the property director or artisan to be able to see beyond the basic form of a piece of furniture to "what-it-could-become" is an invaluable skill. It's very helpful to have the vision — and knowledge of period furniture design — to know that a common kneehole desk can be changed into an appropriate period piece by adding a rolltop or cubby-hole topper. Similarly, the period appearance of a chair or sofa can be altered by replacing its legs with ones of a different style/design. Being able to see the form in the furniture and to know how it can be altered by the addition of more detail, moldings, or structural changes allows the prop shop to save money and resources by the creative alteration of stock and/or inexpensively found items.

Carpenter-style furniture (Figure 13.5) can be built using ordinary woodworking tools and techniques. The illustrated table will be very strong if it is assembled with the open doweled joints illustrated in Figure 13.6. Because of its strength and ease of fabrication, the open doweled joint can be used for reinforcing almost any joint in furniture construction.

Prop and Furniture Construction Joints   There are three types of what appear to be semi-complicated wood joints that, because of their strength, are frequently used in property construction. Actually, they're not complicated and they're all easy to make. They are the open doweled joint, the pocket hole joint, and the biscuit joint.

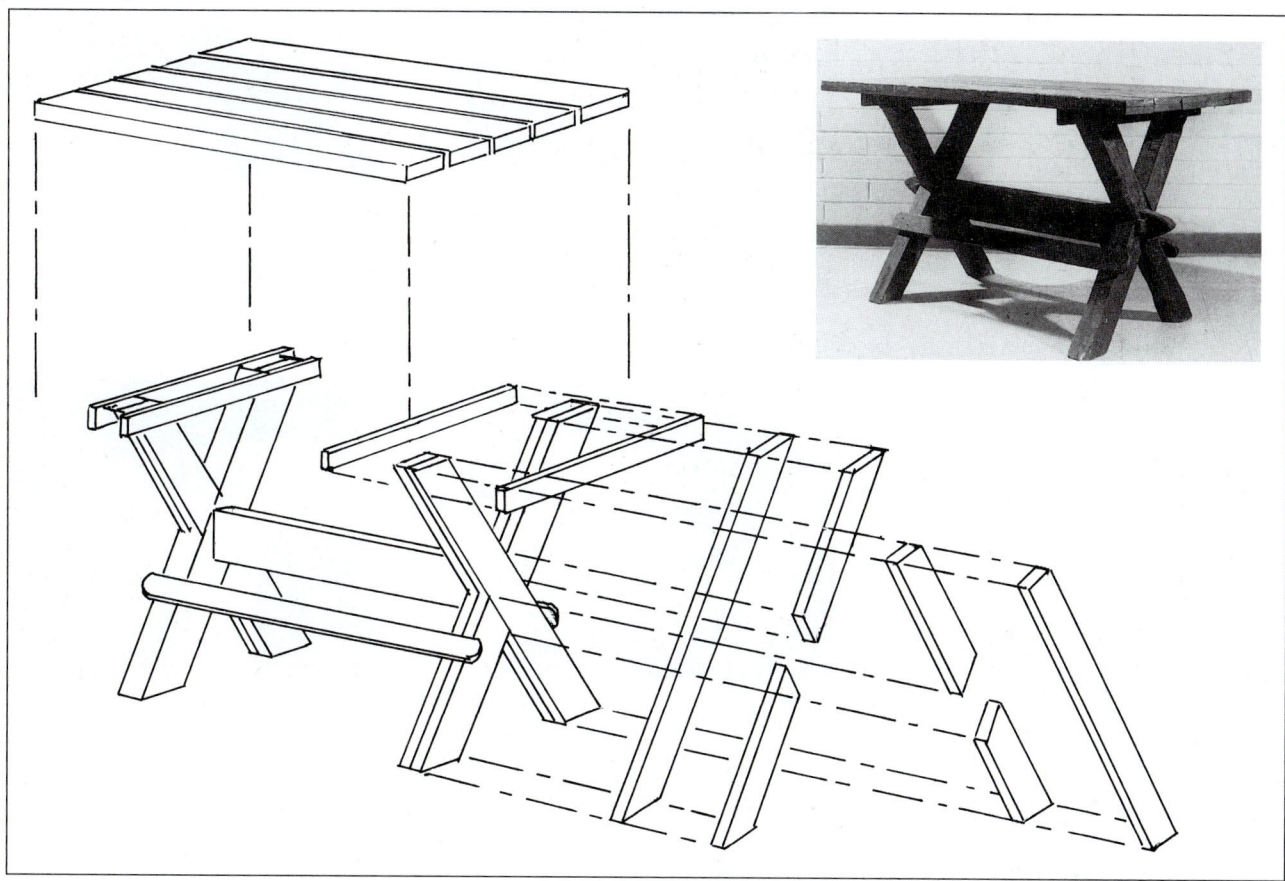

FIGURE 13.5
Exploded view of a carpenter-style table and the finished product. Courtesy of J. Michael Gillette.

Open Doweled Joint   The extremely strong doweled joint, which was introduced in Chapter 11, "Scenic Production Techniques," is used extensively in the furniture industry. The closed doweled (Figure 13.6A) is preferred for assembling fine furniture because the dowel is hidden inside the wood. The open doweled joint (Figure 13.6B) is just as strong and is very easily made. The basic technique for making this joint is detailed in Figure 16.6C–F. The open doweled joint can be used for making many furniture joints and has many other uses in prop construction. Even if the joint is on exposed wood that will be seen by the audience the dowels will rarely be noticed, even in arena productions, because the spectators won't be close enough to see the exposed dowel, particularly if the joint has been sanded, filled with wood putty, stained, **grained,** and varnished.

Pocket Hole Joint   The pocket hole joint is a very strong joint that is held together with specially designed screws. It has the advantage over doweled joints that, if the pieces are not glued together when the joint is made, it can be taken apart without damaging the wood. The pocket hole joint is used extensively in the commercial furniture and cabinet industries and is extremely useful in a variety of applications in property construction.

To construct a pocket hole joint a commercially available **jig** and specialty drill bit are used to drill a pocket hole at a shallow angle into the face of one of the pieces to be joined. Examples of the jigs, clamps, drill bits, and long-shafted square-headed screwdriver bits typically used to construct these joints are shown

grained: A past-tense verb form referring to the "dry-brush wood grain" painting technique described in Chapter 12, "Scene Painting."

jig: A device used hold pieces together in proper positional relationship.

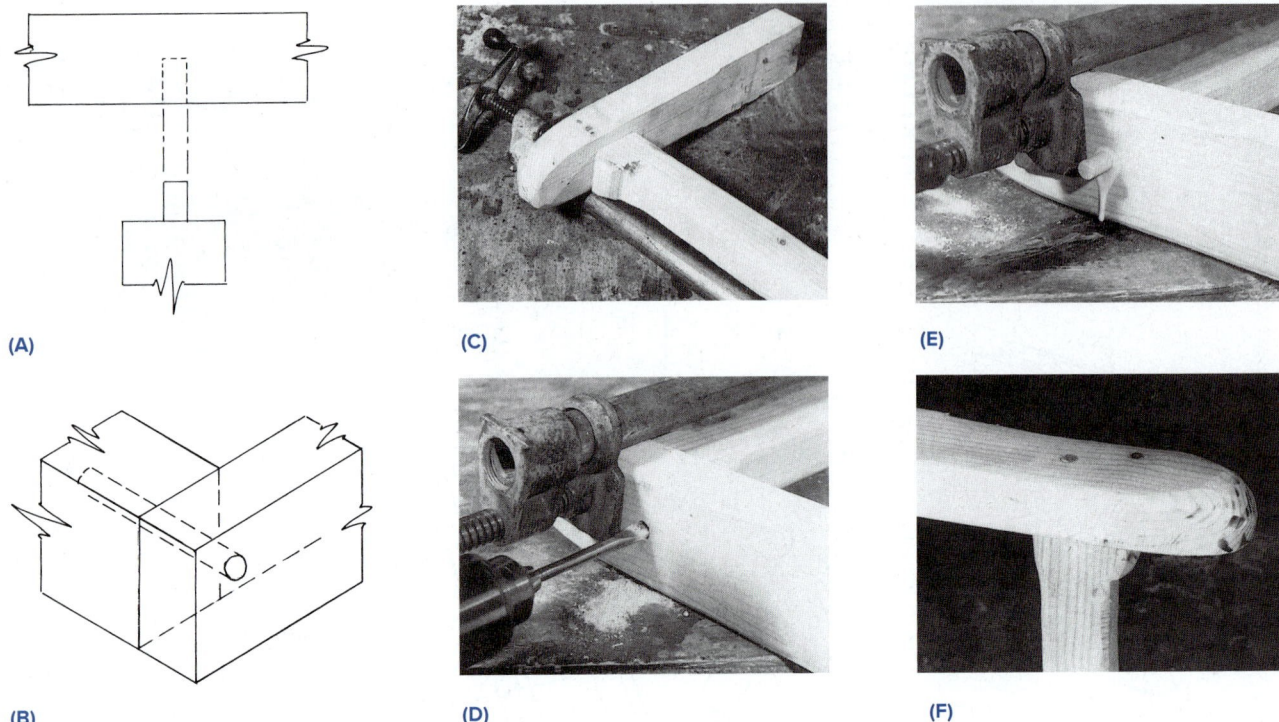

(A)

(B)

(C)

(D)

(E)

(F)

FIGURE 13.6
Open doweled construction technique. (A) Closed doweled joint. (B) Open doweled joint. Clamp together the parts to be joined (C), and drill a hole through the top piece and approximately 1 to 1½ inches into the second piece (D). Squirt glue into the hole and insert a dowel the same diameter as the hole (E). The finished open dowel joint (F) creates a very strong joint. C–F, Courtesy of J. Michael Gillette.

self-tapping: Screws that drill their own pilot holes as they are power-screwed into wood or metal. The screws have an auger-like tip that drills a smaller diameter hole than the screw threads.

carcass: The foundation structure of something, for example, the framework of a cabinet.

in Figure 13.7A. Figure 13.7B illustrates the jig being used to drill the shallow-angled pocket hole. After the pocket hole is drilled the pieces to be joined are clamped together, and the screw is placed in the pocket hole and power-screwed into the second piece of wood as shown in Figures 13.7C and D. These specially designed, **self-tapping** screws have a wide flat head that bears against, rather than biting into, the wood at the bottom of the pocket hole. The unique design of the screw head works like a mini-clamp and is what gives the joint its strength. Information about the types and styles of jigs, clamps, and supplies as well as more how-to information can be accessed by doing an online search for "pocket hole screws."

Biscuit Joint   The biscuit joint, Figure 13.8, is frequently used to edge-join pieces of wood. It can also used to make edge-to-face joints. A typical application would be when making a table and several planks need to be joined edge to edge to make the table top. The biscuit joint is also used to make the edge-to-face joints typically found in cabinet **carcasses.**

To make a biscuit joint, a biscuit cutter, illustrated in Figure 13.8A, is used to cut crescent-shaped holes in the two pieces of wood that are to be joined. Glue is applied to the two faces of the joint and a "biscuit," a flat oval-shaped disk made of compressed wood chips, is inserted into the facing oval slots and the joint is then clamped together. The glue causes the biscuit to swell and tighten. Once the glue has cured, the biscuit joint is incredibly strong as well as invisible.

Wood Turning

Wood turning is done on a lathe. Various prop and scenic items such as furniture legs, decorative poles, banisters, and newels are frequently turned on a lathe.

Because hardwoods such as walnut, oak, mahogany, and cherry have a fairly dense structure, they are usually considered the best candidates for turning, although carefully selected, knot-free, tight-grained pine or fir can be used.

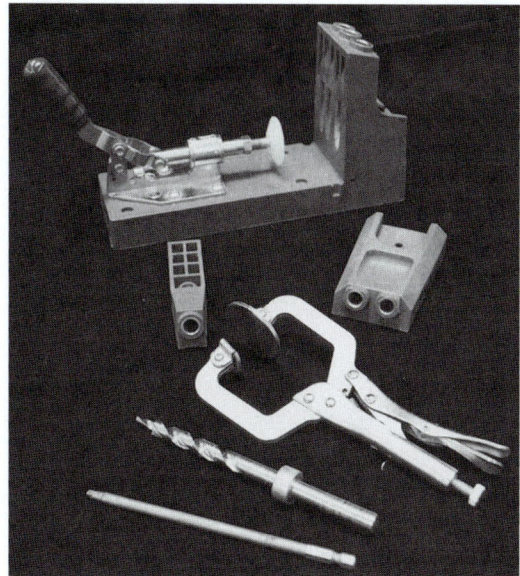

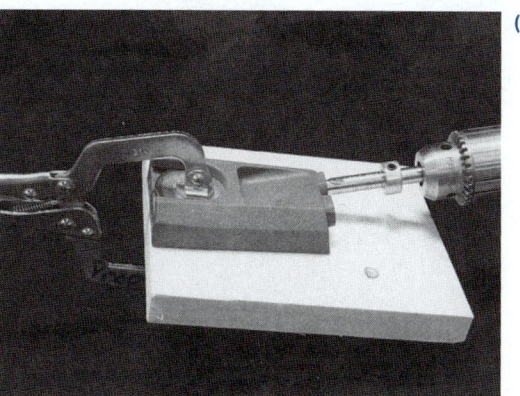

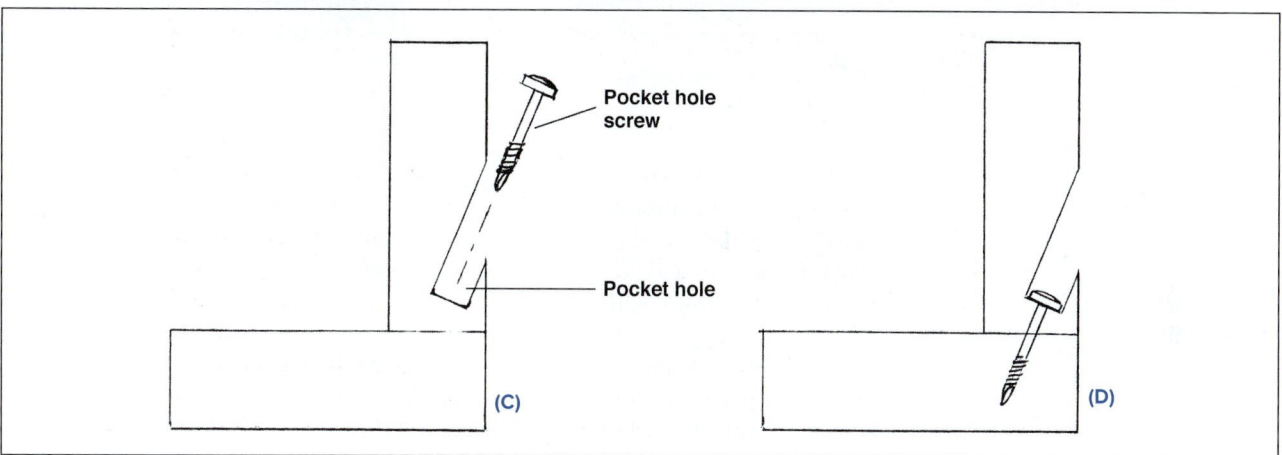

(A)

(B)

Pocket hole
screw

Pocket hole

(C)

(D)

FIGURE 13.7
A pocket hole joint. (A) Jigs, clamps,
drill bit, and screwdriver bit used
in pocket hole joint construction.
(B) A pocket hole being drilled.
(C) A pocket hole screw is
used to hold the joint together.
(D) Completed pocket hole joint.
Photos courtesy of Blaird Wade.
A and B, Courtesy of Blaird Wade.

Wood to be turned is securely mounted on the lathe, and as the lathe spins the stock, it is carved using special chisels called turning tools.

Foam can be turned on a wood lathe by using a slow speed and using sandpaper rather than cutting tools. It can also be shaped with a hot-wire cutter. Urethane foam shouldn't be turned because of the toxic gas it emits when heated. Styrofoam sheets will probably have to be laminated to provide stock of sufficient thickness. Because Styrofoam is not very dense, pieces of ¼-inch plywood of the same size as the ends of the work will need to be securely glued to the ends so that the lathe's **spindle chucks** will have something to bite into to hold the work in the lathe. If the foam turnings are to be very narrow, a wooden armature (a ⅜-inch or ½-inch dowel or ¾-by-¾-inch white-pine stock) may need to be sandwiched into the foam laminate to provide sufficient strength for the unit to be turned. Be sure that the wooden armature is absolutely straight.

Upholstery

Many times the apparent age or period of a fabric-covered piece can be altered simply by changing the upholstery fabric. For example, the relatively square

spindle chuck: A device used to
hold wood in a lathe.

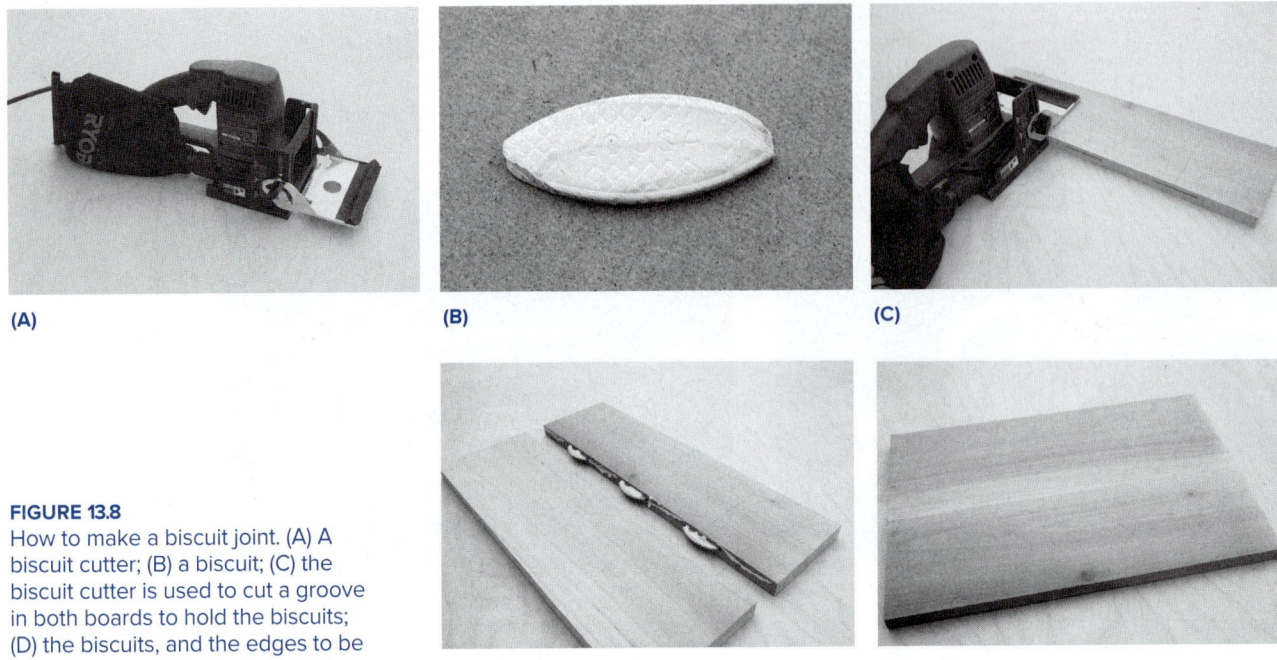

(A) (B) (C)

(D) (E)

FIGURE 13.8
How to make a biscuit joint. (A) A biscuit cutter; (B) a biscuit; (C) the biscuit cutter is used to cut a groove in both boards to hold the biscuits; (D) the biscuits, and the edges to be joined are coated with glue; (E) the finished biscuit joint. A-E, Courtesy of J. Michael Gillette.

silhouette of the tuxedo-style sofa (Figure 13.9) has been in continuous fashion since the 1920s. Although the dust ruffle has been in and out of vogue and floral prints have come and gone, the basic style and shape of the sofa have remained basically unchanged. The fabric covering for **stock furniture** is normally altered in one of two ways: with slipcovers or by reupholstering the piece.

stock furniture: Items owned by the producing organization and held in storage until they are needed for a production.

Slipcovers   A slipcover is upholstery fabric that is tailored to fit a particular piece or type of furniture and is applied over existing upholstery. Slipcovers are normally used on fully upholstered furniture rather than on pieces that have exposed wood. They should be used only if the underlying fabric, padding, and frame are in good condition. Slipcovers can be used on borrowed furniture, because the existing upholstery material is left in place.

FIGURE 13.9
Changing the upholstery can change the apparent period of a furniture piece. ©McGraw-Hill Education.

Reupholstery   Reupholstery involves removing the existing fabric covering and making the item stage ready by making any necessary repairs and

The Wood Lathe

All stationary power tools are inherently dangerous. But they can be operated safely. To do so requires a knowledge of safe work practices and an understanding of how the machine operates. The following precautions should be followed when working with a wood lathe.

1. Never wear loose clothing. It might get caught in the spinning wood.

2. Wear goggles or a face shield.

3. Be sure the wood doesn't have any defects (knots, weak spots) that might cause it to break while spinning.

4. Be sure that all glue joints on stock that is going to be turned are very carefully and thoroughly made and that the glue is completely dry or cured before turning.

5. Center the work, and be sure that it is securely mounted between the spindles.

6. Keep the tool rest as close to the stock as possible. Before starting the motor, rotate the stock by hand to make sure it doesn't hit the tool rest. Adjust the position of the tool rest to keep it close to the stock as the turning progresses.

7. Turn stock over 6 inches in diameter at a slow speed, that from 3 to 6 inches at medium speed, and that under 3 inches a little faster.

8. Don't make any adjustments to the tool rest or other mechanical elements of the lathe while the motor is running.

9. Run all stock at the slowest possible speed until it is rounded.

10. Hold tools firmly with both hands.

11. Remove the tool rest before sanding or polishing the work. If you don't, your fingers may become caught between the stock and the tool rest.

strengthening the piece, restructuring the padding, and replacing the outer covering and decoration. The existing fabric should be carefully removed, as shown in Figure 13.10, so it can be used as a pattern for cutting the new covering material. Once the old fabric is removed, the padding, springs, and webbing should be examined and repaired as necessary. Depending on the age of the piece, the old padding may be urethane foam, cotton batting, or horsehair. Any damaged or compressed padding should be replaced with the same type of material.

When upholstering stage furniture the sofa or chair springs are frequently removed and replaced with plywood. The plywood not only provides a solid base for the padding, it helps strengthen the chair frame and provides some of the extra durability needed for most stage business. A base of urethane foam — urethane foam is available in a variety of densities from most upholstery supply houses — is cut to size and covered with polyester or cotton batting to create the appropriate period shape and feel.

Before applying the new upholstery fabric, any padding/batting should be covered with muslin. The muslin holds the padding and batting in place, allows the upholstery fabric to move freely without snagging the padding, and serves as a base for any future reupholstery jobs.

FIGURE 13.10
Basic reupholstery technique.
(A) A chair in need of reupholstery.
(B) Carefully remove and save the old fabric and torn elements of padding. (C) Apply new padding.
(D) Use the old fabric as a pattern.
(E) Cover the padding with muslin to hold the padding in place and to provide a smooth surface over which the covering fabric can slip. (F) Attach the new fabric with staples or decorative tacks. (G) The finished chair. A-G, Courtesy of J. Michael Gillette.

 (A)

 (B)

 (C)

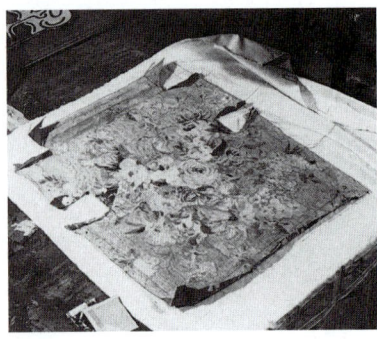 (D)

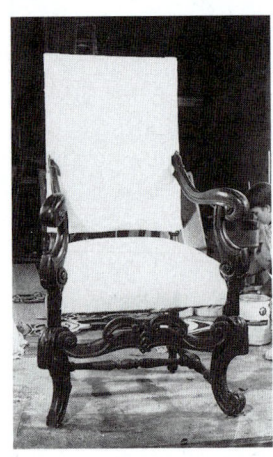 (E)

 (F)

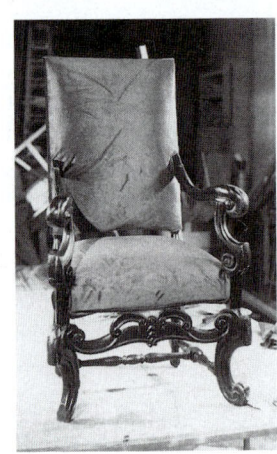 (G)

Upholstery **gimp,** fringe, or trims are often glued or tacked onto the piece to cover the raw edges of upholstery fabric that have been stapled to the frame. The judicious use of glue and/or upholstery tacks will make it easier to remove them when the time comes to, once again, reupholster that piece.

Decorative Curtains and Draperies

Decorative curtains are used by the scenic designer to help **dress** the set. The type and style of drapery or curtain selected should be dictated by the period that is being represented in the design. Background research is done by looking at paintings, drawings, or photographs that show drapery styles of the period being represented. Figure 13.11 illustrates several typical styles of curtains.

A variety of materials are used to make draperies. The specific type of material is dictated by where it is used in the drape. The **valance, drapes** (also called overdrapes), and **sheers** are the primary elements of any window-curtain arrangement. The valance is generally made from heavy drapery material, although it can be made of wood painted or covered with fabric. A wooden valance is called a valance box. Heavy, soft drapery materials like those used for stage drapes (velour, velveteen, corduroy, commando) are generally used for the drapes, and lightweight, translucent materials such as chiffon and netting (see Chapter 18, "Costume Design") are used for making sheers.

gimp: An ornamental flat braid or round cord used as trimming.

dress: To place decorative props such as curtains, doilies, knick-knacks, or magazines on the set to help make the environment look lived-in and provide clues to the personality of the set's inhabitants.

valance: A horizontal element at the top of a drapery arrangement that covers the curtain rod.

drape: A vertical element of heavy fabric that frames the sides of a window or archway; can usually be pulled across the opening.

sheer: A thin gauze curtain that hangs across the opening of a window to soften the "sunlight" and obscure the view into a room.

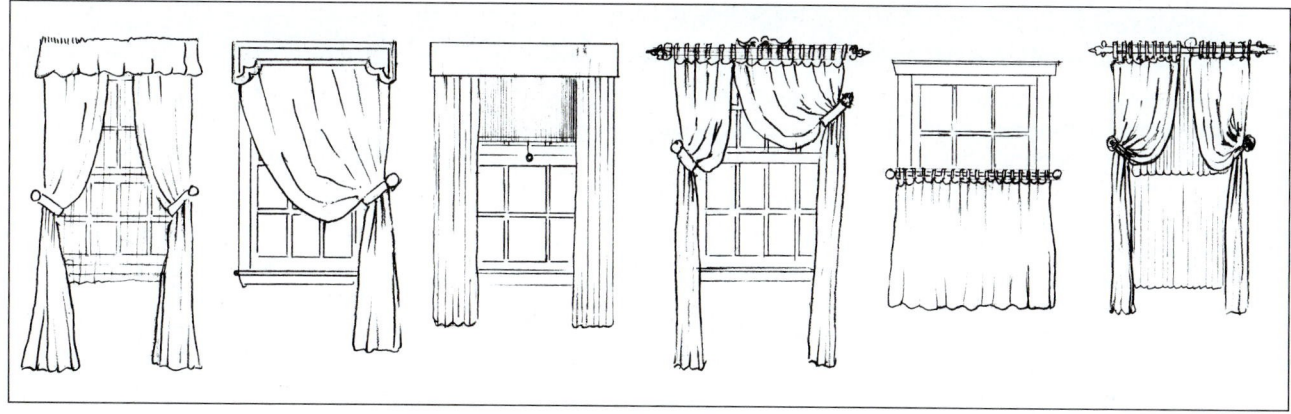

FIGURE 13.11
Several styles of curtains.

Papier-Mâché

Papier-mâché is one of the oldest craft techniques used in the theatre. It is also one of the cheapest. It is used to make, or cover, a wide variety of shapes and objects that range from logs to statues, clubs, and various types of fake food.

Papier-mâché is made by building up a form with successive layers of paper that are bound together with a wheat-paste binder. The normal method of working with it is to tear newspaper into strips about 1 inch wide, dip them in the wheat-paste mixture, and form them over the mold. Between three and six layers of paper are usually applied to the form. After the object has dried (usually 24 to 48 hours), it can be painted with any of the paints used in the shop.

Craft stores frequently sell a prepared mixture of very finely shredded paper and wheat paste. You only need to add water to this papier-mâché mix to create a pastelike substance that can be used for sculpture or as a smooth finish coat over rough objects. It can also be formed in molds.

paperclay: A nontoxic modeling material that can be sculpted, molded, or shaped, and air dries to a hard finish that can be carved or sanded.

The disadvantages of papier-mâché have resulted in it rarely being used in the theatre today. It's fragile, so things made out of papier-mâché don't stand up very well to anything other than very limited-run productions. It takes a fairly long time to dry. Its native finish is pretty crude unless you coat it with something like **paperclay,** which then allows you to apply a number of different paints/coatings with finish reflectivities ranging from matte to gloss. Even with these disadvantages, if you have the time to work with it, and you're looking for a formable material that is very inexpensive, papier-mâché may be just what you're looking for.

Vacuum Forming

Vacuum forming, or vacuforming, is the process of shaping plastics through the application of heat and vacuum pressure. Shapes can be formed with a vacuforming table of the type shown in Figure 13.12.

The vacuum-forming machine consists of a heating oven, a forming table, and a pump to evacuate air from a tank to create a vacuum reservoir. A sheet of plastic is heated by the oven until it becomes limber. While it is still hot, it is placed over a mold on the forming table, and the valve to the vacuum reservoir is released. The pressure of the outside air trying to reach the vacuum reservoir forms the plastic around the mold. When the thermoplastic cools (in a few seconds), it retains the shape of the mold.

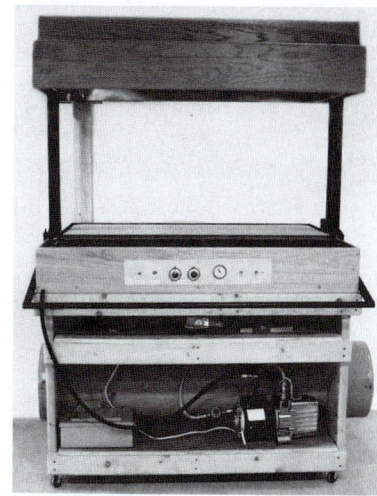

FIGURE 13.12
A vacuforming table. Photo courtesy of Jim Guy.

This very flexible system can be used to form decorative items for both properties and scenery. Small decorative relief panels glued onto basic frames

PRODUCTION INSIGHTS
Drapery and Upholstery Materials

All materials used for stage draperies have roughly the same characteristics. They generally have a soft, nonreflective surface and are available in a variety of colors. Upholstery and decorative drapery materials are not nearly so limited. They are available in a variety of finishes and a panoply of colors.

Factory flame-retardant treatment for stage drapery and flat-covering materials is required by law. When you purchase stage drapes, or material from which to make stage drapes, be certain that the supplier provides a certificate of flame-retardant treatment and keep it on file as it is a distinct possibility that a fire marshal may ask to see it. If the materials aren't flameproofed when you buy them, they will have to be treated by hand, and most flameproofing solutions, if applied by hand, will darken the fabric in an uneven pattern.

Velour

Velour is a cotton-backed material with a deep surface pile generally made from cotton, rayon, or nylon. It is available in a variety of weights ranging from 12 to 25 ounces per square yard and widths from 45 to 54 inches. The material is available in a wide variety of colors, has a rich, lustrous appearance, and absorbs light well. It is generally the preferred material for stage drapes as well as rich, heavy decorative curtains and some upholstery applications. Crushed velour, in which the nap is compressed to create an irregular textural pattern, is a common upholstery material.

Velveteen

Velveteen possesses the same general characteristics as velour, but it is much lighter — 6 to 8 ounces. It has a lustrous pile finish and is generally available in 45- to 48-inch widths from local fabric stores. It is normally used for decorative curtains and upholstery. The material, which wrinkles easily, is not durable enough to be used for stage drapes.

Plush

The pile of plush is softer and longer than that of velveteen but has the same characteristically silk-like sheen. Available in a variety of colors and widths from 45 to 54 inches, plush can be purchased from local fabric and upholstery shops. It is used as an upholstery or drapery material.

Commando

Commando cloth, also known as duvetyn, is a lightweight cotton fabric with a very short, feltlike, almost matted pile. It is available in two widths and weights: 36-inch (lightweight) and 48-inch (heavyweight). The heavyweight material is good for stage drapes but is a little stiff to be used for decorative drapes. The lightweight is suitable for decorative drapes but is a little too delicate for the rugged treatment that most stage drapes receive. Neither type is particularly appropriate for upholstery applications. Commando cloth is available in a variety of colors and can be purchased from scenic-fabric supply houses.

Cotton Rep

Cotton rep is a tough cotton fabric with a ribbed finish that is similar to a very-narrow-wale corduroy. It reflects light more than other drapery materials do. Rep is available in a wide range of colors from scenic-fabric supply houses. It can be used for stage or decorative drapes.

Damask

Damask achieves its rich appearance from the raised patterns of high-luster yarn that are normally woven into the matte finish of the background cloth. The heavy material is available from local fabric houses in a wide range of colors and in widths ranging between 45 and 54 inches. It is primarily used for decorative drapes and upholstery.

Brocade

Brocade is similar to damask but lighter in weight. The pattern, which can be either raised or flat, is generally created through the use of high-luster yarn that contrasts with the matte finish of the background. 45 to 54 inches wide, brocade is available in a wide range of colors and patterns in fabric and drapery shops. It is primarily used for decorative drapes and upholstery.

Satin

Satin is a heavy, stiff fabric with a smooth, shiny finish on the front and a dull finish on the back. If it is patterned, the design is generally printed on, rather than woven into, the fabric. Available in a wide range of colors and pattern designs, it is normally between 45 and 54 inches wide and can be purchased at local fabric and drapery shops. It is used for decorative drapes and upholstery.

Corduroy

Corduroy is a cotton material whose pile ridges, called wales, alternate with a low-luster backing. The width of the wale varies from only $\frac{1}{32}$ to approximately $\frac{3}{16}$ inch. The weight of the material also varies considerably, with the lighter-weight versions suitable for costumes and the heavier weights more appropriate for upholstery. Corduroy is available in a wide selection of colors and in fabric widths from 45 to 54 inches. It can be purchased from local fabric and upholstery shops. Waleless corduroy (similar to a very-short-nap velour) or very-narrow-wale corduroy can be used as a substitute for velvet in draperies, costumes, and upholstery; the wide-wale fabrics are primarily used for upholstery purposes.

or box forms can be used to create very realistic looking items like decorative attachments for screens, stoves, and desks. Appropriately designed vacuum-formed panels can also be used to create scenic items like wall panels and cornices. Generally speaking, the vacuum form machine is used in those situations where one basic form has to be repeated a gazillion times and that form either can't be purchased or is simply too expensive to purchase in quantity.

High-impact polystyrene 0.020 inch thick is the most commonly used material in vacuum forming, because it is thick enough to be reasonably strong after it has been stretched over the mold during forming. The material can be painted with acrylic vinyl, casein, and most oil- or lacquer-based paints. Other types of plastic that can be vacuum formed include thin sheets (0.010 to 0.025 inch thick) of acrylic, vinyl, and cellulose acetate butyrate (CAB). (See Chapter 10, "Tools and Materials," for a discussion of the various types of plastics.) Plans for vacuum-forming machines are available at several online sites.

Molds

In property, costume, and scenic production, molds can be used to create multiple copies of a wide variety of objects ranging from fake loaves of bread to costume jewels and decorative panels. But a word of caution seems advisable. Making molds and casting objects in those molds generally subscribes to Murphy's Law: if something can go wrong it will. If only a few copies of something are needed it's usually faster, cheaper, and easier to simply buy whatever it is. But, at the same time, mold-making and casting provides the property artisan with a technique can be used to create multiple copies of intricately detailed small articles.

Molds can be divided into two categories — open and closed. The only significant difference between the two is that the open mold has an open top or port, whereas the closed mold is enclosed on all sides and has one or more ports into which the casting material is poured.

Molds can further be subdivided into rigid and flexible. Rigid molds (Figure 13.13 top) are generally made from such materials as wood, plaster of paris, fiberglass, or rigid urethane foam. Flexible molds (Figure 13.13 bottom) can be made from a variety of synthetic materials such as room-temperature-vulcanizing (RTV) silicone rubber. RTV silicone rubber and other mold-making materials can usually be found at local craft or art supply shops.

FIGURE 13.13
Rigid (top) and flexible (bottom) molds. Courtesy of J. Michael Gillette.

SDSs — A Reminder

It's axiomatic that in technical theatre we're almost always working in a hurry. There's so much to do and, usually, not enough time to do it. But just because you're in a hurry, don't try to take a shortcut when it comes to safety issues.

The materials typically used in property construction — exotic combinations of adhesives, paints, resins, coatings, and so forth — create what is potentially the most hazardous working environment that you'll encounter anywhere in theatre. Be sure the area in which you're using any of these materials is ventilated according to SDS and OSHA standards. Also be sure that you read the SDSs for any material you're working with and follow the safety instructions therein. If the data sheet for the material with which you're working recommends wearing a mask or respirator with a specific type of filter, be sure to wear it! 'Tis better to be safe than sorry.

In order to remove the cast object from the mold, the inside of the mold must be treated with a release agent before being filled with the casting material. The release agent needs to be compatible with the type of material being cast. A silicone release agent, commercially available in spray cans, will work well for polyester, acrylic, and epoxy resins, but the heat generated by the urethane casting resins requires that a urethane mold release be used with both pour-in-place and spray foams. Both types of release agent are generally available at craft or hobby shops.

Many molding and casting products release gas or fumes during the mixing or curing process. When working with any of these materials it is important that all recommended safety procedures are followed carefully. Information for the safe use of each product is normally printed on the container labels. It is also available on the SDSs that can be obtained from the dealer or online. Good ventilation is necessary for all of them. Most of these materials necessitate the wearing of disposable latex or vinyl gloves. Face shields, respirators, and protective clothing should be worn when working with the more hazardous products. But again, the specific safety equipment required, and its specifications, are detailed on the relevant container labels and SDSs.

Making a Mold   Rigid molds of objects that don't have a great deal of detail can be made fairly quickly by coating the **model** with a urethane release agent and then covering it with either pour-in-place or spray urethane foam (rigid formulation), as shown in Figure 13.14. This type of mold works well for objects that are free from **undercuts,** such as bricks and planks. Rigid molds can also be made in the same manner from plaster of paris or fiberglass.

If there are undercuts on the object being cast, a flexible mold is needed. This type of mold can be made with RTV silicone rubber, as shown in Figure 13.15.

A flexible mold that reveals a great deal of detail of the object being cast can be made by coating the model with silicone release, followed by several layers of liquid latex. Three to five coats are generally required. After the latex has dried, the inside of the box is coated with urethane release agent or lined with polyethylene film (urethane won't adhere to polyethylene), and flexible urethane foam is poured into the mold box. The flexible urethane foam will bond with, and provide a strong backing for, the latex mold.

Casting Molded Objects   It is fairly easy to cast objects from molds. The inside of the mold is coated with an appropriate release agent, and the molding material is poured into the mold and allowed to dry or set. After the material has cured (the time required varies depending on the material, heat, and humidity), the cast object is taken out of the mold. Depending on the complexity of the mold and the material being cast, some finishing details such as sanding or trimming may be required.

In order to paint the cast object, you will generally need to remove all traces of the release agent. Read the label on the release agent's container to determine the type of cleaner that will be needed.

Fake Food

model: An object that is being used as the subject of a mold casting.

undercut: An indentation in a form that leaves an overhang or concave profile — for example, the nostrils in a mask of a face.

Food that isn't going to be consumed onstage — fake food — can be made using a variety of interesting techniques. Casting and molding techniques can be used to produce realistic reproductions of almost all foods. The basic form of many foods such as cakes, pastries, meat and fruit can be cut from Styrofoam, "frosted" with latex caulk, and finished with paints and spray varnishes to mimic the surface of

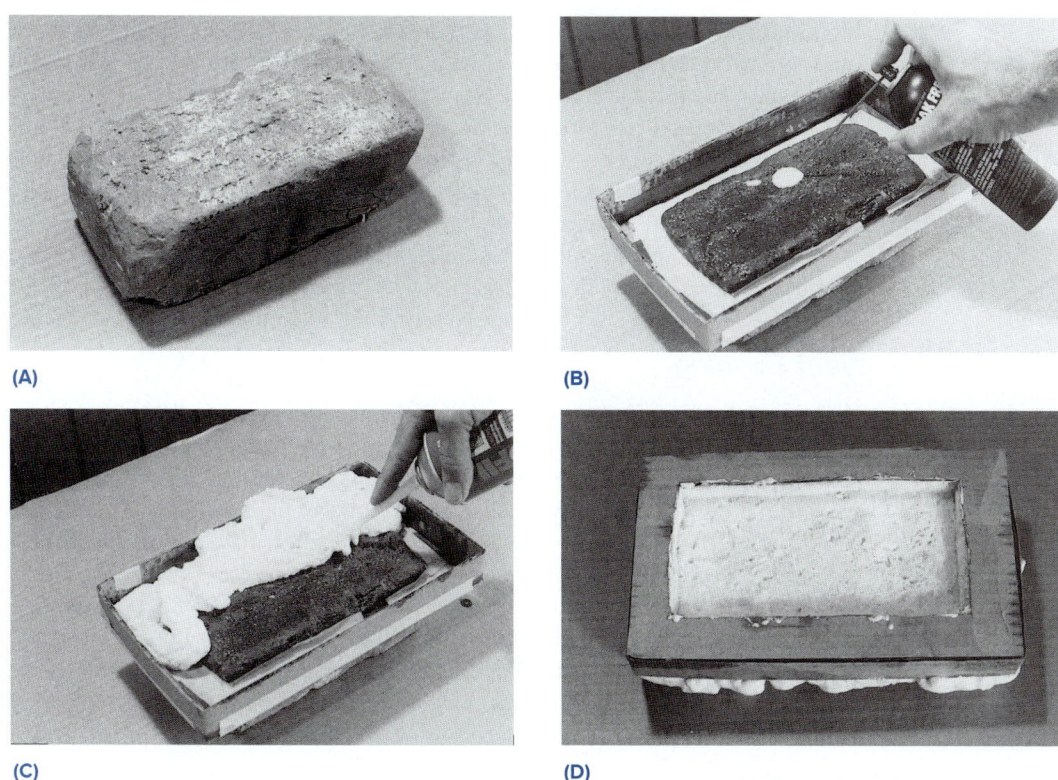

(A)

(B)

(C)

(D)

FIGURE 13.14
Rigid mold-making technique.
(A) The object being cast: a brick.
(B) Attach a collar to create a box for the mold, and coat the brick and box with a silicone release agent.
(C) Coat the brick and box with spray urethane foam (rigid formula).
(D) The finished mold. Be sure to read, and follow, all safety directions on the labels and SDSs for the materials with which you're working.
A-D, Courtesy of J. Michael Gillette.

(A)

(B)

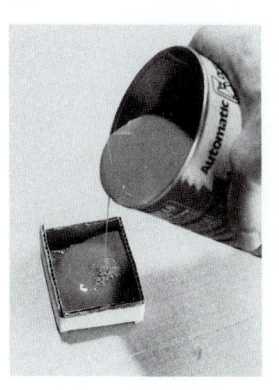

(C)

(D)

FIGURE 13.15
Flexible mold-making technique.
(A) The object being cast: a brooch.
(B) Place the brooch in a cardboard box, and spray both with a silicone release agent. (C) Pour RTV rubber into the box until it covers the top of the brooch to a depth of about ⅛ inch. (D) The finished mold and the brooch. A-D, Courtesy of J. Michael Gillette.

the original. Actual pastries such as rolls and cookies will last through a short-duration run if thoroughly sprayed with several layers of shellac. Rubber bands lightly sprayed with floral paint to resemble fettuccini, when topped with a delicious red "latex sauce" and some papier-mâché meatballs, can appear to be a convincing Italian dinner. Wet thick plaster can be quickly shaped to resemble scoops of ice cream. After it has cured, just add a dark brown latex topping and you have a chocolate sundae.

All it takes to create a variety of fake foods is a little imagination and some common materials found in most scenery and/or prop shops.

Heat Forming

Heat forming generally refers to warming plastic until it becomes flexible enough to bend. Sheet and rod acrylic or PVC can be heated and formed without any preparatory work. Tubes should be filled with sand before they are heated, to prevent them from crimping or collapsing as they are being bent.

If the pieces of acrylic or PVC are small enough, it will be possible to heat the plastic in the oven of a kitchen stove. Remove any paper or protective covering from the plastic, and put the plastic on a cookie sheet. Preheat the oven to 300°F, and heat the plastic for a couple of minutes, or until it is limber enough to bend. The plastic can be formed over a mold or clamped in position until it has cooled. Be sure to wear heat-resistant gloves when you are heat-forming plastics.

Fiberglass

Fiberglass is formed by coating glass-fiber reinforcement with polyester or epoxy resin, as illustrated in Figure 13.16. Polyester resin is normally used, because it is less expensive. The most common types of glass reinforcement are (1) a woven glass-fiber cloth in either sheet or tape form and (2) a glass mat that closely resembles felt cloth. The great strength of fiberglass results from the tensile strength of the glass reinforcement being locked into place by the resin.

Because of safety issues involved in the use of catalyzed polyester resin (see the box "Catalyzed Polyester Resin") most theatrical fiberglass projects now use Aqua Resin rather than polyester or epoxy resin. Aqua Resin and similar brands of water-based resin pose none of the health or safety risks of MEK-catalyzed resins. Water-based resins have the same working properties and are used in exactly the same manner as polyester resin. The only exception involves large structures where strength becomes an issue. Aqua Resin and most other

FIGURE 13.16
Fiberglass construction techniques. (A) "Flesh out" a wooden skeleton with newspaper to create the basic form. (B) Cover the armature with aluminum foil. (C) Drape fiberglass cloth over it to create the line of the sculpture, and coat it with catalyzed resin. (D) The finished form. It can be reinforced with additional coats of glass cloth or mat as necessary and painted or finished as desired. A-D, Courtesy of J. Michael Gillette.

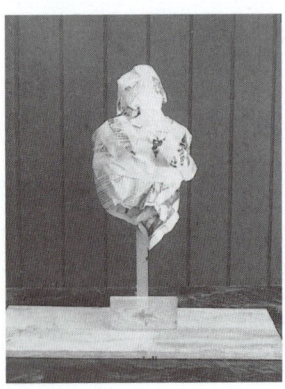

(A)

(B)

(C)

(D)

water-based resins are not as strong as either polyester or epoxy resin. A tech sheet detailing the specifications and working characteristics of Aqua Resin can be found online.

For most applications in property construction, the cloth or mat is draped over an **armature** and held in place with clothespins, wire, or tape. It is also possible to form the fiberglass by using molds.

After the glass-fiber cloth is formed, it is saturated with a coating of resin. A second layer of cloth or mat can be added for additional strength after the resin has cured for 12 to 24 hours. Lightly sand the surface between coats. Generally, two to three coats will be strong enough for most scenic or property applications. Another advantage of the use of Aqua Resin is that most water-based paints will adhere to its cured surface. If polyester resin is used, it generally has to be first painted with a lacquer-based primer before most stage paints can be applied.

CNC Machines

CNC machines are computer-controlled **milling** machines. Because of their high cost and the need to have someone on staff who can program the machine, most prop shops share a machine with the scene shop or outsource the work to a local machining company.

In the prop shop, CNC machines are used to make multiple copies of highly detailed props or relatively simple shapes like carved wooden dishes and bowls. In the scene shop, they are also used to make multiple copies of shapes such as banisters, cornice pieces, and the like.

Building one of these units in the shop can significantly reduce the high cost of CNC machines. Plans are available online from a number of sources.

PRODUCTION INSIGHTS
Catalyzed Polyester Resin

Polyester resin does not dry the way paint or varnish does. It will remain in its liquid state until a catalyzing agent, methylethylketone (MEK), is added and thoroughly stirred into the resin. The catalyst initiates a change in the molecular structure of the resin from liquid to solid. MEK is highly toxic. Be sure to read, and follow, the SDS regarding appropriate safety equipment, working procedures, and shop ventilation when working with this chemical.

When the resin "kicks off" (begins to change its physical state), heat is released. If you carefully follow the suggested recipe that is printed on the resin container, you should have between 10 and 20 minutes to work with the catalyzed resin.

When the resin kicks off, it turns to a jellylike consistency very quickly. From this point, it will take 12 to 24 hours for it to fully cure.

Disposable paper cups make excellent mixing containers for resin, because you can throw them away after the resin has kicked off. Apply the resin with natural-bristle brushes, because it will dissolve synthetic bristles. Most home center stores have stocks of cheap natural bristle brushes — usually white in color. These brushes aren't much good for painting, but they are ideal for applying catalyzed resin because you can throw them away after use. Thoroughly clean any application equipment with acetone before the catalyzed resin gels; you won't be able to clean it after the resin has begun to cure.

armature: A basic skeletal form that holds the covering materials in the desired shape or alignment.

milling: The cutting, drilling, shaping, and finishing of wood, plastic, or metal.

The design and construction of stage properties is a genuinely fascinating field. If your interest in this field has been piqued, you should undertake further study of the almost innumerable design and craft areas such as painting, furniture construction, upholstery, electricity, metalworking, ceramics, and sewing that are part of this theatrical specialty.

Selected References

Gottshall, Franklin H. *How to Design and Construct Period Furniture*. Reprinted by Bonanza Books, original copyright 1937.

Kenton, Warren. *Stage Properties and How to Make Them*. Drama Book Specialists, 1978.

Meyer, Franz Sales. *Handbook of Ornament*. Dover Publications, 1957.

Meyers, L. Donald. *The Furniture Lover's Book: Finding, Fixing, Finishing*. Sunrise Books, E. P. Dutton, 1977.

Neuman, Jay Hartley, and Lee Scott. *Plastics for the Craftsman*. Crown Publishers, 1972.

Chapter 14

Lighting Design

This chapter has been updated thanks to significant input from Michael McNamara, professional lighting designer and educator. The authors wish to publicly thank him for his extensive knowledge and expertize on this subject and for his contributions to this chapter.

Any dramatic production, unless it is performed outdoors in the daytime, needs some kind of artificial light. On the other hand, if illumination were the only function of stage lighting, you could hang a bank of fluorescent lights over the stage and forget about all the dimmers, control boards, cables, instruments, and other complicated paraphernalia of stage lighting.

Obviously, there is something more to stage lighting than simply bathing the stage with light. Effective stage lighting not only lets the spectators see the action of the play but also ties together all the visual elements of the production and helps create an appropriate mood and atmosphere that heighten the audience's understanding and enjoyment of the play.

Controllable Qualities of Light

The late Tharon Musser, a prominent professional lighting designer, once said, "If you ask most people who walk in and tell you they want to be lighting designers, what kind of weather we are having — what's it like outside? — half of them won't know how to describe it, if they remember it at all. They simply don't know how to see."[1] Learning how to see — to understand how light shapes and modifies people and objects — is absolutely essential in learning to understand lighting design.

A lighting designer can "see" how the lighting should look for a production only if he or she has an understanding of the controllable qualities of the medium. The qualities of light that the lighting designer can control are divided into four categories: distribution, intensity, movement, and color.

Light and Perception

Before you can design with light you need to understand how light influences human perceptions and understanding. We all know what light does — it makes things visible. But to know how lighting design works it is essential to fully comprehend the following concept: our impressions and understanding of what we're looking at are determined, to a great extent, by the way that object is

[1] Musser, Tharon, *Lighting Dimensions*, 1977.

illuminated. The angle of the light, its intensity, color, and sharpness or diffusion all affect our perceptions. Almost everyone has heard of the phrase "the ever-changing face of the mountains." But, if you stop to think about it, unless there is some cataclysmic disaster, the features of any particular mountain or mountain range change very little over hundreds or thousands of years. But the light striking those mountains changes significantly over the course of a day. The play of highlight and shadow shift continuously as the sun moves across the sky. Clouds or fog soften or obscure part of the range. A hillside that is in full sun in the morning may be in deep shadows in the afternoon. At sunset the whole mountain can be bathed in a beautifully soft peach twilight. The manner in which the sun illuminates the mountain controls not only what we see but, to a great extent, how we feel about what we're seeing.

Intellectually everyone understands that the physical structure of the mountains hasn't changed. But our individual perception, our personal reaction to those mountains, is based on a complex process involving both our intellectual recognition and emotional reaction to what we're seeing.

Our emotional reaction to anything is controlled by two primary elements: instinct and learned behavior. An example may help explain the process. Imagine it's a nice sunny day. You're walking on a sidewalk next to a small park. A low stone wall is between you and the park. The park is visually pleasant — a thick carpet of grass under a canopy of large shade trees. A young couple sits on a blanket quietly talking. Across the street are several stores — a bookshop, a clothing store, a bank, and a drugstore on the corner.

Now, imagine that you're on the same sidewalk at 2:00 A.M., on a moonless night. It's really dark. The only light comes from the window of the all-night drugstore across the street at the far end of the park. Walking beside the stone wall you hear a noise coming from the park. You peer into the darkness. Starlight filters through the leaves. You see something move but can't see what it is. You quicken your pace as you cross the street then almost break into a run as you dash into the drugstore.

As mentioned earlier, our emotional reaction to anything we see is controlled by two primary elements: instinct and learned response. Instinctively, most people are afraid of the dark. This response was genetically programmed into our ancestors hundreds of thousands of years ago when our progenitors were roaming the plains and woodlands looking for food. Our primary defense against being eaten by something larger, faster, and stronger was to be able to see it. If we couldn't see it, it might "get" us. Humans don't see well in the dark, so those of our ancestors who avoided dark places generally had a better chance of surviving to pass on their gene pool than those who indiscriminately wandered off into the dark. With each succeeding generation this healthy act of self-preservation became more and more reinforced in our genetic makeup.

The second contributor to our reaction to what we see is learned response. From the time we're infants we are busy learning. Almost all of that early learning is experiential — learning by experience. That information is stored in the brain. What we learn experientially is a major contributor to how we will react in any given circumstance. On a cloudy summer day I've occasionally looked outside and absently thought, "It looks like it going to snow." Logically, I know that it can't snow, but there was something about the "look" of the clouds — their shape, color, movement — that reminded me of the way it looks before a snowstorm. Our subconscious mind is constantly comparing incoming information — what we're currently seeing — with memories of what we've experienced in the past in its ongoing struggle to help our conscious minds make sense of our surroundings.

An interesting example of this learned response took place during the University of Arizona production of *Terra Nova,* which is primarily set in Antarctica and chronicles Scott's ill-fated trip to the South Pole. (See Figures 6.14 through 6.21 on pages 103–107.) The director wanted the light for the Antarctica scenes to be "white and painfully bright." At first I left the lights uncolored, but the white light seemed warm rather than color. Before the next rehearsal I put a light blue **color media** into all the lights. At rehearsal that night almost all the people in the audience, including myself, complained of being chilly or cold. The thermostat in the theatre hadn't been changed from the previous day. The only difference was the light blue color in the lights. My assumption was that our subconscious minds saw the pale blue light, compared it with memories of "the color of cold," and convinced our conscious minds into thinking that the theatre actually was cold. After opening night we had numerous complaints from the paying audience that the theatre was "too cold." We raised the thermostat a few degrees even though the production occurred in late September in Tucson when the average temperature was in the high nineties. Such is the power of the mind.

The reasons that we design the lighting for an event or place are to influence the audience's perception and understanding of what they're seeing. That is the reason that lighting is thoughtfully designed for theatre, films, and television as well as for rock concerts, theme parks, and retail stores. Lighting influences our perceptions and understanding. Machiavellian, isn't it?

Distribution

Distribution is a catchall term that refers to several elements: (1) the direction from which the light approaches an area, actor, or object; (2) the shape and size of the area that the light is covering; and (3) the quality of the light — its diffusion or clarity.

Intensity

Intensity is the actual amount, or level of brightness, of light that strikes the stage or actor. Intensity can range from total darkness to painfully brilliant white light.

Movement

Movement can be divided into three general categories: (1) the timed duration of the light cues; (2) the movement of onstage lights, such as a lantern or candle that an actress carries across the stage; and (3) the movement of an offstage light source, such as a followspot or intelligent/moving lights.

Color

Color, which was discussed at length in Chapter 6, is an extremely powerful tool of the designer. The judicious use of appropriately tinted light can greatly assist the audience's understanding of, and reaction to, the play.

Functions of Stage Light

To increase the audience's understanding and appreciation of a play, stage lighting needs to perform several basic functions.

color media: Colored plastic, gel, or glass filters used to modify the color of light.

FIGURE 14.1
Selective focus with light. Notice how your attention moves from person to person in the photo on the left, whereas your attention is directed to the highlighted actress in the photo on the right. Courtesy of J. Michael Gillette.

Visibility

A reasonably accurate adage in the theatre holds that "if you can't see 'em, you can't hear 'em." Stage lighting needs to make everything on stage — the actors, costumes, and setting — clearly visible to the spectators. At the same time, however, the concept of "designed," or controlled, visibility dictates that those actors and objects be seen only in the manner that the designer and director intend. One of the real challenges of lighting design is to create a selective visibility that subtly directs the spectators' attention. The number of lighting instruments and other sources used to light a scene, the color of those lights, and their direction and intensity all affect visibility.

Selective Focus

Selective focus means directing the spectators' attention to a specific place. The lighting designer can selectively focus attention in a number of ways, but the primary method is by manipulating our instinctive response to light. Everybody has a strong instinct to look at an area of brightness or movement in an otherwise neutral scene. By simply making one part of the stage brighter than the rest of the set, the lighting designer forces the spectators to look there (Figure 14.1). This technique of emphatic focus is amply demonstrated, for example, whenever a followspot is used in a musical number. Color can also be used to focus attention. Most people have a more positive emotional response to warm colors than cool. By lighting a scene with warm colors, the audience may feel more accepting of it. (See the section "Meaning of Color" in Chapter 6 for additional information on this subject.)

Modeling

Modeling is the revealing of the form of an object through the pattern of highlight and shadow that is reflected from that object to the eye. The distribution and intensity of the light will, to a great extent, determine our visual understanding of that object. If you have ever yelped, "But that doesn't look like me!" when confronted by a flash-lit snapshot of yourself, you have had a demonstration of this effect. The light from a camera-mounted strobe approaches us from a very unnatural angle — straight from the front and parallel with the floor. Light coming from this direction fills in the areas where we normally expect to see shadows — under the eyebrows, cheekbones, nose, and jaw line. It also puts highlights in rather unexpected places. Because of this redirection of the expected pattern of highlight and shadow, the picture doesn't look like the face that we remember.

Direction is the primary element used in modeling, although intensity, movement, and color all affect modeling to a lesser degree. A change in any or all of these variables will inevitably result in an apparent change of form and feeling of the object being lit.

Mood

Creating a mood with light is one of the easiest and, at the same time, most difficult aspects of stage lighting. It is relatively easy to create a spectacular sunset effect or a sinister feeling of lurking terror; the difficulty comes in integrating these impressive effects with the other elements of the production. Effective stage lighting is subtle and rarely noticed. Although it is fun to create a sunset or similar breathtaking visual display, the opportunity to do so legitimately does not present itself in many plays. Within the parameters of the production concept, stage lighting is usually designed to enhance the mood of the play as unobtrusively as possible.

Designing with Light

Before you can create with light, you have to *see* the light. Let's explore (with visual aids) the effects that can be achieved by manipulating the first two controllable qualities of light — distribution and intensity — to affect the four functions of light: visibility, selective focus, modeling, and mood.

The series of photographs in Figure 14.2 illustrates how varying the direction of light affects the face of an actress. Each photograph is accompanied by a drawing that shows the relative **plan angle** of the light. The **sectional angle** of the light is 45 degrees and shows the angle of the light relative to the actor's face.

Surrounding an actor with a number of light sources provides the potential for modeling with light. In Figure 14.3 the direction of the light varies, but the intensity remains the same. A front light (Figure 14.3A) by itself is unflattering; it tends to flatten and compress facial and bodily features. Both side lights (Figure 14.3B) and top lights (Figure 14.3C) create highlights along the edges of the head and body but cause deep shadows across the face and front of the body. A combination of side and top lights (Figure 14.3D), together with a front light that fills in the shadows created by the side and top lights, reveals the form of the model by surrounding her with light.

When lit from the side-front at about 45 degrees in both plan and section (Figure 14.3E), the model is smoothly illuminated, but her facial and bodily features are slightly compressed. If a top light or back light is added to the side-front light (Figure 14.3F), the resultant rim or edge light creates a highlight that adds depth to the face and body. As you can see, the greatest potential for modeling is achieved when the model is surrounded with light.

Key and Fill

The terms *key light* and *fill light* (borrowed from film and television) are frequently used to describe the relationship between the direction and relative intensity of light striking an object. The key light is the brightest light on the scene, and the fill light is used to fill the shadows created by the key light.

plan angle: The ground plan view of an object.

sectional angle: The angle of intersection between the axis of the cone of light emitted by an instrument and the working height — usually the height of an average actor's face (about 5 feet 6 inches) — of the lighting area.

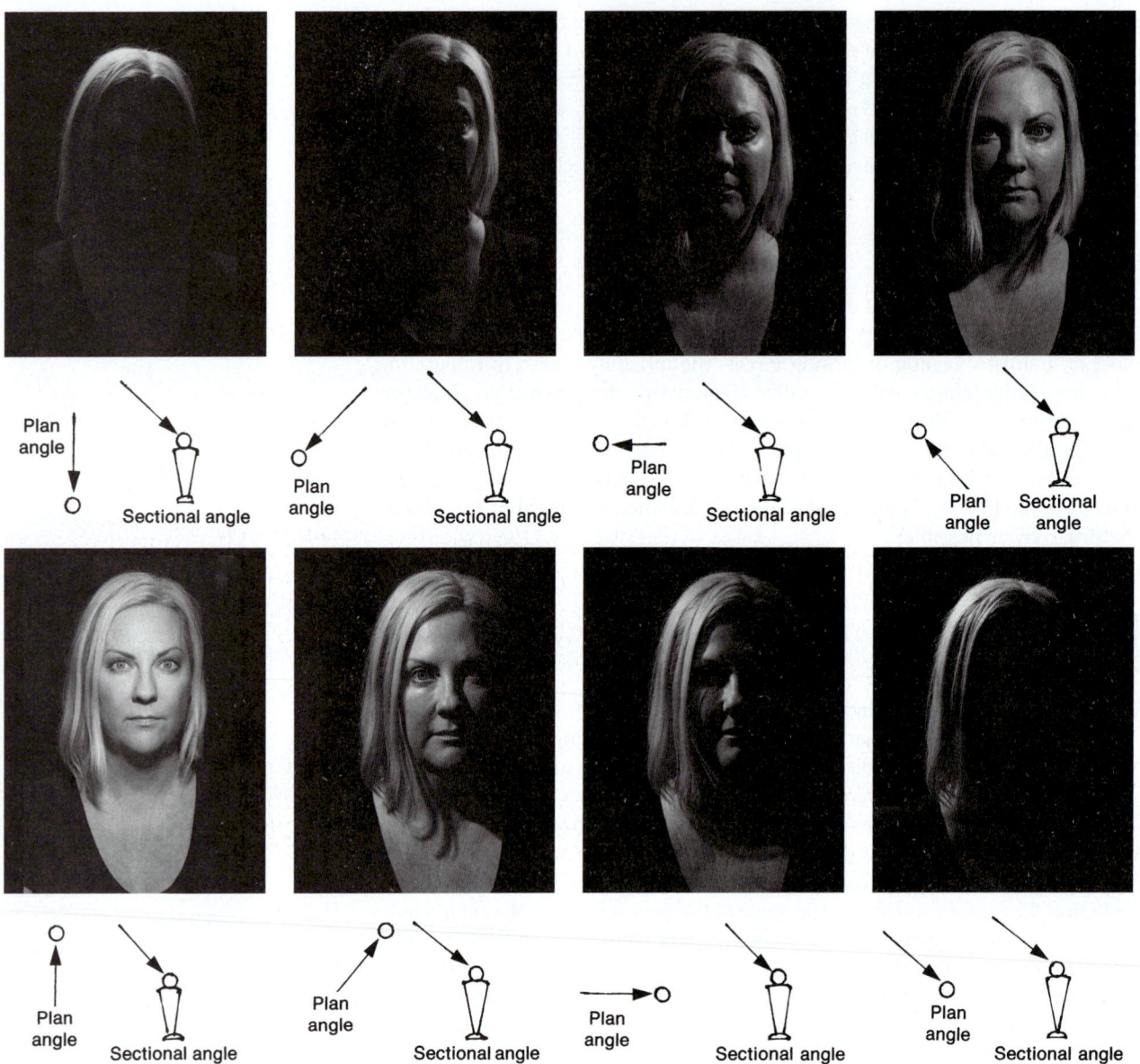

FIGURE 14.2
Effects of varying the direction of light. Courtesy of J. Michael Gillette.

Psychological Effects of Light

In lighting design, just as in literature, the concepts of good and evil are often associated with light and darkness. When a scene is lit with dark and murky shadows, most people instinctively react with a sense of foreboding. The suspicion that something could be lurking unseen in the shadows is almost universal. When a scene is brightly lit, we instinctively relax, because we realize that nothing can sneak up on us unseen.

The direction from which light strikes an object has a direct effect on our perception of that object. Light striking a face from a low angle (Figure 14.4A) effectively creates a "monster" light, because such light does not normally occur in nature. Any light that places the face in heavy shadow, such as the back light shown in Figure 14.4B, will create an uneasy reaction in viewers, because they cannot see the facial expression of the person in the shadows and so cannot read his or her intentions.

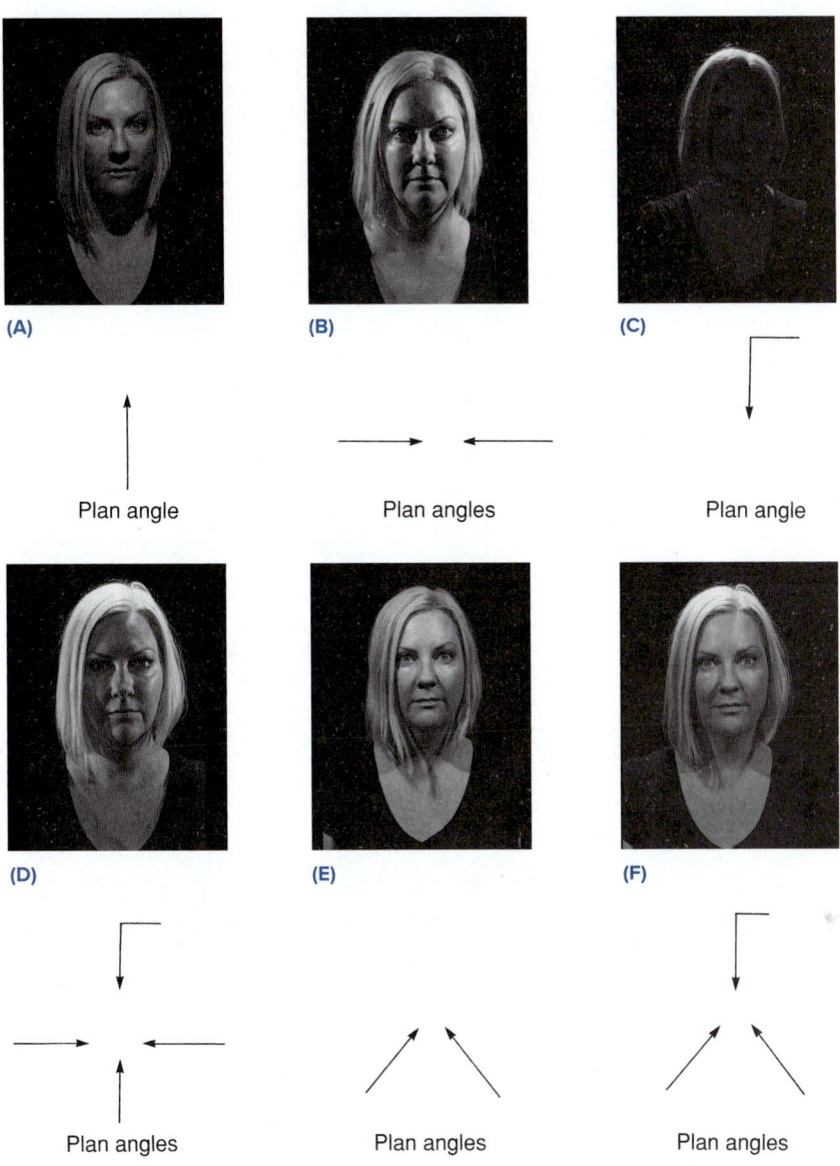

FIGURE 14.3
Surrounding an actor with light creates the most potential for modeling. A-F, Courtesy of J. Michael Gillette.

(A)

(B)

FIGURE 14.4
Psychological effects of varying the angle of light. Photos courtesy of J. Michael Gillette.

Those who are interested in learning more about lighting design should become more fully aware of these instinctive, and learned, responses. More information on the psychology of color can be found in Chapter 6, "Color."

 ## The Light Plot and Related Paperwork

Because the product of lighting design — light — is probably the most intangible and abstract of all the theatrical design elements, some specialized paperwork is needed to help in carrying out the design.

The Light Plot

The light plot is a scale mechanical drawing — a "road map" — that indicates where the lighting instruments should be placed (Figure 14.5). More

FIGURE 14.5
The light plot for the Canadian Opera Company Hummingbird Centre production of *Il Trovatore*. Lighting design by Joan Sullivan-Genthe. Associate lighting designer: Michael McNamara. Drafting by Joshua Windhausen. Courtesy of Michael McNamara.

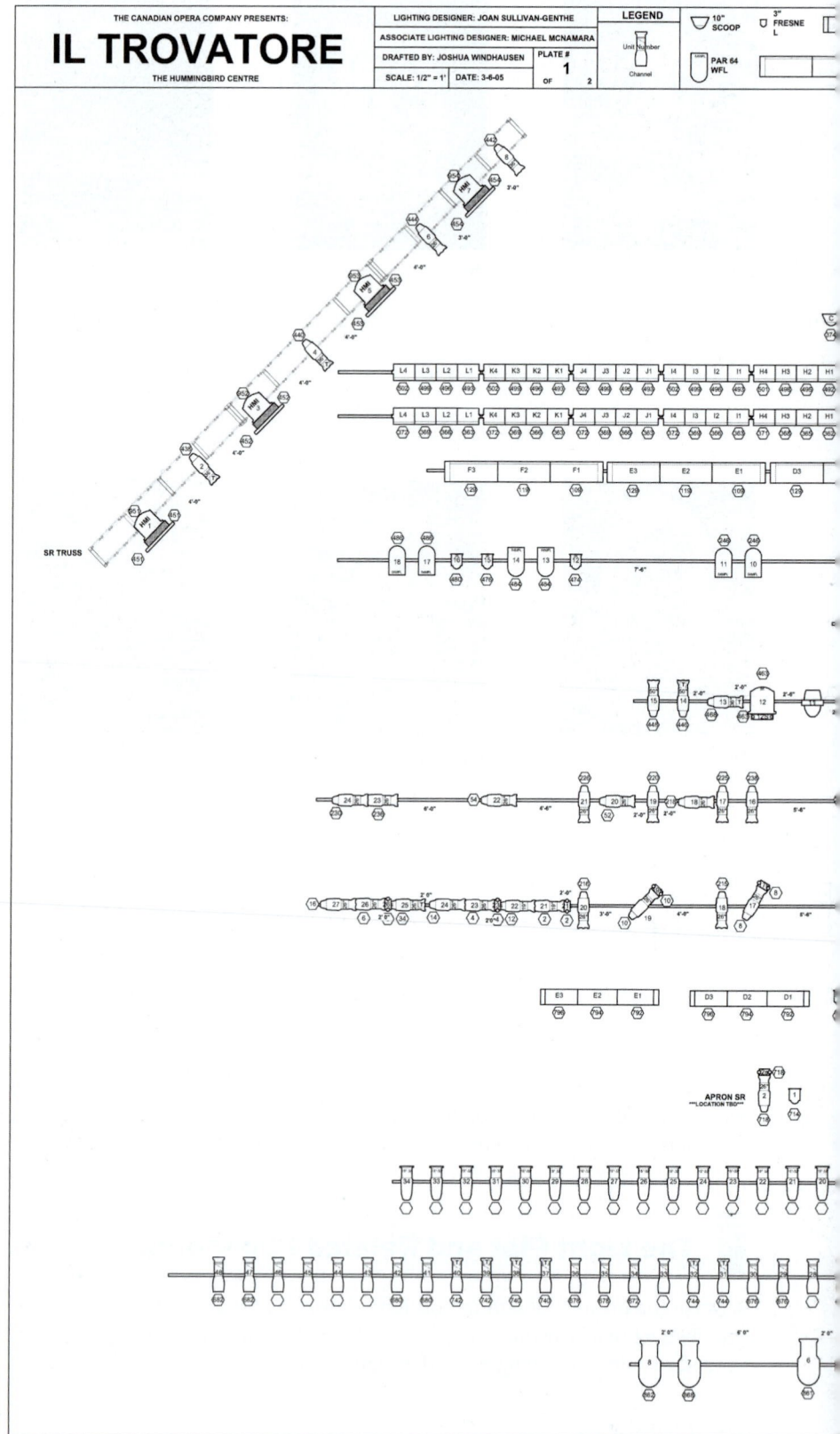

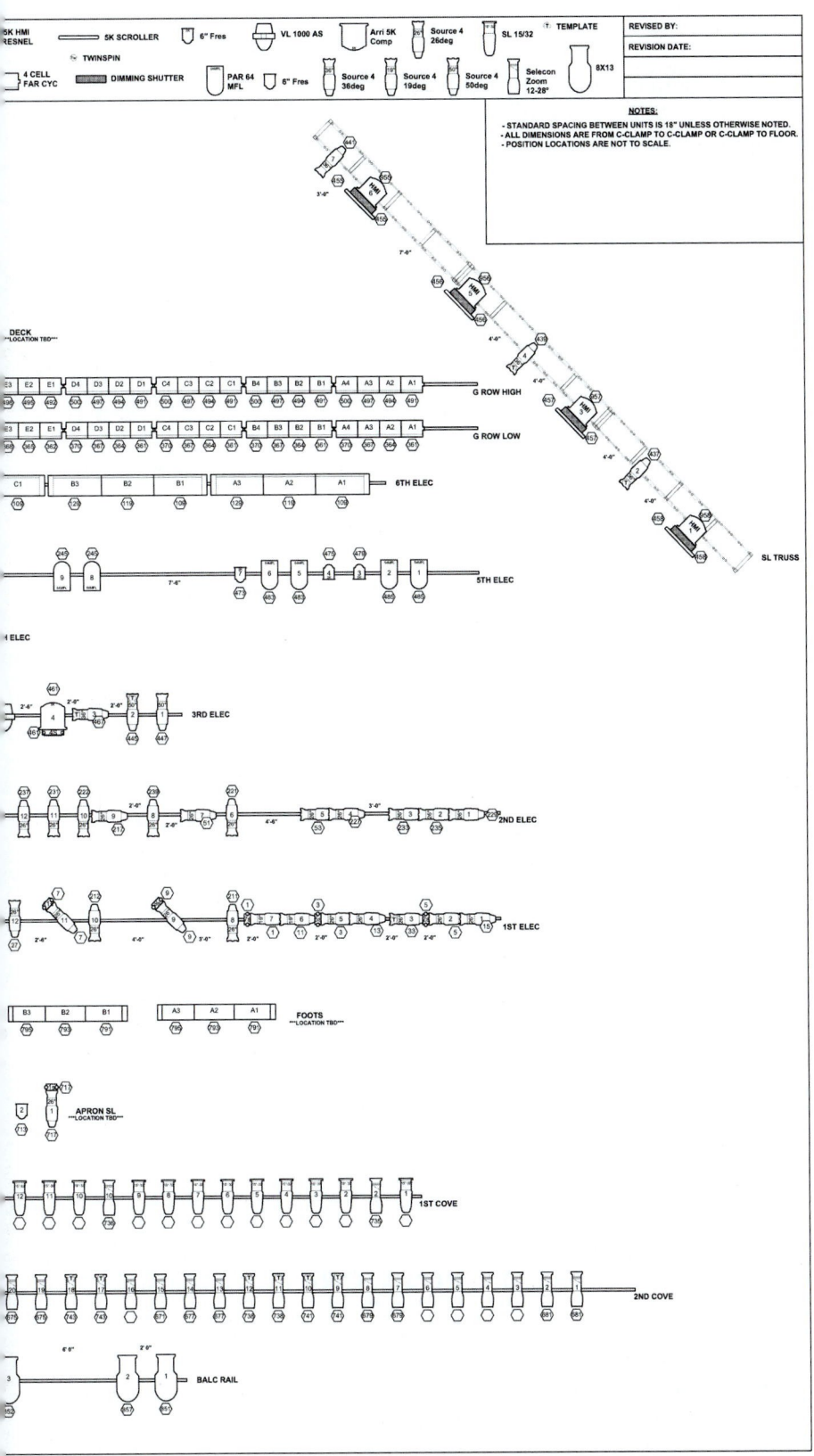

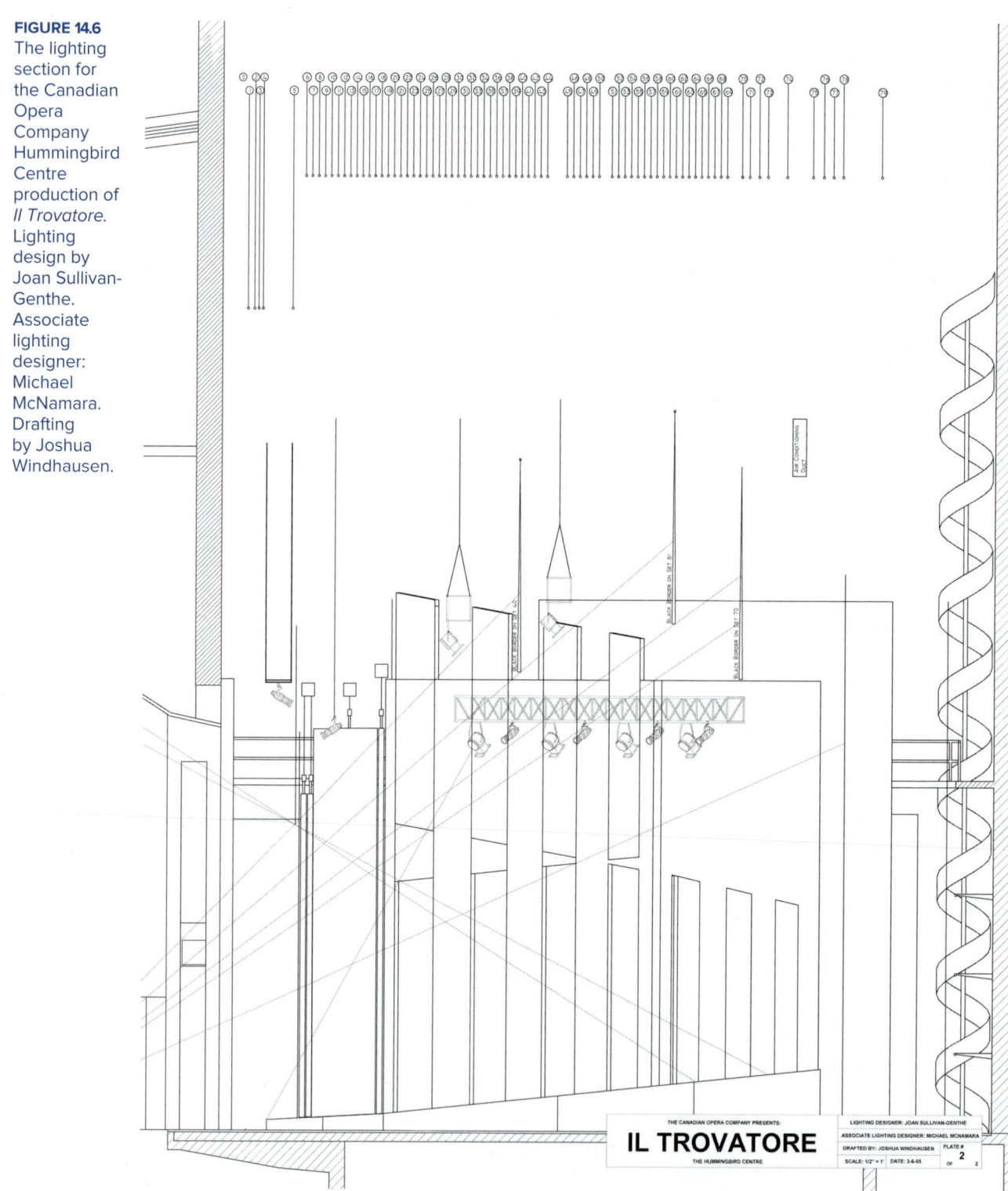

FIGURE 14.6
The lighting section for the Canadian Opera Company Hummingbird Centre production of *Il Trovatore*. Lighting design by Joan Sullivan-Genthe. Associate lighting designer: Michael McNamara. Drafting by Joshua Windhausen.

specifically, it is a "composite plan drawing that provides the most descriptive possible view of the luminaries so that the production staff can most efficiently execute the design intent."[2] According to the United States Institute

[2] Source: "USITT RP-2, Recommended Practice for Theatrical Lighting Design Graphics - 2006," United States Institute for Theatre Technology, June 15, 2006, 1.

for Theatre Technology's (USITT) "Recommended Practice for Theatrical Lighting Design Graphics – 2006." The latest version of the standard is included as Appendix A. The following discussion of lighting design graphics is based, to a large extent, on the recommendations contained in the USITT standard.

Although there is no universally accepted style of drafting light plots, some general information must always be included. Depicting the location of all lighting instruments being used in the production is the primary purpose of the light plot. The lighting designer specifies, to scale (usually ½ or ¼ inch to 1 foot), where the instruments should be placed. The USITT suggests ½ inch scale but leaves the final decision up to the lighting designer. It's a good idea to check with the master electrician to see what scale he or she prefers. The master electrician uses this scale drawing as a guide in hanging and circuiting the plot.

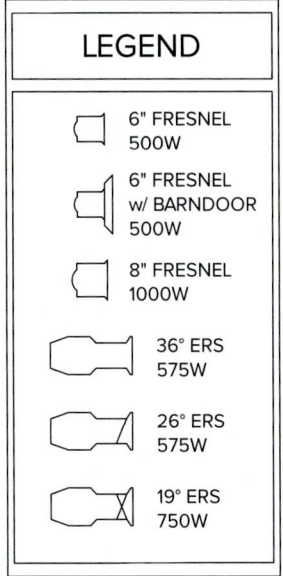

FIGURE 14.7
A sample legend.

The Lighting Section

The lighting section is a scale drawing, normally in the same scale as the light plot, that isn't really a sectional drawing at all. It is a composite side-view drawing (if the set is basically symmetrical) that shows the position of lighting equipment in relation to the set and the physical structure of the theatre (Figure 14.6). If the set is significantly asymmetrical, then two sections will normally be drawn, one looking stage right from the **centerline,** the other looking stage left. This drawing, used primarily by the lighting designer, has several purposes: to check sight lines of the lighting instruments, to assist in determining the appropriate trim height for the borders, and to ensure that the lighting equipment won't interfere with any scenic elements or vice versa. The trim height of the borders is normally determined in consultation with the scenic designer and technical director.

The Legend

A legend, or instrument key (Figure 14.7), provides complete identification information about each instrument used on the plot. In addition to identifying the particular type or style of instrument that is denoted by each symbol, the legend should also contain an explanation of the peripheral information (Figure 14.8) that is associated with each instrument symbol. The types of peripheral information that can be used with each lighting instrument symbol are explained here. The 2006 USITT lighting standard suggests that not every peripheral category needs to be included. Keep the clutter to a minimum. Include just enough peripheral information so the master electrician (ME) and crew can effectively hang the plot.

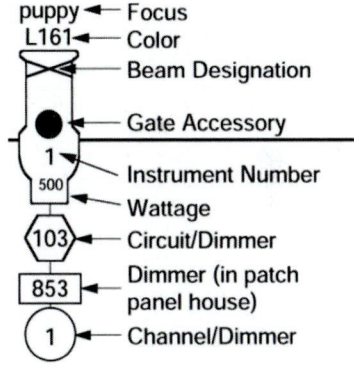

FIGURE 14.8
Recommended instrument notation style.

Focus Area The focus area for each instrument is identified by a letter placed in front of the lens housing of the symbol for that instrument. This letter corresponds to the same letter that identifies a specific lighting area on the light plot.

Color The color number refers to the specific color media that will be used in that particular instrument.

Beam Designation This symbol is used to designate the beam angle – the width of the cone of light expressed as an angle – emitted by an ellipsoidal reflector spotlight. (See Figure 14.7 and the graphics on page 351 for examples.) This symbol generally isn't used with fresnels.

centerline: A leader line that runs perpendicular to the set line from the midpoint or center of the opening of the proscenium.

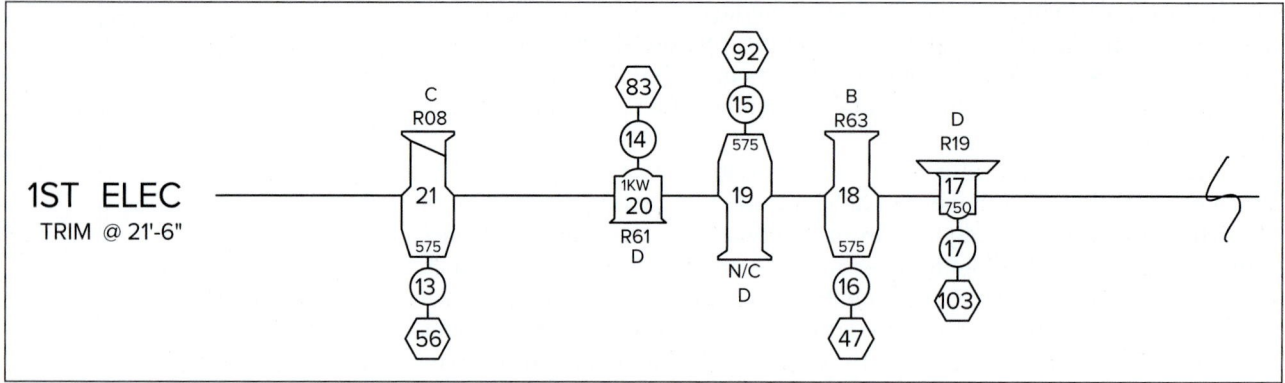

FIGURE 14.9
Instruments are numbered according to two factors: the pipe on which they are hanging and their position relative to other instruments on the pipe.

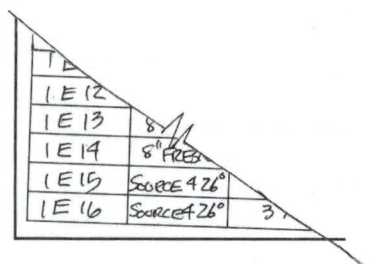

FIGURE 14.10
Details of instrument-notation technique.

instrument schedule: A form used to record all of the technical data about each instrument used in the production; also known as a hookup sheet.

pipe: A counterweighted batten or fixed metal pipe that holds lighting instruments.

first electric: The onstage pipe for lighting instruments that is closest to the proscenium arch.

electric: Any pipe that is used to hold lighting instruments.

dimmer: An electrical device that controls the intensity of a light source connected to it.

Gate Accessory Used to indicate if an ellipsoidal reflector spotlight (ERS) has an accessory, such as a gobo or other device, placed in the instrument's gate accessory slot.

Instrument Number Each instrument needs to be assigned an identification number so that it can be cross-referenced with the **instrument schedule,** or hookup sheet. Figure 14.9 shows how lighting instruments are numbered on the light plot. The specific number recorded for each lighting instrument on the instrument schedule is determined by two factors: (1) its hanging location and (2) its position relative to the other instruments on that **pipe.** The first segment of the number is an abbreviation of its hanging location. The number "1E," illustrated in Figure 14.10, indicates that the instrument is hanging on the **first electric.** The second part of the number indicates the instrument's sequential position on the pipe. In a proscenium theatre, the numbering of any **electric** starts at the left end of the pipe when viewed as if you were standing with your back against the upstage wall of the stage house. The box "Drafting for Lighting Design" explains the USITT-recommended method for numbering instruments for all of the hanging locations in the theatre.

Wattage This number refers to the wattage of the lamp used in that fixture. It is only used if there are multiple wattages for the same fixture.

Circuit and/or Dimmer Number This identifies the stage circuit into which the instrument should be plugged. The appropriate circuit or **dimmer** number can be assigned in this space by the lighting designer, or the space can be left blank to be filled in by the electrician when he or she hangs and circuits the instrument.

Dimmer This identifies the specific dimmer that will control this instrument. If the theatre is equipped with a patch panel, the circuit number is usually assigned to the circuit/dimmer space (see previous section), and this space is used for the assignment of the specific dimmer used with this instrument. Again, the dimmer number can be assigned by the lighting designer but is frequently left to the discretion of the master electrician.

Channel/Dimmer If the theatre has a computer board, this space is normally used for the assignment of the control channel related to this specific instrument.

The earlier-referenced stipulations should be thought of as guidelines and not as rules that must be slavishly followed. The only *real* criteria pertaining to

PRODUCTION INSIGHTS
Drafting for Lighting Design

As we have seen, the lighting designer uses two principal mechanical drawings to record the information that is needed to hang, circuit, and focus the lighting design: the light plot and the lighting section. The purpose of these drawings is to guide the master electrician and crew. The amount and kind of information shown on the paperwork associated with a lighting design vary greatly from production to production and designer to designer. But a set of basic criteria pertains to the drawings associated with any lighting design. The following information is based on the 2006 USITT "Recommended Practice for Theatrical Lighting Design Graphics." The 2006 standard is included as Appendix A at the end of this book.

1. The light plot and lighting section should be drawn to scale.

2. The light plot should show the location of the lighting instruments in relation to the set and the physical structure of the theatre. Instrument symbols should be scale representations of the size of the actual instruments they represent to precisely detail the amount of space they will occupy. They should also be drawn in the same scale as the rest of the drawing.

3. All drawings should adhere to the tenets of good mechanical-drafting techniques (see Chapter 7, "Mechanical Drafting").

4. The darkest lines on the plot should represent instrument symbols and related information, architectural lines should be of medium darkness, and set lines should be the lightest.

5. The instrument key or legend should be used to explain all symbols used on the plot. It should minimally contain

   - Symbol identification for all instruments and devices shown on the plot and controlled by the lighting console, including the instrument manufacturer and wattage.

   - A representation of the typical instrument notation method used.

   - A drawing of the technique used to represent "two-fers."

6. The instrument symbol should include

   - An instrument number as an aid to location.

   - A symbol for attached hardware (such as templates, irises, color scrollers, top hats, barn doors, and so forth).

   - The channel, the circuit and/or dimmer number, and the color notation.

   - A symbol for lamp axis alignment on PAR cans.

   - The method used to illustrate "two-fers."

7. The designation and numbering of hanging positions and instruments in proscenium configurations include the following conventions:

   - Onstage pipes should be numbered from downstage to upstage.

   - Onstage booms should be numbered from downstage to upstage.

   - Box-boom or torm positions should be numbered consistently within each plot.

   - All lighting positions should be designated by stage directions.

   - Front of house (FOH) ceiling positions should be numbered from the apron to the rear of the house as should FOH boom positions, side coves, ladders, or ports.

   - Balcony rails should be numbered from the floor to the ceiling.

   - Pipe grids in "black box" type theatres should be numbered on the x or y axis of the grid and lettered on the opposing axis.

   - Nonconventional black box lighting positions should be identified by compass directions.

   - Trim heights should be indicated from the stage floor or the deck to the pipe with a note on the plot to verify that the measurement is from the "stage floor" or "deck."

   - Instruments on stage electric pipes should be numbered from stage left to stage right.

   - Instruments on booms should be numbered from top to bottom.

   - Strip lights should be labeled (using numbers or letters) from stage left to stage right.

8. Acceptable locations for title blocks are in the lower right-hand or left-hand corners or centered on the bottom of the plate.

what information is located in which position, and inside of what type of circular/square/hexagonal space, is that there be consistency, and that that visual logic be applied to all symbols throughout all the drawings for a single design. Realistically, there are so many variables possible for each lighting design that it is just doesn't make sense to have a nonadjustable standard. The rule of thumb is this: Put in enough information so the ME can hang the plot, but not so much that it will make the plot cluttered.

The Instrument Schedule

The instrument schedule, also known as the hookup sheet or hookup, is a specification sheet that contains everything you might want or need to know about every instrument used on the production (Figure 14.11). It identifies each instrument by its instrument number and specifies its type, hanging location, focus area (called "purpose" in Lightwright), dimmer, lamp wattage, color, and circuit. A section for special remarks is used to note anything else that might be appropriate, such as focusing notes, auxiliary equipment that needs to be attached to the instrument, and so forth.

IL TROVATORE **CHANNEL HOOKUP** Page 1
03 Dec 2005

Canadian Opera Company
Production: Stephen Lawless
LD: Joan Sullivan-Genthe & Michael McNamara

Hummingbird Centre
ALD: Wendy Greenwood
ALD: Heidi Lingren

Channel	Dim	Position	Unit	Type & Accessories & Watts	Purpose	Color & Tmp
(1)	1st ELEC		7	ETC S4 19° 575w	X FAR W	
	1st ELEC		7s	Wybron C-Ram II S4 Scroller	1E #7 Scroller	SCROLL 1
(2)	1st ELEC		21	ETC S4 19° 575w	X FAR W	
	1st ELEC		21s	Wybron C-Ram II S4 Scroller	1E #21 Scroller	SCROLL 1
(3)	1st ELEC		5	ETC S4 26° 575w	X CEN W	
	1st ELEC		5s	Wybron C-Ram II S4 Scroller	1E #5 Scroller	SCROLL 1
(4)	1st ELEC		23	ETC S4 26° 575w	X CEN W	
	1st ELEC		23s	Wybron C-Ram II S4 Scroller	1E #23 Scroller	SCROLL 1
(5)	1st ELEC		2	ETC S4 26° 575w	X NR W	
	1st ELEC		2s	Wybron C-Ram II S4 Scroller	1E #2 Scroller	SCROLL 1
(6)	1st ELEC		26	ETC S4 26° 575w	X NR W	
	1st ELEC		26s	Wybron C-Ram II S4 Scroller	1E #26 Scroller	SCROLL 1
(7)	1st ELEC		11	ETC S4 26° 575w	P2 FAR W	
	1st ELEC		11s	Wybron C-Ram II S4 Scroller	1E #11 Scroller	SCROLL 1
(8)	1st ELEC		17	ETC S4 26° 575w	P2 FAR W	
	1st ELEC		17s	Wybron C-Ram II S4 Scroller	1E #17 Scroller	SCROLL 1
(9)	1st ELEC		9	ETC S4 26° 575w	P2 CEN W	
	1st ELEC		9s	Wybron C-Ram II S4 Scroller	1E #9 Scroller	SCROLL 1
(10)	1st ELEC		19	ETC S4 26° 575w	P2 CEN W	
	1st ELEC		19s	Wybron C-Ram II S4 Scroller	1E #19 Scroller	SCROLL 1
(11)	1st ELEC		6	ETC S4 19° 575w	X FAR C	L161
(12)	1st ELEC		22	ETC S4 19° 575w	X FAR C	L161
(13)	1st ELEC		4	ETC S4 26° 575w	X CEN C	L161
(14)	1st ELEC		24	ETC S4 26° 575w	X CEN C	L161
(15)	1st ELEC		1	ETC S4 26° 575w	X NR C (Slash Slider)	L161
(16)	1st ELEC		27	ETC S4 26° 575w	X NR C (Slash Slider)	L161
(21)	1st ELEC		15	ETC S4 26° 575w	XO RIGHT	
	1st ELEC		15s	Wybron C-Ram II S4 Scroller	1E #15 Scroller	SCROLL 1
(22)	1st ELEC		14	ETC S4 26° 575w	XO LEFT	
	1st ELEC		14s	Wybron C-Ram II S4 Scroller	1E #14 Scroller	SCROLL 1
(27)	1st ELEC		12	ETC S4 26° 575w	42 Cell	L161
(33)	1st ELEC		3	ETC S4 26° 575w	Temp X Mid Cen	R99+R99, T: R7806
(34)	1st ELEC		25	ETC S4 26° 575w	Temp X Mid Cen	R99+R99, T: R7806
(51)	2nd ELEC		7	ETC S4 26° 575w	X FAR IN 2	G841
(52)	2nd ELEC		20	ETC S4 26° 575w	X FAR IN 2	G841
(53)	2nd ELEC		5	ETC S4 26° 575w	X CEN IN 2	G841
(54)	2nd ELEC		22	ETC S4 26° 575w	X CEN IN 2	G841

FIGURE 14.11

The instrument schedule contains all the technical data about each instrument used in the production. Source: Joan Sullivan-Genthe.

Lighting Symbols

Because so much data must be included on a light plot or vertical lighting section, the United States Institute for Theatre Technology has developed a system of symbols for use on these drawings. The following information on lighting symbols is based on those recommendations. The full lighting graphic standard can be found in Appendix A.

Instrument Notation

The normal procedure in drawing a light plot is to use symbols to represent the various types of lighting instrument being used. Some of the USITT-recommended symbols are illustrated in the accompanying figures. A great deal of information is usually associated with each lighting symbol.

Lighting Templates

Lighting templates are only used when hand-drawing light plots. They provide uniform symbols for the stage lighting instruments and practical lamps used in most productions. The photos on the facing page show examples of both plan and sectional lighting templates.

Templates are readily available in scales of ¼ inch to 1 foot and ½ inch to 1 foot (with the latter being the most commonly used scales for drafting light plots).

Lettering

The lettering used on the drawings associated with lighting design needs to follow the same criteria of clarity and uniformity outlined in Chapter 7, "Mechanical Drafting."

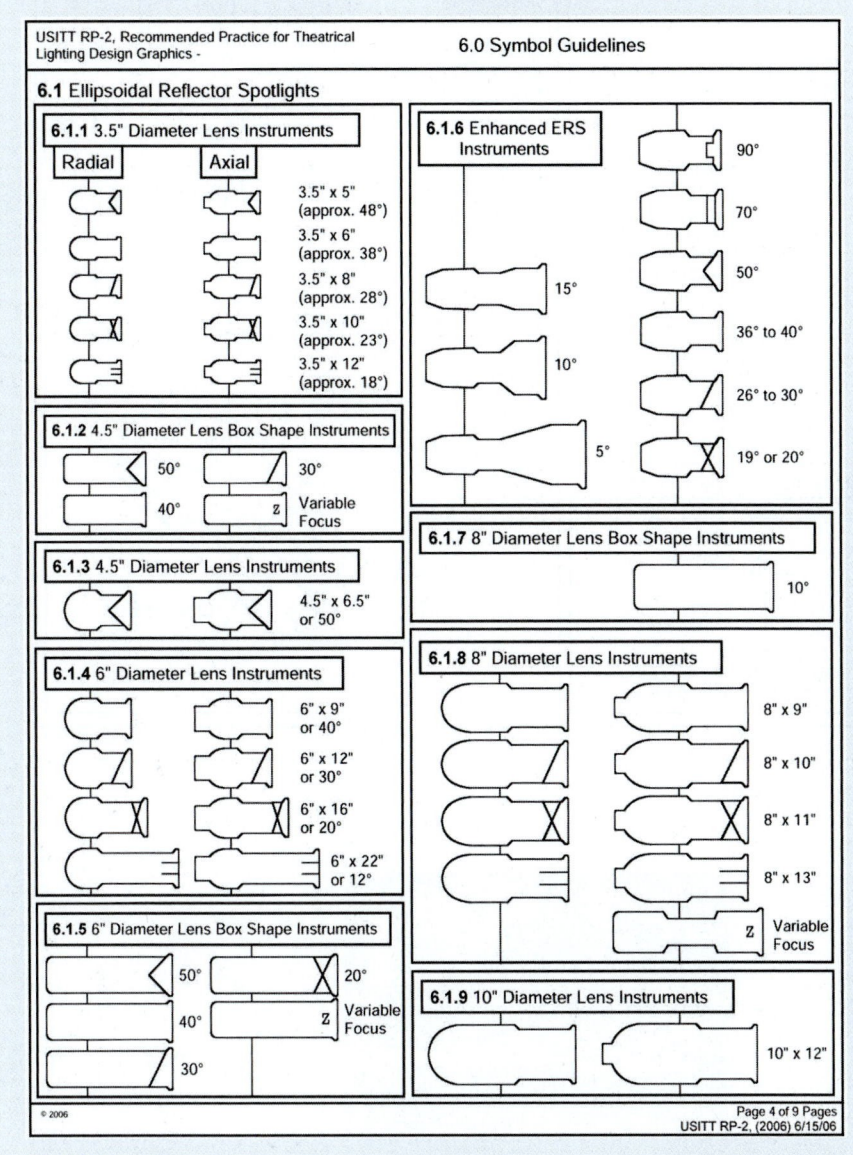

Symbols.

(continued)

PRODUCTION INSIGHTS

Lighting Symbols   continued

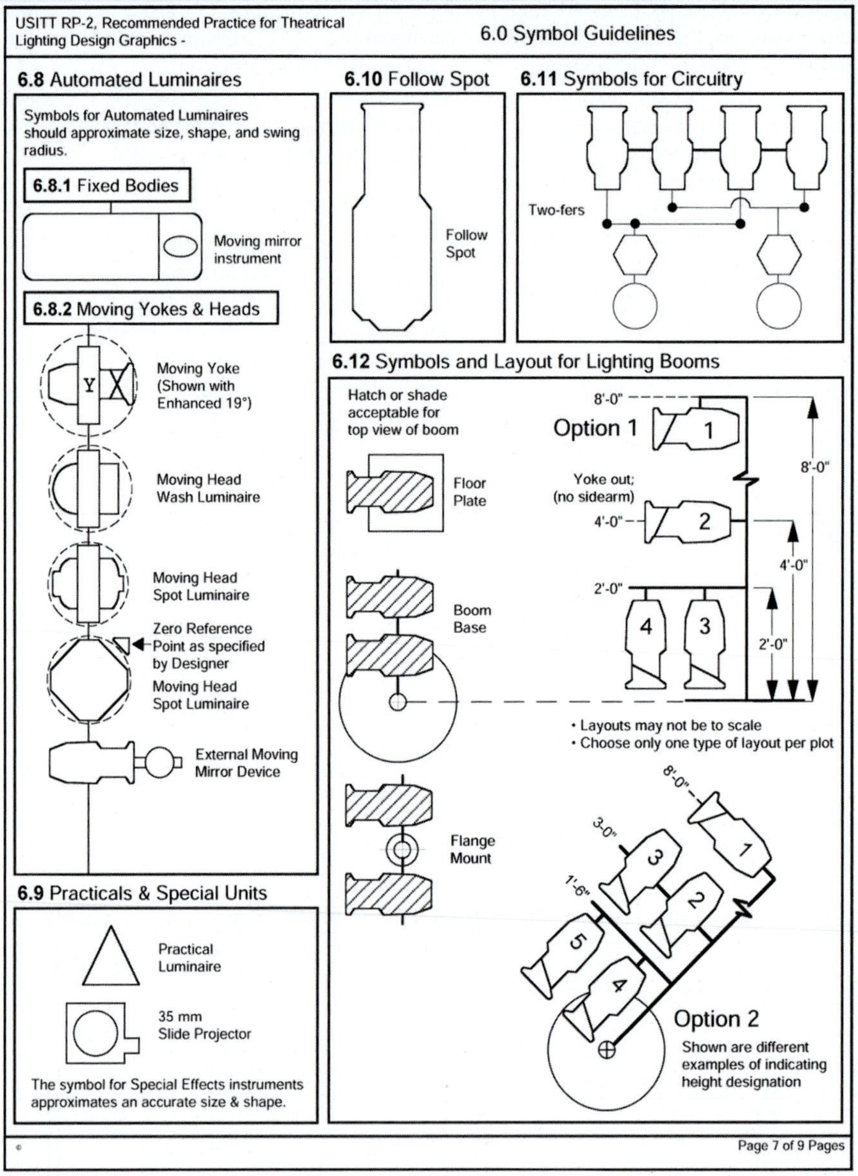

USITT RP-2, Recommended Practice for Theatrical Lighting Design Graphics -

6.0 Symbol Guidelines

6.8 Automated Luminaires

Symbols for Automated Luminaires should approximate size, shape, and swing radius.

6.8.1 Fixed Bodies

Moving mirror instrument

6.8.2 Moving Yokes & Heads

Moving Yoke (Shown with Enhanced 19°)

Moving Head Wash Luminaire

Moving Head Spot Luminaire

Zero Reference Point as specified by Designer

Moving Head Spot Luminaire

External Moving Mirror Device

6.9 Practicals & Special Units

Practical Luminaire

35 mm Slide Projector

The symbol for Special Effects instruments approximates an accurate size & shape.

6.10 Follow Spot

Follow Spot

6.11 Symbols for Circuitry

Two-fers

6.12 Symbols and Layout for Lighting Booms

Hatch or shade acceptable for top view of boom

Floor Plate

Boom Base

Flange Mount

Option 1

Yoke out; (no sidearm)

8'-0"
8'-0"
4'-0"
4'-0"
2'-0"
2'-0"

• Layouts may not be to scale
• Choose only one type of layout per plot

Option 2

Shown are different examples of indicating height designation

Page 7 of 9 Pages

Symbols.

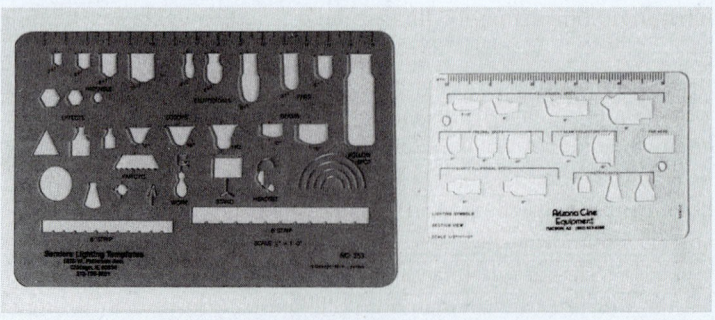

Lighting templates. Courtesy of J. Michael Gillette

All of the paperwork required in connection with a lighting design can be generated with computer programs. CAD programs can be used to draw the light plot and sectional. Database programs such as Lightwright can be used to compile the instrument schedule and hookup sheet, or you can use a generic database or spreadsheet program such as Excel to create your own instrument schedule. If a software program has been specifically developed for lighting design, it may link these two elements. With a linked program, such as Vector-works Spotlight or LD Assistant, if you change anything — instrument location, color, channel, circuit number, and so forth — on either the plot or hookup sheet, the program will automatically change the same data in the other program. The data contained on the instrument schedule can also be used to generate a wealth of other information such as **cut lists, hanging cards,** and so forth.

More information on light plot drafting can be found in Chapter 7, "Mechanical Drafting."

The Image of Light

The image of light is a metaphor. It could be a picture that appears in your mind. It could be a jumble of ideas, images, sounds, and/or musical themes. Or it could be a list. Whatever form it takes, the image of light summarizes your thoughts and ideas about the lighting for a specific production. The following discussion makes reference to the image of light as a picture. For the majority of lighting designers these images are pictorial, but they can also be auditory, emotional, or abstract. The form it takes really doesn't matter. What *is* important is that some type of concept — an image of light — be developed.

An analysis of the image of light for its distribution and intensity is probably the prime determinant for understanding where to place the fixtures in your lighting design. To analyze the image of light for its distribution and intensity, you have to be able to analyze it in a way that will suggest the angles and relative intensities of the various sources proposed by your image of light. However, all is not lost if you cannot actually *see* some type of image in your mind's eye. If you create a nonvisual image (a phrase, melody, or some set of stimuli) that provides you with a central thought or concept, it can be analyzed for its quality of light.

Analysis of the image of light for its component colors is easier than the analysis for distribution, if for no other reason than that people usually have an emotional reaction to a play that can be translated into specific colors.

With the notable exception of productions that use moving light fixtures, movement is probably the most easily adjusted of the qualities of light. The timing of the cues is customarily conceptualized during the design period, implemented during the lighting rehearsal, and adjusted during the technical and dress rehearsals. It normally isn't of primary concern to the designer during the selection phase of the design process.

The Lighting Key

The analysis of the image of light to determine its controllable qualities is not just an idle intellectual exercise. Nor should the **lighting key** — which will be explained in detail a little later in this section — be considered some kind of inviolable rule. It's a guide, an ideal. If circumstances — a wall, ceiling, or something else in the way — prevent hanging fixtures that exactly mimic the key, don't

cut list: A list of all the color media to be used on every fixture during a production. Typically listed by required number, gel-frame size, color. For example: 20 — 6" — Roscolux 09.

hanging cards: Small segments of the light plot, typically pasted onto cardboard so it can be carried in an electrician's pants pocket, that detail all of the hanging information about a specific location such as the first electric or down left boom.

lighting key: A drawing depicting the plan angles of the sources illuminating the image of light; can also be used to show the color(s) of those lights.

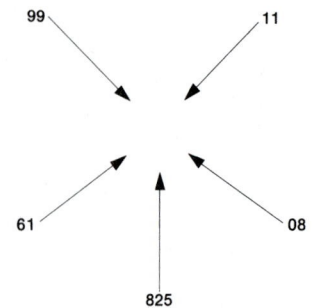

FIGURE 14.12
A lighting key.

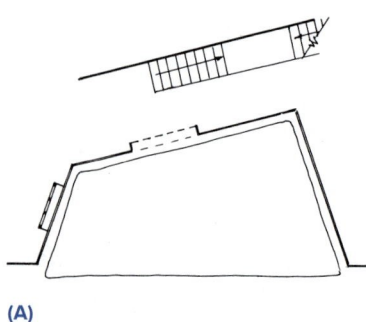

(A)

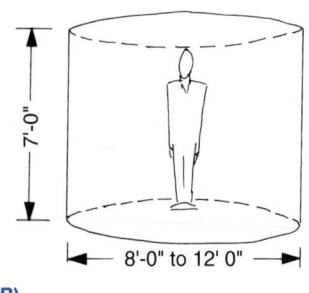

(B)

FIGURE 14.13
Acting (A) and lighting (B) areas.

look: The visual appearance.

beam angle: That point in the cone of light emitted by an instrument where the light is diminished by 50 percent when compared with the output of the center of the beam.

field angle: That point in the cone of light where the output diminishes to 10 percent of the output of the center of the beam.

sweat it. Just try to replicate it as closely as possible. The lighting key is just a tool used to help create the same lighting **look** throughout the acting area. The lighting key (Figure 14.12) is a drawing that indicates the plan angle and color of the various sources illuminating the image of light. The lighting key is used by the designer as a tool to help determine the hanging positions of the fixtures.

Acting and Lighting Areas To fully understand the purpose and function of a lighting key, it will be necessary to digress momentarily and discuss acting areas and lighting areas. Acting areas are those spaces on the stage where specific scenes, or parts of scenes, are played. The shape and size of an acting area (Figure 14.13A), although roughly determined by the shape of the setting, are specifically determined by the blocking patterns used by the actors. A lighting area (Figure 14.13B) is a cylindrical space approximately 8 to 12 feet in diameter and 7 feet tall — an area that can comfortably accommodate two actors with their arms extended.

To achieve a smooth wash of light throughout an acting area, it is necessary to overlap individual lighting areas by approximately one-third, as shown in Figure 14.14. This overlapping of adjacent areas takes advantage of the optical properties of the **beam angle** and **field angle** of the stage-lighting instruments to create a smooth wash of light throughout the acting area.

It should be noted that not every acting or lighting area will utilize every element of the lighting key. For example, things like ceilings and walls may interfere with placing of some instruments when trying to replicate the lighting key. In those cases, be adaptable. Place the blocked fixtures in a next-best-available position, or don't use them at all.

Support lights are lights that support on-stage sources such as glowing fireplaces, light streaming into an interior from outside, light enhancing candle glow, and so forth. Support lights do not subscribe to the lighting key. Their guideline is simple: Put the light in a position that will best create the illusion that the source is creating the light.

Creating the Lighting Key The process of converting the image of light into a lighting key is best explained through example. To illustrate this process,

PRODUCTION INSIGHTS
Beam and Field Angles

The field angle for an ERS is defined as the point at which the cone of light emitted by the fixture diminishes to 10 percent of its maximum output (measured at the center of the beam). The beam angle is defined as that point where the light diminishes to 50 percent of its maximum output. In practical terms, for older model ERSs, this relationship between the beam and field angles means that when the lighting areas are overlapped by roughly one-third, the beam angle of each instrument lights the central, or "un-overlapped," portion of each lighting area, and the field angles of adjacent lighting areas overlap. The result is an additive effect that brings up the intensity level of the overlapped areas to approximately that of the area covered by the beam angle. The beam angle in newer generation ERSs is significantly wider so they don't have to be overlapped as much to achieve uniformly smooth coverage. But some overlap is still required.

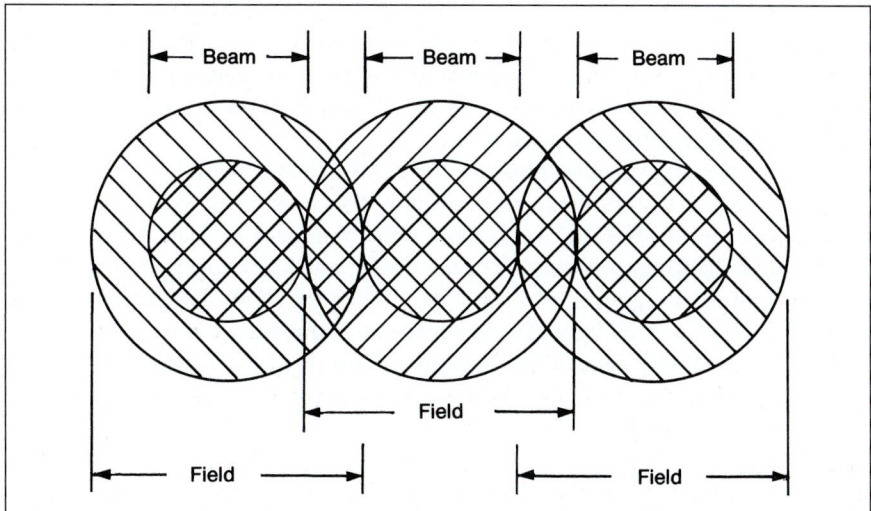

FIGURE 14.14
Lighting areas are overlapped in an acting area to facilitate the creation of a smooth wash of light.

we will create a lighting key for *The Playboy of the Western World* by John Millington Synge.

Let's assume that the overall image of light for this production could be stated as "a bright, twinkling Irish morning." That feeling — which is an emotional response to the script and input from the other members of the design team — evokes a visual image codifying the designer's reaction to the entire play. An analysis of the "twinkling Irish morning" image leads the designer to believe that the concept can best be reached by creating the following: (1) a light and cheery atmosphere, (2) no shadows, and (3) predominate use of thin tints of springlike colors.

Let it be quickly stressed that these descriptions are simply *one* of many possible analytic conclusions that could have been reached: one analysis by one designer that resulted in one conclusion. It is not *the* conclusion, nor is it intended to be the desired image for any particular scene. It is simply an example of the reality that, for many designers, it helps to keep an "overarching visual theme" in their minds when designing the lights for any production.

If an actor in our play were surrounded with light, as shown in Figure 14.15, we would have achieved one of our stated objectives — no shadows. If we adjusted the dimmers that control those lights to a fairly bright setting, we would achieve another of our objectives — a bright atmosphere. By selecting happy, springtime, pastel colors, we would also meet the third objective — a cheery springlike atmosphere.

With this brief analysis of the image of light, we have already determined a great deal of the information that is needed for completing the basic lighting key for our production. Specifically, we have determined the distribution for the basic lighting of each lighting area (four diagonal cross lights) and the basic range of the color palette (pastel tints). Let me reiterate that this particular solution is not the "correct" analysis of the image of light. There are myriad other possibilities, all of them equally "correct." You could have light from more or fewer directions (Figures 14.16A and B). You could also interpret the concept of "springtime pastel colors" to mean thin tints of cool colors as opposed to warm — it just depends on your personal understanding of the idea of a springtime atmosphere and the mood of the play.

With the foregoing proviso firmly in mind, we make the conscious decision that our lighting key is going to be based on a five-sided distribution pattern

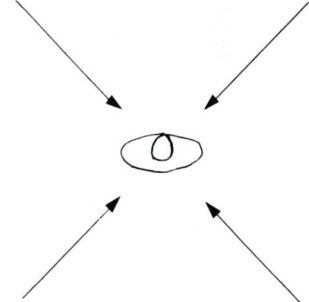

FIGURE 14.15
Four-source lighting key for *The Playboy of the Western World.*

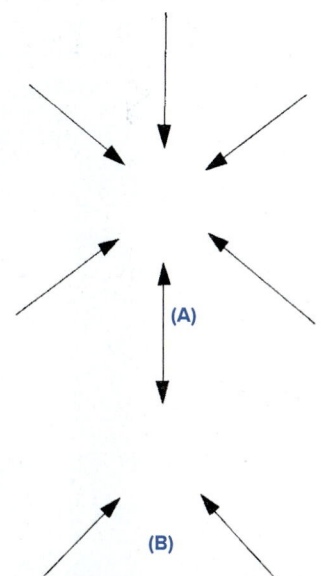

FIGURE 14.16
Six- and three-source lighting keys for *The Playboy of the Western World.* See text for details.

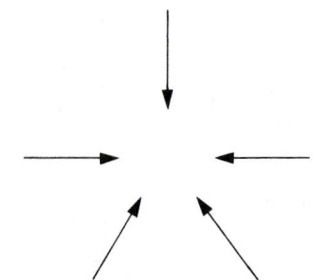

FIGURE 14.17
Five-source lighting key for *The Playboy of the Western World.*

(Figure 14.17). We made this decision because this pattern will provide a smooth, shadowless light that will support our interpretation of the image of light. Additionally, the top or back light (the arrow at the top of the pentagon) will provide a nice rim or halo light around the head and shoulders of the actors to keep them from visually blending into the set.

Before selecting specific colors for the lighting instruments, you must study the color palettes of the scenic and costume designers. This "color study" normally occurs during the various production conferences as each designer (scenic, costume, lighting) presents his or her design and color concepts. The reason that the lighting designer must know what colors the other designers are using is fairly simple. Colored light can drastically alter the apparent color of the sets and costumes, and it isn't in the interests of a unified production concept (or the lighting designer's physical well-being) to change the other designers' work without their knowledge and consent.

During the initial conferences of our hypothetical *Playboy* production, the design team decided that the play would be produced in a realistic style. Based on this concept, the lighting designer will want the set to appear as though it were being lit by the source lights that are located on the set. To determine the nature of these sources, and their locations, it will be necessary to look at a scenic rendering or model of the set. The scenic sketch (Figure 14.18) shows that there are oil lamps on the counter and each table, there is a peat fire glowing in the fireplace, and the window and door are open. Each of these sources would provide light of differing hues. The sunlight, according to our analysis of the image of light, is bright and cheerful. The fireplace is warmer and redder than the sunlight, and the oil lamps give off a soft, amber glow.

Using this analysis and information as a guide, and assuming that our lighting instruments do not have built-in color change capability and therefore require standard color media, Roscolux 61, Mist Blue, is selected to represent

FIGURE 14.18
The set design for *The Playboy of the Western World.* Courtesy of J. Michael Gillette.

the bright, clean sunlight. Roscolux 02, Bastard Amber, is chosen for the fire-light, and Roscolux 09, Pale Amber Gold, is selected to represent the color emitted by the oil lamps. (Roscolux colors, a common brand of theatrical light-ing-instrument media, are being used to identify the specific hues selected for this exercise. These colors are identified by the manufacturer with a name and number.)

Now that the colors have been selected to represent the various sources, they need to be applied to the lighting key. The application of color to the basic distribution pattern of the lighting key should support the thesis that the source lights are providing the light for the environment of the play. To achieve this goal, the lighting designer should color the light from stage left to represent the fireplace color, Bastard Amber, because the fireplace is on the stage-left side of the set. The oil-lamp color (Pale Amber Gold) is used from a direction (stage right) that supports the visual impression that the oil lamps are primarily on the downstage-right part of the set. The light approaching the stage from an upstage direction should represent the sun-light (Mist Blue), because the window and doorway are on the upstage wall of the set.

Figure 14.19 shows the colors assigned to the specific distribution pattern that we had previously determined from our analysis of the image of light. The stage-left side light is assigned Bastard Amber, to support the concept that the fireplace is lighting the room from this direction. The top-back light is col-ored with Roscolux 61, Mist Blue, because this supports the idea that any light approaching the stage from this direction would be sunlight coming through the window or door. The stage-right side light and the stage-right front light are col-ored with Pale Amber Gold, to support the notion that the primary source light for this side of the stage comes from the oil lamps.

This leaves the stage-left front light as the only uncolored instrument. Because there is no specific source light coming from this direction, it will be necessary to refer back to the image of light to determine the appropriate color for this instrument. The image of light specifies that the atmosphere should resemble a "twinkling spring morning." Roscolux 51, Surprise Pink, is selected for use from this direction, because this bright, cheerful color will blend with the Pale Amber Gold (used in the other front light) to produce a warm white light that supports the concept of a cheery morning that is dictated by the image of light.

Using the Lighting Key to Draw the Light Plot

The shape of the acting areas determines the number and arrangement of the lighting areas. In our hypothetical production of *The Playboy of the Western World,* the whole set is a single acting area. In order to draw the light plot, it will be necessary to subdivide that acting area into lighting areas, as shown in Figure 14.20.

To create a smooth wash of light over the entire acting area, the lighting designer needs to replicate the lighting key — as much as possible — in each of the lighting areas. Figure 14.21, on page 359, demonstrates this process for a single lighting area.

Unfortunately, it isn't always possible to achieve an exact duplication of the lighting key in every lighting area, because the walls of the set prevent the use of side light in the lighting areas that are adjacent to the walls, and the ceiling inter-feres with a great deal of the top and back light. More challenges are imposed by the physical limitations of the auditorium, which generally inhibit some of the front-of-house hanging positions.

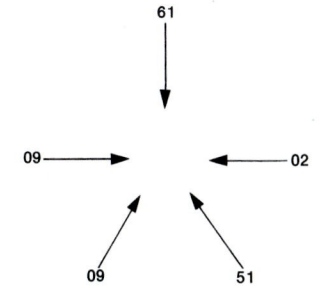

FIGURE 14.19
Five-source lighting key, with color, for *The Playboy of the Western World.*

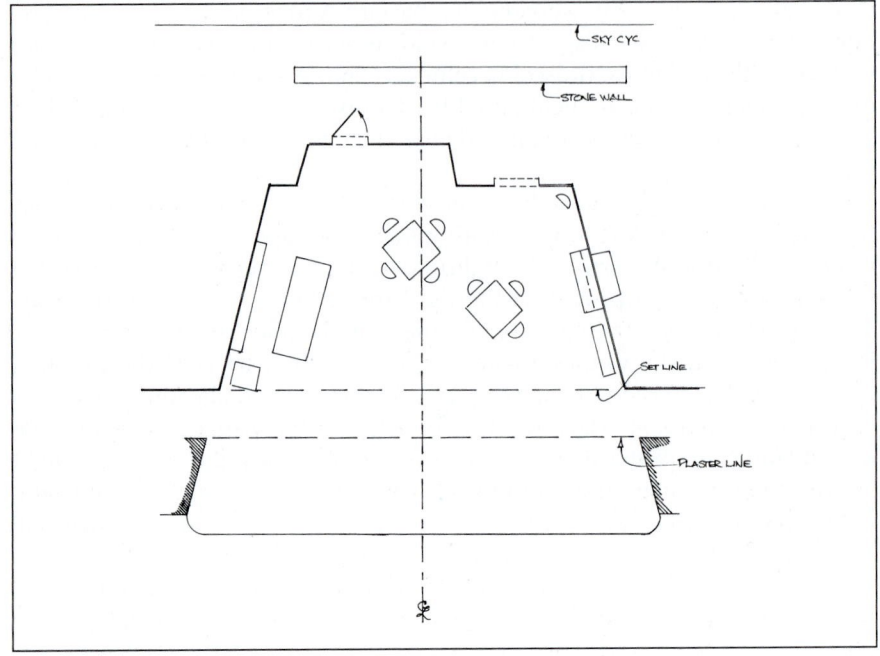

(A)

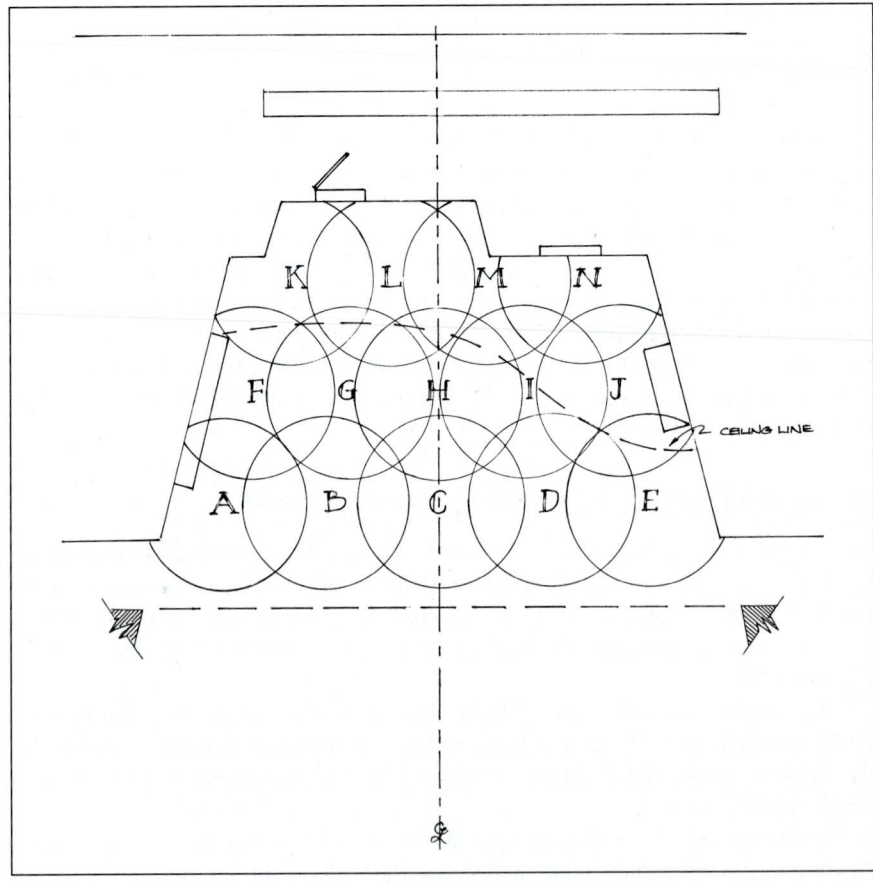

(B)

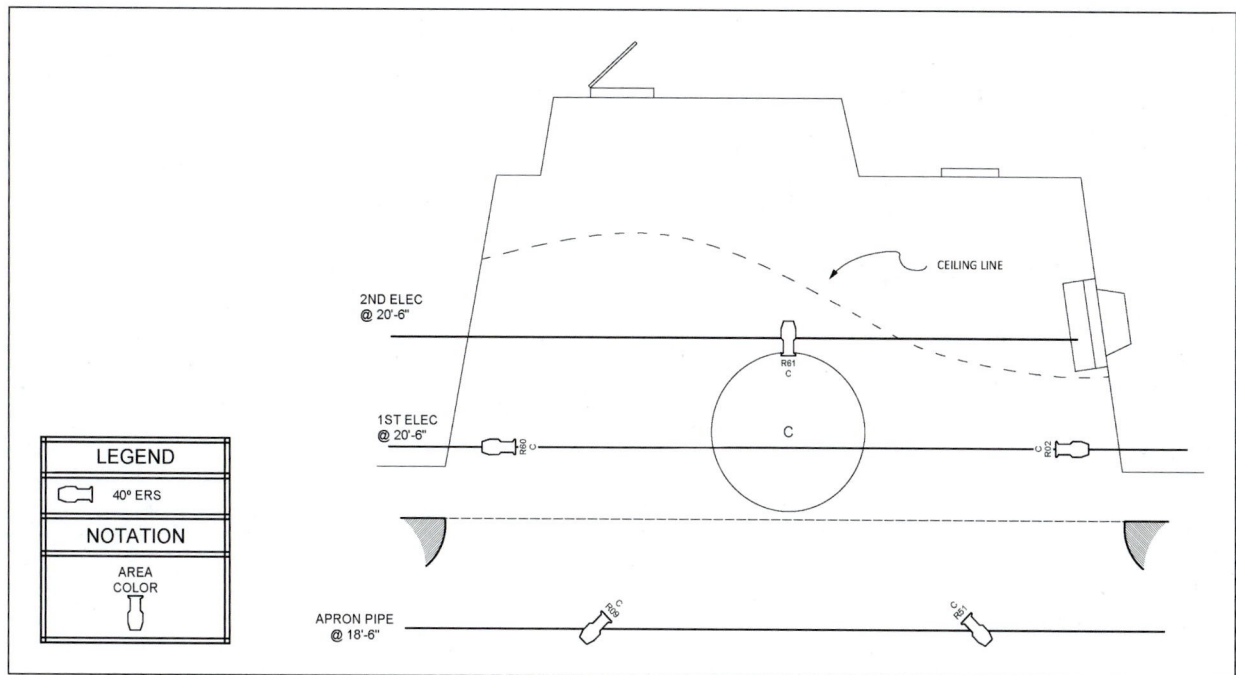

LEGEND

40° ERS

NOTATION

AREA
COLOR

2ND ELEC
@ 20'-6"

1ST ELEC
@ 20'-6"

APRON PIPE
@ 18'-6"

CEILING LINE

FIGURE 14.21
Replication of the lighting key in a lighting area for *The Playboy of the Western World.* Courtesy of J. Michael Gillette.

When a situation occurs that makes it difficult to place an instrument exactly where it is needed, the lighting designer must make a design decision. If a fixture can't be placed where it will replicate the angle specified in the lighting key, the compromise solution needs to be guided by the principles outlined in the lighting key and the designer's interpretation of the image of light. For example, it isn't possible to use direct stage-left side light for Area J (see Figure 14.22 on page 360), because the wall gets in the way. Two possible compromise solutions to this challenge might be: (1) Put an instrument on the stage-left end of the first electric, as shown in Figure 14.22; (2) eliminate the instrument. The choice of which solution to use should be guided by your interpretation of the image of light and the lighting key.

To complete this first layer of the lighting design, it will be necessary to duplicate, as closely as possible, the lighting key in every lighting area. It won't be possible to achieve this ideal if the walls and ceilings are in the way. The realistic goal is to replicate the key as much as possible given the dictates imposed by the set and any other "light-interrupting" circumstances. This process of replication results in a basic light plot that creates the atmosphere and look suggested in the image of light.

Layering

A lighting design exists in time as well as space. It ebbs and flows as the mood of the play changes. Creating a temporal development in the lighting design requires that some method of creating that time-based element be designed into the light plot.

Layering provides the means to that time-based element. It is primarily an organizational tool of the lighting designer. Specifically, it refers to the process of designing layers of light. During the performance these layers will be used in various combinations to create the different looks suggested by the lighting design concept.

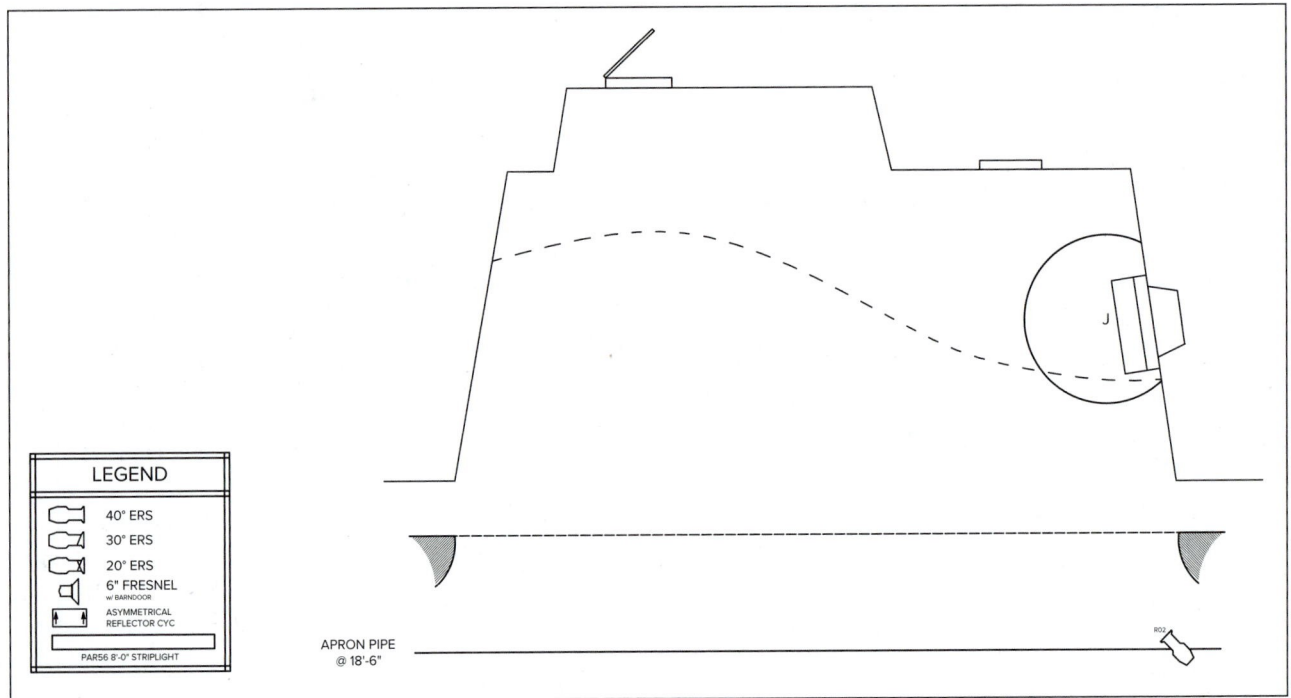

LEGEND

	40° ERS
	30° ERS
	20° ERS
	6" FRESNEL w/ BARNDOOR
	ASYMMETRICAL REFLECTOR CYC
PAR56 8'-0" STRIPLIGHT	

APRON PIPE
@ 18'-6"

FIGURE 14.22

Replication of the lighting key for *The Playboy of the Western World* in a lighting area that is difficult to light.

The first layer of light for our hypothetical production of *Playboy* was created when we implemented our interpretation of the image of light — "a bright, twinkling Irish morning." That image works well for Acts II and III, which take place in the morning and afternoon, respectively. However, Act I takes place in the early evening. The "twinkling morning" look simply doesn't translate as night. To create an appropriate look of early evening for Act I, it will be necessary to do one of two things: (1) Create a completely separate lighting key and design for Act I; or (2) create some supplemental "early evening" lighting that can be used in conjunction with the basic "twinkling Irish morning" lights.

Once again, we'll assume that we're not using LED fixtures or color scrollers/changers and the fixtures will require standard color media. From an aesthetic standpoint, a completely separate plot for Act I would be the preferred solution, but a separate design would necessitate a very large instrument inventory and, for most producing organizations, that isn't a realistic option.

The supplemental lighting solution would achieve relatively similar results with a considerably smaller number of instruments. The instruments used to create this second layer of light need to be positioned and colored to create the look of "indoor evening" in the pub, where the principal sources of light are oil lamps and the peat fire. Any light coming in the window and door should have the appearance of "night light" rather than daylight.

Because this second layer of light needs to be integrated with the "twinkling Irish morning" lights to achieve the look of "early evening," it will be necessary to select angles and colors that work to support the premise that the pub is actually lit by the oil lamps and the peat fire.

The second layer could be a created with a wash of "night" color (Roscolux 79, Bright Blue) that would flood the stage from the front-of-house positions, as shown in Figure 14.23A on page 361. By balancing the intensities of the night colors with those of the first layer, we can ensure that the blue lights won't override the basic modeling and colors of that first layer — which is the core of the

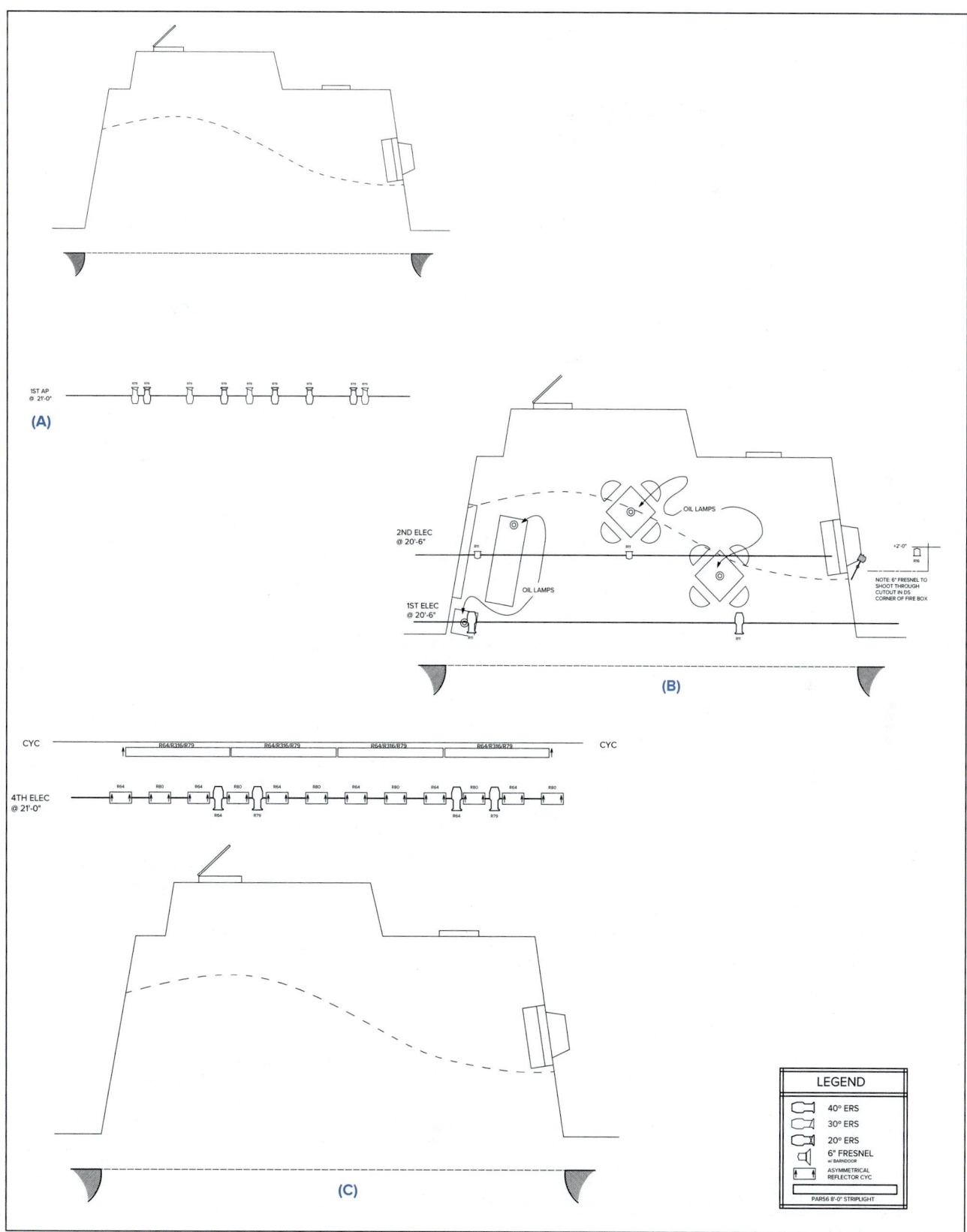

FIGURE 14.23
Layering can be used to supplement the basic design key. (A) instrumentation for the night wash. (B) Effects/source light instrumentation. (C) Supplemental "day" and "night" instrumentation. See text for more details.

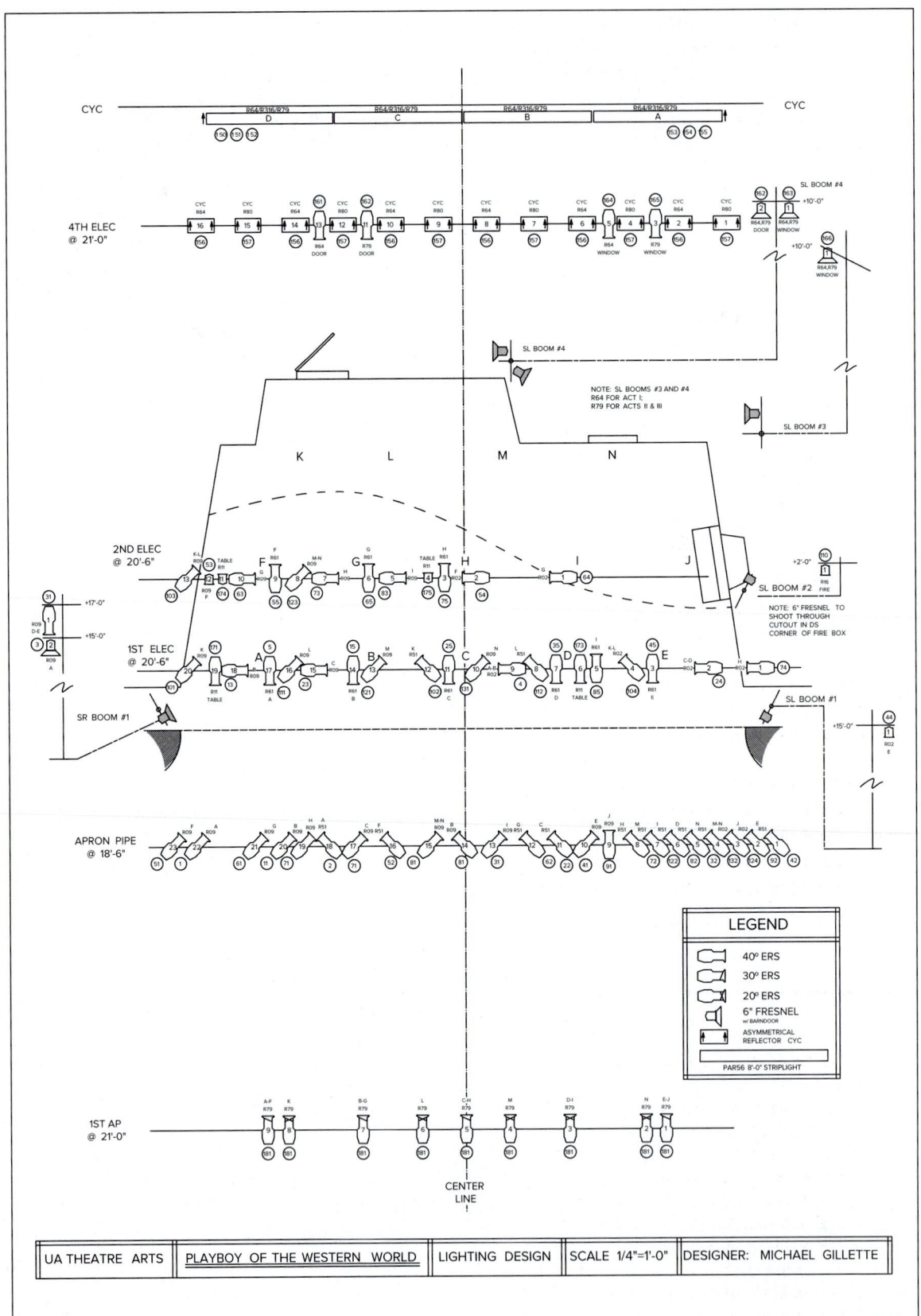

FIGURE 14.24
Light plot for a proscenium production of *The Playboy of the Western World.*

whole design. They will, however, provide a blue wash over the whole acting area that will fill any shadow or underlit areas with a blue light to help create the illusion of nighttime.

Additional instruments could be hung to augment the color selected to reinforce the source lights — the oil lamps and peat fire — created in the first layer of the plot. The instruments in this third design layer, shown in Figure 14.23B, would typically be colored in more fully saturated hues than their "first layer" counterparts, and would be hung in positions to support the effects of the source lights.

A fourth layer of light, Figure 14.23C, shows the location of those instruments used to create the "daylight" and "night light" coming through the window and door.

As indicated at the beginning of this discussion, layering is primarily an organizational tool of the lighting designer. It isn't necessary to divide your thinking about the design into segments, but many designers find that this compartmentalization of the design into specific segments, or layers, makes it easier to concentrate on solving the challenges imposed by the individual elements of the design. Figure 14.24 shows the finished light plot for *The Playboy of the Western World.*

Designing Lights for Thrust and Arena Stages

Designing lights for an arena or thrust stage is not significantly different from designing for a proscenium theatre. The only substantive difference is the location of the audience. In the thrust configuration, as you will recall, the audience sits on three sides of the stage, and in an arena theatre it surrounds the stage. It is the lighting designer's responsibility to light the stage so that all spectators, regardless of where they are sitting, are able to see the production equally well. Again, this ideal may not be obtainable. Dictates imposed by the set as well as sight line restrictions in the auditorium can make it impossible for every spectator in every seat to see and hear equally well.

We can use our hypothetical production of *The Playboy of the Western World* to demonstrate the relative lack of difference between designing lighting for the three modes of stages. Figure 14.25 on page 363 shows a sketch of the modified

FIGURE 14.25
Scenic design for a thrust production of *The Playboy of the Western World.* Left, Courtesy of J. Michael Gillette.

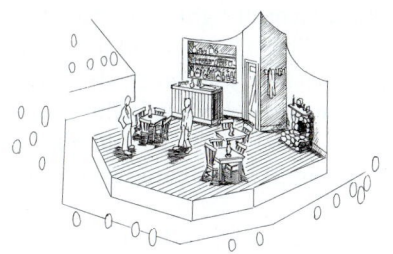

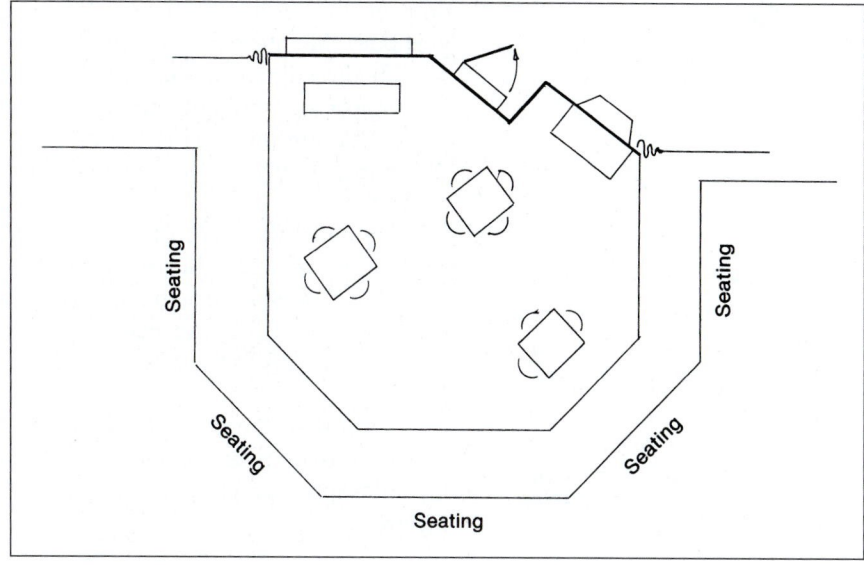

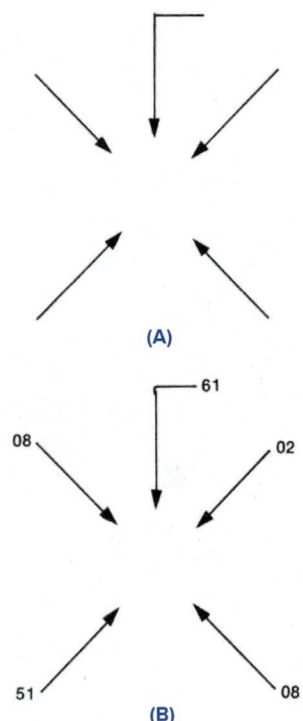

FIGURE 14.26
Lighting key for thrust production of *The Playboy of the Western World.* See text for details.

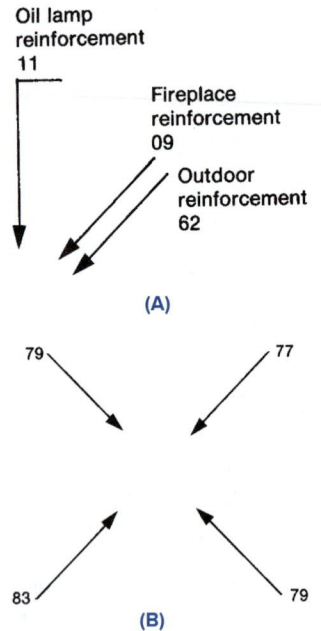

FIGURE 14.27
Additional layers for lighting key for thrust production of *The Playboy of the Western World.* See text for details.

scenic design that would work for a thrust production of our play. Note that the side walls have been removed so that the spectators sitting on the sides of the thrust stage can see all of the action. Also notice that because the walls are gone, the ceiling has been eliminated.

The image of light remains the same as before, simply because the concept of how we are going to produce the play hasn't changed. The distribution of the design key has been slightly modified because of the position of the audience relative to the stage. We are still surrounding the actors with light to re-create our "bright, twinkling Irish morning" as shown in Figure 14.26A. The color of the design key also remains relatively unchanged, although we will lower the saturation of the "warm" color because of the proximity of the audience, as shown in Figure 14.26B.

The second layer for our thrust production could concentrate on enhancing the source lights — oil lamps, fireplace, window, and door (Figure 14.27A, page 364). The third layer (Figure 14.27B) would concentrate on creating the "night" wash.

The lighting design for an arena production of our play would be very similar to the thrust design. The set for the arena production is shown in Figure 14.28 on page 365. Notice how all of the walls that might in any way interfere with the spectators' sight lines have been removed. The scenic design has been essentially reduced to a furniture arrangement, with just enough set left to provide a hint of what the cottage or pub actually looks like. The set has been shifted to a diagonal angle so that the entrances are lined up with the auditorium entryways.

The distribution of the lighting key for the arena production is slightly different from the other two configurations (Figure 14.29A, page 365). The color portion of the design key is also different, but only because we want everyone looking at the play to get the same atmospheric feeling. For the proscenium and thrust productions, we were able to have the light coming from the direction of the door and window gelled with colors that would support the "outdoors" look of the light coming through the window and door. Because we now have the audience surrounding the stage, however, we need to create the same feeling of "interior" lighting from all angles. These changes are shown in the color selection for the design key illustrated in Figure 14.29B.

Similarly, the "night" layers must place lights in positions that will enhance the idea of "night" for the entire viewing audience, as shown in Figure 14.30A on page 365. In this particular design, the third layer of light is used to support both the internal and external source lights. These lights need to be reasonably directional, as shown in Figure 14.30B, because the sources that they are reinforcing (sunlight, moonlight, peat fire) are also directional. The instruments that are reinforcing the oil lamps are placed over the general area of the lamps, simply because the light from the oil lamps illuminates everything around it.

The only other type of design modification that needs to be made when working in an arena theatre is that the instruments are probably hung considerably closer to the actors than in either a thrust or proscenium configuration. Because of this you may want to use less-saturated color, as the closer the instrument is to the actor, the stronger the effect of any color used in that fixture.

Other than these relatively minor adjustments required by the positioning and proximity of the audience, there really aren't any significant changes in philosophy, practice, or techniques when designing for thrust or arena theatres.

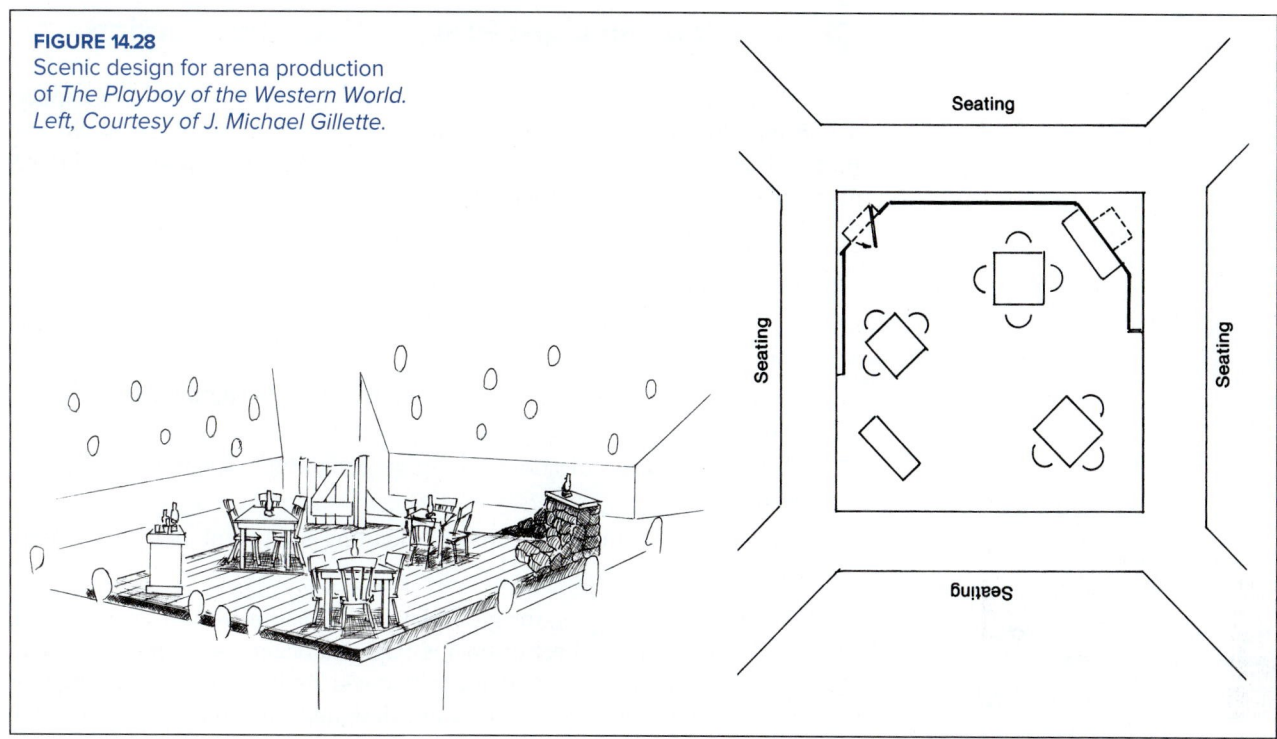

FIGURE 14.28
Scenic design for arena production of *The Playboy of the Western World. Left, Courtesy of J. Michael Gillette.*

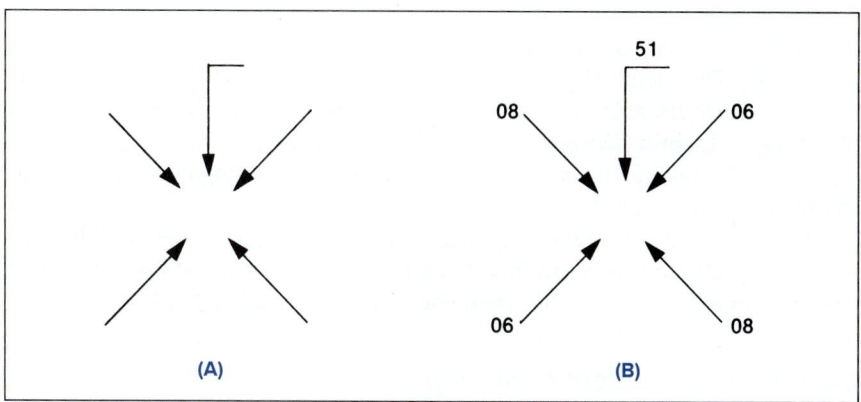

FIGURE 14.29
Lighting key for arena production of *The Playboy of the Western World.* (A) Lighting key. (B) Lighting key with color. See text for details.

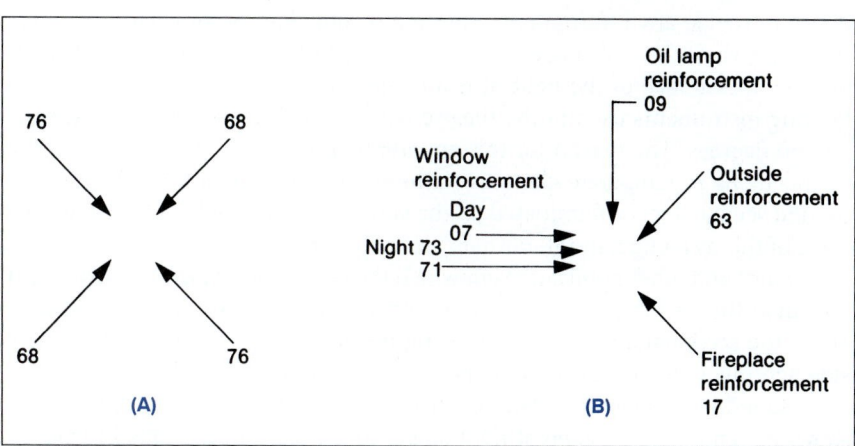

FIGURE 14.30
Additional layers for lighting key for arena production of *The Playboy of the Western World.* (A) Lighting key, with color, for the night reinforcement. (B) Lighting key, with color, for source reinforcement. See text for details.

Drawing the Light Plot and Lighting Section

The lighting designer needs to acquire several specific drawings or computer files from other members of the production design team before he or she can start to draw the light plot. In addition to sketches, models, or photos of the scenic models, the lighting designer will need:

1. The ground plan(s) of the scenic design

2. The sectional(s) of the scenic design

3. A scale ground plan of the stage and auditorium including any permanent hanging positions

4. A sectional of the stage and auditorium including any permanent hanging positions

5. A layout of, and specifications for, the stage lighting system(s) of the theatre

6. An accurate inventory of the theatre's lighting equipment and/or a lighting rental budget.

If hand-drawing the plot, the ground plans of the theatre and set are traced, using a thin line, onto a sheet of tracing paper to begin the layout of the light plot. If computer-drafting, and assuming that you are in possession of computer files for the theatre structure and the scene designer's drawings, you overlay the various elements of the plan files — using appropriate line weights — to create the basic layout information required to begin drawing the light plot. The layout of the stage lighting system, items 4 and 5 above, provide information about the location of the various stage circuits (connecting strips, floor and wall sockets, and so on). The sectionals of the set and the stage and auditorium are used to create the basic visual information necessary for the lighting section. See the box "Drafting for Lighting Design" on page 349 for some of the drafting conventions. Appendix A contains the complete USITT guide for drafting conventions used in theatre lighting design.

Information regarding the lighting key, beam and field angles, and lighting areas was presented earlier in this chapter. However, some additional technical information may prove helpful when you start to draw the light plot.

Determining the Sectional Angle

The lighting key codifies the plan angle and color for each instrument, but it doesn't provide any information about the sectional angle for each instrument. Although the sectional angle should be determined from an analysis of the desired appearance of the light, it is a reality that the sectional angles of most lighting instruments used in the theatre will usually be somewhere between 30 and 60 degrees. The reason for this apparently arbitrarily selected angle is that people living in temperate climates — where some 95% of all humans live — are used to seeing objects illuminated by the sun within this angle range, so we perceive of this as being natural, normal, and appropriate.

Dance and other applications in which the revelation of form is more important than the visibility of the face are notable exceptions to this generalization about the sectional angle. Dance lighting normally makes very effective use of side lighting with an angle of approach parallel with the stage floor.

Figure 14.31A shows the plan view of a single lighting instrument. Figure 14.31B shows a sectional view taken at right angles to the axis of that same instrument. Because the lighting instruments are usually hidden from the spectators' view, the

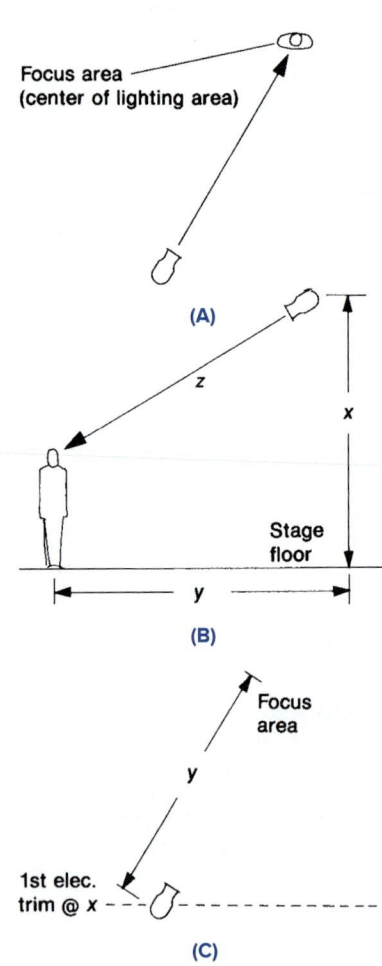

FIGURE 14.31

A sectional view of the hanging position of a lighting instrument provides an accurate picture of the angle from which the light will strike the actor. See text for details explaining A, B and C.

lighting designer will set a specific trim height (height above the stage floor) for the instrument. Because any point along the axial line will produce the "correct" sectional angle, the sectional line can be extended until it reaches the predetermined trim height (x). At that point, a vertical line can be dropped to the stage floor, and the distance from that point to the center of the lighting area can be measured (y). This information is recorded on the light plot by placing the symbol for the instrument at the measured floor distance from the center of the lighting area, as shown in Figure 14.31C. The trim height for the pipe is placed on the plot, at the end of the pipe.

At this point, it should be noted that lighting instruments normally are focused at "head height," as illustrated in Figure 14.31B, and not a circle on the stage floor.

The **throw distance,** (z) in Figure 14.31B, represents the distance light travels from the fixture to the center of the lighting area at head height. It is one of the factors used when selecting instrument size.

Selecting Instrument Size

At the same time that the sectional angle is being determined, the lighting designer can also determine the appropriate size of instrument to use. From the beam and field angle information, available online from the lighting instrument manufacturers, templates of the beam and field angles can be constructed for each instrument. These are simple triangular, scale, acetate, or cardboard templates that contain the throw distance and the beam and field angles of the light emitted by each instrument.

A three-dimensional CAD program such as Vectorworks can also be used to determine the appropriate size of instrument needed for a given situation. The program has a vast library of lighting instruments that may be placed in selected positions and at various trim heights — called "trims" — and "turned on" to light 3-D human figures to help identify the most appropriate lens size, as shown in Figure 14.32. If the first-selected virtual fixture doesn't supply the desired coverage, it can be quickly exchanged for another one for further testing.

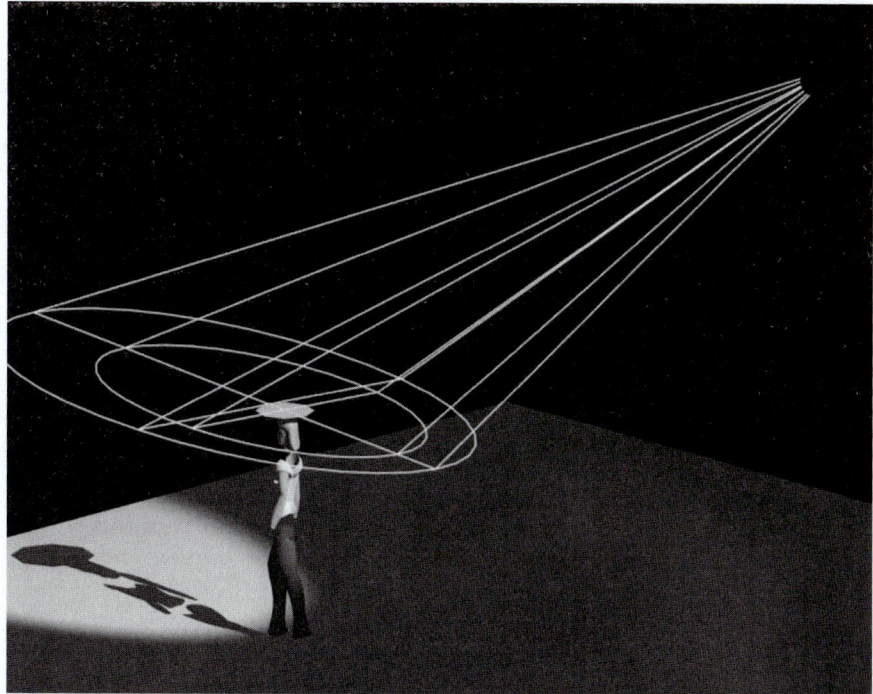

FIGURE 14.32
The fixture required to create a beam spread of a certain diameter at a throw distance of a specific length can be determined using the 3D graphics in a CAD lighting program such as Vectorworks. Screenshot courtesy of Vectorworks.

throw distance: How far light from an instrument travels from its hanging position to the center of its focus area. Courtesy of Michael McNamara.

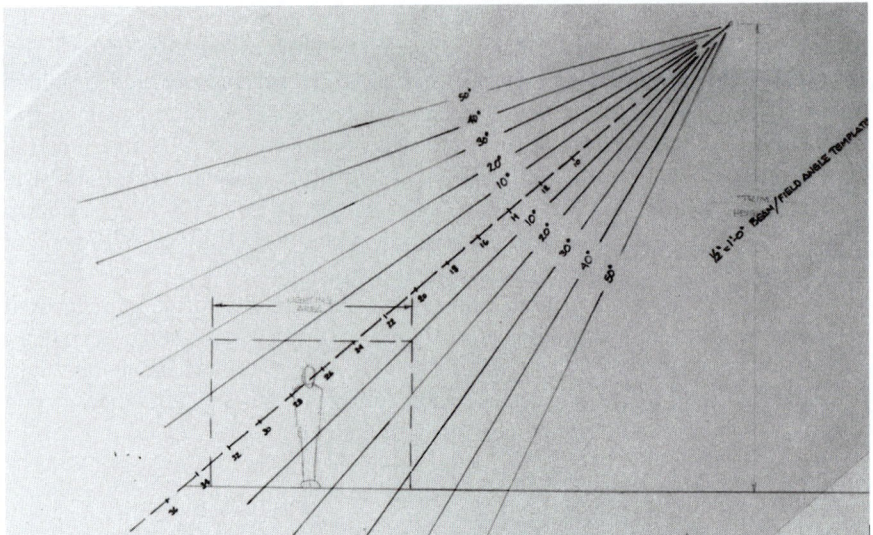

Figure 14.33 shows how to use the beam and field angle template. After the **working sectional** for the instrument has been drawn, the apex of the template is placed at the specified trim height for the instrument. The appropriately sized instrument will have a field angle that slightly overlaps the lighting area and a maximum throw distance that is longer than the required throw distance.

This method of instrument selection is suggested only as a general guide. In the final analysis, the designer needs to make instrument selections based on what is aesthetically appropriate for the particular situation.

 ## Rehearsal and Performance Procedures

It has been said that any lighting design is only as good as its paperwork. The light plot, lighting section, and instrument schedule are only about half of that paperwork. The remainder is associated with recording the **channel** or dimmer intensity levels and other data used when running the lights for a show. In this case, the term "paperwork" is a partial misnomer. While cues for manually operated light boards are still recorded on paper, cues for computer boards are stored in the computer's hard drive. The following section will discuss "keeping track of the cues" for both manual and computer boards.

Manual Preset Boards

Very few manual preset light boards remain in operation in the United States. The current industry standard lighting console is the computer board. Nevertheless, it is still relevant to study the paperwork associated with manual preset boards if for no other reason than many of the principles and techniques used with manual boards have informed the operational techniques of computer consoles. The operational principles of preset boards are discussed in Chapter 16, "Lighting Production."

There are a series of rehearsal and performance procedures, forms, and practices used to keep track of the lighting for any production. Every time there is a change in the lighting — even if it involves only one fixture — those changes

working sectional: A drawing showing the sectional angle for a lighting instrument; used to determine its trim height; not to be confused with the lighting section.

channel: In a channel control system, an individual control to which (typically) any number of dimmers can be assigned.

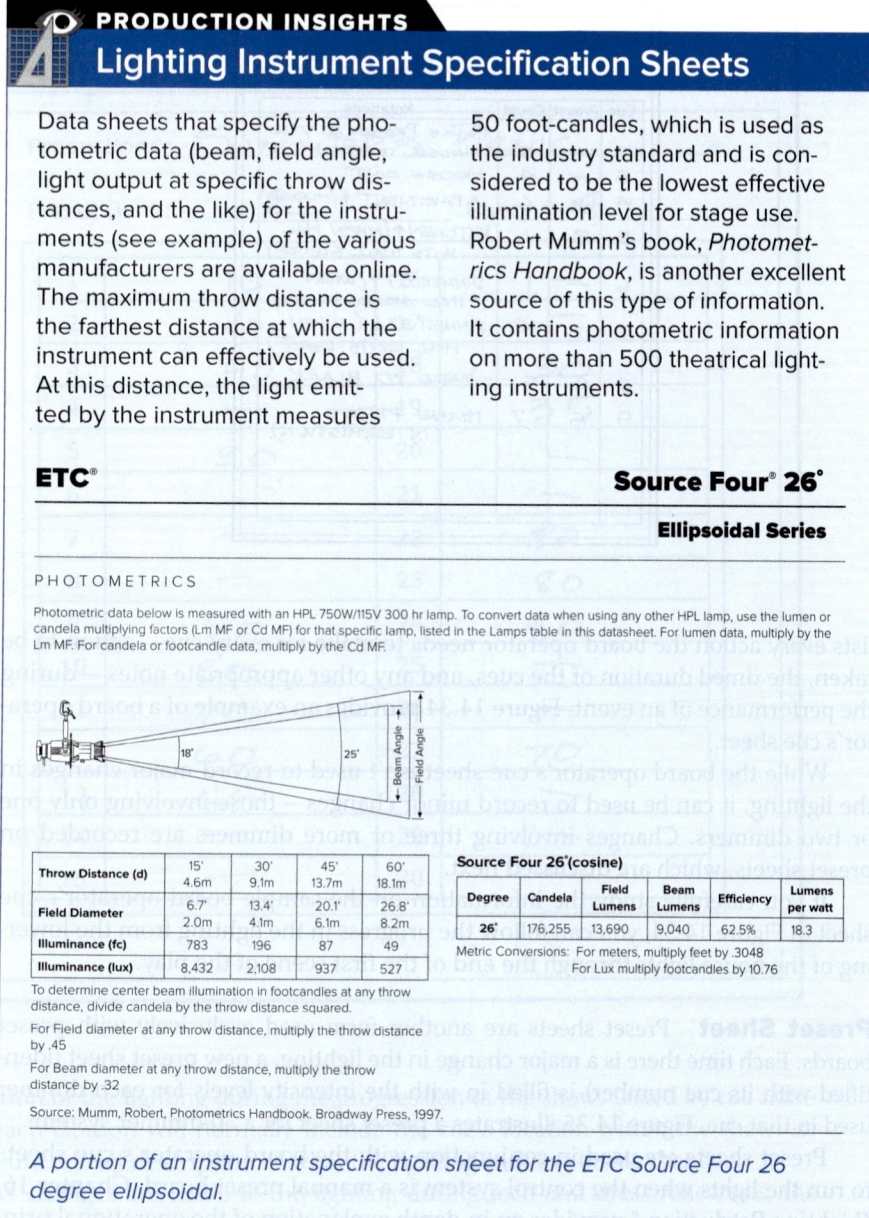

PRODUCTION INSIGHTS

Lighting Instrument Specification Sheets

Data sheets that specify the photometric data (beam, field angle, light output at specific throw distances, and the like) for the instruments (see example) of the various manufacturers are available online. The maximum throw distance is the farthest distance at which the instrument can effectively be used. At this distance, the light emitted by the instrument measures 50 foot-candles, which is used as the industry standard and is considered to be the lowest effective illumination level for stage use. Robert Mumm's book, *Photometrics Handbook*, is another excellent source of this type of information. It contains photometric information on more than 500 theatrical lighting instruments.

ETC®   **Source Four® 26°**

Ellipsoidal Series

PHOTOMETRICS

Photometric data below is measured with an HPL 750W/115V 300 hr lamp. To convert data when using any other HPL lamp, use the lumen or candela multiplying factors (Lm MF or Cd MF) for that specific lamp, listed in the Lamps table in this datasheet. For lumen data, multiply by the Lm MF. For candela or footcandle data, multiply by the Cd MF.

Throw Distance (d)	15' 4.6m	30' 9.1m	45' 13.7m	60' 18.1m
Field Diameter	6.7' 2.0m	13.4' 4.1m	20.1' 6.1m	26.8' 8.2m
Illuminance (fc)	783	196	87	49
Illuminance (lux)	8,432	2,108	937	527

Source Four 26°(cosine)

Degree	Candela	Field Lumens	Beam Lumens	Efficiency	Lumens per watt
26°	176,255	13,690	9,040	62.5%	18.3

Metric Conversions: For meters, multiply feet by .3048
For Lux multiply footcandles by 10.76

To determine center beam illumination in footcandles at any throw distance, divide candela by the throw distance squared.

For Field diameter at any throw distance, multiply the throw distance by .45

For Beam diameter at any throw distance, multiply the throw distance by .32

Source: Mumm, Robert, *Photometrics Handbook*. Broadway Press, 1997.

A portion of an instrument specification sheet for the ETC Source Four 26 degree ellipsoidal.

need to be recorded to ensure that the intensity settings for every dimmer or channel and the timing of every **lighting cue** remain the same from rehearsal to rehearsal and performance to performance.

The forms and practices suggested in this section are not sacrosanct; they are just one of many methods that can be used to record the information needed to consistently run the lighting for any production. Any well-organized system that works for both the lighting designer and electrician can be used. The important point is the necessity of having a clear, systematic method to record the necessary information.

Board Operator's Cue Sheet

The **board operator**'s cue sheet is the manual board operator's bible. Used exclusively with manual boards, the board operator's cue sheet sequentially

lighting cue: A command to take some type of action involving lighting, usually, to raise or lower the intensity of one or more instruments.

board operator: An electrician who runs the lighting control console during rehearsals and performances.

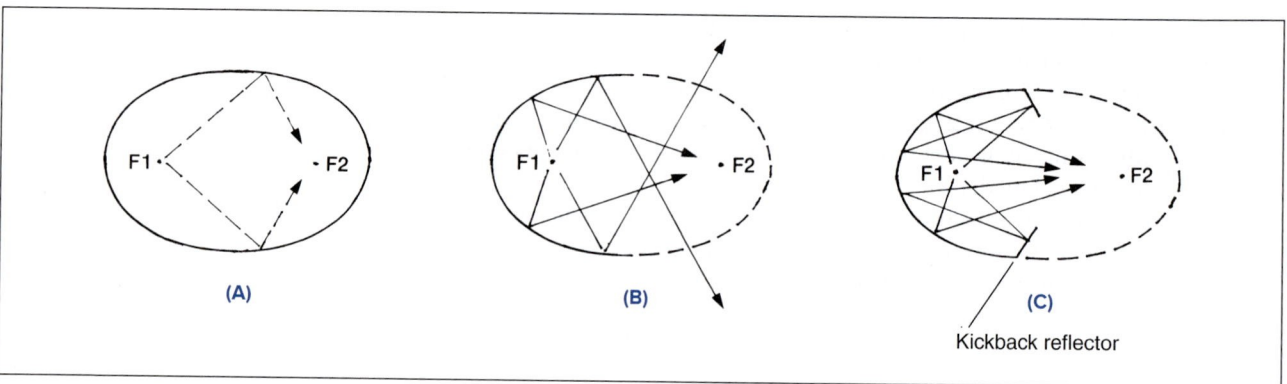

(A)   **(B)**   **(C)**

Kickback reflector

FIGURE 16.14
(A & B) The optical properties of a conical ellipse. (C) Redirecting light with the kickback reflector increases the total light output of the fixture.

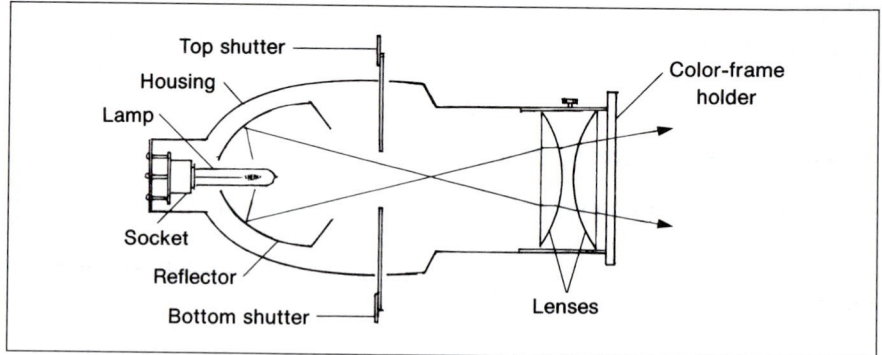

FIGURE 16.15
Cutaway view of an ERS.

zoom ellipse: An ERS with movable lenses that allow the focal length to be changed.

FIGURE 16.16
ETC Source Four Zoom ™ spotlight. Photo courtesy of ETC (Electronic Theatre Controls, Inc).

elliptical reflector shown in Figure 16.14A has two focal points, F1 and F2. Light emitted by a light source at F1 will reflect off the walls of the conical ellipse and pass through F2. If half of the elliptical reflector were removed (Figure 16.14B), light emitted from the source at F1 would again pass through F2, although some of the light would pass out of the open end of the reflector and be lost.

The ERS operates on this basic principle of gathering light from one focal point (F1) and focusing it on the second focal point (F2). Some ERSs have a kickback reflector placed at the open end of the conical ellipse to redirect any spill light back into the reflector, as shown in Figure 16.14C. The shutters, made of stainless steel or some other highly heat-resistant metal, are located in a plane close to the second focal point to shape the light.

Light from the ERS lamp filament passes through the shutter aperture — the opening between the shutters — toward the lens train. ERSs use a variety of plano-convex and double-convex lens configurations, either individually or in combination, to achieve the desired beam spread and throw distance criteria (Figure 16.15).

The **zoom ellipse,** more officially known as the variable-focal-length ERS (Figure 16.16), is an extremely versatile instrument. This variation of the standard ERS has lenses that can slide forward or backward to change the focal length of the instrument. Changing the focal length affects the beam and field angles of the instrument, with those angles widening as the focal length becomes shorter. The field angle of most zoom ellipses can be varied between approximately 20 and 50 degrees.

The ETC Source Four® and the Source Four® Jr. families of ERSs use cold mirror reflectors. These reflectors, made of heavy Pyrex glass, have an applied

TABLE 16.2

Beam/Field Angles for Typical ERSs*

Instrument Type	Beam Angle	Field Angle	Maximum Effective Range**
6 × 16	9	18	60
6 × 12	11	26	50
6 × 9	16	37	35
20	10	20	70
30	12	30	60
40	15	40	55

* All data are approximate but typical. Specific data vary with manufacturer.
** Determined by point at which output diminishes to 50 footcandles.

FIGURE 16.17
Light is bounced off a cold mirror reflector in the Selecon Pacific ERS. Product image supplied courtesy of Philips Selecon

shutter cut: The shadow line created by the edge of the shutter when it is inserted into the beam of light emitted by an ERS.

color frame: A lightweight metal holder for color media that fits in a holder at the front of a lighting instrument.

gobo: A thin metal template inserted into an ERS to project a shadow pattern of light.

dichroic coating that reflects visible light while transmitting infrared (heat) wavelengths. This means that the majority of the heat generated by the lamp *passes through* the reflector and is vented out the rear of the instrument rather than being reflected with the rest of the light. The result is less heat deterioration of the shutters, iris, and gobos, as well as longer color media life.

More innovative ERS design is evident in the Pacific family of fixtures by Philips Selecon. This instrument has a unique shape because it is designed to reflect light off of a dichroic cold mirror before the light strikes the gate as shown in Figure 16.17. The cold mirror reflects visible light but passes infrared (heat) and ultraviolet light through the mirror. A heat sink vents the infrared heat outside of the housing. The net effect is a much cooler beam of light which, in turn, results in longer shutter and color media life. Additionally, the lens tube rotates 360 degrees, which allows the shutters to be positioned to make the most appropriate **shutter cut.**

Table 16.2 lists the beam and field angles in degrees of arc for several varieties of ERSs. As mentioned in Chapter 14, "Lighting Design" the beam angle (Figure 16.18) is that point where the intensity of the cone of light emitted by the instrument diminishes to 50 percent of its intensity as compared with the center of the beam. The field angle is that point where the light diminishes to 10 percent of the output of the center of the beam. As the optical design of theatre lighting instruments has improved, the beam angle has expanded to the point where it is now almost as wide as a fixture's field angle in many manufacturers' ERSs.

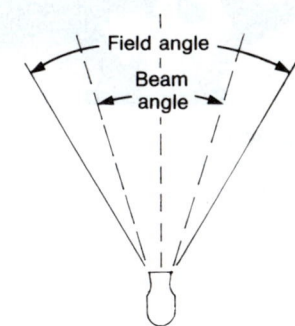

FIGURE 16.18
Beam and field angles.

Accessories

The most basic accessory designed for use with an ERS is the **color frame** (Figure 16.19), a lightweight metal holder for plastic colored media. The color frame is inserted into the holder on the front of the ERS to color the light.

The **gobo** (Figure 16.20), also known as a pattern, template, or cookie, is a lightweight metal cutout that turns the ERS into a pattern projector. Most ERSs are equipped with a built-in pattern slot located adjacent to the shutter plane. A wide variety of commercially designed gobos, usually made of stainless steel, are available from scenic and lighting supply houses. Gobos can be constructed from heavyweight disposable aluminum cookware (roasting pans, pie plates), as shown in Figure 16.21. Depending on the heat generated by the fixture's lamp,

FIGURE 16.19
A color frame. Courtesy of J. Michael Gillette.

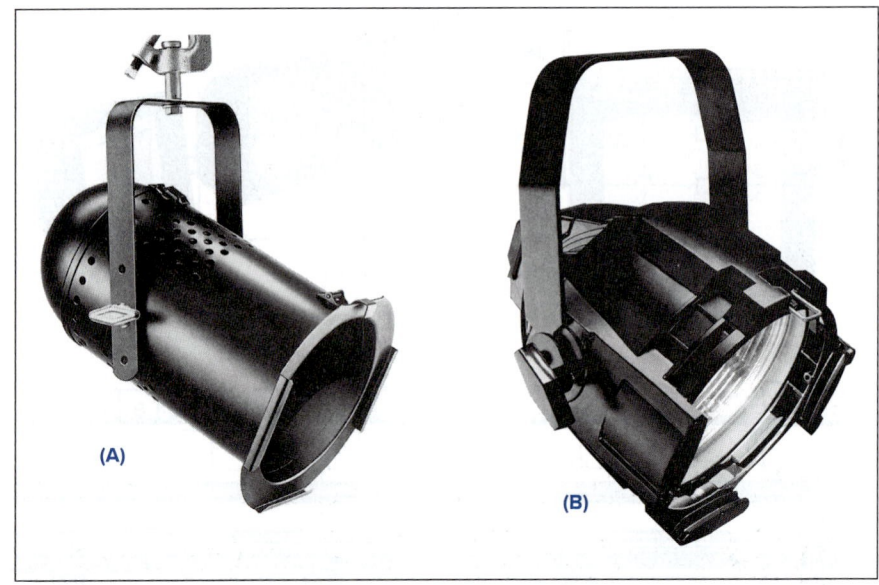

(A)

(B)

TABLE 16.3

Beam and Field Angles for Various PAR 64 Configurations

PAR 64 Lamp	Beam Angle (in degrees) (height × width)	Field Angle (in degrees) (height × width)
Very Narrow	6 × 12	10 × 24
Narrow	7 × 14	14 × 26
Medium	12 × 28	21 × 44
Wide	24 × 48	45 × 71

The light source for a standard PAR can (Figure 16.35A) is a parabolic aluminized reflector (PAR) lamp. The lamp's reflector, filament, and lens are integrated into a single, sealed-beam unit. The PAR can housing doesn't do anything other than safely hold the PAR lamp and color media. The most common size of PAR lamp used in stage lighting is the PAR 64, a 1000-watt lamp about 8 inches in diameter. The variety of beam and field angles available in PAR 64 lamps are described in Table 16.3.

The Source Four PAR (Figure 16.35B) produces the same quality of light as PAR lamps. But the comparisons stop there. The Source Four PAR doesn't use PAR lamps; its housing has a permanently attached parabolic reflector; it uses the same HPL family of lamps as the Source Four ERSs; and it employs interchangeable lenses to change the beam spread, shape, and texture. PARs are rapidly being replaced with LED wash fixtures that do many of the same things.

Followspot

The followspot is used when a high-intensity, hard-edged beam of light is required to follow a moving performer. Followspots are manufactured in a variety of sizes and styles (see Figure 16.36). The smallest followspot is a tungsten-halogen model capable of a useful light throw of about 35 feet. The larger models use high-intensity xenon, HMI, or unencapsulated arc-lamp sources and have a useful light throw of up to 300 to 400 feet.

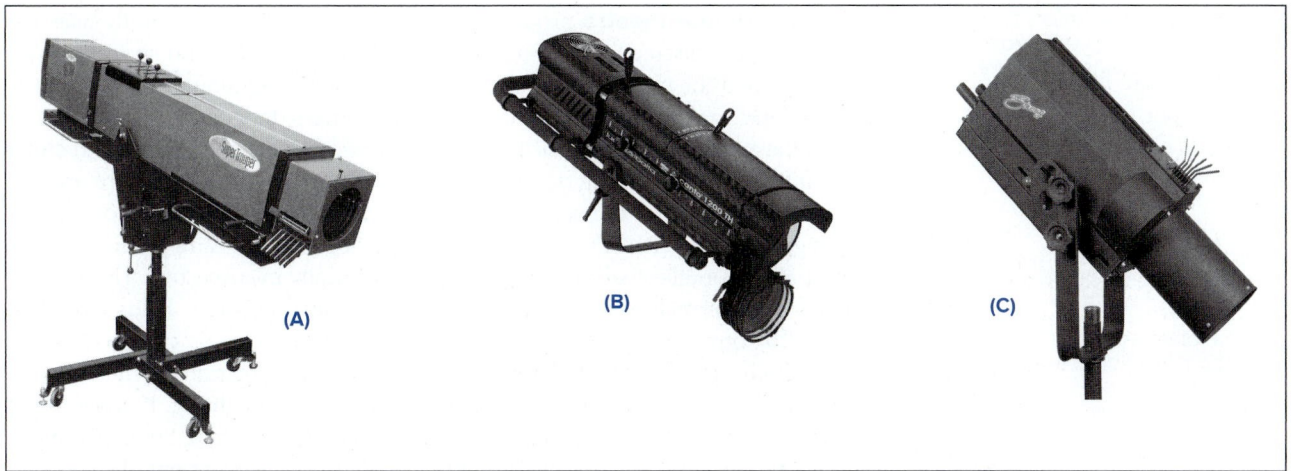

(A)   (B)   (C)

FIGURE 16.36
Followspots: (A) The Strong Super Trouper (with xenon lamp); (B) the Strong Canto 1000 (tungsten-halogen lamp); (C) the Strong Truss Trouper (metal halide lamp). Courtesy Strong Lighting, Inc.

All followspots function on the same general principles, illustrated in Figure 16.37. They have an illumination source — tungsten-halogen, HMI, xenon, or arc. In addition, short-range LED-lamped followspots are beginning to be made. Many have a forced-air cooling system that helps to dissipate the heat generated by the light source.

The iris and **shutter** are internal control devices used to shape the beam of light. By manipulating them simultaneously, the operator can create a variety of beam-edge patterns.

All followspots have some type of lens or reflecting system to gather and shape the light. Portions of the system can be adjusted to focus the light and adjust the crispness of the edge of the beam.

Most followspots are equipped with a mechanical dimming device called a douser. Because the intensity of some of the light sources used in followspots (arc, encapsulated arc, xenon, HMI) cannot be adjusted, the douser provides the only way of smoothly dimming those sources. The douser can also be used to achieve a slow fade-in or fade-out of the light. Followspots are also equipped with a color boomerang, which holds five or six movable color filters. A diffusion filter is frequently inserted into the light *before* the color filters to diffuse and soften both the color and hardness of the light.

shutter: A lever-actuated device used to control the height of the top and bottom edges of a followspot beam; also called a chopper.

Intelligent Fixtures

One of the primary functions of an effective lighting design is the establishment of a mood that supports the production concept. To creatively, and effectively,

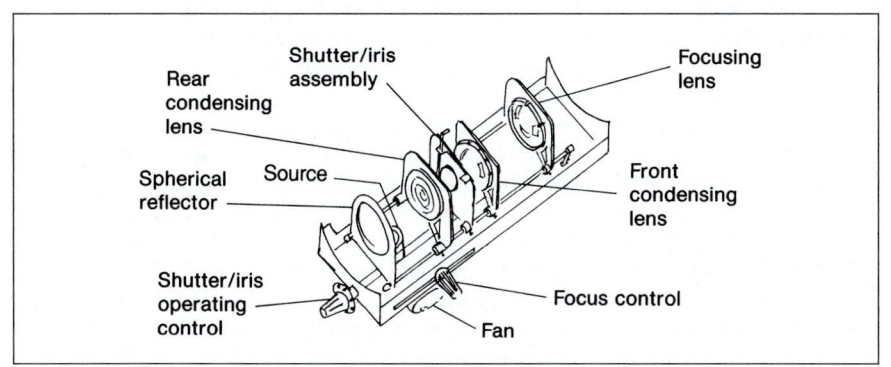

Rear condensing lens

Shutter/iris assembly

Focusing lens

Spherical reflector

Source

Front condensing lens

Shutter/iris operating control

Focus control

Fan

FIGURE 16.37
Cutaway drawing of a followspot.

legitimate theatre: Refers to plays that rely on the spoken word to convey the message. Does not include musicals, reviews, dance, opera, or concerts.

concert: In this context, primarily refers to touring rock and country western shows.

club: In this context, refers to night clubs in which high-energy music (live or recorded) is the prime attraction.

pan: To rotate an object, such as an ERS, about its vertical axis.

light a **legitimate theatre** production, the lighting designer generally uses the basic tools just discussed — ERSs, Fresnels, PARs, cyc lights, and so forth. With this equipment he or she can create the normally subtle lighting that supports the production concept and covertly affects the audience's understanding of the play.

In the application of its basic principles, lighting design for **concerts** and **clubs** is no different than lighting design for legitimate theatre. However, there are two substantial differences: the nature of the production concept and the impact of the lighting on the audience. Production concepts for legitimate theatre productions are almost always intellectual, cerebral, and metaphorically introspective. The production concept for rock concerts and clubs is almost always visceral, bold, and extroverted. The atmosphere at a rock concert or club is about as far removed as you can get from a production of Shakespeare, Williams, or Stoppard. The music is fast, hard, and loud. The atmosphere is high energy. So is the lighting. It is overt and spectacular, and the way it affects meaning and mood is anything but subtle. Basic area lighting is normally done with multiple washes of heavily saturated color from or other wash fixtures. Moving light fixtures provide punch, emphasis, and focus. As more designers have had a chance to learn the capabilities of these versatile fixtures, they have learned that these instruments don't always need to be used to spectacular effect. They can also be very effective if used subtly. Consequently, when budgets permit, they are becoming increasingly common in legitimate theatre.

The common feature of all intelligent fixtures is movement: Light beams **pan** the stage, zoom in and out, change shape, change color, diffuse, and sharpen; gobos materialize, spin around, change patterns, then disappear. This is an exciting and active class of instrument.

Instrument Maintenance

To function effectively, the various instruments discussed in this chapter must be maintained in good working order, and as with any delicate piece of equipment, they must be handled with care.

The position of the lamp filament and the reflector must be kept in alignment, particularly in a non-LED lamped ERS and the Source Four PAR fixtures. If this relationship is disturbed, the light output from the instrument will be greatly reduced, and the hot spot will be moved from the center of the beam. One of the significant advantages of the PAR 64 is that the filament and reflector are permanently aligned during the manufacturing process, so when the lamp in a PAR can is changed, there is no need to check the relationship. LED-lamped fixtures, having no filament to align with the reflector, do not have this issue.

The lenses and reflectors need to be kept clean and free from dust and fingerprints, and all nuts and bolts on the housing, yoke, and pipe clamp should be maintained so that the instrument can be locked securely into place.

When not in use, instruments should be hung on pipes or on rolling racks so that they won't be knocked over. If the theatre does not have an instrument storage cage, the instruments can be stored on a counterweight batten above the stage.

ERSs should be stored with the shutters pushed all the way in to prevent them from being accidentally bent. When the instruments are in storage, care should be taken that the electrical pigtails are not pinched between the yoke and the instrument housing. The electrical plug and pigtail must be kept in good working order.

Followspots are mounted on a yoke and swivel-stand base that must move smoothly to follow the action of a performer. The base and yoke need to be properly lubricated, usually with graphite rather than oil or grease, and all nuts and bolts must be properly tightened.

There are a plethora of moving light fixtures available, as shown in Figure 16.38. Obviously, they don't all function in the same way, nor do they all have the same features. But generally they all use the same principles of operation. Almost all functions — pan, **tilt,** mechanical dimming, color changing, gobo movement and changing, beam spread, beam diffusion, and so forth — of these instruments are controlled by very precise electric **step motors.** Some of these instruments contain up to twenty separate motors to control the various functions.

Control of these step motors would be almost impossible without the development of USITT DMX512, a digital control protocol employed by nearly all intelligent fixture and control manufacturers, as well as the manufacturers of "regular" stage lighting systems. (See the box "USITT DMX512" on page 410.) Digital control allows control signals for all functions of these instruments to be fed to the fixture through one low-voltage control cable. A separate 120 or 208/220 VAC power line is required to power the lamp and control motors.

Tungsten-halogen and encapsulated arc lamps are most commonly used with these instruments, although, here too, LED-lamped fixtures are rapidly becoming more common. T-H lamps can be dimmed, but encapsulated arc lamps, which are used because of their very high output, cannot be dimmed. They require mechanical dimming or dousers which can be precisely regulated with the step motors.

Many intelligent instruments have internally mounted gobos and gobo changers. In some fixtures the gobos can be made to spin either forward or backward. Again, the functions of inserting, changing, and spinning the gobos are controlled by step motors.

There are two methods used to move the beam of light around the stage: moving the mirror or moving the fixture's head. Moving-mirror units, also called scanners, are very effective at creating the spectacular "look-at-me" color-changing,

tilt: To rotate an object about its horizontal axis; to pan vertically. The instrument is suspended from a yoke, which allows the fixture to both pan and tilt.

step motor: An electric motor whose movement consists of discrete, angular steps rather than continuous rotation. Precise movement is achieved by programming the motor to run, in either direction, for a specific number of steps.

(A)

(B)

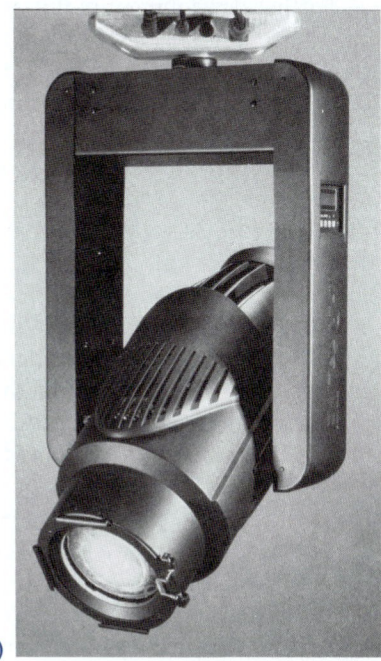

(C)

FIGURE 16.38
Types of moving light fixtures. (A) Martin T-Rex. (B) VL1100 ERS Luminaire by Vari-Lite. (C) VL 550 Wash Luminaire by Vari-Lite. A, Courtesy of Martin Professional A/S. B and C, Courtesy of Vari-Lite.

CYM color mixing: Color mixing using the secondary colors of light — cyan, yellow, and magenta.

heat sink: A metal device that absorbs heat from an operating unit and dissipates it into the air.

non-dim: An undimmable power source — usually 120 VAC — whose off-on switch is controlled from a lighting console.

pattern-shifting effects more suited to dance clubs than the stage. Theatre applications generally need fewer freeform effects and more beam-spread and edge control than scanners provide. For this reason, moving-head fixtures are used more frequently in the theatre.

The Chauvet Intimidator Scan 305 IRC (Figure 16.38A) is a moving-mirror effects generator. It is a compact LED scanner that can run with or without DMX and is capable of changing colors and patterns.

The Philips Vari-Lite VL1100 ERS (Figure 16.38B) is an automated zoom ERS. The head of the unit zooms, pans, and tilts, has **CYM color mixing,** rotating gobos, adjustable diffusion, and either framing shutters or an iris. Available with arc or incandescent sources, the arc version is equipped with a douser.

The head of the Philips Vari-Lite VL 550 Wash (Figure 16.38C) pans and tilts; it has an incandescent source, CYM color mixing, variable diffusion, and interchangeable front lenses to control light quality and beam spread.

While the use of intelligent fixtures is generally limited by both budgets and aesthetic need, these instruments have already become a staple in the equipment inventory of many, if not most, medium- and large-sized theatres. Their use is very exciting and will continue to evolve, particularly with the increasing presence of LED fixtures in this category.

LED Fixtures   High-output LEDs currently are being used in many types of theatrical lighting instruments. The advantages/disadvantages of LEDs were discussed earlier in this chapter. But there are several characteristics that make this source very intriguing to those in the lighting industry.

Because of their small physical size, a number of individual LEDs can be clustered together to effectively create a single lamp of sufficient output to be useful for stage lighting. These LED clusters have already been used as sources in PARs, striplights, and ERSs, and are increasingly being used in moving fixtures. Further development in this area is challenged by one of the by-products of LED clustering — heat. Individual LEDs don't generate much heat, but, when clustered together, heat can build to destructive levels, particularly for those LEDs in the center of the cluster. Current fixture design removes this heat with **heat sinks.** Effective heat dissipation will continue to be a primary, but solvable, design challenge as higher wattage, brighter LEDs, which generate even more heat, are developed.

LEDs require 24-volt DC current instead of the 120-volt AC power used by most stage lamps. Most, if not all, LED fixtures have power converters built into their housings. Feeder power for those units can be supplied from a **non-dim** or by plugging the unit into any 120 VAC source. For fixtures that don't have "onboard" power conversion technology, independent power supplies like the one shown in Figure 16.39 provide the required 24-volt DC power.

Dimming and color mixing instructions for LED fixtures is normally supplied from the primary lighting board. Instruments with onboard power conversion have control data fed directly to them. Fixtures without the onboard power conversion normally route the light board control signals into the power supply and a cable that carries both the power and control data interconnects the power supply and the fixtures.

Because LEDs can be designed to produce light in a very narrow color range it is possible, by using separately controlled red, blue, and green LEDs in the same housing, to produce more than 16 million different colors.

The Spectra PAR 100 (Figure 16.40A) is a 100-watt fixture with PAR light qualities and red, blue, green, and amber color mixing. The Coemar ParLite Led VariWhite (Figure 16.40B) is a washlight that can vary the color temperature

FIGURE 16.39
The LED 300 power supply is used to distribute control data and 24-volt DC power to LED-lamped fixtures. Image published with permission of Doug Fleenor Design, Inc.

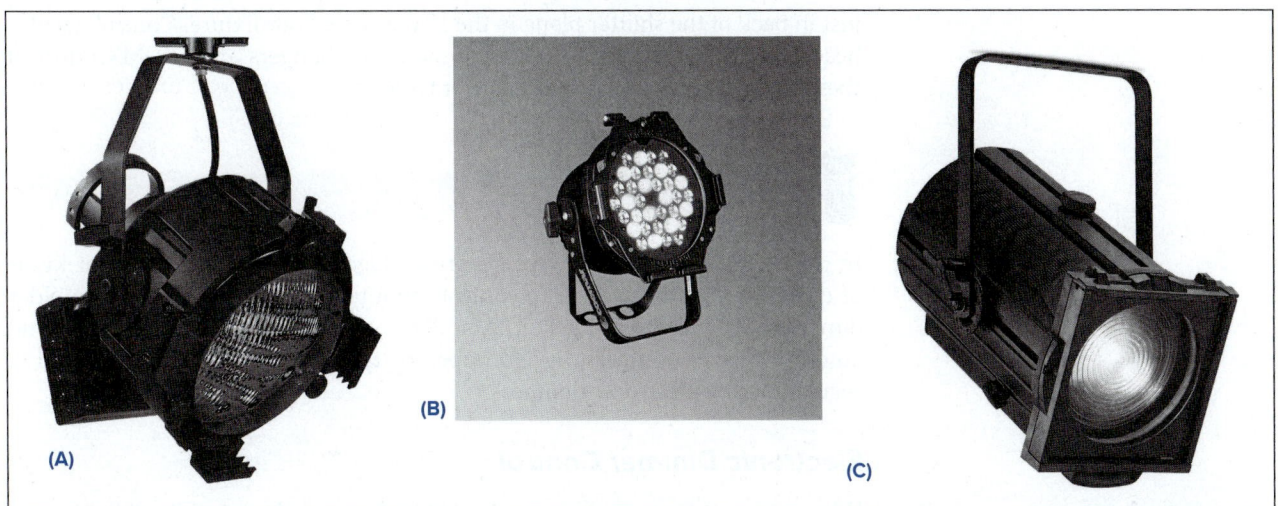

FIGURE 16.40
LED light fixtures. (A) LED Spectra Par 100. (B) Coemar's ParLite Led VariWhite Daylight. (C) Rama LED Fresnel MKII. A, Courtesy of Altman Lighting Co., Inc. B, Coemar S.P.A. C, Courtesy Philips Lighting.

of its white light by plus or minus 10 percent. Philips Selecon Rama Fresnel LED (Figure 16.40C) is advertised as an LED-sourced replacement for a 750-watt 6-inch Fresnel spotlight. It can vary the color temperature of its white light from 2700 to 3500 degrees Kelvin.

The high-output, color-mixing capabilities of LED sources, as well as their inherent lower electrical consumption, are primary reasons that many people in the lighting industry, not only those in theatre, but media and architectural lighting as well, are excited about the developments in this area. As their performance improves and their prices drop, LED-lamped fixtures are moving toward becoming the standard source for stage lighting equipment. It will be exciting to watch this evolution in the coming years.

Color Changers   While becoming increasingly rare with the explosion of LED-sourced fixtures, non-LED color changing is accomplished with either a color scroller or a dichroic color changer. The color scroller, Figure 16.41A, normally is used with traditional, nonintelligent, ERSs, Fresnels, or PARs that don't have internal color-changing capabilities. The color scroller fits in the gel frame holder on the front of the instrument and contains a roll of plastic color media that, if stretched out, would look like a series of different-colored gels taped together. A dichroic color changer generally uses three dichroic filters — normally the secondary colors (cyan, yellow, and magenta) — to change the color of the light. The individual filters can be partially or fully inserted into the fixture's beam of light. The degree of insertion determines the color and level of saturation of the resulting hue. The three filters are used in combination to produce virtually any possible hue. The Seachanger module (Figure 16.41B) fits

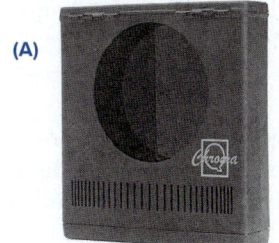
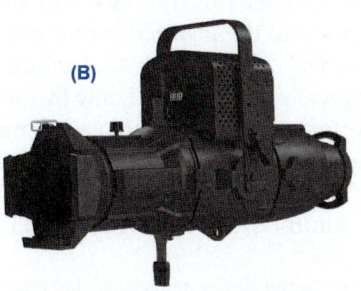

FIGURE 16.41
Color changers utilize two different types of systems to change the color of the light output. Color scrollers, such as the Universal™ color changer by Chroma-Q® (A), use a scroll of colored plastic media. (B) The Seachanger by Pixelteq, Inc. uses dichroic filters. A, Photo ©Chroma-Q. B, Courtesy MEOPTA U.S.A., Inc.

just in back of the shutter plane in the ETC Source Four fixture. Control data for Seachanger, color scrollers, and dichroic color changers are by DMX. Most of these units also require separate power feeds.

 Dimmers

In the relatively brief history of electrical stage lighting, many different kinds of dimmers have been used to control the intensity of instruments. The older dimmers, such as the salt water, saturable core, thyratron tube, resistance, and autotransformer dimmers, have dropped by the wayside. The only types still in regular use are electronic dimmers.

Electronic Dimmer Control

When you move a controller to increase or decrease the intensity of lights connected to an electronic dimmer, you are using a low-voltage control circuit to manipulate the high-voltage output of that dimmer. Formerly, analog control systems were the only method available for controlling SCR dimmers. Now digital control is the universal standard.

To appreciate why "digital is better," you first need to understand how both analog and digital systems work and the basic differences between them.

Analog systems work on the following principle: Output varies as a continuous function of input. For example, increasing or decreasing the output of the control circuit causes a corresponding increase or decrease in the output of the dimmer. This control signal is sent from the light board over a control **line** to the dimmer. Because the analog system requires a continuous signal, every dimmer in the system must be connected to the light board by its own control line.

Digital systems work on a different principle: Output varies in discrete steps. At first glance the difference in operating principles between analog and digital systems appears relatively inconsequential. But the differences are significant. To understand why, we first need to understand how digital information differs from analog. As stated earlier, analog information is continuous. Digital information isn't. Digital information is **discrete.** It is neither continuous nor variable. Digital information exists as binary code — a string of zeros and ones to which meaning can be attached.

The finite nature of the digital signal is very important. It enables digital information to be made up into discrete information or instructional packages. These packages, called data packets, can contain any information that we want them to. Further, they can be sent to specific locations. Figure 16.42 is a diagram of a light board and three dimmers using digital control. The light board continuously sends information — instructional packages — to all three dimmers. However, the dimmers "read" only those instructions that are addressed to them. For example, dimmer 1 reads only instructional packages addressed to itself. It pays no attention to the instructions for any other dimmer. Dimmers 2 and 3 react the same way, reading only that information addressed to them. Because each instructional package is read only by the dimmer to which it is addressed, different information can be sent to each dimmer.

The process of sending two or more messages simultaneously on the same channel is called **multiplexing** and is the primary advantage of digital over analog control systems.[3] Figure 16.43 shows both types of control systems.

line: The wires in low-voltage control systems are frequently called "lines" rather than "wires."

discrete: Separate and complete; in this case, pertaining to information represented by binary code.

multiplex: (1) To transmit two or more messages simultaneously on a single channel. (2) To carry out several functions simultaneously in an independent but related manner.

---

[3] Analog signals can also be multiplexed, but the quantity of signals that can be multiplexed and the quality of the individual signals are lower than with digital.

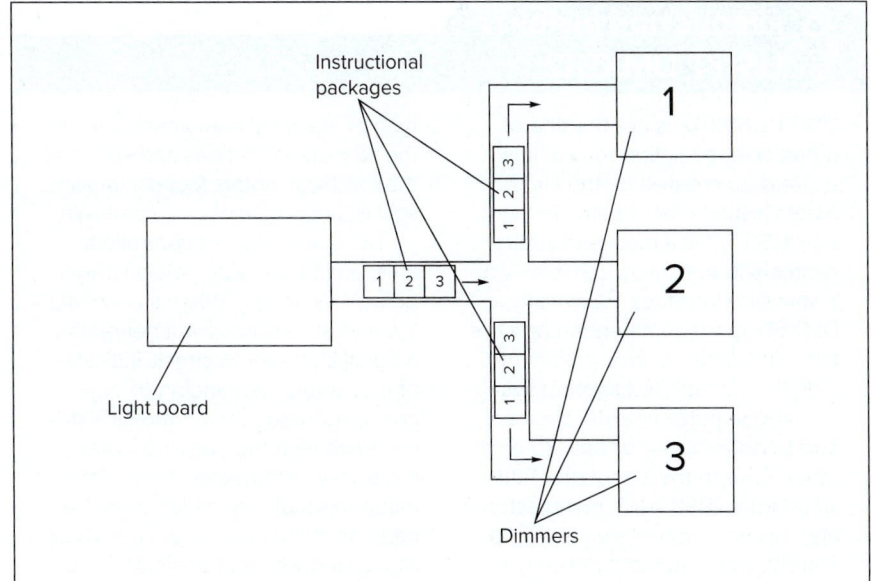

FIGURE 16.42
Digital instructional packages are
continuously sent to all dimmers.
The dimmers read only those
instructions addressed to them.

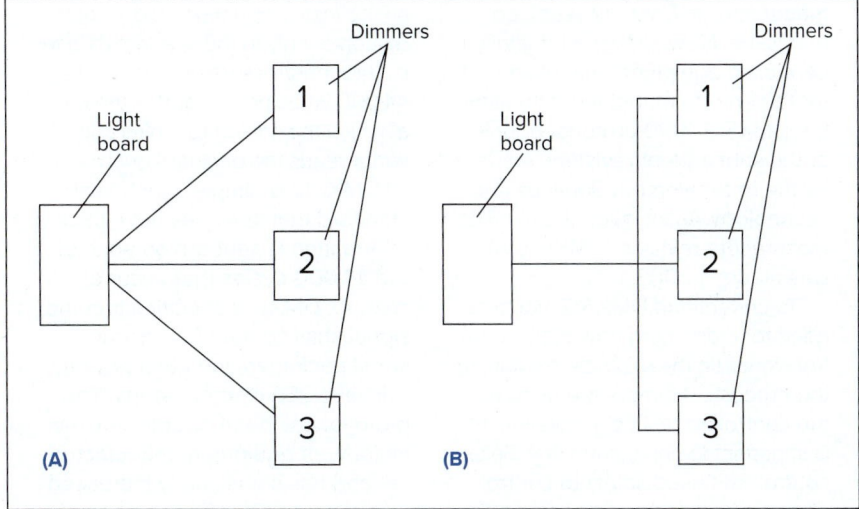

FIGURE 16.43
Schematic drawing of lighting
control systems: (A) analog and
(B) digital.

Figure 16.43A is an analog system. It requires that each dimmer be connected to the light board by its own control line. Figure 16.43B is a digital system. Notice that there is only one control line connecting all three dimmers to the light board. This is because the multiplexed instructional packages are sent to all dimmers but are read by only those dimmers to which they are addressed.

Saving on costs in the wiring of control circuits isn't the only advantage that digital control offers. Multiplexing offers another distinct advantage with digital control. Some moving light fixtures require dozens of control channels to function as designed. Digital control requires only one control cable to provide instructions to all of the functions. An analog system would require that dozens of separate control lines be connected to the instrument. The final advantage that digital offers over analog is precision of control. Digital instructional packages are finite. Once encoded, they don't change. While analog signals can be remarkably

PRODUCTION INSIGHTS

USITT DMX512

USITT DMX512 is not the title of a bad science fiction movie. It is a standard created by the United States Institute for Theatre Technology (USITT) "as a means to control dimmers from lighting consoles via a standard interface."[1] Basically, DMX512 is a recommended practice that allows the various pieces of a digitally controlled lighting system — computer boards, dimmers, and peripherals — to "talk" to each other. Prior to the adoption of this standard in 1990, each manufacturer had its own proprietary method of control, which made it difficult, if not impossible, for the customer to use a light board from one manufacturer to control dimmers, or any other equipment, made by another manufacturer. DMX512 resolved that issue. Now almost all digitally controlled equipment manufactured for the entertainment industry uses the DMX512/1990 protocol or one of the subsequent revisions made by the Entertainment Services and Technology Association (ESTA). The most recent revision (DMX512-A) was made in 2008.

To understand DMX512, you first need to understand how digital control works. (In the example explaining the process, dimmers are used as the controlled device. However, it is important to understand that digital control isn't used solely to control dimmer output. It also can be used to manipulate the functions of any type of electrical equipment, such as the stop/start functions and speed of the electrical motors found in moving light fixtures and motion control units.)

The signal of most controllers — for example, the slide pots on a light board — is analog. When a controller is set to a specific level, it generates a signal that is an electronic indication of that setting. An analog-to-digital converter reads the controller's signal. Each time the converter reads the signal, it translates that information into binary code, adds the address of the dimmer or equipment associated with that particular command, and sends this "instructional package" to all the dimmers and equipment in the system. Each dimmer and piece of equipment receives all the instructional packages, but responds only to those addressed to it. This send/receive process occurs 44,000 times per second — the rate at which the analog-to-digital converter reads the original signal.[2]

DMX512 is simply a technical standard that specifies how much information is sent out on each of the 44,000 cycles that occur every second. DMX512 specifies that the signal shall contain 512 instructional packages and each package will have 256 discrete steps. This protocol has been adopted by the majority of equipment manufacturers and has significantly increased the compatibility of equipment used in the entertainment industry.

[1] Bennette, Adam, "Recommended Practice for DMX512: A Guide for Users and Installers," PLASA/USITT, 1994, p. 7.

[2] Some systems create the control signal digitally, which eliminates the need for the analog to digital conversion. These signals also are scanned and distributed 44,000 times a second.

accurate, they aren't as accurate as the unchanging digital code. For all of these reasons, digital is now the mode of choice in almost all dimmer control applications.

Silicon-Controlled Rectifier Dimmer

The silicon-controlled rectifier (SCR) dimmer, Figure 16.44, is reliable and efficient. It is still considered by many to be the workhorse of the lighting industry, although the sine wave dimmer (discussed in the next section) has uses in certain applications.

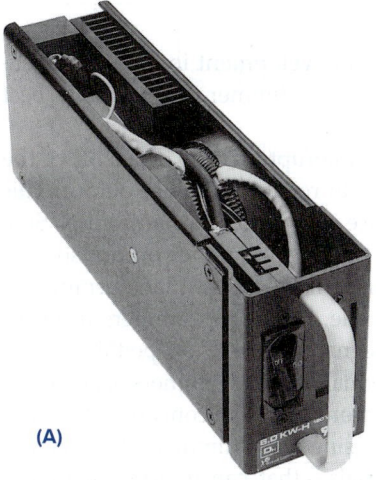

(A)

(B)

FIGURE 16.44
SCR dimmers. (A) An SCR dimmer.
Courtesy of Philips Strand Lighting.
(B) The ETC Sensor3™ Portable
Pack — a six-dimmer portable
module. Courtesy of ETC (Electronic
Theatre Controls, Inc.).

The SCR dimmer operates on a gating principle, which is simply a rapid switching on and off of the power. That principle is explained in the box "Gating Principle" on page 414.

The SCR is a solid-state power transistor, which means that it has no moving parts and no filaments to burn out. The electronic circuitry necessary to switch the SCR to a conducting state is also fairly simple. These properties result in a dimmer that is rugged, long lived, compact, relatively lightweight, moderate in cost, and reasonably quiet in operation.

With the rapid advancements being made in the electronics industry, discoveries will undoubtedly lead to even more efficient dimmers for non-LED fixtures. At present, however, the SCR dimmer is recognized as the best solution.

Safety Tip

Dimmer Maintenance

The greatest enemy of an electronic dimmer such as the SCR is heat. To dissipate the heat, some dimmers are equipped with large heat sinks. Heat sinks are metal — usually aluminum — structures that absorb the heat generated by an SCR and radiate it to the atmosphere. Other dimmer packs are equipped with fans.

It is vital for the longevity of dimmers that they have plenty of air circulating around them. Don't pile anything on top of a dimmer. If you are working with portable dimmers, be sure that the dimmer pack is raised off the ground so that air can circulate under, as well as over, the case.

If your dimmer system is equipped with fans, be sure that they are running smoothly and that the air filters are clean. The dimmers will frequently function for several hours even if the fan isn't working, but the heat buildup will cause a rapid deterioration of the electronic equipment that will usually lead to premature dimmer failure.

PRODUCTION INSIGHTS
Gating Principle

If, in a given period of time, you turn a lamp on, then off, then on, off, on, and off, you effectively control the amount of light it puts out for that specific amount of time. If the lamp is turned on, and left on, for one second, it burns at full intensity for that one-second period. If you turn the lamp on for half a second and turn it off for half a second, it burns at half intensity for the one-second span. If you turn the lamp on for three-quarters of a second and off for one-quarter of a second, it burns at three-quarters intensity for the one-second span. In each of these cases, you will obviously see the lamp being switched on and off. But if the time span for the on-off cycle is reduced to $1/120$th of a second, you perceive the on-off sequence as being a continuous level of illumination — an average of the on-off cycle ratio.

The SCR dimmer operates on this principle. The SCR is actually an electronic switch. The switch, or gate, opens and allows current to pass through the SCR when it receives the proper electronic command. The gate stays open until the power to the SCR is turned off. Sixty-cycle alternating current (AC), the standard current in the United States, alternates its polarity 120 times a second, or twice in each cycle, as illustrated in Figure A. Each time that it alternates its polarity, or crosses the zero point on the graph, there is no voltage. The effective result of this "no voltage" situation is that the electricity is turned off. If a command is fed to the SCR to start conduction at the beginning of the cycle, point A in Figure B, the SCR will conduct for the full half cycle, or until the electricity is shut off

when it changes polarity at point B. Similarly, if the command specifies that the SCR is to begin conducting halfway through the cycle (Figure C), the transistor conducts for only half the cycle, or half as long.

By varying the time that the SCR is able to conduct electricity, you vary the intensity of any lamp load connected to it. This means that if the SCR conducts for a full half cycle, the lamp will glow at full intensity for the duration of that half cycle. If it conducts for only half of the half cycle, the lamp will be perceived to be glowing at half intensity. Similarly, a quarter-cycle electrical conduction means the lamp will appear to be glowing only one-fourth as brightly. Because each SCR conducts for only half a cycle, two SCRs, one for each half cycle, are necessary to make an effective dimmer.

The gating principle

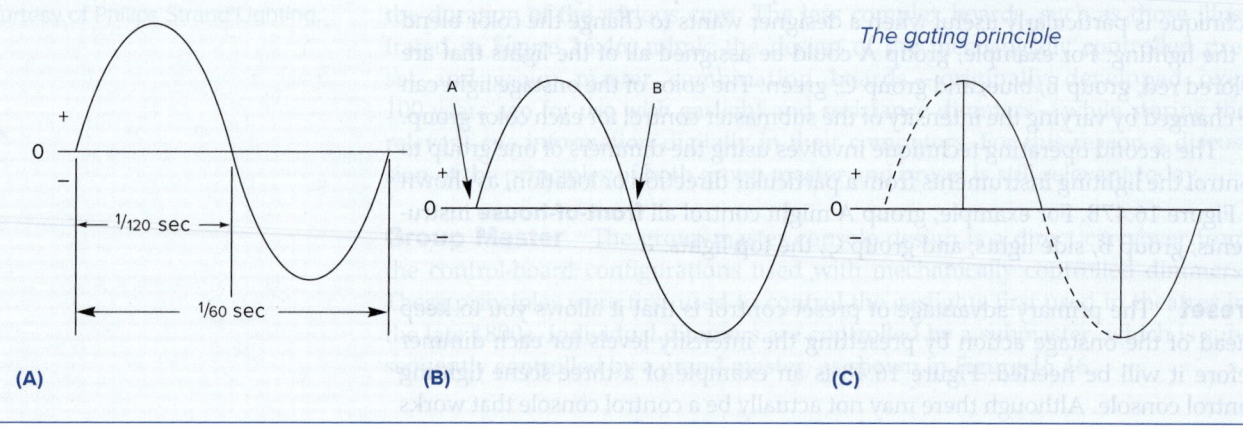

(A)   (B)   (C)

cue is called, the operator cross-fades between faders B and A, which results in activation of the dimmer intensity levels associated with Preset Scene III.

To preset the intensity levels for the fourth cue, the operator presets the appropriate intensity levels on Preset Scene I as soon as he or she has cross-faded into the second cue. To run the remaining cues in the show, the operator repeats the process of presetting intensity levels on open, or nonactive, preset scenes as often as necessary. Many preset control consoles have mechanically or electronically interlocked faders, so when either fader A or B fades up, the other fader automatically dims down.

A fusion of the principles of preset and group-master control provides an extremely flexible lighting-control system. The relatively simple consoles shown in Figure 16.49 combine the principles of preset and group master control without too many additional bells and whistles. The advanced computer boards that

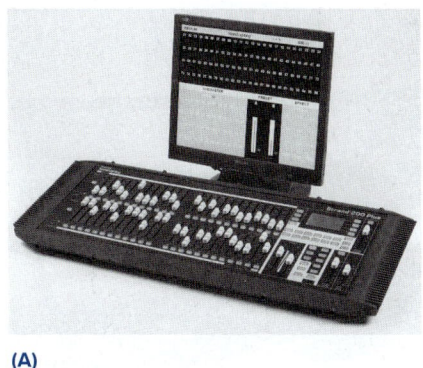

(A)

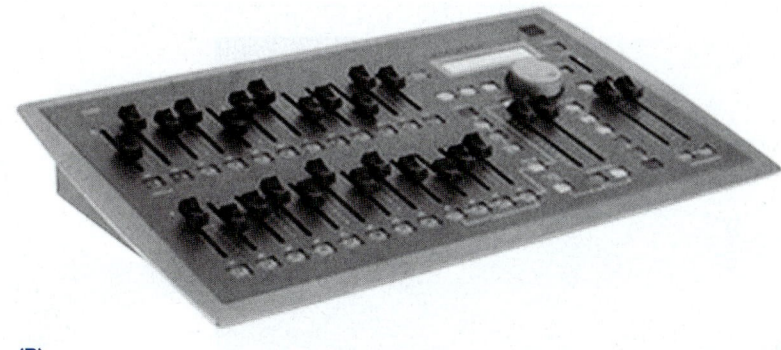

(B)

FIGURE 16.49
Combination boards. (A) Strand 200 plus 24/48 console. (B) ETC SmartFade ® Lighting control console. Courtesy of Philips Strand Lighting and ETC (Electronic Theatre Controls, Inc.).

will be discussed a little later use not only preset and group master principles but have a plethora of other features as well.

Wireless Dimmer Control

The dimming control techniques discussed up to this point all require that a control cable — over which the control signals are sent — be connected from the control console to the dimmer. Wireless dimmers don't require this control cable because the digital control information is sent to the dimmer by radio. For example, to speed up the process of equipment setup and strike, many touring productions are now using wireless control instead of cabling to connect control consoles and dimmer packs.

Some wireless dimming systems use self-contained, battery-powered, component units small enough to be placed inside portable props or, in some cases, hidden in costumes. They are used in special situations such as portable torches or similar situations where a power cord trailing from the prop or costume as it moves around the stage would create physical and/or aesthetic hazards.

The wireless dimmer's control signal typically originates at the theatre's "regular" lighting console. The signal is sent from that console to a wireless transmitter. Because the transmission distance between most of these wireless transmitters and their receivers can be somewhat limited, the transmitter is generally hidden either onstage or placed in the wings in close proximity to the stage. Each battery-powered wireless dimmer has a miniaturized receiver associated with it. The receiver gets the "radioed" control information and uses that to control the dimmer output. The dimmer then operates whatever device is connected to it.

Computer Memory

All contemporary light boards — computer boards — function in fundamentally the same way: a computer electronically stores the intensity levels of all dimmers for each cue. Even the most basic computer boards have a minimum of about 300 memories for cue storage. More expensive boards (Figure 16.50) may have sufficient storage capacity for up to five thousand or more cues. The latest generation of computer boards frequently can be used to control automated lighting fixtures in addition to nonmoving stage lights. Several manufacturers offer

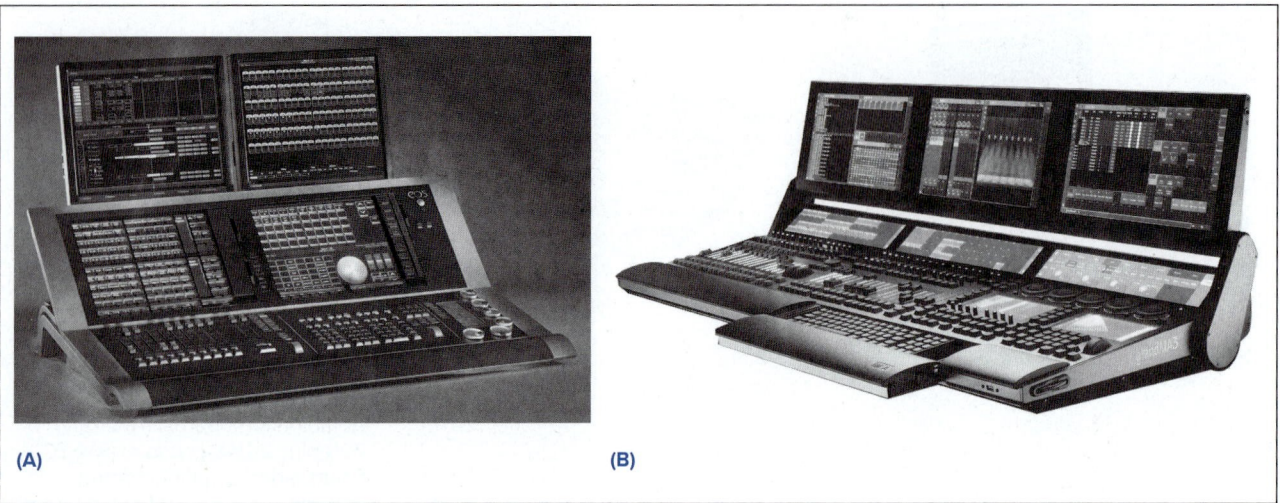

FIGURE 16.50
Computer boards. (A) The ETC Eos®
lighting control console. (B) The
granMA3 full size. A, Courtesy of
ETC (Electronic Theatre Controls,
Inc.). B, ©MA Lighting.

a Windows-based lighting control software program that is used with *your* PC.
You use your own PC with the company's software and output control devices to
control most existing electronic dimmers.

Because computers lose their memory when the power is turned off, these
systems may have an internal battery backup that provides enough power so
that the system can retain its memory for a reasonable length of time. This
period varies from several hours to several weeks, depending on the model and
manufacturer.

Because of **volatility** almost all computer boards have some method of storing the cuing and programming information. Most boards store cueing information on a hard drive built into the console. While even the smallest-capacity hard
drive will store all the cues for just about any show, it is vital to back up the hard
disk in case it **crashes.** The current generation of lighting consoles use USB
flash drives for backup. Prior generations used 3½-inch floppy disks and other
now-obsolete storage media.

Regardless of whether a lighting console uses a hard drive or removable
storage for its primary memory, be sure to make backup copies of all show files.
Most designers believe that running the backup at the end of each rehearsal or
board session provides adequate protection.

Computer Board Control Capabilities

All computer boards have control capabilities that duplicate those of preset systems. But what makes computer control so dynamic is that these boards have
numerous capabilities that simply cannot be duplicated by preset or any other
extant control systems.

As previously explained, analog control systems require that a pair of wires
be connected directly from each dimmer to a potentiometer, or "pot," on the
control console. In these systems increasing or decreasing the level of a specific
dimmer's control pot determines the intensity of any instruments connected to
that dimmer. In a digitally controlled system, a single set of control wires runs
between the control board and all of the dimmers. The control circuit of each
dimmer is wired in parallel with every other dimmer, and that single set of control wires runs from the dimmer racks to the digital control board. Information

volatility: Nonpermanence; in
computers, a volatile memory will be
lost if the computer loses its power
supply.

crash: In reference to hard drives, to
become inoperative. Data normally
cannot be retrieved from a hard
drive that has "crashed."

about intensity levels is distributed to all dimmers simultaneously, with the individual dimmers reacting only to information that is addressed specifically to them.

The digital control method just described allows much greater control flexibility than previous systems. To facilitate this flexibility, almost all computer boards employ an electronic patching system, generally referred to as **soft patch.** To set the level of a dimmer, you assign it to a control channel then adjust the channel level to the desired setting. Soft patch allows you to assign any number of dimmers — from one to all the dimmers in your system — to one particular channel. In practical application there are two primary techniques used with channel control — one dimmer per channel and ganged dimmers per channel. The one-dimmer-per-channel approach lets you adjust each dimmer, and the instruments connected to it, individually. The ganged-dimmers-per-channel approach involves assigning the dimmers — for example, the six dimmers controlling the blue lights on the cyc — to a single control channel. Another way of controlling the blue cyc lights would be to assign the channels controlling each of the "blue light dimmers" to a **group.** The intensity levels of the lights assigned to the individual dimmer channels can be adjusted so the blue wash can be balanced as desired, and then the group is used to raise or lower the intensity of the lights without changing the balance.

soft patch: An electronic patching system in which one or more dimmers can be assigned to a control channel, which in turn controls the intensity level of those dimmers.

group: The grouping of two or more dimmers/channels under one controller.

PRODUCTION INSIGHTS

Computer Boards: A Comparison of Features

Smaller Systems

1. memory for up to several hundred cues

2. capability of controlling 100–150 dimmers

3. maximum of one video screen for displaying various system functions

4. a timed fader

5. some type of group or submaster control

6. control of dimmer intensity by individual sliders

7. keypad for addressing memory and functions

8. limited backup system in case of main-computer malfunction

These smaller, less expensive systems work well in theatres that have modest production demands.

Larger Systems

1. memory for approximately 10,000 cues

2. control of up to 10,000 addresses/dimmers

3. expanded functions

   A. two or more video screens, some of which may be touchscreens, to display more functions simultaneously

   B. advanced backup systems

   C. sophisticated group or submastering

   D. more control functions to permit simultaneous cues at different fade rates

4. dimmer and other functions addressed through a keypad or touchscreen

5. remote capabilities

6. self-diagnostic program to identify malfunctioning component in case of breakdown

7. moving light control software and encoders

8. networking capabilities, both wired and wireless

These larger and more expensive systems work well in facilities that have extensive production programs.

fade-in: A gradual increase; in lighting, usually from darkness to a predetermined level of brightness. Synonymous with fade-up.

fade-out: A gradual decrease; in lighting, usually from a set level of brightness to darkness.

split time fade: A fade in which the fade-in and fade-out are accomplished at different rates or speeds.

delay: Refers to the time interval that the second part of a split time fade follows the first.

cueing: Designing the light cues. Manipulating, and recording, the distribution intensity, movement, and color of the lights for each cue to create the appropriate look for that moment in the play.

All computer boards have some type of timer or time-function capability. The timer is used to assign a fade time to a cue. For example, you could assign a time of 5 seconds to a cue so it takes 5 seconds to execute that particular cue, whether it is a **fade-in** or **fade-out.** Most boards facilitate **split time fades** that allow you to, in one action, fade out one cue in a given time while fading in the next cue at a different rate.[4] When executing a split time fade you frequently want to **delay** the start of the following cue. With this capability the designer can with one board action — pressing the "execute" or "go" button — execute a 15-second fade-out on a scene and, after an 8-second delay, begin a fade-in, (also known as a fade-up), of another cue with a completely different fade rate. Unfortunately, the terms used to describe various board actions — such as "delay," "follow," and "wait" — are not common throughout the industry. The manuals for each board will provide the terminology specific to each different board.

The capabilities outlined earlier provide the basic building blocks of creative lighting control for the designer. Many computer boards have additional capabilities that enhance the designer's ability to control and manipulate light. It is important to become familiar with the specific capabilities and functions of as many computer boards as possible, because an understanding of those capabilities of the equipment will inform the designer's approach to **cueing** the show.

Cables and Connectors

A flexible system of distributing electricity to lighting instruments is necessary, because the hanging position of the lights will be changed for each production. This section discusses the types of cables and connectors that make up this flexible distribution system, as well as several methods of circuiting, or connecting, the lighting instruments to the dimmers.

Electrical Cable for Stage Use

The National Electrical Code (NEC) stipulates that the only electrical cables approved for temporary stage wiring are types S, SO, ST, and STO. These cables have stranded copper conductors and are insulated with rubber (S and SO, shown in Figure 16.51) or thermoplastic (ST and STO). S and SO cables are more commonly used than ST and STO, because their thick rubber jacket can withstand more physical abuse than the thin, heat-resistant thermoplastic insulation of the ST and STO cable. Type S cable is generally used for stage lighting, because SO costs more and its only advantage is that it is impervious to oil and gasoline.

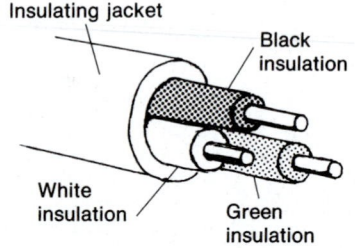

Insulating jacket
Black insulation
White insulation
Green insulation

FIGURE 16.51
An electrical wire.

Wire Gauge

The American Wire Gauge (AWG) system rates wire according to the amount of current that a conductor of a particular size and composition can safely carry. The rated current capacity for any given gauge should never be exceeded. Most cables have the gauge and wire type imprinted every foot or so on the insulating jacket.

---

[4] Split time fades technically separate the times of the channels increasing in intensity from those decreasing in intensity. But the visual results described are the same.

(B) (C)

(A)

(D)

FIGURE 16.52
Typical electrical connectors used in the theatre. (A) A twist-lock; (B) grounded pin connector; (C) Lex powerCON extension cable utilizing Neutrik powerCON 20 amp connectors (D) grounded parallel blade (Edison) connector. Photos A, B, and D, Courtesy of J. Michael Gillette, and (C) courtesy of Lex Products.

The amount of current that can be safely carried varies greatly, as we saw in Table 15.1 in Chapter 15, "Electrical Theory and Practice." There is no standard size of cable for theatre use, because load requirements differ from one theatre to another. However, the NEC stipulates that receptacles used to supply incandescent lamps on stage must be rated at not less than 20 amperes and must be supplied by wires of not less than 12 gauge. Practical or decorative lamps are the only exception to this rule. These lamps may be wired with cable of smaller capacity as long as the lamp load doesn't exceed the rated capacity of the cable. This means that you can use 18-gauge wire (also known as lamp or zip cord) as long as the lamp load doesn't exceed 360 watts (assuming the system voltage is 120 volts: $W = VA$; $360 = 120 \times 3$).

Safety Tip

Cable and Connector Maintenance

The following steps are suggested to keep cables and connectors in good operating condition and in compliance with NEC and federal regulations.

1. When a cable is not in use, coil it and hang it on the wall of the lighting storage room. The cable will stay neatly coiled if the connectors are plugged together or if it is tied with heavy twine or narrow rope.

2. Check cables and connectors periodically, and replace any items that show signs of cracking, chipping, or other deterioration. Cracks in the insulation of cables and connectors increase the chances of someone's receiving a shock from the device. Also, dust can accumulate in the crack and may cause an electrical fire.

3. Always disconnect a plug by pulling on the body of the connector, not the cable. Pulling on the cable puts an unnecessary strain on the cable clamp and will eventually defeat the clamp. When the cable clamp no longer functions, pulling on the cable places the strain directly on the electrical connections.

4. Keep the connectors clean. Remove any corrosion, paint, grease, or other accumulations as soon as they become evident. These substances can act as insulation between the contacts of the connector and, if flammable, pose a fire hazard.

5. All elements of a cable should be of the same electrical rating; for example, 12-gauge (AWG) cable (capable of carrying 20 amperes of current) should have only 20-ampere-rated connectors, and so forth.

Cable storage.

(A)

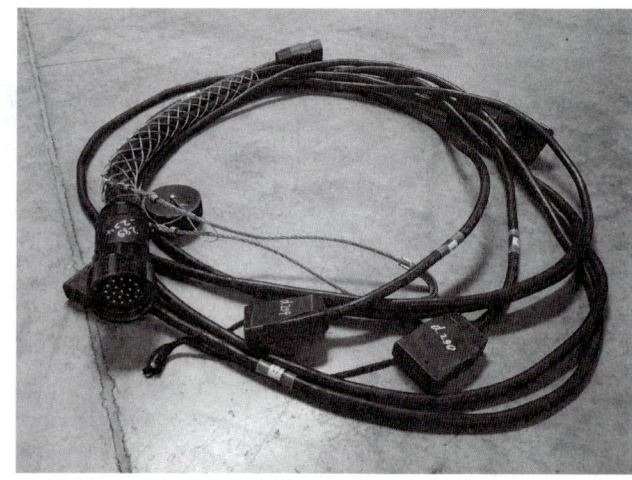

(B)

FIGURE 16.55
Multicables. (A) A typical multicable. (B) A multicable break-out. See text for details. A and B, Courtesy Michael McNamara.

multicable: A cable with typically six "two-conductor-with-ground" circuits enclosed in a single outer jacket. One end terminates in a male Socapex connector, the other in a female Socapex connector.

Socapex connector: A 19-pin connector used with multicables. Typically has six hot pins, six neutral pins, six ground pins, and one left open. Used to create the six electrically isolated circuits found in multicables.

breakout: Device used to connect multicables to lighting fixtures. One end terminates in a male Socapex connector, the other in, typically, one female twist-lock or stage pin receptacle per circuit in the breakout.

breakin: Device used to connect dimmers to multicables. One end terminates in a female Socapex connector, the other in a male plug per circuit, with each plug being compatible with the output receptacles on the dimmer packs.

load-in: The moving of scenery and associated equipment into the theatre and their positioning (setup) on the stage.

load-out: The removal of scenery and associated equipment from the theatre. Term usually used when transferring scenery/equipment to another venue or facility. Not used when referring to the striking of the set/equipment at the end of a production run.

connecting strip: Electrical gutter or wireway that carries a number of stage circuits; the circuits terminate in female receptacles.

auditoriums, music halls, and other facilities where the lighting installation has been guided by criteria other than the needs and requirements of the creative use of designed light.

Spidering and Multicables

Spidering, also known as direct cabling, originally involved running a cable from each lighting instrument or group of instruments directly to the dimmer to which it is assigned. It got its name from the tangled web of cables created by circuiting a production in this manner.

Much of the untidy appearance of spidering can be reduced through the use of **multicables**. A typical multicable (Figure 16.55A) is composed of six separate "two-conductor-with-ground" circuits enclosed in a single jacket. A **Socapex connector** is attached to each end of the multicable — male on one end, female on the other. The nineteen-pin Socapex connector allows the six grounded circuits inside the multicable to remain electrically isolated from each other. Typically, several multicables are strung together to reach from wherever the dimmers are located to a position close to where the fixtures are hanging.

Breakouts (Figure 16.55B) are used at the onstage end of the multicable to connect to the lighting fixtures. From the breakout, standard cabling is used to connect to the individual lighting fixtures. **Breakins** are used to connect the dimmers to the multicable.

Multicables can greatly speed up the time required for **load-in** and **load-out**. Multicabling is typically used in those situations where there are no permanent circuiting options, such as theatres with no permanent lighting system, or for road shows or concert productions that want the lighting to retain the same look as the show moves from venue to venue.

Distribution Systems

An electrical distribution system that utilizes **connecting strips** and multicables creates two advantages for theatres with extensive production programs: (1) The light plot can be hung and circuited quite rapidly, and (2) the system provides a great deal of flexibility.

In most contemporary theatres, the majority of stage circuits are contained in connecting strips, illustrated in Figure 16.56. The connecting strips are distributed

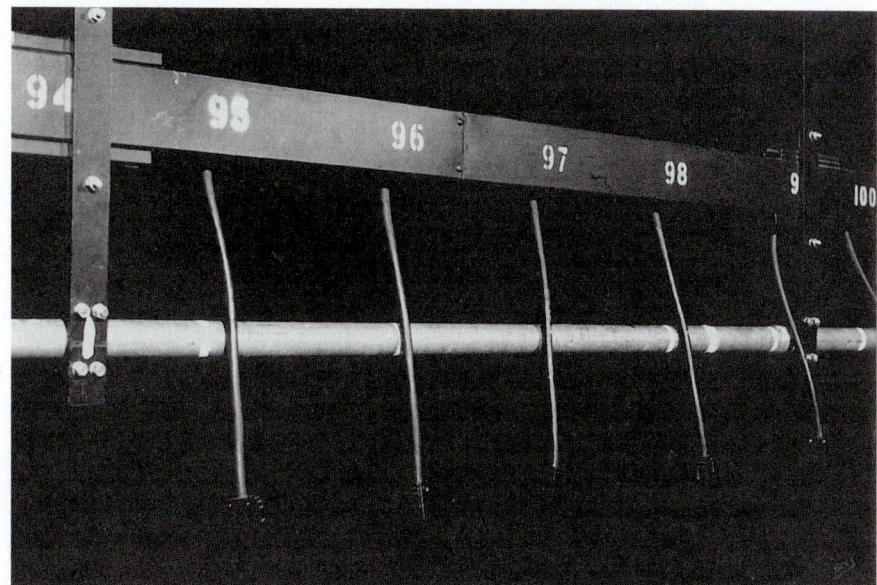

FIGURE 16.56
A connecting strip. Courtesy of
J. Michael Gillette.

FIGURE 16.57
(A) Drop box; (B) floor pocket;
(C) wall pocket. A–C, Courtesy of
J. Michael Gillette.

(A)

(B)

(C)

in a variety of positions about the stage and auditorium — counterweighted battens over the stage; various front-of-house positions (ante-proscenium cuts or slots, coves, boxes); and various locations on the walls of the stage house. This function — placing outlets in various locations throughout the theatre — can also be accomplished with multicables. But regardless of whether connecting strips or multicables are used to reach a specific location, each circuit output is a receptacle usually mounted at the end of a 2- to 3-foot pigtail, although connecting strip receptacles are sometimes flush-mounted on the gutter itself.

Additional stage circuit are often contained in **drop boxes, floor pockets**, and **wall pockets** (Figure 16.57). Drop boxes (Figure 16.57A) are small connecting strips fed by cables that are attached to the grid above the stage. They usually contain four to eight circuits and are equipped with one or two pipe clamps so that they can be easily attached to pipes or booms. Floor and wall pockets (Figures 16.57B and C) are recessed into the floor or wall and typically contain three to six circuits.

All of the circuits contained in connecting strips, drop boxes, and floor or wall pockets have certain properties in common. Each circuit is basically a long extension cable that, at the stage end, terminates in a female receptacle. The offstage end of each circuit terminates in a variety of locations depending on the type of system being used.

drop box: A small connecting strip, containing four to eight circuits, that can be clamped to a pipe or boom.

floor pocket: A connecting box, usually containing three to six circuits, the top of which is mounted flush with the stage floor.

wall pocket: A connecting box similar to a floor pocket but mounted on the wall.

In the dimmer-per-circuit system, which is standard in modern theatrical lighting, the electrical flow runs straight from the dimmers to the individual stage circuit outlets. The onstage end of each circuit terminates at an outlet on a connecting strip, floor pocket, or similar location. The other end of the circuit is directly wired to a dimmer.

In most theatres, a variety of methods are used to connect the dimmers to the fixtures. It all depends on the individual situation. For example, a theatre may have an extant dimmer-per-circuit system, but for a particular show, the lighting designer wants to put fixtures in a location that doesn't have any available circuits. In that case, multicables are run to the fixture locations from either the dimmer mainframe or portable dimmer packs. In those situations, all the dimmers — both mainframe and dimmer packs — are typically controlled by one computer console.

In some older venues, the onstage circuits may still terminate at a patch panel. Patch panels and connecting strips were the standard until the early 1990s. The patch panel, although archaic, is not obsolete. For this reason, it is still included in this textbook, but that material has been moved to Appendix D.

Computer boards make controlling a large number of dimmers easy. This is a major reason that some form of dimmer-per-circuit distribution system with computer control is the most common lighting system used in theatrical lighting.

Selected References

Bellman, Willard F. *Lighting the Stage: Art and Practice.* Harper & Row, 1974.
Gillette, J. Michael. *Designing with Light.* Mayfield Publishing, 4th ed., 2003.
Parker, W. Oren, Harvey K. Smith, and R. Craig Wolf. *Scene Design and Stage Lighting.* Holt, Rinehart and Winston, 6th ed., 1990.

Chapter 17

Projections and Media

(This chapter has been extensively updated thanks to significant input from Jake Pinholster, a professional projection specialist/media designer and educator. The author wishes to publicly thank him for his knowledge and expertise on this subject and for his contributions to this chapter.)

Projections can significantly enhance the visual texture of the stage picture. They can provide seemingly unlimited depth or create an aura of surrealism as one image dissolves into another. They can replace or complement the other visual elements of the setting or they can provide a visual accent.

Projections have become an integral part of many works simply because contemporary playwrights are using an increasing number of cinematic devices and writing styles in their works. Once-radical playwrighting concepts such as quick cutting between locations or video sequences integrated into the script are not that unusual. Projections can solve many of these design and staging challenges.

However, projections aren't a universal panacea. They are just another tool the designer uses in the never-ending quest for a visually evocative expression of the production concept.

 ## Film-Based Media

Over the past 20 years film media — slides, film, and large-format projectors — have become almost completely obsolete. The manufacturing of film and slide projectors is almost nonexistent, and it is becoming increasingly difficult to find repair parts. Additionally, the increasing costs of both film and its processing, when coupled with a precipitous decline in the number of processing facilities, has basically meant the death of this once vibrant market segment.

Generally, the only exception to the use of film-based media projection are the PANI and PIGI **scenic projectors** (Figure 17.1). These high-output projectors have a very wide projection field that still makes them useful in support of opera. They are rarely used in other forms of theatre.

 ## Digital Projectors

Fortunately, digital projection has come to the rescue. Declining equipment costs and increasing ease of use of digital equipment, as well as the development of high-performance digital projectors and computer-based playback systems have made digital projection the standard in the field of projected media.

scenic projector: A high-wattage instrument used for projecting large-format slides or moving images.

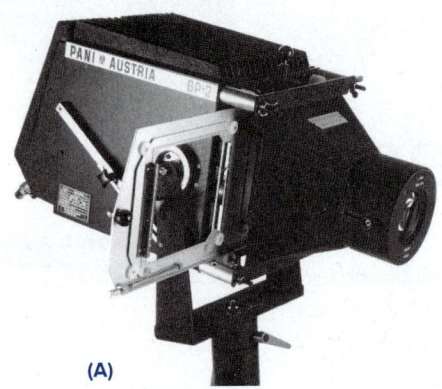

(A)

(B)

FIGURE 17.1
Scenic projectors are composed of the lamp housing, the optical train, and a slide. (A) © Pani Team (B) PIGI Projector, Photo courtesy of ETC (Electronic Theatre Controls, Inc.)

In many applications, the word *projection* is not totally applicable any more because concert tours, television events, and high-end theatrical productions are moving toward emissive surfaces like LED displays, which completely remove projectors from the process.

Anyone who has ever given a presentation using PowerPoint has some familiarity with digital projection. Digital projectors have made their way into classrooms, boardrooms, retail outlets, and many other venues in our daily lives. The heavy use of projectors for consumer and commercial use has led to huge drops in the price of these technologies.

There are two types of digital projectors appropriate for theatrical use: liquid crystal display (LCD) and digital light processors (DLP) projectors.

Liquid Crystal Display (LCD)

LCD was one of the first technologies developed for digital projection. Light from the lamp or lamps is separated into the primary colors (red, blue, green) with two successive **dichroic filters** as shown in Figure 17.2. Each color of light is focused onto panels filled with liquid crystal that responds to the electronic video signal by making some pixels in the panel opaque where the component colors are not present in the image. After passing through the panels, the light is recombined into a single image before being focused by the projection lens on the screen surface.

LCD projectors have the advantage of being extremely economical, but the technology has some drawbacks. The inherent nature of the LCD panels themselves gives the projectors poor color rendering, particularly of reds and oranges. The panels also yellow and fade over time, requiring expensive repairs. Despite these imperfections, LCD projectors are very popular for many applications, particularly offices, schools, and universities.

dichroic filter: A filter that passes a specifically selected wavelength of light and reflects all others. A red dichroic filter allows red light to pass but reflects all other wavelengths.

digital micromirror device (DMD): DMDs are optical semiconductors whose rectangular surface is typically covered with from several hundred thousand to several million micromirrors. The number of micromirrors corresponds with the number of pixels in the image display.

Digital Light Processor (DLP)

DLP projectors are relatively new, and are based on a proprietary technology called **digital micromirror devices** (DMDs) that, at the time of this writing, are the sole domain of Texas Instruments, Inc. (See the box, "Digital Micromirror Devices," for additional information.)

DMDs are similar to LCDs in that the light to be projected is divided into red, blue, and green (RBG) segments, but instead of being directed through individual LCD panels, the light is reflected off micromirrors. Tiny piezo electric

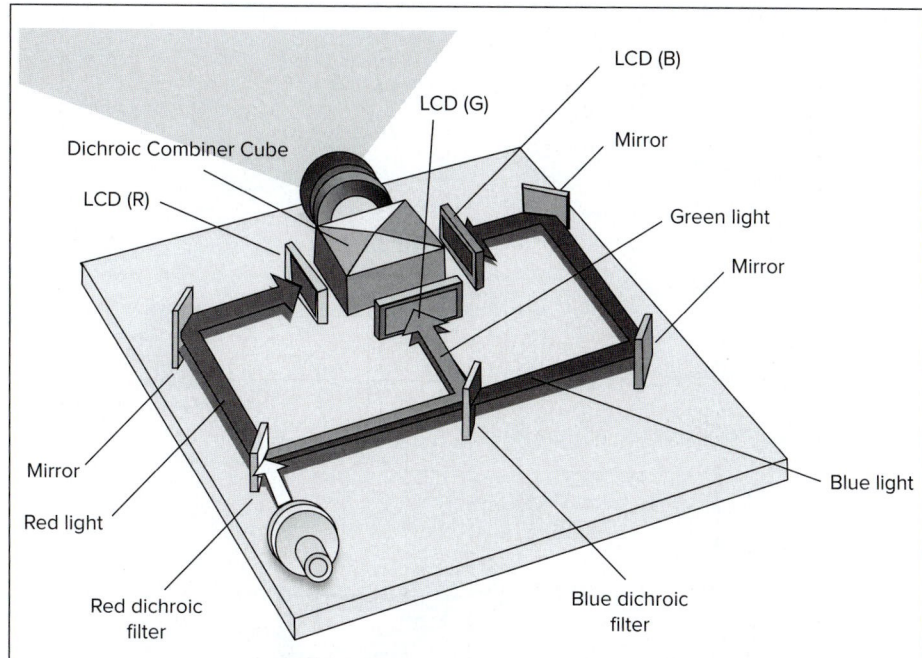

Dichroic Combiner Cube

LCD (G)

LCD (B)

LCD (R)

Mirror

Green light

Mirror

Mirror

Red light

Blue light

Red dichroic filter

Blue dichroic filter

FIGURE 17.2
Operating principles of an LCD projector.

filaments flip each tiny mirror "on" or "off" in time with the video signal for each individual pixel.

There are two models of the DLP projectors: single chip and three chip. The single-chip model uses a spinning color wheel with red, green, and blue divisions to split the light for processing by a single DMD.

The three-chip system is more robust. It is similar to LCDs in its use of a prism and **dichroic mirrors** to direct the component colors of light to three

PRODUCTION INSIGHTS
Digital Micromirror Devices (DMD)

Digital micromirror devices (DMDs) are optical semiconductors whose rectangular surface is typically covered with several hundred thousand micromirrors. The number of micromirrors in the DMD's array corresponds with the number of pixels in the image display.

In a three-chip digital light projector (DLP), the image to be projected is split into red, blue, and green light (RBG). Each of those three colors is directed at an individual DMD.

The hundreds of thousands of tiny aluminum mirrors on the surface of each DMD either reflect or redirect the light, depending on the micromirror's position. An electronic signal is used to tilt the mirrors 10 to 12 degrees to the side, effectively deflecting the light. When "upright," the mirrors reflect the light from the projector lamp through the lens onto the screen. When deflected, no light is sent to the screen. By rapidly switching the position of the mirror, the total intensity of reflected light in a given period of time can be controlled — using the gating principle discussed in the Production Insights box, "Gating Principle," on page 414 in Chapter 16, "Lighting Production." This rapid switching occurs at blazing speed. Manipulating the RBG proportions for each of the hundreds of thousands of pixels in the projected image is how both the image and its color are formed.

dichroic mirrors: A mirror that reflects a specifically selected wavelength of light and allows all others to pass through the mirror. A red dichroic mirror reflects red light and allows all other wavelengths to pass through it.

FIGURE 17.3
Operating principles of a DLP projector. A beam splitter redirects light toward a blue dichroic mirror (M1). Blue light is reflected to the D1 and the remaining light passes through the mirror. M2 reflects the red portion of the spectrum to D2 and passes the remaining light (green) to D3. Light from the 3 DMDs is recombined and sent through the lens to the screen.

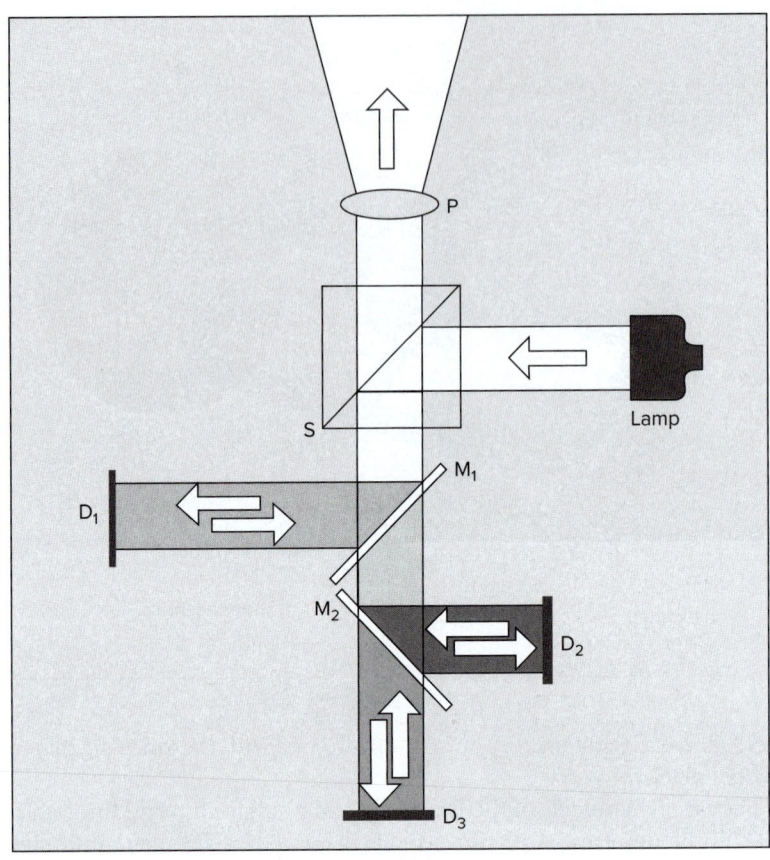

separate DMDs (Figure 17.3). The light reflected from the three DMDs is recombined and focused through the lens of the projector.

DLP projectors have excellent color rendering, project fast motion images well, and can last many years without fading or decay of the image. However, as of this writing, they are still extremely expensive in the more robust three-chip models that are the mainstays of the staging and rental projector markets. Very bright, very capable DLP projectors are still outside the range of most schools, universities, and regional theatres. This may change over the next several years.

Digital Projector Characteristics

The brightness projected by digital projectors is measured in **lumens.** There are various procedures for measuring the light output (**luminous flux**) of a projector. Interestingly, many manufacturers do not use the standardized procedure developed by the American National Standards Institute (ANSI). Even with the ANSI label, there is no guarantee that the projector will operate at the specified brightness outside the laboratory, because the age of the lamp, the age of the LCD panels (if applicable), and the type and range of the lens can greatly affect the brightness of the projector.

Zoom lenses are very popular for use with digital projectors because of their versatility, but due to the physics of light and lenses an appreciable percentage of the light is lost whenever the lens is at either end of its range (widest or narrowest). Other factors also influence apparent brightness: The lightness or

lumens: The unit measurement of light output.

luminous flux: The output of a light source. Measured in lumens.

darkness of the projection surface greatly affects the amount of light reflected from it; the level of **ambient lighting** can drown out or enhance the brightness of the projections; and even the lighting from the previous scene can affect the audience perception of the current imagery.

Because of the myriad factors affecting perceived brightness, the guidelines for determining projection brightness are rules of thumb at best.

When using a light gray projection surface in a situation with moderate ambient lighting, a reasonable brightness level would be 50 to 70 ANSI lumens per square foot measured at the screen. In a best-case scenario, this number would be more like 100 lumens per square foot. On the other hand, with a little creativity and juggling of the variables, a good designer can work with a brightness level of much less.

Contrast Ratios

The term *contrast ratio* refers to the difference between the lights and darks in a projected image. The manufacturers usually determine these ratios by measuring the brightness at both the edge and center of the image at full white and then full black and using those numbers to determine the ratio.

The important thing for designers to remember is that a good contrast ratio can be even more important than brightness: The quality of an image, particularly on a light surface, depends on the contrast inherent in the image. A poorquality projector with a low contrast ratio can spill light everywhere and prevent the subtleties of the design from being seen.

Resolution and Format

Due to the constant evolution of video technologies for both professional and consumer markets, there are many different formats and **resolutions** available for digital projectors. Table 17.1 lists a number of the most popular image

ambient lighting: Surrounding environmental light; light in the projection environment from sources other than the projector.

resolutions: A term defining the sharpness of a digital/video image; determined by the number of pixels used to create the image; the more pixels the sharper the image.

TABLE 17.1

Protocols for Commonly Used Image Formats

Code	Name	Aspect Ratio	Width in Pixels	Height in Pixels
XGA	eXtended Graphics Array	4:3	1024	768
XGA+	eXtended Graphics Array Plus	4:3	1152	864
WXGA	Widescreen eXtended Graphics Array	16:9	1280	720
WXGA	Widescreen eXtended Graphics Array	16:10	1280	800
SXGA (UVGA)	Super eXtended Graphics Array	4:3	1280	960
SXGA	Super eXtended Graphics Array	5:4	1280	1024
HD	High Definition	16:9	1360	768
HD	High Definition	16:9	1366	768
WXGA+	Widescreen eXtended Graphics Array Plus	16:10	1440	900
HD+	High Definition Plus	16:9	1600	900
UXGA	Ultra eXtended Graphics Array	4:3	1600	1200
WSXGA+	Widescreen Super eXtended Graphics Array Plus	16:10	1680	1050
FHD (Full HD)	Full High Definition	16:9	1920	1080
WUXGA	Widescreen Ultra eXtended Graphics Array	16:10	1920	1200
WQHD	Wide Quad High Definition	16:9	2560	1440

pixel: The smallest "picture unit" in a digital image. The actual size varies with the size of the image, but pixels are extremely small relative to image size.

throw distance: The distance from the projector to the screen.

screen diagonal: The diagonal dimension of a screen.

formats. Various manufacturers use one or more of the following variables to define image format: resolution, aspect ratio, and refresh rate.

Resolution Resolution is defined as the total number of **pixels** in the image. It is determined by multiplying the image width (in pixels) times the image height. For example, an image that is 2,500 pixels wide by 1,500 pixels high would have a resolution of 3,750,000 pixels, or 3.8 megapixels.

Aspect Ratio Aspect ratio is defined as the proportion of the width of the image compared with its height. The two most standardized aspect ratios are indicative of the two industries that are colliding in the modern projector market: 4:3 was the ratio of early television; 16:9 was a standard for film for a long time.

Refresh Rate Refresh rate is the number of times per second that the image is renewed with new information from the incoming video signal. This can also be thought of as frame rate, though the terminology *frame* is descended from film and is not a truly accurate depiction of the way video images are produced.

Image Size and Lenses

Digital projection lenses are identified by a number expressing the proportion of the **throw distance** to the **screen diagonal.** For example, a good medium-range, fixed-focal-length lens would be identified by the number "1.8:1" printed on the lens barrel. Similarly, a medium-range zoom lens might be identified by the numbers "1.5-2.3:1." These numbers mean that a projector using this zoom lens can be placed anywhere between 1.5 and 2.3 times the screen diagonal away from the projection surface and still project an image of the desired size. For instance, if the screen diagonal is 10 feet, a projector with a 1.5-2.3:1 lens could be located anywhere between 15 and 23 feet away from the screen, and the image could be adjusted to fit on the screen.

Most projector manufacturers provide lens calculation tools for their products either on their website or make them available as downloadable programs. There are available aftermarket tools, including several apps for smartphones, that will do lens calculations for you. However, it is helpful to know how to do lens calculations manually.

Three variables are used to determine the proper lens for any given projection situation: the planned image size, the projector's throw distance from the projection surface, and the capabilities of the lens being used. If you know two of those variables, you can find the third. Most of the time you will know the size of the screen image you want to project. The critical dimension in terms of screen size is the screen diagonal.

The length of the screen diagonal can be calculated. If you think of the height and width of the desired screen size as the two legs of the triangle, Pythagoras' theorem ($A^2 + B^2 = C^2$) can be used to find the length of the hypotenuse (the screen diagonal), as illustrated in Figure 17.4.

To find the appropriate lens to use for a 9 × 12 foot screen when the projector is 27 feet from the screen, first determine the diagonal dimension of the screen, (the screen diagonal), by plugging the two known variables into the equation:

$$A^2 + B^2 = C^2$$
$$9^2 + 12^2 = C^2$$
$$81 + 144 = C^2$$
$$\sqrt{225} = C^2$$
$$15 = C$$

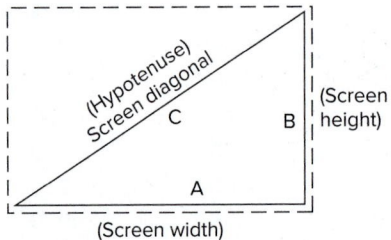

FIGURE 17.4
A method for determining the length of the screen diagonal. See text for details.

The screen diagonal for the 9 × 12 screen is 15 feet.

To find the lens proportion needed to project the desired image size, divide the throw distance by the screen diagonal.

Lens proportion = Throw distance ÷ Screen diagonal

Lens proportion = 27/15

Lens proportion = 1.8

The correct lens would be to either select a fixed-focal-length lens with a 1.8:1 proportion, or a zoom lens whose range brackets the calculated 1.8 lens proportion.

By algebraically manipulating the formula and inserting a known lens proportion, you can calculate the throw distance required to project an image of specific size.

Throw distance = Screen diagonal × Lens proportion

Throw distance = 15 × 1.8

Throw distance = 27 feet

It is important to keep in mind that most projectors have an aspect ratio that is either 4:3 or 16:9. If your desired image size is not in those proportions, then this proportion will define the limiting dimension. For example, if your desired image size is 9 feet × 10 feet, then the closest appropriate image size at a 4:3 aspect ratio is 9 feet × 12 feet.

When renting projection equipment, the size of the image you want to project is generally known, as is the throw distance. In those cases, most rental houses will have a range of lenses available for high-end projectors that will work for your design parameters.

Projection designers for lower-budget producing organizations will also know the size of the image they want to project, but their available projectors either don't have interchangeable lenses or the purchase or rental of multiple lenses is outside the budget. In those situations, lens calculations must essentially be reverse engineered to find the ideal placement position for the projector.

Additional Functions and Concerns

Digital projector specifications can be loaded with a great many confusing metrics and features. However, beyond the characteristics discussed earlier, there are only a few projector characteristics that are important.

Noise   Digital projectors make noise. Current technology requires the use of internally mounted fans to cool the high-brightness lamps used to produce the image. As when trying to accurately determine image brightness, there is a high degree of manufacturer and situational variability in how noise level is measured and how it will affect the acoustic environment of the room. However, when comparing projectors in the same range of brightness and resolution, it can be an important determining factor, particularly if the production is a quiet drama, musical, or opera where the level of background noise in the room can be particularly important. The position of the projector can also be very important in this equation. If the projector position can be somehow "sound masked" from the audience, then the noise can be reduced. If the projector is being used in a rear projection scheme, noise is usually a non-issue.

Control   Most current digital projectors can be controlled remotely via either serial control or network control.

native: In this context the term refers to the control protocol originally installed on an electronic device (e.g., digital projector, lighting control board, and so forth) by the manufacturer.

Serial control protocols such as DMX512, RS232, and RS422 are all used to control digital projectors. RS232 and RS422 are typically used in business applications. DMX512 — the protocol standard for theatrical light boards — is used in many projection setups when the projection equipment is going to be controlled through the light board. However, very few projector models are equipped with **native** DMX512 control. Using a lighting console to control these projectors requires a console capable of RS232 output or an accessory that can translate between protocols.

Network control is relatively new, but comparatively simple. Each projector is assigned an IP (Internet protocol) address and plugged into a network. With this setup, controlling a projector is as simple as plugging the projector's IP address into a browser on a computer connected to the same network and bringing up the Web page with embedded control of zoom, focus, shutters, and so forth, for the projector.

Shutters and Dowsers   With the current state of video technology, all digital projectors are incapable of rendering a completely black image without the use of a dowser. As long as the projector is turned on, it will project a dim light, even when projecting a completely black image or empty signal. This is particularly problematic when there is a blackout onstage. A dim rectangle of light will still be clearly visible on the stage. This phenomenon is known as "video black" or sometimes "video gray," and it is a frequent problem for projection designers.

Many manufacturers install mechanical dowsers or shutters inside the projector's housing. Most are simply mechanical flaps driven by servomotors into the beam of light. A few manufacturers (notably, Barco) have begun making their dowsers more useful for theatrical applications by making them capable of producing smoothly timed fades between full brightness and total darkness. A few models have even added direct control via DMX512 connections on the projectors themselves.

 ## Projection Surfaces

One of the most common misconceptions about working with digital projections in the theatre is that "screens" will always be a part of the equation. It is more useful to think of the projected image as a cone or pyramid of light that intersects the stage. Any surface that the projected image strikes becomes a small "screen" that reflects the projections.

Actors' bodies, painted scenery, dust motes, smoke, and fog can all been used as projection surfaces. However, they don't work nearly so well as scenic elements specifically designed for use as projection screens. There are two basic types of screen materials: front and rear.

Front-Screen Materials

Front-screen projection materials are those surfaces that are designed to reflect light. The best front-projection materials are slide or movie screens. They are white and highly reflective, and the surface is often designed to focus the reflected light in a specific angular pattern. However, unless you want a large white screen sitting onstage, it is essential that the screen be lit with either a projection or color wash at all times.

A smooth, white, painted surface (muslin, hardboard, and the like) provides a low-cost alternative to the commercial projection screen. Although the

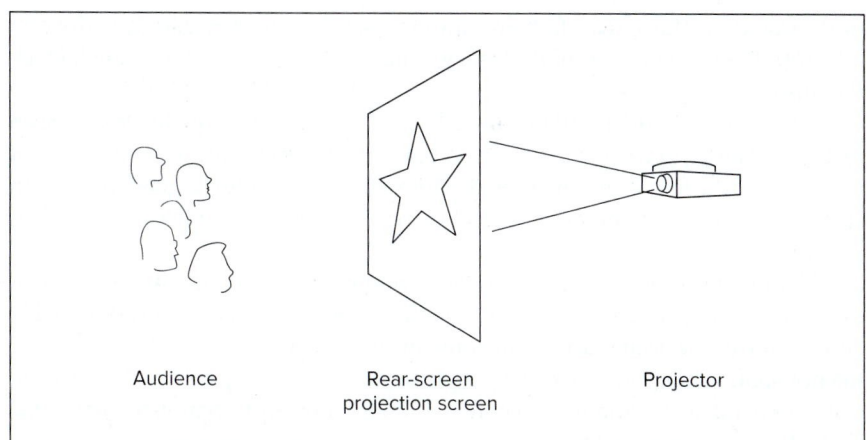

FIGURE 17.5
A typical rear-screen projection setup.

Audience   Rear-screen   Projector
                projection screen

reflected image won't be so crisp as that from the projection screen, it will be more than adequate for most theatrical purposes. When the projections or color washes are turned off, however, the challenge of what to do with the "great white blob" continues. Unless you are planning on using continuous projections or removing the screen from the set, it is frequently desirable to have the projection screen blend into the surrounding scenic elements until it is time to use it. In these cases, the surfaces of the set itself can be used instead of a projection screen. When you are projecting on scenery, the sharpness and brightness of the reflected image will be directly related to the hue, value, and texture of the paint used on the scenery.

Rear-Screen Materials

A major challenge of front-screen projection — actor shadows on the projection surface — is eliminated with the use of rear-screen projection. In this technique, illustrated in Figure 17.5, the projector is placed behind the screen, and the image is transmitted through the screen to the audience.

A significant challenge of rear-screen projection is created by the hot spot. If the projector is located within the audience's sight, the audience will see a small, intensely bright circle of light caused by actually seeing the projector lens through the screen material, as illustrated in Figure 17.6. The hot spot can be eliminated in one of two ways. You can position the projector so that the hot spot is out of the audience's sight line, or you can use a screen material that eliminates the hot spot.

Commercial rear-screen materials transmit clear, crisp images while diffusing or eliminating the hot spot. Rosco Labs produces several types of reasonably priced flexible plastic rear-screen materials in rolls 55 inches wide. Wider screens, with invisible seams, can be made by butting strips of the material edge to edge and taping the joints with No. 200 Scotch transparent plastic tape. Unless the atmosphere is of low humidity, however, the tape seams are only a temporary solution. Heat welding of the seams will provide a permanent bond.

If the projector can be placed in a position that will eliminate the hot spot, a variety of translucent materials can be used to receive the projected image. Scenic muslin and other fabrics of similar weight and weave transmit light quite well. The muslin[1] can be painted with dye — *not* paint — if it is necessary

FIGURE 17.6
A hot spot, caused by seeing the lens of the projector through the screen, will result unless special rear-screen projection material is used. Courtesy of J. Michael Gillette.

[1] Muslin will transmit a crisper image if it is primed with a starch solution of one cup of starch per gallon of hot water.

or desirable for the screen to blend into the set. Dye is transparent and won't interrupt the transmission of the image, whereas paint is opaque and will block the image.

Nylon tricot, sold in 108-inch widths, also provides a quality rear-screen material. The nylon can be stretched tight to eliminate any wrinkles, and if painted with a few coats of diluted white glue it provides a good projection surface that transmits more light, and therefore a more "readable" image, than muslin.[2]

Plain white shower curtains provide another effective, low-cost rear-screen material. The plastic transmits light well, the larger-sized shower curtains are big enough for many scenic uses, and some of the shower curtains actually diffuse the hot spot. White (not clear) polyethylene plastic sheeting, sold as plastic drop cloths in paint stores and home centers, is another effective rear-screen material (if the hotspot can be hidden).

Reflective Characteristics of Screen Materials

Surfaces with low saturation, high value, and little texture generally provide the best reflective surfaces for projected images. However, the materials and techniques used to finish surfaces on which projections are going to be shown create differing reflective characteristics. The following are guidelines to help in the process of creating effective projection surfaces.

- **Surfaces cannot reflect colors they do not contain.** This is a simple operation of the physics of light and color. A deep red curtain will not properly display an image of deep green trees because the red cloth will absorb the green light from the projection. (See the discussion of color mixing in light in Chapter 6, "Color.") In almost all instances, neutrally colored, non-saturated surfaces make the best projection surfaces.

- **Light transmitted or absorbed is light not reflected.** By definition, dark surfaces absorb more light that light surfaces. However, darker surfaces give an excellent image quality in terms of contrast, but the projector lamp must be very bright to yield an acceptable level of image brightness. Projections on black velvet curtains can look fantastic — almost supernaturally vibrant. But to be visible, the projected light must be at least 300 lumens per square foot or more at the surface, which requires an extremely bright projector. Similarly, the use of semi-transparent or translucent fabrics or plastics can achieve handsome effects, but the light passing through those materials is light not reflected to the audience, so again, the projector lamp must be substantially brighter than if the image was being reflected from a solid-material screen. A caveat: Beware of light passing through translucent screen materials. It may light things behind the screens that should remain hidden from the audience.

- **The texture of the surface becomes the nature of the image.** Textiles with heavy, visible weaves impart their texture to the image, sometimes resulting in problematic moiré effects when interference occurs between patterns on the surface and the grid of pixels in the image. Highly polished, mirror-like surfaces reflect imagery with the same uneven glare and reflective qualities you see from those surfaces in bright sunlight. Finally, soft or fuzzy fabrics will soften the reflected light, preventing in-focus imagery from being properly represented.

---

[2] This method was suggested by Professor Richard Gamble at Florida Atlantic University.

Creative projection designers know that not all surfaces have to be manufactured. Some of the most effective and magical projections use unconventional surfaces as simple as painted scenery or as complex as amorphous surfaces like fog or water.

Experimentation and prototyping are the keys in these explorations. Projection designers and video artists have used many unusual materials to great effect: hanging fields of string, shaped costumes, foliage. Working with other designers to discover interesting opportunities to experiment with new surfaces can yield great rewards.

Keystoning

Keystoning refers to the wedge-shaped image created when a projector is pointed at a surface that is not perfectly perpendicular to the axis of projection. The term *keystoning* originated because the wedge-shaped image resembles a keystone — the wedge-shaped stone at the top of a stone arch.

With slide or film-based projectors, there are only two methods for correcting the image distortion: (1) Tilt the projection surface so it becomes perpendicular to the axis of the projected image or (2) compensate for the distortion in the artwork itself by introducing a distortion in the opposite direction. The first solution is often unfeasible. The second solution is extremely complex. Additionally, if the angular relationship between the projector and the surface changes, every piece of artwork will have to be redone.

Digital projection provides a number of simpler solutions for correcting keystoned images. Many digital projectors can internally correct for keystoning. The highest quality projectors compensate optically, by manipulating the lenses and mirrors within the unit. A more prevalent method is digital correction in which the projector's processing units correct for the keystoning before projecting the image. Some projector models even do these compensation calculations automatically through the use of onboard sensors and levels.

Because most digital projectors were not designed for theatrical use, the algorithms of their onboard keystone correction systems can't deal with the extreme angles frequently encountered in the theatre. The result is that the many of these projectors do not completely correct the keystoning. Fortunately, some playback software (covered in the next section) includes keystone correction features that can solve the challenging projection angles frequently encountered in theatre.

Projection Mapping

Projection mapping refers to a variety of techniques that allow media to be projected in non-rectangular patterns — to "break the tyranny of the white rectangle." These techniques allow designers to understand where every pixel of the projection image will fall so the imagery can be placed to intersect and interact with the projection surfaces in new and interesting ways.

The angles used in projection mapping frequently create severe keystoning and geometry correction issues. A number of playback software programs have been developed to combat these issues. Platforms such as Dataton Watchout, Figure 53's QLab, and the Hippotizer media server by Green Hippo have been developed specifically for the entertainment technology industry and deal with both keystone and geometry correction challenges.

Focus Grid

The simplest of these methods is referred to as the process of "shooting a focus grid." This method requires that the projector be placed in its production location and focused as intended for use during the performance. A computer is attached to the projector, set to the native resolution of the projector, and connected to feed images from its primary screen to the projector's output. This allows images created on the screen to be projected onto the stage.

Using a full screen grid in Adobe Photoshop or similar software, the designer can effectively "draw" a projected image onto the stage. This grid is stored in the computer and is used to make any necessary keystone/geometry corrections to the planned images.[3] This technique works well with flat surfaces and relatively simple shapes. To adapt imagery to more complex surfaces, more advanced techniques are used.

3-D Modeling

More complex geometries require more complex tools. It is possible to map projections to virtually any surface — to make them appear as a skin upon the **incident objects** — by using 3-D CAD models of the objects.

The artwork is applied as materials or textures to the surface of the virtual objects in a CAD program such as Autodesk Maya and then rendered from the perspective of a virtual camera placed in the same relative position in virtual space as the projectors will be relative to the objects in actual space. This technique is quite complex in execution, but the effects can be amazing, as the current popularity of architectural projection mapping festivals and events demonstrate.

As technologies evolve, some playback platforms are even beginning to incorporate this functionality into their systems, so that 3-D objects can be imported into the platforms and imagery mapped to them in real time.

 ## Playback

Digital projectors require digital imagery as content. Unlike with slides and other film-based projection media, the display — or "playback" — of digital imagery is not dependent on its format. Digital pictures produced by or scanned into a computer can be easily moved between systems and devices. This has led to a massive diversification of the methods and tools that can be used to control playback of imagery in theatrical production situations.

Slide-Based Digital Systems

Most people are already familiar with a slide-based digital system: Microsoft PowerPoint. All slide-based systems operate in a similar fashion: The space bar or mouse button is clicked, and the next image is displayed. However, as these programs have evolved and computers have become more powerful, their abilities have multiplied. Many are capable of producing slow, smooth fades; using

---

incident object: The object on which light is falling.

[3] A step-by-step tutorial for "shooting the focus grid" can be found at http://livedesignonline.com/gear/0811-projection-focus-grids/.

transparency; and incorporating video content. Apple's Keynote is a particularly powerful and flexible choice for production playback, but it is still unwieldy and hard to use when it is compared to other, more purpose-built systems.

Cue-Based Systems

Cue-based systems for video playback evolved out of systems used for digital sound playback, like SFX by StageResearch, Inc. (Figure 17.7). (Note that SFX is used to playback *sound* cues, not projection cues. But SFX is the programming model on which typical projection cue-based playback systems are based.)

In cue-based systems, the cues are normally maintained in a list that will be played in sequential order. When a cue is activated the digital image or video content plays at level settings that have been previously determined for each cue. These settings — such as fade times, opacity, playback speed, and so forth — are typically set by entering numerical values into dialog boxes for each of the cue's properties. Numerical control makes these systems very precise but somewhat non-intuitive to program. Very complex sequences of cues can be notoriously hard to program properly and efficiently. QLab software by Figure 53 (Figure 17.8) is a very adept and economical example of a cue-based playback system.

Timeline Systems

Timeline systems for video playback are very similar to the nonlinear editing systems used in video editing and for creating traditional animations.

Timeline systems operate on the principles of **keyframes** and **tweening,** where the designer/programmer sets the parameters of sequences with keyframes and the computer fills in the images between keyframes in a process called tweening. Tweening is used to create cues, whether they are fades, moves, changes in color, changes in scale, and so forth. One of the most popular and powerful examples of a timeline-based playback system is Watchout by Dataton (Figure 17.9).

keyframe: A point in time that marks the beginning or ending of an action. The intermediate action — the action between two key frames — is filled in frames referred to as "in-betweens." Used in traditional and computer animation.

tweening: The process of filling in the "in-between" images between two keyframes to give the appearance that the first image smoothly transitions into the second image. Accomplished with software programs in computer animation.

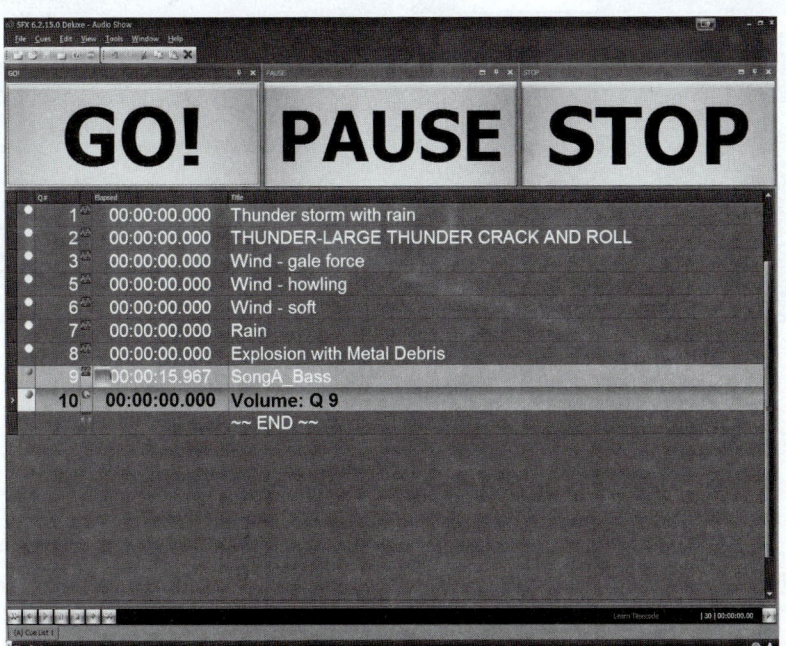

FIGURE 17.7
A screenshot of SFX *sound-cue* playback software. SFX is the program on which many cue-based *projection* playback programs are modeled. Courtesy of Stage Research, Inc.

FIGURE 17.8
A screenshot of QLab® 4 — a cue-based projection playback system based on the techniques developed for the SFX sound-cue playback program. Courtesy of Figure 53.

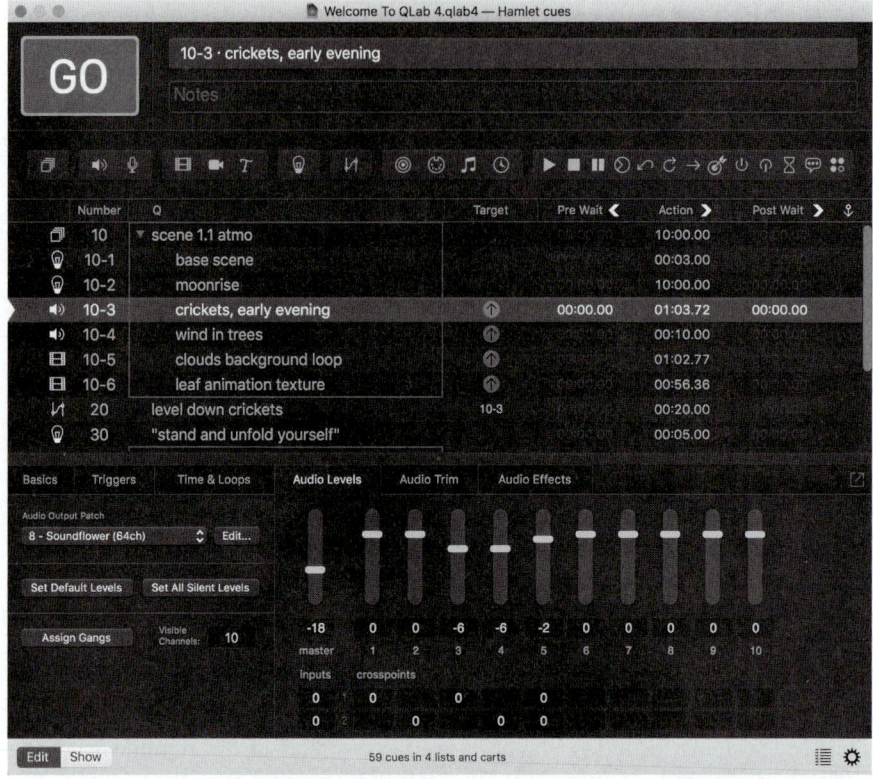

FIGURE 17.9
A screenshot of Watchout 6.1 — a timeline-based projection playback system. Courtesy of Dataton AB.

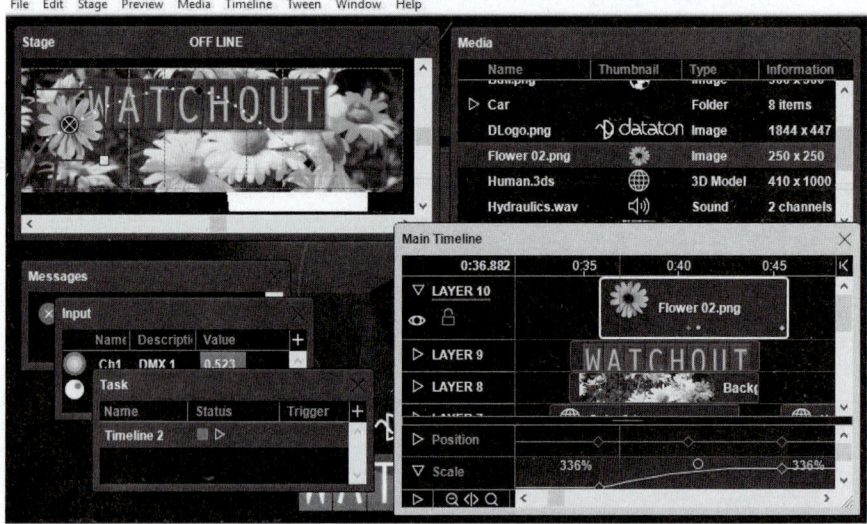

Media Servers

Media servers are video-processing computers used to feed animated images to high-powered, moving, digital projectors. The first media server was the Catalyst, developed for the concert and entertainment lighting industries by High End Systems. It was originally paired with an articulating mirror and turned a high-powered projector into a very fancy moving light. It used a moving light programming console to control layers and objects within its software as if they were automated luminaires, enabling DMX control of attributes such as opacity, scale, rotation, playback speed, and so forth.

All other media servers are based on these same operating principles. It rapidly became obvious that media servers were capable of much more sophistication, and products like Green Hippo's Hippotizer and Pandoras Box by coolux have added many more advanced features, including the ability to map imagery to 3-D objects or merge multiple projectors into a single image.

Display Technologies

The market for display technologies is constantly expanding and evolving — and that means more than just digital projection.

The consumer electronics market is continually driving the development of flat panel displays like HD LCD televisions and plasma displays. These have little use in most theatrical applications.

Of more interest to the entertainment industry is the development of large-format LED displays. Most of us are familiar with these LED "walls" or signs from their applications in commercial signage, awards shows, major concert tours, football stadiums, and basketball arenas. These giant, reconfigurable displays are constantly becoming both cheaper and more flexible. They are still largely out of the reach of most regional theatres and university theatre programs. However, they are an important part of the larger industry and, as such, it is worth a designer's time to become familiar with their particular attributes.

The Future

Other technologies are just being developed that could have a massive impact on the future of projections and media on the stage.

For example, a new type of LED, called an organic LED (OLED), has the potential to be developed into large-scale flexible displays that can be hung like fabric and configured into any shape.

Laser projection promises the possibility of projection without lenses and with true black (through an infinite contrast ratio). Laser images can be projected from almost any distance and from almost any projection angle.

Although the array of technologies available can be dizzying, it is an exciting time to be a projection/media designer.

Chapter 18

Costume Design

(This chapter has been updated thanks to the input of Patrick Holt, professional costume designer and educator. The author wishes to publicly thank him for his extensive knowledge and expertize on this subject and for his contributions to not only this chapter, but his work on Chapter 19, "Costume Construction," and Chapter 20, "Makeup," as well.)

There may be some truth to the adage that "clothes make the man." A study, summarized in the book *The Four Minute Sell,* by Janet Elsea, indicates that during the first four minutes of contact with a stranger our understanding of that person's nature and personality will be based on three primary, but unequal, factors: appearance, 55 percent; tone of voice, 38 percent; and what the person is saying, 7 percent.

Costume designers are aware of these factors, either intuitively or from training. They know that when an actor walks onto the stage for the first time, the audience's feelings about the character will be based, to a great extent, on the information that guides all first impressions.

What is a costume? According to Barbara and Cletus Anderson in their text *Costume Design,* "Anything worn onstage is a costume, whether it be layers of clothing or nothing at all."[1] More specifically, this definition includes all clothing, underclothing, hairdressing, and makeup, and accessories such as hats, scarves, fans, canes, umbrellas, and jewelry worn or carried by each character in a production. The design and appearance of all these costume elements is the province of the costume designer.

Most people agree that the costume worn by an actor profoundly affects the audience's perceptions of the character being created by that actor. If that assumption is correct, then it would logically follow that the costume designer's job entails the manipulation of the design of each character's clothing to project some specific personal information about that character and, if appropriate, to affect the physicality of the actor by inhibiting or limiting, in a manner appropriate to the characterization, the way an actor moves, speaks, stands, or sits on the stage. How the costume designer does that is the subject of this chapter.

 ## The Nature of Costume Design

In fashion design, primary attention is given to creating a striking visual design that gives little, if any, thought to the character or personality quirks of the individual person who ultimately will wear the clothes. While fashion designers

[1] Barbara and Cletus Anderson, *Costume Design* (New York: Holt, Rinehart, Winston, 1984), p. 20.

The Design Process in Costuming

This discussion applies the principles of the design process to costume design. A review of Chapter 2 may be appropriate if you are hazy on the fundamentals of this problem-solving technique.

Commitment

In order to accomplish your best work, you have to promise yourself that you will perform the task to the best of your ability.

Analysis

The type of information that is needed to clarify and refine the challenge is gathered by reading the script and asking questions of the other members of the production design team. Typical questions that relate specifically to costume design include:

1. What is the costume budget?
2. What is the production concept?
3. Is the play a period piece? What is that period? Is *our* production being faithful to that period or are we using a different period?
4. When is the first dress rehearsal?
5. Does the director want a costume parade?
6. What does the set design look like? What is its color palette?
7. What is the lighting designer's color palette?

Some questions will be answered when you study the script. Others will be discussed and answered during the production conferences, in which the director and all designers freely exchange ideas and information.

The second phase of analysis involves discovering areas and subjects that will require further research. Note these areas so you can investigate them during the next phase of the design process.

Research

Research is divided into two separate areas: background research and conceptual research. The primary function of background research is to answer the questions generated during the analysis phase. The vast majority of costume designs are based on a fairly realistic interpretation of the style of clothing worn during some particular period of history. For this reason it is particularly important in costume design to consult primary research materials whenever possible.

Primary research items include clothing and accessories actually made during the period under investigation. The reason for primary research is to obtain the most accurate information about the period silhouette, the type and nature of the fabrics used, and construction techniques. Nothing tells you more about the design and construction of a dress of the 1890s than examining a dress made in the 1890s.

If primary resources are not available for examination, then the costume designer's research naturally expands to include online or "eyeballs on" examination of photographs of actual garments of the period, museum displays of actual clothing and accessories, paintings appropriate to the time and locale of the intended production, and texts on the history of clothing and costumes.

The further back one goes in history, the greater will be the variations in the style of clothing from region to region and country to country. Before 1800 land transportation was by foot, horse, carriage, or cart. Travel between continents was by sailing ship. With the development of steamships, railroads, and the telegraph, the time that it took for information to travel from one place to another shrank from months and years to merely minutes and days. Consequently, the readily identifiable regional variations in the style of clothing began to diminish as the interchange of ideas, goods, and services became easier.

Digital communication has reduced that information time lag even further so it now takes just seconds for information to get anywhere on the planet. Even so regional differences in dress are still alive and well. But the current variations in clothing between regions and countries are generally more subtle today than they were even fifty years ago.

During conceptual research, you need to visualize as many potential solutions to the design challenge as possible. Sketch a lot of ideas. Gather fabric samples that might be appropriate for material from which to construct the various costumes, and attach them to the sketches.

Incubation

Rest. Relax. Get away from the project. Work on something else. Go for a walk. Go to the library. Go see a play or movie. Do anything but work on or think about the project.

Selection

When you come back to the project your subconscious will generally have developed a plan or concept. You pick-and-choose from those ideas to develop the overall costume concept for the production. You will also need to select the appropriate design idea that will be used for each individual costume in the production.

Implementation

The implementation phase in costume design involves the drawing and painting of costume renderings, the selection of the appropriate fabrics for each design, and sometimes the supervision of the construction of each garment. (To be technically correct, the costume designer is responsible for the appearance, not the construction, of the

(*continued*)

PRODUCTION INSIGHTS

The Design Process in Costuming   continued

finished costume. It is the costumer, not the costume designer, who is responsible for the supervision of the actual making of the costumes. In some production companies, these lines of responsibility become fuzzy.)

Evaluation

After the show has opened take an objective look at the communication process that has taken place between you and the other members of the production design team as well as your own use of the

design process. The purpose of this evaluation is to discern ways in which you could improve your communication with other members of the production design team as well as your use of the design process.

---

generally break their collections into two categories — haute couture and ready-to-wear — with each carefully designed for a particular season of the year as well as the social/economic level of clientele, the purpose of costume design for the theatre is somewhat different. Its needs are more specific. Each costume that an actor wears in a play is generally designed to visually reinforce the emotional, mental, and physical traits of a unique character at a particular time in a specific play. That costume also needs to be designed to fit, and work with, the body of one individual actor. To be effective, the costume designs for a production need to (1) reflect the production design team's agreed-upon interpretation of the production concept (discussed in Chapter 1, "Production Organization and Management"); (2) exhibit a unity of style among all the costume designs for that production; (3) provide a visual reflection of the personality and nature of each character at a given time in the play; and (4) provide visual information about the world of the play including locale, period, season, time of day, culture, as well as the play's socioeconomic, religious, and political environment.

After the production design team agrees on the style of the production concept — the compositional characteristics that will be used as the unifying elements in each designer's work — the costume designer uses those compositional principles as guides in creating the costume designs for the production. The particular style selected might be based on the line and color palette used in a specific painting by a particular artist that was discovered while doing background research. Or it might be synthesized from the works of several artists, filmmakers, or composers. It could even be a subjective reaction to seemingly random thoughts, textures, and colors. The actual elements used in its creation aren't important. What is important is that the production design team agrees on, and understands the meaning of, the stylistic guide called the production concept.

Costume Design for the Theatre

All costumes for a production need to be thought of as equally important. Whether they are designed for the lead (Figure 18.1) or an **extra** (Figure 18.2), or whether the costumes are to be built "from scratch," pulled from a theatre's stock (or rented) and altered, all costumes are equally important.

In terms of design parameters, costume design is identical to the other design areas in the theatre. The two primary sources of information about a production — how this particular performance is going to be interpreted and performed — are the script and the production concept. The script contains general information about the play — the historical period of the play, the socio economic status and occupations of the characters, the season and climate. Specific information about the characters — personality traits, character quirks — is frequently revealed in the script by what the characters say about themselves and what others say about them. All of this information can be, and frequently is, modified,

extra: A nonspeaking part. A person who provides "visual dressing" for the scene.

FIGURE 18.1
Costume design by Peggy Kellner
for Mrs. Mullin in *Carousel*. Courtesy
of Peggy Kellner.

sometimes extensively, by the production concept adopted for that specific production. The production concept, generally voiced initially by the producer or director, evolves during conversation in the meetings of the production design team until it becomes a unified thought that is the focus point — the "this-is-the-way-that-we're-going-to-do-it" image — used by all members of the production design team as they go about their individual tasks.

The designs for all costumes for any given production need to be guided by the designer's interpretation of the script and the production concept. Doing so helps assure that those designs will visually reinforce the agreed-upon production concept as well as assisting the audience to understand the nature and personality of each character in the production.

The Psychological Meaning of Clothes

What a person wears, and how it is worn, says a great deal about that person and the society in which he or she lives. In contemporary Western countries, corporate businesspersons traditionally wear conservatively cut, somber-colored suits and ties. A man or a woman who wants to fit into that environment would generally buy only those clothes appropriate to the fashion and wear them as prescribed by the style.

A certain type of clothing can be worn to conform to or rebel against a certain segment of society. During World War II, American pilots demonstrated their collective individualism by wearing their hats at jaunty angles rather than the "hat bill level and two fingers above the bridge of the nose" prescribed by the military dress-code manual. A visit to a contemporary American high school would reveal numerous distinctive styles of dress — "goth," "preppie," "stoners," "skaters," and "jocks" — that visibly demonstrate the peer groups to which the various students belong.

Clothes can also be visible clues to the wearer's emotional state. An introvert would probably wear something that would make him blend into the crowd, whereas an extrovert might wear something that would make her stand out and be noticed. Similarly, someone who is gloomy might wear something dark and dreary to reinforce and visually announce that mood, whereas a cheerful, happy individual might dress in bright and cheerful colors.

Objective Information Provided by Clothes

In addition to providing psychological clues, clothing can provide a variety of objective information about a person.

BALM
IN
GILEAD
PATRICK HOLT

DOPEY
ACT I

(A)

WARLOCK

(B)

(C)

(D)

FIGURE 18.3
The silhouette of a costume can provide visual clues about character and historical period. Costume designs by Patrick Holt for (A) Dopey in Act I in the North Carolina School of the Arts production of *Balm in Gilead* and (B) Warlock in *Faust*. A, B Courtesy of Patrick Holt. (C) Asolo State Theatre's (Sarasota, Florida) production of *Charley's Aunt*. Costume design by Catherine King, scene design by Gordon Miconis; photo courtesy of Gary W. Sweetman. (D) Jeri Leer, Candy Buckley, Linda Gehringer (left to right) and Michael O'Hara (background) in Dallas Theatre Center's production of *The Three Sisters*. Designed by Leo Akira Yoshimura; photo by Linda Blase.

Historical Period   The shape or silhouette of garments can provide clear indications of their historical period. Theatrical costumes may be faithful to their historical period, or the costume designer may choose to use history as a reference point from which to create a design that is more meaningful to the production concept for a particular play. Either way, the historical silhouette can be a primary indicator of the historical period of the play, as shown in Figure 18.3.

Age   In any period the color, style, and fit of clothes provide a great deal of information about the age of the wearer. While the clothing of each period has its own characteristics that differentiate between youth and age, one generalization holds true for almost all periods: Young people tend to reveal more of their bodies than do their elders. Two theories suggest the reasons: Young people generally are more interested in attracting romantic partners than are their elders, and exposed skin attracts notice; young bodies with smooth skin and superior muscle tone are generally more attractive to look at than the skin and muscles of their elders, on whom time and gravity have taken their toll. For example, miniskirts, short-shorts, halter tops, and muscle shirts are all clothes of youth. Put these clothes on an out-of-shape middle-aged or elderly body and the almost universal viewer response will be that that person is trying to recapture, or doesn't want to let go of, his or her youth, or they are mentally unbalanced.

Gender   Throughout history, with a few exceptions, clothes have almost always clearly indicated the gender of the wearer. When specifying gender differentiation, fashion design has almost always provided a visual reflection of the society from which it sprang. For example, during the Victorian and Edwardian periods, women were fully covered from neck to foot, but there was visual emphasis on the hair, bust, and bustle, providing a visual reflection of the Victorian ideal of woman as wife and mother. The 1920s saw a revolt against the strict Victorian codes and the bold (for the time) assertion that women were individuals who could possibly have a life outside the traditional roles of wife and mother. A primary fashion statement of the 1920s, the flapper style, reflected the societal reevaluation of the role of women with its boyish look of short hair, flat bosom, and slender hips.

Socioeconomic Status   Social status has always been indicated with clothes. Someone dressed in shabby, ill-kempt clothes of rough homespun materials would rarely be mistaken for a member of the upper class. A woman dressed in beautifully fashioned linens, silks, and satins would rarely be mistaken for a servant. Prior to about 1930, the cut and fit of many upper-class clothing styles actually precluded the possibility of manual labor. The upper classes didn't work, so their clothes were designed to reflect and enforce their lives of leisure. Generally, servants' clothes have always been similar to those of their masters, but the designs have been simpler, the cloth plainer, and the colors more drab.

Occupation   Similar to the clues that clothing provides about a character's socioeconomic status, clothes can also tell us about a person's job. Uniforms are obvious indicators of occupation. Police officers, military personnel, chefs, maids, workers in franchised businesses such as McDonald's and Pizza Hut are all readily identifiable. Sometimes the identification is not so clear. But we would probably identify a man in a flannel shirt, jeans, and heavy boots, with a tool pouch hanging from his belt, as some kind of workman, not a corporate lawyer. If he *were* a corporate lawyer, then we probably would instantly label him as eccentric.

Climate and Season   If we see someone bundled up in a heavy fur coat, we assume that the weather is cold. Dark hues, heavy fabrics, and multiple layers are also strong indicators of cold climate. Light colors, lightweight fabrics, and fewer clothes provide good indications that the weather is warm. Interesting inferences can be made about the personality of a character who dresses "out of season," such as the Reverend Hale, who, in James Michener's novel *Hawaii*, wears long underwear and a woolen frock coat while living in the tropical heat and humidity of the Hawaiian islands.

General Considerations for Costume Design

A variety of diverse considerations and sources of information affect the work of the costume designer.

Analyzing the Script

The costume designer reads the script to gather various kinds of information about the play and the characters in it.

The script provides specific factual information about the historical period in which the play is set: the time of day, season, climate, and time span covered by the play; the sex, age, socioeconomic status, occupation of each character; and so forth. In addition to discovering this historical data, the costume designer gleans the emotional quality of the play and learns about the interrelationships existing between the various characters in the play from reading the script.

The analysis of the script expands beyond the printed page to include the views and interpretations of the producer, the director, and the other designers. Any or all of these other members of the production design team may see the relationships between the characters differently than you do. Their opinions must be acknowledged and evaluated.

All of this information provides the essential background material that the costume designer uses to create designs which effectively reflect the personality and characteristics of each role in the play.

Chapter 2, "The Design Process," contains a specific script-analysis discussion and suggests a procedure that can be used to create effective costume designs. The Production Insights box, "The Design Process in Costuming," found earlier in this chapter, illustrates the use of the design process in costume design.

Other Conceptual Considerations

While an analysis of the script provides a substantial beginning point in the conceptualization of each costume design, several other considerations must be addressed by the costume designer during the design process.

Stereotypical Costuming   The actor, not the costume, is the primary vehicle for conveying a character's nature and personality. For this reason, costume designers normally avoid stereotypical designs that clearly proclaim who or what a character is — a gangster in dark pinstripe suit, black shirt, and white tie or a prostitute in a tight, bust- and thigh-revealing red dress. The obvious exception to this principle involves those vehicles or production concepts which are based on flat, two-dimensional cartoonish characters, as in musicals such as *Li'l Abner* or *Guys and Dolls*. The use of design features that hint, rather than scream, at the true nature of the character allows the actor to develop the character with the aid of the costume, rather than being upstaged by it. But it shouldn't be assumed that designers never use stereotypes as the basis for a design. Sometimes stereotypes are used to quickly define a character or to deceive the audience into making incorrect assumptions about a character. In reality stereotypical design, and the decision of when and how often to use it, is simply another tool in the designer's arsenal or bag o' tricks.

Character Evolution   Costumes need to match the growth and change that characters experience during the course of the production. In Carson McCullers's *The Member of the Wedding,* the character of Frankie matures and changes from a child into a young adult over the course of the play. The costumes that she wears should reflect this maturation process. Similarly, costumes worn by characters who experience emotional or intellectual growth should reflect those changes. A young woman who evolves from a flirt into a serious businesswoman might start out dressed in light-colored, ruffled tea dresses and finish the play costumed in dark-hued business suits.

Costume Stylization   The type and degree of stylization dictated by the script and production concept must be recognized by the costume designer. Stylization is a complex subject perhaps best described by example. What follows is a sampling of some of the types of stylization that can be used. None of them should be thought of as "right" or "correct." They simply show some of the myriad styles that can be created. Obviously, any particular style that is adopted should be a reflection of the production concept for that particular production. Some plays set in contemporary America are populated by ordinary characters using vernacular language. These slice-of-life dramas may be appropriately costumed with clothes purchased or faithfully copied from fashions available at JC Penney, Saks Fifth Avenue, or a local Salvation Army store. These costumes should reflect the everyday world of the play. Verse dramas, on the other hand, are populated by people who speak in heightened language. The thoughts, speech, and actions of Shakespearean characters, for example, are frequently more lofty, or at least more exaggerated, than ours. If produced in a straight period style, faithful to an author's original setting and intent, the characters' costumes should mirror their eloquence and grand thoughts. Similarly, plays in which the protagonist struggles against the gods or the cosmos are not "ordinary" or "normal" in their scope. The costume design for such a production can reflect the "supernormal" world of the play. Many contemporary productions of Shakespeare and other classical works are performed quite effectively in modern dress. The production concept adopted for any production should dictate the design style. For example, the costume design for a Brechtian play presented in minimalist style could be reflected in the simplicity of the designs regardless of whether the costumes were period or contemporary.

Interpretation of Period   Costumes make a statement that visually unifies the historical period, the style of the script, and the production concept. However, any historical period, regardless of whether it is one or forty years long, has a plethora of design styles, and each of those styles has an overwhelming number of subtle variations. If the costume designer were to randomly select costume elements from the entirety of the period, the result would be a visual hodge-podge. Therefore, the costume designer needs to distill that mound of information into a few typical lines, colors, textures, and details that represent the essence of the period. Once that visual theme is established, then variations can be created within it to reflect the traits of the individual characters in the play. This distilled line is frequently an interpretation of the historical data. Character traits, or merely the importance of a character within a scene, sometimes require a departure from historical accuracy of the costume. Sometimes historical accuracy itself can cause visual problems. The **detailing** on gowns of Elizabethan nobility was incredibly ornate. If accurately reproduced for the stage, it could result in a visual "war" between the various trim designs. Simplification of the trim could increase the significance of what is selected and, depending on the production concept, perhaps create a design more appropriate to the production.

Interpretation of Color and Fabric   Historical research will acquaint the costume designer with the color and types of fabrics used in a particular historical period. This information needs to be manipulated during the design process. While historically accurate data may form the root of the design, the colors and fabrics selected must be appropriate to the production concept and the individual characterizations. Typically, the designer will select a range of colors, textures, and fabrics appropriate to the period and production concept and then develop variations within those themes for individual characters.

Practical Considerations

In addition to historical, analytical, and conceptual considerations, the costume designer must be aware of a number of practical matters before the designs can be finalized.

Needs of the Actor   The actor's needs can be divided into two categories — physical and psychological. The physical needs are fairly simple: The costume should fit, it should be reasonably comfortable, and it shouldn't inhibit any necessary and appropriate motion. Because people today are not used to the physical constraints imposed by many fashion modes of the past, the costume designer needs to adapt the costume design to accommodate the actors, while still retaining the historical silhouette and line of the costume. The circumference of the hem of the hobble skirt (shown in Figure 18.4) was so small that women wearing them could take only very tiny steps; it was all but impossible to move up or down stairs. For stage use hobble skirts, and similar movement-inhibiting clothes, are usually designed with authentic lines but with slight modifications to allow for a little more freedom of movement.

Because a costume is designed to provide a visual statement about the character's personality and station in life, the simple act of putting it on psychologically helps the actor to become the character. And it works. Just ask any actor.

Production Venue   Costume design is also influenced by the production venue. The small, delicately tinted pastel embroidered flowers on a peasant blouse detail, totally appropriate to the character and clearly visible in a production staged in an intimate arena theatre seating 125 people, would be completely lost in a large proscenium theatre seating 3,000 or 4,000.

Budget   Obviously, the amount of money in the costume budget, and the time and staff available to design and construct the costumes, have a direct effect on design choices.

Construction Demands of the Design   Construction demands in costume design are generally predicated on the number of costumes in the production, the complexity of the individual designs, the budget, and the expertise of available personnel. Costumes for professional productions are constructed

FIGURE 18.4
A hobble skirt. Costume design by Peggy Kellner for *Hotel Paradiso*, Old Globe Theatre, San Diego, California. Courtesy of Peggy Kellner.

detailing: Trim, appliqués, buttons, ribbons, braid, and so forth attached to a garment to enhance its appearance.

under contract by a costume production house or the resident costume crew, although contemporary tailored clothes such as men's suits are frequently purchased. Because of time, fiscal, or other constraints, some of the costumes for educational and regional professional company productions may be rented or **pulled** from stock and modified. When a production uses a combination of rented, pulled, and constructed costumes, the designer needs to pay extra attention to creating a unified overall design and a visual blending of the costumes acquired from these disparate sources.

Renting Costumes   Carefully tailored, period-specific items such as military uniforms and expensive men's suits are frequently rented. An advantage of renting uniforms is that the costume houses often have the appropriate accessories, such as swords, decorations, headgear, and footwear.

Buying Costumes   When producing a contemporary production, costume designers frequently buy clothes "off the rack" and modify them as necessary to fit the production concept and the specific actor. For productions that are set in the past twenty to thirty years, costume designers can browse through used-clothing stores and pick up many appropriate garments.

Modifying Stock Costumes   Educational and regional professional companies frequently have a stock of costumes that have been used in previous productions. Costumes can be pulled from stock and modified by dyeing and/or the addition or deletion of trim and accessories. Significant variations in the appearance, and apparent period, of a costume can be made by something as simple as creating a lace **overlay** for the **bodice** of a gown. Similar changes can be effected by changing from lace to fur trim or vice versa.

 ## Organizational Paperwork

Because there are frequently between twenty and one hundred costumes per production, the costume designer must use a variety of organizational paperwork to keep track of the myriad details during all phases of production.

The costume designer must keep track of amazing amounts of detail regarding every costume in the production, so it is essential that he or she make copious and complete notes. An ever-increasing number of software programs aid the costume designer and the costume shop personnel in keeping track of all these details. Reviews and content of some of these products may be found on the USITT website: www.usitt.org.

In Chapter 2, it was suggested that designers carry a notebook for jotting down ideas. In addition to using a notebook, costume designers often jot notes in the margins of the script because of the frequent references to specific items worn by the characters.

Most costume shops have an organizational tool that is frequently referred to as the "costume bible."[2] This book holds all the information regarding the planning and construction of a particular show. If the production company or construction shop is working on more than one show at a time, each show normally will have its own "bible." While the specific information contained in the

pull: To remove a costume from storage for use in a production.

overlay: A garment, usually made of lace or a similar lightweight, semitransparent fabric, designed to lie on top of another garment.

bodice: The upper part of a woman's dress.

---

[2] Information extracted from Rosemary Ingham and Liz Covey, *The Costume Designer's Handbook*, 2nd ed. (Portsmouth, N.H.: Heinemann, 1992), p. 157; Rebecca Cunningham, *The Magic Garment: Principles of Costume Design* (Prospect Heights, Ill.: Waveland Press, 1994), p. 229.

"costume bible" obviously varies from company to company, it will normally include the following:

cast list and production contact sheets
measurement sheets
calendars and deadlines
costume plots and lists
budget sheets, including an area to keep a running total of costs
rental contracts and pull lists
copies of renderings
swatches and dyeing instructions
production notes from the stage manager

Many of the items listed will be discussed a little later in this chapter.

Costume Chart

The costume chart (Figure 18.5), also known as the actor's scene chart, is used to visually plot what each character (or actor if he or she is playing multiple roles) wears in each scene in the play. Generally, two versions of the costume chart are created. For early discussion and budget purposes, a preliminary costume chart can be created early in the design process to help organize the designer's ideas and thoughts while analyzing the script and noting the needs of the production. Another chart is based on the final designs and is a helpful aid to those running the show and stage management.

FIGURE 18.5
A sample costume chart. Design by Dianne J. Holly.

Romeo & Juliet	I:1	I:2	I:3	I:4	I:5	II:1	II:2	II:3	II
Romeo	Cream sweater, Beige silk slacks, Beige shoes, socks & belt	Same		White linen suit, Black knit shirt, Black belt & shoes	Add mask and cape	Same	Same	Same	S
Juliet			Peach kimono, Beige slip		White dress, White petticoat, White shoes, Nylons, Mask		Kimono, Slip		
Nurse			Day dress, Nylons, Shoes, Necklace		Eve. dress, Shoes same, Jewelry, Mask?		Voice only		
Capulet	2 pc. gray silk suit, Gray striped shirt, Rose tie & handkerchief, Black shoes	Same			D. breasted tux., Cummerbund, Tux shirt, Black bow tie, socks, & shoes, Wht. handkerchief, Cuff links, studs				
Lady Capulet	Blue knit dress, belt & shoes, Slip, nylons, Necklace, Earrings, purse, Bracelet, fur		Same		Black velvet gown, Earrings, Bracelet, Black shoes, Mask				
Mercutio	White tux shirt, Black leather pants, Black boots			Same, Add blue cape, Baldric sword	Same, Add mask	Same			
Time of Day	Sunday about noon	Sunday, minutes later	Sunday late afternoon, early evening	Sunday late afternoon, pre-party	Sunday night, party, visual climax	Sunday night, late post-party			

There are numerous ways to make a costume chart. It can be hand-drawn by gridding off squares on relatively large sheets of paper, or the information can be entered into a computer database and printed either as a large chart or as individual sheets that can be organized in a three-ring binder. In either case the character's names are listed on the left side, and each act (or each scene if the acts are subdivided into scenes) is noted across the top of the page. All costume items, including accessories, are noted in the scene in which they are first worn. Subsequent costume changes are noted in the appropriate scene.

As an organizational device, some costume designers attach color samples to each listing so that they can see the development of the overall color scheme of the production, as well as trace the color progression of individual characters at a glance. Wardrobe personnel use the costume chart as a guide when dressing the actors, and directors and actors use it to help keep the costumes organized in their minds.

Costume List

Frequently created simultaneously with the costume chart, the costume list (Figure 18.6) specifies every element, including accessories, of each costume worn by every actor. Broken into two sections, men and women, in larger productions it is further subdivided into Principal Men, Chorus Men, Extra Men, Principal Women, Chorus Women, and Extra Women as necessary. Each costume is numbered so that the total number of costumes in the production is readily apparent. Other information, such as any necessary quick changes, is also noted.

PRINCIPAL MEN

Romeo
1. Cream sweater, beige silk slacks, beige shoes, beige socks, beige belt
2. White linen suit, black knit shirt, black belt, black socks and shoes
3. Mask, cape MEDIUM QUICK CHANGE

Capulet
4. Two-piece gray silk suit, gray/white striped shirt, rose tie and handkerchief, black socks/shoes
5. Double breasted tux, cummerbund, tux shirt, black bow tie, black socks/shoes, white handkerchief, cufflinks and studs (gold)
6. Pajamas, robe, slippers

Mercutio
7. White tux shirt, black tux trousers, dinner jacket, black boots
8. Blue cape, baldric sword

Extra Men
18. Guard I — dark gray suit, black shoes, black shirt, black tie
19. Guard II — dark gray suit, black shoes, black shirt, black tie
20. Servant I — black dress pants, white shirt, black bow tie

PRINCIPAL WOMEN

Juliet
9. Pink kimono, beige slip
10. White dress, white petticoat, white shoes, nylons mask
11. Cream skirt, yellow sweater, cream nylons/shoes, straw hat

Nurse
12. Day dress, nylons, shoes, necklace
13. Evening dress, matching shoes, jewelry, mask
14. Shawl

Lady Capulet
15. Blue silk dress, matching belt, slip, nylons, blue shoes, necklace, earrings, bracelet, fur
16. Black velvet gown, earrings, bracelet, black shoes, mask
17. Pink nightgown, blue robe, blue slippers

Extra Women
21. Servant I — black maid's uniform, black shoes, nylons
22. Servant II — black maid's uniform, black shoes, nylons

FIGURE 18.6
A sample costume list.

This list is extremely useful to the designer when estimating costs or when dealing with a costume house that may build the costumes or with a business from which certain costumes may be rented. The costume list is also used by the dressers/wardrobe maintenance crew as a checklist to verify that all elements of each costume are together and that each costume is placed in its proper location prior to each performance.

Character–Actor Dressing List

This list is used by the actors and **dressers** during dress rehearsals and performances. Primarily posted in the actor's dressing room, it can also be located wherever the actor makes a costume change (dressing-room locker, makeup mirror, offstage costume-change enclosure). It details everything, including accessories, that the actor wears in each scene, as shown in Figure 18.7.

FIGURE 18.7
A sample character–actor dressing list.

```
                    DRESSING LIST

PLAY:    Romeo & Juliet

ROLE:    Capulet

ACTOR:   Carl Douglas

DRESSER:  Ted Freeman
_____

I: i — 2-piece gray suit
        Gray/white striped shirt
        Rose tie & handkerchief
        Black shoes
        Black socks

I: ii — Same

I: iv — Double-breasted tux
        Black cummerbund
        Tux shirt (ruffled front)
        Black bow tie
        White handkerchief
        Gold cufflinks & studs
        Black patent leather shoes
        Black socks

III: i — Same as I: i

III: iv — Same as I: i

III: v — Pajamas
         Robe
         Slippers (no socks)
```

dressers: Costume-crew personnel who assist actors in putting on their costumes.

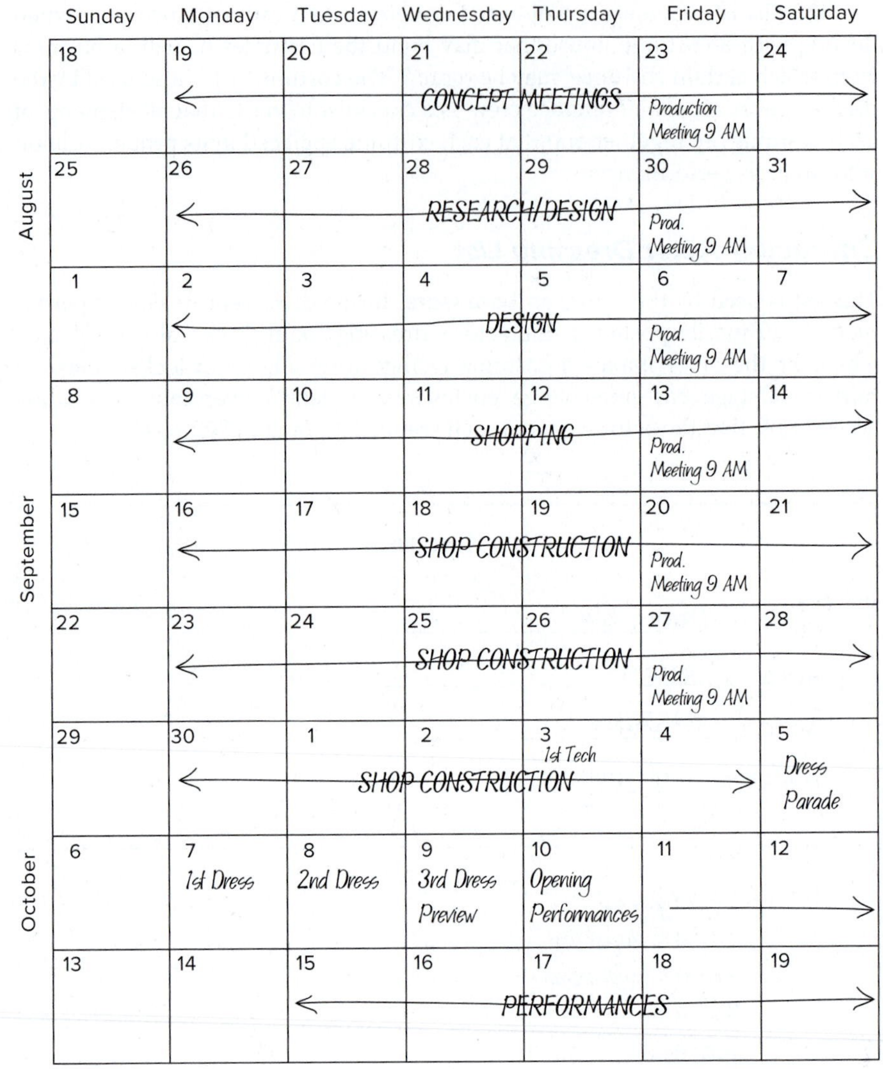

	Sunday	Monday	Tuesday	Wednesday	Thursday	Friday	Saturday
August	18	19	20	21	22 ← CONCEPT MEETINGS	23 Production Meeting 9 AM →	24
	25	26	27	28	29 ← RESEARCH/DESIGN	30 Prod. Meeting 9 AM →	31
September	1	2	3	4	5 ← DESIGN	6 Prod. Meeting 9 AM →	7
	8	9	10	11	12 ← SHOPPING	13 Prod. Meeting 9 AM →	14
	15	16	17	18	19 ← SHOP CONSTRUCTION	20 Prod. Meeting 9 AM →	21
	22	23	24	25	26 ← SHOP CONSTRUCTION	27 Prod. Meeting 9 AM →	28
October	29	30	1	2 ← SHOP CONSTRUCTION	3 1st Tech	4 →	5 Dress Parade
	6	7 1st Dress	8 2nd Dress	9 3rd Dress Preview	10 Opening Performances	11	12 →
	13	14	15 ←	16	17 PERFORMANCES	18	19 →

Costume Calendar

The costume calendar (Figure 18.8) helps the costume designer budget time and provides a visualization of how much time is to be devoted to each phase of the costume design and construction process. To be effective it must include all facets of the process: readings/conferences, research, design, fabric shopping, construction, and rehearsals leading up to the opening performance.

The forms listed in the preceding sections are almost indispensable to the costume designer, but they can also trap the unwary. It is sometimes easy to lose sight of the fact that any theatrical production is always a work in progress. In even the best-planned production, designs are rarely finalized in the preliminary stages. Adjustments to the costume chart and costume list are frequently made during dress rehearsals. Accessories that were agreed on by both the director and costume designer during the design phase may need to be changed once they're seen onstage during dress rehearsals. Whole costumes may need to be replaced. If the director is truly prepared, and if the agreed-on production concept is fully understood by all concerned, then these adjustments should be minimal and not overly disruptive. Experienced costume designers know and understand these needs, plan for them, and adapt as necessary.

Visual Presentation of the Costume Design

At some point, costume designers need to begin to codify their thoughts about the costume designs. This is when they start drawing. Costume designers create several types of drawings: preliminary sketches, the costume layout, and the final costume sketch or rendering.

A vital element in all costume drawings is that the sketches should do two things: show the nature and personality of the character at the time in the play when the illustrated costume is being worn; evoke the mood and spirit of the play. Obviously, these demands require that costume designers be able to draw the human body and clothes with ease and confidence. Chapter 22, "Drawing and Rendering," provides an introduction to the subject of figure drawing, but students who are truly interested in pursuing costume design are strongly encouraged to take courses in figure drawing, watercolor rendering, as well as computer drawing and painting in the appropriate departments of their colleges or universities.

Preliminary Sketches

Frequently the most exciting time in the creation of costume designs, the preliminary-sketch phase, is that time when the first visible results of the creative process appear on paper. These sketches, often rapidly drawn in pen or pencil on the pages of a sketch pad or notebook, are the first tangible results of the synthesis of the costume designer's thoughts, ideas, impressions, and research. Normally not fully completed drawings, they are rough sketches, equivalent to the thumb-nail sketches of the scenic designer, showing the silhouette and perhaps a little detail of the costume, as shown in Figure 18.9. Frequently, costume designers will cover one or more pages of the sketch pad with numerous variations of the same design as they try out different ideas and concepts in search of an appropriate and meaningful design.

As these first sketches are distilled toward their final form, the costume designer will show them to the director and other members of the production design team so that they all can be assured that their work is progressing toward the same goal. During these production conferences, it is typical for adjustments to be made to the design concepts and also quite normal for the sketches to be revised. Some designers make multiple photocopies of the pencil sketches so that they can present a variety of color schemes by coloring the photocopies with markers or watercolor pens. The sketch can also be scanned into a computer and modified in line, color, or texture as was discussed in Chapter 9. Sometimes a solution is not readily apparent, in which case the designer goes "back to the drawing board" and continues making new design choices and sketches based on the input from the production design team.

Costume Layout

The costume layout, Figure 18.10, is a group of small figures, simply and clearly drawn, that illustrate the costume designs for a number of characters. Normally sketched in pencil or ink, the costumes may be fully or partially colored with pencils, markers, dyes, or pigment (see Figures 6.24 and 6.25, page. 111, for costume

(A)

(B)

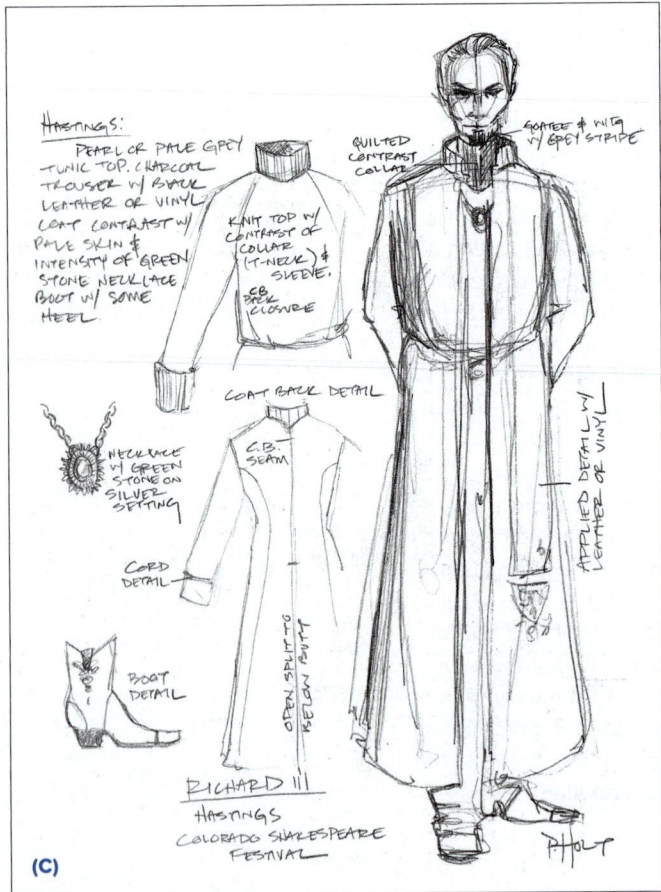

(C)

FIGURE 18.9
Preliminary costume sketches for (A) extras in *Carousel*, designed by Peggy Kellner. Courtesy of Peggy Kellner. (B) the Tinker in *Young Abe Lincoln*, designed by Kathi Perkowski Mills. Courtesy of Kathi Perkowski Mills. (C) Hastings in the Colorado Shakespeare Festival's production of *Richard III*. Designed by Patrick Holt. Courtesy of Patrick Holt.

FIGURE 18.10
(A) Costume layouts for the finale in the American Southwest Theatre Company's production of *Barnum,* designed by Kathi Perkowski Mills. Courtesy of Kathi Perkowski Mills. (B) Costume layouts for Crystal, Chiffon, and Ronnette from the Arizona Repertory Theatre's production of *Little Shop of Horrors.* Costume design by Patrick Holt. Courtesy of Patrick Holt.

layouts in color). If the cast for the play is small and the costume changes are few, one layout may suffice, but more frequently several layouts will be necessary. Characters are normally grouped in some logical sequence. For a musical, all dancers might be on one layout, while the leads may be grouped on another, and the secondary characters and extras are on yet another. Alternatively, a series of individual rough sketches for each design can be drawn and checked, as a group, by the designer to see if there are any misfits or irregularities. These preliminary sketches, frequently with color swatches from the paint department of a local home improvement center attached, are shown at an early production meeting so the director and other designers can see the direction the costume designer is thinking in terms of both color and style.

Regardless of the method used, the purpose of the costume layout drawings is to provide an overall view of the costume concept for the entire production and to give an indication of how the various costumes will look, or work, together.

Costume Sketch

Created by the costume designer, the costume sketch or plate is a full-color drawing that should give a strong indication of character, and the costume should look like it is being worn by the specific character for whom it was designed. Drawn with a single character per plate, as shown in Figure 18.11, the sketch should be large and clear enough to provide accurate information about the line and detail of the garment, yet not look cramped on the plate. Generally, a

FIGURE 18.11
Costume sketch. Esmerelda in the North Carolina School of the Arts production of *Camino Real*. Designed by Patrick Holt. Courtesy of Patrick Holt.

figure between 10 and 15 inches tall will satisfy those demands, although larger or smaller figures can be used as necessary. Swatches of the fabrics to be used in the construction of the costume frequently will be attached to the drawing. Notes about the costume are often penciled into the margins of the plate. If the design is complex, pencil sketches showing other views of the garment may be drawn on the plate or provided on additional sheets. Research materials that indicate construction details frequently provide more accurate information for the cutter/ draper than any pencil sketches. If available, photocopies of these research materials are frequently provided with the costume rendering. Basically, any information that will help construct the costume as the designer envisions it can, and should, be provided with the costume sketch or rendering. Finally, each plate should identify the play, the name of the character, and the scene(s) in which the costume is worn.

The costume sketch or plate is a working drawing that must communicate in a variety of ways with a number of production staff. The costume sketch conveys the designer's design concepts to the director and producer for approval of the design. It is used by the scenic and lighting designers to provide information about the costume color palette and fabrics, and by the costumer and shop staff as the master construction guide.

Specific information on the pragmatic aspects of designing, drawing, and coloring costume designs is given in other chapters. Figure drawing and rendering techniques are covered in Chapter 22, "Drawing and Rendering," while design elements and color are discussed in Chapter 5, "Style, Composition, and Design," and Chapter 6, "Color."

Costume design is a challenging and rewarding craft. To be able to design effectively, you must be imaginative, be able to draw and paint with ease and authority, and have a thorough understanding of fabrics and their characteristics, as well as an encyclopedic knowledge of the history of clothing. While the acquisition of this required body of knowledge may seem daunting, your reward comes from watching the costumes you've designed help actors create beautifully drawn characters in a well-produced production.

Selected References

Anderson, Barbara, and Cletus Anderson. *Costume Design*. Holt, Rinehart and Winston, 1984.

Barton, Lucy. *Historic Costume for the Stage*. Baker's Plays, 1963.

Cunningham, Rebecca. *The Magic Garment: Principles of Costume Design*. Waveland Press, 1994.

Ingham, Rosemary, and Elizabeth Covey. *The Costume Designer's Handbook*. Heineman, 1992.

Pecktal, Lynn. *Costume Design: Techniques of Modern Masters*. Watson-Guptill, 1993.

Prisk, Berneice. *Stage Costume Handbook*. Greenwood, 1979.

Russell, Douglas. *Costume History and Style*. Prentice-Hall, 1982.

Russell, Douglas. *Stage Costume Design: Theory, Technique and Style*. Prentice-Hall, 2nd ed., 1985.

Chapter 19

Costume Construction

The realization of a costume design — the process of creating a costume that brings the visual and evocative intentions of the costume designer's sketch to life — is the responsibility of the costume shop personnel. The specific job responsibilities of the various costume shop positions are detailed in Chapter 1, "Production Organization and Management."

Building a costume isn't simply a matter of going down to the fabric store, buying a pattern and some fabric, and then going home and making a dress. The process of constructing a costume is much more complex. While there are many obvious similarities between costume construction and home sewing, the differences are considerable. The needs of a costume are different and unique. Drama deals with heightened emotions. While maintaining a period silhouette, costumes also must accommodate the range of motion and rigors imposed by the physicalization of those heightened emotions — running, jumping, leaping, falling, rolling, fighting, dancing, and any number of other activities. Street clothes simply aren't intended for that kind of abuse. At its best costume design helps explain the play's characters to the audience by providing visual clues to each character's emotional state, social rank, and financial status. The line, color, and fabric of street clothes more typically reflect prevalent fashion trends. Costume construction is concerned with the processes, materials, and techniques used in making costumes and costume accessories. Specifically, the field requires knowledge of the **hand** of fabrics used in theatrical costumes; techniques of making and adjusting patterns; sewing; fabric painting, dyeing, and distressing; as well as such specialty skills as jewelry-, shoe/boot-, wig-, and armor-making techniques.

 ## Organization of Costume Shops

In the Broadway theatre, all of the technical personnel are hired for a single production. After the producer has approved the designs and the costume construction bids, the costumes are built by a professional costume house. During construction the costume designer is in frequent contact with the shop supervisor to answer any artistic and practical questions about the costumes. When dress rehearsals begin, the costumes are moved into the theatre dressing rooms or costume storage area; their use and maintenance is coordinated by the wardrobe supervisor (also known as the wardrobe master or mistress) and the dressers or **wardrobe crew or staff.** In unionized professional theatre, the costume running crew personnel belong to a different union than do the construction crew personnel.

The organization of the costume shops of regional professional theatres, university theatre arts departments, and community theatre groups is not significantly

hand: The quality and characteristics of a fabric that can be evaluated or defined by a sense of touch.

wardrobe crew or staff: Those crew members such as dressers and wardrobe-repair personnel who work during the dress rehearsals and performances.

different from the organization of a professional costume house because both are frequently working on more than one production at the same time.

The Costume Shop

Because of the wide variety of materials used in the construction of costumes, many types of tools and basic equipment are necessary in any well-equipped costume shop.

Basic Equipment

While costume shops come in a variety of shapes and sizes, all must be equipped with certain basic equipment.

Cutting Tables Used for laying out patterns and fabrics, cutting tables should be 42 to 50 inches wide (to accommodate all but the widest fabrics), about 36 inches high (so people of average height won't have to bend over while working on the table), and 6 to 8 feet long. The tabletop should be covered with cork or a muslin-covered composition board such as Homosote or Upson board. The cork or composition board make it easy to push pins into the surface (to hold patterns and fabrics in place), and both the cork and muslin surfaces effectively make the table skid-resistant (so slick material won't slide off). The large area under the table is normally used for storage.

Dress Forms Dress forms, also known as dressmaker's dummies, are extremely useful in the costume shop. These rigid forms, which are padded so material can be pinned directly to them, are used for draping as well as pinning and adjusting cut pattern pieces. Available in standard men's and women's sizes, a well-equipped shop will have a variety of sizes (Figure 19.1). Foam mannequins should be used only if commercial dress forms cannot be afforded. Adjustable home sewing dummies usually are more trouble than they are worth but can be used if other forms are not available.

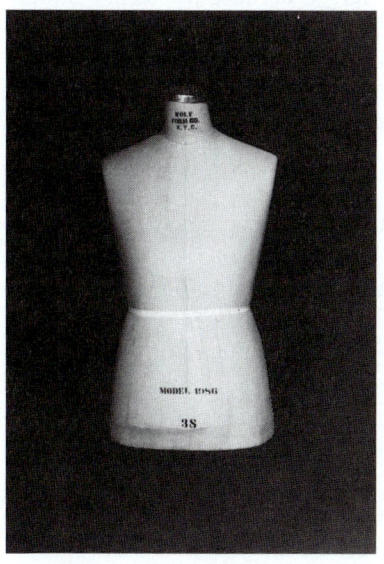
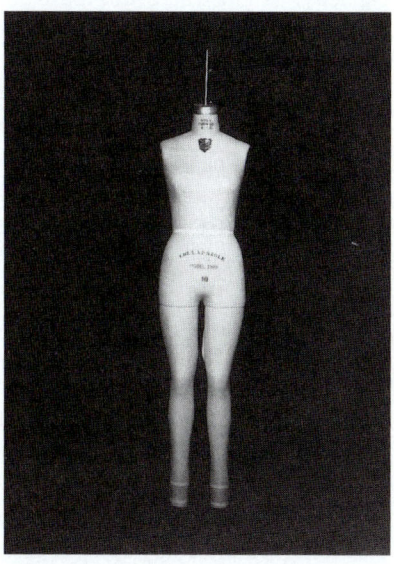

FIGURE 19.1
Two types of dress forms, or dressmaker's dummies. They are available in a variety of sizes for both men and women. Courtesy of J. Michael Gillette.

FIGURE 19.2
A jacketed steam kettle, normally used in restaurant kitchens, works very well as a dye vat. Courtesy of J. Michael Gillette.

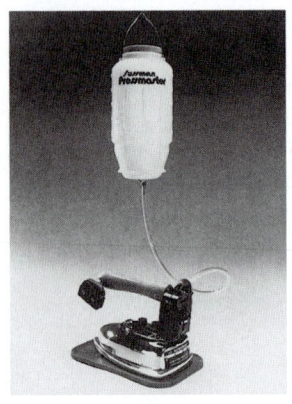

FIGURE 19.3
A heavy-duty steam iron. mr.steam® Courtesy of Sussman.

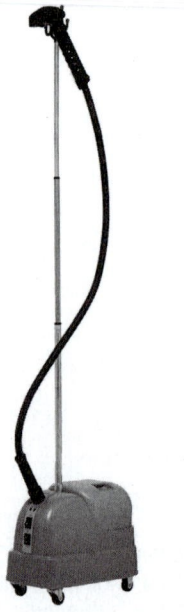

FIGURE 19.4
Portable steamer. Courtesy Chandler Machine USA.

Fabric Storage   Large pieces of scrap fabric should be stored for future use in bins or drawers identified as to fabric type and color. Additional bin/drawer storage should also be available for storing accessories as jewelry, millinery, parasols, and so forth. Shelf storage should be available for bolts of fabric such as muslin and rolls of brown paper (both regularly used in pattern-making) and for special-purchase items such as close-out specials and remnants.

Washing Machine and Dryer   Used for cleaning washable costume elements during dress rehearsals and performances, and for dyeing fabrics, large-capacity, heavy-duty machines with a variety of settings are best. It is preferable to have one set for washing and one for dyeing. However, if one set is used for both dyeing and cleaning, both the washer and the dryer must be kept scrupulously clean, including the drain hoses, so that leftover dye won't spot, stain, or discolor clothes that are being washed and dried. Again, it is infinitely preferable to have two sets of machines: one for dyeing and one for washing.

Dye Vat   Commercial dye vats are expensive, but jacketed steam kettles, shown in Figure 19.2, cost less and work almost as well. The dye vat should be able to minimally heat 20 to 40 gallons of water to boiling. Budget permitting, it is preferable to use a commercial dye vat because they do a superior dye job. Whether using a commercial dye vat or soup kettle it is always better to use a steam-jacketed version because the heat surrounds the vat/kettle rather than just coming from the bottom. The surrounding heat typically results in more uniform dyeing of the fabric.

Hot Plate   A hot plate useful for boiling water for dyeing when the amount of fabric to be dyed does not warrant the use of the dye vat.

Stove   A residential-type stove can be used in place of a hot plate for boiling water. Additionally, the stove's oven can be used for heating certain types of plastics and craft materials frequently used in the construction of costume ornamentation and accessories.

Irons   Heavy-duty industrial steam and dry irons with a multigallon water capacity, as illustrated in Figure 19.3, are preferred because the steam is more concentrated and the irons last longer than those designed for home use. Each iron should be equipped with a metallic or heat-resistant rest on which the iron can be placed when heated but not in use. Distilled water should be used to avoid mineral buildup in the iron and the possibility of inadvertently staining the costumes.

Ironing Boards   Large, heavy-duty industrial ironing boards with sturdy tip-resistant bases are desired. Smaller specialty boards, such as sleeve boards, and needle boards for pressing velours and velvets are highly desirable.

Steamer   Portable steamers (Figure 19.4) generate a stream of steam that is useful for taking wrinkles out of materials that cannot be ironed easily such as velvets, velours, and corduroys. Portable steamers are also useful in millinery for shaping felt.

Sink   A sink with cold and hot water is essential for cleaning equipment and providing water for a variety of costume shop activities.

FIGURE 19.5
A movable clothes rack.

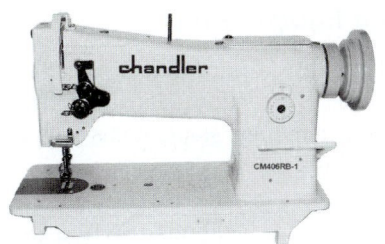

(A)

(B)

FIGURE 19.6
Sewing machines: (A) A heavy-duty machine. (B) A power machine. A, Courtesy of J. Michael Gillette. B. Courtesy Chandler Machine USA. C, Courtesy Juki America, Inc.

Mirror   A full-length three-way mirror is extremely useful during fittings. It allows the costume designer, crew members, and the actor to see the costume from all directions and aids checking fit and finish while the costume is being worn.

Racks   Large-castered, sturdy, movable clothes racks (Figure 19.5) can be moved to convenient locations and used to hang clothes under construction, in storage, or in production.

Tables and Chairs   These are extremely useful for doing hand sewing and other detail work. Stitchers, who frequently sit in these chairs doing handwork for, literally, hours at a time, will be very happy campers if some thought, and funding, is given to providing them with comfortable, ergonomically designed, chairs.

Sewing Machines   A variety of sewing machines are used in the costume shop. Every shop will need at least three or four straight-stitch machines and one zigzag machine. Commercial-grade zigzag machines are normally capable of straight stitching as well, so they can be used for both purposes. The more exotic specialized machines can be added to the shop's inventory as finances permit.

Straight-Stitch Sewing Machines   Heavy-duty, commercial grade (not light-duty homemaker models) straight-stitch machines are used for the majority of the machine sewing in the costume shop.

Zigzag Sewing Machines   There is also a need for one or more heavy-duty machines capable of making zigzag, buttonhole, and similar specialty stitches. These machines, shown in Figure 19.6A, can be used for straight stitching as well.

Walking-Foot Machine   Also called power machines (Figure 19.6B), these high-speed, straight-stitch machines have the power to stitch any fabric from chiffon to leather with equal ease.

Serger   The serger, also called a merrow machine, or overlock (Figure 19.7), sews a seam, cuts both pieces of fabric about one-quarter inch from the seam, and makes an overcast stitch on the edge of both pieces of fabric to prevent it from raveling — all in one operation. Again, as with all shop machines, the heavy-duty, industrial grade models are preferred.

Blind-Stitch Machine   This is a specialty sewing machine used to make hems quickly with an easily removable stitch. The blind stitch is now available on most straight-stitch and zigzag machines.

FIGURE 19.7
A serger or merrow machine.
Courtesy of J. Michael Gillette.

Sewing Equipment

The following is a nonexhaustive list of basic sewing supplies commonly used in costume construction. Many of these items are illustrated in Figures 19.8 and 19.9. To save money, staple items such as needles, pins, and fasteners should be bought in bulk.

FIGURE 19.8
Hand tools commonly used in costuming. Courtesy of J. Michael Gillette.

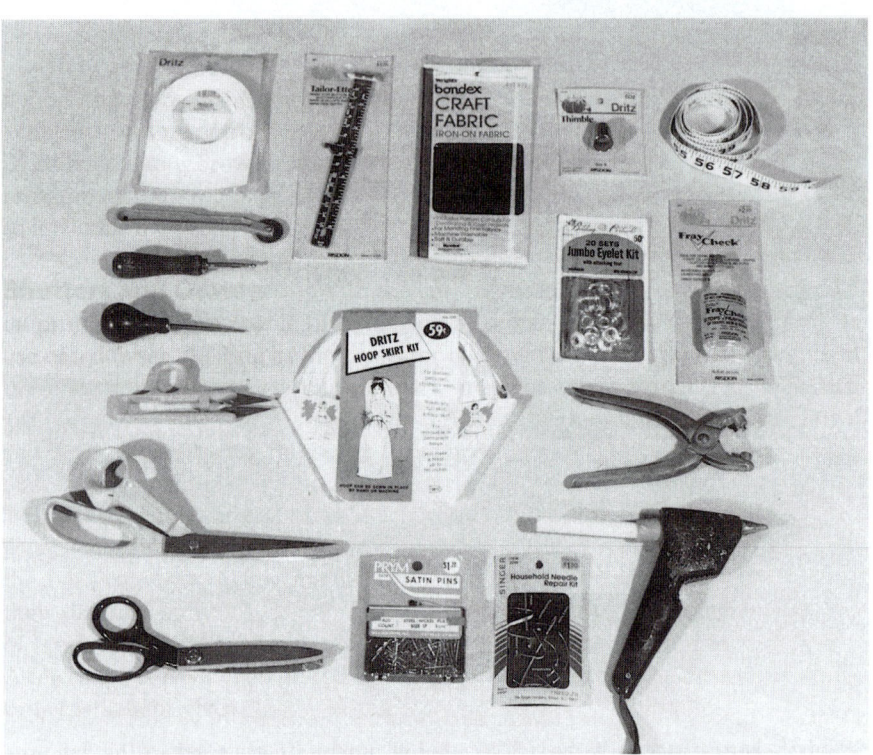

FIGURE 19.9
Fasteners used in costuming. Courtesy of J. Michael Gillette.

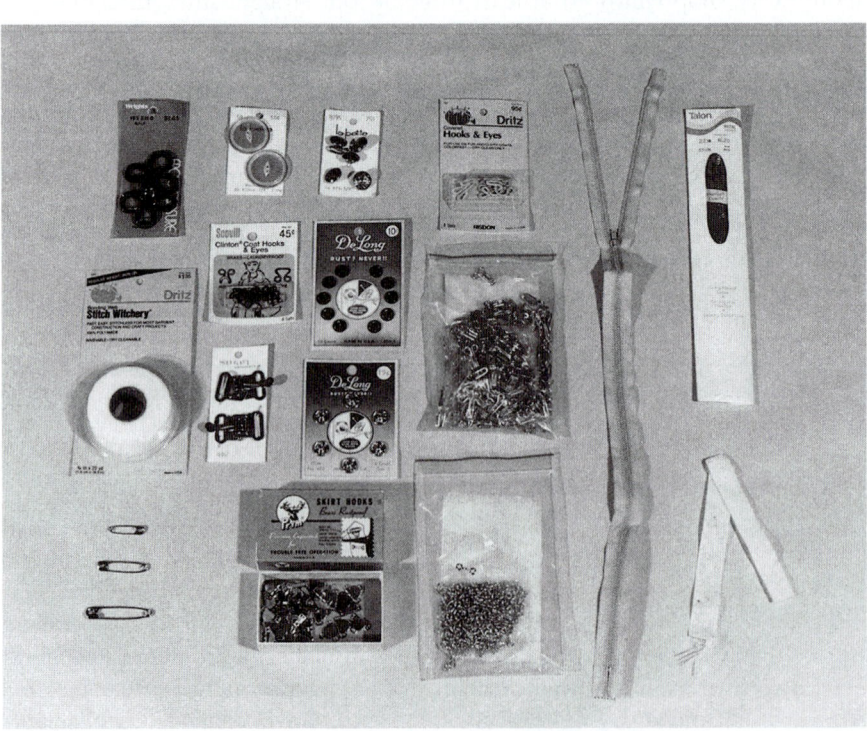

Measuring Devices   Accurately inscribed 60-inch, plastic tape measures are used for the majority of measuring in the costume shop. Aluminum rules, 48 to 72 inches long, are helpful for laying out large garments such as skirts and capes.

Hand Needles   Long-eyed needles are used because they are the easiest to thread. Sizes 5 to 10 are the most commonly used. Heavy materials require heavy-duty needle types such as carpet and darning, as well as straight and curved upholstery needles.

Machine Needles   Medium-sized universal-pointed needles are used for the bulk of the sewing in the costume shop, although lightweight and heavy needles are used for sheer and heavy weight fabrics. Ball-pointed needles are used on knit and polyester fabrics, while sharp-pointed universal needles are used on the rest.

Thread   To save money, many costume shops prefer to match the value of thread to costume rather than match color. These shops use only black, white, and gray thread. However, if the audience is particularly close to the stage, they may match the color of the topstitch thread to the fabric. Heavy-duty carpet and button threads are also used for special applications.

Thimbles   A plastic or metal cap for the end of the finger, thimbles are used to protect the finger when pushing a needle through the fabric. Thimbles in a variety of sizes are normally stocked in the costume shop.

Straight Pins   Rustproof pins of medium size are used to pin fabric together and pin patterns to most fabrics. Silk pins are available for use with sheer fabrics. Larger pins are useful when working with heavier fabrics.

Safety Pins   Large sizes are most frequently used, although there is a need for all sizes.

Tracing Wheels   These are toothed wheels used with tracing paper for transferring markings from a pattern to fabric. Available with several "tooth" designs, the regular V-toothed wheel works well in most applications, although the very sharp stiletto-toothed wheel works better with heavy fabrics.

Tracing Paper   A heavy paper with transferable color, it is used with the tracing wheel to transfer markings from patterns to fabric. Several colors are normally stocked so a hue that contrasts with the color of the fabric can be used.

Tailor's Chalk   Manufactured in chalk and wax bases, tailor's chalk is available in white and colors. It is used for transferring pattern lines and for marking fabric during fittings.

Shears and Scissors   The cost of fabric-cutting shears is directly related to their quality. Buy the best you can afford — as the more expensive ones generally stay sharp longer — and use them for fabric cutting only, as cutting other materials dulls the blades. Bent-handle shears with 8-, 10-, or 12-inch blades are best for fabric cutting. Less-expensive shears and scissors in a variety of sizes should be kept on hand for cutting other things.

Seam Rippers   The small ones seem easiest to use, although this is usually a matter of personal preference.

Single-Edged Razor Blades These are sometimes unadvisedly used as a substitute for a seam ripper. Murphy's Law would indicate that when so used, the fabric will be cut more often than the thread.

Snaps All sizes from tiny to huge, in both black and silver, should be kept in stock in the costume shop.

Hooks and Eyes Again, all sizes from small to large, in both black and silver, should be kept on hand, although the larger sizes — 3 through 5 — seem to be used most often.

Zippers Although zippers will frequently be bought for a specific costume, a stock of metal dress zippers in both black and white, from 7 to 22 inches long, should be kept on hand. White zippers can be dyed to match the color of the costume.

Velcro This is used as a substitute for snaps, hooks and eyes, zippers, and buttons, particularly when a very quick change is expected. Manufactured in 12-yard rolls, many shops maintain a supply of both black and white Velcro. Although the white doesn't dye particularly well, it can be tinted to approximate the hue of the costume fabric.

Hot Glue Gun This electrically heated pistol-gripped device melts sticks of glue and dispenses the glue in a narrow line. Arguably the most versatile tool in the costume shop, it can be used as a substitute for sewing in some projects and is almost indispensable in jewelry and ornamentation making, parasol repair, and similar types of work.

Seam-Binding Tape This includes any of the twill and/or bias tapes that are sewn to the cut edges of fabric to prevent seams from raveling. It is useful in ¼-, ½-, and 1-inch widths. Finishing seams with seam-binding tape is not necessary if a serger is used.

 ## Fabrics

Fabric is the basic material from which costumes are made, so it is imperative that the costume designer understand fabric materials. Each type and weight of fabric has its own intrinsic characteristics. Some fabrics are crisp and stiff, and when draped they fall in stiff, angular lines. Other fabrics are soft and limp, and when draped they flow into smooth, sensuous curves. The costume designer must select the specific fabric or material that will most appropriately re-create the visual impression conveyed by the costume sketch.

The hand of a fabric — its characteristics that can be determined by a sense of touch — is of prime importance in determining the suitability of a fabric for a particular costume. The hand of any fabric is determined by the type of fiber from which it is constructed; the weave or structure of the fabric; how, and with what, the fabric is treated; and how it is finished.

Fabric Fibers

Two general types of textile fibers are used in the manufacture of cloth: natural and synthetic. Each type of fiber has its own distinctive characteristics.

Natural Fibers

Cotton   Cotton — the white fiber contained in the seed pod, or boll, of the cotton plant — has been used in making cloth for more than 3,000 years. Cotton **breathes** well, readily accepts dyes, and wrinkles easily unless treated. Cotton thread is characterized by ribbonlike twists. Available in a huge number of weaves and **blends,** the varieties of weights, textures, and finishes of cotton fabrics are truly amazing. Mercerization is a caustic soda treatment applied to cotton that causes the fibers to swell and straighten out slightly. Mercerized cotton is more lustrous and dyes better than unmercerized cotton.

Linen   The oldest textile fiber known, linen, derived from the flax plant, is stronger than cotton, has a silky luster, is a good conductor of heat, is lint-free, but does not dye well because of the hardness of the fiber. It washes easily, is hard to stain; shrinks and creases easily.

Silk   Silk is the natural substance from which silkworms spin their cocoons. Silk is expensive, strong, lightweight, pliable; has good elasticity; is lustrous; holds heat; and takes dye extremely well. There are two basic forms of silk filament: cultivated and wild. Wild silk filament is brown and has a rough texture. Cultivated silk filament is smoother, more lustrous, and grayish-yellow. There are two ways of collecting the filament from the cocoon — reeling and spinning — and each method affects the appearance of the silk. Reeling yields longer filaments with less twisting than spinning, resulting in a stronger, more lustrous filament.

Wool   One of the oldest fibers used in textiles, wool is made from the fleece of sheep. There are two primary types of woolen yarns: woolen and worsted. Woolen yarns are loosely twisted, soft, and weak with a fuzzy, textured surface. Worsteds are more tightly twisted and stronger and have a smoother surface. Worsteds tend to breathe well, whereas the softer surface of woolen yarn traps air, making it a good insulator. Wool readily absorbs moisture and dyes. However, the boiling water used with most dyes can cause substantial shrinkage as well as texture changes. Woolen and worsted fabrics don't readily wrinkle, and most wrinkles **hang out** easily. Wool fabrics can be shaped with steam, which makes them ideal for making form-tailored garments.

Synthetic Fibers   Synthetic fibers are chemical compounds that are changed into hardened filaments by a variety of patented processes. Unless treated further, these fibers have a tendency to be slick, smooth, and dense. In general, synthetic fibers do not absorb moisture or breathe as well as natural fibers, so they tend to trap body heat inside the costume. On the positive side, most synthetic fabrics have an inherent resistance to wrinkling and are quite durable.

Two or more synthetic and/or natural fibers are often blended to form a fabric that will take advantage of the best attributes of each while deemphasizing their negative aspects. These blended fabrics are usually wrinkle-resistant and durable.

The care of any fabric, as well as its fiber content, must by law be indicated on the **hang tag** of the bolt of fabric. Synthetic fabrics that have approximately 40 to 50 percent natural-fiber content (cotton, linen, wool, and so forth) generally breathe well. Fabrics that are 100 percent synthetic generally do not breathe well. The costume designer and the costumer should be acquainted with the care of any fabric used in a stage costume, because those garments will normally need to be cleaned or washed and pressed frequently during the run of the production.

Acrylic   Acrylics are made from compounds based on coal, petroleum, and other materials. The acrylic fiber is soft and lightweight. Commercially, acrylic

breathes: A term that defines a material's ability to transmit heat, air, and water vapor.

blend: A combination of more than one type of fiber, blends are created to take advantage of the best properties of all fibers in the blend.

hang out: In this instance, hang out means that most wrinkles will disappear from the fabric if it is hung up.

hang tag: The small label usually attached to the cardboard core of a bolt of fabric that indicates the percentages of various component fibers.

cotton linters: The short hairs covering the cotton seed.

yarns are frequently made into sweaters, blankets, and socks. Factory dyes are colorfast, but the material does not dye well in the costume shop. It is wrinkle-resistant, holds its shape well, and needs little if any ironing. Common trade names include Acrilan, Orlon, and Creslan.

Nylon   A slurry of air, water, and coal is heated and extruded through spinner-ettes to produce the continuous-filament fiber known as nylon. Nylon is light, strong, extremely elastic, and resistant to abrasion. Wrinkles easily fall out of fabrics made from nylon. Nylon fiber doesn't conduct heat well or absorb moisture, so the fabric's heat-transmission characteristics depend on the weave: Smooth, tight weaves trap heat; loose, open weaves do not. Some nylon fabrics dye well, others do not. Common trade names include Antron, Capriolan, and Qiana.

Polyester   Another petroleum-based product, polyester fibers are highly resis-tant to wrinkling, are very strong, are commercially colorfast and reasonably stain-resistant, but they do not dye well in the costume shop. Polyester fibers are made into many types of light-, medium-, and heavyweight fabrics and, blended with cotton, create a fabric with excellent wash and wear characteristics and breathability. Trade names include Dacron, Kodel, and Quintess.

Rayon   Rayon was one of the first synthetic fabrics. It is made from regenerated cellulose, a viscous solution of **cotton linters** and wood pulp that is extruded through spinnerettes to form a continuous fiber. Rayon dyes easily, has excellent colorfastness, works well when blended with other fibers, and is very absorbent. Similar in many characteristics and weaves to silk, rayon can frequently be used as a low-cost alternative to silk. Common trade names include Avril, Celanese, Fibro, and Zantrel.

Acetate   Similarly to rayon, chemicals are added to the regenerated cellulose solution to create cellulose acetate before the fibers are extruded. Acetates have little strength, must be ironed with low heat, don't hold a crease well, but have good draping characteristics and wrinkle resistance. Triacetates solve the heat-toleration and crease-retention problems associated with acetates while retain-ing their better qualities.

Weaves

Numerous types of weaves are used in making fabrics, and each type produces specific textural and visual effects. The fiber content of the threads woven into the fabric greatly affect the appearance and hand of the resultant material.

The threads running the length of the fabric are called the warp, and the threads running the width of the fabric are called the woof, fill, or weft. Some common ways that those threads are configured are shown in the weave pat-terns illustrated in Figure 19.10. Each pattern produces fabric with specific characteristics.

Plain Weave   In the plain weave, the fill passes over one warp thread and under the next. In the next row this pattern is alternated, as illustrated in Figure 19.10A. The visual effect of a plain weave is a simple, uncomplicated fabric. Variations of the plain weave include the ribbed weave, in which the fill yarn is much bulkier than the warp.

Basket Weave   In the basket weave, a variation of the plain weave, two or more fill yarns are passed over an equal number of warp yarns, as shown in Figure 19.10B. Oxford cloth is an example of a basket weave. Variations of the basket weave are numerous.

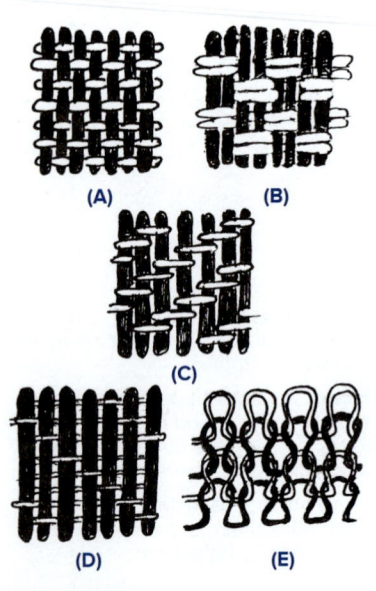

FIGURE 19.10
Types of weave patterns: (A) plain weave, (B) basket weave, (C) twill weave, (D) satin weave, and (E) plain knit.

Twill Weave   The most durable of all weaves, twill is created when the fill yarn is interlaced with the warp to create diagonal ridges in the fabric, as shown in Figure 19.10C. Depending on the design of the weave, the **wales** may run diagonally from left to right, right to left, or both ways. Herringbone, in which the direction of the diagonal wales changes directions every few rows, is a common variation of the twill weave.

Satin Weave   The satin weave produces a smooth, very rich-looking fabric. This lustrous look is achieved by passing warp threads over a specific number of fill yarns, passing under one, then repeating the pattern (Figure 19.10D). The number of skipped threads, or floats, varies between four and twelve but remains constant for any particular piece of fabric. The lustrous sheen of satin has a definite direction, and patterns need to be cut keeping the direction of the fabric in mind.

Pile Weave   Lustrous velvets and velours have a plush texture and appearance that is extremely rich. The fabric is created by weaving an extra warp or fill yarn between the warp or fill of the base material. This extra yarn is looped higher than the base material and may, or may not, be cut. Velvets, velours, terrys, plush, velveteens, and corduroys are all variations of the pile weave, and they all have directional characteristics (like satin), so care must be taken to match the direction when cutting the fabric.

Plain Knit   Technically not a woven fabric, knits are constructed from a series of interlocking loops, and each row of loops is dependent for its support on the rows of loops below and above it, as shown in Figure 19.10E. There are many types of knits, and they are all very elastic and porous.

Fabrics and Nonfabric Materials Used in Costume Construction

Fabrics

A number of fabrics are used in the construction of stage costumes (and street clothes, for that matter). This list is not exhaustive, but it does provide examples of the types of fabrics typically used in costume construction.

Brocade   Available in light, medium, and heavy weights, brocade has a slightly raised pattern and is made from high-luster yarn that is woven into the matte finish of the background cloth. These patterns are reversed on the back side of the fabric. Usually made from rayon or silk, the fabric normally has a rich, reflective, multitextured surface.

Buckram   An open-weave material, buckram is a stiff fabric that has been sized with a heavy glue. Available in light, medium, and heavy weights, buckram is used as a foundation for millinery and other costume elements needing stiffness. Buckram can be shaped and molded because it becomes limp when dampened but regains its stiffness when dry.

Canvas   Normally a cotton or cotton-synthetic blend, canvas is a heavy, plain-weave fabric used as lining material or other applications where its semistiff, extremely durable characteristics might prove helpful. Duck and sailcloth are lighter-weight versions.

wale: Visible, usually narrow, ridges in the surface of a fabric caused by a variation in the weaving pattern.

PRODUCTION INSIGHTS

Fabric Finishes

Irrespective of the type or fiber content of a fabric, most textiles are treated with either a functional or a decorative finish or with both.

Functional Finishes

Functional finishes are normally applied to the fabrics before they leave the mill:

1. Permanent-press processes enable permanent creases to be put into trousers and other garments while all but eliminating wrinkles from the finished fabric and clothes.

2. Mercerization is a chemical process that adds strength and shine to cotton thread.

3. Flameproofing is a chemical treatment of cloth that prevents it from supporting flames. It does not, however, prevent the cloth from charring and smoldering.

4. Preshrunken cloth, particularly cotton, has been bathed in water.

5. Cloth can be impregnated with antibacterial agents to reduce the severity of stains from perspiration and other natural substances.

Decorative Finishes

Decorative finishes alter the appearance of the fabric. These treatments include bleaching, dyeing, printing, and texturing. Although the vast majority of these treatments are applied to fabrics before they leave the mill, some decorative treatments, such as dyeing and fabric painting, are frequently performed in the costume shop.

Chiffon   Chiffon is a sheer, usually translucent, cloth frequently made from rayon or silk with soft, diaphanous draping qualities.

Corduroy   A medium to heavy material, most frequently made from cotton or cotton-synthetic blends, corduroy has raised ridges (wales). The material is fairly stiff and doesn't drape well. Waleless and pinwale (very narrow) corduroy can be used as low-cost substitutes for velvet and velour, although they don't have the softer draping qualities of those fabrics.

Crepe   This is a thin, crinkle-finished fabric with a low luster and soft draping qualities. Rayon, silk, and fine cotton crepes are most frequently used for lingerie, blouses, and flowing gowns.

Crinoline   This tight-weave material has permanent sizing to provide stiffness.

Denim   A fairly coarse twill weave of cotton or cotton-synthetic blend, this slightly stiff fabric is primarily used for blue jeans and similar working-class clothes.

Drill   Similar to denim but of smoother surface and more luster, drill is a twill weave of cotton or cotton-synthetic blends.

Felt   Felt is a woolen, cotton, or rayon material made from fibers that have been matted or pressed together under pressure. Shaping is best accomplished with wool felt. When steamed it becomes limp and can be shaped and formed. It will retain the molded shape when dry. Felt is primarily used for hats and trimmings.

Flannel   A lightweight material woven with soft-finish threads of wool, wool blend, or cotton, flannel is normally used for men's and women's suits, trousers, and shirts.

Gabardine   This is a light-, medium-, or heavy weight, hard-surfaced twill-weave material made from wool, cotton, synthetics, or blends. It is used for inexpensive suits and outerwear.

Jersey   A knit fabric with excellent draping qualities, jersey is manufactured in a variety of fibers — wool, cotton, rayon, and blends — in a full range of weights.

Linen   Its irregular yarns of linen and linen-synthetic blends give the fabric a nubby, soft-luster surface. It is primarily used for tropical suits and sportswear.

Muslin   A plain-weave durable cotton with moderate sizing, unbleached muslin is commonly used as a lining material. It is also used for making patterns.

Net   Net is a stiff, very-open-weave material commonly made from cotton, rayon, or nylon. Nylon net is the most stiff and is used where light, airy stiffening — ballet skirts, stiff veils — is desired.

Pellon   This is the brand name of a nonwoven stiffening material. Similar to felt in manufacturing method, Pellon is used as a stiffening interfacing material and in petticoats. Pellon does not soften when dampened and will retain its stiffness through many cleanings.

Sateen   A satin-weave cotton fabric of low luster, sateen is primarily used as a lining material.

Satin   This high-luster, satin-weave fabric is made from silk, rayon, and other synthetics. Available in a variety of weights and subcategories, satin is used for a variety of purposes from evening wear to draperies.

Taffeta   This plain-weave, smooth-surfaced, high-luster fabric is normally made of rayon but is occasionally available in silk. *Moire taffeta* has a nonrepetitive pattern pressed into the surface of the cloth that creates an interesting surface treatment. It is used extensively in eighteenth- and nineteenth-century clothes.

Velour   A pile-weave fabric normally made of cotton or cotton–nylon blends, velour has a soft, reflective quality. Heavyweight velour is normally used for upholstery and drapes, while lightweight velour is used for sportswear.

Velvet   Velvet is a pile-weave fabric normally made of rayon or nylon, also available in silk. It drapes sensuously and has rich, light-reflective characteristics. Available in a variety of weights, the heavier are used for capes, drapes, and upholstery, while the lighter weights are typically used for evening wear.

Nonfabric Materials

A variety of materials other than cloth are used in costume construction. Some of these materials are substituted for fabric, and others are used to bind various costume materials together. This list is neither exhaustive nor exclusive. Almost any material can be, and has been, used to make costumes. In addition to the cloth and fabric materials that form the basis of most costumes, any number of decorative materials can be appliquéd to the fabric to enhance its appearance. The only limitations on appropriateness are commonsense rules of safety for the actors and those around them, and the suitability of the material to the design concept for that particular costume.

(A)

(B)

FIGURE 19.11
Uses of Sculptor Coat. (A) Helmet construction. (B) Sculptor Coat was used as an adhesive to glue the elements of this hat together. Courtesy of J. Michael Gillette.

Leather   Leather is often used for hats, shoes, and certain period pieces such as vests, armor, and belts. In the United States most leather is treated cowhide, although leather can be made from the hide of almost any animal. Leather has a smooth side and a rough side. The side that is used by the costumer is solely dependent on the particular look that is wanted. Most leather can be dyed with special leather dyes and sprays. It can be machine-stitched using a heavy-duty sewing machine equipped with a leather needle. It can also be hand-stitched. The surface of the leather can be tooled, and a variety of tools (awls, leather punches) can be used to punch holes in the material.

Leather can be formed into curves for such items as helmets and breast-plates by steaming it and forming it to an appropriately shaped mold. Leather can be rather heavy, is extremely durable, and holds heat well. Complete costumes constructed of leather can become very warm and uncomfortable.

Plastic Coatings   Sculptural Arts Coatings of Greensboro, North Carolina, produces a line of water-base, low-emissivity craft products, paints, and finishes that can be used for myriad projects in the costume as well as scene and prop shops.

Helmets can be made with Sculptor Coat by coating a head form with a release agent (Vaseline), then forming a felt foundation over the head form. The felt is coated with a mixture of Sculptor Coat, plaster, and water. When the surface is dry, it can be sanded or worked with power tools (angle grinder, sander) and finished to a high metallic sheen using acrylic paint and plastic varnish as shown in Figure 19.11A. Figure 19.11B shows millinery that has been glued together using Sculptor Coat. Forms for other objects can be made from just about anything — Styrofoam, Ethafoam, foam rubber, metal, wood, hard plastics. A cheesecloth covering, applied with a layer of Sculptor Coat, will increase the strength of the form. Filling the texture of the underlying fabric will probably take an additional coating or two of Sculptor Coat. Textural additives such as white paper towels, sand, dirt — anything that will help you achieve the surface look you envision — can be built up on the form by applying the material after wetting it with Sculptor Coat, by working it into the still-wet surface, or by mixing it with the Sculptor Coat before applying it. Basically, any type of material — rigid or flexible — can be bonded together and finished with the products in this line and still retain the structural qualities of the original material. Similar materials are produced by other manufacturers such as Rosco. See the discussion of "texturing" in Chapter 12, "Scene Painting."

Plaster Bandage   Plaster-impregnated gauze can be used to make built-up forms such as masks and small armor pieces. Available from surgical supply houses and some drugstores, it is the material that doctors use to make casts. It is water-soluble, creates no toxic or noxious fumes, and can be formed easily. After the material has dried, it can be sanded and painted with both water- and oil- or lacquer-based paints.

Thermoplastics   These are stiff plastics that soften in hot water and can be molded before they cool and stiffen. They are available in pellet, mesh, and fabric forms. They can be molded on the face and body for masks and armor, and finished with most paints.

Fiberglass   Fiberglass is an extremely strong material formed of two parts: glass fibers in the form of mat or woven cloth and a resin coat that cures into a hard plastic. It can be used for constructing armor and helmets, while the resin can be used by itself in the production of jewelry. More information about fiberglass can be found in Chapter 13, "Stage Properties." Rose Brand Fabric

FIGURE 19.12
Metal is frequently used in the fabrication of decorative items such as appliqués and buckles. Courtesy of J. Michael Gillette.

has introduced Aqua-Resin, a water-base, two-part resin. Other brands of water-based resins are available in many hardware stores and home centers.

Metal Aluminum, copper, and brass appliqués and jewelry are often used in the construction of various accessories for gowns, armor, buckles, and similar applications. Metal appliqués (Figure 19.12) can usually be found in fabric stores, while thin sheet metal can be found in craft shops. The sheet metal can be formed using standard woodworking tools, and the copper and brass sheets can be soldered. All three metals can be fastened with pop rivets or glued with appropriate cyanoacrylate cements such as Super Glue or Krazy Glue. (See Chapter 10, "Tools and Materials," for more information on adhesives.)

Garment Construction

While there are certainly many similarities between clothing construction in the fashion industry and costuming, there is one substantial difference. The goal in garment industry is to make multiple copies, in a number of different sizes, of a single design. That single design is also intended to fit a variety of body types. The goal in costume construction is much more specific — to make one-of-a-kind garments for one specific body. Additionally, the design of the costume must help reveal the personality of the character for whom it was created.

Patterns

Arguably, the most important step in the realization of a costume is the creation of the pattern from which the costume will be constructed. "The three main goals of drafting and/or draping a costume pattern are (1) to manipulate a flat piece of cloth by cutting and shaping so it conforms to a specific three-dimensional body, while (2), at the same time, accurately translating a sketch prepared by a costume designer into reality, and (3) creating a costume that serves all the various needs of the script, the actor, and the production."[1]

There are two main methods of patterning: flat patterning (drafting) and draping. This section will provide a brief explanation of both. Neither flat patterning nor draping should be considered as a preferred method of patterning. Both have advantages, and both should be learned. Some shapes are more easily constructed by draping than flat patterning. Tailored or form-fitting garments, such as men's suits and uniforms, are generally better suited to flat-pattern methods. But it is possible to create tailored garments by draping. The patterning method used in any particular situation is determined by the working preferences of the cutter/draper.

Flat Patterning   One of the primary jobs of the cutter is to create the flat patterns from which costumes are frequently made. Pattern making is both an art and a craft. So it is reasonable to assume that there is really no single "correct way" to make a pattern. Every cutter develops personal methods and techniques of working. But there is a general process that most cutters follow when creating a flat pattern, and that process will be explained here. But remember that this method is neither "right" nor "correct." It is simply one way of going about the process of making a flat pattern.

Because a flat pattern is created for one particular actor, it is necessary to get a set of very specific measurements for that actor. Those measurements are detailed in the measurement chart shown in Figure 19.13. From those measurements the cutter develops a basic pattern. The basic pattern, also called a body block or block, is laid out on wide brown wrapping or butcher paper. This isn't the final pattern for the costume because it doesn't provide any period details. It is simply a generic pattern designed to fit cloth to a particular actor's body. After the block is drawn on paper, it is transferred to medium-weight muslin, cut out, and stitched together. The actor then comes into the costume shop for a fitting (Figure 19.14); or, if the actor is unavailable, the muslin mockup is fit to a tailor's dummy with measurements that very nearly approximate those of the actor, and any necessary adjustments are made. These adjustments are normally transferred back to the paper pattern. This provides a finished basic pattern that fits the actor's body. This is the pattern from which the costume pattern is developed.

The costume pattern is developed by modifying the block to exhibit the design characteristics of a particular style or period as interpreted by the costume designer. For example, the sleeve block provides the pattern for a basic sleeve that fits the actor and allows full range of arm motion. But it doesn't say anything about period or style. By studying the costume designer's sketch, and from conversations with the designer, the cutter will know what the sleeve, and the rest of the costume is supposed to look like, including its period and style. There are many excellent books that contain historical costume patterns. As indicated in Chapter 18, "Costume Design," there are also numerous other sources that the costume designer consults to develop an understanding of the look of clothes from a given period and place. The cutter gleans information from these sources as well. But the cutter's research focuses more on how to construct the costume than on its design. Using information from all of these sources, the cutter modifies the sleeve block to create a pattern that both fits the

[1] Rosemary Ingham and Liz Covey, *The Costume Technician's Handbook,* 3rd ed. (Portsmouth, N.H.: Heinemann, 2003), p. 97.

FIGURE 19.13
Costume-measurement chart.

MEASUREMENT CHART

Name: _____ Height: _____ Weight: _____

Bra Size: _____ Dress Size: _____ Tights/Pantyhose: _____ Leotard: _____

Men's Shirt: _____ Trousers: _____ Men's Suit: _____ Shoe: _____

Chest/Bust	Ribcage (Underbust)	Head (Circ)	Head (Temple to temple, around back of head)	Head (Forehead to nape)	Head (Ear to ear; over head)
CF Neck to waist	F Shoulder to waist	Center of shoulder to bust point	Bust point to bust point	Underbust to waist	Neck at base Neck at midpoint
F Chest width (armscye to armscye)	X Both shoulders (Front)	CB Neck to waist	B Shoulder to waist	B Chest width (X shoulder blades)	X Both shoulders (Back)
Arm length to wrist	Arm length to elbow	Men's sleeve (CB neck to wrist)	Left shoulder	Right shoulder	
Armscye	Bicep	Elbow	Wrist	Overhand	
Waist	Hips	Thigh	Knee	Below knee	Calf
Waist to hip (on side)	Waist to above knee	Waist to below knee	Waist to ankle	Waist to floor	Outseam
CB Neck to floor	CF Neck to floor	Side neck to floor	CB Waist to floor	CF Waist to floor	Inseam
Crotch depth (Seated)	Crotch or 1/2 girth	Full girth (for leotards)			
Glasses?	Contacts?	Pierced ears?	Tattoos?	Other Notes	

actor and realizes the designer's intent. This process is repeated until the cutter has a complete pattern for the entire costume.

Using the initial costume pattern, the costume technicians normally make a muslin mockup of the costume and fit it to the actor. Any modifications to the mockup are transferred to the paper pattern. While it is possible to use the adjusted muslin mockup as a pattern for cutting the final costume material, this normally isn't done because the muslin can be stretched or pulled out of shape. Because the paper doesn't distort, it provides a much more accurate pattern.

Draping   Draping is the process of pinning fabric directly to a tailor's form and creating pattern pieces or a garment by manipulating the fabric until the desired look is achieved. Draping requires that you have a tailor's form whose dimensions closely match those of the actor for whom the costume is being made. While draping can be used to create tailored clothes, it is more frequently used to create untailored, three-dimensional elements such as bustles.

Depending on the particular production circumstances, drapers will either make a pattern of the object, or they will skip the pattern step and simply use the costume material to create the draped design. The choice isn't always made to save time. The way a particular fabric drapes is dependent on its physical characteristics — the type of weave, its tightness or looseness, the weight and stiffness of the fabric, and so forth. If the draper is going to make a pattern, the pattern material needs to closely approximate the physical characteristics of the "final" material so that it will hang and drape like the final material. You don't want to use a lightweight, soft material to drape a pattern that's going to be finalized in a heavy brocade simply because the two fabrics don't hang or drape the same way.

Pattern-Drafting Software   There are numerous programs available for flat pattern drafting, but none, as of this writing, that are useful for draping. The advantages of these flat-pattern programs over hand-drafting are similar to those listed for other drafting programs — faster layout, greater accuracy, much faster revisions, and data transfer. The primary disadvantage is also the same — a very steep initial learning curve. To be useful to a cutter/draper, a pattern-drafting program must allow the operator to either modify the program's existing patterns and/or create original patterns. One program, Custom Pattern Maker, allows the operator to draft original patterns on a body block using the same processes that were described earlier. It also allows the operator to alter the measurements of any existing pattern. Because the pieces of a complete pattern are usually large, plotters and large-format printers are typically used to print patterns.

 ## Special-Effects Treatment of Fabrics

Fabric Dyeing

Before beginning the discussion on dyes and dyeing it is necessary to consider the safety issues surrounding this subject. Dyes are inherently dangerous. Powdered dyes can be inhaled. So can the vapors from dyes that are in solution.

Companies that manufacture dyes, or import them for sale in the United States, are required to have Safety Data Sheets (SDSs) for each color of every dye they make or sell. That may seem excessive. It isn't. Why? Different chemical compounds are used to create different dye colors. And the level of toxicity of a specific dye depends entirely on the chemicals used to make it. Unfortunately, companies who buy in bulk and then repackage dyes into smaller quantities for sale to the general public, and costume shops, aren't required to provide the buyer with the SDSs for these materials. But be persistent. Find out who the bulk manufacturer was. Contact the company. Try an online search. The bottom line in the safety issue is you. Be smart with your own safety. Don't use dyes that you don't know how to handle safely. Some of them are benign, some are mildly hazardous, and some are carcinogenic. And you can't tell which is which without the safety information.

Fabric must be washed and rinsed before it is dyed. If the material was heavily sized, it should be soaked in a light soda ash solution before it is washed. Dyes go into solution best when initially mixed with boiling water. The working temperature of the dye solution depends on the type of dye and material being dyed. Tightly woven fabrics do not dye as well as those with looser weaves. The color-fast characteristics of any dyed fabric are enhanced if the material is thoroughly rinsed after it has been dyed. (Be sure to review the Safety Tip at the bottom of this page.)

Types of Dyes   There are a large number of fabric dyes that can be used in the costume shop. Because no single dye works equally well on all types of fabrics, this section will discuss the characteristics of several common dyes. The description of the effects and characteristics of these dyes is necessarily vague simply because the exact impact that a particular dye will have on a specific fabric depends on many variables — the saturation and heat of the dye solution; the amount of time the material is left in the dye solution; the type and amount of **setting** agent in the dye; the type, blend, and finish of the fabric; and so forth.

Union Dyes   Union dyes contain several types of dyes and are designed to be moderately effective on many fabric types. Union dyes are exemplified by household dyes such as Rit or Tintex that are available in most fabric stores. If used with boiling water, union dyes will work well on most natural-fiber fabrics and rayon if you are trying to achieve a tint or medium shade. Slightly more intense colors can be achieved by using more dye than is called for in the instructions, but it is almost impossible to achieve a deep shade of full saturation using union dyes. When dyeing cotton or linen, you can enhance the setting of the dye by adding salt to the solution. When dyeing wool or silk, add vinegar to the dye. Union dyes are not particularly effective on synthetic materials other than rayon. To maintain color intensity, wash union-dyed materials in cold water or have them dry cleaned.

Aniline Dyes   All-purpose or **unified aniline dyes,** also known as acid dyes, create strong colors of light to full saturation on natural-fiber fabrics and a few synthetics. Either salt or vinegar (½ cup per teaspoon of dry dye) is used in the dye solution as a setting agent. A little alcohol is added to the dry dye to form a paste,

Safety Tip

Most of the dyes used in the costume shop recommend heating the dye anywhere from 100°F to boiling. Heated dye solutions give off vapors that are hazardous to some degree. In addition to reading the directions of the dye containers, also read the SDSs for the specific dyes that are being used. Be sure to follow the recommendations for safe handling of wet and dry dyes, protective clothing and eyewear, respirators, ventilation, and related safety issues.

setting: To help lock the dye into the fiber of the fabric; to reduce or prevent the dye from being rubbed off the fabric.

unified aniline dye: A coal-tar– derivative dye formulated to work on both animal- and plant-derivative fibers.

then boiling water is added to the paste. In general, 1 teaspoon of dry dye will make 1 quart of full-strength dye, although the ratio of the mixture can be varied.

Disperse Dyes Designed for use with synthetics like acetate, nylon, and polyester, disperse dyes have intense color and are quite colorfast if the dye solution is almost boiling when the fabric is dyed. A little liquid detergent in the dye solution helps the dye penetrate the fabric fibers.

Fiber-Reactive Dyes These dyes are arguably the most useful for fabric painting of natural-fiber fabrics because they produce intense, colorfast colors when the temperature of the dye bath is lukewarm or cool. Salt is used as the setting agent.

Spray Painting

Any type of spray painting — aerosol spray cans, air brushes, air or airless spray guns — releases atomized paint or dye into the air. This constitutes a potentially serious health hazard.

Always spray paint in an environment where the paint or dye mist can be controlled. An exhaust ventilation system — a location where the spray mist is being evacuated and replaced with clean air — offers the best spray mist control. A paint booth — a walk-in, enclosed environment that exhausts contaminated air, filters it before releasing it into the environment, and replaces the contaminated air with fresh air — provides the most effective protection. A paint station is basically a desktop version of a paint booth with one wall removed. A typical paint station is enclosed on top, bottom, and three sides, with a powered exhaust vent usually located in the top. Fresh air is drawn into the unit from the open side, which is also where you stand to work. The final type of exhaust ventilation system is location with an exhaust hood above a designated workspace. Because this system is entirely open it is critical that the fan be powerful enough to not only suck in the contaminated air, but also prevent any overspray from escaping the updraft.

A dilution ventilation system, rather than exhausting contaminated air, mixes fresh air with the contaminated air to dilute the level of contaminants to acceptable levels. Less effective than the exhaust ventilation system, this type of system should be used only for diluting the vapors of nontoxic materials. Again, consult the SDS for the material with which you're working to see if a dilution ventilation system is even recommended. If it isn't, don't use the material in that environment.

Weather permitting, you can also take the work outside. There are two dangers inherent to working outside: (1) you may pollute the environment; (2) if there's no breeze, the spray may simply hang in the air as it would indoors with no ventilation. To counter that challenge, just set up a fan to blow across the work area. If a breeze is blowing, stand on the "up wind" side of the work so the spray isn't blown onto you.

Regardless of the type of ventilation system you use, be sure to wear the appropriate type of respirator for the materials with which you're working. Respirators filter out a substantial level of contaminants. But not every respirator filters out every type of contaminant. Filters are "contaminant specific." Consult the SDSs for the dyes or paints with which you're working and wear the recommended respirator, with the recommended filter, and wear the recommended safety apparel. If an appropriate respirator or filter can't be found, *do not do the work until one is found.*

As with so much in safety-related issues, be sure to apply a heavy dose of common sense when working with any hazardous materials. If you're spraying *anything,* you don't want to inhale it, and you don't want the spray to land on your skin. So wear recommended type of respirator/filter and protective clothing, and work only in an environment that has a recommended, and functioning, ventilation system.

Fabric Painting

Fabric can be painted for a variety of reasons, but it is normally painted to create added texture, enhance the fabric's three-dimensional qualities, age the fabric, and create or reinforce a pattern.

Fabric can be painted with almost anything that will adhere to or penetrate the fabric fibers. Union dyes, aniline dyes, acrylic fabric paints from craft stores, leather and vinyl spray paints, spray enamels, textile inks, **French enamel varnish (FEV),** permanent markers, shellac and bronzing powders can all be used effectively in fabric painting.

Fabric dyes and paints are applied with a variety of applicators. Brushes are frequently used with both wet and dry brush techniques. Larger brushes can also be used for spattering when texturing or aging costumes. Sponges and rag rolls can be used to apply texture. (See Chapter 12, "Scene Painting," for information on these painting techniques.) Automotive-paint stores sell compressed-air touch-up spray guns that have small, removable glass paint canisters. These spray paint and dyes effectively. Air brushes, which can be equipped with a variety of nozzles, can spray any of the liquid media in patterns ranging from a sharp line to a fan-shaped mist. Stencils can be cut and the pattern sprayed, brushed, or sponged onto the fabric. Stamp stencils, made from sponges or hard foam, can be used to apply a repetitive pattern. Hot glue guns can be used to apply ornamentation or decorative patterns to the fabric. These patterns can be painted after they've cooled.

The actual effects that each of these processes will have on fabric can be learned only through experimentation. However, some general guidelines may be helpful. Almost everything but dye will stiffen the fabric to some degree. When brushed or sprayed, the color of most dyes will not be as intense because the water is not boiling. After brushing or spraying, most dyes can be set if they are steamed in a steam cabinet. Alternatively, pressing the garment with a steam iron also works but exposes the presser to any gasses released in the process. Be sure to read the SDSs for any types of dyes you're using and follow their safety recommendations. Be sure to use a **pressing cloth** between the iron and the fabric to prevent the fresh dye from adhering to the sole of the iron. French enamel varnish produces brilliant color, but the shellac stiffens the fabric. Increased flexibility with no significant loss of brilliance can be achieved if you substitute flexible clear-acrylic textile medium — found in the fabric-painting supplies at most craft stores — for the shellac in an FEV mixture. Most of the pigments applied in fabric painting will lose their saturation and brilliance with washing or dry cleaning.

Costume Aging

While the techniques discussed in fabric painting can be, and frequently are, used to make costumes look old, abused, and worn, there are times when it may be necessary to severely distress the costume. Garments generally show their age at those points where the fabric receives the greatest stress — seats, knees, elbows, cuffs, hems, collars. The fibers in these places can be roughed up with sandpaper or a wood file. Old sweaters, coats, and pockets also show their age by stretching out of shape. This type of aging can be simulated by wetting the fabric (after the garment has been constructed) and pulling and stretching it out of shape until it is dry. Dirt-colored paints or dyes — primarily shades of brown for light fabrics and off-white for darker fabrics — can be rubbed into worn areas. Many painter/dyers assemble a "morgue" of photos of old clothing and use these examples as they distress costumes.

Again, experience is the best teacher. Get into the costume shop and learn by doing. Besides, it's fun.

French enamel varnish: A mixture of dye and shellac; made by mixing alcohol-based leather dye (e.g., Fiebing's Leather Dye) with shellac that has been reduced (1:1) with denatured alcohol.

pressing cloth: A cloth placed between the iron and the fabric being pressed.

The Costume Shop Can Be Hazardous to Your Health

There are a wide variety of safety hazards in the costume shop. Some of them are readily apparent — sharp scissors and needles, sewing machines, hot irons, and boiling water. Others, such as fabric lint and chemical fumes, are a lot less apparent and potentially much more dangerous.

A variety of noxious and toxic chemicals are used in finishing textiles. Every time you work with fabric — unroll it, smooth it out, cut it, and sew it — small amounts of lint are released into the air. That lint continues to float until it settles to the ground or you and your coworkers inhale it. Potentially hazardous chemical vapors are released from paints, dyes, glues, and adhesives. Neither the chemically coated lint nor the chemical vapors are good for your health, and the long-term effects of continuous exposure to some of them could be harmful.

To reduce these hazards, the costume-shop area needs to be well ventilated. Frequently, the shop is in the basement, and many of those buildings were constructed before OSHA's safety guidelines became law, so little or no thought was given to proper ventilation. If the air is not constantly changing and/or being filtered, make sure that there are fans to do so. Move fresh air into the workplace, and move stale, contaminated air out.

Frequently, the dye vat will be set up in a small room separate from the rest of the costume shop. It should be well ventilated. Be sure to wear a proper respirator while working with the heated dye water.

All costume shops should maintain an up-to-date list of the Safety Data Sheets (SDSs) for any hazardous materials used in the shop. Because reality has a way of intruding on even the best of intentions, the shop's list may not be completely up to date. The best way to get the most current information available is to conduct an online search. Go to the website of the manufacturer of the specific product for which you're searching. If the SDS information isn't available on the website, contact the manufacturer by e-mail — the address is usually located on the website homepage — and ask for a copy. If none of that works, do an online search for "SDS." The results will reveal a number of websites with links to the SDSs for a large number of manufacturers' products and materials, as well as instructions for reading and understanding the frequently obtuse "legalese" used to write SDSs.

Following these safety tips, plus using your common sense and becoming familiar with the safety tips listed in Chapters 8, 9, 10, 13, and 14, should help make the costume shop a safe and enjoyable place in which to work. If you see something that doesn't look, sound, feel, or smell safe, it probably isn't. Report it to your supervisor. Remember that safety is everybody's business.

Costume Crafts

Costume crafts is a broad catch-all term that refers to all those costume items that the actor wears that are not the basic garment. It includes, but is certainly not limited to wigs, hats, shoes, belts, braces, gloves, ties, purses, stockings, socks, scarves, shawls, handkerchiefs, jewelry, eyeglasses, parasols, walking sticks, canes, masks, armor, spats, gun holsters, swords, and scabbards. Costume artisans who work in the area of costume crafts need to be creative problem solvers, and they require many of the same skill sets as property artisans. They need to have a thorough understanding of not only the principles of design, but how to look at a design and be able to visualize a way to construct whatever is needed. They need to be skilled in not only flat patterning, draping, and the other

FIGURE 19.15
The ass's head from the Colorado Shakespeare Festival production of *A Midsummers' Night Dream.* Costume design by Mary McClung. Printed with permission of Mary McClung.

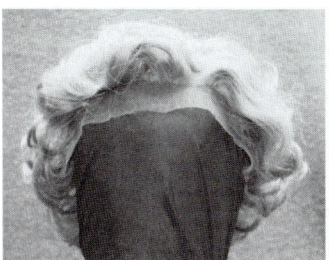

FIGURE 19.16
Fronted wigs have a ventilated section attached to the front of the wig. Courtesy of J. Michael Gillette.

FIGURE 19.17
Hard-front wigs do not have a ventilated transition section. Courtesy of J. Michael Gillette.

traditional skills required for costume construction; they also need to have a thorough understanding of fine metalworking and leatherworking, as well as a variety of painting, dyeing, and distressing techniques, molding/casting, and so forth.

Some of the more complex costume crafts items, such as the ass head for *A Midsummer's Night Dream* (Figure 19.15), could easily fall into that "is-it-a-costume-or-a-prop?" twilight zone area between costumes and props. That's why it is so important to have good communication between the various production shops. Fantasy items such as the *Midsummer's* ass head could realistically be built by either costume or property artisans. It should be obvious that the decision as to which shop will build this type of item needs to be made early in the production process.

The remainder of this section will discuss some of the more prominent costume crafts areas.

Wigs

A wig is an important element of the costume. It is frequently necessary to use a wig to achieve the correct hair style, either male or female, for a particular historical period. A well-dressed wig can be used to enhance the appearance of contemporary costumes as well. Wigs used in the theatre are generally divided into two basic categories: fronted and hard-front.

Fronted wigs are those that have a section of ventilated hair added at the hairline to create the illusion of hair growing out of the scalp, as illustrated in Figure 19.16. The lace used for this ventilated section is quite delicate. Care must be taken when working with it so it is neither torn nor pulled out of shape. Water-based spirit gum can be used to secure the lace to the forehead, although a well-fitted wig should not require gluing. However, if spirit gum is used, the lace should be carefully cleaned and any spirit gum residue removed after each use.

A hard-front wig, Figure 19.17, does not have a ventilated front piece, so the wig hair begins abruptly rather than having a more natural-looking appearance. Hard-front wigs are very effective if they are styled in a manner that hides the hard edge of the artificial hairline, as shown in Figure 19.18. Hard-front wigs can also be changed into fronted wigs simply by attaching a ventilated section

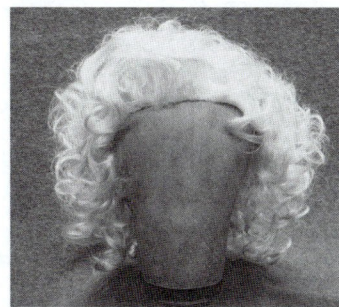

(A)

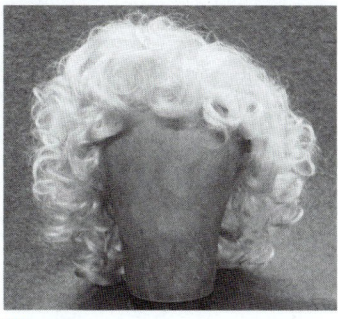

(B)

FIGURE 19.18
Wig styling can ease the visual transition of hard-front wigs. (A) The hard edge revealed. (B) Hair styled to conceal the hard edge. Courtesy of J. Michael Gillette.

to the front of the wig using hair from the wig to make the ventilated section. Ultimately, the choice of whether to use a fronted or hard-front wig will be determined by budget, the expertize of the theatre's wigmaker, and the hair style required for the particular character being portrayed.

Period wigs can be rented from many theatrical-costume supply houses, or they can be made in the shop using natural hair or synthetic hair such as horsehair rayon or dynel. Sometimes yak hair is used because of its coarse texture. Wigmaking is a difficult craft that requires a great deal of patience and experience. However, excellent results frequently can be achieved by restyling contemporary wigs. Long-haired wigs of either synthetic or (preferably) human hair can be purchased at local wig shops, and they can be styled to achieve most of the period looks shown in Figure 19.19. Frequently, these wigs are manufactured

FIGURE 19.19
A progression of hair styles. Drawings by Peggy Kellner.

Sumerian 2900–2685 B.C.

Egyptian wig 1555–7330 B.C.

Second-century Greek

French c. 1150

Italian c. 1488

Spanish c. 1613

French c. 1660

French c. 1778

English c. 1831

American Gibson style c. 1895

American c. 1926

American bubble c. 1963

Assyrian

Roman

French c. 1150

Burgundy c. 1448

Elizabethan Van Dyke beard

English c. 1670

American c. 1776

English c. 1831

American mutton chops and handlebar moustache c. 1884

American Valentino look c. 1930

American crew cut c. 1942

American flower child c. 1960s

with an overabundance of hair. If a natural rather than "wiggy" look is desired, the wig stylist removes about one-third of the hair from the commercial wig. This hair is used to ventilate a piece of netting attached to the front of the wig foundation. (The ventilating process is explained and illustrated in Chapter 20, "Makeup.") The modified commercial wig looks quite natural, and the ventilated portion creates a realistic hairline.

The wig stylist, who works under the supervision of the costume designer, consults the costume designer's sketch to determine the designer's concept for the hair style. He or she will also need to consult primary source materials (paintings, photos, and so on) for additional information on the look and style of hair in the period being used.

Hair pieces or extensions provide another way of creating a period hair style that uses the actor's natural hair, and hairline, as the basis of the design.

Human-hair wigs can be coiffed with conventional curlers, electric rollers, or curling irons. Synthetic wigs can be dressed by using hair styling products such as gels and mousses, rolling the hair on a cold curling iron or cold rollers and gently heating the hair with the warm air from either a handheld or cap-style hair dryer. Most professional costume shops dry both synthetic and human-hair wigs in commercial wig-drying cabinets where the temperature and drying time can be controlled.

To dress a wig, most wig masters will pin the wig to a **canvas head block** that is clamped to a working surface such as a table or counter. If the wig has a ventilated front, the leading edge of lace should be secured to the head block so it will retain its shape. The edge of the lace is covered with a piece of twill tape or ribbon and pinned to the head block every half inch as demonstrated in Figure 19.20.

Securing a wig to an actor's head is a multistep process, as illustrated in Figure 19.21. If the actor has long hair, it will frequently need to be pinned up under the wig cap in pin curls and secured with bobby pins. The pin curls should be evenly spaced so when the wig cap is fitted the pin curls do not alter the actor's natural head shape. To help anchor the wig to the head, pin curls are normally placed at each temple, on top of the crown, and on both sides of the nape of the neck as shown in Figure 19.21A. A **wig cap,** available in mesh as well as solid cotton fabrics and in a variety of colors, is used to compress the actor's own hair. The color of the wig cap, as well as any **bobby pins** and **hair pins**, should closely match the color of the wig. The wig cap, Figure 19.21B is secured to the pin curls with hair pins. Any stray hair is then tucked up inside the wig cap. In the event that the actor's hair is too short for pin curls, foam medical tape can be wrapped around the actor's head like a head band, but above the hair line, to create the necessary anchoring points. The wig is then placed on the actor's head, Figure 19.21C, and secured by pinning through the wig foundation and wig cap, Figure 19.21D, and into the foam medical tape or the strategically placed pin curls. A properly fitted wig, Figure 19.21E, fits the actor's head and looks very natural. Wig dressing is an exacting craft and should be attempted only under the supervision of someone with experience in the field.

Millinery

In the same manner as wigs, hats are frequently a requirement for completing the costume in many periods of history (see Figure 19.22). Traditionally, hats have been made using one of three basic techniques: pulled felt, covered buckram, and braided straw.

Pulled felt hats, like a man's bowler or top hat, are created by steaming an existing broad-brimmed felt hat, or a felted hood or body, until the felt is limp

FIGURE 19.20
A wig pinned to a head block for styling. Courtesy of J. Michael Gillette.

canvas head block: A block of material in the shape of a head, covered with canvas. Wigs are pinned to it for styling and storage.

wig cap: A skull cap of thin, tight-fitting mesh material. Used to cover and compress the wig-wearer's hair.

bobby pin: A hair pin made of springy flat metal wire bent in a tight U shape. The legs — one straight, the other wavy — touch each other and provide the clamping power to hold the hair in place. Generally used with shorter hair.

hair pin: A piece of round metal wire bent in a slightly opened U shape. Used with longer hair than bobby pins.

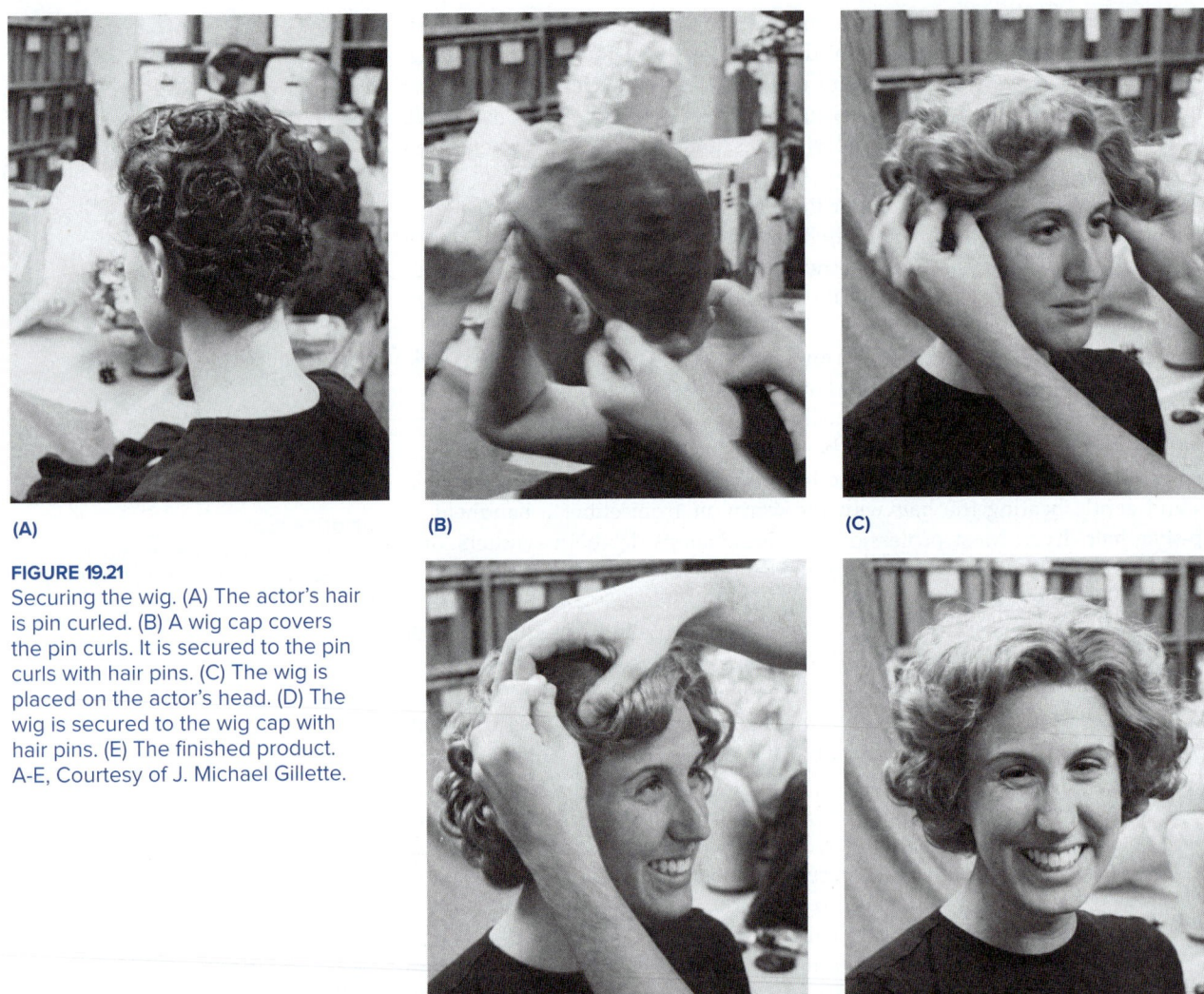

(A)

(B)

(C)

(D)

(E)

FIGURE 19.21
Securing the wig. (A) The actor's hair is pin curled. (B) A wig cap covers the pin curls. It is secured to the pin curls with hair pins. (C) The wig is placed on the actor's head. (D) The wig is secured to the wig cap with hair pins. (E) The finished product. A-E, Courtesy of J. Michael Gillette.

and pliable then pulling and stretching it until the desired shape is achieved. The shaping/drying process is aided by using an electrically heated hat block or hat mold (Figure 19.23). Once the felt cools the application of a sizing solution to the felt helps the form keep its shape. When the shape of the crown and brim have been finalized the pieces are joined.

Buckram is a fairly stiff, loosely woven and sized material used to make hat foundations. To make a covered buckram hat, like the saucy little number that Eliza Doolittle wears in most productions of *My Fair Lady*, the decoration, crown, and brim shape are patterned and then cut from buckram. The pieces are joined and then covered with fabric that fits snuggly to the buckram hat form. The hat's edges — the brim and crown — are frequently finished with grosgrain ribbon or bias-cut strips of fabric, and the inside of the hat is normally lined as well.

Woven hats, such as the men's straw boater illustrated in Figure 19.22, can usually be purchased from costume supply houses. If the commercially available styles won't work for your particular design concept, woven hats can also

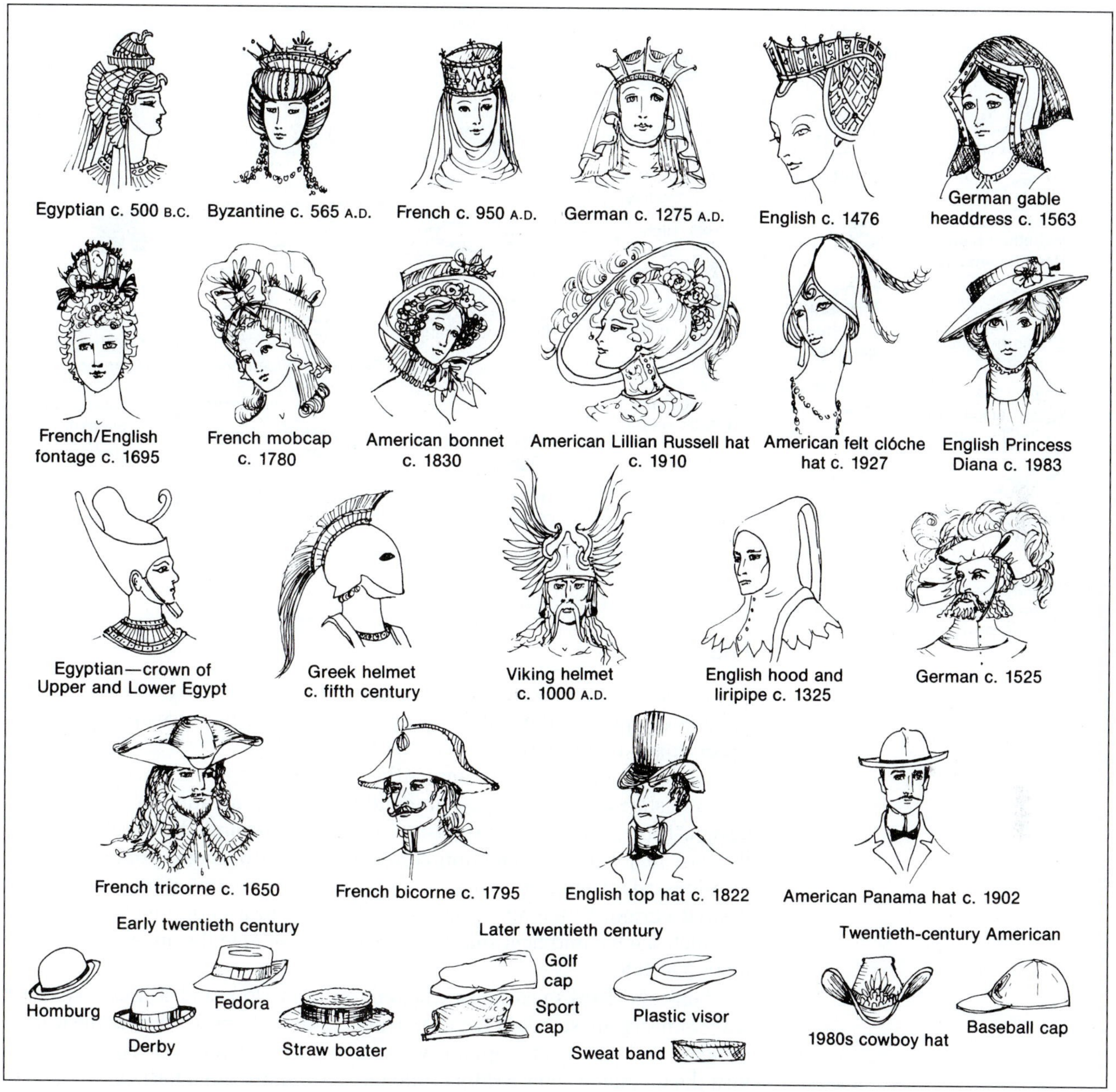

Egyptian c. 500 B.C.   Byzantine c. 565 A.D.   French c. 950 A.D.   German c. 1275 A.D.   English c. 1476   German gable headdress c. 1563

French/English fontage c. 1695   French mobcap c. 1780   American bonnet c. 1830   American Lillian Russell hat c. 1910   American felt clóche hat c. 1927   English Princess Diana c. 1983

Egyptian—crown of Upper and Lower Egypt   Greek helmet c. fifth century   Viking helmet c. 1000 A.D.   English hood and liripipe c. 1325   German c. 1525

French tricorne c. 1650   French bicorne c. 1795   English top hat c. 1822   American Panama hat c. 1902

Early twentieth century   Later twentieth century   Twentieth-century American

Homburg   Fedora   Derby   Straw boater   Golf cap   Sport cap   Sweat band   Plastic visor   1980s cowboy hat   Baseball cap

FIGURE 19.22
A progression of styles in hats, headdresses, and crowns. Drawings by Peggy Kellner.

be built by joining concentric circles of woven straw to create the desired brim width, crown height, and shape and then joined together.

There are endless possibilities for what can be placed on an actor's head. The range is from a simple leather-thong headband to an amazingly complex Las Vegas showgirl headdress complete with flashing lights. When creating large and/or outlandish hats and headdresses a great deal of consideration must be given to their structural stability, centering, and support.

A number of excellent source books, including books that provide patterns for various period headdresses, are listed in the Selected References. Almost any period hat can be constructed using these patterns and the materials available from a well-supplied fabric shop, mail-order millinery store, or Internet supplier.

FIGURE 19.23
A hat mold. Courtesy of J. Michael Gillette.

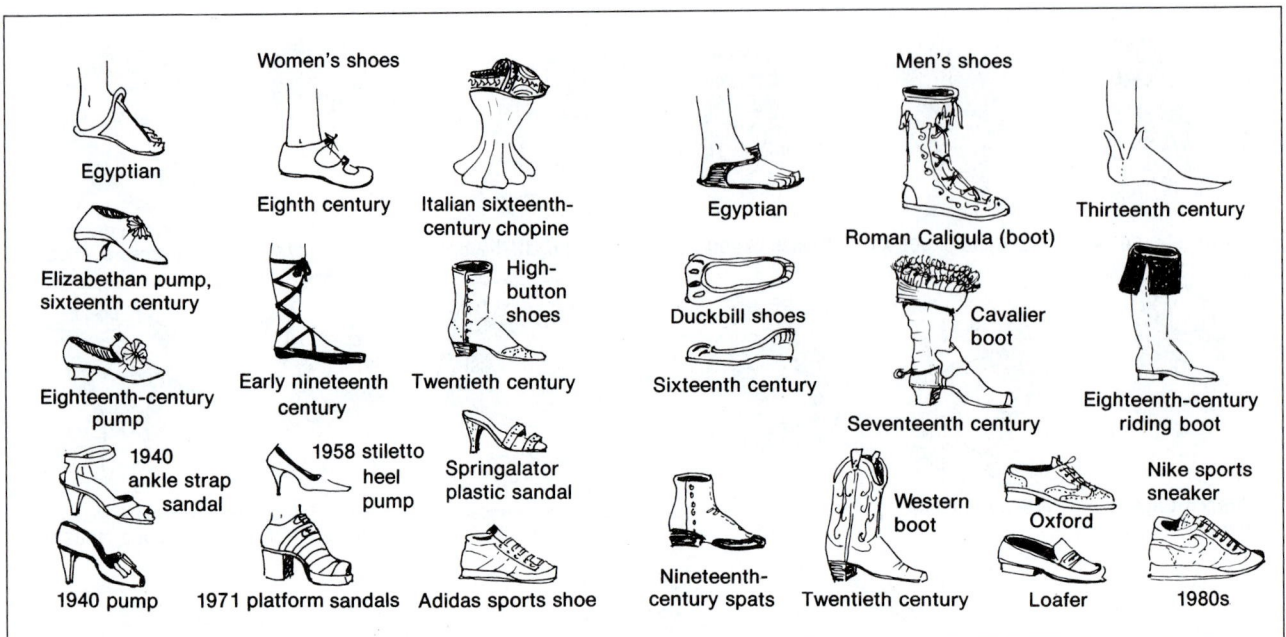

FIGURE 19.24
A progression of period shoe styles.
Drawings by Peggy Kellner.

Footwear

Just as many costumes would not be complete without a wig or a hat, no costume is complete without the appropriate footwear. Examples of shoes from various periods are shown in Figure 19.24.

Although the ideal solution to this challenge is to contract with a cobbler or a shoe company to custom-build footwear of an appropriate style and design, this prohibitively expensive solution is beyond the fiscal means of the vast majority of production companies. Instead, many producing organizations adapt modern shoes by adding elements more appropriate to the desired period. When adapting a modern shoe to a period look, select one in which the toe and heel shape most closely resemble the appearance of the intended style.

Soft- and hard-soled house slippers, in both cloth and leather, with and without heels, are standard items in many costume shops. By dyeing the leather or fabric and adding appropriate accessories such as buckles or bows, you can turn the ubiquitous house slipper into footwear appropriate for many male and female fashion periods. Period-specific boots can frequently be made by sewing a leather boot top to a leather slipper.

Jewelry

A variety of techniques can be used to create jewelry and ornamentation such as buckles, crowns, brooches, and so forth. When making these objects, it is important to adhere to the shape, size, and materials of historical antecedents, but how it will look from the back of the house is more important. "Simplicity and the right amount of exaggeration are the key to good stage jewelry and ornament."[2]

---

[2] Douglas A. Russell, *Stage Costume Design,* 2nd ed. (Englewood Cliffs, N.J.: Prentice-Hall, 1985), p. 157.

The basic shape of the object to be created can be formed out of wood, metal, thermoplastic, or any other material appropriate to the object being built.

Bits of cording, lace, or other objects can be glued on to add texture. The object is painted flat black, brown, or deep blue, and the raised areas dry-brushed with metallic paints such as silver or gold to add luster and highlights. If a deep, high-sheen surface is required, water-base fiberglass resin can be used for the dark base coat. The resin can be colored with pigments, dyes, and/or bronzing powders. Rhinestones or colored glass "jewels" can be hot-glued onto the finished form. (Chapter 13, "Stage Properties," discusses a number of craft processes that are useful in the construction of jewelry and other costume accessories.)

Every costume shop should have a collection of "junk jewelry." These rings, brooches, necklaces, and similar pieces, which almost always look fake and gaudy up close, project a rich, elegant look from the stage.

Armor

Body armor such as breastplates and helmets are frequently made from Fabric Form, fiberglass, or several types of thermoplastics. (See Chapters 10 and 13 for discussions of fiberglass, thermoplastics, and vacuum-forming techniques.)

Fiberglass armor is frequently formed by building up the basic shape on a clay-covered armature, covering the mold with aluminum foil, and applying the material to the form to create the basic rigid shell. Decoration is then applied by hand. When casting items that are fairly detailed and need to be uniform in appearance — military helmets, breastplates, leg shields, and so on — a rigid plaster-of-paris mold of the clay-covered armature is frequently cast. The mold will reveal all the detail on the clay original, particularly if fiberglass construction is used to create the object. After the release agent is applied to the mold, a gel coat of appropriately colored, catalyzed water-base fiberglass resin is applied to capture the detail. After the gel resin has set, glass mat or cloth is applied to the gel coat, while it is still in the mold, to build up the strength of the piece.

Armor can also be formed from thermoplastic materials such as those illustrated in Figure 19.25. These thermoplastics, available from medical supply houses under such trade names as Veraform, Polyform, and Hexcelite, become limp and formable when heated in 160-degree water for approximately 30 seconds. They can also be heated with handheld hair dryers. The nontoxic (unless burned) material can be worked, formed, and fused for approximately 2 to 4 minutes before it must be reheated. These materials are very durable and cost-effective, as any waste scraps can be heated and fused together to form workable-sized pieces. As with fiberglass, thermoplastics can be formed on or in a mold. If care is taken to insulate the actor — a sweatshirt or cloth of similar thickness is usually enough — the warm thermoplastic can be formed directly on the actor's body.

Masks

Masks are made from a wide range of materials and fabrics, but like armor the base layer of most masks is constructed on a clay or plaster mold. Masks used to be built on a mold using papier-mâché, as shown in Figure 19.26, but now thermoplastics, fiberglass, and plaster bandages are more commonly used to form rigid shells, while synthetic latex, netting, and various foams are used to create flexible elements, as shown in Figure 19.27. Rather than using a generic face mold, you can make an exact fit for a specific actor if the thermoplastic or plaster-bandage material is formed directly on the actor's face or from a life mask.

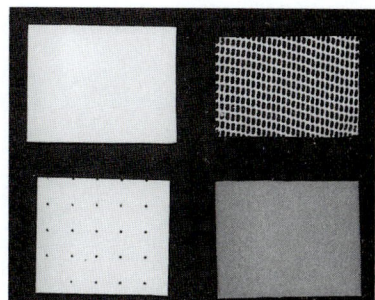

FIGURE 19.25
Low-temperature thermoplastics used in mask and costume construction. Courtesy of J. Michael Gillette.

FIGURE 19.26
Papier-mâché mask construction technique. (A) Cover the armature – in this case a life mask – with aluminum foil. (B) Cover the armature with several layers of glue-soaked newspaper strips. (C) Allow the papier-mâché to dry on the armature (24–48 hours). (D) Finish as desired. A-D, Courtesy of J. Michael Gillette.

(A) (B)

(C) (D)

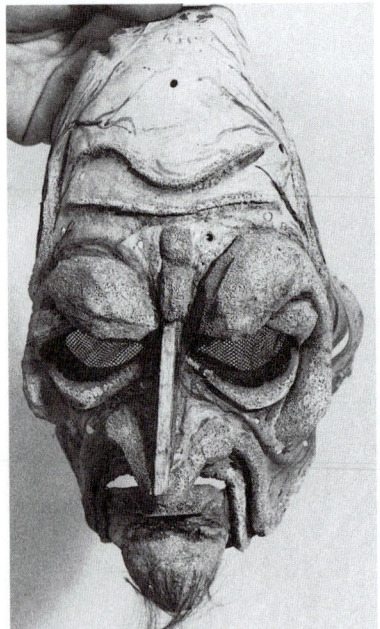

FIGURE 19.27
A mask made from plastic furnace filter foam hot glued onto a latex / gauze / Celastic base. Courtesy of J. Michael Gillette.

(Life mask construction techniques are detailed in Chapter 20, "Makeup.") The painting, texturing, aging, and appliqué techniques discussed in the jewelry- and armor-making sections of this chapter, and elsewhere in the text, are equally applicable to the construction of masks.

Selected References

Ingham, Rosemary, and Elizabeth Covey. *The Costume Technician's Handbook.* Heineman, 3rd ed., 2003.
Waugh, Norah. *The Cut of Men's Clothes 1600–1900.* Theatre Arts Books, 1964.
Waugh, Norah. *The Cut of Women's Clothes 1600–1930.* Theatre Arts Books, 1968.

Chapter 20

Makeup

Makeup is a vital element in creating the total appearance of the actor. To a great extent, the makeup design gives the audience its primary clue to the age, health, and vitality of the character. Although the overall appearance of the actor is the costume designer's domain, a makeup designer, working with the costume designer, is frequently responsible for the design and execution of the makeup.

Stage makeup enhances the illusion that the actor has become the character. In almost every production some of the actors, for one reason or another, do not facially resemble the characters they are playing. Makeup can help solve this challenge by providing actors with the means to change their appearance. Through the skillful application of the various techniques of makeup, young faces can be made to look older, older faces younger, pretty faces less attractive, blemished skin clear, and rather plain faces ravishingly attractive. On a more mundane level, bright stage lights tend to lighten skin tones, so makeup is also used to put color back in the cheeks of the actor. By thoughtful design, that color can be made more appropriate to the character than are the actor's natural skin tones.

A great deal of the communication process that transfers information from the actor to the audience takes place visually. To fully understand what the actors are saying (actually, what they are meaning), the audience must be able to read the actors' facial expressions. But makeup does more than simply exaggerate the facial features of the actor. Effective makeup will both exaggerate or minimalize the actor's natural features as well as project the character (not the actor) to the audience.

In the past thirty-five or so years makeup design, as well as the technology of makeup, has changed. Prior to roughly the mid-1980s, actors generally covered their entire faces and necks with a foundation of either greasepaint or pancake makeup. This was, at best, uncomfortable. In many cases it caused skin problems. As street makeup — makeup worn by the "average woman on the street" — evolved into products that were healthier for the skin so did theatrical makeup. Simultaneously, the style basis for general theatrical makeup design has become more natural looking. There are exceptions, such as specific character makeup, but the general makeup design trend is toward a more naturalistic style.

Designing the Makeup

It is the makeup designer's responsibility to create a design that will help transform the actor into the character. In order to accomplish this goal, it's necessary to understand what the character should look like. Looking at the costume sketches and analyzing the script for information about the appearance is essential. Research information can help. Richard Corson, in his excellent text, *Stage Makeup,*

PRODUCTION INSIGHTS
The Design Process in Makeup Design

This discussion applies the features of the design process to makeup design. Another tour of Chapter 2 would be appropriate if you think that you don't fully understand the fundamentals of this problem-solving technique.

Commitment

To do your best work, you must promise yourself that you will perform the work to the best of your ability.

Analysis

The first phase of the analysis step involves clarifying and refining the challenge, "What should the makeup look like for this show?" Answers to this question are found by reading the script and asking questions about the characters, costume designs, budgets, schedules, and so forth. Some of these questions will be answered when you study the script. Others will be answered during the production conferences, in which the director and designers freely exchange ideas and information.

The second phase of analysis involves discovering areas and subjects about the appearance of the character(s) that will require further research. You will investigate these areas during the research phase of the design process.

Research

Research is divided into two areas: background research and conceptual research. Background research involves finding answers to the questions raised during your analysis of the challenge. In makeup design, a primary research source is the designer's analysis of the script and conversations with the costume designer. Of equal importance is the background-research phase, when you analyze each character in terms of those elements that affect their appearance.

Conceptual research is the process of putting together as many potential solutions to the design challenge as possible. This is the time that the makeup designer draws the preliminary makeup sketches. The best designs are normally achieved when the designer creates several variations of each design.

Incubation

After doing the preliminary sketches, you should move on to some other project or activity. This will give your subconscious mind a chance to sort through the material and synthesize the best design choice.

Selection

After incubation, focus on the project again and consciously make your final design choices.

Implementation

The implementation phase involves the actual production of the design sketches as well as the application of that design on the actor.

Evaluation

Evaluation involves objectively studying your application of the design process to the creation of the makeup design. Honestly analyze your work. Did you do enough background research? Did you spend enough time analyzing the challenge? The answer to these and similar questions should tell you ways in which you could improve your communication with other members of the design team as well as your own use of the design process.

suggests that *genetics, environment, health, disfigurements, fashion, age,* and *personality* are the main influences that affect physical appearance.[1] Genetics is the prime determinant of anyone's physical appearance.

[1] Richard Corson, *Stage Makeup,* 8th ed. (Englewood Cliffs, N.J.: Prentice-Hall, 1990), p. 19.

It's axiomatic that it's impossible to do too much research for makeup design. One of the best ways to do this is to create a morgue which, in this case, is a collection of a wide variety of images. The morgue shouldn't just be of pretty faces. It should include as many categories as you can think of: young, old, happy, sad, frumpy, grumpy faces; faces with cuts and bruises; animal and fantasy faces. It should include anything that you think might inspire you as you go through the process of trying to conjure up a design. Maybe even pictures of trees, flowers, or rocks. Whatever works for you. These images can be collected from online sources as well as photos from magazines and books. Just be sure to *copy* the images from books and magazines rather than tearing out the pages. That's just rude. With this morgue you'll have a wide variety of visual images at your disposal when it comes time to create a makeup design.

If, when doing research for a makeup design, you discover that makeup was not worn by people from the socioeconomic strata of that particular character, the design challenge will be to create and execute a makeup design that makes it appear that the actor is not made up at all.

Genetics determines height, skeletal structure, and hair and eye colors, while basic skin color is determined by genetics and shaped by environment as well.

Exposure to the elements — sun, wind, water, temperature — affects the color and texture of skin, so whether a character spends the majority of time indoors or outdoors, and the climate in which he or she lives, will definitely help shape his or her appearance.

Disfigurements may be genetically or accidentally caused. Richard III's disfigurements are noted in the script of *Richard III* by Shakespeare. Obviously, those deformities must be created in the costume and makeup. But a broken nose or a scar, uncalled for in the script, may aid in projecting the nature of a particular character to the audience.

Research will tell the makeup designer the particular makeup fashions of the period in which the play is set. Unless it is desired to have the character seem eccentric, out of fashion, or weird, the makeup should generally adhere to the fashion of that period.

A character's appearance also reveals something about his or her age and general health. Young, healthy skin usually has good color and a firm, smooth texture, whereas older skin or that of an ill person tends to be pallid, wrinkled, and less firm.

Personality is also revealed by facial appearance. Although we may do it subconsciously, almost everyone monitors the faces of people with whom they're talking to determine that person's mood. An arched eyebrow, eyes that suddenly narrow, a smile that turns into a frown communicate specific meanings. In the same manner, the shape of the face at rest communicates information about the personality of the character. If the mouth is set in a perpetual frown, we tend to assume that the person is serious and/or grumpy. If there are "smile lines" at the edges of the eyes and mouth, we tend to think of the person as happy. Makeup designers use these visual clues to help the actor reveal the character of the roles he or she is playing.

The process of creating makeup designs is similar to that followed by other designers. The script is read; production meetings are attended; individual conferences are held with the director, costume designer, and actors; research is

FIGURE 20.1
Preliminary makeup sketches show the idealized design of what the makeup should look like. Courtesy of J. Michael Gillette.

ALDONSO   ACT III

BEARD MUCH WHITER THAN ACT I

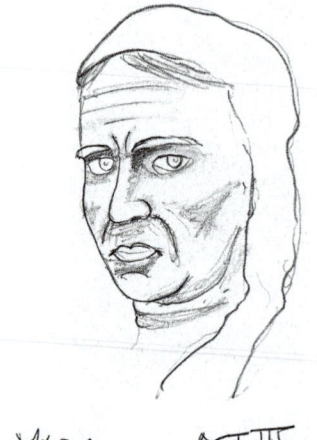

MARIA   ACT III

done; sketches of the designs are created; and finally, the makeup is applied to the actors. The specific steps that the makeup designer follows are outlined in the box "The Design Process in Makeup Design" on page 490.

Makeup Drawings

There are several types of drawings used by the makeup designer. Preliminary sketches are quick sketches (Figure 20.1) drawn in any medium, that show what the makeup should look like. If the makeup artist is inexperienced in sketching, worksheets with predrawn frontal and profile views can be used, as shown in Figure 20.2.

When the design is finalized, it should be adapted to the actor. This can be accomplished by placing tracing paper over a photo of the actor, tracing his or her natural features onto the paper, and then adapting the makeup to the actor's face, as shown in Figure 20.3. This process can also be accomplished by scanning the two images into a software program such as PhotoShop and printing a composite image.

Working drawings in makeup are similar to working drawings in other design areas. They detail information that shows the actor or makeup artist how to apply the makeup. The working drawing in Figure 20.4 shows frontal and profile views of the makeup design and contains written notes specifying techniques and materials to be used to re-create the design on the actor's face. Whether drawn in black and white or color, the most important point is that these drawings fully explain how and what makeup should be applied.

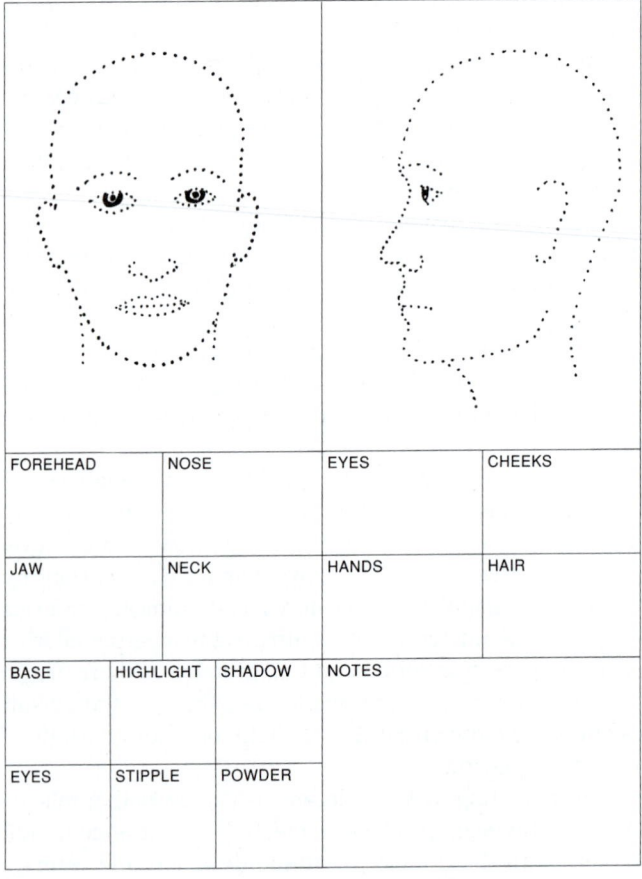

FOREHEAD	NOSE		EYES	CHEEKS
JAW	NECK		HANDS	HAIR
BASE	HIGHLIGHT	SHADOW	NOTES	
EYES	STIPPLE	POWDER		

FIGURE 20.2
Predrawn makeup worksheet.

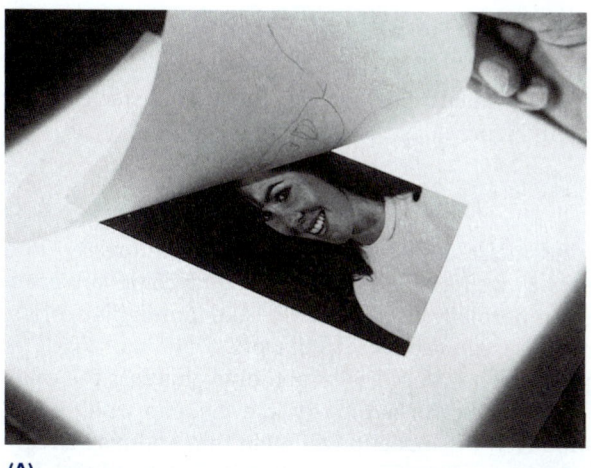

(A)

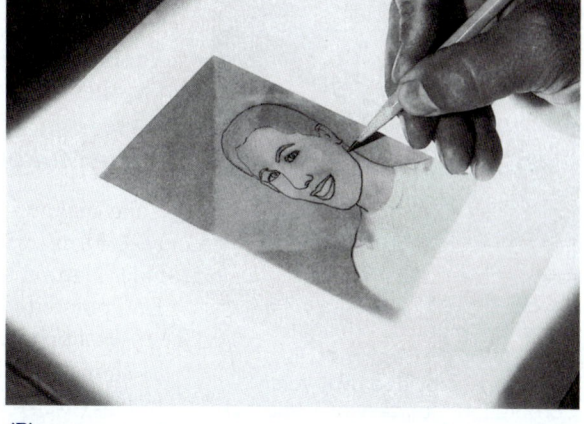

(B)

(C)

(D)

FIGURE 20.3
The makeup design is adapted to the actor's face by (A) transferring the outline of the actor's face to tracing paper from a photo and (B–D) redrawing the idealized design on the representation of the actor's face. Courtesy of J. Michael Gillette.

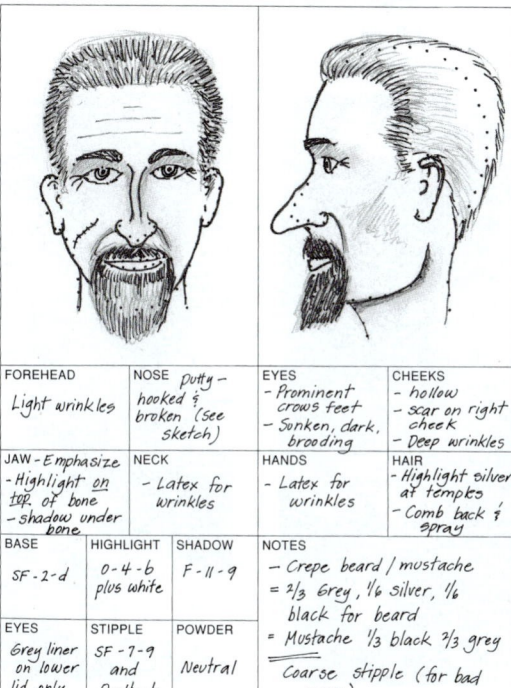

FOREHEAD	NOSE *putty – hooked & broken (see sketch)*	EYES - Prominent crows feet - Sunken, dark, brooding	CHEEKS - hollow - scar on right cheek - Deep wrinkles
Light wrinkles			
JAW - *Emphasize* - Highlight <u>on top</u> of bone - shadow under bone	NECK - Latex for wrinkles	HANDS - Latex for wrinkles	HAIR - Highlight silver at temples - Comb back & spray

BASE	HIGHLIGHT	SHADOW	NOTES
SF - 2 - d	0 - 4 - b plus white	F - 11 - 9	- Crepe beard / mustache = ⅔ Grey, ⅙ silver, ⅙ black for beard
EYES	STIPPLE	POWDER	= Mustache ⅓ black ⅔ grey
Grey liner on lower lid <u>only</u>	SF - 7 - 9 and 0 - 4 - b	Neutral	<u>Coarse stipple</u> (for bad acne)

FIGURE 20.4
Makeup working drawing.

FIGURE 20.5
A well-equipped makeup table. All makeup shown here and in the following illustrations was generously provided by Kryolan Corporation. Courtesy of J. Michael Gillette.

sweat off: When an actor's face perspires, some makeups will run. These makeups are said to "sweat off."

set: To prevent smearing or smudging. Once a greasepaint makeup design is finished, it is locked in place with a coating of powder.

Types of Makeup

Various materials are used for makeup base, liners, beards, mustaches, and prosthetic devices, as shown in Figure 20.5.

Cake Makeup

Cake makeup — both dry and moist — is pigmented material compressed into cake form. A variety of bases as well as highlight and shadow colors are available. Natural silk sponges are normally used to apply cake-foundation colors. Flat, pointed, and eyeliner brushes are used for detail work.

To apply cake makeup, dampen the applicator and draw it across the cake, as shown in Figure 20.6. If the applicator is too dry, the makeup won't easily transfer to the face. If it is too wet, the makeup will seem thin and may streak. Best results are achieved if the face is cleaned of any other makeup and moisturizers before application of the cake makeup. Normally, the entire face is covered with a smooth, translucent foundation color, and highlights and shadows are applied over the foundation. However, highlights and shadows can be applied *under* the foundation to achieve muted effects or to cover a heavy beard or pigmentation abnormality. If a heavy, opaque quality is desired, it is normally built up with several light applications rather than a single heavy one. Blending between colors once they're on the face is normally achieved by brushing lightly with a clean, slightly dampened brush. Cake makeup does not require powdering. Kryolan Aquacolor is a brand of cake makeup in common use today. It is heavily pigmented, so not much has to be used, it blends easily, is available in a wide variety of colors, and doesn't **sweat off.**

Creme Makeup

This moist, nongreasy foundation makeup is applied with a sponge, a brush, or the fingers, as shown in Figure 20.7. It is compatible with cake makeup but does require powdering to be **set.** Creme makeup is also available in stick form that is generally referred to as crayons.

(A)

FIGURE 20.6
Application of cake makeup. (A) A damp sponge is drawn across the cake. (B and C) A smooth translucent foundation color is applied to the face and neck. Makeup by Amy Lederman, professional makeup artist. Photos Courtesy of J. Michael Gillette.

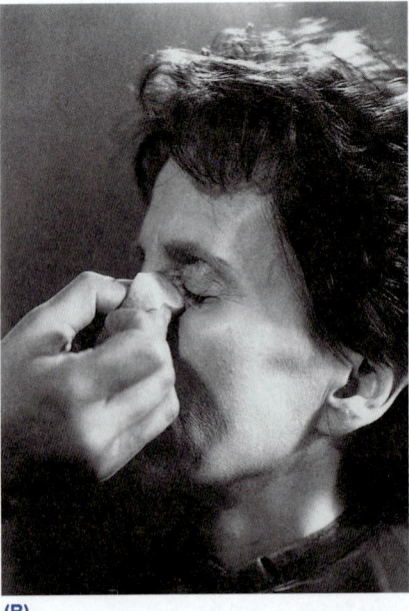

(B)

(C)

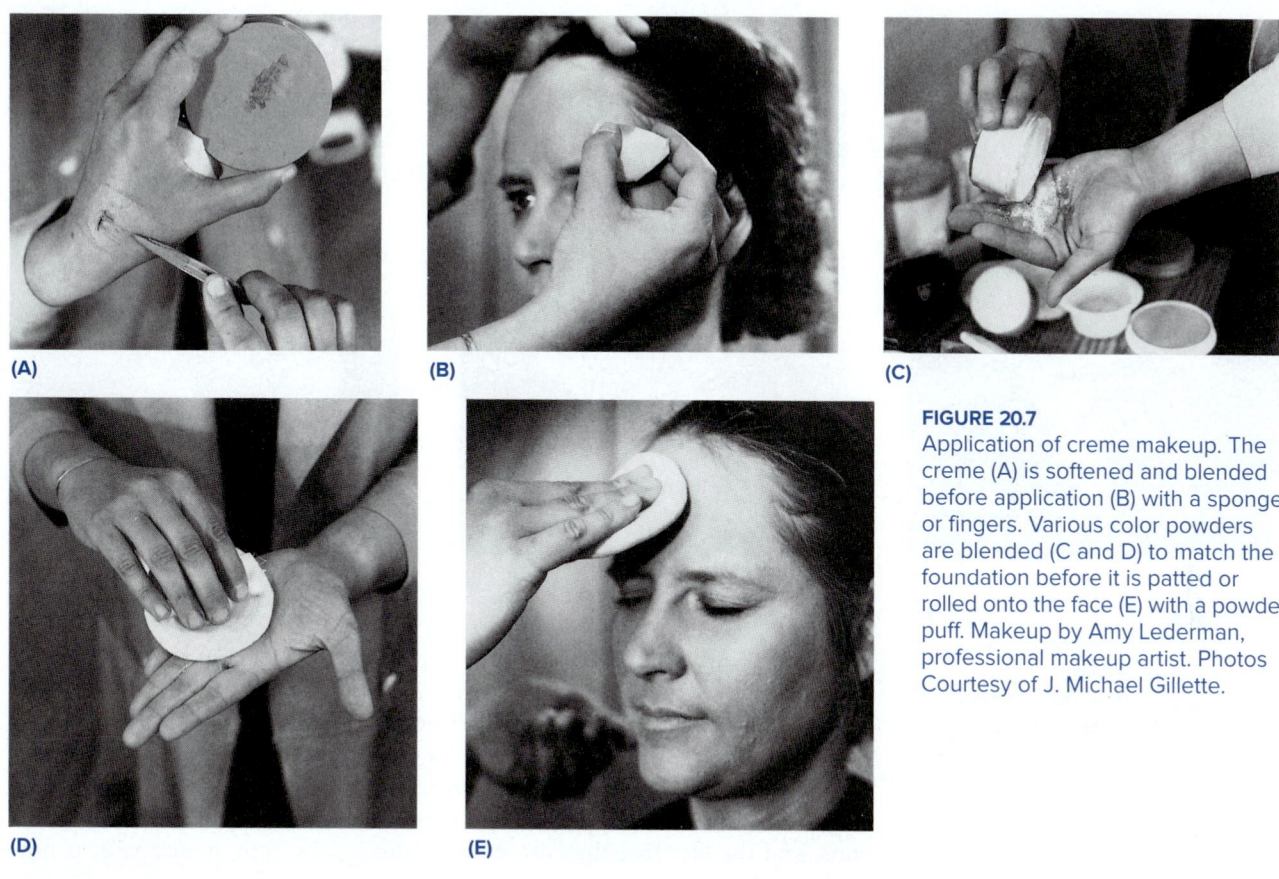

(A)   (B)   (C)

(D)   (E)

FIGURE 20.7
Application of creme makeup. The creme (A) is softened and blended before application (B) with a sponge or fingers. Various color powders are blended (C and D) to match the foundation before it is patted or rolled onto the face (E) with a powder puff. Makeup by Amy Lederman, professional makeup artist. Photos Courtesy of J. Michael Gillette.

Liquid Makeup

Liquid makeup manufactured for theatrical purposes is pretty much limited to body makeup. However, a variety of liquid bases formulated for street wear work perfectly well for the stage. The only problem with the use of liquid bases is that they dry quickly, which makes them difficult to blend if more than one color is being used.

Dry Makeup

This category includes all makeup that is dry when applied to the skin. Dry makeups, such as face powders and pressed powder rouge, are normally used to supplement other types of makeup such as cake, creme, and greasepaint.

Face powder is primarily used to set creme and greasepaint makeup or to reduce shine, although it can be used by itself as a "quick" foundation. It is applied by pressing on the face with a powder puff. Any excess powder is removed by gently brushing with a soft powder brush or clean rouge sponge.

Dry rouge is a pressed cake form of face powder. It is normally applied with a rouge brush, cotton ball, or powder puff.

Greasepaint

Until the development of quality creme and cake makeup, greasepaint was the most commonly used type of theatrical makeup. Opaque and cream based, it is available in jars, tubes, sticks, and tins in a wide variety of colors.

After the skin has been cleansed, soft greasepaint is applied to the face and neck in little dots, then blended with the finger tips to create a smooth

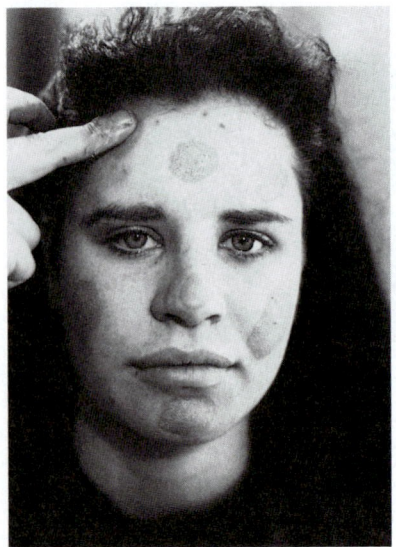

(A)

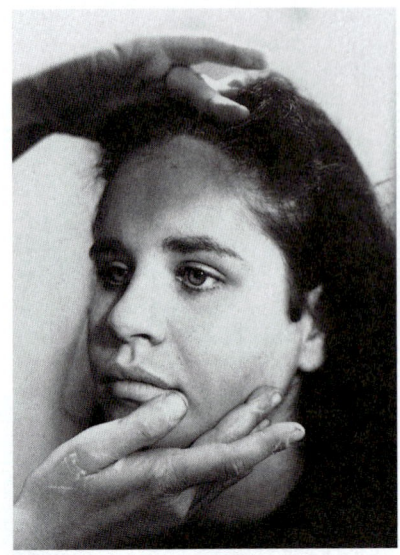

(B)

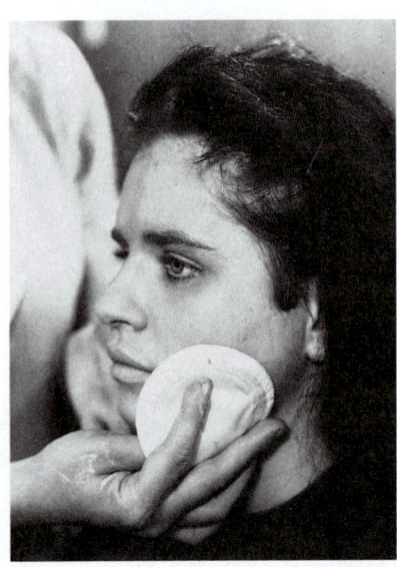

(C)

FIGURE 20.8
Application of greasepaint. The grease-paint is applied in dots (A), then blended to form a smooth foundation (B) and set with powder (C). Makeup by Amy Lederman, professional makeup artist. Photos Courtesy of J. Michael Gillette.

translucent foundation, as shown in Figure 20.8. Greasepaint creates a greasy, shiny base that does not take highlights and shadows well and requires a coating of powder to set the makeup. If successive layers are to be built up, as when **stippling,** each layer needs to be set with powder. Another drawback to greasepaint is that it clogs the pores, which promotes facial perspiration. Because of the ease of application of creme cake, liquid, and powder foundations, and the fact that they are much easier on the skin, greasepaint is now rarely used.

Rubber-Mask Greasepaint

This specialty greasepaint, made with a castor-oil base, is primarily used to cover latex. Unlike regular greasepaint, it is applied by gently patting or stippling with a sponge, and it must be thoroughly powdered before any additional makeup can be applied. Like greasepaint, rubber-mask greasepaint is now rarely used because foam latex — as opposed to "regular" or "unfoamed" latex — is the current "material of choice" for the construction of makeup prosthetics. Foam latex can be made up using regular creme or powder-based makeup.

Makeup Removers

Makeup removers such as Kryolan's Makeup Remover and Mehron's Liquefying Cream are sold by those manufacturers for use with their products. All-purpose makeup removers such as Ben Nye's Quick 'n Clean Makeup Remover take off both makeup and spirit gum. Spirit gum can also be removed with spirit-gum remover. Cleansing creams, cold cream, and baby oils remove most makeups but may be slightly harsher on the skin than are the more specific commercial products.

stippling: A texturing technique in which makeup is applied by touching the skin with a textured surface, usually a stippling sponge. Similar to stippling in scenic painting.

 ## Application Techniques

Several application techniques can be used with all types of makeup.

Highlights and Shadows

To a great extent, humans perceive the three-dimensional quality of objects by "reading" the patterns of highlight and shadow created by light falling on the object. Ever since birth we've subconsciously studied the patterns that light creates on faces. We've all learned experientially that highlights are reflected from protruding structures such as the bridge of the nose, cheekbones, and the eyebrow ridge. Therefore, when looking at a face we *expect* to see highlights in those areas. Similarly, we *expect* to see shadows in areas shaded from the light such as eye sockets and under the jaw.

Makeup artists, by painting artificial highlights and shadows on an actor's face, manipulate the audience's perception of that face. For example, the eye socket is a natural shadow area. By painting the eye socket with a color that is lighter than the foundation color, the apparent depth of that eye socket is reduced, as shown in Figure 20.9A and Figure 20.9B. Darkening the eye-socket

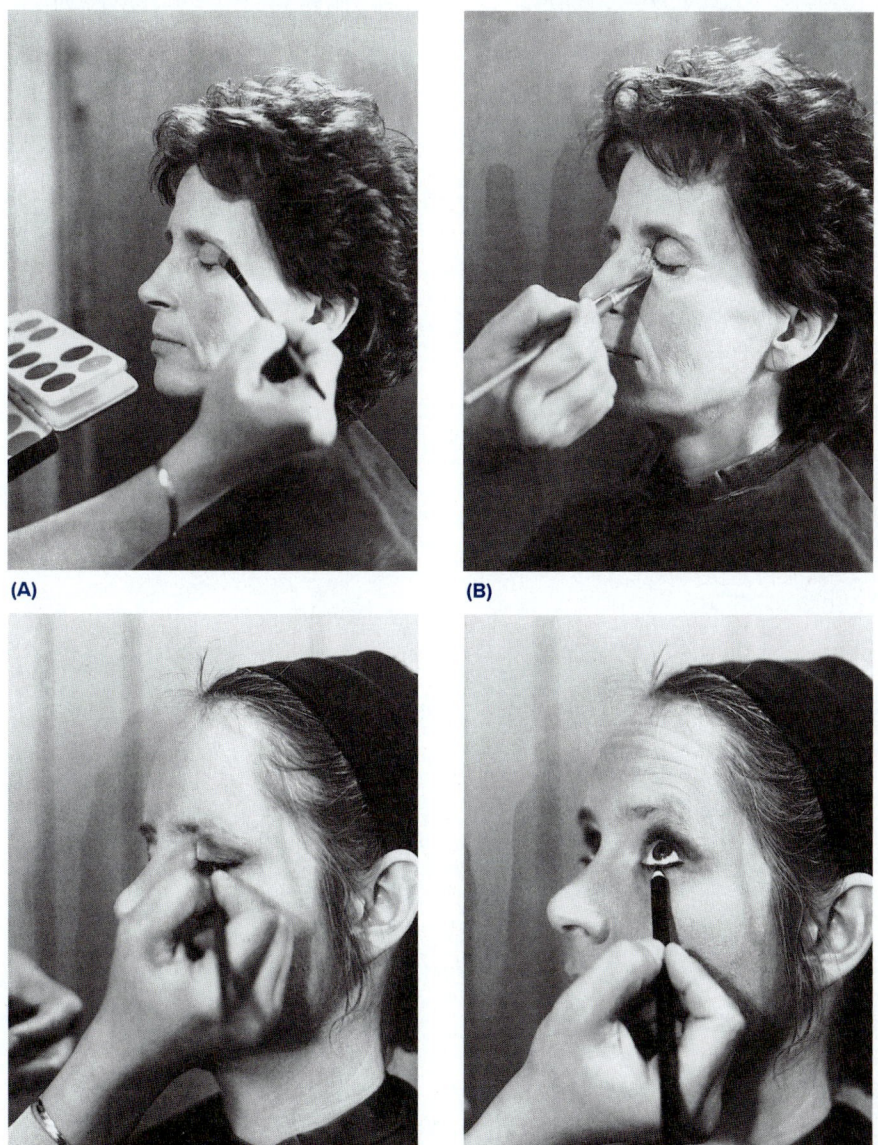

(A)

(B)

(C)

(D)

FIGURE 20.9
Application of highlight and shadow. (A and B) Use of highlight to decrease natural shadows. (C and D) Use of shadow and liner to emphasize eyes. Makeup by Amy Lederman, professional makeup artist. Photos Courtesy of J. Michael Gillette.

color and the use of eye liner will increase its apparent depth. Darkening the eye-socket color also increases its contrast with the white of the eye, which focuses more attention on the eye, as shown in Figure 20.9C and D. A straight nose can be made to appear crooked by painting the bridge with a crooked highlight, and a crooked nose can be made to appear straight by painting a straight highlight line.

Because there are few harsh angles, such as creases or deep wrinkles, on most faces, almost all junctures between highlight, base, and shadow are soft edged. A soft edge is created by blending — stroking with a brush from the lighter color to the darker, as shown in Figure 20.10. If a hard-edged line is needed, simply brush the shadow color into place with the edge of a small flat brush and don't blend it, as illustrated in Figure 20.11.

FIGURE 20.10
A soft edge is created by blending the shadow color with the base. Makeup by Amy Lederman, professional makeup artist. Photos Courtesy of J. Michael Gillette.

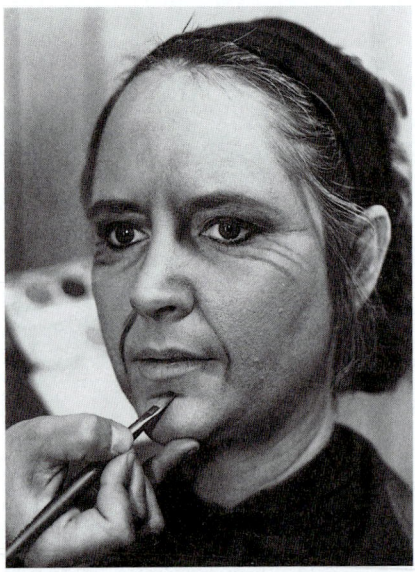
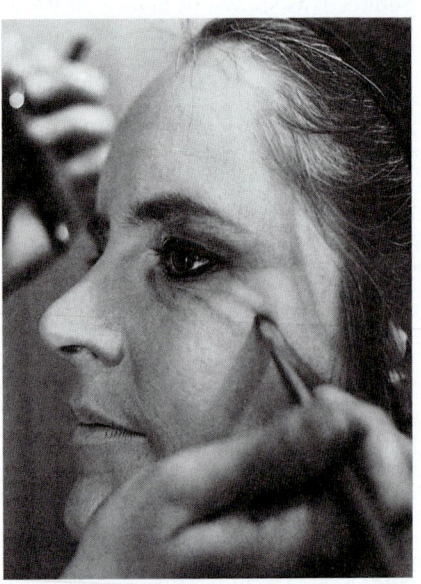

FIGURE 20.11
A hard edge is created by not blending the highlight color. Makeup by Amy Lederman, professional makeup artist.

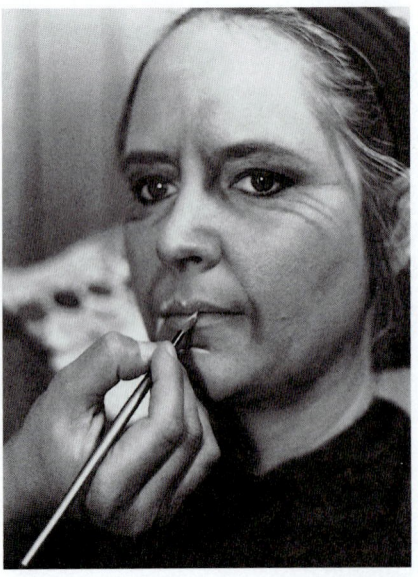
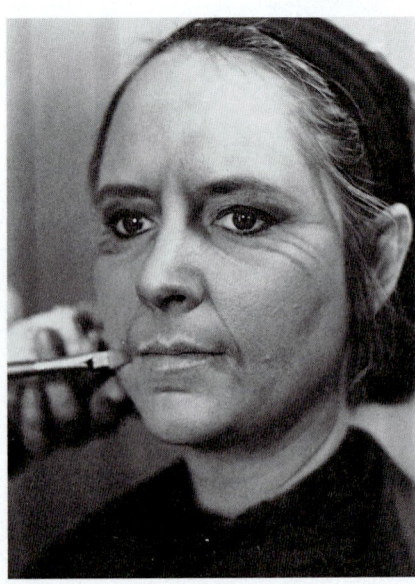

Highlight and Shadow Colors

Facial highlights are simply those areas that reflect more light than the surrounding skin reflects, whereas shadows are those areas that reflect less. Therefore, the highlight color is simply a lighter version of the foundation, whereas shadow color is darker. The amount of difference between the foundation color and its highlight and shadow hues is dependent on a number of variables — principally whether the foundation color is light or dark, skin condition, and age. For normal effects on Caucasian skin, highlights and shadows will be just a bit lighter and darker, respectively, than the foundation. As the value — relative lightness or darkness — of the skin tone decreases — becomes darker — the contrast between the highlight/shadow colors needs to increase in order to project a realistic effect. Increasing the contrast between the highlight/shadow colors and the foundation will increase the apparent age of the skin.

Stippling

Stippling is a method of applying makeup by daubing or patting rather than stroking. Normally accomplished with a sponge, and occasionally with a brush, stippling roughens the apparent skin texture, as shown in Figure 20.12. The roughness of that texture depends on two elements: the surface texture of the applicator and the contrast between the stipple color and the foundation. Generally, the larger the pores of the applicator, and the more contrast between the stipple color and the base, the rougher the apparent texture.

Black stipple sponges, red rubber sponges, natural sponges, and household sponges can be used for stippling. The stipple color is applied to the sponge, then pressed onto the face. The use of two or more stipple colors (rather than one) will create a more natural look. Large textural elements such as freckles are normally applied with a small, flat makeup brush.

Shadow or highlight areas that are too dark, bright, or intense can be toned down by stippling them with the base color.

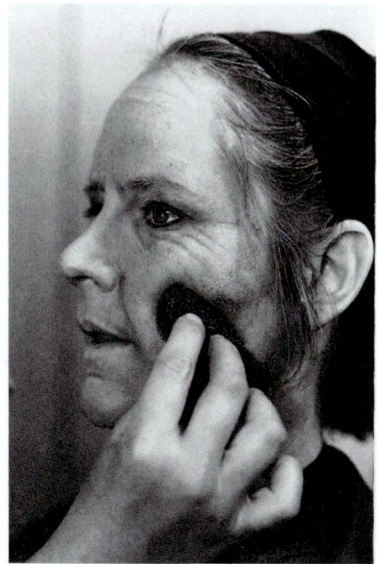

FIGURE 20.12
Stippling made with contrasting highlight and shadow colors gives the appearance of rough skin texture. Makeup by Amy Lederman, professional makeup artist. Photo Courtesy of J. Michael Gillette.

Corrective Makeup

Corrective makeup is similar in purpose and design to everyday, or street, makeup. Its purpose is to enhance the natural appearance of the actor. Corrective makeup normally begins with a foundation color of one or more colors that are specified on the makeup worksheet.

After the foundation has been applied, the face's natural structure is either emphasized or de-emphasized through the application of highlights and shadows. The highlights are normally applied where highlights would naturally occur, such as the bridge of the nose, the cheekbones, and the top of the eyebrows. Shadow colors are applied to natural shadow areas, such as wrinkle lines, eye sockets, and cheeks.

Three-Dimensional Makeup

Three-dimensional makeup involves the use of various materials to alter the shape of the actor's face, neck, or hands. A variety of materials and processes can be used to achieve these effects.

Nose Putty

Nose putty can be used to alter the shape of the nose, chin, and other nonflexible areas of skin, as illustrated in Figure 20.13. When working with nose putty, be sure the application site is free from all makeup and grease. Apply just enough K-Y jelly or cleansing cream (not petroleum jelly) to your fingers to prevent the putty from sticking to them, and knead the putty until it is soft. Press the putty onto the skin to firmly attach it, then shape it and smooth it into the surrounding skin. Adhesion will be increased if a coat of spirit gum is applied to the skin and allowed to dry until it is very tacky before the nose putty is applied. When it is properly shaped, stipple the putty to give it skin texture, then apply makeup to

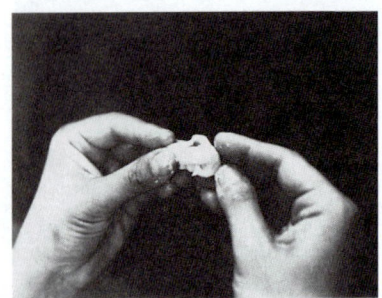

(A)

FIGURE 20.13
Application of nose putty. (A) The nose putty is kneaded until soft and pliable. (B) Spirit gum is applied to the nose and allowed to dry until tacky. (C) The nose putty is applied and shaped. (D) The nose putty is patted with a black stipple sponge to give it texture. (E) Foundation makeup is applied. Makeup by Amy Lederman, professional makeup artist. Photos Courtesy of J. Michael Gillette.

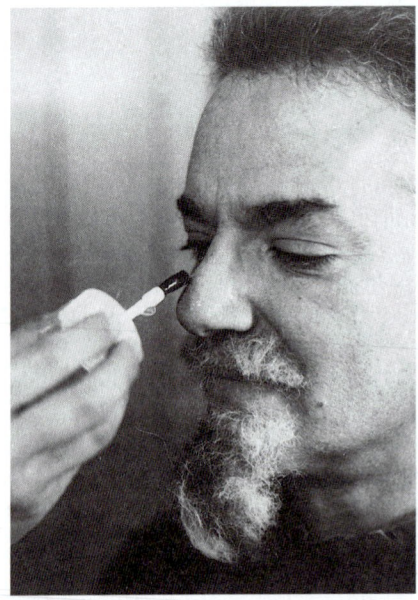

(B)

(C)

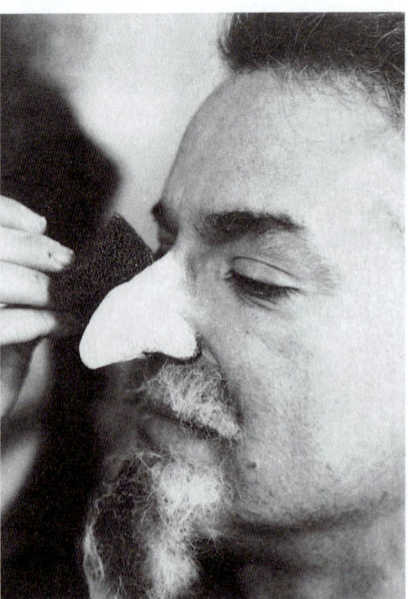

(D)

(E)

match the actor's natural skin tone, powder if necessary, *then* apply the foundation color and any appropriate highlight or shadow colors.

To remove nose putty, pull or scrape it off and gently massage makeup remover onto the area until the remaining putty is softened enough to be removed with tissues.

Derma Wax

Derma wax is softer than, but does not adhere as well as, nose putty. It is used for similar modifications of hard structures such as noses and chins. The application of derma wax follows the same procedure as nose putty except that the coating of spirit gum is required to firmly attach the derma wax. Increased adhesion will result if cotton fibers are embedded in the spirit-gum layer. When the spirit gum is very tacky, press a cotton ball into it. When the spirit gum is dry, pull the ball off. Some cotton fibers will remain. Work a small amount of derma wax into the cotton fibers, then apply the remaining wax and build up the desired shape.

Derma-wax structures can be pulled off and the residue removed with an all-purpose makeup remover or with spirit-gum remover and makeup remover.

Gelatin

Gelatin, such as unflavored Knox gelatin available in grocery stores, when mixed with hot water to form a thick paste that solidifies when cool, can be used to form three-dimensional shapes such as warts, moles, and scars. If mixed with cool water, the gelatin will have a more grainy texture. Gelatin adheres to thoroughly grease-free skin and is more flexible than either nose putty or derma wax, so it can be used on fleshy, flexible skin such as cheeks.

A working paste is formed by mixing the gelatin one to one with very hot tap water. The paste must be applied when warm and shaped quickly with an orange stick, modeling tool, or similar applicator before it cools. Successive layers can be built up until the desired shape is achieved, as shown in Figure 20.14. If the edges start to peel, they can be glued down with spirit gum. Shapes can

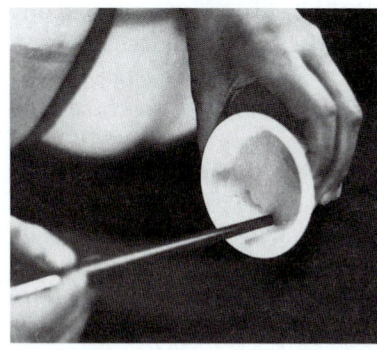

(A)

FIGURE 20.14
Application of gelatin. (A) Gelatin is mixed with water and (B) applied to grease-free skin. (C) The gelatin mole is colored and stippled with a brush. Makeup by Amy Lederman, professional makeup artist. Photos Courtesy of J. Michael Gillette.

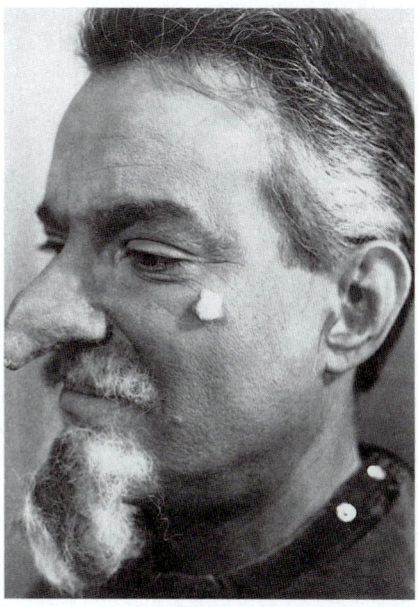

(B)

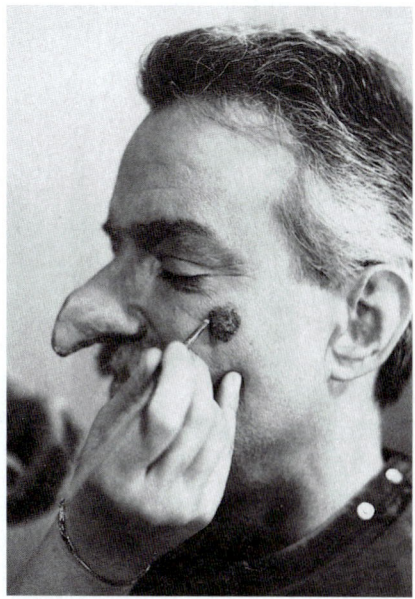

(C)

bald cap: A latex cap that covers a person's hair.

eyebrow mask: A thin piece of plastic film or latex glued over the eyebrow. Also known as an eyebrow block.

block out: To cover with soap, spirit gum, wax, material, or preformed plastic film so that no hair is evident.

also be preformed either in a mold or on a flat glass surface and attached to the skin with spirit gum, which improves adhesion. The gelatin forms can be covered with any type of makeup.

The disadvantages of gelatin forms are that they can melt when heated and perspiration loosens them, although the perspiration problem can be overcome with spirit gum.

Latex

Several types of latex systems are used for a variety of purposes such as forming prosthetic pieces, creating wrinkles, and applying crepe hair. Liquid latex is available in clear and flesh-colored formulations. Foam latex is a soft, flexible expanding foam that is poured into molds to form prosthetic pieces. It is made by mixing liquid latex with foaming, gelling, and curing agents. The mixture is poured into a cast and baked in a low-temperature oven. Specific instructions come with foam-latex kits, which are available from theatrical supply houses that handle makeup.

Liquid latexes specifically designed for forming in molds should not be applied directly to the skin as they may cause irritation or burning. Liquid Plastic Film, manufactured by Kryolan, is a clear liquid plastic, available in two formulations, that is used in the same way as liquid latex. Glatzan L is used for making **bald caps, eyebrow masks,** eye pouches, and so forth. It should not be applied directly to the skin. A variety of manufactured latex pieces (noses, chins, pouches, warts, and so forth) are available from makeup manufacturers or distributors such as Paramount, Bob Kelly, and Kryolan.

Liquid latex is frequently used to create wrinkles. The skin to be aged is pulled tight, and clear latex (white when liquid, clear when dry) is stippled onto the skin with a sponge or fingers, as shown in Figure 20.15. When the stretched skin is released, wrinkles magically appear. Additional coats of latex on the stretched skin will deepen the wrinkles. Kryolan's Old Skin Plast can be used as a substitute for liquid latex. An age makeup can be applied either under or over the latex. If the makeup is under the latex, apply the latex carefully to avoid smearing. If makeup is being applied over the latex, you can tint the latex with appropriate hues of food coloring to approximate the actor's natural skin tone.

A cautionary note when using liquid latex: Before you apply latex to any hairy parts such as the backs of hands, beards, stubble, eyebrows, or soft, downy facial hair, you need to understand that when you pull off the latex, most of the hair will come with it. To avoid this problem, either **block out** or shave off the hair before applying the latex.

If deep wrinkles are desired, torn (not cut) facial tissue can be applied to the stretched skin of the face with either latex or spirit gum. When the tissue has dried on the stretched skin, a coat of latex is applied over the tissue. The use of a hair dryer will speed the drying process. Work a small area at a time, and be sure that the skin is stretched until the latex is dry. If even deeper wrinkles are desired, soft paper toweling can be substituted for the tissue. After the whole face is covered with the tissue (or paper towels) and latex, a rubber-mask greasepaint or greasepaint foundation with appropriate highlights and shadows is applied over the latex. Additional skin texture can be created by stippling with latex or a honey-thick mixture of latex and gelatin.

Prosthetics

Prosthetic devices—latex noses, chins, bald caps, eyebrow blocks, and so forth—can be purchased or made in the shop. If purchased, generic shapes such

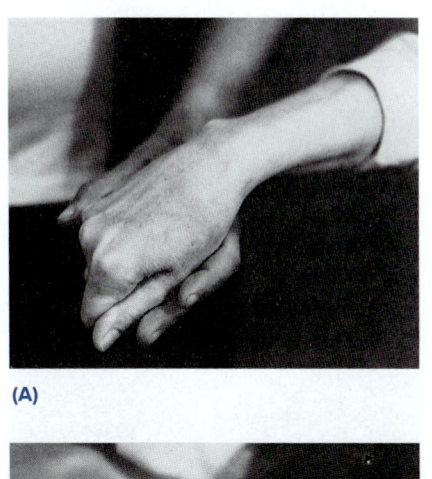

(A)

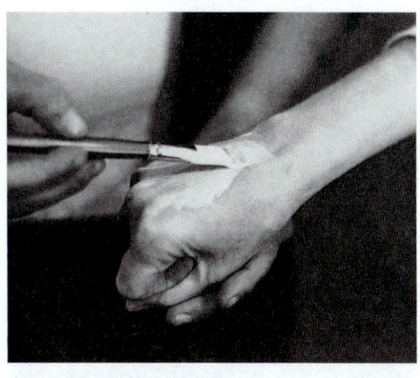

(B)

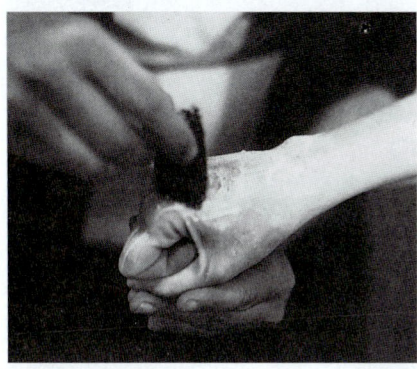

(C)

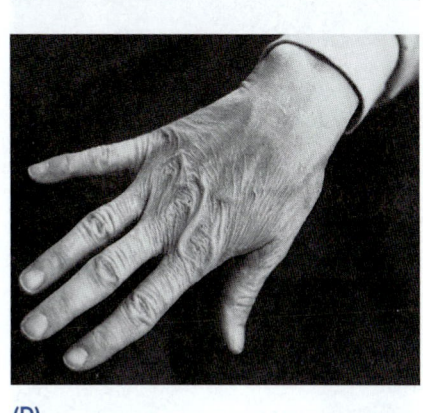

(D)

FIGURE 20.15
Making wrinkles with liquid latex.
(A) The skin is stretched tight and
(B) painted with latex. (C) The moist
latex is stippled to give it texture.
(D) The dried latex causes wrinkles.
Makeup by Amy Lederman,
professional makeup artist. Photos
Courtesy of J. Michael Gillette.

as bald caps and eyebrow blocks normally can be made to fit well. However, items such as noses and chins that must fit well because of the movement of the fleshy parts of the actor's face are frequently better created on the actor's face or cast from a **life mask** of the actor.

The process of creating a life mask using dental alginate, or *moulage* (a rubbery casting material that can be purchased from makeup suppliers or dental supply stores), is shown in Figure 20.16. After the negative mold is removed from the subject's face, you'll want to make a positive mold immediately because the alginate mold shrinks quickly. The positive mold, which is the life mask, is normally made from dental stone or plaster and is illustrated in Figure 20.17 on page 505. When the life mask is fully cured — two to five days, depending on temperature and humidity — it should be sealed with several coats of shellac.

life mask: A plaster mask of a person's face. A negative mold is made by covering the person's face with plaster of Paris. The negative mold is used to make a positive cast that is the life mask.

Safety Tip

Using Liquid Latex

If any burning, itching, or irritation is felt when applying liquid latex directly to the skin, don't apply any more. Each company (Bob Kelly, Kryolan, Mehron, Ben Nye, Joe Blasco, among others) manufactures its liquid latex with slightly different formulations. The chances are good that if one type irritates your skin, another won't. Try a different product until you find one that doesn't irritate your skin. Also, remember that some liquid latexes are not designed to be applied directly to the skin. Be sure to read the instructions on the bottle or can before applying the liquid latex to your skin.

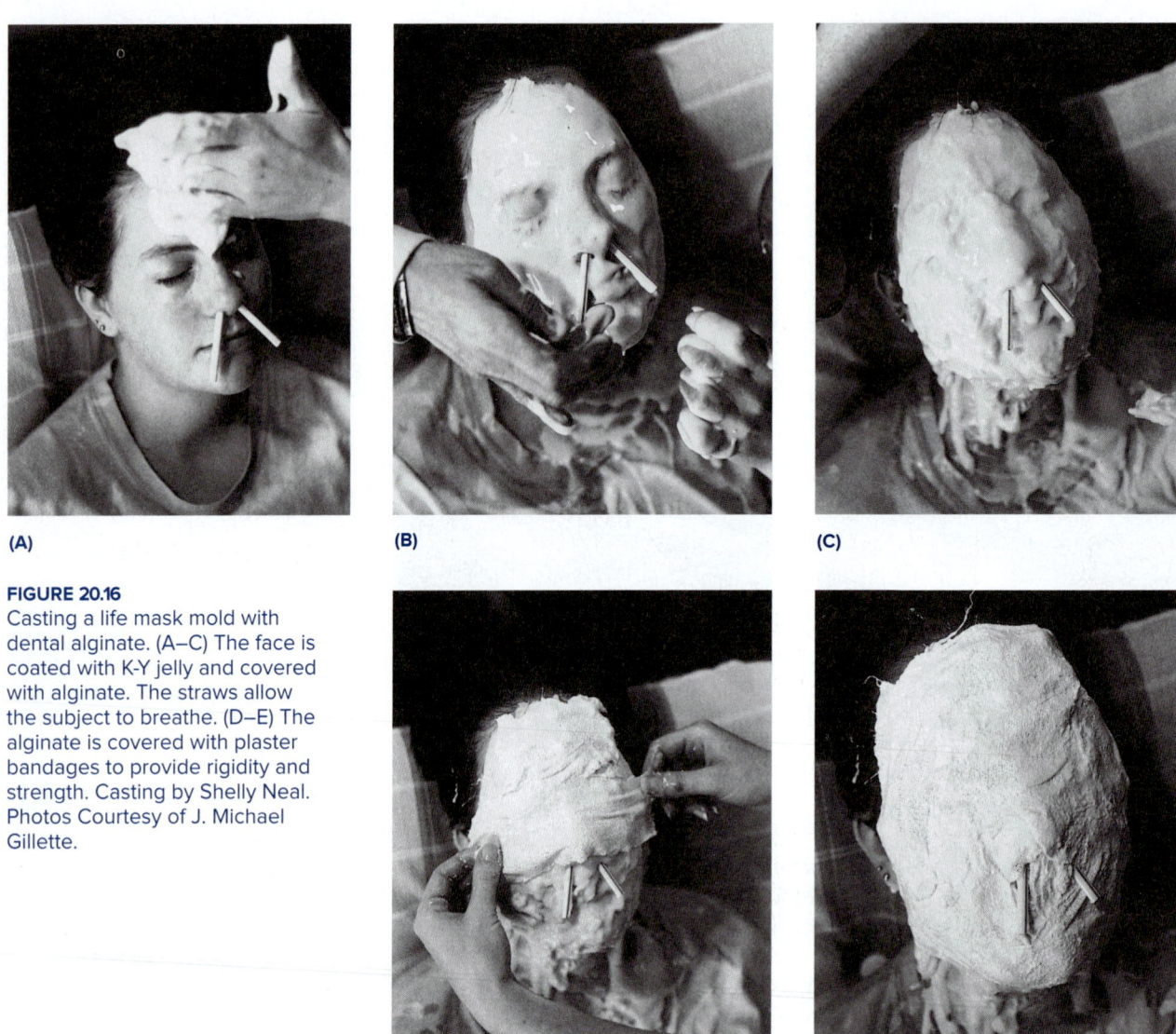

(A)

(B)

(C)

(D)

(E)

FIGURE 20.16
Casting a life mask mold with dental alginate. (A–C) The face is coated with K-Y jelly and covered with alginate. The straws allow the subject to breathe. (D–E) The alginate is covered with plaster bandages to provide rigidity and strength. Casting by Shelly Neal. Photos Courtesy of J. Michael Gillette.

After the life mask has been sealed, clay can be used to sculpt such features as noses, eye pouches, eyebrow blocks, or anything else. Small plaster or moulage casts can then be made of these features, as shown in Figure 20.18, and these molds used to cast the features in latex. When making these small prosthetic molds, be sure to thoroughly apply a thin layer of K-Y or petroleum jelly to the life mask to prevent the new mold material from sticking to it.

Two forms of latex are used for creating prosthetics — the previously described liquid latex and foam latex. Probably the easiest method of casting prosthetics is the slush method, illustrated in Figure 20.19 on page 506. While holding the negative plaster mold in your hand, pour in a little liquid latex and rotate the mold to coat the inside. Pour in a little more and repeat the process. Be sure that the edges are the thinnest part and that enough thickness has been built up so that the object will retain its shape when you remove it from the mold. The mold should be dusted with baby powder to prevent the latex from sticking to the mold. Because dried latex will also stick to itself, you'll also need to thoroughly powder the cast object and continue to dust both sides of it as you work it loose from the mold. Additional techniques for casting with molds are discussed in Chapter 13, "Stage Properties."

Latex prosthetics can be attached to the skin with either latex or spirit gum. Latex can be used if you don't intend to reuse the piece and the skin you're attaching it to doesn't perspire much. (Perspiration weakens the adhesive power of the latex.) If you are planning to reuse the piece, attach it with spirit gum. Spirit gum is applied to the inside edges of the piece (Figure 20.20 on page 507), allowed to dry until very tacky, then firmly pressed into place with the fingers. An orange stick can also be used to press down the edges.

It should be noted that some people have adverse reactions to both spirit gum and/or liquid latex. There are alternative adhesives that can be used to attach prosthetics such as water-based spirit gum as well as a number of different formulations of medical adhesives.

Latex prosthetics require special treatment during makeup. Rubber-mask greasepaint is blended into the other makeup used on the skin, or if several pieces are being used, it might be easier to cover the whole face with rubber-mask

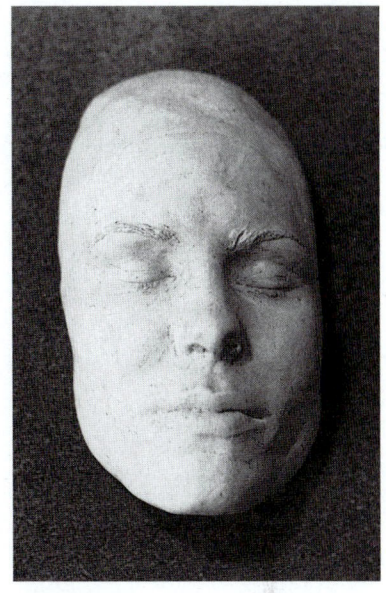

FIGURE 20.17
A life mask. Casting by Shelly Neal. Photo Courtesy of J. Michael Gillette.

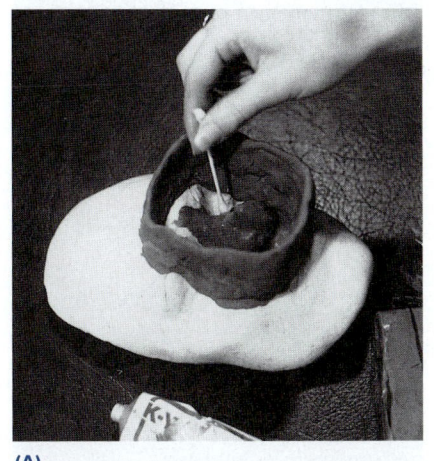

(A)

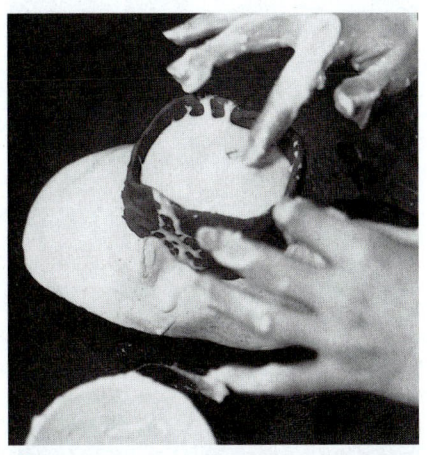

(B)

(C)

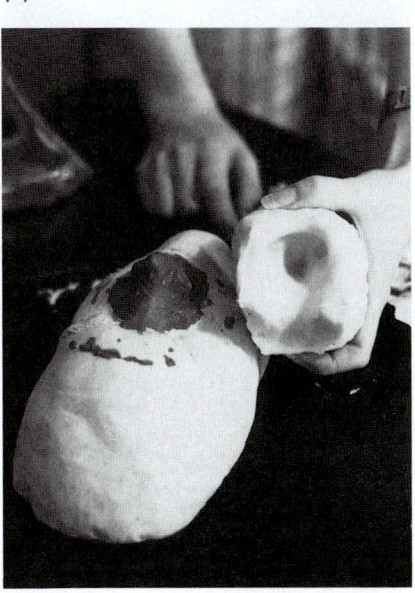

(D)

FIGURE 20.18
Casting a nose from a life mask. (A) A clay dam is built around the area to be cast and coated with K-Y jelly. (B) The dam is filled with plaster (if there are no undercuts in the form), alginate, or moulage. (C) The dam is peeled away and (D) the casting removed. Casting by Shelly Neal. Photos Courtesy of J. Michael Gillette.

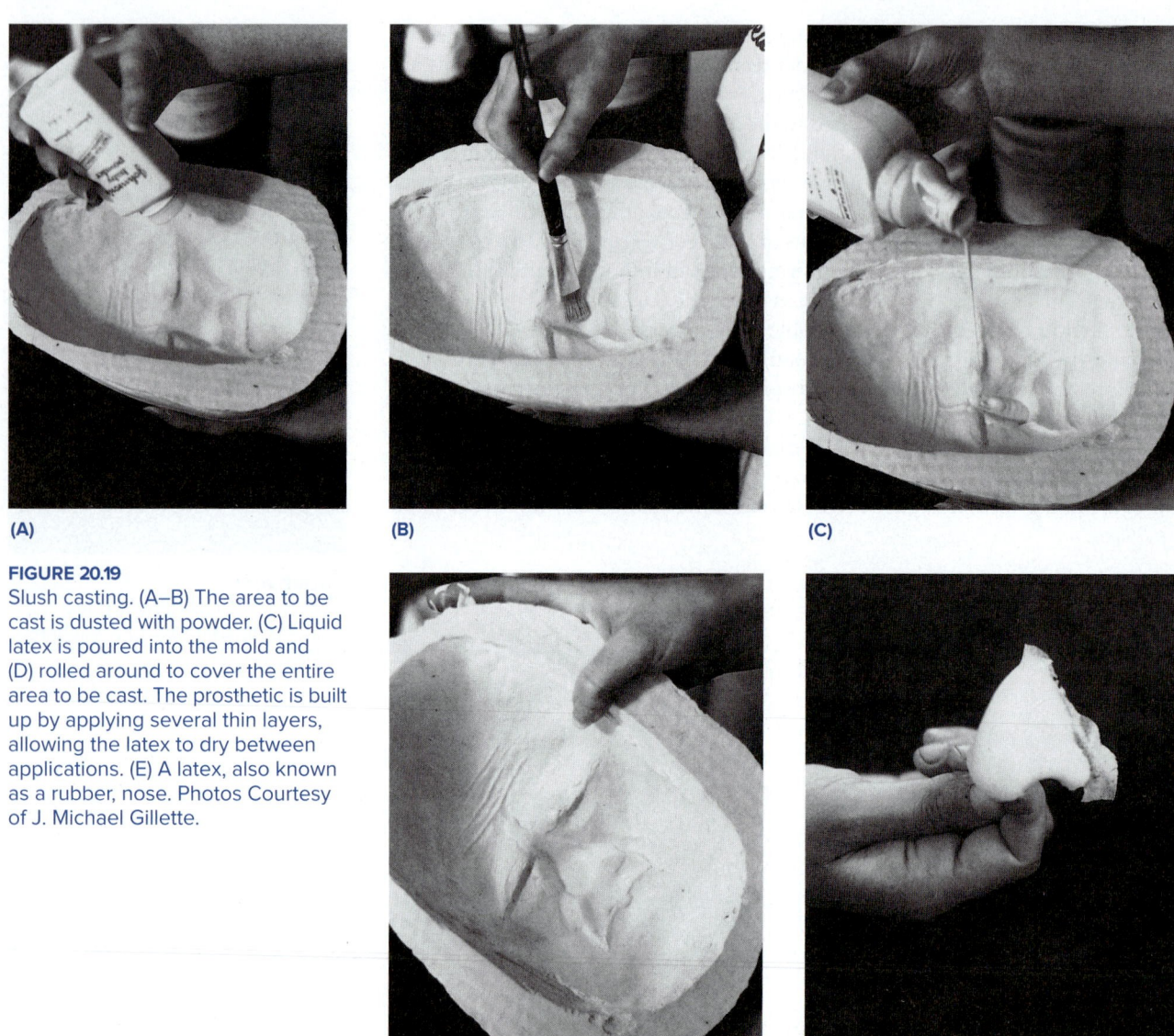

(A)

(B)

(C)

(D)

(E)

FIGURE 20.19
Slush casting. (A–B) The area to be cast is dusted with powder. (C) Liquid latex is poured into the mold and (D) rolled around to cover the entire area to be cast. The prosthetic is built up by applying several thin layers, allowing the latex to dry between applications. (E) A latex, also known as a rubber, nose. Photos Courtesy of J. Michael Gillette.

greasepaint rather than try to blend several types of makeup together. Regular greasepaint and creme makeup can also be used to cover latex prosthetics, but because they are a little more viscous they are harder to apply and blend smoothly. Stippling with several colors can help blend between the prosthetic device and the actor's skin.

If you're planning to reuse the piece, remove it by loosening the adhesive with spirit-gum remover, peel back the edges, and apply more remover. Repeat this process until the piece can be lifted off, then clean off any residual spirit gum with additional remover.

Beards and Mustaches

False beards and mustaches used to be laboriously constructed using crepe hair as illustrated in Figure 20.21 on page 508. Crepe hair is rarely used in theatrical makeup anymore, with the general exception of creating the illusion of beard

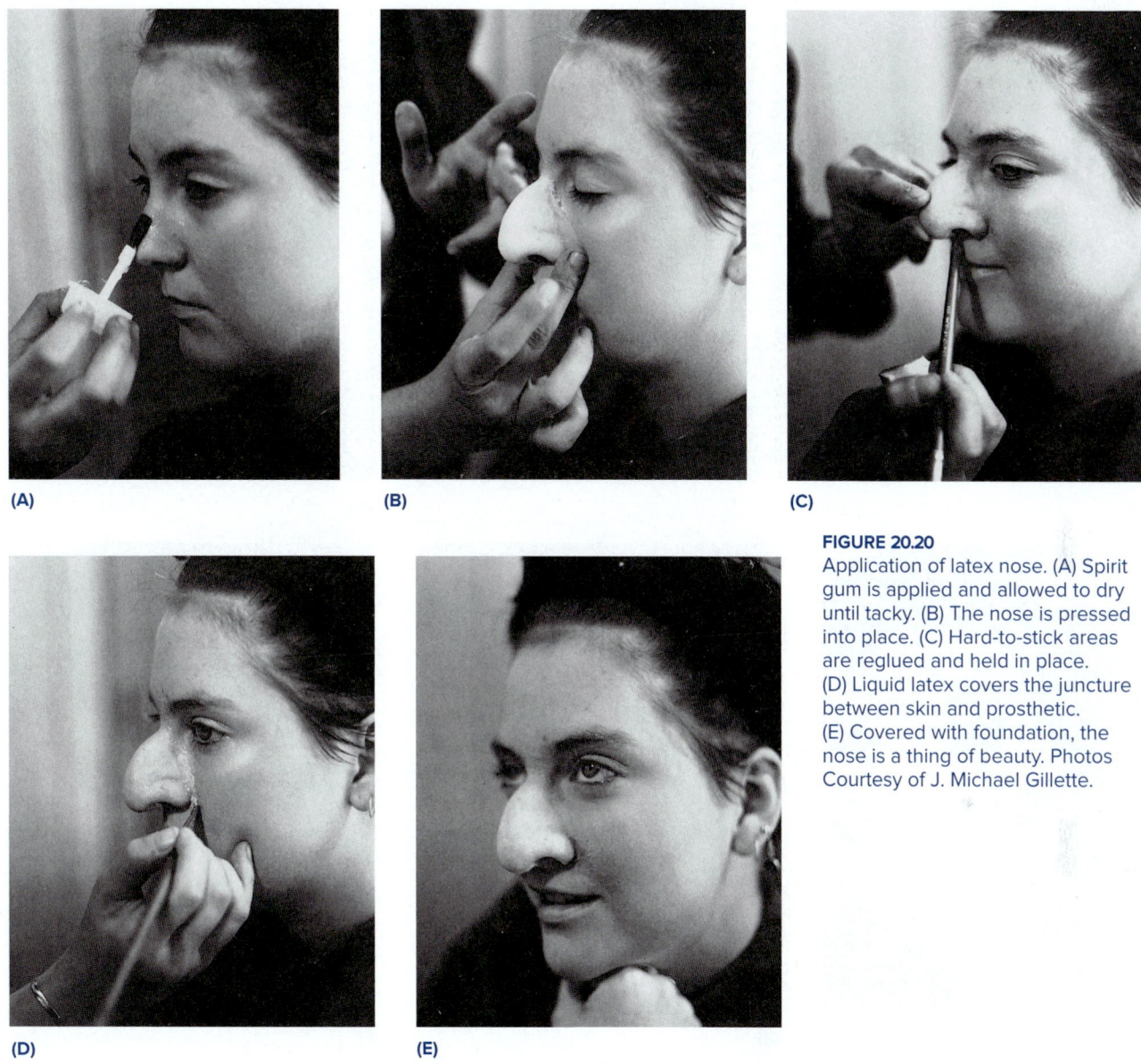

(A)   (B)   (C)

(D)   (E)

FIGURE 20.20
Application of latex nose. (A) Spirit gum is applied and allowed to dry until tacky. (B) The nose is pressed into place. (C) Hard-to-stick areas are reglued and held in place. (D) Liquid latex covers the juncture between skin and prosthetic. (E) Covered with foundation, the nose is a thing of beauty. Photos Courtesy of J. Michael Gillette.

stubble. In this case the crepe hair, which is sold in tightly braided strands that can be straightened by unbraiding and pressing with a steam iron, is very finely cut and glued to the beard area with spirit gum or medical adhesive. Because real beards contain whiskers of numerous tones, shades, and colors, be sure to use at least three or four different tones or colors if using this technique.

The demise of crepe hair was primarily caused by the general availability of excellent, very realistic, premade beards, mustaches, sideburns, and eyebrows. Almost all of these appliances are made using the ventilating process — hand-tying individual hairs onto a very fine net. Generally made from synthetic or very coarse human hair, they are available in a wide variety of colors, sizes, and designs from supply houses. An online search should reveal numerous sources. A commercially available ventilated mustache is shown in Figure 20.22. The ventilating process is illustrated in Figure 20.23 on page 509.

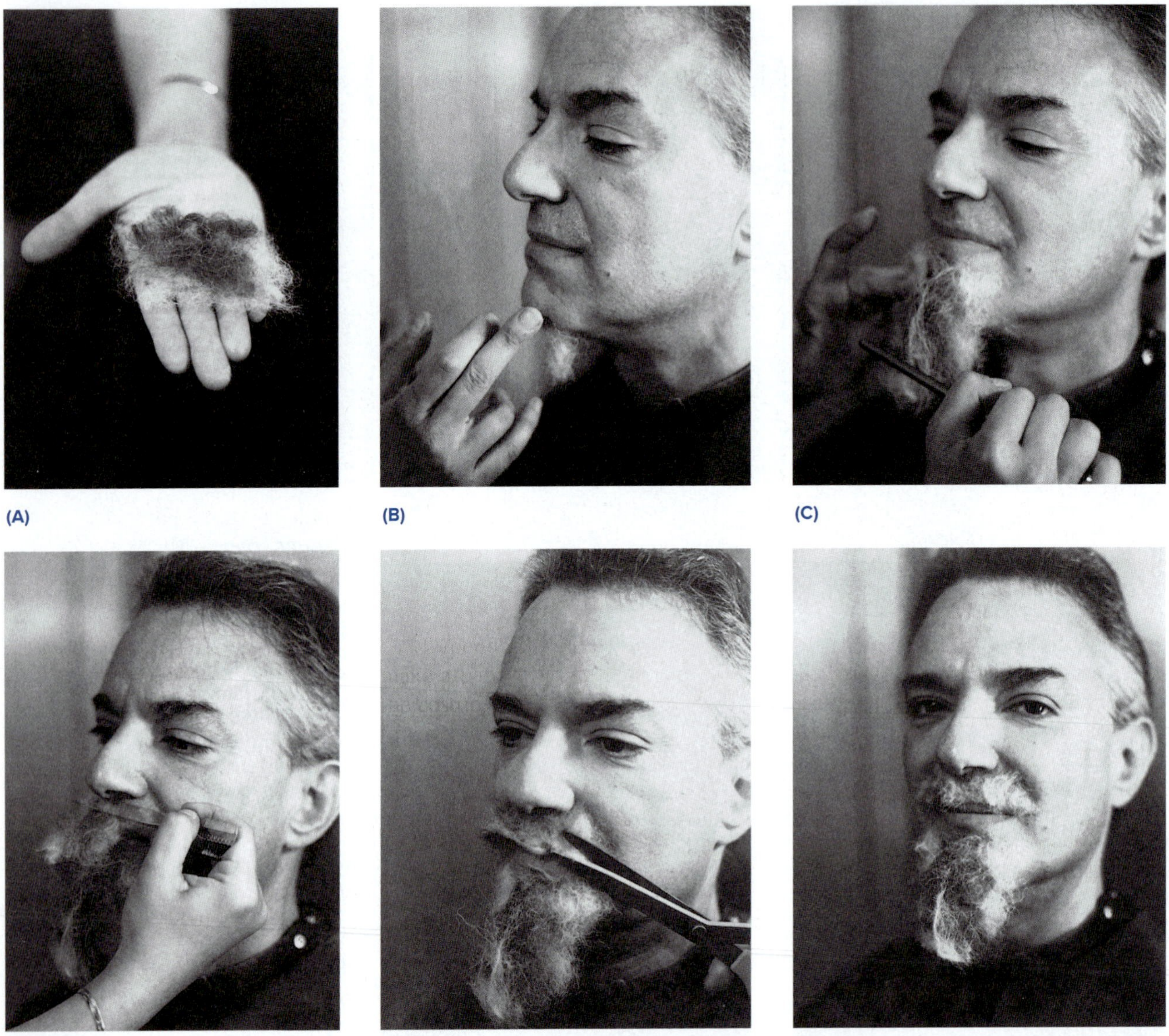

(A)

(B)

(C)

(D)

(E)

(F)

FIGURE 20.21
Application of a crepe-hair beard. (A) The crepe hair is straightened, colors blended, and cut to a length about twice as long as its final form. (B–D) The crepe hair is attached with spirit gum and (E–F) trimmed to the desired shape. Courtesy J. Michael Gillette.

FIGURE 20.22
A ventilated mustache from Kryolan. (A) Front view and (B) rear view showing the lace backing. Courtesy J. Michael Gillette.

(A)

(B)

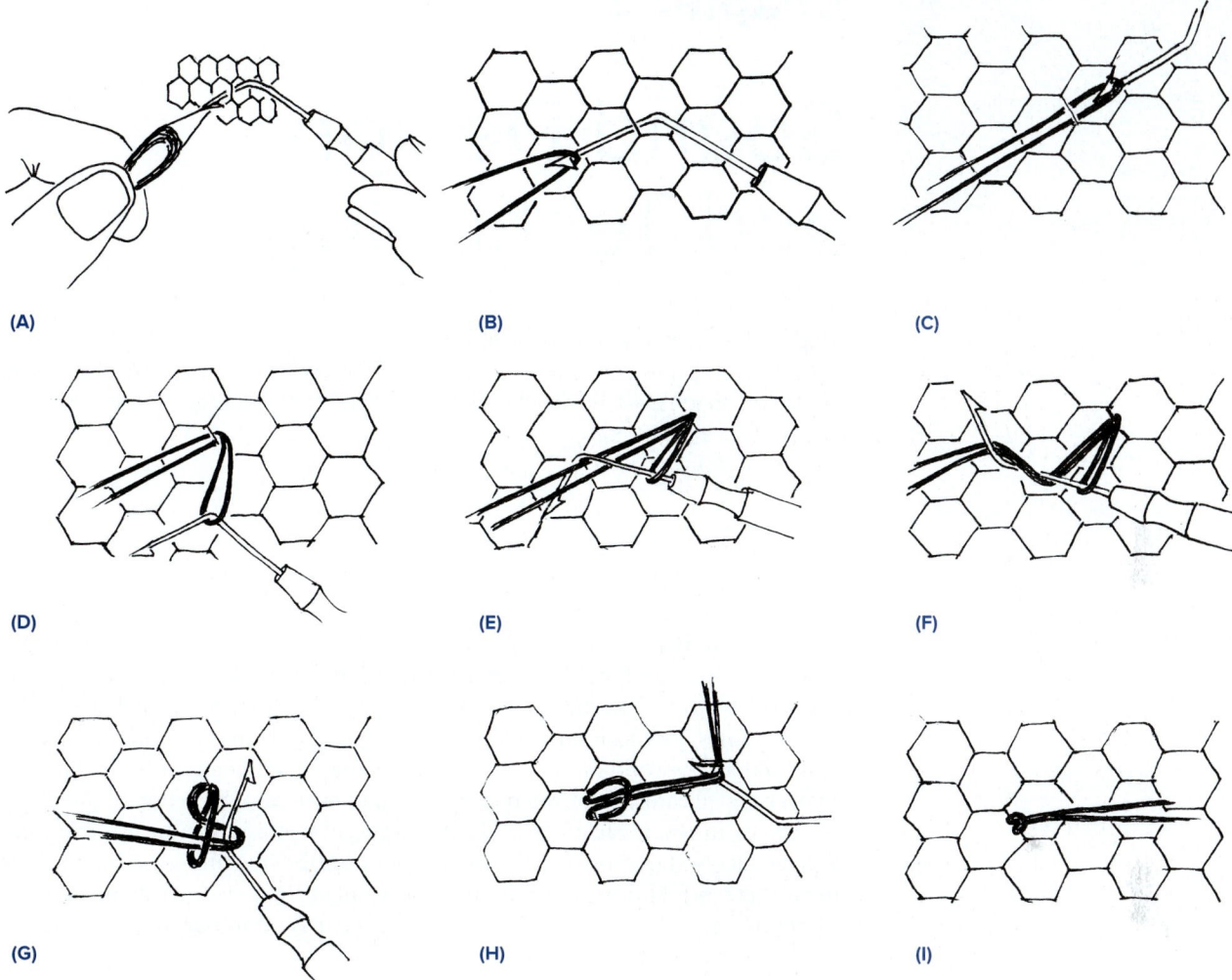

(A)   (B)   (C)

(D)   (E)   (F)

(G)   (H)   (I)

Ventilated pieces are normally attached with spirit gum. Generally the spirit gum is applied to clean skin and allowed to dry until tacky, and the gauze or lace netting is pressed into it using a clean, slightly moistened cloth. Any hairs that are glued down can be lifted using a pointed, stiff object such as an orange stick or eyebrow brush. As the netting is delicate and can easily tear, removal of the piece requires the copious use of spirit-gum remover and patience.

Selected References

Corey, Irene. *The Mask of Reality*. Anchorage Press, 1968.
Corson, Richard. *Stage Makeup*. Prentice-Hall, 8th ed., 1990.

FIGURE 20.23
The ventilating process. A few hairs are caught with the tip of the ventilating hook (A) and pulled through the lace backing (B) to form a loop (C). The hook is then rotated around the strands (D–F) and pulled through the loop (G–H) to form a knot (I). This process is repeated with additional strands to tie the hair to the lace backing. While tedious and time consuming, ventilating does create the most realistic beards, mustaches, and wigs.

Chapter 21

Sound Design and Technology

(This chapter has been updated thanks to significant input from Heath Hansum, professional sound designer and educator. The author wishes to publicly thank him for his extensive knowledge and expertize on this subject and for his contributions to this chapter.)

Nothing in theatre production is arbitrary. Everything is planned. The actors are selected because the director believes they have "that magical something" that will allow them to become the characters. The color, textures, and shape of the sets, costumes, props, and lighting are all designed to help the audience become immersed in the world of the play. The choreography of scene shifts and lighting changes are all carefully planned to pull the audience into the action of the play.

Sound in the theatre is exactly the same. Everything you hear during the performance — the actors' voices, the pre-show music, the underscoring musical themes, the rumblings from the rabble just outside the door, distant thunder, telephones and doorbell chimes — are designed with one purpose in mind: to immerse the audience in the play.

In *Sound and Music for the Theatre,* Deena Kaye and James LeBrecht define sound design as ". . . the creative and technical process resulting in the complete aural environment for live theatre."[1] Just like the other design areas, sound design is both creative and technical. A successful design requires both a quality plan and skilled technicians to implement it.

Sound in the Theatre

What is sound design? It is effective blending of three elements — music, effects, and reinforcement — to create an aural environment supportive of the production concept for a given production. This section will introduce you to each of those elements.

Music

Music, whether obtained from a music library or composed specifically for the production, refers to all pre-show, post-show, and intermission music, as well as the themes used to underscore moments or scenes within the play.

---

[1] Deena, Kaye, and James LeBrecht, *Sound and Music for the Theatre,* 3rd ed., Focal Press, 2009, p. 1.

Music is often used to elaborate the emotional intensity of moments in a play. Characters in musicals frequently burst into song when their emotions become too strong for ordinary speech. **Underscoring** can be used to intensify the emotions of a character or scene. Because people tend to remember things as an amalgam of the senses involved in an experience, once a melody has been heard, it often reminds the audience of those earlier events and emotions when heard again later.

Sound Effects

Sound effects include not only specifically identifiable sounds such as doorbells, telephone rings, and dog barks, but unidentifiable noises like crashes, bangs, and bumps as well. This category may also include tracks of environmental sounds designed to suggest an urban environment or an approaching thunderstorm.

Sound effects can be produced live or be recorded. **Foley effects** such as footsteps, whistles, gongs, improvised drums, and even coconut halves clapped together to create the sound of a passing horse have been used since theatre began and can add a "presence" to the effect that can't be duplicated with recorded sound.

Sound Reinforcement

A play or musical is doomed if the audience can't hear or understand the dialogue or lyrics. A good sound reinforcement system will amplify, process, and balance the voices of the actors, singers, orchestra, and effects to achieve this result. And it will magically do all of this in such a way that the audience is unaware that a sound system is even being used.

Some actors may have weaker voices than others. Wireless mics and the clever balancing of reinforcement levels can reduce, if not solve, that challenge.

Without reinforcement, an orchestra's sound will frequently overwhelm the singers' voices. Judicious balancing of both the voices and the orchestra can make the singer's voices clearly heard over the orchestra.

There are more uses for reinforced sound than simply "making things louder." Voices can also be processed to enhance their quality. Reinforcement systems can also free directors to stage actors where they'll create the desired stage picture rather than having to worry about whether or not they can be heard.

underscoring: Using music or sound to reinforce the emotional content of a scene or moment.

Foley effects: Named for sound-effects artist Jack D. Foley. Foley was famous for his work creating sound effects for films using everyday items to simulate sounds, such as flapping gloves for bird flight and celery for breaking bones.

The Nature of Sound

Sound is a pressure wave that moves, in air and at sea level, at about 1,130 feet per second. That's the physical reality. But an understanding of three separate processes — generation, transmission, and reception — is needed to understand how sound works.

Figure 21.1 illustrates how a pressure wave is generated when a drum is struck with a drumstick. When the drumhead is struck, the air immediately adjacent to the drumhead is compressed, creating a compression wave. That compression wave is transmitted through the air until it is received by the ear. The ear converts that force into a neurological impulse, which is sent to the brain, where that stimulus is interpreted as a drumbeat of a particular tone and quality.

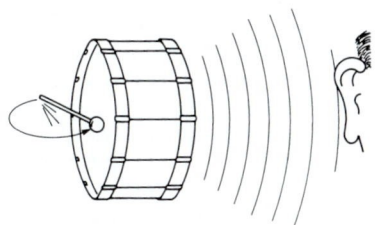

FIGURE 21.1
The transmission of sound in the air.

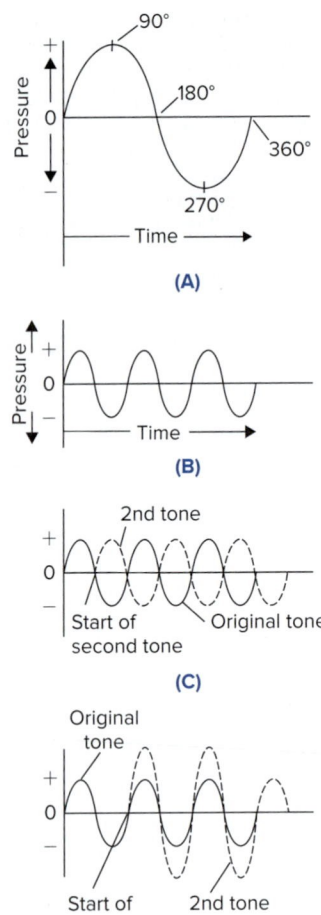

FIGURE 21.2
(A) Position on a wave is noted by its phase angle. Effects of phase alignment: (B) A three cycle tone. (C) Phase cancellation effects. (D) Additive phase effects.

phase: A method of notating position in a cyclic behavior such as wave movement; often expressed in degrees. A full or complete phase equals 360 degrees. The phase value at the beginning of each full cycle is zero; halfway through the cycle its value is 180 degrees. A full cycle equals 360 degrees.

sine wave: A waveform whose change over time can be graphically expressed as a sine curve.

pitch: The characteristic tone produced by a vibrating body; the higher the frequency of vibration, the higher the pitch.

The Sound Wave

As described earlier, sound waves are created by the cyclical compression and decompression of molecules in the medium through which the sound is traveling. In air, when a sound is instigated, the air pressure increases as the air molecules press against adjacent molecules until the sound reaches its loudest moment (a pressure peak). The pressure then decreases until it reaches the maximum level of decompression. Then the compression cycle starts again. That cyclic action describes the behavior of sound waves.

Figure 21.2A illustrates the trace for one full **phase** (or cycle) of a sound wave. It begins at the zero line, goes through the positive (compression) phase, and then crosses back into the negative (rarefaction) phase before returning to zero. In this example, the full phase is shown as a **sine wave**. In reality, a full phase can take numerous other wave shapes — square, rectangular, sawtooth, and so forth. Irrespective of the specific shape a sound wave takes, the same terms are used to describe its phase.

It's important to know a signal's phase — both when the signal is an actual sound wave and when it's an electronic version — a sample — of that sound wave. That's because the intensity of the sound will be affected if the signals are out of phase. Multiple instances of the same signal at slightly different arrival times (we're talking micro- and milliseconds) can significantly affect the resultant signal.

The way that phase affects a signal is best explained by example. Figure 21.2B represents three full cycles of a tone. Figure 21.2C shows another tone — the dashed line — of the same frequency and intensity being initiated 180 degrees out of phase of the first one. Theoretically, this should result in no sound being heard. Practically, this phase cancellation results in a significant reduction in intensity but not a complete loss of sound. If the initiation of the second tone is delayed one full phase — 360 degrees — the resultant waveform would theoretically be twice the intensity of the original, as illustrated in Figure 21.2D. Practically, due to a number of variables, the resultant sound won't be twice as loud, but it would definitely be louder.

There are a number of variables that are frankly beyond the scope of this introductory material. But suffice it to say that the net effect of either electronic or physical signals being out of phase is distortion. In addition, distortion is a change in the shape of the waveform that causes an undesired change in the sound.

Frequency

Frequency is the rate at which an object vibrates. Frequency is often referred to as **pitch** by musicians, while engineering types generally refer to it by its cyclic rate per second, measured in Hertz (or Hz).

At one time or another, most of us have strung a rubber band between our fingers and strummed it. The rubber band vibrated and made a sound. As we stretched the rubber band tighter the number of oscillations increased and the pitch got higher. That demonstrates the direct relationship between frequency and pitch: As frequency increases, pitch increases.

To better understand the concept of frequency and its effect on pitch, let's assume that when the drumhead discussed earlier was struck with the drumstick, it took one second to complete 20 full vibrations, as shown in Figure 21.3A. We would hear or feel it as a very low sound. If we were able to tighten the drumhead so it vibrated at a frequency of 200 Hz (Figure 21.3B), we would hear a higher pitched sound.

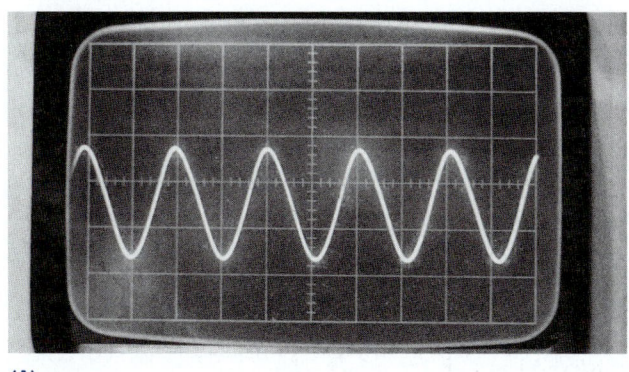

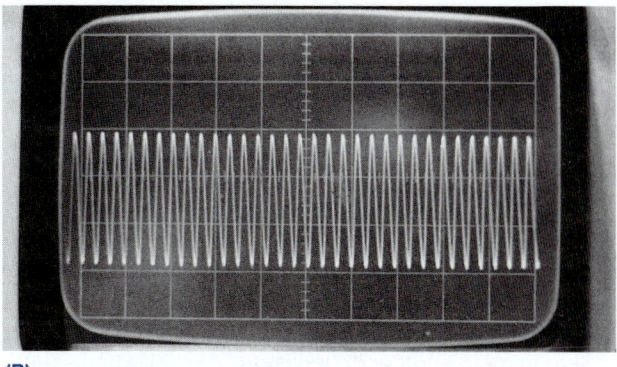

(A)   **(B)**

FIGURE 21.3
The higher the frequency, the higher the pitch. (A) A 20-cycle (Hz) sound; (B) a 200-cycle (Hz) sound.

Most humans were born with the ability to hear frequencies ranging between 20 and 20,000 Hz. As we age — and as we make poor decisions regarding hearing protection — we lose the ability to hear the higher frequencies. Figure 21.4 shows the frequencies produced by some readily identifiable sound sources.

intensity: An objective statement of the power of sound.

loudness: A subjective term describing an individual person's perception of sound intensity.

Intensity

Although there is a rough correlation between the terms **intensity** and **loudness,** there are technical differences between the two. Intensity refers to the measurable quantity of the power of sound, normally expressed in **decibels** (dB).[2] Loudness is a subjective term that describes a person's perception of sound intensity and varies by frequency and individual. What is "loud" for one person may not be for another.

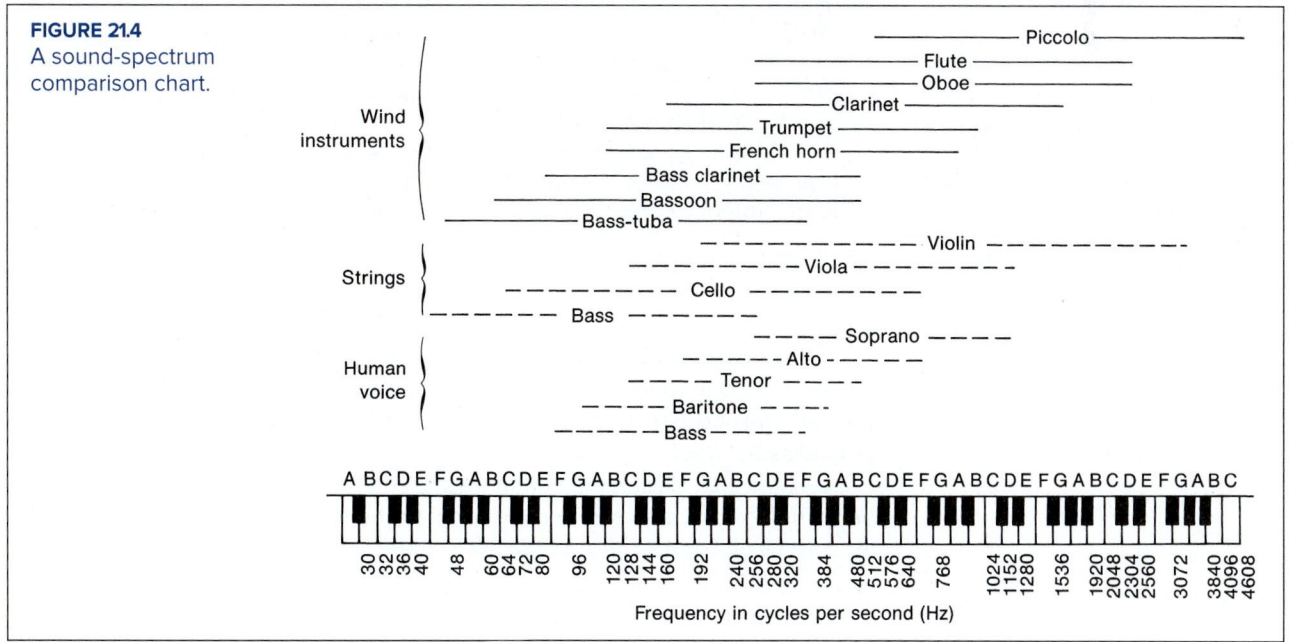

FIGURE 21.4
A sound-spectrum comparison chart.

[2] The term decibel is actually 1/10 of a Bell, the original unit of measurement for sound pressure. The name Bell was chosen to honor Alexander Graham Bell, inventor of the telephone. But calculations using the Bell quickly became cumbersome, so it was decided to use "deciBell" as the term of choice. At some point "deciBell" was revised to the now-familiar "decibel." The capital B was left in the abbreviation (dB) to honor Mr. Bell. Cool, eh?

PRODUCTION INSIGHTS
Decibels Can Be Confusing

The term *decibel* can be really confusing. Most of that confusion stems from not fully understanding the term's definition and how it is used in actual practice. And that confusion is perfectly understandable.

We're all used to a "measurement" being made from one absolute point to another: to measure the length of a board, you measure from one end of the board to the other. Sound intensity isn't measured that way. Sound intensity is measured as a ratio comparing two different sound levels.

To illustrate this point, the figure on the right side of this box diagrams the relative loudness levels of a variety of sounds. Notice that the intensity level for "threshold of hearing" is defined as 0dB. That doesn't mean, there is no sound. 0 dB is not an absolute. The intensity level that someone begins to hear varies, sometimes significantly, from individual to individual. The figure at the right indicates that normal conversation has a sound intensity of somewhere in the 65 dB range. That's not an absolute number either. It's movable. So while you can accurately say, "Normal conversation is 65 dB louder than the threshold of hearing," that's not a statement of absolutes. The statement is actually comparing one sound level to another.

To further confuse the issue, decibels are used to measure both the intensity of the actual pressure waves that sound generates and the electronic signals that represent those sounds. The intensity of airborne sound waves is noted as dBSPL (decibels sound pressure level). The intensity of the electronic signals are identified with a number of different suffixes that specify what is actually being measured — dBV (decibels voltage), dBm (decibels milliwatt), and so forth.

There are two ways to solve this perplexing annoyance. You could memorize the fact that the measurement of intensity in sound is a ratio comparing two sound levels and also memorize any decibel suffixes you encounter. The other more preferable way is to sufficiently immerse yourself in the subject until you fully understand not only the terms but the math used to determine those relationships.

For the introductory level provided by this textbook, understanding that sound intensity is a ratio comparing two sound levels is probably sufficient. If you want to get further involved in this genuinely exciting field — and I encourage you to do so — you'll have to delve deeper into this subject. There are numerous online sites and more advanced textbooks that provide full explanations of this subject.

Decibels	
130	Jet plane at 100 feet Threshold of pain
120	
110	Loud rock band at 5 feet
100	Thunder
90	
80	Loud street traffic at 5 feet
70	Normal conversation at 5 feet
60	
50	
40	Quiet street noise
30	Quiet residence
20	Quiet whisper
10	
0	Threshold of hearing

The rule of thumb for describing the power needed to generate a sound that will be perceived to be twice as loud as an existing sound is as follows: Intensity (power) must be increased ten-fold (+10 dB) for a sound to be perceived as twice as loud as the original sound.

As indicated earlier, the unit of measurement for sound intensity is the decibel (dB). Decibels are used to measure both the intensity of sound waves in the air and the electronic representations of those sound waves.

Timbre

Timbre refers to the distinctive quality of a sound. It is what makes one voice sound different than another, or a trumpet sound different than a violin. This qualitative difference is based on the harmonics made by the sound-producing body.

Pure sounds, as shown in Figure 21.5A, rarely occur in nature. Most natural sounds (voices, violins, surf noises) produce a variety of overtones, or harmonics, as shown in Figure 21.5B. These harmonic frequencies are based on the pitch of the fundamental, or base frequency, illustrated in Figure 21.6.

The amplitude, or loudness, of each harmonic will be less than the loudness of the fundamental frequency, and the amount of each harmonic in the final tone will be determined by the physical structure of the source. The reason that no two voices or instruments sound exactly alike is that each voice or instrument structure has physical variations that affect the amplitude of the various harmonics it produces.

Sound Systems

This section explains how the components of a sound system are strung together and how each of those components works.

Sound System Configuration

There are three basic types of sound systems used in the theatre: sound reinforcement, sound recording, and sound playback. Figure 21.7 shows block diagrams of those three systems. Much of the same equipment is used in all three configurations, just arranged in slightly different order.

Figure 21.7A shows the equipment configuration for a single-channel sound reinforcement system. A **microphone,** which is a type of **transducer,** picks up the sound. The microphone converts the sound into a very weak electrical signal. That signal is sent to a **preamplifier** in the **mixer.** The preamp boosts the power of the signal to **line level** for **signal processing** by the

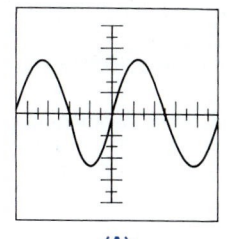

(A)

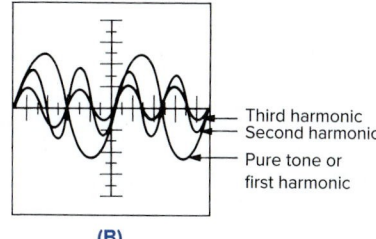

(B)

FIGURE 21.5
(A) A pure tone and (B) its harmonics.

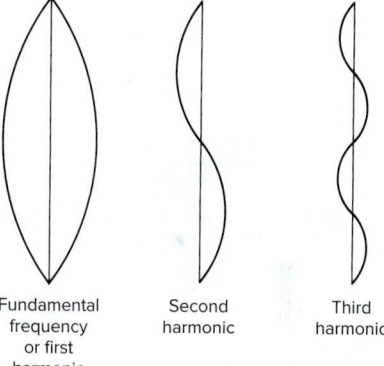

FIGURE 21.6
The loudness of a harmonic will be less than its fundamental frequency.

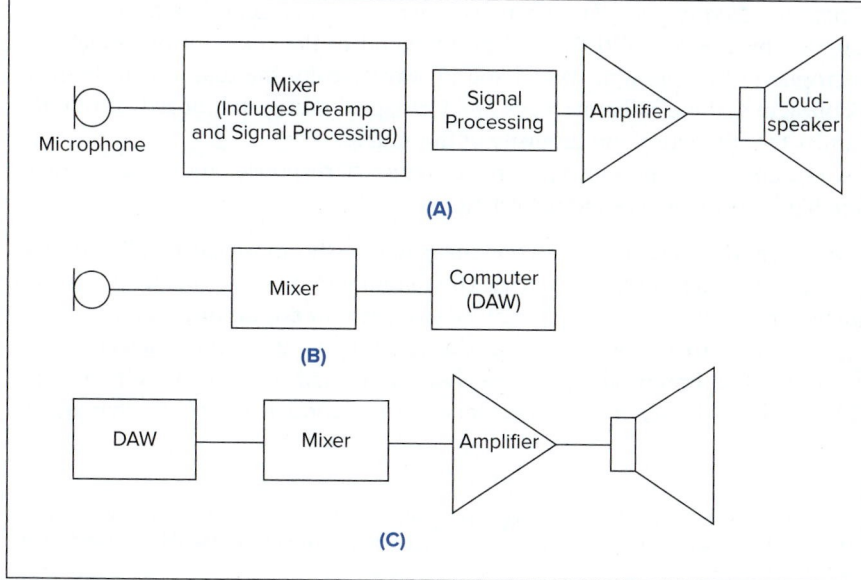

(A)

(B)

(C)

FIGURE 21.7
(A) A block diagram of a single channel sound system. (B) Block diagram of a single channel sound recording system. (C) Block diagram of a single channel sound playback system.

microphone: A transducer that converts sound waves into electrical energy.

transducer: A device that converts one form of energy into another.

preamplifier: A device that increases the power of a weak signal for use by subsequent stages in an electronic circuit.

mixer: A device used to combine two or more input signals to create a blended output signal. Multichannel mixers blend numerous input signals and routes them to multiple output channels.

line level: The standard operating voltage used by mixers and signal processors.

signal processing: The manipulation of transducer input signals to change, blend, and enhance the resultant output signal(s).

power amplifier: A device used to boost the signal received from the mixer to a level that will drive a loudspeaker.

capacitor: An electronic component composed of two conductive plates separated and insulated from each other. Used to store an electrostatic charge.

mixer. After the sound has been processed, it is sent to the **power amplifier.** The power amp substantially increases the power of the signal and sends it to the loudspeaker.

Figure 21.7B illustrates a single-channel version of a sound recording system. In this example a signal is generated by the microphone and boosted to line level by the mixer's internal mic preamp. The strengthened signal may be processed[3] in the mixer before it is sent to a computer equipped with digital audio workstation (DAW) software for recording. An electronic instrument such as a guitar or keyboard could be substituted for the microphone in this example.[4] Any type of transducer can be used to generate the signal that ultimately will be recorded.

Figure 21.7C illustrates a single-channel version of the third type of theatrical sound system — the playback system. The initiating transducer in a playback system is typically a DAW that plays the music and/or effects files. That signal is sent through the mixer for processing, then on to the amplifier/loudspeaker and out into the auditorium.

Sound System Components

Every sound system works on the principles outlined in the previous section. The operating principles of the various pieces of equipment that make up those sound systems will be covered in this section.

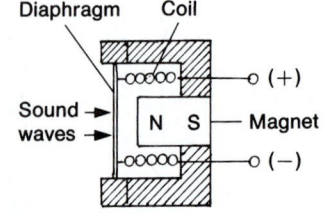

Diaphragm   Coil

Sound →
waves →

N S — Magnet

(+)
(−)

FIGURE 21.8
A dynamic microphone.

Microphones   Microphones (mics) used in the theatre are quantified by four different characteristics: element style; pickup pattern; physical design; and their connectivity — how they connect to the rest of the sound/recording system — either wired or wireless.

Element style refers to the manner in which the mic converts acoustic energy into an electrical signal. The types most commonly used in the theatre are dynamic and condenser microphones. Ribbon, electret, piezoelectric, and carbon microphones are less frequently used.

Dynamic Microphone   The heart of a dynamic microphone is a magnet surrounded by a wire coil (Figure 21.8). One end of the coil is firmly attached to microphone's diaphragm. When sound waves strike the diaphragm, both the diaphragm and the coil move back and forth, generating an induced current that mimics the frequency and intensity of the source.

Dynamic microphones have good frequency response, are rugged, and are suitable for onstage use and recording.

Condenser Microphone   The condenser mic is the most electrically complex microphone used in theatre sound. The diaphragm, which is made of thin conductive material, forms one plate of a condenser[5] or **capacitor.** A constant voltage is applied across these plates as shown in Figure 21.9. When a sound wave strikes the diaphragm, the pressure changes the space between the two plates. This causes a change in the capacitance of the condenser, which changes the

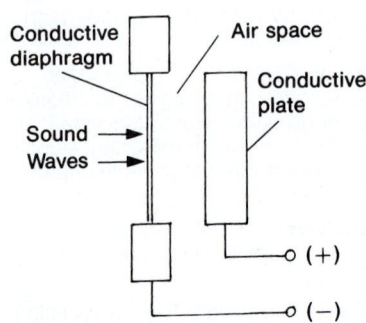

Conductive
diaphragm

Air space

Conductive
plate

Sound →
Waves →

(+)

(−)

FIGURE 21.9
A condenser microphone.

[3] Normally, when making a live recording, very little processing is done to the signal so its original sound will be preserved. Original signals are typically processed only during the re-recording/cue construction process.

[4] Substituting a guitar or keyboard for a microphone typically requires additional equipment to be inserted in the circuit between the instrument and the mixer to ensure the compatibility of their signals.

[5] Although the word *condenser* is an obsolete term for capacitor, it remains as the name-of-choice for this type of microphone. Go figure . . .

PRODUCTION INSIGHTS
Balanced and Unbalanced Lines and the Direct Box

Two types of cables are used for distributing the electronic signal between the various pieces of a modular sound system: **unbalanced lines** and **balanced lines.** When implemented correctly, balanced lines are much less susceptible to hum and noise than unbalanced lines.

An unbalanced line (Figure A) is a sound cable in which a single insulated conductor is wrapped in a braided or foil shield. A thin, outer plastic, insulating jacket protects the shield. Both the conductor and shield carry the signal, while the shield connects to the ground. Unbalanced connections are susceptible to hum and noise of nearby electromagnetic fields that can be induced in the shield and become part of the signal. Unbalanced lines are also very susceptible to **ground loops**.

A balanced line is a sound cable with two conductors wrapped in a braided or foil shield surrounded by an outside insulating jacket (Figure B). The two conductors carry the signal, and the shield is connected to ground. The balanced line creates a circuit that is immune to the effects of magnetically induced interference, and it can be configured to eliminate ground loops. In professional sound systems, virtually all microphone and line level signals are connected using balanced lines.

Another device that reduces hum and distortions in sound circuits is the direct box. The direct box (Figure C) accepts inputs from both balanced and unbalanced lines but only outputs a balanced signal. The direct box also has circuitry that eliminates potential ground loops by electronically breaking the ground connection between the interconnected devices.

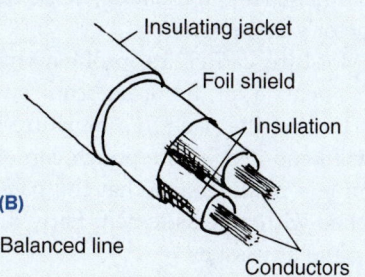

(A) Unbalanced line — Insulating jacket, Braided shield, Insulation, Conductor

(B) Balanced line — Insulating jacket, Foil shield, Insulation, Conductors

(C)

voltage applied across the two plates. Those voltage variations mimic the pattern of the sound waves generated by the source.

The condenser microphone has excellent frequency response and **dynamic range.** Condenser mics require a power supply, which can be supplied by a small battery inserted into the microphone or from **phantom power** supplied by the mixer.

Ribbon Microphone   Ribbon microphones have excellent frequency response. They use an extremely thin strip of corrugated metal suspended between the poles of a magnet to **transduce** the sound, as shown in Figure 21.10. The air pressure of the sound waves move the metal ribbon back and forth to generate an induced voltage between the two ends of the ribbon. That voltage mimics the frequency and intensity of the sound source.

Ribbon microphones have a history of being quite delicate — to the point where even blowing into the mic could break the ribbon. Although most often associated with recording, newer designs use a much more resilient film that can withstand the rigors of live stage use.

Microphone Pickup Patterns   Microphones discriminate in what they hear according to their **pickup patterns.** Pickup patterns, also known as polar patterns, depict the intensity of the microphone output (measured in dB) relative to the angle from which the sound arrives.

unbalanced line: A sound cable in which a single insulated conductors is wrapped in a braided or foil shield.

balanced line: A sound cable in which two insulated conductors are wrapped in a braided or foil shield.

ground loop: An unwanted current generated when two supposedly isolated circuits use a common ground. Ground loops are a major source of noise and hum in sound systems and can be a potentially lethal shock hazard.

dynamic range: Sensitivity to changes in loudness; the ratio between the largest and smallest intensity levels of sound. Measured in decibels.

phantom power: A method of supplying DC power through the microphone cable to operate condenser microphones.

transduce: Convert one form of energy into another.

pickup patterns: The visual pattern illustrating the intensity of a microphone's output (measured in dB) relative to the direction from which the sound arrives.

lavelier: Small mic (usually) clipped to the shirt, lapel, or other inconspicuous place on the actor's/talent's clothing.

input: Information put into a system for processing.

output: Information produced by a system.

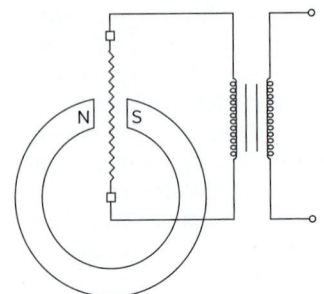

FIGURE 21.10
A ribbon microphone.

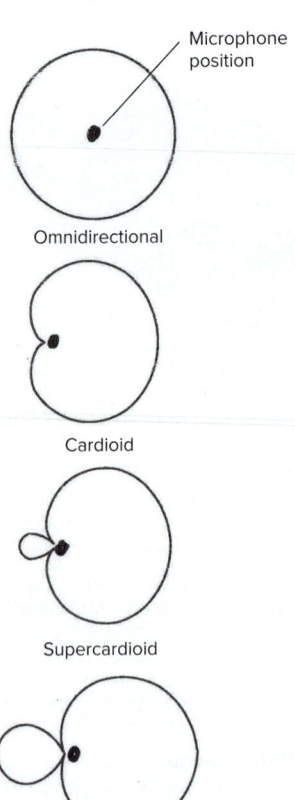

Omnidirectional

Cardioid

Supercardioid

Hypercardioid

Figure Eight
or Bi-Directional

FIGURE 21.11
Microphone pickup patterns.

Microphone pickup patterns range from omnidirectional to figure eight, as shown in Figure 21.11. High-quality dynamic or condenser microphones with cardioid pickup patterns are generally the most useful in the theatre.

It's almost impossible to tell what kind of pickup pattern a microphone has just by looking at it. Quality microphones will have the manufacturer's name and model number indicated somewhere on the microphone. This information can be used to find the mic's specifications and pickup pattern on the manufacturer's website.

Wireless Microphones Wireless microphones come in several styles — hand-held, head-worn, and **lavelier**. They all use a low-wattage FM radio transmitter to broadcast the microphone's signal to a receiver, which feeds the signal to the mixer.

Head-worn mics (Figure 21.12) are very small microphones typically taped to the actor's forehead just below the hairline, over the ear, or on the cheek at the hairline. Performers in musicals frequently wear boom microphones (Figure 21.13) to get the mic close to their mouths to enhance the quality of the pickup. The microphone is connected to a battery pack/transmitter, which transmits the signal to the mixer. The wire for all head-worn mics is typically hidden in the actor's hair while the battery pack/transmitter is usually hidden somewhere in the actor's costume.

Moisture can create problems when using wireless mic bodypacks. If an actor sweats a lot, he or she can "sweat out" the pack, or cause it to malfunction. Putting the pack in a moisture-resistant pouch made of a waterproof fabric will keep it dry. The pouch can either be sewn into a hidden pocket in the costume — making sure that the pack can be easily removed for servicing — or attached with an elastic belt. Early discussions with the costume shop can usually avoid any issues.

Mixers Mixers perform three main functions in sound systems: signal routing, processing, and gain control. This process is best explained by example. Figure 21.14 shows the setup of a hypothetical mixer's **input** and **output** channels for a one-person show. While most mixers have eight or more inputs only two are being used in this example. The performer's wireless mic is connected to one input. The playback computer's music and effects files are fed into a second input.[6]

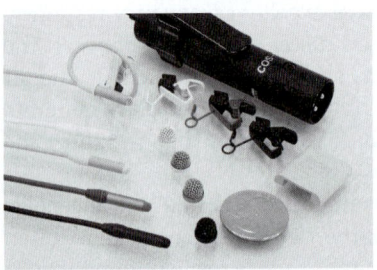

FIGURE 21.12
Sanken COS-11D head-worn wireless microphone. Courtesy of Sanken.

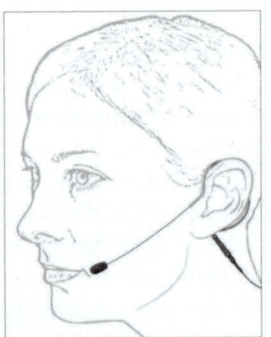

FIGURE 21.13
Countryman E-6 boom mic. Courtesy of Countryman Associates.

[6] A playback computer typically uses several playback channels depending on the style of audio interface used. In this example only one channel is being indicated to simplify the explanation.

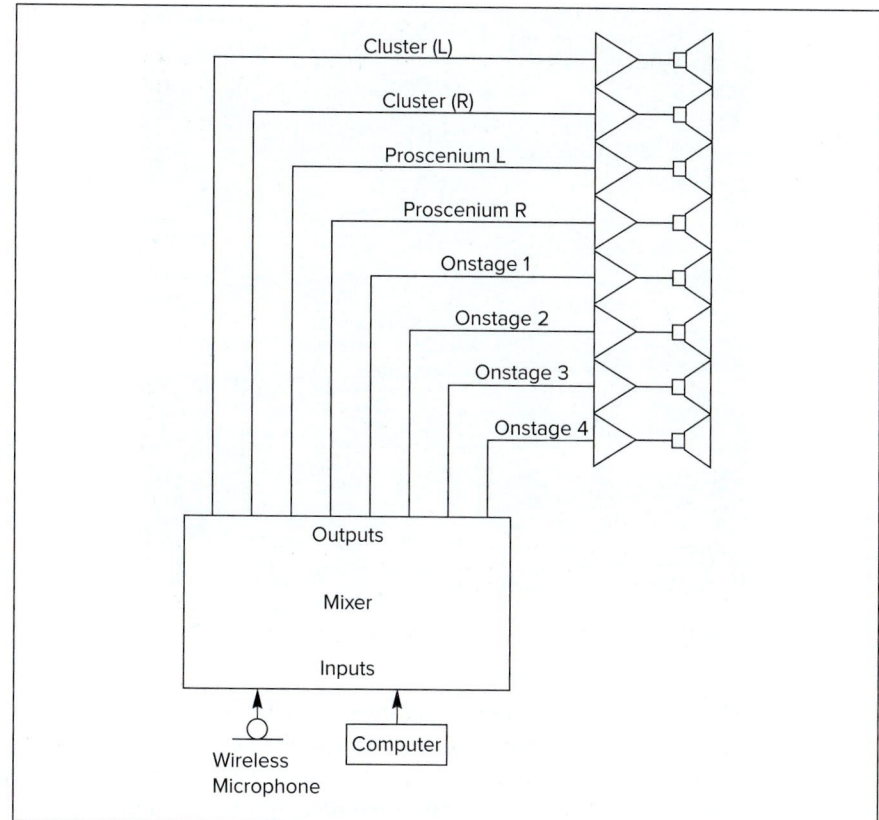

FIGURE 21.14
Block diagram of a hypothetical mixer with two inputs and eight outputs.

Two of the eight output channels are connected to the hypothetical speaker cluster at the top of the proscenium arch. One is connected to the speaker stack on the left side of the proscenium and another to the speaker stack on the right side of the proscenium. The last four are connected to onstage loudspeakers.

The mixer allows any of the input signals to be routed to any of the loudspeaker locations. For example, a hypothetical, not-very-realistic, example illustrates the point. A soundboard operator could make an actor's voice seem to coincide with her location by adjusting the strength of the signal sent to the various loudspeaker locations. As the actor moves around the stage, the sound operator could "follow" her with the sound by increasing the proportion of the mix being sent to loudspeakers nearest her location. Again, this is an illustrative example and is rarely, if ever, done. But it does illustrate how sound can be moved from speaker to speaker to seemingly "move" the sound around the stage. Any music or effects cues can be sent to any of the speaker groupings to achieve an intended directional effect.

There are two types of audio mixers: analog and digital. They perform the same tasks, but the digital models convert all signals to a digital format. Most digital mixers have some sort of memory that enables them to recall routing, **processing**, and gain settings so that information can be repeated from performance to performance.

Most mixers are equipped with both microphone and line level inputs. The microphone inputs feed directly to **onboard** preamps that boost the mic's signal to line level. The line level inputs are used to connect **outboard** devices such as disc players, computers, and signal processors to the mixer. A typical analog audio mixer is shown in Figure 21.15. Figure 21.16 illustrates a typical medium-format digital mixer.

onboard: Devices with discrete functions mounted within the housing of a larger unit.

outboard: Separate stand-alone units.

FIGURE 21.15
Mackie 1642-VLZ3 Mixer Courtesy
of Mackie/Loud Technologies.

FIGURE 21.16
The Yamaha QL-5 is a digital
audio mixer Courtesy of Yamaha
Commercial Audio Systems.

boosting: Increasing.

attenuating: Decreasing.

compressor: An electronic device
or software that automatically
reduces signal amplitude when a
predetermined intensity level is
reached.

gate: A device or software that
automatically increases the gain of
an input signal (effectively turning
it on or off) when a predetermined
intensity level is reach.

signal delay: Software that holds
a signal for a specified amount of
time before sending it on to the next
device in the system.

processing: Term used in
sound production. Refers to the
manipulation of an input signal to
achieve a desired output result.

equalizer: An electronic device used
to adjust different audio frequencies.

reverb: An electronically produced
echo effect.

compression: The process used
to attenuate loud spikes in an
electronic signal.

gate: An electronic device used
to active/deactivate (typically) a
microphone when its signal reaches
a predetermined level.

Nearly all audio mixers contain equalizers used to shape the frequency response of the signal by **boosting** or **attenuating** relatively narrow frequency ranges of the input signal. In addition to equalization, each channel of a digital mixer is normally equipped with a **compressor,** a **gate,** and **signal delay,** devices that are also used to shape the sound.

Processing In sound production **processing** refers to the manipulation of an input signal to achieve a desired output result. Processors are the equipment that performs that function. The most commonly used processors in the theatre are equalizers, delay, reverb, gate, and compression.

Equalizers are used to compensate for situations — such as equipment or facility issues — where certain frequencies are either too loud or not present enough. The equipment — and term — originated in the "olden days" of analog telephones when equalizers were used to even out the frequencies lost in transmission. Equalizers are used in the theatre to do the same thing but with much more accuracy and clarity. The most commonly used styles of equalizers in the theatre are the graphic and parametric.

Delay is used to time-align the sound emitted from two different sources. For example, if two separate loudspeakers are presenting the same content, but one is farther away, it may be useful to "delay" the signal to the closer loudspeaker so its sound arrives at the listener at the same time as the sound from the more distant speaker.

Reverb — short for reverberation — refers to the application of a simulated acoustic environment to a sound. Reverb would be called for if you wanted to make a whisper appear as if it were coming from inside a large empty room. It can be used to simulate the sound reflecting off a surface, perhaps several times over. A related term — verb — includes things that are not actually reverb, but instead are effects such as pitch shift, flange, or chorus.

Compression and **gate** are used to control the dynamic range of a sound.

Compression is used to attenuate loud spikes in a signal. Compression is accomplished with a comp/limiter — a device that automatically fixes the gain at a specified ratio. This is useful for protecting speakers (and ears) from a damagingly loud signal.

Gate deals with the "quiet end" of a signal. Once a signal level drops below a set threshold, the gate closes — infinitely reduces the gain — so no sound passes. For instance, picture a panel discussion with several panelists — all with separate microphones — seated at a table. One panelist not speaking might be making low-level noises (shuffling papers, pouring water, and so forth). That sound wouldn't be loud enough to allow the gate to open. But when he or she spoke directly into the mic, the gate would open and sound would be normally processed.

Most of the processors described above are built into digital consoles. However, if used as standalone devices, they are generally placed between the mixer and the amplifiers. In certain circumstances, a processor may be used as an "insert" to restrict the effect to a single channel.

Crossovers There are two types of crossovers — active and passive. The purpose of both is to split the audio signal into the frequency components suitable for each type of loudspeaker in the system to reproduce. For example, in a two-way crossover network (either active or passive) the signal might be split at 1,200 Hz, sending the frequencies below 1,200 Hz to the amplifier powering the woofer and the signals around 1,200 Hz to a high-frequency horn driver.

Active crossovers are placed before the amplifier, as illustrated in Figure 21.17, and may also contain equalizers, **digital delays,** and limiters to process the output from the mixer before it reaches the power amp. Active crossover networks are sometimes called bi-amp or tri-amp systems, depending on the number of power amps associated with them.

Passive networks are placed after the amplifier, as illustrated in Figure 21.18. They are typically located inside the speaker cabinet. They don't have any additional signal processing functions other than splitting the signal. (That's why they're called passive.)

Power Amplifier The only reason for the power amplifier's existence is to boost the low-voltage signal it receives from the input source to a higher-voltage signal capable of efficiently driving the loudspeakers.

The power rating of the power amplifier is one of its most important statistics. It isn't uncommon to find amplifiers rated beyond 1,000 watts RMS in

digital delay: A device used to time-align the sound emitted from two different sources.

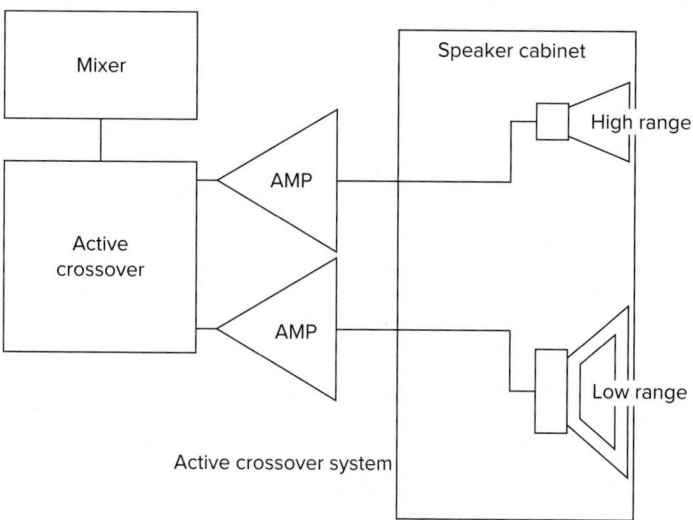

FIGURE 21.17
Active crossovers are typically located after the mixer and before the power amp.

FIGURE 21.18
Passive crossovers are placed after the power amp. They are typically located inside the speaker cabinet.

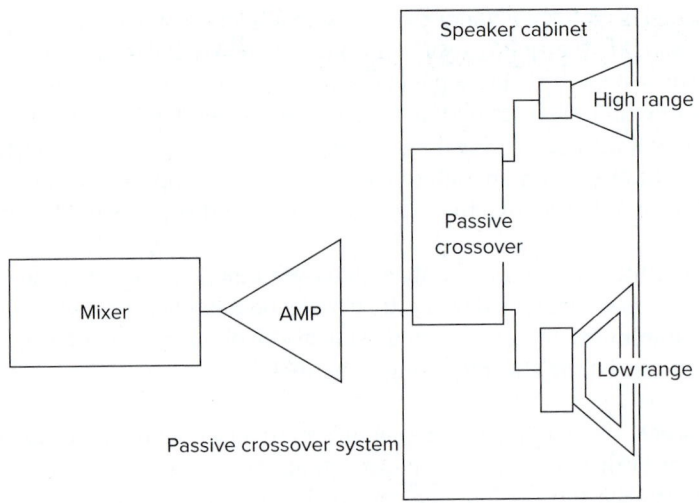

the theatre. An example will help illustrate why this is important. An average-sized auditorium may require 100 watts of power to play a musical selection at a reasonable listening level. If there is a momentary peak in the music that is ten times larger than the normal signal (which is fairly typical), it will take ten times the power (1,000 watts) from the amplifier to prevent the music from distorting and sounding fuzzy and muddy rather than clear and crisp.

Power amps must also be sized appropriately for the speakers they will be driving. An amplifier that is too large can overheat and damage the loudspeaker. An amplifier that is too small for the speakers will distort the signal peaks while trying to drive the loudspeaker to its rated power maximum. However, a little extra amp power above anticipated demands will provide **headroom** — the ability for a power amp to handle brief high demands without distorting the signal.

Power amplifiers are often standalone single-purpose devices, but it is not uncommon to find amps with built-in signal processing designed to match a particular speaker. Power amps can also be built into a speaker cabinet to create a powered loudspeaker. These will be discussed in a later section.

Loudspeakers and Speaker Systems   Literally hundreds of varieties of loudspeakers have been created for countless applications. The loudspeakers described in this section are the types most commonly found in theatrical settings.

Loudspeakers, like microphones, are a type of transducer. They generate sound the same way as the microphone — but in reverse. Loudspeakers create sound when an electrical signal moves a flexible membrane back and forth to compress air and create sound waves — as illustrated in Figure 21.19.

The signal activates an electromagnet attached to the loudspeaker frame. The electromagnet generates a magnetic field that corresponds in intensity to the frequency and loudness of the electrical signal emitted by the amplifier. The variation in this magnetic field causes a voice coil (attached to the rear of a flexible cone) to move the cone forward and backward in a pattern that mimics the frequency and loudness dictated by the electrical signal.

Loudspeakers (also called speakers) work most effectively and efficiently when they are designed for a relatively narrow frequency range. Speakers are generally classified as low-frequency (**woofers**), middle-frequency (**mid-range**), and high-frequency (**tweeters**). Almost all woofers are cone-type loudspeakers.

headroom: A power amp's ability to handle brief high demands without distorting the the signal.

woofer: A low-frequency speaker, with a frequency range from 20 to approximately 1,200 to 1,500 Hz.

mid-range: A speaker designed to reproduce the middle range of audible frequencies — roughly 200 to 1,000 Hz.

tweeter: A high-frequency speaker generally designed to reproduce from approximately 1,000 to 20,000 Hz.

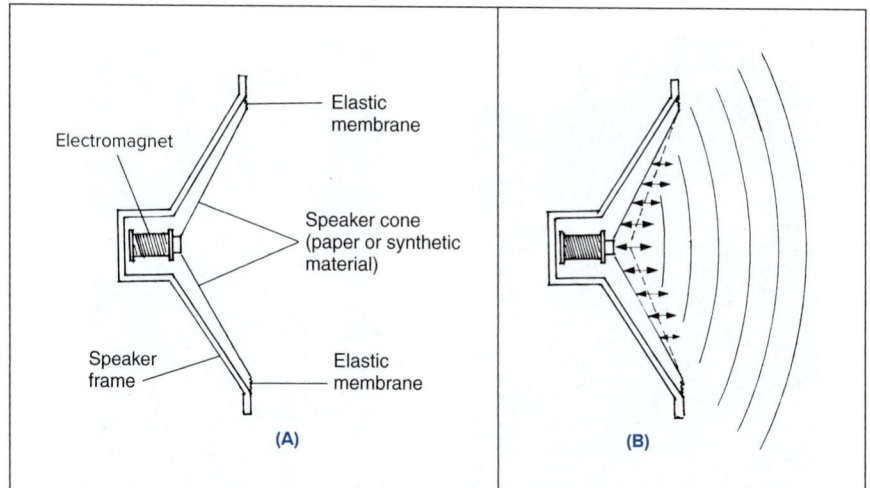

FIGURE 21.19
How a loudspeaker converts electrical energy into mechanical energy. (A) The structure of a typical loudspeaker. (B) The cone is moved forward and backward by the magnet to produce sound.

Mid-range speakers and tweeters are also made with cones, but loudspeakers for live performances are typically manufactured using **pressure drivers** and **horns** due to the high sound pressure levels and carefully controlled coverage angles required.

The pressure driver (also known as a driver), illustrated in Figure 21.20, creates sound in the same way as a cone speaker — a signal drives an electromagnetic voice coil, which is attached to a diaphragm that compresses air to create sound waves. The primary difference is that the diaphragm in the pressure driver is made from very thin metal such as titanium instead of paper or a synthetic material. The metal is more capable of producing loud mid- and high-frequency sounds without damage. The horn directs the sound from the driver in a particular dispersion pattern such as 40 degrees vertical by 90 degrees horizontal. Horns typically disperse sound over a range of 40 to 120 degrees. Examples of horns are shown in Figure 21.21.

Powered Loudspeakers   Powered loudspeakers — also called self-powered speakers or active speakers — have built-in power amplifiers and signal-processing capabilities. Active speakers provide outstanding speaker overload protection, and nullify the need to think about amplifier/speaker power ratings. They just require the output level of the mixer to match the input requirement of the

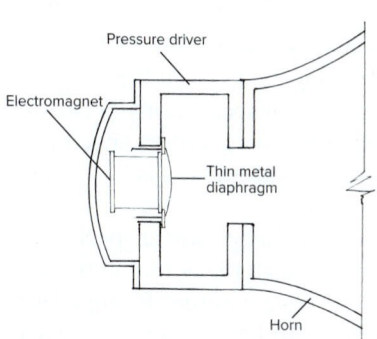

FIGURE 21.20
How a pressure driver works.

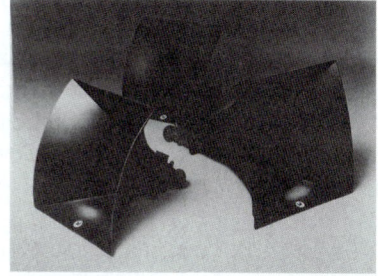

FIGURE 21.21
Acoustical horns. Horns produce a fairly linear frequency response within the coverage angles of the horn. Courtesy of JBL by Harman.

pressure driver: A unit housing a large magnet that vibrates a very thin metallic diaphragm to create mid-range and high-frequency sounds.

horn: A dispersion device attached to the front of a pressure driver to direct the sound emitted by the driver into a specific pattern.

FIGURE 21.22
The QSC-K8 is a powered
loudspeaker. Courtesy of QSC.

FIGURE 21.22
The QSC-K8 is a powered
loudspeaker. Courtesy of QSC.

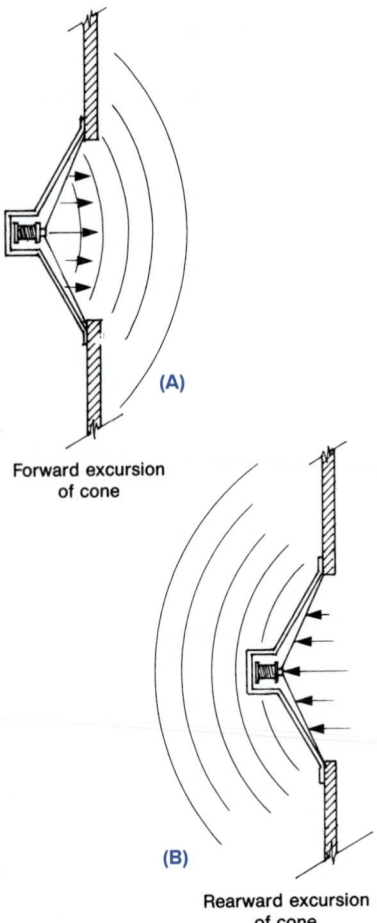

(A)

Forward excursion
of cone

(B)

Rearward excursion
of cone

FIGURE 21.23
A loudspeaker compresses air on
(A) its forward excursion and (B) its
rearward excursion.

impedance: Resistance in an
AC circuit.

amplifier/loudspeaker. An example of an active speaker — the QSC-K8 — is
shown in Figure 21.23.

Speaker Cabinets Most low-frequency speaker cabinets are designed to
enhance the reproduction of low-frequency sounds because low-frequency
sounds require more power to produce than mid- or high-frequency sounds.

When the cone of a woofer moves forward, it compresses air, which produces sound waves as shown in Figure 21.23A. When the cone moves backward,
the same amount of air is compressed and produces the same amount of sound
waves as shown in Figure 21.23B. If the speaker were mounted in a hole in a wall
between two rooms, it would produce the same frequency, quality, and intensity
of sound in both rooms.

Any speaker cabinet is designed to do one of two things: either absorb the
sound radiating into the space in back of the woofer or redirect that sound to
reinforce the sound coming from the front of the speaker.

Practically speaking, for live sound systems, the power handling capabilities
of speakers should be about half the RMS wattage rating of the amplifier. For
example, if the loudspeaker system can handle 200 watts of steady power, the
amplifier should be rated at about 400 watts RMS.

Loudspeaker Hookup Methods This discussion needs to begin with
another caveat: If you don't know what you're doing, don't do it. It is very easy
to damage either the power amplifier or loudspeakers if speakers are hooked up
incorrectly. Be sure to read (and follow) the manufacturer's recommended practices before connecting any speakers to a power amp and *definitely* before turning
the power on.

To ensure the best quality sound from the system the speaker or speaker system **impedance** (normally 4, 8, or 16 ohms) must match the output impedance
of the amplifier; in other words connect a speaker system of specific impedance
to the power amp's output with the same number. (And don't forget the caveat:
Read and follow the manufacturer's instructions if you don't know *exactly* what
you are doing.)

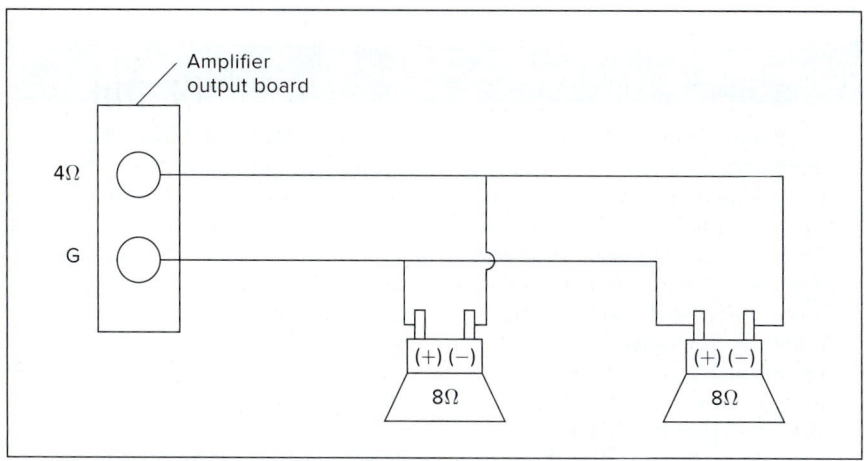

FIGURE 21.24
Parallel wiring of speakers.

Sometimes it is desirable or necessary to drive more than one speaker with a single amplifier.[7] This can be accomplished by wiring the speakers in parallel, as shown in Figure 21.24.

To calculate the total impedance when two loudspeakers of the *same* impedance are wired in parallel, divide the rated impedance of one of the loudspeakers by the number of loudspeakers to be wired in parallel. For example, two 8-ohm loudspeakers, wired in parallel, have an impedance of 4 ohms. And remember the caveat: If you don't know what you're doing, don't do it. Learn how to do whatever it is properly. Read the manufacturer's instructions and check with your supervisor.

Power amplifiers should be connected to the speakers with professional grade audio hookup cable. **Signal loss** can occur when the resistance in those cables is too high. To avoid signal loss use the following rules of thumb: When the **cable run** between the power amp (or wall-mounted speaker outlet) and the speaker is less than 50 feet, make the connection with 14-gauge audio hookup cable; runs between 50 and 150 feet require 12-gauge cable. Use high-grade connectors as well. If possible, avoid using ¼-inch phono-style or banana plug-style connectors and opt for a locking connector such as the Neutrik SpeakON.

Recording and Playback Equipment

Sound score material, whether effects or prerecorded music, is gathered from a variety of sources — live recordings, CDs, online sources, and so forth. Once it has been gathered or recorded, it is normally downloaded to a computer's internal hard drive, external hard drive, or server and then edited using one of the many available digital audio workstation (DAW) software programs. These programs are used to record, process, mix, and prepare the sound score for playback.[8]

There are many DAW packages available, such as Pro Tools by Avid, Logic by Apple, Cubase by Steinberg, and Ableton Live. Figure 21.25 is a screenshot of another DAW package, the Digital Performer by Mark of the Unicorn (MOTU).

---

[7] Sound systems rarely have more than two loudspeakers wired in parallel because the resulting impedance would be too low for the amplifiers to drive the speakers correctly. If driven with this imbalance, the speakers may distort the sound or overheat.

[8] DAW software is not designed for production playback. Other software is used for that purpose.

signal loss: Degradation in the quality of the sound represented by the signal.

cable run: The length of audio hookup cable needed to connect a power amp to a speaker.

PRODUCTION INSIGHTS
Connecting Sound Equipment

You want to playback some sound cues you've stored on a computer. You connect a computer to a mixer, connect the mixer to a power amp, and then connect the amp to a loudspeaker. You turn everything on and press play. No sound comes out. Why? It could be due to a variety of reasons, but one of the most common, and most commonly overlooked, causes has to do with signal compatibility. What's that, and why does it matter?

There are two signal forms used in electronic equipment: analog and digital. Electronic equipment (mixers/processing equipment/amplifiers) won't function properly if its **input signal** is in the wrong form. To wit, digital equipment won't provide distortion-free output without a properly formatted digital input signal. Ditto for analog equipment — it needs an analog input signal. To recap, for any electronic equipment to work properly, it must receive its input signal in the correct form — either analog or digital.

You also need to understand the following truths about the equipment used in recording and playback: It's difficult to tell simply by looking at a device what kind of input signal it requires or what form of output signal it delivers. You need to consult the manufacturer's information sheet for that particular manufacturer's make, model, and serial number. Failing that, consult with your supervisor. You need to know: (1) the form of input signal the machine requires and (2) what form of output signal it delivers.

If the manufacturer's sheet doesn't specify the signal form (or your supervisor doesn't know), the chances are reasonably good that that particular device has built-in input and output **signal converters** — electronic devices that change the signal form from analog to digital or digital to analog depending on the specific needs of the equipment. If that's the case, just hook the equipment together with good-quality connecting cables and everything should work out — unless Murphy's Law[1] is in effect.

You may encounter a situation where you have a device with a digital output and the input of the next device is analog — and neither device has built-in signal converters. In that case, an appropriate standalone signal converter — either analog to digital or digital to analog — can be placed between the two devices. Simply plug the output of the first device into the converter's input and plug the converter's output into the next device. That will assure the signal stream is compatible. In addition, as mentioned elsewhere in this chapter, be sure to use high-quality cables and connectors when patching any of these devices together.

In any case, when hooking up a sound device **equipment stream**, DO NOT turn any of the equipment on until a supervisor has checked the equipment and connections and determined that everything is genuinely compatible. This stuff is expensive and can be easily damaged via incorrect hookups. It is better to be safe than sorry.

[1]Murphy's Law: An adage that states, "Anything that can go wrong will go wrong."

input signal: The electronic signal being sent to a device.

signal converter: An electronic device that changes the signal form from digital to analog or analog to digital.

equipment stream: In a sound system the connected devices — computer/mixer/amp/loudspeaker and so forth — through which the signal travels.

The use of DAW-equipped laptops as a supplement to, or replacement for, dedicated computer sound consoles/desktop computers is increasing in sound design. The laptop gives the sound designer the flexibility to sit in the auditorium and make on-the-fly adjustments to existing cues during sound and tech rehearsals.

Live Recording

Sometimes it is necessary to record live music. Figure 21.26 is a block diagram that illustrates the setup for a typical recording session. Each sound source (microphone, electronic instrument, and so forth) is connected to an input on the mixer and appropriate recording levels[9] are set. The signals from the mics and instruments are fed through the mixer to the DAW workstation and

[9] In almost all cases, an "appropriate" recording level can be described as follows: "as loud as possible without introducing distortion."

FIGURE 21.25
A DAW sound cue from the Indianapolis Repertory Theatre production of *I Love to Eat*. Sound design by Richard K. Thomas.

recorded. Playback signals for the performers/musicians are routed from the DAW through the mixer to the monitoring amplifiers/speakers and to the performer's headphones.

To preserve the quality of the original sound, live recordings are typically made without signal processing. Each mic or instrument is almost always recorded on a separate track.

Once a good **take** has been recorded, additional tracks — called **overdubs** — are laid down with background vocals, lead guitar, and so forth. Each of the overdubs is recorded on a separate track in the DAW.

Live recording of sound effects is usually much simpler and often requires just a single microphone and portable recording device such as the H4n recorder

take: A recording made in one uninterrupted session.

overdub: An additional recording that will be added to the original recording.

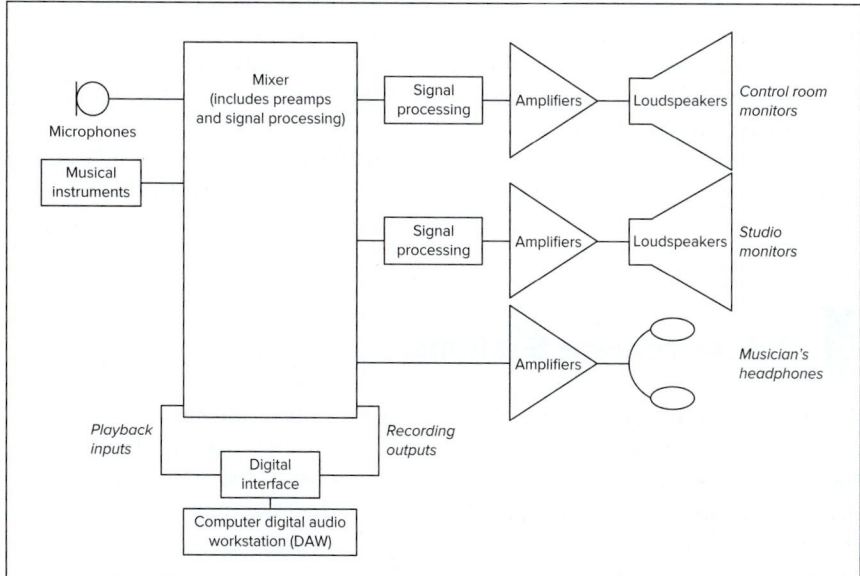

FIGURE 21.26
A block diagram of how a mixer is used in recording.

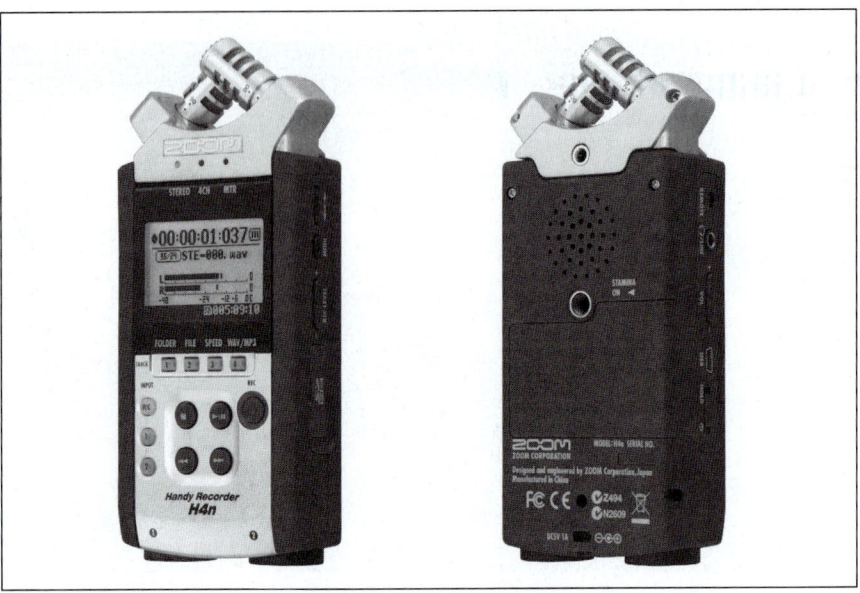

shown in Figure 21.28. It's an easy way to capture that 'perfect' squeaky door or tractor-engine sound. This type of setup is also handy for quick voice recording.

Mixdown

The **mixdown** session is used to construct the sound cues for the production. For each cue, the sound designer creates the desired balance between all of the individual tracks used on that cue, and then mixes those tracks down to the requisite number of final tracks.

The actual number of final tracks produced for any cue varies and depends entirely on the needs of the production. For example, a cue of a dog barking somewhere in the distance normally requires only one track. That cue would be played through a loudspeaker placed where the sound would be coming from.

A different cue in the same show might require the audience to be engulfed in the middle of a raging storm. The final mixdown for that cue might use as many as four or five tracks. Each of those tracks would play through strategically placed stage and house speakers to make the audience feel as if they were actually immersed in the storm.

Once all the show cues have been constructed, a copy of the sound **cue file** is stored in the computer's hard drive where it can be accessed by the playback software.

 Reinforcement Systems

At its best, sound reinforcement is transparent — after the first moments the audience should forget that it is being used and will escape into the world of the play. When sound reinforcement is obvious — when the actor's voices seem disembodied or louder than they should be, or when the orchestra drowns out the singers — reinforcement prevents the audience from entering the world of the play.

mixdown: The editing process of merging multiple tracks into (typically) a two-track recording.

cue file: A file containing the production sound cues in sequential order.

PRODUCTION INSIGHTS

Sit in the House!

The sound operator should be sitting *in* the house when he or she is running the sound for any show. Why? So they can hear the sound that the audience is hearing. That's the only way they can adjust the sound to keep the loudness and mix balance the same for every performance.

The only thing constant is change. That's as true in the theatre as it is in life. Every performance is different. The acting will vary slightly from performance to performance. The audience changes as well. The number of patrons will be different; what they're wearing will change; the ambient noise they make will change; the amount of coughing, murmuring, and sneezing all conspire to change the auditorium's acoustic environment for every performance. The sound operator needs to not only be aware of this reality; he or she needs to be able to *hear* it directly so adjustments can be made to the loudness and balance of the mix.

Sound mix position at the Goodman Theatre. Courtesy of David Naunton.

Even if your performance space doesn't have a nicely finished, house-located, sound operating station as shown above, sound operators must have their ears (and preferably the rest of their body) in the house so they can hear the results of their on-the-fly adjustments to the sound mix and readjust accordingly. A table at the back of the auditorium isn't ideal, but it is certainly better than sitting in a glass-enclosed booth at the back of the theatre where you can't hear what the audience is hearing.

In many productions the actors and singers will wear wireless microphones. Performers not wearing wireless mics are typically picked up with floor mics (Figure 21.28).

The operating principles for reinforcement mixers are identical to those used in recording. But the sheer quantity of inputs and outputs increases the complexity of reinforcement mixers, as does the need to be able to make on-the-fly adjustments. Figure 21.29 is a block diagram of a typical sound reinforcement system.

FIGURE 21.28
A Crown PCC 160 microphone. These are sometimes used as floor pickup microphones. Courtesy of Crown International by Harman.

FIGURE 21.29
A block diagram of a sound reinforcement system.

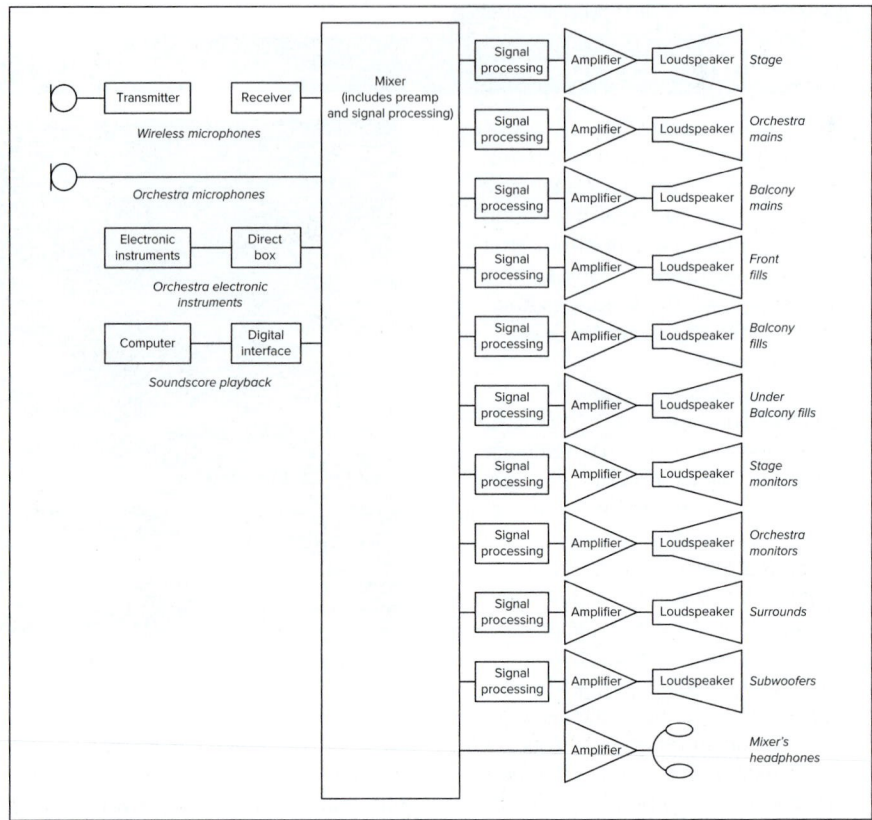

Loudspeaker Placement

The aural environment created by any particular sound cue is determined by two factors: where the loudspeakers are placed, and how many speakers or used for playback of that cue. Single speakers localize the sound. Multiple speakers generally project a feeling of spaciousness.

The purpose of any loudspeaker is primarily a function of where it is placed.

Onstage Loudspeakers — Onstage effects loudspeakers are typically located somewhere within or adjacent to the set and serve a variety of purposes.

Reinforcement Speakers – **Reinforcement loudspeakers** are located close to the actors and make the reinforced sound seem more believable. They are ideally located downstage of the dramatic space — to avoid feedback issues — but as close to the actors as possible.

Onstage Effects Speakers — Sound that is fed through an actual onstage radio or TV rarely sounds real. To make the sound seem "more real," a loudspeaker is normally placed inside — or somewhere close to — the radio or TV's location. In addition to the issue of **perceived veracity,** a reinforcing sound's location is equally important, especially in smaller theatres where the audience can clearly identify a sound's location. If the sound for a radio sitting stage left comes from stage right, the audience's focus on "the world of the play" will be broken.

Stage Foldback Monitors — In musical productions, onstage (or just offstage) loudspeakers are often used so the actors can hear the orchestra, which is critical for timing and pitch alignment between the singers and music. These loudspeakers are typically hung on overhead pipes or attached to a side-light boom or truss and focused onto the stage rather than toward the auditorium. To prevent feedback, little, if any, of the actors' vocals are fed to these foldback speakers.

perceived veracity: Imagined truth; the dichotomy between what is perceived as being real and what is fact. In this case, the sound produced by an onstage radio's actual speaker is often perceived as unreal. Audiences *expect* that radio to sound like it does in their home or cars. Meeting that expectation in the theatre almost always requires the use of a support loudspeaker.

reinforcement loudspeaker: Loudspeaker used to reinforce actors' voices.

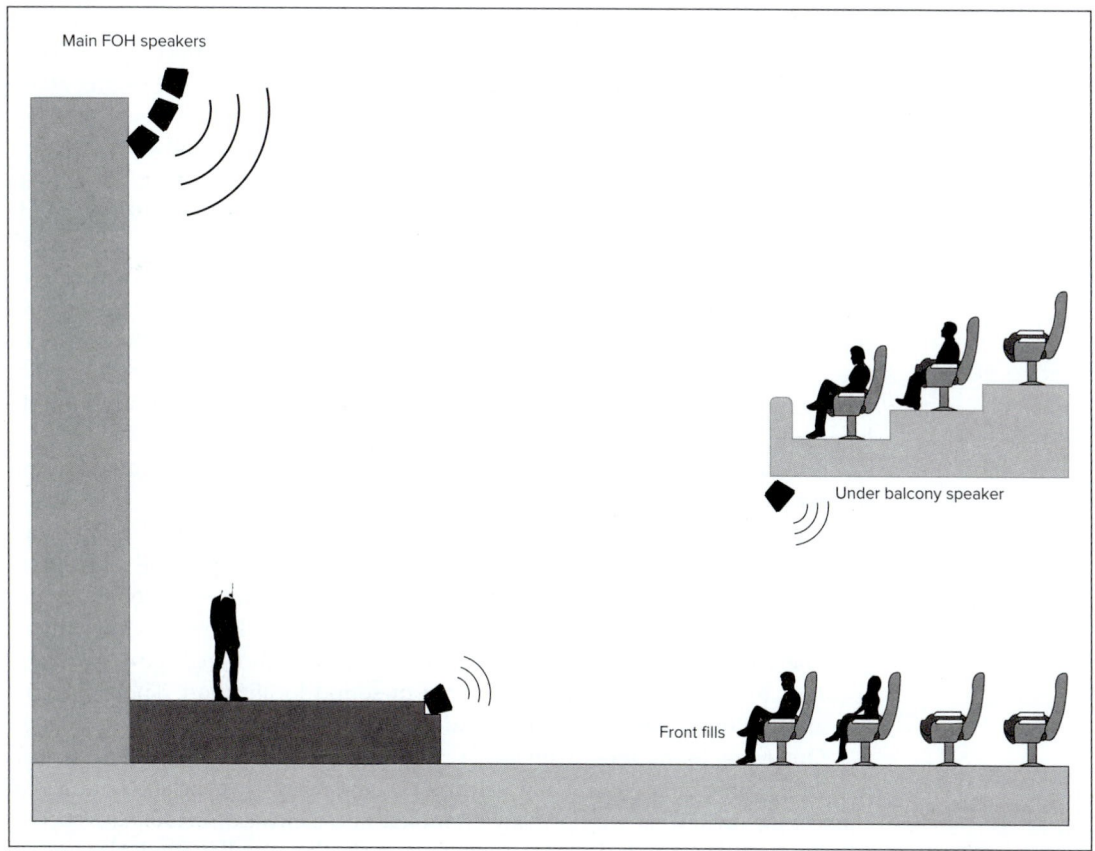

FIGURE 21.30
Front-of-house (FOH) speakers provide coverage for the seats closest to the stage. Front-fills and under-balcony speakers provide coverage for seats that may be missed by the main FOH speakers hanging above the proscenium arch.

Front-of-House (FOH) Loudspeakers – Front-of-house loudspeakers are typically hung above, or on either side of, the proscenium arch, as shown in Figure 21.30. The front-fill speakers provide coverage for the seats closest to the stage that may be missed by the main FOH cluster located above the proscenium arch. Typically, vocals come from a center cluster hung just above the proscenium arch (or directly over the thrust or arena stage) and the front-fill speakers, while the music comes from the speakers on the left and right sides of the auditorium.

Under Balcony Loudspeakers – In theatres with a balcony, direct sound from the FOH positions frequently has difficulty reaching the seats beneath the balcony. To fill this direct sound shadow area, sound designers often mount a series of small loudspeakers underneath the balcony lip to provide direct sound to those under balcony seats, as illustrated in Figure 21.31.

FIGURE 21.31
Aviom A320 Personal Monitor Mixer. Courtesy of Aviom Products.

Balcony Delay Loudspeakers — In some larger theatres the balcony can be so deep that sound from the main cluster cannot reach them effectively. Balcony delay loudspeakers, usually hung from a truss or directly from the ceiling above the balcony, can solve this problem. The sound from the balcony delay speakers is delayed so it arrives in sync with the sound from the FOH loudspeakers.

Front Fill Loudspeakers — Front fill loudspeakers are small loudspeakers that are placed just under and across the front lip of the stage. They help provide reinforcement for the closest seats and help pull the sound image down from the center cluster so the sound — when properly balanced between the front fill speakers and the cluster — appears to be coming from the stage rather than the speakers. The number of front fill loudspeakers required is determined by the horizontal coverage pattern of the loudspeakers. Again, a careful balance between the FOH and front fill loudspeakers will help make the sound appear to be coming from its appropriate location.

Surround Loudspeakers — Surround speakers are normally located around the periphery of the auditorium.

There are two versions of surround sound systems. The first uses a large number of smaller, relatively low powered loudspeakers to provide a feeling of non-localized sound — as though the listener was being immersed in the sound. This type of system enhances the sense of space in the auditorium.

The second type of surround system uses fewer, more high-powered loudspeakers to provide a well-defined sense of sound localization. These systems can make a sound appear to zip around the auditorium.

Orchestral Monitors — In an ideal situation every member of the orchestra can hear every other musician equally well and everyone plays on time and in tune. Fat chance. Pit orchestras are normally crammed into awkward, inadequate spaces. To compensate, the sound designer will frequently place small individual monitors close to the musicians (or provide headphones) so they can hear each other.

Networked pit monitor systems, such as the one shown in Figure 21.31, allow each member of the orchestra to create their own custom mix of what sounds — singers, other orchestra members, and so forth — they want to hear. Although systems like this are becoming more reasonable in price, they are usually reserved for larger touring and Broadway productions.

Rehearsal and Performance Procedures

There are a number of specific steps that most sound designers take when beginning the implementation phase of the design process in sound design.

Cue Sheets — Cue sheets are created to identify and describe each sound cue. They serve a two-fold purpose: The sound designer uses them to codify his or her thoughts about the design, and they're used to inform the other members of the production team about each cue's meaning, intent, and purpose.

The sample cue sheet shown in Figure 21.32 includes everything needed to understand the intent of each cue: where the cue is located in the script, when it will happen, what it will sound like, how long it will last, and which speakers will be used.

Sound Cue Preparation — The actual construction of the individual sound cues is relatively straightforward. After all the sounds have been gathered or recorded the sound designer creates the cues with the DAW software during a mixdown session. Each cue is recorded as a separate file with its own cue number and a brief description of its contents such as, "Q300 Distant Dog Howl," then stored in the show's sound cue folder.

PRODUCTION INSIGHTS
The Design Process in Sound Design

Commitment

If you don't fully accept the challenge and promise yourself that you will do your best work, you will end up with a mediocre product.

Analysis

In defining and refining the challenge of sound design, read and analyze the script according to the guidelines suggested in Chapter 2. Ask questions of the other members of the production design team: What is the budget for sound? What equipment does the theatre own? What is its functional status? Are there any local shops where equipment can be rented? Will the actors' voices and/or the orchestra need to be reinforced? What is the rehearsal schedule for sound? When will the director want each element of the sound design available for use in the rehearsal process? What is the tech schedule for implementation of sound?

As the sound designers analyze the script and production concept they begin to assemble a sound and music palette for the show. This is simply a list of every piece of music and sound effect that is required in the show, as shown in the accompanying figure.

Research

Background research for sound design is no different than any other design area. Both music and sound effects appropriate to the period and style of the production must be researched. Additionally, the sound designer delves into the world in which the author lived; the music, culture, and social world of the period in which the play was

***I Love to Eat* Sound and Music Palette**

SFX					
Q010, 540	Oven Timer	Egg Timer	Microwave Timer	Eggs Breaking	Water boiling
	steaks sizzling	champagne corks popping	wooden spoons stirring	knives chopping in different rhythms	whisks
	electric mixers	Cuisanarts	Blenders	Pots and pans clanking like cymbals	
Q010, 080, 270, 275, 300, 330, 360, 380, 390, 410	Canned Applause, Laughter				
Q030,040, 090 470, 510	Mr. Beard's Phones				
Q050	The markets of Cote d'Azur				
Q060, 260, 310, 320	Cow Bell/Glass 1, 2				
Q070	TV Theme Voiceover (Rick Lee?)				
Q190	Ocean Sounds, children playing on beach, seagulls				
Q200	Swimming, Being Underwater				
Q210	Ships Horn				
Q220	Baritone Practising (Vergene?)				
Q230	World's Fair Crowd				
Q280	Fire Engine Siren				
Q340	Rimshots, slide whistles and cow bells				
Q370	Mouton Cadet Stinger				
Q450	Cocktail Party				

MUSIC		
Q010	*Nessun Dorma* by Jussi Bjorling, on The Very Best of Jussi Björling (EMI Classics)	
	Amazon Link:	Ultimate-Collection/dp/B00000J911/ref=sr_1_3?ie=UTF8&qid=131 1444105&sr=8-3
Q020, 090, 420, 520	Scene Change	
Q110, 130, 180,420, 430, 480, 490, 500	The Fat Man Upstairs	
Q050	Cote d'Azur	
Q070, 265, 290, 350, 400	I Love to Eat Theme Music	
Q120	The Sun Whose Rays (sheet music)	
	Source ($1.99):	http://everynote.com/opera.show/5784.note
Q160	Stravinski's Firebird (need better quality recording)	
Q170	Savorite Recipes (Bitches Brew, already have)	
Q230	Sousa Band	
Q240	Accordian/French Singer	
Q250, 440	Maria Callas	
Q460	*Good Morning Blues* by Lester Young and the Kansas City Five	
	Amazon Link:	http://www.amazon.com/Kansas-City-Sessions-Lester-

First Impressions
Frying bacon and eggs in the nude
A six foot wide pan to make an enormous crepe suzette
Plunging champagne in hot sausages and hot sauerkraut, champagne spurting
Saw Madame Butterfly at age of six
American food-you didn't make appreciative sounds
Feel raw eggs in the bowl

A sample from the preliminary sound and music palette from Indiana Repertory Theatre production of I Love To Eat. *Sound design by Richard K. Thomas.*

(continued)

written and their relationship to the script; and when appropriate, the production history of the script as well as the audience for whom the production is to be performed.

Music research involves analyzing the demographics and average age of the anticipated audience and trying to estimate their musical tastes. Knowing who the audience is, and what their musical tastes might be helps the sound designer select music that will enhance (rather than alienate) the audience's involvement with the play.

Research into sound effects may be a little more arcane than research in music, because recorded sounds don't always sound the way you think they would. The recorded sound of water rushing down a mountain stream, when played back, may sound exactly like someone crumpling up a piece of cellophane, water running from a spigot, or a flushing toilet. The sound designer needs to be aware of this reality and be prepared to deal with it by using his or her imagination.

It is vital that the sound designer understand the psychological purpose and desired impact of each sound effect as well as the nature of that particular sound. If the script calls for a horn honking, the sound designer needs to create a scenario about the sound that considers the tempo, rhythm, phrasing, dynamics, and spatial requirements of the scene. He or

she needs to know a great deal of specific information about the horn. Is it attached to a vehicle? What kind, type, and year of vehicle is it? Is the driver casually honking, or is he (or she) really mad and insistent? Is the vehicle nearby or far away? Is it moving or standing still? Consider expanding your thinking beyond the bounds of realism and using a sound that gives the psychological essence of a honking horn, rather than simply using the sound of a real horn. These and similar questions need to be discussed with the director before the sound designer can begin to produce a genuinely original sound that helps pull the audience into the play.

Every resident theatre company should have a good basic library of sound effects. Sound effects libraries such as Sound Ideas, Valentino, Hollywood Edge, and BBC can be researched for any strange and/or unusual sounds. Another outstanding resource is Sounddogs.com, which includes virtually every sound library in existence and allows you to "try before you buy"; it fully licenses individual sound effects, which can keep costs under control.

Conceptual research in sound design means creating, either mentally or by recording, as many potential solutions to each sound cue as possible. For the preshow music, select from the work of a number of composers. With sound

effects, let your ideas flow, even if some of them seem to be strange, bizarre, and unworkable. Just dream them up. Do not judge them at this point.

Incubation

Let the ideas sit unattended for a while. Do something else.

Selection

Import the sound and music palette into your DAW. Organize the library, and make sure that it includes everything you might use in the production. It should be much larger than what you will eventually use. You don't want to be searching for sound in the heat of composing the sound cue. Choose the specific music and sound effects that you intend to use for each particular cue. It is rare that any of these prerecorded effects can be used without editing. It is totally normal to edit and mix two or three separate effects together to create a new effect that is appropriate for a specific cue.

Implementation

Stop talking and start creating!

Evaluation

After the show opens, review your use of the design process to see how you can improve both your use of the process and your communication with the other members of the design team the next time you get an assignment.

Because playback software plays the cues sequentially, the sound cues need to be numbered in the order they will be played during the performance. Notice that the cue numbers in the sample cue list (Figure 21.33) leave room between the extant cues for additional cues to be added. In the sound playback sequence — the cue list that's used during the show — the cues provide a wealth of information as to the cue's content (Figure 21.34).

Block Diagram — The block diagram (Figure 21.35) of the sound system details every piece of equipment used in the sound design, it's physical location, the make and model number of each piece of equipment, and how each piece

| Preliminary Sound Cue Sheets (Revised -7/24/11) | | | *I Love to Eat* | | | Page 1 |
Cue	Page	Cue Line	Sound	Message	Time	Spkr
10	1	Stage Manager	Overture	See description at start of play.	3:00	Mains
20	3	With Lighting Change	Scene Change 1*	A short sustained sound that just hints at the main theme: *Alone*. Emotionally, it takes us to the 1984 present, but hints at the crisis building between the man talking to the audience and the man upstairs.	0:06	All
30	3	Hello.	Phone 1	1984 phone. Wired. Cell phones were only available in cars: http://features.blogs.fortune.cnn.com/2011/07/03/mobile-phones-hot-new-industry-fortune-1984/. Should be touch tone though, as rotary's pretty much ended by 1984: http://www.phworld.org/pictures/weco/	0:07	Live? Need to see How IRT typically handles this.
40	4	Someone might call.	Phone 2		0:07	Live?
50	5	South of France- *magnifique*	The Markets of Cote d'Azur	Faint sound of Julia Child's voice from the phone is overtaken by the first statement of the 'memory" theme. In this version romantic--not sentimental, but not too big; perhaps a gentle wave washes us into and out of this.	1:00	Mains
60	7	...show on television	Cow Bell/Glass 1	Cow Bells Clanking followed by Glass breaking. Cow bells with a note attached land on the stage.	0:10	Stage
70	7	...refer to was -	TV Theme 1	Includes VO: "Elsie Presents: I LOVE TO EAT. Delivered by -- BORDEN'S. And featuring James Beard..." Also, need to get model asap. Found some Elsie the Cow commercial musit at: http://www.youtube.com/watch?v=RIqQSG3J2I4	0:15	Mains

FIGURE 21.32

A sample sound cue sheet from the Indianapolis Repertory Theatre production of *I Love to Eat*.

connects to every other piece of equipment in the system (including the names/locations of all **patch points**.)

The sound system installer relies on this diagram to properly install the sound system and will make notes on the drawing to document the **as-built** for the show.

patch points: The physical locations in the theatre — stage, auditorium, and so on — where any connections are made between pieces of sound equipment.

as-built: A document that describes any deviations made from the original plans during construction. Sound design as-builts are typically made by notating on the original drawing any deviations made from the original specifications.

Basic Acoustics

Acoustics is the study of the generation, transmission, and reception of sound. In the theatre, acoustics is concerned with the study of those qualities of the stage and auditorium space that affect the audience's hearing and understanding of the sound (language music, and effects) of the play.

Since it's highly unlikely that a performance will include every audience member listening to the production through individual headphones, the acoustics of the performing space must be considered when planning the sound

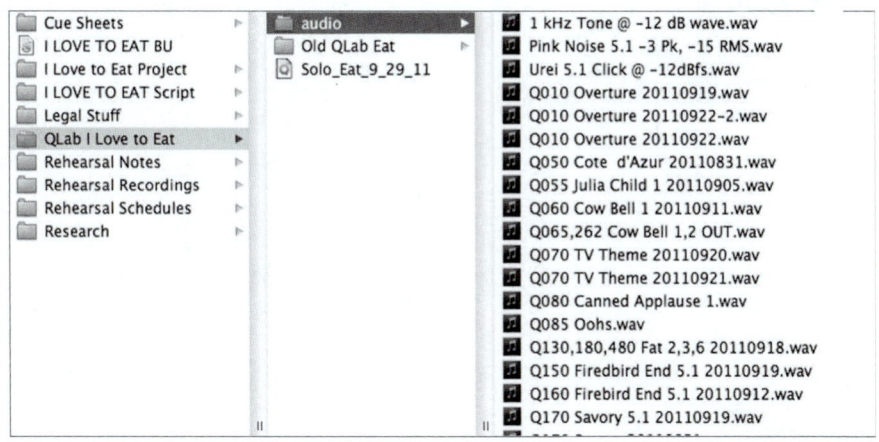

FIGURE 21.33

Notice that the cue numbering (right-hand column) is not sequential. This leaves room for new cues to be inserted when necessary. (A portion of the sound cue list [Show Directory] from the Indianapolis Repertory Theatre production of *I Love to Eat*.)

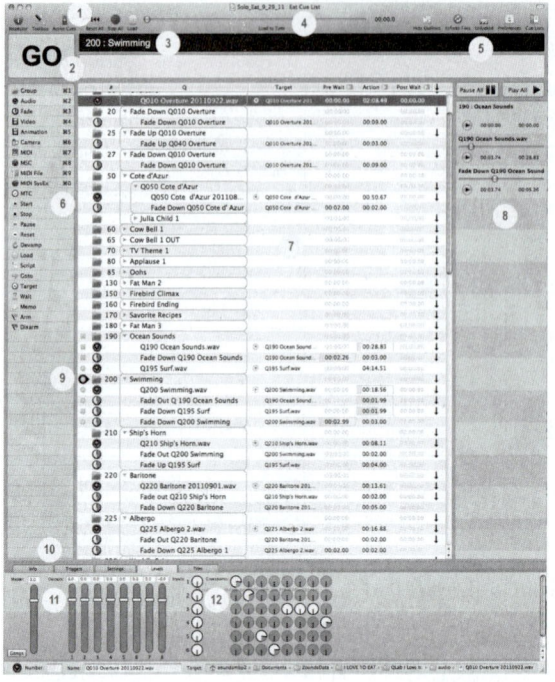

design. A theatre with good acoustics will allow every member of the audience to hear, and understand, the words being spoken by an actor standing anywhere on the stage. Figure 21.36 demonstrates how the average audience member hears several copies of a sound originating on the stage.

The primary sound, coming directly from the speaker to the listener, arrives first — because it travels the shortest distance. Each reflection, represented by R1 to R5, arrives at a slightly different time. This creates a conundrum. The multiple arrival times are beneficial for music because it makes the sound seem fuller, more alive. However, when trying to *understand* — not just hear — what the speaker is saying, the multiplicity of arrival times frequently makes the spoken word more difficult to comprehend.

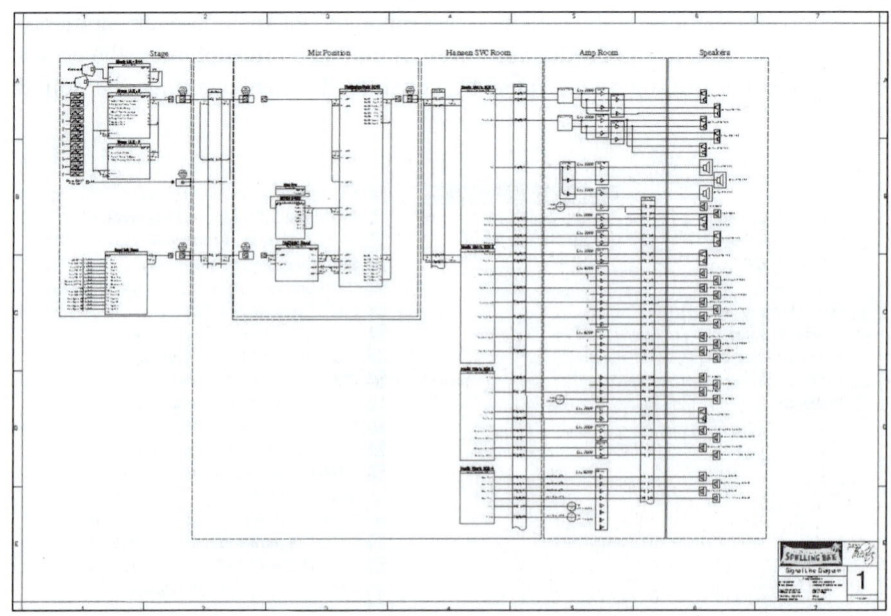

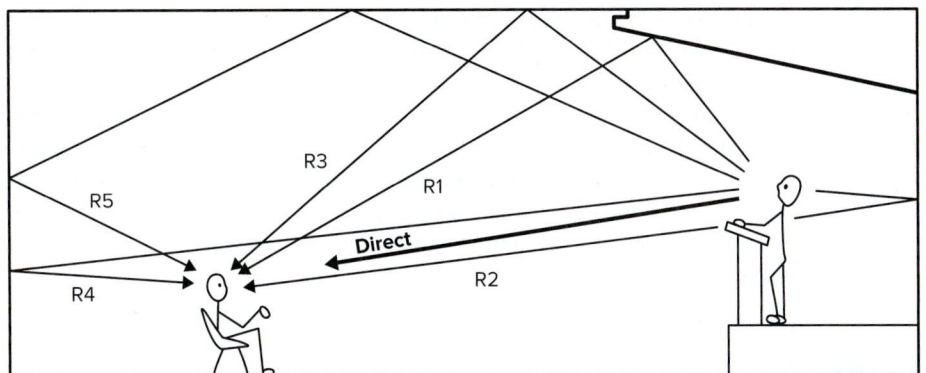

FIGURE 21.36
The average audience member hears several copies of a sound originating from a speaker on the stage. R1-R5 illustrate the differentiations in the reflected sound's arrival time. See text for additional details.

An almost limitless number of factors determine the acoustics of an auditorium. The room's shape vitally affects the reflection of sound. If the walls are parallel, the sound will bounce back and forth between them, reducing the intelligibility of the spoken word. To reduce that reflection many architects slightly curve the auditorium walls so that no wall will be parallel with any other.

The materials used to finish the walls, ceiling, and floor of the auditorium also have a great impact on the reflection of the sound. In general, hard-surface materials (wood, metal, plaster, and the like) reflect sound, and soft- or open-surface materials (cloth, foamed or loosely spun insulation, and the like) absorb sound.

Acoustically balancing a theatre for both speech and music is an almost impossible task. An auditorium that is well balanced for the spoken word needs an approximate **decay time** of less than 1 second for good intelligibility. Music sounds better if the decay time is stretched to 1 to 2 seconds to give the instrument sounds time to blend.

Because it isn't possible to create a theatre equally well balanced for speech and music, some type of compromise needs to be made. It's rare to find a performing space where music is never played. Most theatres serve multiple purposes — theatre, lectures, concerts, and musicals, with the occasional opera thrown in for interest.

Fortunately, some effective solutions to this challenge have been developed. The Constans Theatre at the University of Florida (Figure 21.37) uses adjustable acoustical baffles mounted in various positions on and over the stage as well

decay time: The time it takes a sound to become inaudible.

FIGURE 21.37
The carpeting on the wall and the alternating vertical wood strips and cloth effectively reduce reverberation in the Constans Theatre, University of Florida.

dry: Acoustically absorbent; dead.

speaker routing: The particular speaker through which an audio signal will be played.

show file: All the data associated with an individual sound cue.

as in the auditorium walls and ceiling to allow the theatre to be "tuned" for the appropriate degree of reverberation for the type of group (nonmusical theatre, musical theatre, opera, orchestra) performing on the stage.

Another solution is to adjust room acoustics with an artificial reverberation system such as Meyer Sound's Constellation system. These systems use many microphones strategically located throughout an acoustically **dry** auditorium to pick up the sounds, which are then processed by sophisticated computers. The processed signals are then sent to loudspeakers located throughout the listening area and balanced to create an artificial reverberation.

 ## Installation, Verification, and Calibration

Once the sound system has been designed for a particular production, it becomes the responsibility of the Head Sound Engineer — if there is one — to ensure that the equipment is installed and tested properly, that everything works as intended, and finally, that the system has been calibrated for optimal performance. If the budget hasn't allowed for a sound engineer, then the installation, verification, and calibration of the system becomes the responsibility of the sound designer.

The processes involved in installation, verification, and calibration of sound systems are significantly beyond the scope of this introductory text. If you're interested in learning more about this subject you should consult Bob McCarthy's excellent book, *Sound Systems: Design and Optimization* (3rd Edition, Focal Press, 2016).

 ## Sound Design Playback

The types of equipment used to play back sound are dictated by the budget and the needs of the production. Non-musical plays may require nothing more than a couple front-of-house speakers for pre-show/intermission music and one or more onstage "spot" speakers for sound effects. Broadway-style musicals may use scores of speakers, several mixers, a sophisticated reinforcement system, and dozens of wireless microphones.

Computer Playback

Playback software, such as Stage Research's SFX and Figure 53's QLab or Meyer Sound's Matrix 3, is used to play the sound cues back during the show.

In addition to its audio content, each cue contains information that controls its loudness level, fade rate, **speaker routing,** and so forth. Most playback programs store this information in a **show file.**

Playback Mixer

The audio outputs of the computer will typically be routed through a digital mixer before they're sent on to their various speaker destinations.

The digital playback mixer serves multiple functions. It can rout the signal directly to its appropriate output without additional processing. It can add delays to the output signals so the loudspeakers can be optimally aligned with each other; it can tweak the equalization of the output signals to smooth out the interaction between multiple loudspeakers.

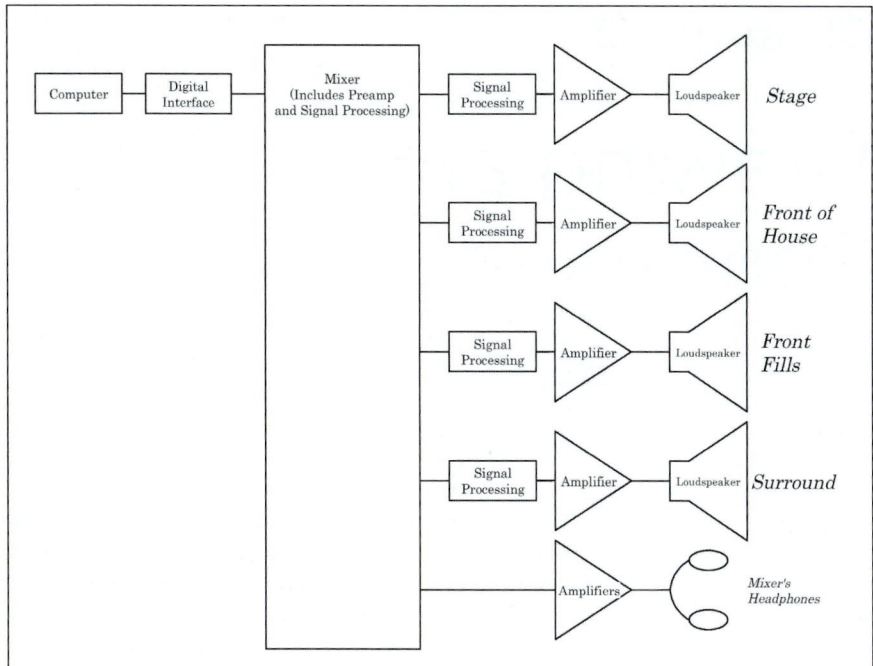

FIGURE 21.38
A playback sound system. Note that only one input channel is shown.

To account for the vagaries in background noise that occur from performance to performance, one of the mixer's faders can be assigned to globally control all the outputs. This allows subtle boosts or attenuations to all sources in the system without changing the balance between them.

A block diagram of a typical playback system is illustrated in Figure 21.38.

The contemporary theatre is truly an exciting place to be for someone interested in sound design, simply because what were formerly regarded as "rules" for the "proper" use of sound and music in the theatre no longer apply. They have been replaced with an exciting atmosphere of experimentation and dynamic growth.

Selected References

Beranek, Leo L. *Music, Acoustics and Architecture*. Robert E. Krieger Publishing, 1979.
Burris-Meyer, Harold, and Edward C. Cole. *Theatres and Auditoriums*. Reinhold, 1949.
Burris-Meyer, Harold, and Lewis Goodfriend. *Acoustics for the Architect*. Reinhold, 1957.
Collison, David. *Stage Sound*. Drama Book Publishers, 1982.
Davis, Don, and Eugene Patronis. *Sound System Engineering*, 3rd ed. Focal Press, 2006.
Davis, Gary, and Ralph Jones. *Sound Reinforcement Handbook*, 2nd ed. published by Hal Leonard Corporation (for Yamaha), 1989.
Eargle, John, and Chris Foreman. *Audio Engineering for Sound Reinforcement*. Hal Leonard Corporation, 2001.
Heil, Bob. *Practical Guide for Concert Sound*. Melco Publishing, 1976.
Huber, David Miles, and Robert E. Runstein. *Modern Recording Techniques*. Focal Press, 2010.
Kaye, Deena, and James LeBrecht. *Sound and Music for the Theatre*. Focal Press, 2009.
Leonard, John A. *Theatre Sound*. Theatre Arts/Routledge, 2001.
McCarthy, Bob. *Sound Systems: Design and Optimization*. Focal Press, 2010.
Mullin, Donald C. *The Development of the Playhouse*. University of California Press, 1970.

Chapter 22

Drawing and Rendering

Drawing and rendering are the primary visual-communication methods used by theatrical designers. Every designer must be able to draw and render with ease and facility. During the production meetings, designers frequently communicate their ideas with quickly drawn pencil sketches — the costume designer's preliminary sketches and the scenic designer's thumbnail sketches. After the concepts have been discussed and developed, the designers create renderings that provide color representations of the appearance, character, and flavor of the designs. As discussed in several earlier chapters, sketches can be produced either by hand or with a computer. The choice is up to the individual designer and the particular circumstances.

It is important that you have an understanding of a variety of the computer drawing/rendering programs as well as CAD. Obviously, it's advantageous — and certainly should be a goal if you want to be employed in any technical/design area — for you to become proficient in the programs commonly used in your chosen technical/design area. But it is absolutely essential that you be able to draw and paint — well and with ease and facility — by hand. This chapter will demonstrate some of the materials and techniques that are common to this skill.

There are literally as many styles of drawing and rendering as there are designers. Every good designer will ultimately develop a distinctive style for creating scenic, costume, or property sketches. Rest assured, however, that no beginning designer ever just sat down and magically began to draw and paint. Personal style develops after a great deal of time, practice, and effort. Before you begin to practice, you need to learn about the basic materials and techniques of sketching and rendering.

 Materials

Designers use a wide variety of materials to create their hand-drawn sketches and renderings. These materials can be roughly divided into two categories: the material being applied — pencils, inks, paint, pastels, or markers — and paper.

Pencils

Almost any pencil can be used for sketching, but different pencils have different characteristics. Hard-lead drafting pencils such as a 3H, 4H, or 5H make crisp, sharp-edged lines, whereas soft-lead drawing pencils such as the 3B or 4B make darker, wider, and softer-edged lines. Ordinary pencils such as the Number 2 tooth-marked Ticonderoga used for taking notes in class can also be used for sketching.

Which type of pencil you choose depends on the subject matter you'll be drawing, the type of paper on which you'll be working, and personal preference. However, it is important to practice with all types of pencils on all types of papers. Experimentation is the only way to learn about the different characteristics of each type of pencil and paper, which works well with which, and which ones you prefer.

There are two general types of colored pencils — hard and soft. As might be expected, the hard pencils produce sharp lines and are good for linear effects, whereas the softer pencils, such as Eagle Prismacolor, produce softer lines. Watercolor pencils can be used to produce a pigmented line which, when overlayed with a water wash, creates a tint of the same hue.

Inks

Some designers use inks for making preliminary and thumbnail sketches and outlining detail on renderings. Frequently, these ink drawings are made with inexpensive drawing and drafting pens such as those manufactured by Pilot, Expresso, and Itoya-Nikko. These pens are available in a variety of nib widths and flexibilities. Traditional artist's pens and inks are also preferred by some designers because of the larger variety of nibs that are available. Bottles of drawing inks, manufactured by Pelikan, Carter's, and Higgins, are available in a relatively narrow range of colors.

Paint

Costumes and scenic sketches or renderings have traditionally been painted with transparent watercolor paints. Although this practice continues, many designers use other materials as well.

Watercolor Watercolor paint is a pigment mixed with water to create a transparent paint. It is the traditional medium for theatrical rendering, because transparent watercolor provides the sketches with a luminescent quality which closely approximates the appearance that costumes and scenery will have under stage lights. If too much pigment is added to the mix, the watercolor becomes opaque, the dried surface of the painting will have an uneven gloss, and the luminescent quality of the rendering will be lost.

Watercolor pigments are available in three types — tube, cake, and liquid — as shown in Figure 22.1. The tube colors are emulsified pigments of approximately the consistency of well-chilled sour cream. The cake colors are manufactured in hard blocks of watercolor pigment. The liquid watercolors are packaged in small bottles of highly saturated hues.

Both tube and cake watercolors provide the same high-quality pigment, so the choice of which to use is basically a matter of personal preference. Tube colors are a little more convenient for painting a large expanse, such as a sky in a scenic rendering. Similarly, the cake colors are a little more convenient if you need only a small amount of paint to provide trim color on a costume sketch. The third type of watercolor shown in Figure 22.1, Dr. Martin's Watercolors, is a liquid of extremely strong saturation and brilliance. Because these paints are already liquid, they mix very easily and always remain transparent.

Designer's Gouache Designer's gouache is an opaque watercolor. It is available in tubed form in a wide range of hues similar to those of transparent watercolor. Designer's gouache closely resembles the **matte** reflective properties

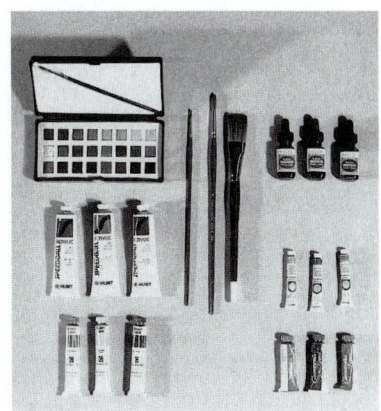

FIGURE 22.1
Watercolor pigment is available in tube, cake, and liquid forms.

matte: Dull, nonreflective.

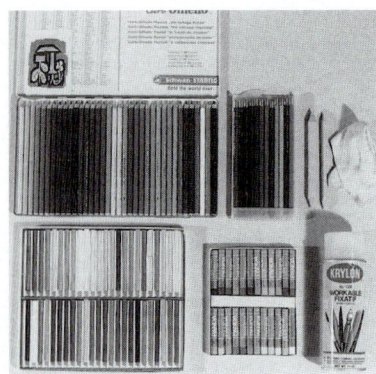

FIGURE 22.2
Pastels, colored pencils, and associated materials.

and colors of scene paint. When thinned sufficiently, the paint becomes transparent. The primary difference between designer's gouache and transparent watercolor is that gouache has a matte finish regardless of whether it is mixed to an opaque or transparent consistency, whereas watercolors seem to have a little more **life**.

Acrylic   Acrylic paint is widely available and very versatile. It can be thinned with water to the consistency of watercolor and can be used for the same purposes. When it is used as a substitute for watercolor or designer's gouache, the only significant difference is that the acrylic leaves a slightly **glossy** surface whereas the watercolor and gouache finishes are matte.

Brushes   It is a truism that you should buy the best brushes that you can possibly afford. With this proviso in mind, most artists would agree that the best watercolor brushes are made from red sable. The next best alternative is the synthetic bristles made to duplicate the characteristics of sable, such as Sabline.

Red sable and high-quality synthetic bristles, such as most manufacturers' student line of brushes, carry watercolor pigment easily, have good **spine**, and cling together when wet. Brushes other than these do not have these qualities, and they will not allow you to do your best work. In all honesty, you're wasting your money and your time if you buy them.

While the number and type of brushes that you purchase are matters of choice, you will need brushes of at least two sizes with which to begin. The size of artist's brushes is indicated by numbers — the higher the number, the bigger the brush. The number is normally printed on the handle of the brush. A No. 3 brush can be effectively used for most detail work, and a No. 7 can be used for laying in most washes. A No. 12 brush is very handy for creating large, smooth washes.

Pastels

There are two primary types of pastel, chalk and oil, as shown in Figure 22.2. Colored pencils are also shown, because even though they are not made of pastel, they are used in basically the same manner. Ultimately, the way in which an artist uses any tool is a matter of personal choice, but each type of pastel has specific working characteristics.

Chalk Pastels   Chalk pastels are formed into square or round sticks that have approximately the same consistency as blackboard chalk. The square sticks are about 3½ inches long, and the round sticks are about 6 inches. The square sticks are generally more useful for theatrical sketching, because you can draw a relatively sharp line with the edges of the stick as well as a smooth wash with the flat surfaces.

Chalk pastels are available in three hardnesses: soft, medium, and hard. The brilliance of the color is linked to its hardness — the harder the stick, the less brilliant its color. Soft- and medium-consistency chalk pastels are extremely useful for laying down a smooth background color or a graded wash (which smoothly varies in hue from top to bottom or side to side). Medium and hard pastels are useful for detail work.

Oil or Wax Pastels   Oil or wax pastels have a slightly greasy feeling, because they are manufactured with a soft wax binder. The wax makes them very easy to blend. If you are planning to use oil pastels in conjunction with watercolors, you will need to remember to "paint first and pastel second," because the wax prevents paint from adhering to the paper.

life: Brilliance, visual depth, and sparkle.

glossy: Highly reflective, mirrorlike.

spine: The relative stiffness of bristles; good watercolor bristles will flex easily but will also have enough spine to remain erect when fully saturated with paint.

PRODUCTION INSIGHTS

Blending with Pastels

Both chalk and oil pastels can be blended using either paper or felt blending stumps. The figures show some blending techniques.

In addition to the commercial paper and felt blending stumps, newsprint, toilet paper, facial tissues, or your fingers can also be used.

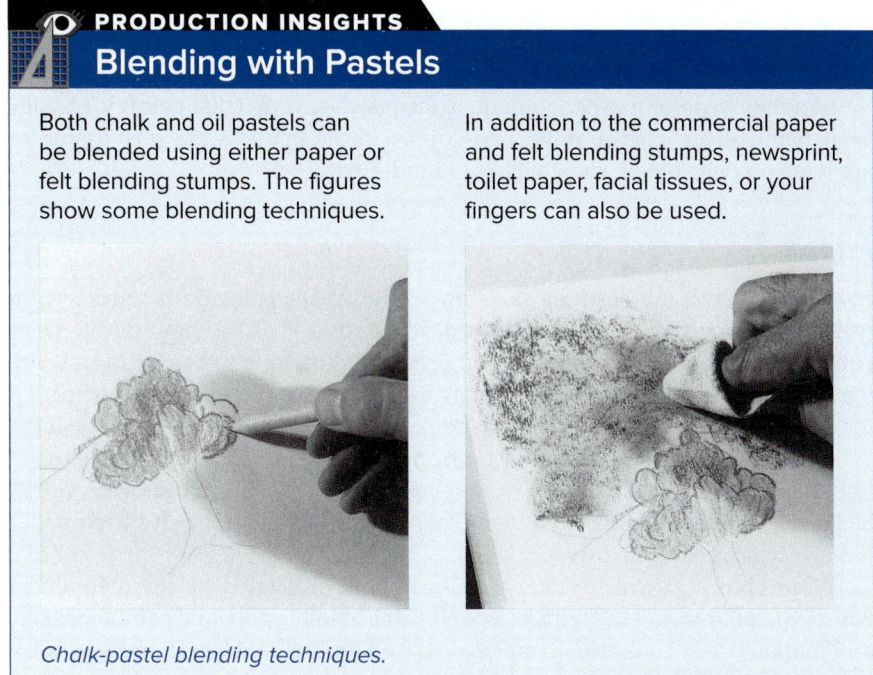

Chalk-pastel blending techniques.

FIGURE 22.3
Markers.

Markers

A number of different markers and marking pens are available. The principal differences are in the shape and material of the tip and the nature and characteristics of the paint or ink contained in the marker (Figure 22.3).

The majority of these markers, such as the Magic Marker brand, contain a permanent semitransparent ink that dries very quickly and is generally available in a limited range of colors. Several lines of artist's markers contain water-color ink that is more transparent than this permanent ink. Watercolor markers are also available in a much wider range of colors. Both types of marker can be used very effectively for detail work on renderings.

Another type of marker contains a lacquer-based metallic paint. Generally available in silver, gold, bronze, and copper, these markers are very useful for applying metallic detail or highlights to renderings.

Paper

Most final scenic and costume sketches are drawn or painted on some type of watercolor paper or **illustration board.** Illustration board is simply watercolor paper that has been mounted on a stiff pressboard backing to keep it from bending or wrinkling. Other types of paper such as charcoal or velvet paper can be used for work with pastels, pencils, and markers, but they don't work well with paint.

There are three primary surface finishes for watercolor papers and illustration board. A **hot-press finish** is very slick and smooth. The **cold-press finish** has a slight texture similar to a heavy bond typing paper. **Rough-finish** paper has a very noticeable texture.

Your choice of which paper to use should be dictated by the medium in which you plan to work. The hot-press finish is good for opaque paints, pencils, and markers. The cold-press papers work well with all media. The rough-finish papers are particularly well suited for pastels and watercolor.

Matte boards (hot-press illustration board with colored surfaces) are also interesting surfaces for designer's renderings, particularly if you are planning on working with any of the opaque media such as designer's gouache, pastels, or pencil.

Newsprint is often used by both scenic and costume designers for their thumbnail and preliminary sketches. It is inexpensive, has a slightly roughened **tooth,** and is a receptive surface for softer pencils, soft-nibbed markers, and soft pastels.

To determine which paper is suitable for a particular project, you will need to develop an understanding of the characteristics of the various papers and their surfaces. This knowledge can be gained only by playing and experimenting with the various media on the different papers and illustration boards.

Computer Drawing

There are a variety of drawing programs, and they contain a number of features. Generally, they can be divided into two generic types: painting programs and drawing programs.

Painting Tools Painting programs such as Adobe Photoshop (Figure 22.4A) and Corel Painter (Figure 22.4B) are generally used for nontechnical drawings such as renderings and sketches. Technically, these programs create bitmap objects. A bitmap object is viewed by the computer as a collection of pixels each pixel corresponding directly to one or more "bits" of computer memory including its color and location within the picture.[1] The structure of a bitmap image facilitates the creation of blended or soft-edged images commonly associated with sketching and painting.

Drawing Tools Objects created with drawing programs such as Strata Studio Pro (Figure 22.5) and/or 3D Studio are object-oriented or vector images. As first discussed in Chapter 7, "Mechanical Drawing," a vector-based program

illustration board: Watercolor paper mounted on a pressboard backing.

hot-press finish: A slick, smooth texture achieved by pressing paper between hot rollers; this treatment leaves a thin layer of oil, which makes the paper unsuitable for use with transparent watercolor; works well with designer's gouache, acrylic, pencils, and markers.

cold-press finish: A slight surface texture achieved by pressing paper between cold rollers; no oil residue results, so the paper can be used with transparent watercolor, designer's gouache, acrylic, markers, or pencils.

rough finish: A pebble-grained texture achieved by cold-pressing paper with a textured roller or by other techniques; suitable for painted and pastel renderings having little intricate detail.

tooth: A term used to describe the surface texture of a paper.

---

[1] Peter Jerram and Michael Gosney, *Multimedia Power Tools,* 2nd ed. (New York: Random House/Verbum, 1995), p. 89.

(A)

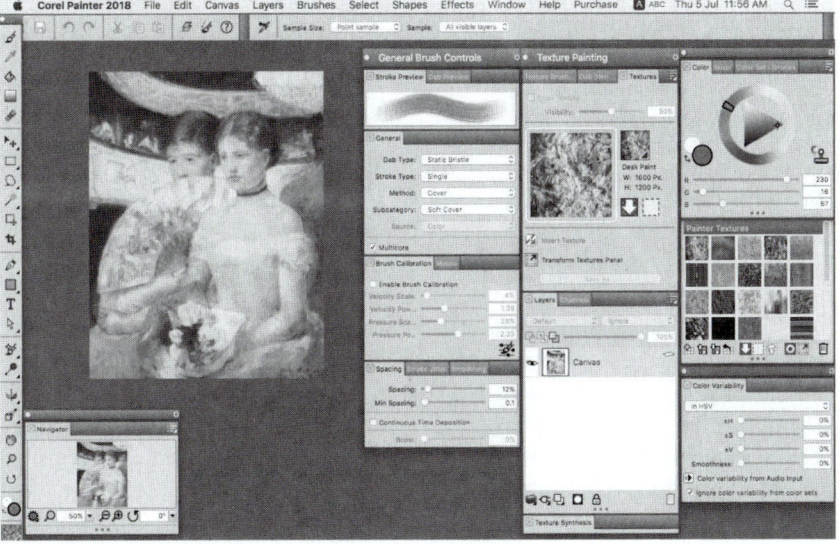

(B)

FIGURE 22.4
(A) On-screen view of Adobe Photoshop, an image editing program. Software: Photoshop by Adobe Systems Incorporated. Photo ©Shutterstock/Youproduction. (B) On-screen view of Painter, an image editing program. Software: Painter™ by Corel Corporation. Photo courtesy of National Gallery of Art, Washington, DC.

views each object in a picture as a mathematical calculation. If you create a background, then draw other objects in the foreground, you can point and click on one of the foreground objects and move it around in the drawing without affecting the background. When an object is moved, the computer recalculates its position.[2] This quality enables the operator not only to change the position of the object within the picture but also to rotate the object about its various axes to see what it looks like from all sides. Vector programs can be used to create sketches and renderings, but their forte is in the creation of drawings which contain multiple objects that may need to be manipulated independently and that require relatively hard-edged lines.

[2] Ibid.

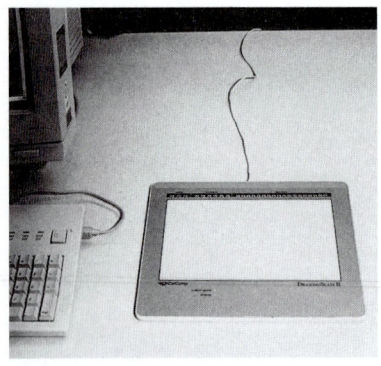

FIGURE 22.6
A digitizing tablet, which can be used to "draw" images on the monitor screen.

digitizing tablet: An electromechanical device that converts the pressure of a stylus on a flat plate (tablet) into binary information that can be understood by the computer.

scan: To use a digitizing scanner to convert existing artwork, photos, or drawings into binary information.

Most of these drawing and painting programs contain both two- and three-dimensional functions in the same program. The actual drawing can be done with a mouse or with a **digitizing tablet** (Figure 22.6). The first digitizing tablets allowed you to draw lines on the pad with a stylus. The line you traced on the tablet was transferred to the monitor screen. You could erase, move, and redraw the lines. The drawings could be stored and/or printed. Newer models of digitizing tablets, now more commonly known as graphics tablets or digitizer tablets, are pressure-sensitive. The pressure sensitivity permits a more natural drawing style closely akin to drawing with a pencil: The harder you press the stylus, the wider and darker the line; the lighter the pressure, the narrower and lighter the line. Both types of digitizing tablets are still available, and both are quite useful.

Most of the current drawing software include color palettes with literally millions of hues. These programs typically have specific surface textures (e.g., wood, cloth, skin, plastic, fur, grass, dull or shiny metal, and so forth) that can be applied to objects you are drawing or modeling. The majority of these programs allow you to design the lighting for your drawings. You can select the location and intensity of the light(s) that are illuminating the object you're drawing. This feature automatically results in the projection of shadows which aid the three-dimensional quality of the drawings.

Drawing programs can be used in several ways. Original sketches can be created with a program such as Poser, or hand-drawn sketches or research illustrations can be **scanned** into the computer. Various color combinations and textures can be quickly "tried out" on the sketches. Three-dimensional drawings allow you to see all sides of costumes and sets from any seat in the house. Computer-drawn sketches generally have not replaced hand-rendered drawings and designs at this time but more designers are using computer sketches than ever before. As the technology advances, it has become more and more difficult to tell the difference between hand- and computer-drawn designs. The advantages that computer drawings offer the designer are many and ever-increasing. Which method is better? It really doesn't matter. The reality is that whichever method provides the best visualization of the designer's intention will be the appropriate method to use. But the caveat "know how to do both" still applies.

PRODUCTION INSIGHTS

The Scanner

A scanner allows you to enter an existing drawing/photo/picture into a computer. You put the picture in the scanner, which digitizes the information and transfers it to the computer and onto the screen. In addition to working with preexisting artwork, you can create an original sketch by hand and scan it; then you can play with its color, outline, and texture to quickly see what effect these changes have on the overall design.

While you can purchase stand-alone scanners, many printers have four-in-one capability — printing, scanning, faxing, and copying. At the time of this writing the stand-alone units generally have better resolution and work a little faster than the four-in-one units.

Drawing and Rendering Techniques

The following suggestions will familiarize you with some of the basic techniques that are used with the various media. Try the suggested application techniques. Doodle with the pencils, paint, pastels, and markers. Have fun with them. After you've worked with each medium separately, try combining them. Whatever else, be sure that you have fun, because you will improve only with practice, and you will practice only if you're having fun.

Sketching

Scenic, costume, and property designers need to be able to make quick, clear sketches. Thumbnail drawings and preliminary sketches are presented and modified during the production meetings, and almost all renderings begin with pencil sketches.

Initially, almost everyone feels intimidated by the idea of sketching. But some simple hints may help you improve your ability to sketch.

In Chapter 5, "Style, Composition, and Design," we learned that lines are evocative, that they contain meaning. But what is that meaning, and how is it expressed? In theatrical sketching, the lines that define the shape, texture, and detail of costumes, sets, and props are actually representations of the materials that will be used to build the designs. This is the first principle of theatrical sketching: Lines must reflect the qualities of the materials they represent. For example, the quality and character of the line(s) used to create a costume sketch should reflect the psychological qualities of the character as well as the weight, texture, and characteristics of the fabric and materials from which the costume will be

(A)

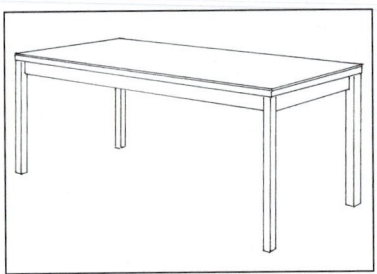

(B)

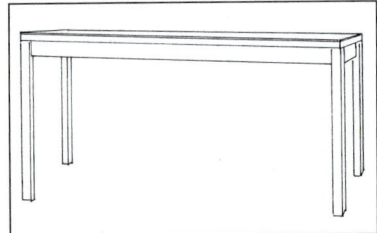

(C)

FIGURE 22.7
Draw what you see, not what you think you see (review the text for details).

made. Similarly, the lines used to describe a set should be evocative of the wood, metal, fabric, and so forth from which it is constructed. This first principle leads to a second: You must be intimately familiar with the physical characteristics of the materials you're drawing. To accurately sketch a chiffon blouse or heavy woolen cape, you must know the hand of those fabrics — what they feel like, their weight, their draping characteristics, and so on. Sets are made from various materials each of which has its own physical characteristics. Some are rigid, others flexible; some are rough, others smooth and polished. The set designer must know and under-stand those characteristics before he or she can create an accurate representation of them.

A related, third principle states that you must know what you're drawing before you can draw it. To draw a chiffon blouse, you must be able to see what it looks like — the shape and fullness of body, sleeve, collar, and cuff; whether it has button closure down the front or back or no buttons at all. To create a real-istic Victorian drawing room, you have to know what one looked like. This type of understanding comes from doing the research described in the design process (Chapter 2, "The Design Process").

When you follow these three principles, something magical happens as you begin to draw. Your brain, programmed with all the background information it needs, guides your hand and a finished representation of the concept, which actually looks like the object you envisioned, just seems to appear on the paper. But this magic doesn't happen instantly. It takes practice — lots of practice. But it is a skill that all designers must master, and it is only mastered through repeti-tive practice.

A sketch does not need to, nor is it supposed to, create a photographic like-ness of a person or object. Sketching creates a simplified view that shows the basic appearance and, of equal importance, the spirit or character of the object.

A major stumbling block that many people encounter when learning to sketch is that they try to draw what they think they see rather than what they actually see. Figure 22.7A shows a photograph of a table. Because people know that the top of a table is its most useful surface, they tend to draw the top of the table as the most dominant visual element, as shown in Figure 22.7B. They're not drawing what they see. If you really look at the photo of the table, you'll see that the top is only a narrow sliver compared with the overall size of the table. Figure 22.7C is a sketch that was made after careful observation of the photo of the table. Notice that even though the sketch doesn't show every detail, it does provide an accurate representation of the table, and it also gives you a feeling about its nature or character.

All sketches are based on three principal elements: thematic lines, line angles and intersections, and proportions. Most objects are composed of more than one thematic or predominant line, like the rocking chair shown in Figure 22.8A. The intersection of these thematic lines allows you to use a fairly easy method to accurately lay out the proportions of an object. While you're noting the angle of intersection of the thematic lines (the chair back, legs, seat, rockers, and the floor), also note the relative position where those line intersections take place. On the rocking chair, notice that the seat intersects the back just a little more than one-third of the way up the back. Also notice that the seat itself is just a little bit longer than the distance from the seat to the rockers. This "ratio technique" generally reduces a beginning artist's anxiety (which allows you to be more creative), because it depersonalizes the sketching process. You're no longer "drawing a chair," you're simply observing lines of intersection and re-creating them. An accurate sketch of the rocking chair, Figure 22.8B, can be made simply by using these observations as a guide. The rest of the detailing of the sketch, Figure 22.8C, is based on the same type of observational techniques. The locations of the various solid and spindle elements of the chair are determined by observing their relative positions on the model and then, using the ratio technique, drawing them on the sketch.

Figure Drawing

It is imperative that designers be able to sketch the human figure easily. For costume designers, this requirement is obvious. If clothes are to fit the body in a natural and realistic manner, the costume designer must draw the figure so that it looks natural and realistic, then the clothes follow easily. For scenic designers,

FIGURE 22.8
Sketching techniques (see text for details).

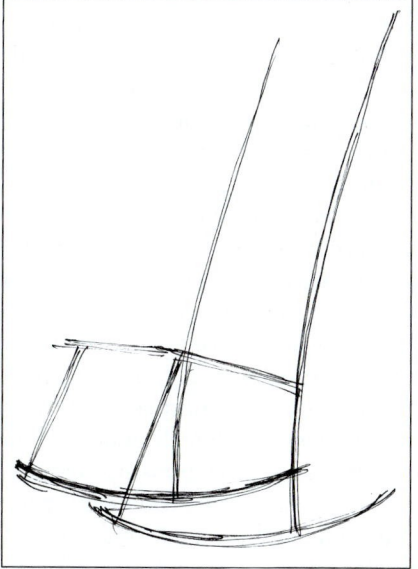

(A)   (B)   (C)

the figure-drawing requirement is less obvious, but many designers like to place a human figure or two in their sketches, models, or drafting plates to provide a readily understandable scale reference.

Some designers believe it is important that a figure have a readily identifiable face. Others do not. However, almost all costume designers agree that a visually dynamic sketch — one in which the figure, and consequently the costume, appears to be in motion — is an important aid in representing the character of the costume.

The quick figure sketch in Figure 22.9 is used to capture the flavor and personality of the character. Accomplished with just a few strokes, the quick sketch is the visual distillation of the designer's thoughts, ideas, and research about the character, and it provides a visual description of that character's personality. In costume design, the quick sketch can be considered analogous to the lighting designer's lighting key in that it provides a touchstone to which the designer refers as the figure and subsequent costume design are being developed.

Every costume design needs to begin with a figure drawing. If the body doesn't look right — isn't in proper proportion, doesn't reflect the personality characteristics of the role — then the design of the clothes placed on that body will be similarly flawed. Proportion is arguably the single most important element in figure drawing. If the proportions aren't correct, the figure won't seem natural. Reasonably normal proportions are achieved if the male is about 8½ heads high and the female about 8 heads high, as shown in Figure 22.10. Study the distances and relationships between the various body parts. The center of the chest is about one head height below the chin, the shoulders are about two heads wide, and so on. A sense of balance and stability is achieved when the figure's head is directly above its center of support, as shown in Figure 22.11. This sense of balance is achieved because the body's mass is evenly divided on

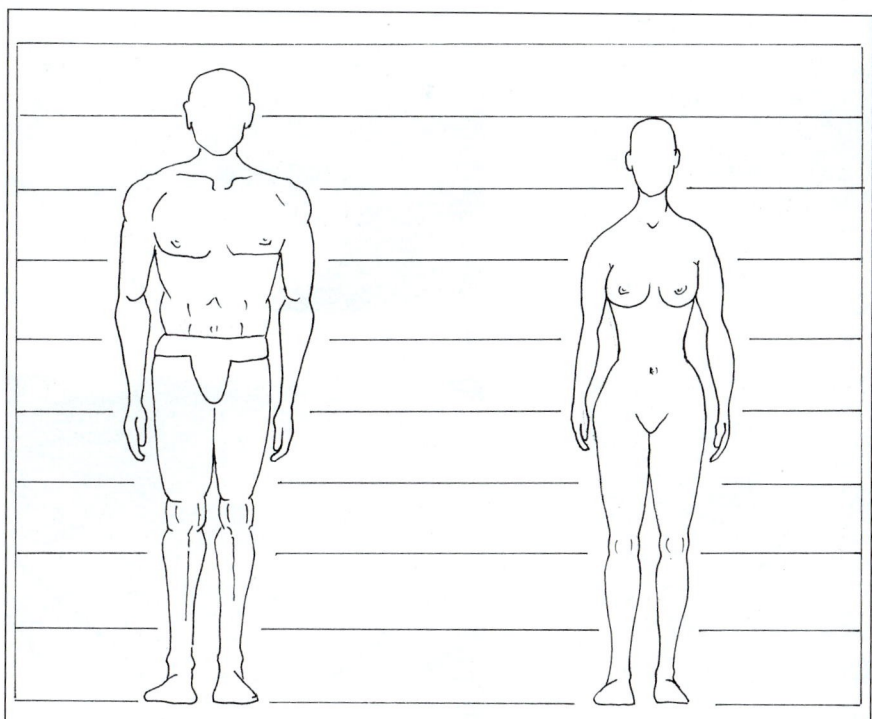

FIGURE 22.10
Proportions of male and female figures.

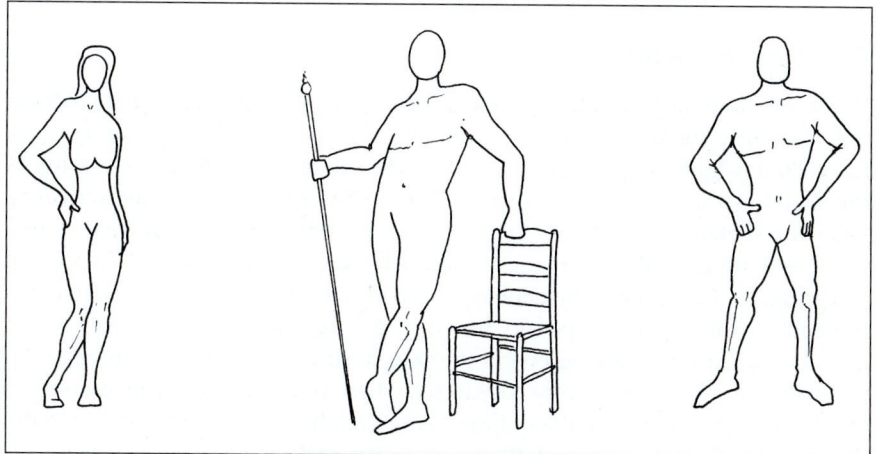

FIGURE 22.11
Costume design figures should appear to be dynamically balanced (see text for details).

either side of the center of balance. Notice also that the body pivots around its natural hinge points — spine, shoulders, elbows, wrists, hips, knees, ankles, and so forth — to create this balance.

To provide the best possible view of the costume, designers draw most costume figures standing with one or both arms extended away from the body in a manner that will provide a view of sleeve detail. Naturally, the particular pose chosen should reflect the personality and nature of the character being portrayed. Deviations from this convention are appropriate when they will provide a better view or understanding of how the costume will look and work in the production.

Proficiency in figure drawing is not achieved easily. It requires study and practice. Designers should become familiar with the skeletal structure of the body and how the various muscle groups work to animate it. And they must practice. Take life-drawing courses, carry a sketch pad, and draw during any idle time.

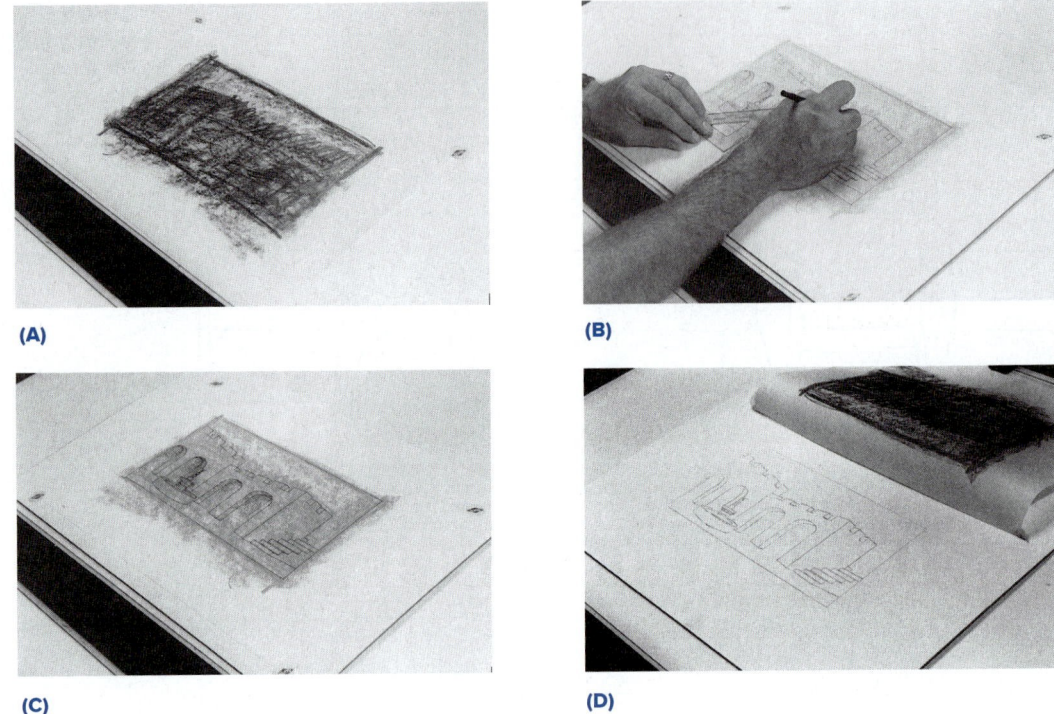

(A)   (B)

(C)   (D)

FIGURE 22.12
Graphite-transfer technique. Cover the reverse side of the sketch with soft graphite and set it (see text for details). (A) Turn the drawing over and trace the sketch (B and C) to transfer the linework to the watercolor paper or board (D).

Graphite Transfers

Watercolor and pastel renderings and sketches usually begin with a pencil drawing. It is fairly standard practice to draw the design on tracing vellum, because the vellum is fairly rugged and will be able to sustain a fair amount of erasing as the sketch is modified. Figure 22.12 explains the process of graphite transfers. After the sketch is completed, turn the vellum over and cover the back side of the sheet with **graphite.** (Soft stick graphite is used for this purpose.) To prevent smearing, set the graphite by daubing thinned rubber cement over it. Use a cotton ball as your dauber. Tape the drawing, face up, to the illustration or watercolor board, and trace the outline of the sketch. (If you use a fine-point ballpoint pen with red ink, it will be very easy to see where you've been as you are tracing the drawing.) As you trace the outline of the sketch, you will be transferring the design to the illustration board. It's much easier, and considerably less messy, to use Saral graphite transfer paper instead.

You may be tempted to use old-fashioned carbon paper that was used for making typed copies instead of using Saral graphite transfer paper or going through the rather laborious task of "graphiting" the reverse side of the tracing vellum. If you are planning on using a transparent medium such as watercolor, try to resist this temptation, because the carbon paper graphite is very dark and will bleed through any transparent paint that you may apply to the paper. If you are planning on working with opaque media, however, the colored transfer papers typically used by costumers to transfer pattern outlines will work very nicely. Colored transfer paper is usually available at most fabric stores.

A light table provides another good way to transfer the original to watercolor paper. The original is taped to the watercolor paper then placed on the light table. Light shines from the table through the "sandwich" allowing you to trace the original sketch onto the watercolor paper.

graphite: A soft carbon similar to the lead in a pencil; sticks can be purchased in most art supply stores.

Scanning

One of the most nerve-wracking experiences in the rendering process is when you've completed your pencil sketch, transferred it to the watercolor paper, and you're ready, for the first time in your life, to add color to the sketch. For many students their first reaction is, "Gulp . . ." A great deal of this stress can be eliminated if, rather than painting the original, you scan the pencil art and print multiple copies on an appropriate paper stock. That way if you botch your first attempt you have backups. Actually, a number of seasoned designers use this technique. They find it useful for trying out different color combinations or application techniques. Experimentation is almost always a good thing. Try mixing pastels (use them for the cyc or background) with watercolor (for details), or add detail to a watercolor sketch with watercolor pencils or artist's markers. After you practice a bit, and experiment with some of the techniques outlined in this chapter, you'll discover that the thought of coloring your sketch isn't nearly as daunting as it once was.

Watercolor

A **wash** can be laid down wet or dry. A wet wash is made by wetting the area to be painted with water before applying the paint, as shown in Figure 22.13. Using your brush, paint the outlined area with water, let it dry until the area has a uniformly dull finish, and then apply the paint. A wet wash conceals brush strokes a little better than a dry wash.

Because watercolor is a transparent medium, you'll need to remember that the whites and light colors are achieved by letting the paper show through the layer of paint. Because of this characteristic, it is normal procedure to build up a watercolor rendering from light to dark. This simply means that you paint the light areas first, then move to those of middle tone, and finish by painting the darkest details or objects. Applying each hue individually is also a normal technique in watercolor painting. After each coat has dried, additional layers can be built up over the original coat to deepen or change its hue or add texture or detail *if* the previous work has been sealed with a **workable fixative.** Fine detail work can either be applied over the watercolor washes after they have dried, and fixed, or the area where the detail is to be applied can be left unpainted when you are putting in the wash. Detail work can also be applied directly on top of a dried transparent wash with opaque media such as designer's gouache, acrylic, pastels, or markers.

If you have some intricate detail that will be silhouetted against a large wash area, you can "paint" the detail area with rubber cement or masking fluid before laying in the wash. Masking fluid is preferred because there's less chance of damaging the paper. After the wash has dried, peel off the dried masking fluid to expose the unpainted paper, and paint in the detail work.

Pastels

The design can be transferred to pastel paper or illustration board using the graphite-transfer technique.

Oil or wax pastels, which are very easy to blend, give a smooth, opaque finish that somewhat resembles a drawing done with crayons. Chalk pastels give a chalkier, luminescent finish. Most theatrical designers prefer working with chalk pastels, because they can be used with watercolor whereas oil pastels cannot. (The oil in the wax pastel causes the watercolor to bead up and dry in little blobs rather than a smooth wash.)

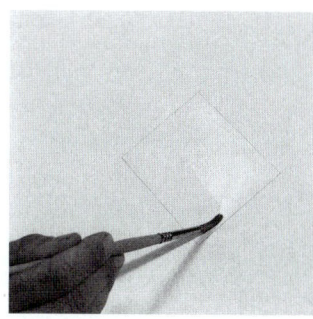

(A)

(B)

(C)

FIGURE 22.13
Applying a wet wash with watercolor. First wet the area with water (A). When the water has partially dried (the paper will have a uniform dull sheen), smoothly spread the watercolor across the area (B) to create a smooth wash of color (C).

wash: The covering of a relatively large area with a smooth layering of paint; a smooth wash consists of only one color; a blended wash is created by smoothly segueing from one color to another.

workable fixative: A spray that seals colors in place. "Workable" indicates that paint can effectively be applied on top of the fixative.

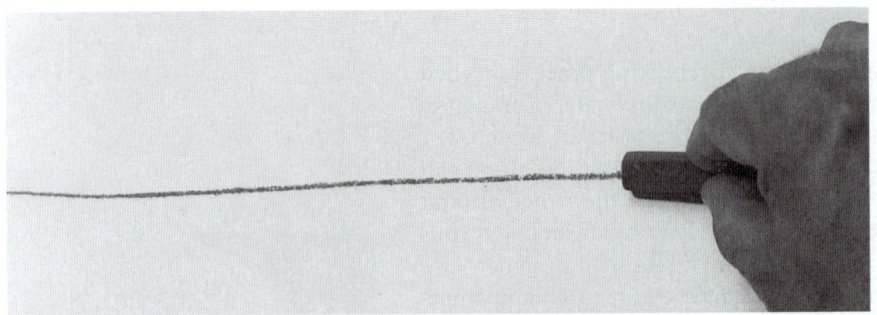

FIGURE 22.14
Pastel-application techniques. (A) A straight line. (B) A smooth wash. Pastels can be used to lay down background washes (C). Be sure to use drafting tape to mask areas to be left "unwashed." Spray the drawing with workable fixative (D) to lock the pastel to the paper.

(A)

(B)

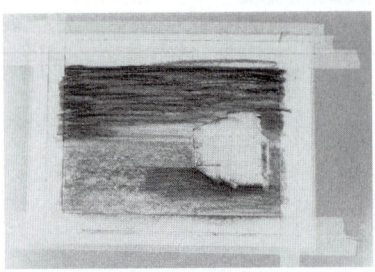

(C)

(D)

How you actually apply the pastel to the paper has a great deal to do with the finished appearance of the design. Chalk pastels will leave a definite line when applied using an edge, as shown in Figure 22.14. A smooth coverage over a large area can be accomplished by using a softer blend (soft or medium hardness) and the flat side of the pastel stick.

Once the pastel has been applied, it can be blended using felt or paper blending sticks, tissue, or your fingers. Stick pastel can also be erased (although not completely) with a kneadable or soft pink eraser.

If you don't want to get the pastel on a particular area of the drawing, mask off that space with drafting tape. Large areas can be effectively masked using paper held in place with drafting tape. Be sure to use drafting tape. Do not masking tape. Masking tape leaves a slightly gummy residue on the paper when it is removed. Additionally, the adhesive on masking tape is sufficiently strong that it can pull the finish surface layer right off the paper!

Chalk pastels are basically colored chalk. The image they leave on the paper is made of chalk dust and is very easy to smear. Although this characteristic is handy for blending two or more colors, a spray fixative is needed to prevent the picture from being smeared after it is finished.

A workable fixative enables you to create several layers on a pastel rendering. If you first draw and blend the background and then spray it with fixative, you can draw the foreground detail without smearing the background work. Each successive layer should be sprayed, and when the rendering is complete, it should be sprayed again. Be sure to use workable fixative; its finish won't affect the application of additional layers of pastel.

Pencils and Markers

Colored pencils and pens as well as watercolor or oil markers can be used to good effect for both scenic and costume renderings.

The watercolor drawing pencils, which are hardened watercolor pigments, can be used to sketch in or add detail. The edge of the line can be softened by painting it with water, as shown in Figure 22.15.

Artist's markers are available in a full range of hues and saturations. The ink has the same transparent properties as watercolor paint, whereas the oil markers are generally translucent or opaque. Either type of marker can be used in a variety of ways to achieve any number of interesting effects.

Combined Media

To be able to select the appropriate visual expression for a specific design concept, a designer should feel free to use and combine a wide variety of rendering materials, styles, and techniques. The rendering for a soft, ethereal, dye-painted

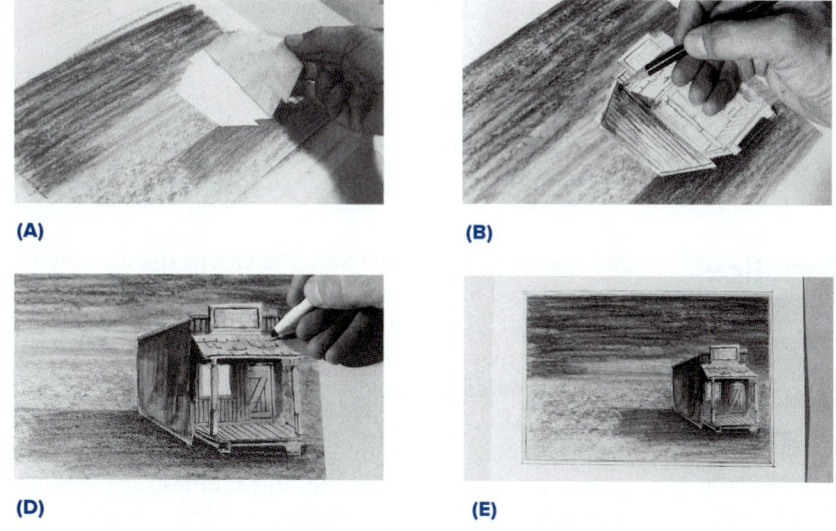

(A)   **(B)**   **(C)**

(D)   **(E)**

FIGURE 22.15
Combining media can produce interesting results. The building masked in the pastel drawing shown in Figure 22.14 is unmasked (A), and the detail is sketched in and colored with watercolor pencils (B), which are blended with a brush and water (C). After the water has dried, additional detail is sketched in with pens (D) and markers to create a drawing with an interesting appearance of depth (E).

scrim is probably best achieved with chalk pastels, watercolors, or a combination of the two. The sketch for a costume with a sequined bodice and a long, flowing diaphanous skirt could be effectively realized with watercolor or designer's gouache and fine-line markers or pen and ink. A nonrepresentational setting of abstract forms in strongly contrasting colors might best be expressed by cutting the forms from colored construction paper and pasting them to a representation of the stage space. Ultimately, the selection of which medium, or combination of media, to use for a specific rendering is the designer's choice, and those choices will be more varied if the designer is familiar with a number of media and rendering techniques.

As with any craft, your personal ability to use this information about rendering will improve only with practice. Take courses in drawing, life drawing, pastel sketching, and watercolor painting in your school's art department to help you learn the many techniques and media that can be used to visually communicate your design ideas. As you become more familiar with the materials and techniques of sketching and rendering, you will discover that your ability to manipulate them is improving as well.

Appendix A

USITT RP-2, Recommended Practice for Theatrical Lighting Design Graphics — (2006)

Preamble

The original Graphics Standards Board noted that a standard is an example for comparison and an authority, which serves as a model. It should be noted that this model cannot hope to cover all possible situations encountered during the drafting of a light plot or section and thus should be viewed as a guide that theatrical lighting practitioners use to create their drawings. This document, therefore, represents a "recommended practice." The terms *instrument* and *luminaire* are used interchangeably throughout the document to designate lighting luminaries while other equivalent designations may also include *fixture, unit* and *lantern*. This document also does not seek to represent a specific manufacturer of lighting equipment but suggests common instruments in general use. The result is a group of generic instrument types that can be adapted to specific uses as necessary rather than an attempt to present a symbol for each luminaire available.

The purpose of this document is to establish a standardized language among lighting designers and anyone else who needs to understand or execute such a design. In practical terms, this document is intended to provide guidelines so that anyone, ranging from technicians who hang the luminaires to other members of the production team, can clearly understand the intent of the lighting designer.

1.0 INTRODUCTION

Legibility and consistency should determine the graphic choices made in the drafting of both CAD and hand-drafted drawings. USITT, or modified ANSI three-line thickness standard drafting practices, may be employed as set forth in the USITT Scenic Design and Technical Production Graphic Standard of 1992 (reissued April 15, 1999). Complex drawings may require the use of three- or four-line thicknesses. Luminaire outlines should take visual precedence over other information on the lighting design drawings.

The graphical representation of a lighting design normally consists of two categories of documents: the Light Plot and the Lighting Section. Preferably, the documents are produced in $1/2'' = 1'-0''$ scale. Other scales, such as $1/4'' = 1'-0''$, $3/8'' = 1'-0''$, 1:25 or 1:50 (if working in SI or metric) may be used after considering the size of the architectural space, the overall size of the document and reproductions, the number of individual luminaries, and the desired legibility of their text and numeric attributes. A complete lighting design requires additional paperwork such as channel hookups and shop orders not addressed in this document. Generally, the light plot should include all information necessary to assure clear understanding of the designer's intentions.

1.1 Special Considerations for CAD drawings

Computer assisted drawings should follow the same recommended practice as those drawn by hand. However, several additional considerations should be made. Layer, class designation, line weight, and color assignment must be coordinated with other members of the production team who are using the same document to create other drawings. This avoids confusion between the draftspersons or the end users. When a lighting graphic symbol is created with "labels," attention must be paid to the relative orientation of both the symbol and its associated text. When a symbol is inserted into a drawing, the associated text should be properly oriented with the rest of the text in the drawing. The luminaire symbols that are included in some computer applications may be specific to various manufacturers' equipment rather than the generic symbols provided in this document. Nevertheless, the size and designation of the luminaires used should follow these generic symbols as closely as possible.

2.0 THE LIGHT PLOT

The light plot is a composite plan drawing that provides the most descriptive possible view of the luminaries so that the production staff can most efficiently execute the design intent. It may consist of more than a single plate; however, all plates should be the same size to facilitate reproduction. Distances between front of house hanging positions and the playing area can be compressed in a light plot.

2.1 Information contained in the light plot

Normally, the light plot should include all information necessary to assure clear understanding of the designer's intentions. The location and identification data of every luminaire, accessory, and specialty unit should be represented on the light plot, along with the following information:

- The centerline
- A lineset schedule when appropriate
- A ruler or some other indicator of distance left and right of centerline in scale
- A ruler indicating on-stage distances up and down stage (or the 90° axis to centerline) in scale
- A drawn representation of the edge of the stage where applicable
- A drawn representation of the edge of the playing area where applicable
- Basic scenic elements
- All scenic masking
- All architectural and scenic obstructions
- The proscenium arch, plaster line, smoke pockets, or other architectural details necessary to orient the lighting design in flexible spaces
- Trim measurements for movable mounting positions should read from the stage level surface (or other common point of reference) to the pipe (or mounting position)
- Trim heights to boom positions measure from bottom of the boom base to the side arm or clamp
- Identification (label) of hanging/mounting positions
- The legend or instrument key designating symbol type and notation in the light plot
- The title block (see Section 4)
- Sightliness

Additional information may include:

- Lighting areas
- Template key
- Color key
- Liability disclaimer
- Union stamp

2.2 Luminaire symbol information

The luminaire symbols used on the light plot should represent the approximate size and shape of the luminaires in scale (except where computer applications supply more specific symbols). The symbol should be placed so that its location reflects its exact hanging point. Unless otherwise noted, the default spacing between typical fixed focus luminaries is 18" (or 45 cm) to allow for adequate focus range of each luminaire. When the symbols are placed in relative locations other than the default, dimension lines or other measuring notations should be added between the symbols to indicate the distance and to facilitate mounting the luminaires. It is acceptable to visually orient the angle of each drawn luminaire to either focus points or 90° axes.

Normally, each symbol should be accompanied by the following information:

- Luminaire number
- Indication of focal length or beam spread as part of the symbol (where appropriate)
- Indication of any accessories such as templates, irises, scrollers, top hats, barn doors, etc.
- Channel (or control designation)
- Axis notation for PAR lamps

Additional information may include:

- Focus
- Wattage
- Circuit and/or dimmer number or space for the electrician to add this information
- Indication of "two-fers"
- Color notation
- Color notation for scrollers
- Template notation

2.3.1 Designation and numbering of conventional mounting positions

- Front of House (FOH) positions begin numbering from the position closest to plaster line.
- Onstage electrics number from downstage to upstage.
- Onstage booms number from downstage to upstage.
- All hanging locations not intersecting centerline are subnamed by their location relative to centerline. Ladders, box booms, booms, and such are divided between stage left and stage right; stage left listed first.

2.3.2 Numbering luminaires within conventional mounting positions

Each luminaire receives a unique whole number. If a luminaire has an attachment that alters the beam of an instrument, the attachment will often not receive its own whole number but rather the host instrument's number. Luminaires that are inserted between previously numbered fixtures are assigned the lower luminaire's unit number plus an additional letter (e.g., 3A or 3B). At the designer's discretion, decimal or letter suffixes may also be added to a luminaire's number. In common practice, multi-circuited luminaries such as striplights will be assigned a letter with a corresponding number for each circuit (e.g., A1, A2 and A3) while luminaries with multiple control channels or attributes will often be represented through a whole number designation of the unit number followed by a decimal point and number representing specific attributes for the luminaire (e.g., 23.1, 23.2 and 23.3).

- Luminaires on hanging positions perpendicular to centerline (e.g., battens) are numbered from stage left to stage right.

- Luminaires on onstage booms or other vertical hanging positions are numbered from top to bottom, downstage to upstage.

- Luminaires mounted on FOH positions parallel to centerline should number starting with the units nearest to plaster line.

- Luminaires mounted on FOH positions non-parallel to centerline (box booms) should number starting with the units closest to centerline.

2.3.3 Designation and numbering of mounting positions in non-proscenium venues

- Pipe grid positions should be designated by numbers on one axis of the grid and by letters on the other axis.

- Other atypical mounting positions may be designated by compass points or numbering in a clockwise manner.

- Mounting positions that repeat should be numbered from a consistent starting point.

- Other atypical hanging positions should be designated in a fashion that is sensible to the electricians. Luminaires hung in these positions should be numbered in an intelligible fashion compatible with other luminaire designations on the plot.

3.0 THE LIGHTING SECTION

The lighting section is a sectional view in which the cutting plane intersects the theatre, typically along the centerline but may intersect any plane that best illustrates the mounting positions. This drawing provides the most descriptive view of the hanging positions relative to the architectural and scenic elements of the production. While it may be appropriate to compress distance (horizontal or vertical) in a presentational section, doing so in the working version reduces its effectiveness.

3.1 Information contained in the Lighting Section

The purpose of the lighting section is to communicate spatial information and relationships of all other elements relative to the lighting design. The following information should be represented on the lighting section:

- Definition of where the section is "cut"

- Stage floor, deck, or "vertical zero" location (indication of which one is being used as reference zero)

- Proscenium, plaster line, smoke pocket, or the "horizontal zero" location

- Back wall or upstage limitation of the performing space

- Vertical audience sight points and/or sightlines

- Downstage edge of stage floor and/or edge of playing area

- Architectural details necessary to orient the lighting design in non-proscenium spaces

- All hanging positions including side elevation of booms, ladders, etc.

- Trim height for all hanging positions that can change height

- Identification of all lighting positions

- Architectural and scenic obstructions

- Sectional view of scenery

- All masking

- Title block (See Section 4)

- Scaled representation of the luminaire that determines batten height mounted in each position.

- Human figure (or "head height") in scale

Additional information may include:

- Vertical ruler in scale

- Horizontal ruler in scale

- Defined distance to other elements not shown on the drawing (to follow spot booth, other sightlines, etc.)

- Liability disclaimer

- Union stamp

4.0 TITLE BLOCK

Acceptable locations for the title block are:

- Lower right hand corner of the drawing

- Vertical banner on the right side of the drawing

4.1 Information contained in the title block

To be placed in the order deemed most important by the lighting designer:

- Name of the producing organization

- Name of the production

- Name of the venue

- Drawing title
- Drawing number (i.e., "1 of 4")
- Predominant scale of the drawing
- Date the plate was drafted
- Designer of the production
- Draftsperson of the drawing

Additional information may include:

- Location of the venue
- Director of the production
- Other members of the production team
- Lighting assistant and/or Master Electrician
- Date and revision number
- Approval of the drawing
- Contact information (telephone and fax numbers, e-mail addresses)

5.0 LEGEND OR INSTRUMENT KEY

Placement is acceptable in any location that does not conflict with other information.

5.1 Information contained in the legend or instrument Key:

- Pictorial representations (symbols) of all luminaires and devices shown on the plot with identifying descriptions of each.
- Beam spread (in degrees or focal length) for each luminaire type if the numeric value is not part of the luminaire's name.
- Designation of all notations associated with each luminaire.
- Color manufacturer designation (e.g., R = Rosco, L = Lee, G = Gam, etc.)
- Template manufacturer designation (when applicable)

- Wattage (total luminaire load) and/or ANSI lamp code
- Symbols for any accessories — templates, irises, color scrollers, top hats, barn doors, etc.

Additional information may include:

- Luminaire manufacturer
- Representation of "two-fers"
- Indication of voltage

6.0 SYMBOL GUIDELINES

These guidelines represent a selection of standard generic symbols that approximate the size and shape of stage luminaires. Further differentiation or notation may be necessary to distinguish between luminaires of approximately the same size. This may include shading the symbol, making the "front" of the symbol a heavier line, and other individual techniques. As manufacturers introduce new luminaries and accessories that are not specified by the current Recommended Practice, a designer may either create new symbols or make variations in existing symbols that approximate the silhouettes and optical qualities of the new equipment. In this case, a clear indication of the new symbol must be included within the instrument Key. Detailed luminaire symbols specific to each manufacturers' products and supplied by computer drafting programs may be substituted, provided they allow the specialized markings needed to exactly specify the luminaire and provided they are properly explained by the instrument key (see Section 5).

These symbols are presented as a guideline. Specific choices should be considered to differentiate between different manufacturers of the same type of luminaire. It is USITT policy not to specify any manufacturers in the symbol guidelines.

Because of the number and complexity of attributes in automated fixtures, each designer must determine a logical notation system for the luminaire used.

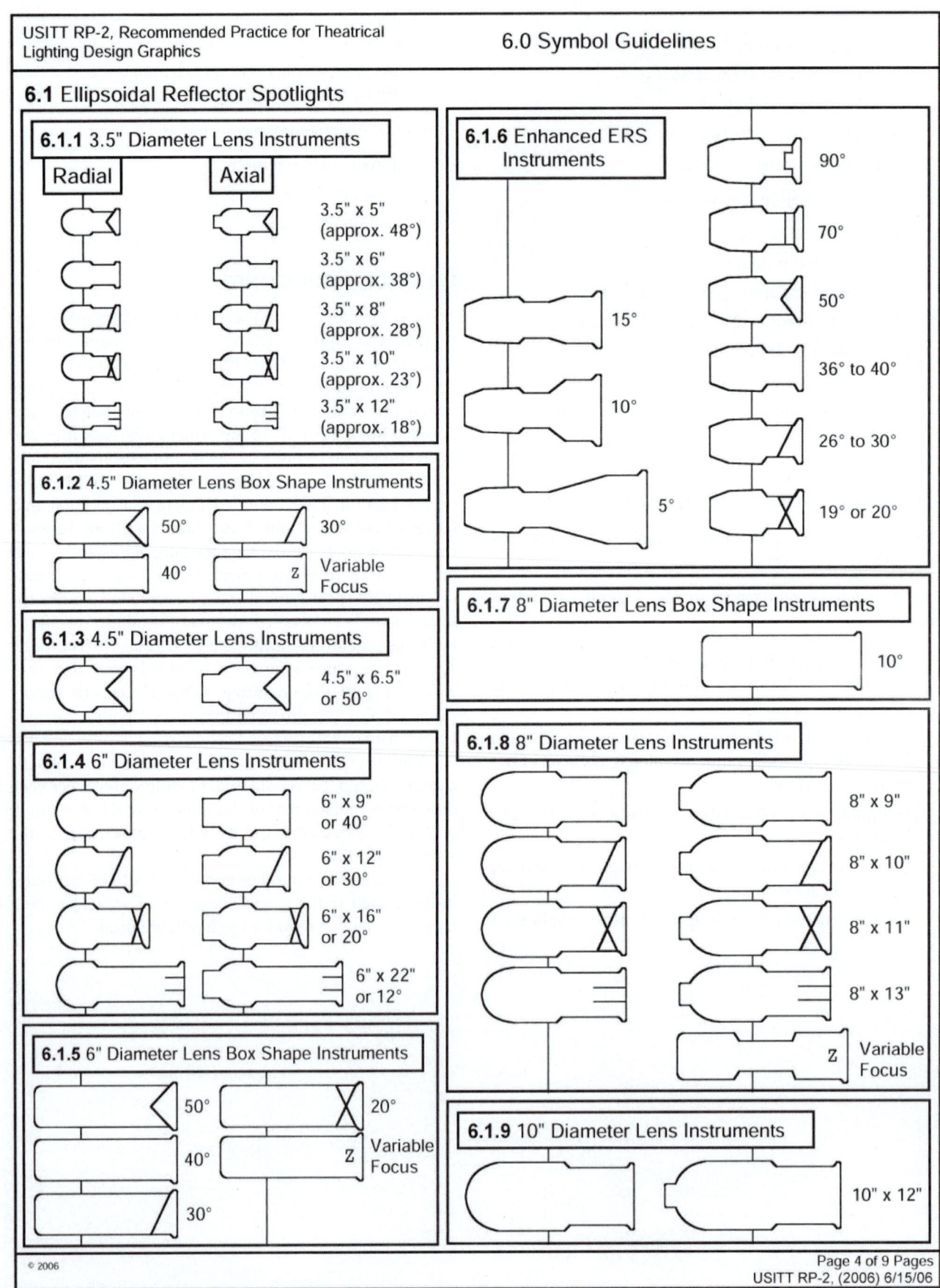

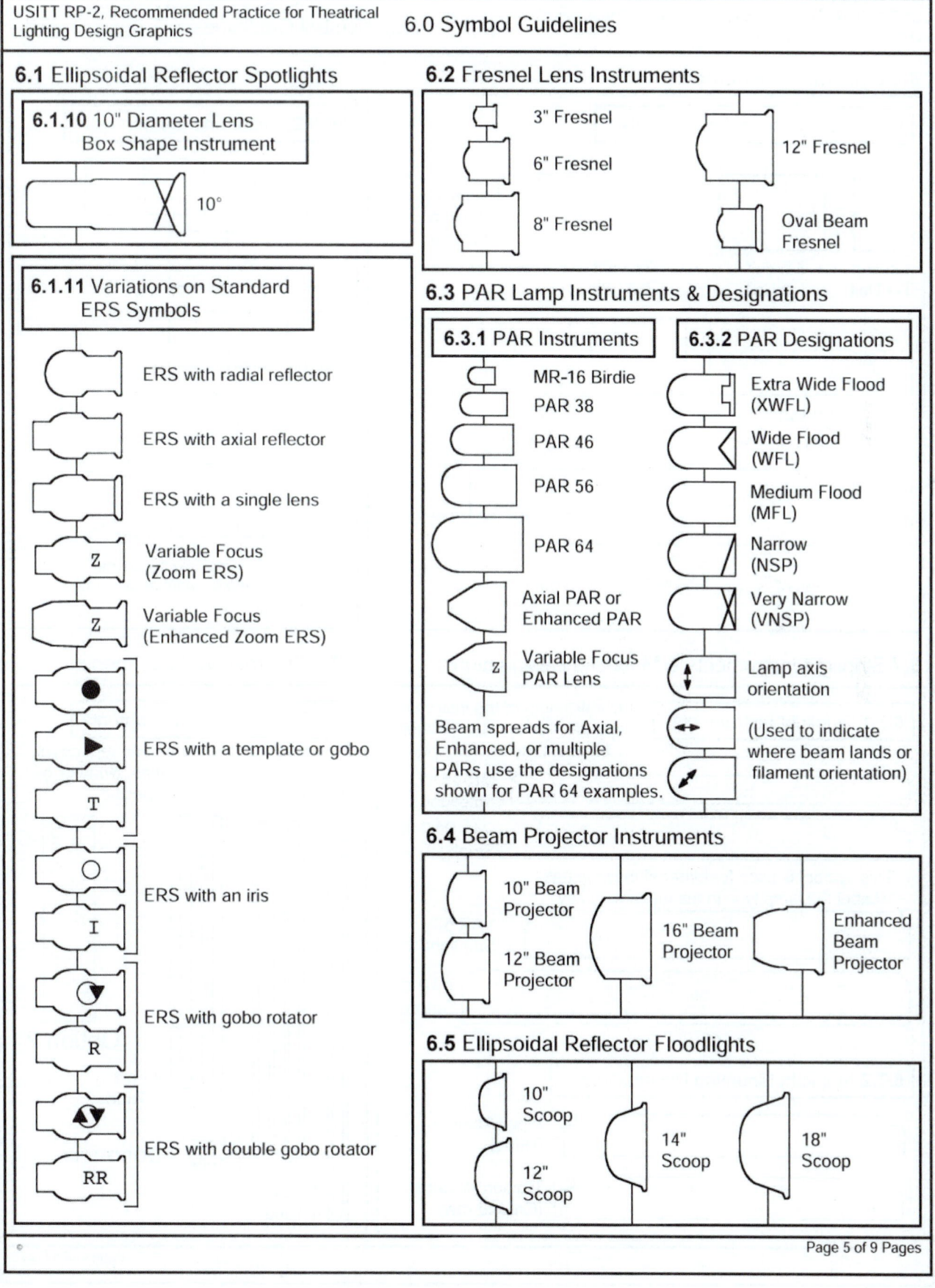

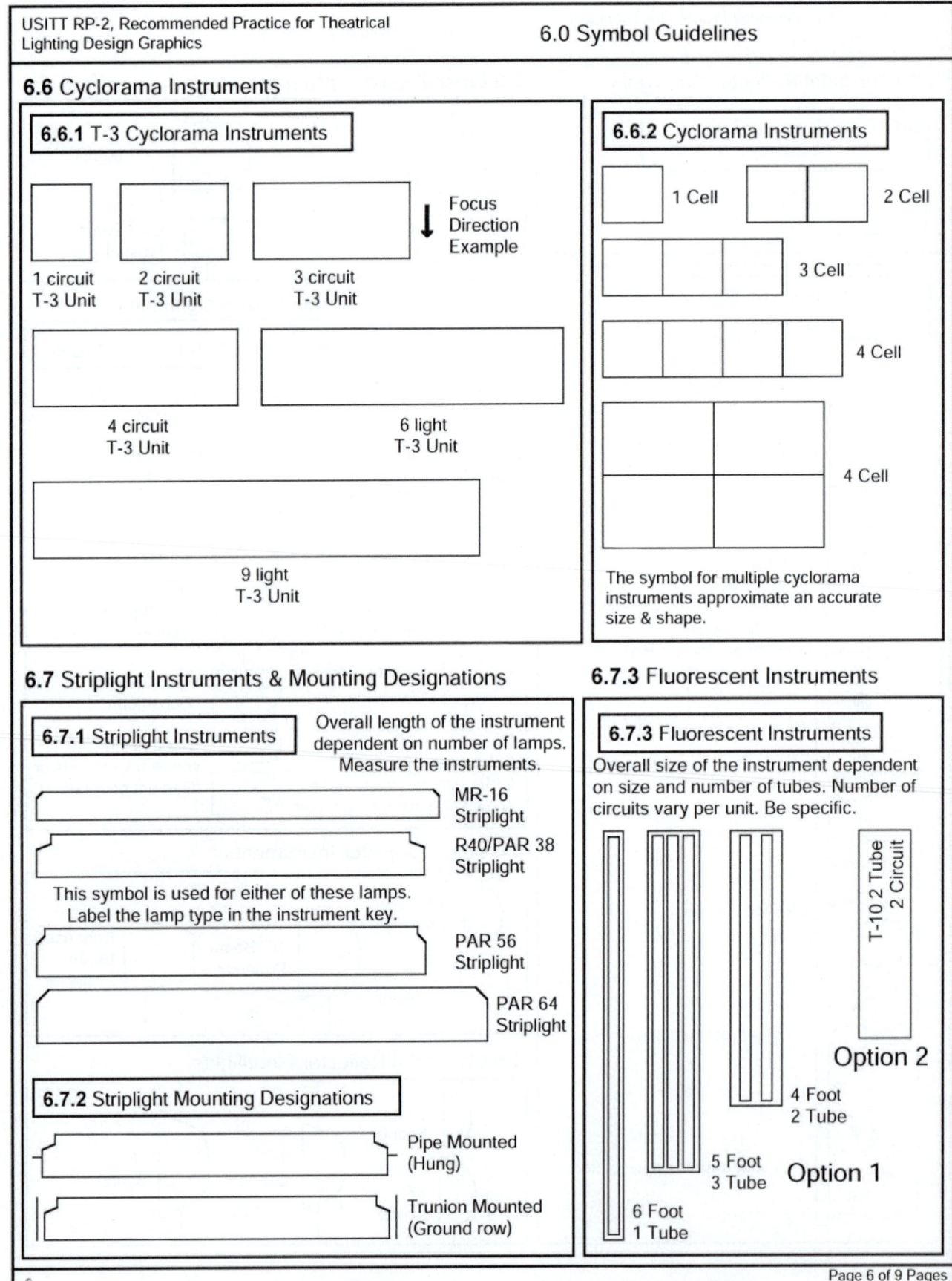

USITT RP-2, Recommended Practice for Theatrical Lighting Design Graphics

6.0 Symbol Guidelines

6.6 Cyclorama Instruments

6.6.1 T-3 Cyclorama Instruments

↓ Focus Direction Example

1 circuit T-3 Unit

2 circuit T-3 Unit

3 circuit T-3 Unit

4 circuit T-3 Unit

6 light T-3 Unit

9 light T-3 Unit

6.6.2 Cyclorama Instruments

1 Cell

2 Cell

3 Cell

4 Cell

4 Cell

The symbol for multiple cyclorama instruments approximate an accurate size & shape.

6.7 Striplight Instruments & Mounting Designations

6.7.1 Striplight Instruments

Overall length of the instrument dependent on number of lamps. Measure the instruments.

MR-16 Striplight

R40/PAR 38 Striplight

This symbol is used for either of these lamps. Label the lamp type in the instrument key.

PAR 56 Striplight

PAR 64 Striplight

6.7.2 Striplight Mounting Designations

Pipe Mounted (Hung)

Trunion Mounted (Ground row)

6.7.3 Fluorescent Instruments

6.7.3 Fluorescent Instruments

Overall size of the instrument dependent on size and number of tubes. Number of circuits vary per unit. Be specific.

T-10 2 Tube 2 Circuit

Option 2

4 Foot 2 Tube

5 Foot 3 Tube

Option 1

6 Foot 1 Tube

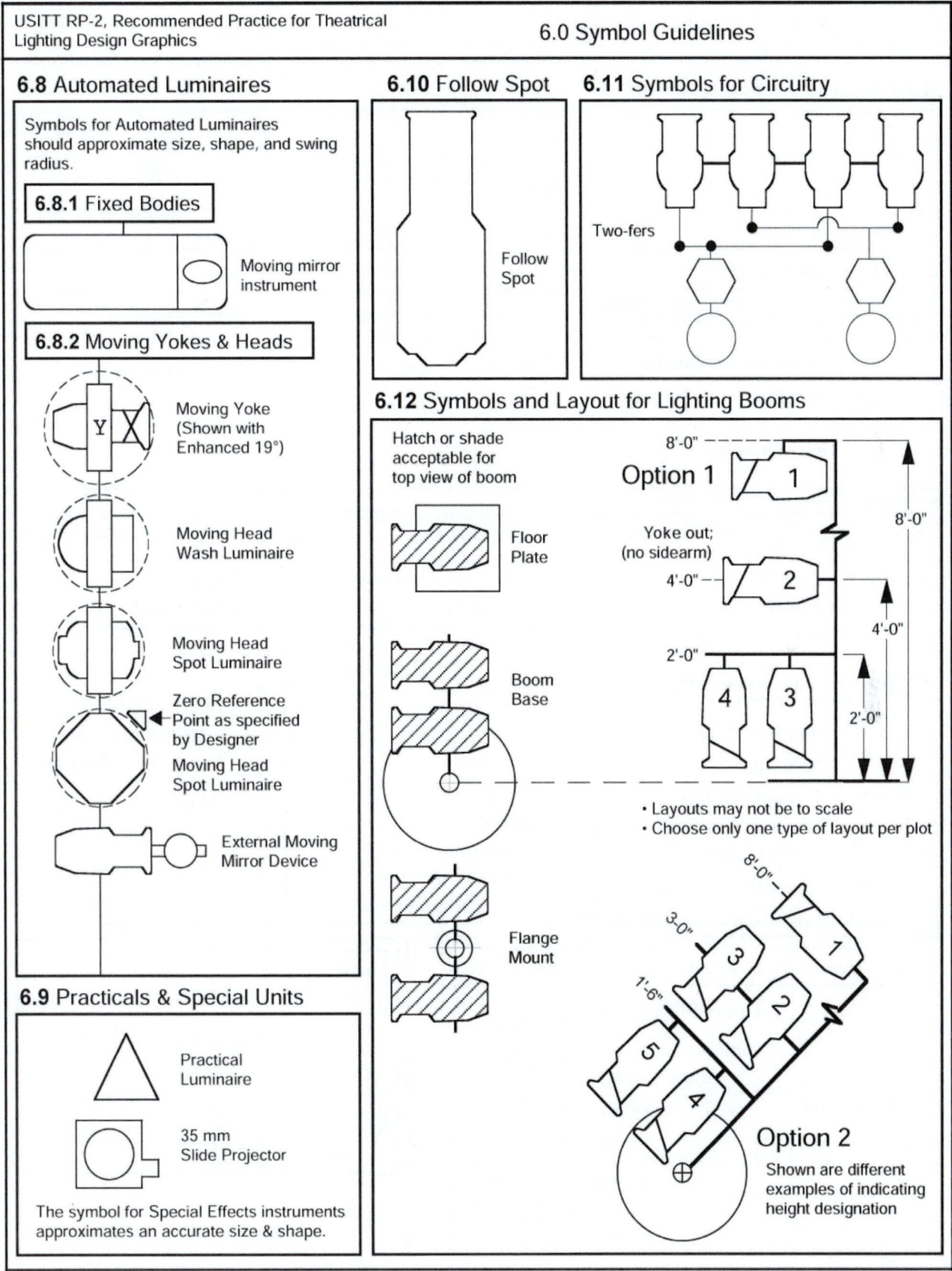

6.0 Symbol Guidelines

6.8 Automated Luminaires

Symbols for Automated Luminaires should approximate size, shape, and swing radius.

6.8.1 Fixed Bodies

Moving mirror instrument

6.8.2 Moving Yokes & Heads

Moving Yoke (Shown with Enhanced 19°)

Moving Head Wash Luminaire

Moving Head Spot Luminaire

Zero Reference Point as specified by Designer

Moving Head Spot Luminaire

External Moving Mirror Device

6.9 Practicals & Special Units

Practical Luminaire

35 mm Slide Projector

The symbol for Special Effects instruments approximates an accurate size & shape.

6.10 Follow Spot

Follow Spot

6.11 Symbols for Circuitry

Two-fers

6.12 Symbols and Layout for Lighting Booms

Hatch or shade acceptable for top view of boom

Floor Plate

Boom Base

Flange Mount

Option 1

Yoke out; (no sidearm)

8'-0"
4'-0"
2'-0"

8'-0"
4'-0"
2'-0"

• Layouts may not be to scale
• Choose only one type of layout per plot

Option 2

Shown are different examples of indicating height designation

8'-0"
3'-0"
1'-6"

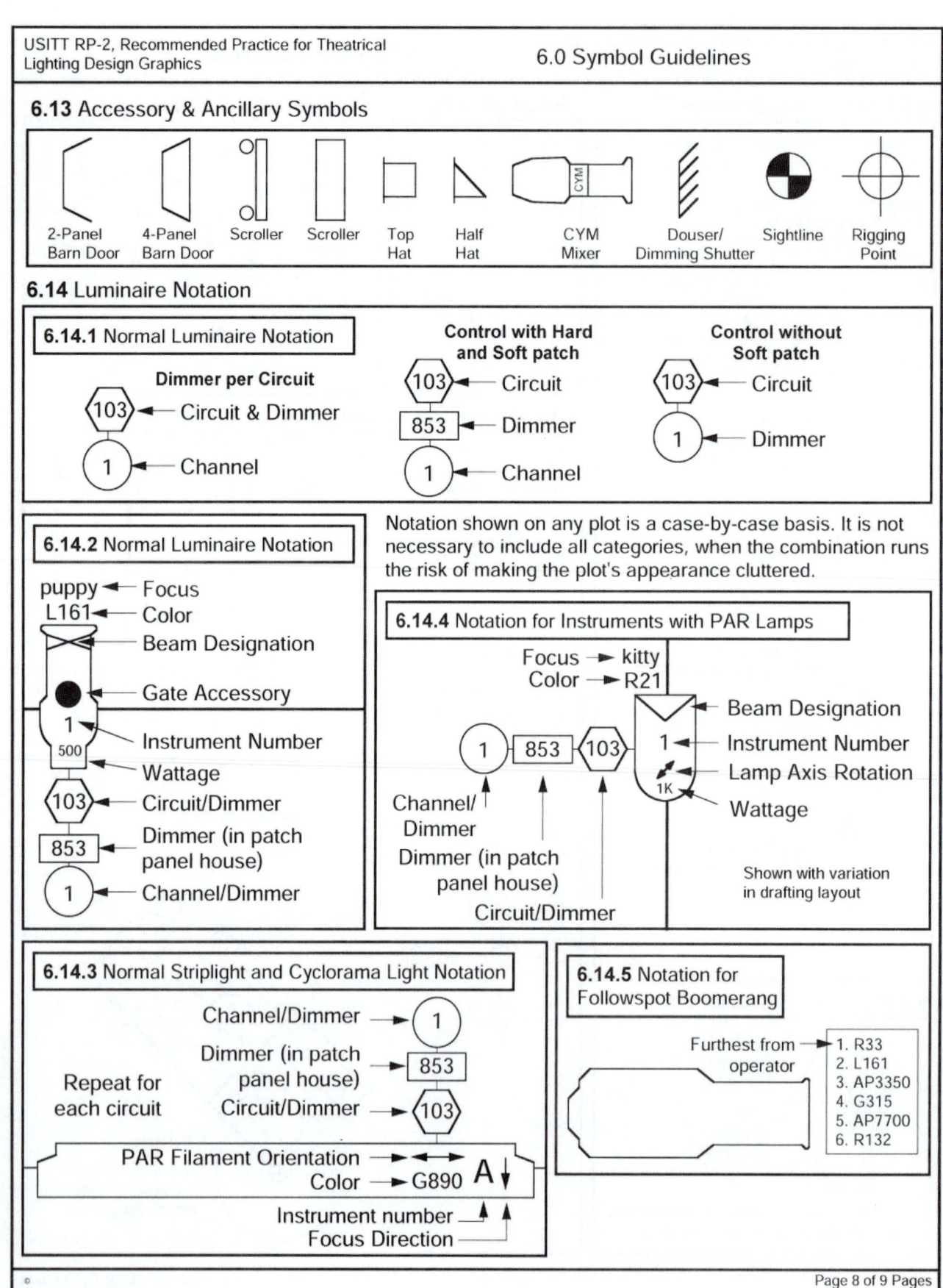

6.13 Accessory & Ancillary Symbols

2-Panel Barn Door | 4-Panel Barn Door | Scroller | Scroller | Top Hat | Half Hat | CYM Mixer | Douser/ Dimming Shutter | Sightline | Rigging Point

6.14 Luminaire Notation

6.14.1 Normal Luminaire Notation

Dimmer per Circuit
103 ← Circuit & Dimmer
1 ← Channel

Control with Hard and Soft patch
103 ← Circuit
853 ← Dimmer
1 ← Channel

Control without Soft patch
103 ← Circuit
1 ← Dimmer

6.14.2 Normal Luminaire Notation

puppy ← Focus
L161 ← Color
← Beam Designation
← Gate Accessory
1 ← Instrument Number
500 ← Wattage
103 ← Circuit/Dimmer
853 ← Dimmer (in patch panel house)
1 ← Channel/Dimmer

Notation shown on any plot is a case-by-case basis. It is not necessary to include all categories, when the combination runs the risk of making the plot's appearance cluttered.

6.14.4 Notation for Instruments with PAR Lamps

Focus → kitty
Color → R21

1 853 103

Channel/ Dimmer
Dimmer (in patch panel house)
Circuit/Dimmer

1 ← Beam Designation
← Instrument Number
← Lamp Axis Rotation
1K ← Wattage

Shown with variation in drafting layout

6.14.3 Normal Striplight and Cyclorama Light Notation

Channel/Dimmer → 1
Dimmer (in patch panel house) → 853
Repeat for each circuit   Circuit/Dimmer → 103

PAR Filament Orientation → ← →
Color → G890   A↓
Instrument number ↑ ↑
Focus Direction

6.14.5 Notation for Followspot Boomerang

Furthest from → operator
1. R33
2. L161
3. AP3350
4. G315
5. AP7700
6. R132

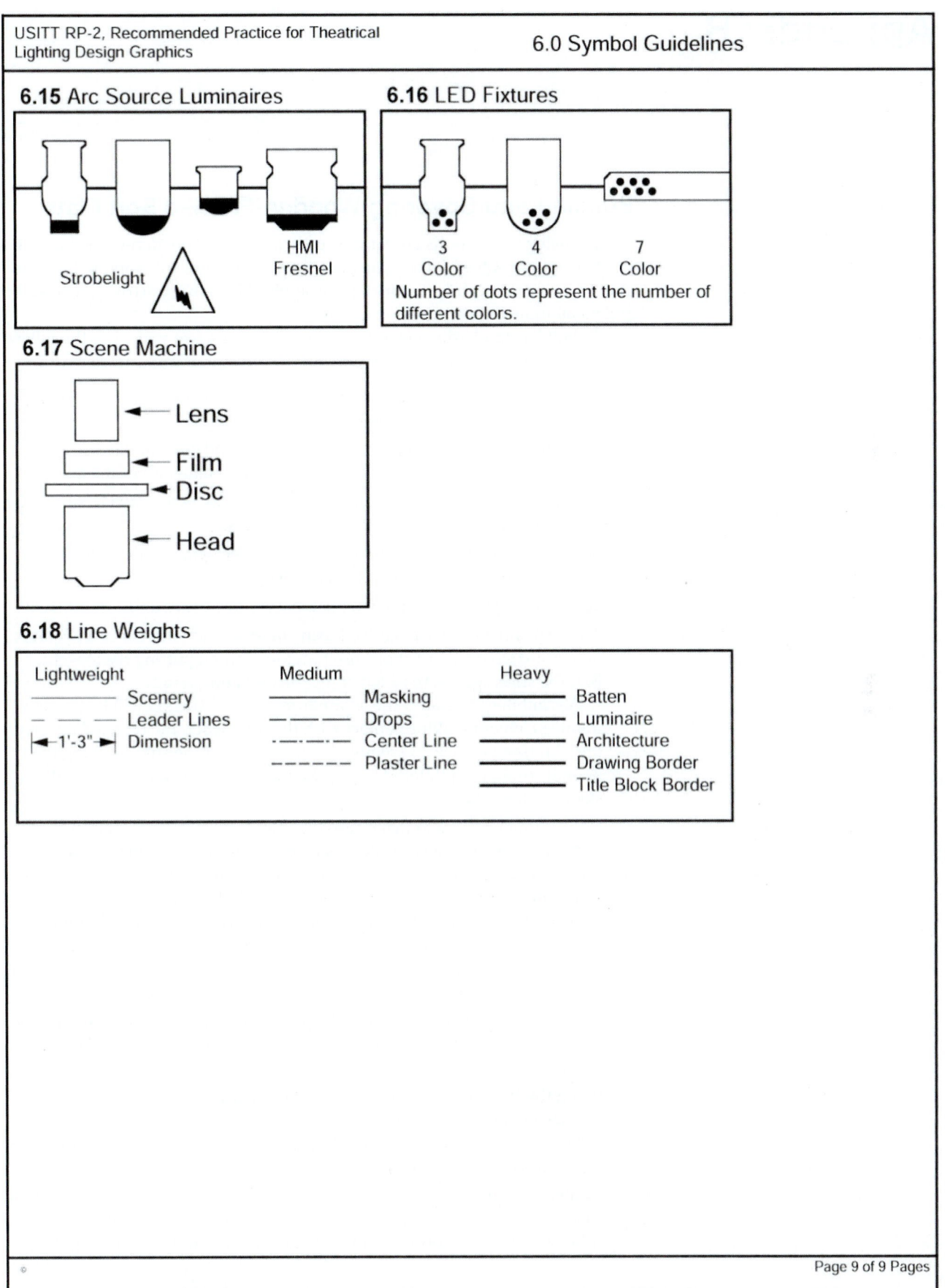

6.15 Arc Source Luminaires

Strobelight

HMI
Fresnel

6.16 LED Fixtures

3
Color

4
Color

7
Color

Number of dots represent the number of different colors.

6.17 Scene Machine

← Lens

← Film

← Disc

← Head

6.18 Line Weights

Lightweight	Medium	Heavy
——— Scenery	—— Masking	—— Batten
— — — Leader Lines	—·—— Drops	—— Luminaire
←1'-3"→ Dimension	·—·—·— Center Line	—— Architecture
	—————— Plaster Line	—— Drawing Border
		—— Title Block Border

Appendix B

Building and Covering Wooden-Framed Soft Flats

The following instructions are for the construction of a wooden-framed flat. But the principles involved — the guidelines for placement of stiles and rails, as well as the spacing of togglebars — are equally applicable to the construction of studio and metal-framed flats.

To build a standard wooden flat 14 feet tall and 4 feet wide, use the following fifteen step procedure:

1. Select good, straight white pine 1×3 or 1×4 ("B or better" or "C select") for the rails, stiles, and toggle bars.

2. Trim and square the end of one of the boards, and cut two pieces 4 feet long for the rails. (Note that the rails are cut the full width of the flat.)

3. Trim and square the boards, and cut the two stiles 14 feet (the height of the flat) minus the combined width of the two rails.

4. Square the boards, and cut two toggle bars 4 feet (the width of the flat) minus the combined width of the two stiles.

5. Before you begin to assemble the flat, cut the keystones and cornerblocks.

6. Although a flat can be assembled using mortise and tenon or halved joints for extra strength, most shops use butt joints when putting flats together. Butt the stiles against the edge of the top and bottom rails.

   Assembling the flat in this manner means that the rail will be the only framing element making contact with the floor when the finished flat is set upright. If the flat were assembled with the end of the stile touching the floor, it would be splintered and broken whenever the flat was moved or skidded along the floor.

7. Use a framing square to make sure that the corner joint between the rail and stile is square. Lay a cornerblock on top of the joint with its grain running perpendicular to the line of the joint (parallel to the grain of the stile), and inset ¾ inch from the outside edge of both the rail and stile. Secure the cornerblocks (as well as the keystones or straps) with coated staples, or power-driven screws. This routine is repeated for each corner of the flat.

8. Center the toggle bars at 4 feet 8 inches and 9 feet 4 inches so that they will be equidistant from the top and bottom of the flat and from each other. Use the framing square to make sure that the toggle bars are square to the stile, and secure them with keystones that are also inset ¾ inch from the edges of the stiles.

9. When the flat is wider than 3 feet, diagonal corner braces made of 1×2s are placed in the upper and lower corners of the same side of the flat. Secure these corner braces with plywood straps ripped in half and angle cut so that they can be inset ¾ inch from the outside edge of the flat.

10. To cover the flat, you will need to turn it over so that it is lying on the corner blocks and keystones (Figure 1A). Stretch a piece of heavyweight muslin (128- or 140-thread count) over the frame. The muslin should be slightly

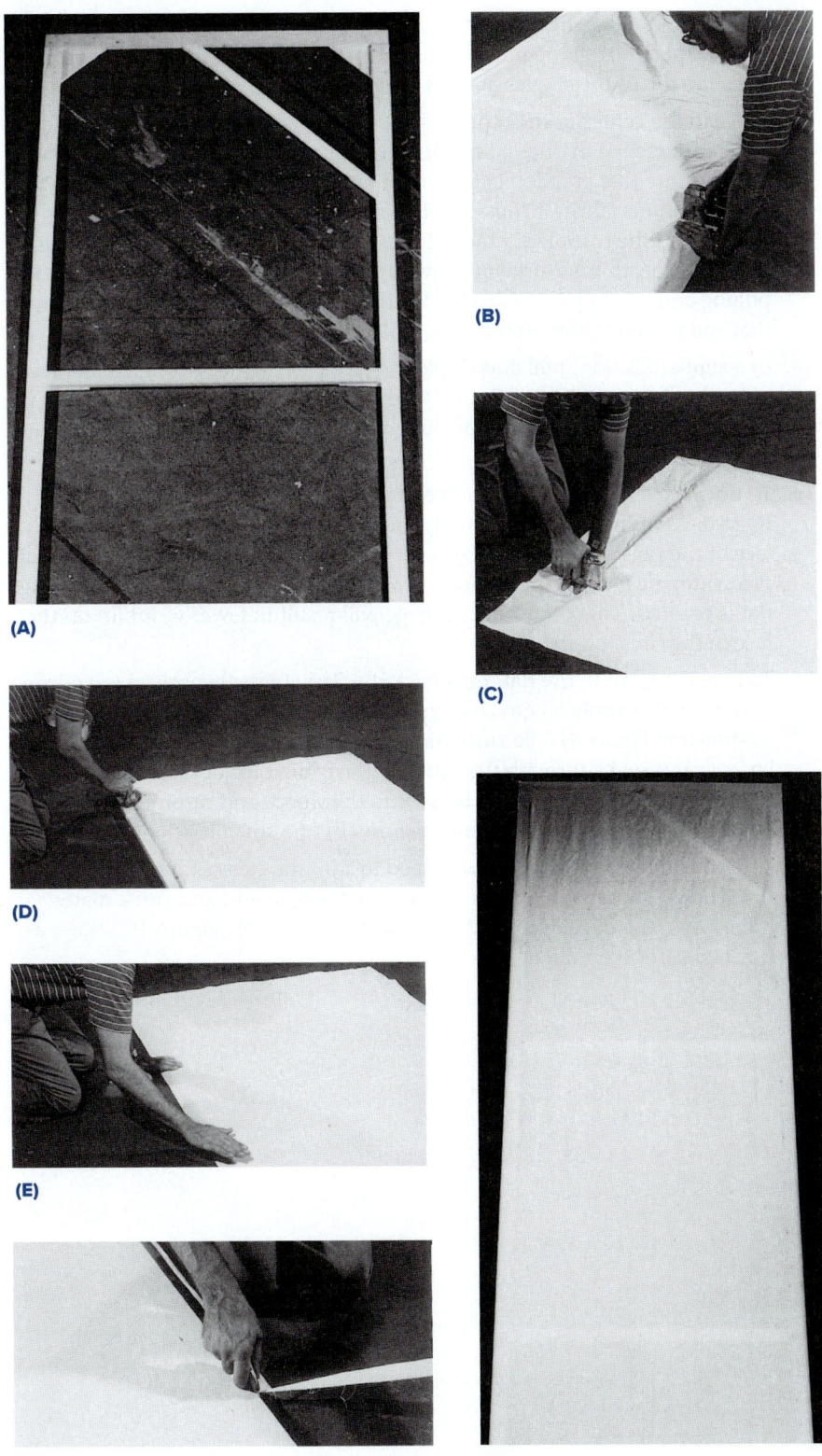

(A)

(B)

(C)

(D)

(E)

(F)

(G)

FIGURE 1
Flat-covering technique. (A) The smooth front side of a flat frame. (B) Lay fabric slightly wider and taller than the flat frame over the frame. (C) Staple the fabric to the inside edge of the face of the flat. (D) Glue the fabric to the frame, and smooth the fabric onto the frame with your hands (E) or a small block of wood. Trim the excess fabric with a matte knife (F) after the glue has dried. (G) The finished flat.

larger than the height and width of the flat, as shown in Figure 1B. Using a hand stapler, attach the muslin along the inside edge of the face of one of the stiles. Place the staples about 1 foot apart.

11. Move to the center of the other stile, and pull the muslin until it barely sags across the face of the flat. Staple it on the inside edge of the face of that stile. Be sure that you don't stretch the muslin until it is tight; you need to allow room for fabric shrinkage when you paint the muslin. (On a 4-by-14-foot flat, the completely tacked muslin should just brush the work surface underneath it.) Work your way toward the end of the flat, alternately pulling and stapling the material. Do this in both directions from the staple that you placed in the center of the stile.

12. In a similar fashion, pull and staple the fabric to the inside edge of the face of both rails, as shown in Figure 1C. If there are any wrinkles or puckers in the fabric, the staples should be pulled and the fabric restretched until the wrinkles are removed.

13. To finish covering the flat, you need to glue the muslin to the frame. Regardless of the shape of the flat, you should glue the covering only to the face of the rails and stiles. If the covering fabric is not glued to any internal pieces (toggle bars, corner braces), it will be able to shrink evenly when the flat is painted. This uniform shrinkage will result in fewer wrinkles on the face of the finished flat.

14. To glue the cloth to the flat, turn back the flap of muslin around the edge of the flat and apply a light coating of glue to the face of the stiles and rails, as shown in Figure 1D. Be sure that you use a thorough but *light* coating, because if it soaks through the muslin, it may discolor or darken the ensuing paint job. Fold the muslin back onto the wood, and carefully smooth out any wrinkles with your hand (Figure 1E) or a small block of wood.

15. After the glue has dried, you will need to trim the excess fabric from the flat. The easiest way to do this is to pull the fabric tight and run a matte knife down the edge of the flat, as shown in Figure 1F. Figure 1G shows a finished soft-covered flat.

Appendix C

Drafting Materials and Instruments

The list of equipment used in hand-drawn mechanical drawing isn't extensive. It includes a drafting board minimally 24 inches high by 36 inches wide (a larger board of approximately 30 by 42 inches will be better if you are also going to be drawing light plots); a good T square with a shaft long enough to reach across the width of the drafting board; one 8-inch 45-45-90-degree triangle and one 12-inch 30-60-90-degree triangle; a pencil compass; an architect's scale rule; an eraser; 2H, 3H, and 4H drafting pencils; and drafting tape.

All hand drafting should be done on good-quality, translucent drafting paper such as Clearprint or a brand of similar quality. Drawings made on this type of paper can be easily bluelined for use by other members of the production design team and the various construction shops. Cheap tracing paper tears easily when an erasure is attempted and becomes brittle and unusable with age. Tracing paper with grids shouldn't be used, as the lines will interfere with the drawings that you will be making on the paper.

DRAFTING BOARD

The size of the drafting board is not too important provided that the board is large enough to accept the dimensions of the stage for which you will be designing drawn to a scale of ½ inch to 1 foot. The board is usually made of white pine and may be covered with a plastic laminate. The ends of the board should be finished smoothly or, preferably, covered with a metal or plastic cap strip. The edges of the board must be absolutely straight so that the head of the T square will ride evenly on them. (See Figure 1.)

If the face of the drafting board is not covered with a plastic laminate, it should be padded with either a sheet of heavy white paper or drafting board padding material. The padding not only makes the drawing easier to see but also prevents sharp pencil points from scoring the wooden surface of the board.

FIGURE 1
Drafting equipment.

T SQUARE

The accuracy of any hand-produced mechanical drawing depends, to a great extent, on the condition of the T square. All horizontal lines are made by placing the head of the T square snuggly against the edge of the drawing board and guiding a pencil along the upper edge of the leg of the T square, as shown in Figure 2A. Vertical lines are drawn by placing the base of the triangle against the leg or shaft of the T square and guiding a pencil along the vertical edge of the triangle, as shown in Figure 2B. If the head of the T square is not firmly attached to the shaft at a true right angle, neither vertical nor horizontal lines will be accurate. Other types of equipment, such as the Mayline parallel (Figure 2C), the track drafting machine (Figure 2D), and the elbow drafting machine (Figure 2E), perform the same function as the T square but are considerably more expensive. As might be expected, the parallel and drafting machines are generally easier to use and more accurate than the T square.

TRIANGLES

Triangles can be purchased in many different sizes, but the 8-inch 45-45-90-degree and the 12-inch 30-60-90-degree triangles are ideally suited for most drafting purposes. Triangles any smaller than these necessitate shifting both the T square and triangles to a new position to draw a long vertical line. By placing one triangle against another, as shown in Figure 3, and guiding both with the T square, angles of 15 and 75 degrees can be drawn.

The set square, shown in Figure 4, is an adjustable triangle with two parts joined by a plastic protractor reading from 0 to 45 degrees. A threaded bolt and thumbscrew allow the two halves of the triangle to be locked in any desired position.

(A)

(B)

(C)

FIGURE 2
How to use a T square. (A) Pull on the leg to keep the head of the T square flush with the edge of the board when drawing horizontal lines. (B) Hold the triangle snuggly to the leg of the T square when drawing vertical lines. (C) A Mayline parallel rule. (D) A track drafting machine. Courtesy of Alvin & Company, Inc. (E) An elbow drafting machine. Courtesy of Vemco Drafting Products Corporation.

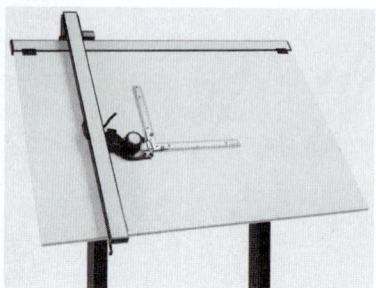

(D)

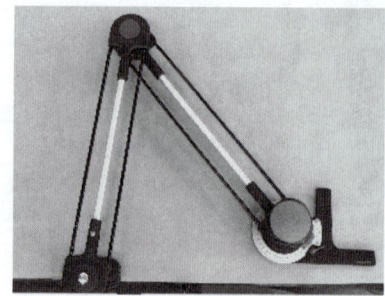

(E)

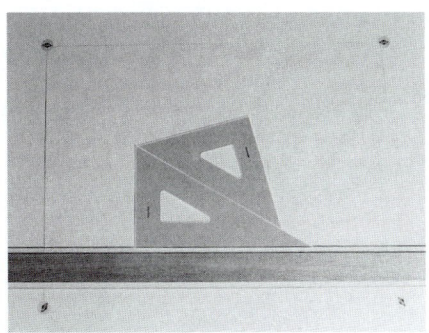

FIGURE 3
How to draw 15- and 75-degree
angles.

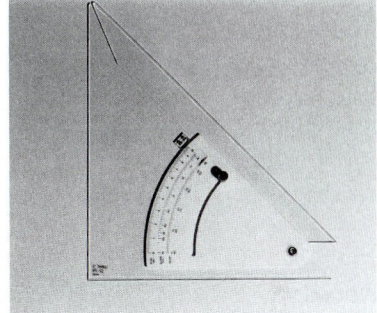

FIGURE 4
A set square.

COMPASS AND CIRCLE TEMPLATE

A medium-quality compass (Figure 5A) is needed for drawing circles and arcs. A substitute preferred by many drafters is a circle template, shown in Figure 5B. When purchasing a circle template, select one with a large number of circle diameters, because a template will almost invariably have every size except the one you want to use.

ARCHITECT'S SCALE RULE

The key to making all scaled mechanical drawings is the use of an architect's scale rule. The scales found on the rule make the process of allowing a fraction of a foot represent a full foot practically painless.

The architect's rule (Figure 6) is made in two shapes, triangular and flat. The triangular rule (which is less expensive) has a standard foot measure on one edge and ten different scales, two on each of the remaining five edges: 1 foot to $\frac{3}{32}$, $\frac{1}{8}$, $\frac{3}{16}$, $\frac{1}{4}$, $\frac{3}{8}$, $\frac{1}{2}$, $\frac{3}{4}$, 1, $1\frac{1}{2}$, and 3 inches. The flat rule may be a little more convenient to use, but it has only eight scales and is more expensive.

The one-half-inch scale, as noted, is the most frequently used in theatrical drafting. This scale reads from right to left on the architect's scale shown in Figure 7A. At the extreme right of the rule is a ½-inch space that has been divided into twelve spaces representing inches, with each scale inch subdivided into halves by shorter lines. Foot measurements are indicated in multiples of two; they read 0, 2, 4, 6, and so on. Odd-numbered foot measurements, not indicated by a numeral, are found by using the marks for the 1-inch scale. These marks fall midway between the numerals of the ½-inch scale. On the ½-inch scale the foot measurements are read to the left of the zero, and the inches are read to the right.

Figure 7B shows how the architect's scale rule is used to measure a line. One end of the line is placed on a full-foot mark, and the other end of the line projects into the inch breakdown of the scale foot. The length of the line is read by counting the number of feet to the right of the zero point on the scale and the number of inches to the left.

DRAWING PENCILS

Most drafting for theatrical work is done with drafting pencils marked 2H (soft), 3H (medium), and 4H (hard). Drawing pencils (those designated by the letter *B*) leave a blacker line, but they smudge easily and quickly leave both the drafter's hands and drawing instruments covered with graphite. It is much easier to handle and manipulate a long drafting pencil than one that has been worn down to a

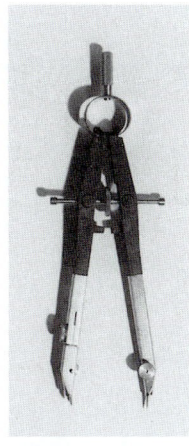

(A)

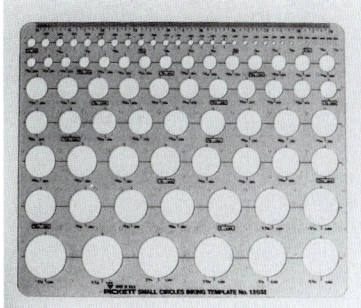

(B)

FIGURE 5
(A) A compass and (B) a circle template.

FIGURE 6
Architect's rules.

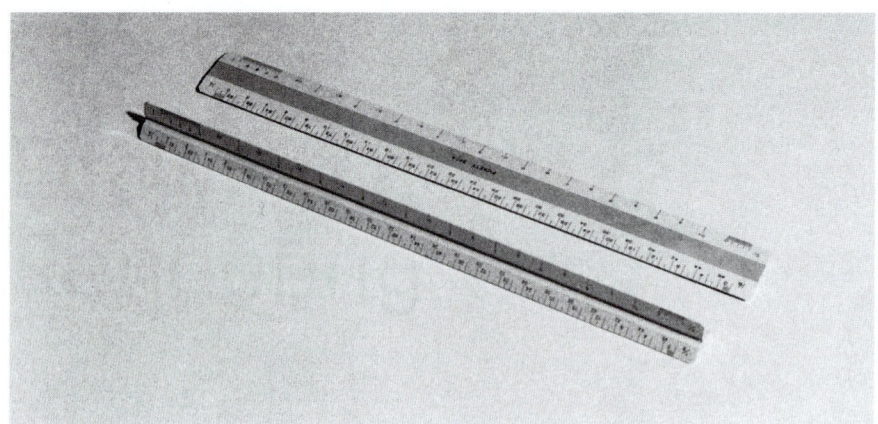

FIGURE 7
(A) A half-inch rule. (B) How to measure the scale length of a line.

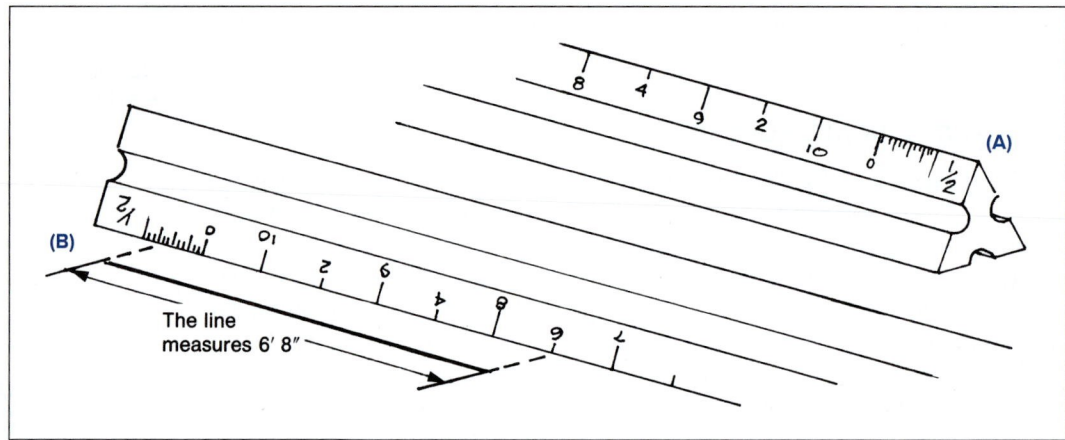

The line measures 6' 8"

FIGURE 8
Auxiliary drafting equipment.

pig: A bag of loosely woven fabric containing powdered eraser material.

stub. A sharp pencil is essential for accurate drafting, because only a sharp point can draw a clean, crisp line of unvarying width. The mechanical push-point drafting pencils, which use leads of diameters that correspond to the widths of the various drafting lines — approximately 0.3 mm for thin lines and 0.5 mm for thick lines — solve a lot of the problems with dull points that seem to plague neophyte drafters. However, whether you choose mechanical or wood pencils is strictly up to you.

ERASER

A soft, pliable, pink eraser or a kneadable eraser (Figure 8) is the best choice for correcting penciled mistakes. Both remove the graphite without discoloring or damaging the paper.

Powdered eraser, contained in either a shaker can or a bag called a **pig,** can be sprinkled on the drafting paper while the drawing is being made. The movement of the T square and triangles over these particles keeps the underside of the instruments clean and prevents a graphite "shadow" from forming on the paper.

DRAFTING TAPE

Drafting tape is used for holding the paper in place on the drafting board. Drafting tape and masking tape look alike. However, drafting tape will not leave a sticky residue on your drawings, whereas masking tape will.

To tape the paper to the board, you will need to adjust it until the upper or lower edge of the paper is parallel with the T square shaft. Use 2- to 3-inch strips of drafting tape to hold down the four corners of the paper, as shown in Figure 9. Commercially available small circular taping tabs can also be used to tape the paper to the drawing board.

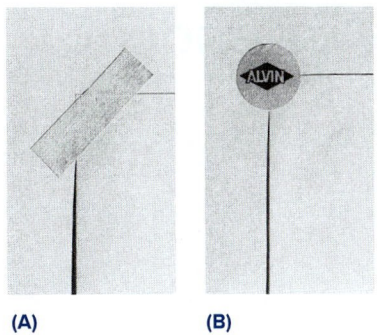

(A)   **(B)**

FIGURE 7.9
(A) Use of drafting tape. (B) Taping tabs.

Appendix D

Patch Panels

The patch panel, Figure A, is an interconnecting device that provides the capability of connecting (patching) any stage circuit into any dimmer.

Figure B describes the basic operation of a patch panel. A lighting instrument is connected to a stage circuit. That stage circuit terminates at the patch panel in a male plug. The dimmer, which is usually located in another part of the theatre, is permanently wired to several receptacles — wired in parallel — on the face of the patch panel. This allows more than one circuit to be patched into each dimmer.

The patch panel is actually simple to operate. What makes it seem so complex is that it contains more than the single circuit and dimmer illustrated in Figure B. Typically, a patch panel contains several hundred stage circuits and between sixty and several hundred dimmers.

Patch panels typically have some type of electrical-overload protection — circuit breakers — in both the stage and dimmer circuits, as illustrated in Figure C.

FIGURE A
A patch panel. Courtesy of Colortran.

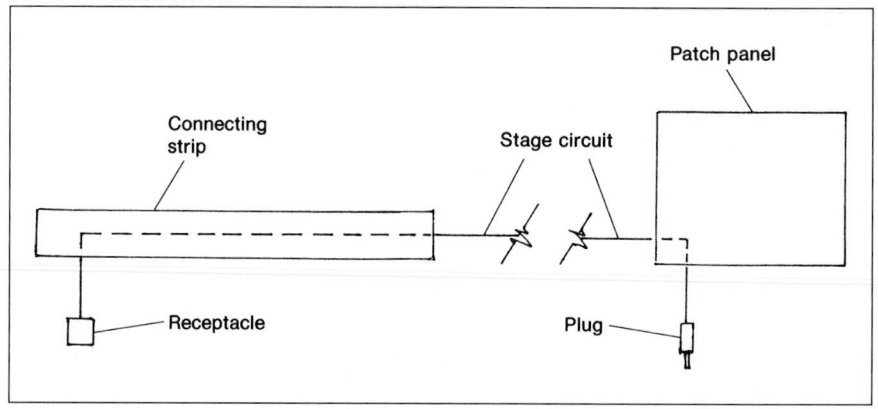

FIGURE B
A lighting instrument is connected to the receptacle; the plug ion the other end of the circuit is patched into the appropriate dimmer at the patch panel.

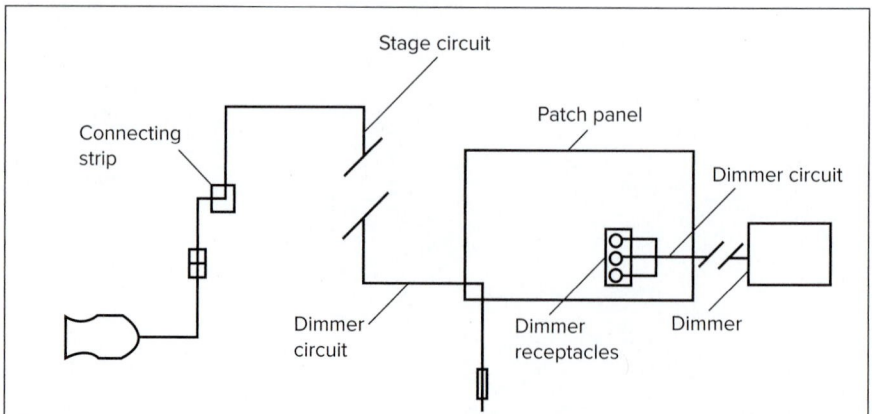

FIGURE C
The patch panel allows you to plug more than one circuit into a single dimmer.

Each circuit breaker automatically breaks continuity — stops the flow of electricity — in its circuit when an unsafe amount of current is sensed in the line. The location of those circuit breakers varies from system to system. Circuit breakers protecting the stage circuits are typically located on the patch panel. However, the breakers for the dimmer circuits may be located either at patch panel or at the dimmers' mainframe location.

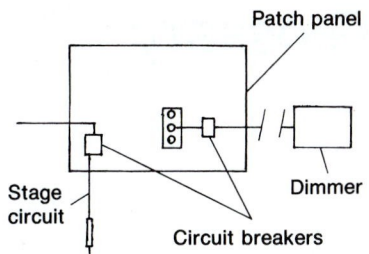

FIGURE D
Circuit breakers provide overload protection for both the stage circuits and the dimmer circuits.

Glossary

1-inch centers: the centers of adjacent elements, such as holes, are spaced 1 inch apart.

4-in/2-out: a mixer device with four inputs and two outputs.

6-inch centers: those spaced 6 inches apart.

18-inch centers: those spaced 18 inches apart.

Accessory: in costuming, anything other than clothing that is worn or carried, including wigs, hats, footwear, jewelry, and similar items.

Acoustics: the sound-transmission characteristics of a room, space, or material; also, the science that studies these qualities.

Acrylic: a plastic most readily identified by its trade name Plexiglas; available in rigid sheets and in liquid form (for use as a casting resin).

Acting areas: those areas of the stage on which specific scenes, or parts of scenes, are played.

Additive color mixing: the transmission of light of varying hues to the eye and the brain's interpretation of the ratio of the light mixture as a specific hue.

Additive manufacturing: creating a manufactured part by adding material instead of cutting it away; applies to 3-D printing.

Adjustable arc-joint pliers: long-handled pliers with a series of jaw pivot points that provide a variety of jaw-opening ranges; used for gripping square and round objects with a great deal of leverage; also known as alligator pliers.

Adjustable-end wrench: generally known by the trade name Crescent Wrench, the adjustable-end wrench has smooth jaws that adjust to fit almost any small to medium-sized nut; used to tighten bolts and nuts.

Adjustable wood clamps: a wooden clamp with two adjustable faces; the jaws can be adjusted to various angles that are useful in holding furniture frames while the glued joints are drying.

Aerial perspective: an optical phenomenon in which objects that are farther away appear less sharply in focus and less fully saturated in color.

Air caster: a nonwheeled caster that lifts objects and holds them up using high-volume, low-pressure compressed air; three to four air casters are used to raise most objects; the one-foot-diameter air caster, load rated at 2,000 pounds, is the standard size used in theatrical production.

Aircraft cable: extremely strong, flexible, multistrand, twisted metal cable; ⅛-inch aircraft cable is frequently used for flying heavy scenery because it has a breaking strength of approximately one ton.

Allen wrench: an L-shaped piece of steel rod with a hexagonal cross-sectional shape; used for working with Allen-head screws and bolts.

Alligator pliers: see adjustable arc-joint pliers.

Ambient: surrounding or background.

Ambient lighting: surrounding environmental light; light in the projection environment from sources other than the projector.

Ampere: the unit of measurement of electrical current.

Amplifier: an electronic device used to boost the voltage, current, or power of a signal; normally used to increase the power to the level needed by the next piece of equipment in the circuit.

Amplitude: synonym for loudness.

Analog: in electronics, a circuit or device in which the output varies as a continuous function of the input.

Analogous colors: colors that are adjacent to each other on the color wheel; also known as related colors.

Aniline dye: transparent pigment made from aniline, a poisonous derivative of benzene; characterized by brilliant hues and full saturation; a strong solution can be made by putting one teaspoon of dye into a quart of boiling water.

Animal glue: a natural glue (a byproduct of the meat-packing industry) used for securing muslin to flat frames and as a binder in dry pigment and binder scene paint.

Anvil: a heavy, solid metal device with variously shaped faces; used in conjunction with a mechanic's or blacksmith's hammer for shaping metal.

Appliqué: a decorative item attached to a basic form.

Apron: the flat extension of the stage floor that projects from the proscenium arch toward the audience.

Arc: an electric current that leaps the gap between two closely placed electrodes.

Arc welder: a welder that uses an electrical arc to melt the metals being welded. The approximately ⅛-inch-diameter electrode melts and flows into the welding zone to provide filler metal.

Arena stage: a stage completely surrounded by the audience.

Armature: a basic skeletal form that holds the covering materials in the desired shape or alignment.

Artistic director: person responsible for the major artistic decisions of a theatrical production company — hiring of production personnel, selection of season, and so on.

As-built: a document that describes any deviations made from the original plans during construction. Sound design as-builts are typically made by noting on the original drawing any deviations made from the original specifications.

Assignable: in this case, the property of being able to be assigned; e.g., an assignable input may be connected to any output or any number of outputs.

Asymmetrical balance: a sense of equipoise achieved through dynamic tension created by the juxtaposition of dissimilar design elements.

Attenuating: decreasing.

Atom: the smallest particle of a chemical element that retains the structural properties of that element.

Atomic theory: a generally accepted theory concerning the structure and composition of substances.

Attenuate: to decrease or lessen.

Auditorium: the seating area from which the audience observes the action of a play.

Auger bits: spiral-shaped bits designed to be used with a brace; used for drilling holes (¼ inch to approximately 2 inches in diameter) in wood.

Backing: flats, drops, or draperies placed on the offstage side of doors and similar openings to prevent the audience from seeing backstage.

Backpainting: literally to paint on the back. You paint the back, or reverse, side of the scenery or drop.

Backsaw: a fine-toothed (twelve to fourteen teeth per inch) crosscut saw with a stiffening spine on its back; used with a miter box to make accurate miter cuts.

Balance: the arrangement of parts of a composition to create a sense of restfulness; also, to adjust the loudness and equalization levels of individual signals while mixing, to achieve an appropriate blend.

Balanced line: a sound cable in which two insulated conductors are wrapped in a braided or foil shield.

Bald cap: a latex cap that covers a person's hair.

Ball peen hammer: a hammer made of hardened steel with a round ball on the back of its head; used for bending and shaping metal and seating rivets.

Baluster: a vase-shaped vertical member that supports the handrail of a staircase rail.

Band saw: a stationary power saw with a narrow continuous loop (or band) blade that passes through a table that supports the work; used for making curvilinear cuts.

Banister: the vertical member that supports the handrail of a staircase rail.

Bar clamp: similar to a pipe clamp except a notched bar is substituted for the pipe.

Barn door: an accessory for a Fresnel spotlight whose movable flippers are swung into the beam to control it.

Base coat: the first coat of the finished paint job; provides the basic color for the ensuing texture coats.

Bass-reflex speaker enclosure: an insulated box with a carefully designed hole or port in front that synchronizes the phase of the rearward speaker excursion with its forward excursion to reinforce the bass frequencies.

Batten: a metal pipe (generally 1¼ to 1½ inches in diameter) attached to the onstage lines from a rope-set or counterweight system. Scenery is attached to the batten.

Batten-clamp drop: a drop that can be quickly attached to or removed from a batten by the use of batten clamps.

Battened butt joint: two pieces of lumber butted end to end with a small piece of similar width attached directly above the joint.

Battery memory: recharging batteries with nickel-cadmium (NiCd) technologies shortens the life of the batteries unless they were fully depleted prior to recharging. Nickel-metal-hydride (NiMH) batteries have the same memory loss issue, just not as severe.

Beam angle: that point where the light emitted by an instrument is diminished by 50 percent when compared with the output of the center of the beam.

Beam projector: a lensless instrument with a parabolic primary reflector and a spherical secondary reflector that creates an intense shaft of light with little diffusion.

Belaying pin: vertical pipes extending above and below the pin rail. Used to secure the loose ends of spot lines.

Belt clamp: a woven nylon belt with a ratchet device to tighten the belt around the work; used to clamp irregularly shaped objects.

Belt sander: a handheld, portable power tool that uses belts of sandpaper for rapid sanding of (primarily) wood.

Bench grinder: a stationary stand- or bench-mounted power tool consisting of an electric motor with shafts extending from either end; various grinding and buffing wheels, as well as wire brushes, can be mounted on the shafts to perform a variety of grinding, buffing, and polishing functions.

Bench sander: a stationary stand- or bench-mounted, power tool that consists of a combination of a belt and a disk sander; used to bevel or smooth the surface or edges of wood and some plastics.

Bevel protractor: measuring device similar to the combination square except that the angle of the blade is adjustable; used for marking angles between 0 and 90 degrees.

Bevel set: a measuring device similar to a tri square except that the angle between the blade and handle is adjustable; used for transferring angles from one piece of work to another.

Bi-amplified: a speaker system with two built-in amplifiers; one driving the woofer, the other driving a combined mid-range/tweeter.

Bidirectional: two directions; a microphone pickup pattern primarily receptive to the front and back.

Binder: an adhesive in paint that "glues" the pigment and fillers to the painted material after the vehicle has evaporated.

Biscuit: thin, oval-shaped, made of compressed wood shavings, expands when wet with glue.

Blackout: When the stage is completely dark. The stage lights are out and no other lights are on.

Bleeding: the capillary migration of an applied dye or paint to an area outside the area to which it is applied.

Blemish (in wood): refers to any defect that weakens the wood by breaking its continuous parallel graining. Examples include knots, missing wood, wane, and so forth.

Blend: a combination of more than one type of fiber, blends are created to take advantage of the best properties of all fibers in the blend.

Blocking: the actors' movements on the stage.

Block out: in makeup, to cover with soap, spirit gum, wax, material, or preformed plastic film so that no hair is evident.

Block plane: a small plane with a shallow (approximately 15 to 20 degrees) blade angle; used to smooth across the grain of wood.

Blueline: to copy drawings made on tracing vellum; the lines are printed in blue or, sometimes, in black; also known as the diazo process.

Blueprint: an obsolete mechanical drawing-reproduction technique in which the background is blue and the lines are white.

Board foot: a unit of measurement equivalent to a piece of stock lumber that is 12 inches long, 12 inches wide, and 1 inch thick.

Board operators: the electricians who run the light board during rehearsals and performances.

Bobbinet: a transparent, open, hexagonal weave material; used as a glass substitute, diffusion drop, net backing for cutout drops, and similar applications.

Bobby pin: a hairpin made of springy flat metal wire bent in a tight U shape. The legs — one straight, the other wavy — touch each other and provide the clamping power to hold the hair in place. Generally used with shorter hair.

Bodice: the upper part of a woman's dress.

Bogus paper: a heavy, soft, absorbent paper; similar to blotter paper.

Bolt cutter: heavy-duty shears with a great deal of leverage; used to cut through bolts and mild-steel round stock up to ½ inch in diameter.

Book: to fold hinged flats together so that they resemble a book.

Book ceiling: two large flats about the same width as the proscenium arch, stored in a booked position in the flies; when needed to create a ceiling, they are opened and lowered onto the walls of the set.

Boomerang: (1) a rolling scaffold with several levels; used for painting vertical scenery; (2) a device to hold color media in a followspot.

Boosting: increasing.

Borderlights: any lights hung above the stage, behind the borders (horizontal masking pieces). In this context the borderlights were striplights — long, narrow, troughlike fixtures usually containing eight to twelve individual lamps.

Borders: wide, short, framed or unframed cloth drops suspended over the stage to prevent the audience from seeing above the stage. In the Restoration theatre, borders normally matched the decorative treatment on the wings and drops. In modern practice, borders are frequently made of black, unpainted velour.

Bottom hanger iron: flying hardware; a metal strap iron with a D ring at the top and a hooked foot at the bottom; used at the bottom of heavy flats to support the load under compression.

Box: to pour paint back and forth between buckets to ensure a complete and uniform mix.

Box-end wrench: a wrench with a closed, toothed head that must be fit over the head of the bolt or nut; used to tighten bolts and nuts.

Box nail: nail with a narrower shaft than a common nail, to reduce the chance of splitting the lumber.

Brace: a hand-cranked drill used for turning auger bits; used for drilling large-diameter holes in wood.

Brace cleat: bracing hardware attached to the stile on the back of a flat to provide means for securing a stage brace to the flat.

Breathes: a term that defines a material's ability to transmit heat, air, and water vapor.

Breakin: device used to connect dimmers to multicables. One end has a female Socapex connector, and the other end — the separate circuits — has plugs compatible with the output receptacles on the dimmer packs.

Breakout: device used to connect multicables to lighting fixtures. One end terminates in a male Socapex connector, and the other end — the separate circuits — typically is equipped with female twist-lock or stage pin receptacles.

Brocade: fabric similar to damask but lighter in weight; woven patterns achieved by weaving high-luster yarn into a matte-finish background can be either raised or flat; used for making costumes, upholstery, and decorative drapery.

Bulb: the Pyrex glass or synthetic quartz container for a lamp filament and gaseous environment; synonymous with envelope.

Burn: to record on a CD.

Butcher paper: a medium-weight brown paper, available in 36-inch-wide rolls; also known by its trade name, Kraft paper.

Butted: to place items end to end.

Butt joint: a wood joint; two pieces of wood are square cut and fit together end to end, end to edge, edge to edge, end to face, or edge to face.

Butt weld: a welded metal joint; the pieces being welded are joined edge to edge.

Cabinet drawing: a type of detail drawing that subscribes to the principles of oblique drawing except that all depth measurements are reduced by one-half or some similar ratio, such as 1:4.

Cable run: the length of audio hookup cable needed to connect a power amplifier to a speaker.

Cable picks: the attachment point for a bundle of (typically) electrical or sound cables to be suspended above the stage or auditorium.

CAD environment: the on-screen digital workspace in which objects are modeled in CAD. Includes the "modeling space," tools, menus, and buttons used to control the program.

Call: to tell specific crew members when to perform their cues.

CAM software: software that uses CAD files of drawings to create commands for a CNC machine to follow.

Canvas head block: a block of material in the shape of a head, covered with canvas. Wigs are pinned to it for styling and storage.

Capacitance: the electrical capacity of a condenser.

Capacitor: an electronic component composed of two conductive plates separated and insulated from each other; used to store an electrostatic charge.

Carcass: the foundation structure of something, for example, the framework of a cabinet.

Cardioid: a heart-shaped pickup pattern that primarily picks up sounds in front of, and slightly to the sides of, the microphone.

Card stock: a thick cardboard, similar in thickness to 3-by-5 notecards and file folders.

Carpenter's level: a 2- to 3-foot piece of wooden, steel, or aluminum I beam with glass-tube spirit levels at either end and the middle; used to determine true horizontal and vertical.

Carpenter's rule: see folding wood rule.

Carpenter's vise: a vise for holding wood; attached to a workbench, one or both faces are covered with hardwood to prevent the vise from scratching, denting, or marring the surface of the work.

Carriage: the part of a stair unit that supports the tread and risers.

Carriage bolt: a bolt whose upper face has a rounded surface and whose under-side has a slightly tapered square collar a little wider than the diameter of the bolt shaft; used to join wood to wood or wood to metal.

Cartooning: the process of transferring line work (and color blocks) from the painter's elevations to the scenery.

Casein: a natural or synthetically derived phosphoprotein — a chief component of milk.

Casein paint: a paint with a casein binder; has good covering power, is water-resistant when fully dry, and can usually be thinned with a ratio of between two and four parts water to one part paint concentrate.

Casket lock: a heavy-duty hidden lock used to hold platforms together and for similar applications.

Cassette tape: audio recorder tape, also used in computer storage.

Caster: a wheel/axle device attached to platforms and the like to make them roll; casters for theatrical use should have hard rubber tires, a load rating of at least 300 pounds, and sturdy construction.

Casting resins: liquid plastics used for creating forms in molds.

Cavea: Roman term for auditorium.

C clamp: a clamp composed of a U-shaped frame with a threaded shaft; work is clamped between a pressure plate at one end of the U and the toe of the shaft; used for a wide variety of jobs, such as holding work together while parts are being assembled or while glue joints are drying.

Ceiling plate: flying hardware; a flat metal plate with an O ring in the center; attached to the primary structural members of ceiling flats to provide a means of attaching the flying lines to the ceiling.

Centerline: a leader line that runs perpendicular to the set line from the midpoint or center of the opening of the proscenium arch.

Center-line sectional: a sectional drawing whose cutting plane is the center line of the stage and auditorium; used to show the height of the various elements of the theatre, stage and any pertinent set pieces, lighting, sound and other equipment.

Center punch: a pointed tool made of hard steel; used for indenting shallow holes in wood and metal.

Centrifugal force: force that moves away from the center; for example, the circular motion of electrons spinning around a nucleus generates centrifugal force.

Chalk line: a metal or plastic housing holding a long piece of twine and filled with dry scenic pigment; used for marking straight lines.

Channel: an individual control in a channel control system. Channel control is an electronic patching method used with computer boards. One or more dimmers can be assigned to a control channel, which in turn controls the intensity level of those dimmers.

Channel control: an electronic patching system in which one or more dimmers can be assigned to a control channel, which in turn controls the intensity level of those dimmers.

Character: the distinctive qualities, traits, and personality of a person, place, or thing. Also, the emotional quality (e.g., soft, hard, harsh, sensuous) of a line.

Cheat sheet: a quick reference to the specific dimmer or channel that controls a specific light; also known as a magic sheet.

Chiffon: a sheer, usually translucent, cloth frequently made from rayon or silk; used for scarves and diaphanous blouses and gowns.

Chopper: *see* shutter.

Chroma: *see* saturation.

Chuck: the adjustable jawed clamp at the end of a drill that holds the drill bits.

Circuit: a conductive path through which electricity flows; also, to connect a lighting instrument to a stage circuit.

Circuit breaker: a device to protect a circuit from an overload; it has a magnetic device that trips open to break circuit continuity.

Circular saw: a portable circular-bladed saw; the angle and depth of cut is variable; used to cross- and angle-cut as well as rip stock and plywood.

Claw hammer: a hammer with two sharply curved claws projecting from the back of its head that facilitates nail removal; used for driving nails.

Cleat: a piece of wood used to brace, block, or reinforce.

Clip art: digitized pictures that can be transferred, or clipped, from the original program into a document on which you are working.

Clothesline: a small-diameter cotton rope; not used for raising or suspending loads, but is the standard rope for lash lines and is used as the operating rope for traveling drapes (travelers).

Clout nail: a wedge-shaped nail made of soft iron used to attach cornerblocks and keystones to the frame of a flat; it is driven through the wood onto a steel backing plate, which curls the end of the nail back into the lumber.

Club: in context, refers to night clubs in which high-energy music (live or recorded) is the prime attraction.

Coated box nail: a box nail with an adhesive applied to the shaft that tightly bonds the nail to the wood.

Cobbler: one who makes shoes.

Cold chisel: a chisel made of hard steel; used for cutting or shearing mild steel and nonferrous metals.

Cold-press finish: a slight surface texture achieved by pressing paper between cold rollers; no oil residue results, so the paper can be used with transparent watercolor, designer's gouache, acrylic, markers, pencils, pastel, and so forth.

Collage: a picture made of various materials (e.g., paper, cloth) glued on a surface; can include drawn or photographic images as well.

Color: a perception created in the brain by the stimulation of the retina by light waves of certain lengths; a generic term applied to all light waves contained in the visible spectrum.

Color frame: a lightweight metal holder for color media that fits in a holder at the front of a lighting instrument.

Color media: the plastic or glass filters used to modify the color of light projected by lighting instruments.

Combination square: a 12-inch steel rule with a movable handle angled at 45 and 90 degrees; used for marking those two angles, and the rule can be used for measuring.

Commando: a lightweight cotton fabric with a short, feltlike, almost matted pile; available in two weights and widths, the heavyweight is suitable for stage drapery; the material face is generally too susceptible to wear for use as an upholstery fabric; also known as duvetyn.

Common nail: nail with a large head and thick shank; used for heavier general construction.

Complementary: two hues that, when combined, theoretically yield white in light or black in pigment; colors that are opposite to each other on a color wheel. In practice, mixing complementary pigment colors results in complex dark grays, not true black.

Composition: an arrangement of parts to create a whole.

Compound curves: a surface that curves in more than one direction (like a ball) or changes the radius of its curve (like a playground slide).

Compression: the process used to attenuate loud spikes in an electronic signal.

Compressor: (mechanical) a pump that drives air into a tank; the output pressure from the tank is controlled by a valve called a regulator; (electronic) an electronic device or software that automatically

reduces signal amplitude when a predetermined intensity level is reached.

Concentric revolving stages: a revolving stage with, usually, two sections, one rotating inside the other.

Concert: in context, primarily refers to touring rock and country western shows.

Condensing lens: a device that condenses the direct and reflected light from a source and concentrates it on the slide-plane aperture of a projector.

Conduit: thin-wall metal (aluminum or steel) tubing; used as a housing for electrical wiring and decorative stage material.

Conduit bender: a tool for bending conduit.

Cones: nerve cells in the retina that are sensitive to bright light; they respond to red, blue, or green light.

Connecting strip: an electrical gutter or wireway that carries a number of stage circuits; the circuits terminate on the connecting strip in female receptacles.

Constructed sound: any sound created by editing, manipulating, or changing previously recorded sounds.

Construction adhesive: also called panel adhesive. An adhesive contained in a caulking tube; dispensed with a caulking gun. Available in a number of formulations for use in gluing wall panels to studs (wood to wood), Styrofoam to wood, wood to metal, and so forth.

Construction calendar: a calendar that details when various technical elements of a production will be constructed.

Construction crew: those who build the set, move it into the theatre, and set it up onstage.

Construction line: in a two-line-weight system, a thick line 0.5 mm thick (in pencil) or 0.020 to 0.025 inch thick (in pen).

Contact cement: an adhesive for bonding nonporous surfaces together; surfaces bond as soon as they come in contact with each other.

Continental parallel: a platform made of a folding framework of nonvariable height; the top and center supports are removable; the frame folds into a more compact unit than does the standard parallel.

Continuous-loop cable: a cable whose ends have been spliced or joined to form the cable into a loop.

Contrast: the juxtaposition of dissimilar elements.

Coping saw: a lightweight handsaw composed of a U-shaped frame with a narrow, fine-toothed (sixteen to eighteen teeth per inch) replaceable blade; used for making curvilinear cuts in thin plywood and lumber.

Corduroy: a cotton material whose pile ridges, called wales, alternate with a low-luster backing; available in a wide variety of wale widths and depths; heavier weights are used for upholstery, while lighter weights are used in costuming; waleless corduroy is similar to a short-nap velour, with similar uses.

Cornerblock: a triangular-shaped piece of ¼-inch plywood used to reinforce the joint between a stile and a rail of a flat.

Corner brace: a diagonal internal framing member that helps keep a flat square.

Corner plate: an L-shaped piece of ¹⁄₁₆-inch galvanized steel, predrilled for use with flat-head wood screws; used to reinforce corners of doors, windows, and so on.

Corrugated fasteners: corrugated strips of metal used primarily to hold lightweight frames together.

Costume designer: person responsible for the design, visual appearance, and function of the costumes, accessories, and makeup.

Costumer: person responsible for the construction of the costumes and supervision of the costume shop.

Cotton canvas: a durable lightweight, coarse-weave material; used for covering platforms and making ground cloths.

Cotton duck: a lightweight cotton canvas; used more in costumes than scenic construction.

Cotton linters: the short hairs covering the cotton seed.

Cotton rep: a tough cotton fabric with a ribbed finish similar to a narrow, short-nap corduroy; good for stage draperies, costumes, and upholstery.

Counterweight arbor: a metal cradle that holds counterbalancing weights used in flying.

Crash: in reference to hard drives, to become inoperative. Data cannot usually be retrieved from a hard drive that has "crashed."

Crepe: a thin, crinkle-finished, soft cloth usually made from rayon, silk, or fine cotton; frequently used for women's blouses.

Crescent wrench: *see* adjustable-end wrench.

Crosscut saw: a handsaw with an approximately 26-inch blade whose angle-sharpened teeth bend outward so that the kerf is wider than the blade; designed to cut across the grain of the wood. Crosscut saws with ten to twelve teeth per inch are suitable for most scenic purposes.

Crossover network: an electronic device that splits the signal from the amplifier into frequency ranges most appropriate

for use by woofers, midrange speakers, and tweeters.

Crowbar: a round metal bar with flattened metal claws similar to those on a claw or rip hammer on one end and a tapered wedge on the other.

Cue: a directive for action, for example, a change in the lighting.

Cue file: a file containing the production sound cues in sequential order.

Cueing: designing the light cues. Manipulating, and recording, the distribution, intensity, movement, and color of the lights for each cue to create the appropriate look for that moment in the play.

Cure: to harden and reach full strength (in reference to adhesives).

Cut awl: a portable power saw with a reciprocating blade mounted in a swiveling head; available with a variety of blades to make intricate curvilinear cuts in materials ranging from fabric to wood, paper, and plastic.

Cut list: A list of all the color media to be used on every fixture during a production. Typically listed by required number, gelframe size, color. For example: 20 — 6″ — Roscolux 09.

Cutoff saw: a semiportable stand-mounted circular-bladed power saw that can be equipped with a wood or metal cutting blade for square and angle cutting of lumber or metal stock; can be set up for cutting either wood (wooden table without holding clamps) or metal (metal table with holding clamps); also known as a motorized miter box.

Cutout line: *see* silhouette.

Cutter: person who pins patterns to fabrics and cuts the material.

Cutting plane: the plane at which an object is theoretically cut to produce the most appropriate view.

CYM color mixing: color mixing using the secondary colors of light—cyan, yellow, and magenta.

Cyanoacrylate cement: a powerful, rapid-bonding adhesive that will bond almost anything; generically known by the trade names Super Glue, Krazy Glue, and so forth.

Cyc light: a lensless instrument with an eccentric reflector used to create a smooth wash of light on a cyc or skytab from a close distance.

Cyclorama: a large drop used to surround the stage.

Dado head: a specialty circular saw blade consisting of a set of toothed blades that sandwich a chisel-like chipper. The blades smooth-cut the outside edges of the kerf while the chipper gouges out the wood

between the blades. The distance between the blades is variable; used with table and radial-arm saws.

Dado joint: a wood joint made by cutting a notch or groove in the face of one piece of lumber to receive the edge of another piece of stock.

Damask: a rich-appearing cloth with raised patterns of high-luster yarn that are normally woven into the matte finish of the background cloth; used for making costumes, upholstery, and decorative drapery.

Dead hang: to suspend without means of raising or lowering.

Dead lift: to lift without counter balancing.

Deburr: to remove protruding, ragged edges on metal caused by drilling or other machining processes.

Decay time: the time it takes a sound to become inaudible.

Decibel: a unit for expressing the intensity of sounds; an increase or decrease of one decibel is just about the smallest change in loudness that the human ear can detect.

Decking: the covering surface of a structure on which people will walk.

Decorative prop: any item that is used to enhance the setting visually but is not specifically touched by an actor, such as window curtains, pictures, doilies, table lamps, bric-a-brac, and so forth.

Delay: refers to the time interval that the second part of a split time fade follows the first.

Demi-mask: a mask, normally mounted on a stick, that covers half the face.

Denim: a coarsely woven cotton or cotton blend twill.

Designer's cue sheet: a form used by the lighting designer to record pertinent information (dimmer levels, timing, "go" point, and so forth) about every cue in the production.

Design style: a recognizable pattern of compositional elements that provides a distinctive reflection of the social and political history of the time.

Detail drawings: drawings that describe the detail of objects. Usually drawn in a fairly large scale, normally between ¾ inch = 1 foot and 1½ inches = 1 foot.

Detailing: trim, appliqués, buttons, ribbons, braid, and so forth attached to a garment to enhance its appearance.

Diagonal cutters: pliers with beveled cutting faces on the jaw rather than flat gripping faces; used for cutting soft wire.

Dielectric material: material that is a poor conductor of electricity but a good supporter of electrostatic fields. In LED technology, these properties help focus the RF energy on the sealed bulb.

Dichroic filter: a filter that passes a specifically selected wavelength of light and reflects all others. A red dichroic filter allows red light to pass but reflects all other wavelengths.

Dichroic mirrors: a mirror that reflects a specifically selected wavelength of light and allows all others to pass through the mirror. A red dichroic mirror reflects red light and allows all other wavelengths to pass through it.

Diffuse: to soften the appearance of light by using a translucent filtering element to scatter the light rays.

Digital delay: a device used to time-align the sound emitted from two different sources.

Digital Micromirror Device (DMD): DMDs are optical semiconductors whose rectangular surface is typically covered with from several hundred thousand to several million micromirrors. The number of micromirrors corresponds with the number of pixels in the image display.

Digital tape recording: a form of recording in which the audio information is stored on the magnetic tape as binary information rather than an analog signal.

Digitizing tablet: an electro-mechanical device that converts the pressure of a stylus on a flat plate (tablet) into binary information that can be understood by the computer. Also referred to as a digitzer tablet or graphics tablet.

Dimension: the relative length and width of a line.

Dimmer: an electrical device that controls the intensity of a light source connected to it.

Dimmer circuit: an electrical circuit terminating on one end at a dimmer. The other end terminates at either a patch panel or onstage. Synonymous with stage circuit when it terminates onstage.

Distortion: an unintended change in the waveform of a sound frequency. Typically results in a falsified reproduction of the original sound.

Director: person responsible for interpreting the script, creating a viable production concept, and directing the actors.

Discrete: separate and complete; in context, pertaining to information represented by binary code.

Distress: to create a worn or aged appearance as with fabric, wood, or metal.

Distributed dimming: a concept in which dimmers are placed at the point of use — close to where the fixture to be dimmed is located — rather than in a centralized dimmer racks.

Double-convex lens: outwardly curved surfaces on both sides of the lens.

Double-headed nails: nails with two heads; they are driven into the wood until the lower head is flush with the surface, leaving the upper head exposed so that it can be pulled out easily; used for scaffolding or any temporary structure that needs to be dismantled quickly.

Double plano-convex lens train: two plano-convex lenses placed with their curved surfaces facing each other; creates a system that has a shorter focal length than either of its component lenses.

Double-sided: covered on both sides.

Double whip: a block and tackle configuration that provides a 2:1 mechanical advantage.

Douser: a mechanical dimming device with movable slats or an iris to block or allow light to pass.

Dowel: a short cylinder of hardwood, usually birch.

Doweled joint: a butt joint that is internally supported by dowel pegs.

Drape: a vertical element of heavy fabric that frames the sides of a window or an archway.

Draw to scale: to produce a likeness that is a proportional reduction of an object.

Dremel tool: a hand-held router similar to a dentist's drill that can be equipped with a number of bits for grinding, cutting, or carving of wood, metal, and plastic.

Dress: to place decorative props such as curtains, doilies, knickknacks, or magazines on the set to help make the environment look lived-in and provide clues to the personalities of the characters who inhabit the set. Also, to work with hair or a wig to create a specific style or look.

Dressers: costume-crew personnel who assist actors in putting on their costumes.

Dress rehearsal: a run-through with all technical elements, including costumes and makeup.

Drill press: a stationary bench or stand-mounted power drill with a variety of speeds. The chuck will generally hold bits up to ½ inch in diameter.

Drive wheel: a motorized rubber-tired wheel driven by a variable-speed electric motor.

Drop: a large expanse of cloth, usually muslin or scenic canvas, on which something (a landscape, sky, street, room) is usually painted.

Drop box: a small connecting strip, generally containing four to eight circuits, that can be clamped to a boom or a pipe.

Drum winch: in this case, a motorized system in which steel cables are wound around a drum or cylinder and the taking up, or letting out, of the cables is controlled by the rotation of the drum. Each drum winch is equipped with a motor, gearbox, and brake.

Dry: acoustically absorbent; dead.

Dry brushing: a painting technique frequently used to. create a wood-grain appearance; done by lightly charging a brush and lightly stroking it across the surface of the work.

Drywall: gypsum board typically used to cover interior walls in home construction; normally ½ inch thick although other thicknesses are available.

Ducted-port speaker enclosure: a speaker enclosure similar in operational theory to the bass-reflex enclosure except that a tube of specific diameter and length is substituted for the open hole, or port; it reinforces bass frequencies.

Dust mask: a device covering the nose and mouth that filters particulate matter from the air.

Dutchman: a 5- to 6-inch-wide strip of cloth of the same material as the flat covering; used to hide the joints between flats in a wall unit.

Duvetyn: *see* commando.

Dynamic range: sensitivity to changes in loudness; the ratio between the largest and smallest intensity levels of sound. Measured in decibels.

Effects head: a motor-driven unit capable of producing crude moving images with a scenic projector.

Electric: any pipe that is used to hold lighting instruments.

Electrical current: the flow or movement of electrons through a conductor.

Electrical potential: the difference in electrical charge between two bodies; measured in volts.

Electric glue pot: a thermostatically controlled pot used for melting animal glue.

Electric hand drill: a portable, hand-held power drill; some models have variable-speed and reverse controls; it generally accepts bit shanks up to ⅜ inch in diameter.

Electricians: those who work on the stage lighting for a production.

Electrician's cue sheet: a form used by the board operator that contains the primary operating instructions for every lighting cue in the production.

Electricity: a directed flow of electrons used to create kinetic energy.

Electric screwdriver: a portable, hand-held power tool that resembles an electric hand drill; equipped with a variable-speed motor, a clutch, and a chuck that holds a screwdriver tip; used to insert and remove screws.

Electron: a negatively charged fundamental particle that orbits around the nucleus of an atom.

Electronics: the field of science and engineering concerned with the behavior and control of electrons within devices and systems, and the utilization of those systems.

Elevator stage: a large elevator used to raise scenic elements or whole sets stored beneath the stage to stage level.

Elevator trap: a small elevator used to shift small pieces of scenery, or an actor, from the basement underneath the stage to the stage or vice versa. Usually no larger than 4 × 4 or 4 × 6 feet. Also known as a disappearance trap.

Ellipsoidal reflector floodlight: a lensless instrument with a conical ellipse reflector; used for lighting cycs and drops; also known as a scoop.

Ellipsoidal reflector spotlight: a lighting instrument characterized by hard-edged light with little diffusion; designed for long throws, it is manufactured with fixed and variable focal-length lenses; the light beam is shaped with internally mounted shutters.

Emery cloth: fabric whose surface has been coated with abrasive grit; used for smoothing wood, metal, and plastic.

Enamel: an oil-, lacquer-, or synthetic-base paint that has a hard surface and excellent covering power. It is usually formulated so that it dries with a smooth satin or gloss finish.

Envelope: the Pyrex glass or synthetic quartz container for a lamp filament and gaseous environment; synonymous with bulb.

Epoxy: an extremely strong, waterproof plastic most frequently used in the theatre as an adhesive and casting resin.

Epoxy-resin adhesive: a two-part epoxy-based adhesive available in a variety of formulations that enable the user to do gluing, filling, and painting.

Equalizer: an electronic device that selectively boosts or attenuates specific frequencies or ranges of frequencies.

Equipment stream: in sound systems, the connected devices — computer/ mixer/amp/loudspeakers and so forth — through which the signal travels.

Extra: a non speaking part. A person who provides "visual dressing" for the scene.

Eyebrow mask: a thin piece of plastic film or latex glued over the eyebrow; also known as an eyebrow block.

Facing: thin hardboard, MDF, or plywood attached to the face of a platform.

Fade-in: a gradual increase; in lighting, usually from darkness to a predetermined level of brightness. Synonymous with fade-up.

Fade-out: a gradual decrease; in lighting, usually from a set level of brightness to darkness.

Fader: a device, usually electronic, that effects a gradual changeover from one circuit to another; in lighting it changes the intensity of one or more dimmer circuits; in sound it changes audio circuits or channels.

Fade rate: the amount of time it takes for a fade — either fade-up or fade-down — to be completed.

False proscenium: a rigid framework covered with drapery material that is used to adjust the height and width of the proscenium arch. Sometimes un-framed drapes are used to create a false proscenium.

Faux finish: using techniques with paints/varnishes to create the illusion of a particular type of surface or material, for example, painting wood to look like metal or stone.

FEL lamp: lamps made in the United States are designated with a three-letter code that specifies all design criteria such as wattage, voltage, filament and base type, color-temperature-rated life, and so forth, FEL specifies a very specific 1,000 watt lamp.

Feedback: the return of information about the result of an activity.

Feedback loop: the flow of information within a control system that allows for self-correction based on differences between the actual output and the desired output.

Felt: a material made by matting together short fibers by the use of heat, water, and light pressure.

Ferrule: the metal part of a brush that binds the bristles to the handle.

Field angle: that point where the light output diminishes to 10 percent of the output of the center of the beam.

Filament: the light-producing element of a lamp; usually made of tungsten wire.

Filler: a material that creates opacity (covering power) in paint.

Filler rod: a metal piece of the same composition as the material being welded; used to replace the metal lost during welding or to fill a hole or groove in the work.

Fillet weld: a welded metal joint; made when the edge of one piece is welded to the face of another; both sides of the joint should be welded.

Fill light: the light or lights that fill the shadows created by the key light.

Finish nail: a nail with a slender shaft and minute head; designed to be driven below the surface of the wood so that the nail head can be hidden.

First electric: the onstage pipe for lighting instruments that is closest, from the onstage side, to the proscenium arch.

Five-quarter lumber: a specialty lumber, straight grained and free from knots, that is 1¼ inches thick.

Fixture: *see* lighting instrument.

Flange weld: a welded metal joint; similar to a butt weld, except the edges of the material are bent up; the weld is made by melting the upturned flanges.

Flannel: a lightweight, loosely woven material usually made from soft-finish wool, wool blend, or cotton thread; used for men's and women's suits, trousers, and shirts.

Flat: a framework, normally made of wood or metal; usually covered with fabric, although a variety of other covering materials may be used.

Flat-head wood screw: common screw with a flat head that is beveled on the underside to easily dig into the wood; used for attaching hardware (hinges, doorknobs) and joining various wood elements together.

Flexible glue: animal glue with glycerine added.

Floor line: the base of the vertical plane in a perspective drawing. For a proscenium sketch, it is usually drawn across the stage in contact with the upstage edge of the proscenium arch.

Floor painting: painting scenery — flats, drops, and so forth — on the floor rather than standing up or attached to a paint frame.

Floor plate: bracing hardware; a block of wood with a non-skid material (foam, rubber) attached to the bottom; the foot of a stage brace is attached to the top of the floor plate, and weights (sandbags, counterweights) are piled on to keep it from moving.

Floor pocket: a connecting box, usually containing three to six circuits, whose top is mounted flush with the stage floor.

Floppy disk: a thin piece of plastic coated with metal oxide, used to record the information stored in a computer's memory.

Fluorocarbons: a family of tough, durable, low-friction, nonstick plastics best known by the trade name Teflon; used in the theatre as a bearing surface where its slippery qualities can be used to advantage.

Flush: smooth, level, even.

Flux: a chemical that reduces surface oxidation and thus aids in soldering or welding.

Fly: to raise an object or person above the stage floor with ropes or cables.

Fly cyc: a single drop, hung on a U-shaped pipe, that surrounds the stage on three sides.

Fly loft: the open space above the stage where the scenery and equipment are flown.

Focal length: the distance from the lens at which light rays converge to a point; for lenses used in stage lighting instruments, the focal length is usually measured in even inches.

Focus: to direct light from the lighting instruments to a specific area.

Folding wood rule: a 6-foot wooden rule, composed of twelve segments that fold into a unit 7½ inches long; used for measuring lumber in scenic construction.

Foley effects: named for sound-effects artist Jack D. Foley. Foley was famous for his work creating sound effects for films using everyday items to simulate sounds, such as flapping gloves for bird flight and celery for breaking bones.

Followspot: a lighting instrument with a high-intensity, narrow beam; mounted in a stand that allows it to tilt and swivel so that the beam can "follow" an actor.

Font: a particular style or design of typeface.

Footlights: lights placed along the front edge of the stage.

Forced perspective: a process that creates apparent depth in a set by angling the horizontal line.

Foreshortening: representing the lines of an object as shorter than they actually are in order to give the illusion of proper relative size.

Form: space enclosed within a line or lines that meet or cross; also, elements that have similar physical characteristics, such as arena theatres, thrust stages, proscenium stages, and so forth.

Found theatre spaces: structures originally designed for some other purpose that have been converted into performing spaces.

Framing square: a large steel L, typically 16 inches on the bottom leg and 24 on the vertical leg; used for checking the accuracy of 90-degree corner joints.

Free electron: an electron that has broken away from its "home" atom to float free.

French enamel varnish (FEV): a mixture of dye and shellac; made by mixing alcohol-based leather dye (e.g., Fiebing's Leather Dye) with shellac that has been reduced (1:1) with denatured alcohol.

Frequency: the rate at which an object vibrates; measured in hertz (cycles per second).

Fresnel lens: a type of step lens with the glass cut away from the convex face of the lens.

Fresnel spotlight: a spotlight that produces a soft, diffused light; the Fresnel lens is treated on the plano side to diffuse the light.

Front elevation: a front view of each wall segment of the set, including all detail such as windows, doors, pictures, and trim.

Front-of-house: the area in an auditorium that is close to the stage.

Front projection screen: an opaque, highly reflective, usually white material used to reflect a projected image; the projector is placed on the audience side of the screen.

Full-scale drawings: scale drawings made actual size.

Full spectrum: containing all the colors of light in approximately the same proportions as sunlight.

Functional model: a three-dimensional thumbnail sketch of a scenic design; normally built on a scale of ¼ or ½ inch to 1 foot; usually made from file folders or similar cardboard; also known as a white model.

Fuse: a device to protect a circuit from an overload; it has a soft metal strip that melts, breaking circuit continuity.

Gaffer's tape: cloth tape, similar in appearance to duct tape. Used for a variety of scenery and lighting shop applications. It is less sticky and easier to tear than duct tape.

Gallery: the elevated walkway where the pin rail is located.

Gantry: a bridge-like structure. In this case, a device mounted above a CNC machine's working surface that is used to support the machine's cutting equipment.

Garbage or slop paint: any paint left over from previous paint jobs; the various paints are mixed and neutralized to create a medium-gray or light-brown hue; frequently used for a prime coat.

Gate: (1) a device or software that identifies a specific signal based on predetermined criteria and sends that signal for further processing; (2) an electronic device used to activate/deactivate a device (typically a microphone) when its signal reaches a predetermined level.

Gauge: a method of describing metal thickness by its weight. Steel, copper, and aluminum all have different gauge numbers. Gauge charts are available online. The rule of thumb for gauge numbers is as follows: The higher the number, the thinner the metal.

Gel: (1) to put a color filter into a color frame and insert it in the color-frame holder of a lighting instrument;

(2) generic name for the plastic color media used in lighting instruments.

Geometry: in CAD drawing, refers to the form/shape of an object being created.

Gesso: plaster of Paris in liquid state; approximately the consistency of sour cream; dries to a hard plaster finish.

Gimp: an ornamental flat braid or round cord used as trimming.

Glaze: a transparent, usually lightly tinted, layer of thin paint.

Gloss: highly reflective, mirrorlike.

Gobo: a thin metal template inserted into an ellipsoidal reflector spotlight to create a shadow pattern of light.

Graded base coat: a base coat that gradually changes hue or value over the height or width of the painted surface.

Grained: A past-tense verb form referring to the "dry-brush wood grain" painting technique.

Grand drape: the curtain that covers the opening of the proscenium arch.

Grand rag: slang synonym for grand drape.

Grand valance: a teaser or border made of the same material as the grand drape. Used in conjunction with the grand drape, it masks the scenery and equipment just upstage of the proscenium arch.

Graphic equalizer: an equalizer with individual slide controls affecting specific, usually fairly narrow, segments of the sound spectrum; so called because the position of the individual controls graphically displays a picture of the equalization of the full sound spectrum.

Graphite: a soft carbon similar to the lead in a pencil; sticks can be purchased in most art supply stores.

Grid: a network of steel I beams supporting elements of the counterweight system.

Grid transfer: transferring a design from an elevation to the scenery by use of a scale grid on the elevation and a full-scale grid on the scenery.

Grommet: a circular metal eyelet used to reinforce holes in fabric.

Grommet set: a hole punch, a small anvil, and a crimping tool; used to seat grommets.

Ground loop: an unwanted current generated when two supposedly isolated circuits use a common ground. Ground loops are a major source of noise and hum in sound systems and can be a potentially lethal shock hazard.

Ground plan: a scale mechanical drawing in the form of a horizontal offset section with the cutting plane passing at whatever level, normally a height of four feet above the stage floor, required to produce the most descriptive view of the set.

Ground row: generally low, horizontal flats used to mask the base of cycs or drops; frequently painted to resemble rows of buildings, hedges, or similar visual elements.

Group: the grouping of two or more dimmers/channels under one controller.

Gusset: a triangular piece of material used to reinforce a corner joint.

Hacksaw: an adjustable frame hand-saw with an extremely fine-toothed (twenty to twenty-five teeth per inch) replaceable blade; used for cutting metal.

Hair pin: a piece of round metal wire bent in a slightly opened U shape. Used with longer hair than bobby pins.

Halved joint: a wood joint made by removing half the thickness of both pieces of lumber in the area to be joined so that the thickness of the finished joint will be no greater than the stock from which it is made; also called a halved lap joint.

Hand: the quality and characteristics of a fabric that can be evaluated or defined by a sense of touch.

Hand drill: a hand-cranked device used for spinning drill bits; used for making small-diameter holes in wood.

Hand power grinder: a portable, hand-held version of the bench grinder; useful on pieces that are too heavy or awkward to be worked with the bench grinder.

Hand power sander: a slightly less powerful version of the hand power grinder; equipped with a flexible disk that provides backing for sanding discs of varying grit; used for rough sanding of wood, metal, and plastic.

Hand prop: a small item that is handled or carried by an actor.

Handrail: the part of the stair rail that is grabbed with the hand; supported by the banister and newel posts.

Hanger iron: flying hardware; a metal strap with a D ring at the top; the hanger iron is attached to the top or bottom of the back of a flat, one end of a line is attached to the D ring, and the other end is attached to a counterweight batten.

Hanging: the process of placing lighting instruments in their specified locations.

Hanging cards: small segments of the light plot, typically pasted onto cardboard so it can be carried in an electrician's pants pocket, that detail all of the hanging information about a specific location such as the first electric or down left boom.

Hanging crew: those responsible for the hanging, circuiting, patching, focusing, and coloring of the lighting instruments; they are under the supervision of the master electrician.

Hanging positions: the various locations around the stage and auditorium where lighting instruments are placed.

Hang out: in this instance, hang out means that most wrinkles will disappear from the fabric if it is hung up.

Hang tag: the small label usually attached to the cardboard core of a bolt of fabric that indicates the percentages of various component fibers.

Hardboard: generic term for composition sheet goods such as Masonite and particle board.

Hard covered: covered with a hard-surfaced material such as plywood. The hard surface is frequently covered with a fabric before painting.

Hard drive: a computer storage device. A spinning magnetic or optical disk on which data are stored and from which data can be retrieved.

Hard teaser: the horizontal element of the false proscenium; usually hung from a counterweighted batten so that its height can easily be adjusted.

Hardware: the physical elements of the computer and the various electronic equipment, printed circuit boards, and so forth inside the computer.

Harmonics: frequencies that are exact multiples of a fundamental pitch or frequency.

Harmony: a sense of blending and unity that is achieved when the various parts of a design fit together to create an orderly, congruous whole.

Head: (1) a housing that holds scenic-projector lenses in fixed positions to project images of a specific size; (2) a high-quality electromagnet on a tape deck or tape recorder that is used to implant, retrieve, or erase electrical data from audio tapes.

Headroom: a power amplifier's ability to handle brief high demands without distorting the signal.

Head block: a multisheave block with two or more pulley wheels, used to change the direction of all the ropes or cables that support the batten.

Header: a small flat that can be placed between two standard-sized flats to create a doorway or window.

Heat gun: a high-temperature air gun, visually similar to a handheld hair dryer.

Heat sink: a metal device that absorbs heat from an operating unit and dissipates it into the air.

Heat welding: the use of a heat gun to fuse two pieces of plastic.

Heavy-duty hand drill: similar to the electric hand drill, but with a heavier-duty motor; the chuck will generally accept bit shanks up to ½ inch in diameter.

Hinged-foot iron: bracing hardware similar to the rigid foot iron but hinged so that it can fold out of the way for storage.

Hole saws: saw-toothed cylinders of hardened steel with a drill bit in the center that is used to center the saw in the work; used with a power drill to make holes from ¾ inch to 2 inches in diameter in wood that is 1½ inches thick or less.

Holidays: sections of a painted surface that appear lighter than the rest of the surface because the area is either unpainted or the paint was too lightly applied. Areas where the painter took a holiday.

Home page: a site or addressable location on the Internet that contains information about (generally) a particular service, interest group, resource, or business.

Homespun: a coarse, loosely woven material usually made from cotton, linen, or wool.

Honeycomb paper: a manufactured paper product with a hexagonal structure similar to a honeycomb.

Hookup sheet: a sheet containing pertinent information (hanging position, circuit, dimmer, color, lamp wattage, focusing notes) about every lighting instrument used in the production. Also known as an instrument schedule.

Horizon line: in perspective drawing, a line representing the meeting of the earth and the sky; normally drawn parallel to the top or bottom edge of the paper.

Horizontal offset section: a section drawing with a horizontal cutting plane; the cutting plane does not remain fixed — it varies to provide views of important details.

Horn: a dispersion device attached to the front of a pressure driver to direct the sound emitted by the pressure driver into a specific pattern.

Hot-melt glue gun: a handheld electric tool that heats sticks of adhesive to make rapid-hold bonds on a wide range of materials, such as wood, plastic, paper, cloth, metal, dirt, sand, and so forth.

Hot mirror: a glass dichroic filter that reflects the infrared spectrum while allowing visible light to pass.

Hot-press finish: a slick, smooth texture achieved by pressing paper between hot rollers; this treatment leaves a thin layer of oil, which makes the paper unsuitable for use with transparent watercolor. It works well with designer's gouache, acrylic, pencils, and markers.

Hot spot: an intense circle of light created when a projector lens is seen through a rear projection screen.

Hot-wire cutter: a tool for cutting foam; it consists of a wire that is heated to incandescence.

House: synonym for auditorium.

Hue: the qualities that differentiate one color from another.

Hypercardioid: a directional, narrow, elongated cardioid pickup pattern that all but eliminates pickup from anywhere except directly in front of, and for a short distance immediately behind, the microphone.

Hyperlink: a link connecting one digital file to another, or a location in a file to a different location in the same or different file. Typically activated by clicking a highlighted word or image on the computer screen.

Illustration board: watercolor paper mounted on pressboard backing.

Image of light: a picture or concept of what the light should look like for a production.

Immersion heater: an electric heater that can be immersed in a bucket of liquid to heat it; used for heating water for starch mixtures, aniline dye, flameproofing solutions, and so forth.

Impact wrench: a power-driven tool that uses sockets to tighten or loosen bolts or nuts; may be either electric or pneumatic.

Impedance: resistance in an AC circuit; the only difference between impedance and resistance is that impedance is defined as resistance to flow in an AC circuit, while "resistance" is defined as resistance to flow in a DC circuit.

Improved stage screw: bracing hardware; an improved version of the stage screw consisting of a steel plug, threaded on the outside and inside, that is inserted into an appropriately sized hole drilled into the stage floor. The screw screws into the plug, and the plug can be removed and a piece of dowel inserted into the floor to fill the hole.

Incident object: the object on which light is falling.

Infinite-baffle speaker enclosure: an air-tight, heavily insulated box that absorbs the sound waves produced by the rearward excursion speaker; it is inefficient and requires a high-wattage amplifier to achieve satisfactory sound levels.

Inert gas: a nonreactive gas. Will not chemically combine to form a compound.

Inertia: the tendency of a body in motion to remain in motion or a body at rest to stay at rest.

Inner above: the elevated area located directly above the inner below in the Elizabethan theatre.

Inner below: the curtained area at the upstage edge of the playing area in the Elizabethan theatre.

Input (general): information put into a system for processing.

Input signal: the electronic signal being sent to a device.

Input voltage: the voltage being fed to a device.

Instrument schedule: a form used to record all of the technical data about each instrument used in the production; also known as a hookup sheet.

Intensity: an objective statement of the power of sound; the relative loudness of a sound.

Iris: a device with movable overlapping metal plates, used with an ellipsoidal reflector spotlight to change the size of the circular pattern of light.

Irregular flat: a flat having nonsquare corners.

Isometric drawing: a scaled mechanical drawing that presents a pictorial view of an object on three axes; the primary axis is perpendicular to the base line and the other two project from its base, in opposite directions, 30 degrees above the base line.

Jack: a triangular brace.

Jig: a device used to hold pieces together in proper positional relationship.

Jog: a flat less than 2 feet wide.

Joint compound: a finishing material the consistency of pudding. Normally used to cover drywall seams.

Joists: parallel beams that support flooring.

Kerf: the width of the cut made by a saw blade.

Keyhole saw: a handsaw with a narrow, tapering blade of ten to twelve teeth per inch; used for making curvilinear cuts in plywood and lumber.

Keyframe: a point in time that marks the beginning or ending of an action. The intermediate action — the action between two keyframes — is filled in frames referred to as "in-betweens." Used in traditional and computer animation.

Key light: the brightest light on a particular scene.

Keystone: a wedge or rectangular-shaped piece of ¼-inch plywood used to reinforce the joint between a stile and toggle bar of a flat.

Keystoning: the linear distortion created when a projector is placed on some angle other than perpendicular to the projection surface.

Kit cut (kit-cutting): to cut *all* the individual pieces needed to make something *before* assembly is started; like a model airplane kit.

Lacquer: refined shellac or varnish with quick-drying additives.

Lag screw: large wood screw with a hexagonal or square head; used in situations where bolts are not practical, such as attaching something to a wall or floor.

Laminating: the process of gluing thin pieces of wood together to make a thicker piece.

Lap joint: a wood joint made when the faces of two pieces of wood are joined.

Lap weld: a welded metal joint; made when the pieces being welded are overlapped.

Lashing: a method of joining scenery; a piece of ¼-inch cotton clothesline (lash line) is served around special hardware on adjoining flats to hold them together.

Lash-line cleat: lashing hardware secured so that the pointed end projects over the inside edge of the stile.

Lash-line eye: lashing hardware with a hole through which the lash line passes, attached to the inside edge of the stile.

Lash-line hook: used for same purposes as a lash-line cleat, but has a hook instead of a point; used on extra-wide stiles or in situations that preclude the use of a lash-line cleat.

Latch keeper: *see* S hook.

Latex: a natural or synthetic liquid plastic with the flexible qualities of natural latex or rubber; bonds well and is flexible.

Latex cement: a milky-white flexible cement.

Latex paint: a paint with a latex binder; has fair to good covering power, may or may not be water-resistant, and can be thinned very little, usually no more than one pint of water per gallon of paint.

Lathe: a stationary, stand- or bench-mounted, variable-speed power tool that rapidly spins wood so that it can be carved with the use of special chisels. Can be used to turn foam.

Lauan: also known as Philippine mahogany; ⅛-inch lauan plywood is strong and quite flexible; commonly used as a flat-covering material and for covering curved-surface forms.

Lavelier: a small microphone, typically clipped to the shirt, lapel, or an inconspicuous location on the actor's/talent's clothing.

Leader line: in a two-line-weight system, a thin line 0.3 mm thick (in pencil) or 0.010 to 0.0125 inch thick (in pen).

Leaf: the movable flap of a hinge.

Legitimate theatre: refers to plays that rely on the spoken word to convey the message. Does not include musicals, reviews, dance, opera, or concerts.

Legs: narrow, vertical stage drapes used for masking.

Lensless projector: a projector that works by projecting a shadow image

without a lens, such as the Linnebach and curved-image projectors.

Lens train: two or more lenses used in combination.

Life: in rendering, the qualities of brilliance, visual depth, and sparkle.

Life mask: a plaster mask of a person's face. A negative mold is made by covering the person's face with plaster of Paris or alginate. The negative mold is used to make a positive cast that is the life mask.

Lift jack: a jack equipped with swivel casters, used to pick up and move platforms.

Lighting area: a cylindrical space approximately 8 to 12 feet in diameter and 7 feet high; lighting areas are located within acting areas to facilitate creating a smooth wash of light within the acting area.

Lighting cue: generally, some type of action involving lighting; usually the raising or lowering of the intensity of one or more lighting instruments.

Lighting designer: person responsible for the appearance of the lighting during the production.

Lighting grid: a network of pipes, usually connected in a grid pattern, from which lighting instruments and other equipment can be hung.

Lighting instrument: a device that produces a controllable light; for example, an ellipsoidal reflector spotlight or a Fresnel spotlight.

Lighting key: a drawing depicting the plan angles of the sources illuminating the image of light; can also be used to show the color of those lights.

Lighting rehearsal: a run-through, without actors, attended by the director, stage manager, lighting designer, and appropriate running crews to look at the intensity, timing, and placement of the various lighting cues.

Lighting sectional: a composite side view, drawn in scale, of the set showing the hanging position of the instruments in relation to the physical structure of the theatre, set, and stage equipment.

Lighting template: a guide for use in drawing lighting symbols.

Light plot: a scale drawing showing the placement of the lighting instruments relative to the physical structure of the theatre and the location of the set.

Limit switch: a switch that opens or closes when contacted by a moving object; used to limit the travel of that object.

Limited run: a production run of predetermined length, for example, two weeks, six weeks, and so forth.

Line: the wires in low-voltage control systems; frequently called "lines" rather than "wires."

Line level: the standard operating voltage used by mixers and signal processors.

Line level setting: the electronic equivalent of a loudness setting for the line level signal. An optimum line level signal would be loud enough to be distinctly heard by the next equipment in line — the power amplifier — but not so loud as to introduce distortion.

Linen canvas: an excellent flat-covering material; extremely durable, it accepts pant very well and doesn't shrink much; expensive.

Line of vision: the vertical line drawn from the observation point (OP) to the floor line in a perspective grid; it represents the line of sight from the observer to the vertical plane.

Liner: in makeup, any saturated color that is used as rouge, as eye shadow, or to create other areas of highlight or shadow.

Lining: painting narrow, straight lines; done with lining brushes and a straightedge.

Livery: identifiable clothing associated with a specific occupation or trade.

Load: a device that converts electrical energy into another form of energy: A lamp converts electrical energy to light and heat; an electric motor converts electricity to mechanical energy.

Load-in: the moving of scenery and associated equipment into the theatre and their positioning (setup) on the stage.

Load-out: The removal of scenery and associated equipment from the theatre. Term usually used when transferring scenery/equipment to another venue or facility. Not used when referring to the striking of the set/equipment at the end of a production run.

Loading platform: a walkway suspended just below the grid where the counterweights are loaded onto the arbor.

Locking pliers: generally known by the trade name Vise Grip, locking pliers are available in a wide variety of sizes and configurations; used for gripping and holding, the size of the jaw opening and amount of pressure applied by the jaws are adjustable by the screw at the base of the handle.

Locking rail: a rail that holds the rope locks for each counterweight set.

Loft block: a grooved pulley mounted on top of the grid, used to change the direction in which a rope or cable travels.

Long-nose pliers: pliers with long tapering jaws; used for holding small items and bending very light wire; also called needle-nose pliers.

Look: the visual appearance.

Loudness: a subjective term describing an individual person's perception of sound intensity.

Loudspeaker: a transducer used to convert an electrical signal from an amplifier into audible sound.

Lumens: the unit measurement of light output.

Luminous flux: the output of a light source. Measured in lumens.

Mac: the hardware, operating systems/software, and peripherals based on the Apple Macintosh computer.

Machine bolt: bolt with a square or hexagonal head used to attach metal to metal.

Machinist's vise: a vise with toothed steel faces; used to hold and clamp metal; can be used to hold wood, but the serrated steel faces will mar the surface unless protective blocks of wood are used to sandwich the work.

Magic sheet: a quick reference to the specific dimmer or channel that controls a specific light; also known as a cheat sheet.

Main drape: synonym for grand drape.

Mallet: a hammer with a wooden, plastic, or rubber head; the wooden and plastic mallets are generally used for driving chisels; all three can be used for shaping thin metal.

Managing director: person responsible for the business functions of a theatrical production company — fund-raising, ticket sales, box office management.

Manila rope: a strong, yet flexible rope; used in the theatre for raising and suspending loads and as the operating line for counterweight systems.

Mansions: small scenic representations of the standard locations (heaven, hell, garden, palace, etc.) used in medieval plays.

Margin line: an extra-heavy-weight line that forms a border for the plate ½ inch in from the edge of the paper.

Mask: to block the audience's view — generally, of backstage equipment and space.

Masonite: a registered trade name for a sheet stock made from binder-impregnated wood pulp compressed into 4-by-8-foot sheets.

Mass: the three-dimensional manifestation of form.

Master electrician: person responsible for ensuring that the lighting equipment is hung, focused, and run according to written and verbal instructions from the lighting designer.

Master seamer: person responsible for costume construction and direct supervision of costume crews.

MDF: medium-density fiberboard. A fine-grained particle board.

Matte: dull, nonreflective.

Matte knife: *see* utility knife.

Mechanical advantage: a measure of force amplification. A ratio comparing "force produced" to "force applied" for a tool or machine.

Mechanical perspective: a drafting technique that provides an illusion of depth.

Mechanic's hammer: a hammer with a heavy, soft metal head; used for shaping metal.

Merrow machine: a machine that, in one operation, sews a seam, cuts both pieces of fabric about ¼ inch from the seam, and makes an overcast stitch on the edge of both pieces of fabric to prevent raveling.

Metal file: any file with very fine teeth; used for smoothing metal.

Microcassette tape: audio recorder tape for use in small cassettes; used in computer storage.

Microphone (mic): a transducer that converts sound waves into electrical energy.

Microwatt: one millionth of a watt.

Mid-range speaker: a speaker designed to reproduce the middle range of audible frequencies — roughly 200 to 1,000 Hz.

MIG (metal inert gas) welder: a welder that focuses a flow of inert gas (usually carbon dioxide or argon) on the welding zone to prevent or reduce oxidation of the weld; the electrode is a thin piece of wire automatically fed through the welding handle from a spool stored in the housing of the power unit.

Mike: (verb) to pick up a sound with a microphone; to place one or more microphones in proximity to a sound source (instrument, voice).

Mild steel: a medium-strength, easily worked ferrous metal that is easy to weld; the metal most commonly used in stage construction.

Milling: the cutting, drilling, shaping, and finishing of wood, plastic, or metal.

Milliner: one who constructs and styles hats.

Miter: an angle that is cut in a piece of wood or metal, usually in pairs, to form a corner.

Miter box: a guide used with a backsaw to make accurate angle cuts in wood.

Miter joint: similar to a butt joint, but the edges to be joined are angle, rather than square, cut.

Mix: to blend the electronic signals created by several sound sources.

Mixdown: the editing process of merging multiple tracks into (typically) a two-track recording.

Mixer: a device used to combine two or more input signals to create a blended output signal. Multichannel mixers blend numerous input signals and routes them to multiple output channels.

Model: an object that is being used as the subject of a mold casting.

Modeled: in this case, to create an accurate representation of an object.

Mold: a matrix used to create a form.

Molding cutter head: a heavy cylindrical arbor in which a variety of matched cutter blades or knives can be fit; used with a table or radial-arm saw to cut decorative molding.

Monkey wrench: a heavy-weight, smooth-jawed adjustable wrench for use on large nuts or work that is too large for an adjustable-end wrench.

Monofilament line: a single-strand, transparent, monofilament line; sold as fishing line in sporting goods stores; also known as trick line.

Mood: the feeling of a play — comic, tragic, happy, and so forth.

Mortise: a square hole; used in conjunction with a tenon to make a mortise and tenon joint.

Mortise and tenon joint: a wood joint made by fitting a tenon (square peg) into a mortise (square hole).

Mortise drill bit: a drill bit housed inside a square hollow chisel; used with a drill press to make square holes.

MOSFET chip: metal-oxide-semiconductor field effect transistor; uses a low-voltage control circuit to rapidly switch a higher voltage current flow on and off.

Motorized miter box: see cutoff saw.

Mouse: an electromechanical device that controls the movement of a cursor on the computer screen; used by the operator to provide directives to the computer program.

Mullion: a vertical crossbar in a window.

Multicable: a cable with typically six "two-conductor-with-ground" circuits enclosed in a single outer jacket. One end terminates in a male Socapex connector, the other in a female Socapex connector.

Multiplex: (1) to transmit two or more messages simultaneously on a single channel or wire; (2) to carry out several functions simultaneously in an independent but related manner.

Muntin: a horizontal crossbar in a window.

Muslin: a flat-surfaced, woven cotton fabric.

Nail puller: a tool with a movable jaw on one end for grasping nail heads and a movable slide hammer on the other to drive the jaws into the wood to grasp the nail; used to pull nails out.

Nailer: a piece of plywood or stock used to join adjacent pieces. When used to prevent movement between adjoining pieces of flooring, the nailers should be attached with screws.

Native: in this context the term refers to the control protocol originally installed on an electronic device (e.g., digital projector, lighting control board, and so forth) by the manufacturer.

Needle-nose pliers: see long-nose pliers.

Neutralization: subtractive color mixing; the selective absorption of light as the result of mixing complementary pigment hues; the creation of gray.

Neutron: a fundamental particle in the structure of the nucleus of an atom; possesses a neutral charge.

Newel post: the post at the bottom or top of a flight of stairs that terminates the handrail.

Nicopress tool: a plierlike tool that crimps Nicopress sleeves onto wire rope or cable to make permanent, nonremovable friction clamps.

Non-dim: an undimmable power source — usually 120 VAC — whose off-on switch is controlled from a lighting console.

Nonrepresentational design: a style in which the portrayed elements do not represent physically identifiable objects.

Nonspecific musical effect: any sound effect that does not reinforce a readily identifiable source such as a doorbell or telephone.

Notched joint: a wood joint made by cutting a notch from a piece of lumber; the size of the notch is determined by the width and thickness of the other piece of stock that the notch will receive.

Noxious: harmful to one's health.

Nucleus: the central part of an atom, composed of protons and neutrons.

Nut driver: tool similar in appearance to a screwdriver with a cylindrical socket instead of a slot or Phillips head; used for tightening small hex (six-sided) nuts.

Objective lens: a device used to focus a projected image on a screen or other surface.

Oblique drawing: a scaled mechanical drawing with one face of the object, drawn as an elevation, placed at right angles to the observer's line of sight; the remaining faces project from the elevation to the right or left using a 30- or 45-degree base line.

Ohm's Law: the law that states: As voltage increases, current increases; as resistance increases, current decreases.

Oil stone: an abrasive composite stone, usually with different grits on opposite faces; used for sharpening knives, chisels, and other cutting tools.

Omnidirectional: in all directions; a spherical microphone pickup pattern.

Onboard: devices with discrete functions mounted within the housing of a larger unit.

On center: the distance from the center of one object to the center of the next.

Open-end wrench: a wrench with non-adjustable U-shaped jaws on both ends; the opening between the jaws is of a specific width to grip bolts and nuts of specific diameters; used to tighten bolts and nuts.

Orchestra: the circular area on which the majority of the action of the play took place in a Greek theatre.

Orchestra pit: the space between the stage and the auditorium, usually below stage level, that holds the orchestra.

Orthographic projection: a series of elevations, drawn to scale, that show each side or face of an object.

Outboard: separate stand-alone units.

Out of phase: two or more waveforms of the same frequency that are out of sync; they do not pass through the same value points at the same instant.

Output: information produced by a system.

Overdub: an additional recording that will be added to the original recording.

Overlay: a garment, usually made of lace or a similar lightweight, semitransparent fabric, designed to lie on top of another garment.

Oxford cloth: a flat-surfaced cotton or cotton-blend material frequently used for making shirts.

Oxidation: a chemical reaction between metal and air that forms a thin, discolored "skin" over the work that effectively prevents heat transfer. Oxidation adversely affects the strength and conductivity of both soldered and welded joints.

Pageant wagon: a staging convention used during the medieval period. Basically, a bare platform backed with a plain curtain mounted on a wagon. The wagon could be pulled from town to town.

Paint chip: a small rectangle of paper or thin cardboard painted in a specific hue.

Paint crew: persons responsible for painting the scenery and properties; they are under the supervision of the scenic artist.

Painter's elevations: elevations of a set painted to show the palette and painting styles to be used on the actual set.

Pan: to rotate an object about its vertical axis.

Panel adhesive: an adhesive product, such as Liquid nails, packaged in a caulking tube and intended to be dispensed with a caulking gun.

Paper clad: both sides covered with paper.

Paperclay: a nontoxic modeling material that can be sculpted, molded or shaped, and air dries to a hard finish that can be carved or sanded.

Papier-mâché: a process of building up a form by laminating wheat-paste-soaked strips of newspaper; also available commercially in a powdered form to make a paste suitable for forming in molds.

Parametric equalizer: an equalizer in which individual frequencies or custom-designed bands of frequencies can be programmed for boost or attenuation.

Paraskenia: long, high walls that extended on either side of and parallel with the skene of the Greek theatre.

PAR can: a holder for a parabolic aluminized reflector (PAR) lamp; creates a powerful punch of light with a soft edge; the PAR 64 is commonly used for concert lighting.

Particle board: a sheet stock composed of small wood chips and sawdust mixed with a glue binder and compressed into 4-by-8-foot sheets; it is quite brittle, so it cannot be used as a load-bearing surface.

Passive crossover: a device that splits the signal into the frequency ranges most appropriate for use by the individual speakers in the system.

Patch: to connect a stage circuit to a dimmer circuit.

Patch bay: a cross-connect or patch panel for sound.

Patch panel: an interconnecting device that allows one to connect any stage circuit to any dimmer.

Patch points: the physical locations in the theatre — stage, auditorium, and so on — where any connections are made between pieces of electronic/electrical equipment.

Pattern maker: person who makes patterns based on information contained in the costume designer's sketch, notes, and instructions.

PC: the hardware, operating systems/software, and peripherals based on the IBM personal computer (PC).

Perceived veracity: imagined truth; the dichotomy between what is perceived as being real and what is fact. In this case, the sound produced by an onstage radio's actual speaker is often perceived as unreal. Audiences *expect* that radio to sound like it does in their home or cars. Meeting that expectation in the theatre almost always requires the use of a support loudspeaker.

Perspective-view base line: the bottom edge of a perspective drawing.

Phantom power: a method of supplying DC power through the microphone cable to operate condenser microphones.

Phase: a method of notating position in a cyclic behavior such as wave movement; often expressed in degrees. A full or complete phase equals 360 degrees. The phase value at the beginning of each full cycle is zero; halfway through the cycle its value is 180 degrees. A full cycle equals 360 degrees.

Phase alignment: when the phases of two or more signals are perfectly aligned; aligned phases eliminates one source of distortion.

Phase angle: a particular point in a phase as measured from the zero point at the beginning of the phase.

Phillips-head screwdriver: *see* screwdriver.

Photomontage: a composite picture made by combining several separate pictures; can include nonphotographic images as well.

Piano wire: extremely strong wire made from spring steel; frequently used for flying scenery because of its strength; should not be sharply bent as this significantly reduces its strength.

Pickup patterns: the visual pattern illustrating the intensity of a microphone's output (measured in dB) relative to the direction from which the sound arrives.

Picture frame stage: a configuration in which the spectators watch the action of the play through a rectangular opening; synonym for proscenium-arch stage.

Picture hook and eye: hooks and eyes that facilitate rapid hanging and removal of decorative draperies.

Piezoelectricity: voltage produced when pressure is placed on certain crystals.

Pig: a loosely woven bag containing powdered eraser material.

Pigment: material that imparts color to a substance such as paint or dye.

Pilot hole: *see* starter hole.

Pinch bar: a flattened metal bar configured like a crowbar.

Pin rail: a horizontal pipe or rail studded with belaying pins; the ropes of the spot line system are wrapped around the belaying pins to hold the batten at a specific height.

Pipe: a counterweighted batten or fixed metal pipe that holds lighting instruments.

Pipe clamp: a threaded pipe with a movable end plate and an adjustable head plate; used for clamping furniture frames and similar wide objects. A bar clamp is similar except that a notched bar is substituted for the pipe.

Pipe cutter: a tool used for making clean right-angle cuts through steel tubing of half-inch and larger diameters.

Pipe wrench: similar in shape to the monkey wrench, the pipe wrench has jaws that are serrated to bite into the soft metal of pipes; used for holding or twisting pipes and their associated couplings.

Pit: (1) the ground in front of the stage where the lower-class audience stood to watch the play in Elizabethan theatres; (2) in twentieth-century theatres, a commonly used abbreviation for orchestra pit.

Pitch (print): the size of a particular typeface.

Pitch (sound): the characteristic tone produced by a vibrating body; the higher the frequency of vibration, the higher the pitch.

Pit orchestra: musicians located in the orchestra pit.

Pixel: the smallest "picture unit" in a digital image. The actual size varies with the size of the image, but pixels are extremely small relative to image size.

Plan angle: the ground-plan view of an object.

Plane: a knife-edged tool used to smooth or round the edges or corners of wood.

Plano-convex lens: a lens with one flat and one outward-curving face.

Plaster line: in drafting, a leader line extending across the opening of the proscenium arch.

Plate: (1) the horizontal pieces at the top and bottom of stud walls; (2) a sheet of mechanical drawings, drawn to scale.

Platea: the open acting area in front of the mansions of the medieval stage.

Playback system: devices used to play recorded sound; usually composed of some combination of a turntable, a tape deck, a CD player, or a computer; an equalizer; an amplifier; and a speaker.

Playwright: person who develops and writes the script.

Plotted: refers to printing a hardcopy (paper) from a CAD file.

Plotter: similar to a printer, a plotter is used to print large-format line art like ground plans and light plots.

Plug: a wooden insert used to replace a knothole or other imperfection in the surface layer of a sheet of plywood.

Plush: fabric similar to velveteen but with softer and longer pile; common drapery and upholstery fabric.

Ply-metal: refers to TEK screws specifically designed to attach plywood to metal. The flat head of the screw is typically driven flush with, or slightly into, the top surface of the plywood.

Plywood: a sheet stock made by laminating several layers of wood; its superior strength is created by alternating each successive layer so that its grain lies at a 90-degree angle to the layers immediately above and below it.

Pneumatic nailer: a compressed-air-powered tool similar in appearance to a pneumatic stapler but using clips of adhesive-coated nails rather than staples.

Pneumatic stapler: a compressed-air-powered stapler capable of driving staples with legs up to 1½ inches long; adhesive-coated staples are generally used for assembling flat frames, putting tops on platforms, and similar functions.

Pointing and clicking: pointing: using a mouse to move the on-screen cursor to a specific location; clicking: using a button on the mouse to initiate an action. Thus, "pointing and clicking" refers to using a mouse to initiate a specific action.

Polyethylene: a class of plastics that, in solid form, have a characteristically slick, waxy surface; polyethylene film is frequently used as a drop cloth and can be used as a projection surface; polyethylene foam, generally known by the trade name Ethafoam, is flexible and is available in sheets, rods, and tubes.

Polystyrene: a class of plastics with a variety of formulations useful in theatrical production; high-impact polystyrene sheeting has a hard surface and is moderately flexible, fairly strong, and somewhat brittle. It is used in vacuum forming; polystyrene foam is commonly known by the trade name Styrofoam; it is available in sheets and is frequently used as decorative trim.

Polyvinyl alcohol (PVA): a water-soluble synthetic thickener/adhesive.

Polyvinyl chloride: a family of plastics that are, in solid form, characteristically strong, lightweight, and rigid; PVC water pipe can be used for a variety of functional and decorative purposes; also available in sheet, rod, and other forms.

Polyvinyl glue: a white liquid adhesive that resembles white glue; has excellent adhesion to porous surfaces and good flexibility.

Pop riveter: a tool used to secure rivets in thin metal.

Position: relative placement of objects within a composition.

Potential: the difference in electrical charge between two bodies; measured in volts.

Power amplifier: a device used to boost the signal received from the mixer to a level that will drive a loudspeaker.

Power hacksaw: stationary power tool for cutting metal; a horizontal reciprocating metal-cutting blade is used to cut through various types of metal stock.

Power pipe cutter: a stationary stand-mounted power tool for cutting and threading metal pipes with diameters from approximately ½ to 2 inches.

Power ramp up: the time it takes for power to increase from "off" to "on." A sudden ramp up causes filament hum. A gradual ramp up reduces the level of hum.

Preamplifier: a device that increases the power of a weak signal for use by subsequent stages in an electronic circuit.

Preset sheet: a form used by the electrician to record the intensity levels for each dimmer during major shifts in the lighting.

Pressing cloth: a cloth placed between the iron and the fabric being pressed.

Pressure driver: a unit housing a large magnet that vibrates a very thin metallic diaphragm to create mid-range and high-frequency sounds.

Primary colors: hues that cannot be derived or blended from any other hues. In light the primaries are red, blue, and green; in pigment the primary colors are red, blue, and yellow.

Primitives: term used in CAD drawing to refer to basic shapes such as squares, cubes, circles, spheres, triangles, and so forth.

Prime coat: the first layer of paint; applied to all elements of the scenery to provide a uniform base for the rest of the paint job.

Processing: in sound production, refers to the manipulation of an input signal to achieve a desired output result.

Producer: person who selects the script, finds financial backing, and hires all production personnel.

Production concept: the creative interpretation of the script, which will unify the artistic vision of producer, director, and designers.

Production design team: the producer, director, and scenic, costume, lighting, and sound designers who, working together, develop the visual/aural concept for the production.

Production manager: coordinator of production scheduling and administrative/logistic details of a multishow theatrical season.

Production meeting: a conference of appropriate production personnel to share information.

Production model: a scale model similar to a functional model but fully painted and complete with furniture and decorative props.

Production style: a recognizable pattern of elements, both visual and intellectual, based on social and political history, used to create the environment for the production of a particular play.

Production team: everyone working, in any capacity, on the production of a play.

Profile: *see* silhouette.

Prompt book: a copy of the script with details about each actor's blocking as well as the location, timing, and, as necessary, action, of all set, prop, light, and sound cues.

Propane torch: an open-flame torch powered by propane gas; used for heavy-duty soldering and heat shaping of thin-gauge steel.

Properties: such elements as furniture, lamps, pictures, table linens, bric-a-brac, and window draperies that provide the finished set with visual character.

Property crew: those who construct or acquire all props and run (organize, shift, store) props during rehearsals and performances.

Property master: one responsible for the design, construction, and finishing of all properties.

Prop table: a table, normally located in the wings, on which hand props are stored between onstage use.

Proscenium: a stage configuration in which the spectators watch the action through a rectangular opening (the proscenium arch) that resembles a picture frame.

Proskenium: a columned arch that supported a porchlike projection from the upper floor of the skene in the Greek theatre.

Prosthetic device: in makeup, a device such as a false nose, beard, or other appliance that is added to the face to change the actor's appearance.

Proton: a fundamental particle in the structure of the nucleus of an atom; possesses a positive charge.

psi: pounds per square inch. A measurement of pressure in the United States.

Pull: to remove a costume from storage for use in a production.

Pulley: a grooved wheel. Used to change the direction of travel of ropes, cables, or belts. Encased in a wooden or metal sheath for use in block and tackle systems. Attached to the motor and drum shafts in belt-drive systems.

Push-drill: a hand-powered drill that uses a springloaded shaft to spin the drill bit when one pushes downward on the handle; for light usage, it uses bits from to inch in diameter; useful for making starter holes.

Push-drill bits: steel bits with sharp points and straight fluted indentations running up the sides of the shaft; used with the push drill to drill narrow holes (to inch in diameter) in wood.

PVA: abbreviation for *both* polyvinyl acetate and polyvinyl alcohol. Both substances are adhesives, but their chemical formulae are different. Polyvinyl acetate is opaque or translucent if thinned. It is the primary ingredient in white glue. Polyvinyl alcohol is a transparent liquid that, in theatrical production, is primarily used as a base in some specialty scene painting techniques.

Pyroxylin: Celastic is the trade name for a pyroxylin-impregnated felt material that becomes extremely limp when dipped in acetone; when the acetone evaporates, the pyroxylin stiffens the felt so that it will hold its molded shape.

Quadraphonic: a sound system composed of four discrete sound channels.

Quality: the nature or intrinsic properties (e.g., straight, curved, jagged) of a line.

Radial-arm saw: a circular-bladed stationary power saw; the motor and blade are suspended from an arm above a table; the height and angle of the blade are adjustable. Primarily used for cross and angle cutting, this versatile saw can be used for ripping and trim molding as well.

Rail: a top or bottom framing member of a flat.

Raked stage: a stage that is higher at the back than the front.

Raster: the projected video image.

Raster file: a dot matrix image composed of colored pixels.

Ratchet winch: a device used for hoisting that consists of a crank attached to a drum. One end of a rope or cable is attached to the drum, the other end to the load; turning the crank moves the load; a ratchet gear prevents the drum from spinning backward.

Rat-tail file: a file with a circular cross-sectional configuration; depending on surface finish it can be used for smoothing wood, metal, or plastic; also known as a round file.

Rear elevations: scale mechanical drawings that show the back of flats depicted on front elevations.

Rear projection screen: translucent projection material designed to transmit the image through the projection surface; the projector is placed in back of the screen.

Related colors: *see* analogous colors.

Rendering: in CAD, refers to the process of applying color, texture, light, and shadow to the object (geometry) model.

Repeatablility: the ability to exactly repeat an action. Usually associated with the precision control offered by computers.

Representational design: a style in which the portrayed elements represent some recognizable object, such as a room, a forest, or a street corner.

Reinforcement: the use of sound systems to amplify and enhance the voices, music, and sounds of a performance.

Reinforcement loudspeaker: loudspeaker used to reinforce actors' voices.

Resistance: the opposition to electron flow within a conductor, measured in ohms; the amount of resistance depends in part on the chemical makeup of the material through which the electricity is flowing.

Resolutions: a term defining the sharpness of a digital/video image; determined by the number of pixels used to create the image; the more pixels the sharper the image.

Respirator: a mask covering the nose and mouth that filters out gases as well as particulate matter; the type of filtering medium used determines the type of gases removed from the air.

Reverb: an electronically produced echo effect.

Reverberate: to reflect in a series of echoes.

Reverberation: a multiple reflection of a sound that persists for some time after the original source has decayed.

Revolve: large, circular platform that pivots on its central axis; also called turntable.

Revolving stage: generally refers to a revolve that is built into the stage floor as part of a theatre's permanent equipment.

Rhythm: the orderly and logical interrelationship of successive parts in a composition.

Rigid caster: a caster that cannot swivel or rotate.

Rigid foot iron: bracing hardware; an L-shaped piece of metal, one leg attached to the bottom of the flat, the other secured to the floor with a stage screw that is inserted through the ring at the end of the leg.

Rip: to saw parallel with the grain. Ripping is generally done with a table saw.

Rip bar: tool similar to a crowbar, but the nail-removing claws have more curl for better leverage.

Rip hammer: a hammar with two relatively straight claws projecting from the back of its head that can be used for prying or ripping apart previously nailed wood; used for driving nails.

Rip saw: a handsaw with an approximately 26-inch blade whose chisel-sharpened teeth bend outward so that the kerf is wider than the blade; designed to cut parallel with the grain of the wood. Rip saws have fewer teeth per inch than a crosscut saw has.

Riser: the vertical face of a stair.

RMS wattage rating: a system (root-mean-square) providing an accurate picture of the energy-dissipation characteristics of sound equipment.

Rods: nerve cells in the retina that are sensitive to faint light.

Roostered: a term used to describe a lighting fixture that is "standing up" on a pipe — like a rooster. The yoke of the fixture is attached to the pipe so it places the fixture above the pipe.

Rope set: a counterbalanced flying system in which ropes are used to fly the scenery. Sandbags are tied to the offstage end of the ropes to counterbalance the weight of the scenery.

Rough finish: a pebble-grained texture achieved by cold-pressing paper with a texture roller or by other techniques; suitable for painted and pastel renderings having little intricate detail; can be worked with other media as well.

Roundel: a glass color medium for use with striplights; frequently has diffusing properties.

Round file: *see* rat-tail file.

Round-head wood screw: screw with a head that has a flat underside and a rounded upper surface; used when having the top of the screw flush with the surface of the work is not desirable, as when attaching thin metal or fabric to a wood frame.

Rough cut: wood, roughly cut, not smooth. A piece of wood's rough-cut dimensions (in inches) are used to identify its size such as a 1×3 or 2×4.

Router: a portable, handheld power tool that uses a chisel-like rotating bit (25,000 RPM) to shape or carve the surface or edge of the piece of wood; primarily used for shaping decorative moldings and trim pieces.

RTV (room temperature vulcanizing) silicone rubber: a compound used to make flexible molds.

Running: controlling or operating some aspect of production.

Running block: a block and tackle system that provides a 2:1 mechanical advantage.

Running crew: those responsible for operating lighting equipment and shifting scenery and props during rehearsals and performances.

Saber saw: a portable power saw with a reciprocating blade; used for making curvilinear cuts in wood and plastic.

Sandpaper: paper whose surface has been coated with abrasive grit; used for smoothing wood and plastic.

Satin: a stiff, heavy fabric with a smooth, shiny finish on the front and a dull finish on the back; if patterned, the design is usually printed on rather than woven in; used for making costumes, upholstery, and decorative drapery.

Saturated polyester: a plastic used to form the fiber from which polyester fabrics such as Dacron are made; also used to form films such as Mylar.

Saturation: the relative purity of a particular hue.

Scaenae frons: an elaborately decorated facade or wall that was located at the rear of the stage in the Roman theatre. Its historical antecedent was the skene of the Greek theatre.

Scale: a black, scaly coat that forms on iron when it is heated for processing.

Scab: a small piece of scrap material.

Scan: to use a digitizing scanner to convert existing artwork, photos, or drawings into binary information.

Scarf joint: two boards joined lengthwise by making a shallow angle cut approximately 18 inches long in the face of each board; the joint is secured by gluing and screwing or bolting.

Scene shop foreman: person responsible for supervising the crews who build and rig the scenery and some of the larger props.

Scenery automation: the use of computer-controlled, motorized devices to shift scenery, almost always in view of the audience.

Scenic artist: person responsible for the painting of the scenery and properties.

Scenic designer: person responsible for the design and function of the scenery and properties.

Scenic projector: a high-wattage instrument used for projecting large-format slides or moving images.

Scoop: *see* ellipsoidal reflector floodlight.

Score: to cut partially through.

Scratch awl: *see* scribe.

Screen diagonal: the diagonal dimension of a screen.

Screwdriver: a tool for inserting or driving screws; the standard screwdriver has a narrow blade for work with standard screws; the Phillips-head screwdriver has a four-flanged tip that matches the crossed slots of the Phillips-head screw.

Screw nail: nail with a threaded shaft that rotates as it is driven into wood; used for jobs that require greater holding power.

Scribe: a sharp metal tool used to mark wood, metal, and plastic; also called a scratch awl.

Scrim: a drop made from translucent or transparent material.

Scumbling: a blending of paints of several hues or values to create the appearance of texture; done with brushes.

Secondary colors: the result of mixing two primary colors.

Secrets: the name used to describe the stage machinery in medieval times.

Sectional: a drawing, usually in scale, of an object that shows what it would look like if cut straight through at a given plane.

Sectional angle: the angle of intersection between the axis of the cone of light emitted by an instrument and the working height — usually the height of an average actor's face (about 5 feet, 6 inches) — of the lighting areas.

Self-tapping: screws that drill their own pilot holes as they are power-screwed into wood or metal. The screws have an auger-like tip that drills a smaller diameter hole than the screw threads.

Set: to prevent smearing or smudging. Once a greasepaint makeup design is finished, it is locked in place with a coating of powder.

Set line: in drafting, a leader line that extends, parallel with the proscenium arch, across the farthest downstage point(s) of the set.

Set prop: a large, movable item, not built into the set, that is used in some way by an actor, such as a sofa, floor lamp, table, and so forth.

Setscrew: typically, a short hex-head machine bolt with the other end cupped or pointed. Screwed through one part of a machine or device — such as socket on a steel-framed platform — to hold another part — the leg — in place.

Setting: to help lock the dye into the fiber of the fabric; to reduce or prevent the dye from being rubbed off the fabric.

Shade: a color of low value; usually created by mixing one or more hues with black.

Sharkstooth scrim: an open-weave material used to make transparent scrims.

Shear force: side-to-side movement.

Sheer: a thin gauze curtain that hangs across the opening of a window to soften the sunlight and obscure the view into a room.

Sheet-metal screw: a pan-head or hex-head screw used for joining sheets of metal.

Sheet stock: a generic term that applies to lumber products sold in sheet form, such as plywood, Upson board, and Masonite.

Shellac: a generally clear glossy coating made of resinous material (lac — the secretions of certain scale insects) suspended in wood alcohol; also known as spirit varnish.

Shift: to change the position of the scenery, props, or stage equipment.

Shift rehearsal: a rehearsal, without actors, where the director, scenic designer, technical director, and stage manager work with the scenery and prop crews to perfect the choreography and timing of all scenic and prop shifts.

Shim: scrap wood or metal used to raise adjacent parts so that they are level or fit together as designed.

Sine wave: a waveform whose change over time can be graphically expressed as a sine curve.

S hook: an S-shaped piece of steel strap used to hold stiffening battens on the back of wall units that are made up of two or more flats; also called a latch keeper.

Show control: the use of computer-controlled, motorized, devices to shift scenery, almost always in view of the audience.

Show file: a sequential listing of the sound cues in the order they will be played during the production.

Show portal: a false proscenium that visually supports the style and color palette of a particular production.

Shutter: a lever-actuated device used to control the height of the top and bottom edges of a followspot beam; also called a chopper.

Shutter cut: the shadow line created by the edge of the shutter when it is inserted into the beam of light emitted by an ERS.

Shutters: movable upstage scenic elements used to create a visual backdrop. Essentially wide painted wings, shutters were mounted in grooved tracks and slid into view from either side of the stage. Performed the same function as, and predated, drops.

Shuttle stage: a long narrow wagon that moves back and forth across the stage, like a shuttle in a loom; used for shifting scenery.

Sight line: a sighting extending from any seat in the house to any position on stage.

Sight-line drawing: a scale drawing (plan and section views) of sightings that extend from the extreme seats (usually the outside seats on the front and last rows of the auditorium) to any position on the stage; used to determine how much of the stage and backstage will be visible from specific auditorium seats.

Signal converter: an electronic device that changes the signal form from digital to analog or analog to digital.

Signal delay: software that holds a signal for a specified amount of time before sending it on to the next device in the system.

Signal loss: degradation in the quality of the sound represented by the signal.

Signal processing: the manipulation of transducer input signals to change, blend, and enhance the resultant output signal(s).

Silhouette: the general outline of form; frequently used to refer to the shape of a garment, set, or prop. The quality and character of the line determines the evocative characteristics of the resultant form. Also known as a profile or cutout line.

Sill iron: a strap of mild steel attached to the bottom of a door flat to brace it where the rail has been cut out.

Single-hand welding: a technique in which one hand holds the welding handle and the other hand is not used.

Single whip: a block and tackle configuration that changes the direction of travel of the line but provides no mechanical advantage.

Size coat: a paint coat used to shrink previously unpainted scenic fabric and to fill the weave of the fabric.

Size water: a mixture of one cup of hot animal glue and one tablespoon of Lysol per gallon of warm water; white glue can be substituted for the animal glue in approximately equal measure.

Skene: originally a wall or facade to hide backstage action in Greek theatres. By the end of the fifth century B.C., the wall had evolved into a two-story building.

Skid: a low-profile substitute for a wagon; usually a piece of ¾-inch plywood on which some small scenic element is placed.

Skin: a top or bottom plywood covering for a platform.

Sky drop: a large drop made to be hung flat, without fullness; used to simulate the sky.

Sky tab: synonym for sky drop.

Slide-plane aperture: the point in a projection system where a slide or other effect is placed.

Slide projector: a reasonably high output instrument capable of projecting standard 35 mm slides.

Slip-joint pliers: common pliers with an adjustable pivot point that provides two ranges of jaw openings; used for clamping, gripping, bending, and cutting light wire.

Slipstage: a stage wagon large enough to hold an entire set.

Smooth base coat: a base coat that has no texture.

Smoothing plane: a large, heavy plane with a blade angle of approximately 25 to 30 degrees; used to smooth parallel with the grain of wood.

Socapex connector: a 19-pin connector used with multicables. Typically manufactured with six hot pins, six neutral pins, six grounded pins, and one pin left open. Used to create the six separate, grounded circuits found in stage multicables.

Socket set and ratchet handle: sockets are cylindrical wrenches used with a ratchet handle; the reversible ratchet handle allows one to tighten or loosen nuts without removing the socket from the nut; used to tighten or loosen nuts and bolts in confined spaces or where other wrenches might not fit.

Soft patch: an electronic patching system in which one or more dimmers can be assigned to a control channel, which in turn controls the intensity level of those dimmers.

Software: the programs (sets of electronic instructions) that perform various functions such as word processing, drafting, and three-dimensional modeling.

Solder: a metal alloy made of lead and tin.

Soldering: the process of forming a low-strength bond in metal by flowing a molten metal over a joint area.

Soldering gun: a quick-heating, trigger-activated soldering iron that physically resembles a pistol.

Soldering iron: a device to heat solder and the item to be soldered to the point where a good bond can be made.

Soldering pencil: a low-wattage soldering iron.

Sole: the bottom plate of a plane, with a slot through which the tip of the blade projects.

Sound crew: those who record and edit sound and who set up and run any sound equipment during the production.

Sound designer: person responsible for the design, recording, and playback of all music and sound effects used in a production.

Sound mixer: an electronic device used to adjust the loudness and tone levels of several sources, such as microphones and recorded sources (computer files/tape playback equipment).

Sound plot: a list describing each sound cue in the production.

Sound score: the music and sound effects used in support of a production.

Sound scoring: background music and/or effects tracks that play at a low loudness level throughout a scene or scenes.

Soundscape: the total auditory experience of the performance including music, effects, and vocal reinforcement; the sound environment.

Source: the origin of electrical potential, such as a battery or 120-volt wall outlet.

Source light: the apparent source of light that is illuminating a scene or an object.

Spackle or spacking: a plaster-like paste used to fill small holes and cracks in walls.

Spade bits: *see* wood bits.

Spattering: the process of applying small drops of paint to a surface; done by spraying paint with a garden sprayer or slapping a lightly charged brush against the heel of one's hand to throw paint drops at the scenery.

Speaker routing: the particular speaker through which an audio signal will be played.

Specifications: clarifying notes that explain the building materials, textures, or special effects to be used in a design or other project.

Spectrometer: a device for measuring specific wavelengths of light.

Spidering: running a cable directly from the dimmer to the instrument; also known as direct cabling.

Spindle chuck: a device used to hold wood in a lathe.

Spine: the relative stiffness of brush bristles; good watercolor bristles will flex easily but will also have enough spine to remain erect when fully saturated with paint.

Spirit: the manner and style in which a play is presented to the audience.

Split time fade: a fade in which the fade-in and fade-out are accomplished at different rates or speeds.

Spoke shave: a small plane with a wide, narrow, slightly rounded sole and a steeply angled (approximately 30 to 35 degrees) blade; it is pulled rather than pushed across the surface of the wood; used to soften or round sharp edges rather than to smooth flat surfaces.

Spot lines: individual rigging lines used to raise/lower scenery. Typically, located for a specific purpose. Normally, motorized and computer controlled.

Spray cone: the shape or pattern of paint emitted from the nozzle of a spray gun.

Spray gun: a pistol-like device that shoots out a cone of paint.

Spreading: *see* bleeding.

Stage: the area where the action of the play takes place.

Stage brace: an adjustable wooden or aluminum pole that is attached to a brace cleat on the back of a flat to hold it vertical.

Stage business: a specific action, also known as a "bit," performed by an actor during the play.

Stage circuit: an electrical circuit terminating on one end in a female receptacle in the vicinity of the stage. The other end is connected to a dimmer or a patch panel. Synonymous with dimmer circuit when it terminates at a dimmer.

Stage crew: those who shift the sets and, sometimes, props during rehearsals and performances.

Stage manager: person who assists the director during rehearsals and manages all backstage activity once the play has opened.

Stage screw: bracing hardware; a coarse-threaded, large, hand-driven screw used to anchor a foot iron or the foot of a stage brace to the stage floor; leaves ragged holes in the stage floor.

Stage worthy: strong enough to withstand the use inflicted on them when used on the stage, for example, sofas/chairs that are stood and/or danced on; tables that break apart during fights, and so forth.

Standard parallel: a platform made of a folding framework of nonvariable height; the top is removable and the frame folds like a giant parallelogram for storage.

Staple gun: a tool with a spring-driven piston used to drive staples; used in upholstery, in attaching muslin to flat, and so forth.

Staples: U-shaped fasteners sharpened at both ends; used to attach wire, rope, cording, chicken wire, screening, and similar materials to supporting wooden frames.

Starter hole: a small hole bored into a piece of wood or metal to hold the tip of a screw or drill bit; also called a pilot hole.

Stencil brush: a short, squat brush with a circular pattern of short, stiff bristles; the bristles are pressed onto, rather than stroked across, the work, to prevent the paint from bleeding under the edges of the stencil.

Stencil paper: stiff, water-resistant paper used for making stencils.

Step-down transformer: a transformer whose output voltage is lower than its input voltage.

Step lens: having the optical properties of plano-convex lenses but the glass on one side of the lens is cut away in "steps."

Step motor: an electric motor whose movement consists of discrete, angular steps rather than continuous rotation. Precise movement is achieved by programming the motor to run, in either direction, for a specific number of steps.

Step-up transformer: a transformer whose output voltage is higher than its input voltage.

Stereo: two distinct sound channels; a stereo system is composed of two discrete monaural systems.

Stiffening batten: a length of 1×3 attached to a multiflat wall unit to keep it from wiggling.

Stile: a vertical side member of a flat.

Stippling: in scene painting, a texturing technique, similar in appearance to spattering, but leaves a heavier texture; stippling is done by touching a sponge, feather duster, or ends of a brush to the surface of the work. In makeup, a texturing technique in which makeup is applied by touching the skin with a textured surface, usually a stippling sponge. Similar to stippling in scenic painting.

Stitcher: one who sews costumes together.

Stock: regular-sized lumber that can be purchased from a lumberyard.

Stock furniture: furniture items owned by the producing organization and held in storage until they are needed for a production.

Stock set: scenery designed to visually support a generalized location (garden, city street, palace, interior) rather than a specific one.

Stop block: a small piece of scrap wood attached to the stile of a flat to prevent flats from slipping past each other when lashed together in an inside corner configuration.

Stop cleat: metal tabs used to prevent flats from slipping past each other when they are being lashed in an outside corner configuration.

Stove bolts: bolts smaller than carriage or machine bolts and with threads on the entire length of the shaft; used for attaching stage hardware, hinges, and similar items that require greater fastening strength than screws do.

Stovepipe wire: soft-iron wire approximately of an inch in diameter and generally black; very flexible but has little tensile strength; used for tying or wiring things together; is not strong enough to be used for flying scenery.

Straightedge: a thin piece of wood, usually 4 to 6 feet long, with a handle attached in the center; used as a guide while painting straight lines.

Straps: rectangular strips of ¼-inch plywood used to reinforce butt joints on the interior support elements (toggle bars, diagonal braces) of flats; substitute for keystones.

Stream-of-consciousness questioning: asking whatever relevant questions pop into your mind in the course of a discussion.

Street makeup: makeup worn in everyday life.

Strike: taking down and/or destruction of the set following the conclusion of a play's production run.

Stringers: structural pieces inside a framework; e.g., the pieces spanning the width of a stressed-skin panel's framework.

Striplight: a long, narrow troughlike instrument with three or four circuits controlling the individual lamps; each circuit is normally equipped with a separate color; used for blending and creating color washes; also known as an X-ray.

Stud: the vertical elements in a stud wall.

Sturd-I-Floor: the tradename of a plywood subflooring used beneath carpet, vinyl flooring, and tile in home construction.

Style: specific compositional characteristics that distinguish the appearance of one type of design from another; for example, realism, expressionism, surrealism, and so forth.

Stylization: the use of specific compositional elements characteristic of a particular style or period that create the essence of that style or period.

Subtractive color mixing: the selective absorption of light by a filter or pigment.

Subtractive manufacturing: cutting away or removing material during the manufacturing process.

Supernumerary: an actor, normally not called for in the script, used in a production; an extra; a walk-on.

Surform blade: a thin, disposable strip of spring steel honeycombed with sharpened protrusions projecting from its surface; the serrated blade face doesn't leave a smooth surface, so the wood generally has to be smoothed with sandpaper.

Surform tools: tools that use the Surform blade — planes, files, routing bits, and gouges.

Sweat off: when an actor's face perspires, some makeups will run. These makeups are said to "sweat off."

Sweep: a wooden curvilinear form frequently used to outline an arch or irregular form in door- and window-flat openings.

Swivel caster: a caster that swivels or rotates around a vertical axis; the bearing plate should have a ball-bearing swivel.

Symmetrical balance: correspondence in size, form, and relative position of parts on either side of a center dividing line; mirror-image balance.

Synthesizer: a musical instrument that creates sound electronically; can be used to create a close facsimile of instrumental, vocal, or natural tones.

Table saw: a circular-bladed stationary power saw; the blade projects upward from the underside of a table; the height and angle of the blade are adjustable; used to rip lumber, plywood, and other sheet goods.

Tack hammer: a lightweight hammer with a small magnetized head for inserting tacks and a large face for seating them; used only with tacks.

Take: a recording made in one uninterrupted session.

Tap and die: tools used to cut threads on pipe and rod stock; the tap is used to cut internal threads; the die cuts external threads.

Tape deck: a magnetic-tape transport mechanism used to record an electrical signal on magnetic tape; also used to play back that signal; does not contain a playback amplifier or speaker.

Tape measure: a retractable, flexible metal rule housed in a plastic or metal case; used for measuring in general stage work.

Tape recorder: a magnetic-tape transport mechanism used to record and play back an electrical signal on magnetic tape; it has a built-in playback amplifier and speaker(s).

Teaser: a short, horizontal drape used for masking the flies; synonym for *border*.

Technical director: person responsible for supervising the construction, mounting, rigging, and shifting of the scenery and properties.

Technical production: all organizational and procedural aspects of the construction, painting, and operation of scenery and properties.

Technical rehearsals: run-throughs in which the sets, lights, props, and sound are integrated into the action of the play.

Tenon: a square tab projecting from a piece of stock; used in conjunction with a mortise to make a mortise and tenon joint.

Texture: the relative roughness or smoothness of the finish of an object.

Theatrical gauze: a fine mesh weave, similar to cheesecloth, but the threads are thicker and the weave is slightly tighter; 72 inches wide; used for apparition effects and applications similar to sharkstooth scrim.

Theatron: the steeply raked seating area for the audience in a Greek theatre.

Theme: the repetitive use of similar elements to create a pattern or design.

Throw distance: (1) in lighting, the distance light travels from a fixture's hanging position to the center of its focus area at head height; (2) in projection, the distance from the projector to the center of the screen.

Thrust stage: a stage projecting into, and surrounded on three sides by, the audience.

Thumbnail sketch: a small, quickly drawn rough sketch, usually done in pencil, that shows the major outline, character, and feeling of an object but doesn't show much detail.

Tie-off cleats: special cleats used in pairs approximately 30 inches above stage level to tie off the line after the flats have been lashed together.

Ties: strips of material (usually 36-inch pieces of ½-wide cotton tape, or 36-inch shoestrings) used for tying stage drapes to battens.

Tilt: to rotate an object about its horizontal axis.

Timbre: the distinctive quality of a sound that distinguishes one voice, musical instrument, or sound from another of the same pitch and intensity.

Tin snips: scissorlike tools used for cutting thin metal.

Tint: a color of high value; usually created by mixing one or more hues with white.

Tip jack: two (or more) large interconnected jacks that are fitted with swivel casters; normally used for moving wall units.

Toggle bar: an interior horizontal framing member of a flat.

Tone: (1) a color of middle value achieved by mixing one or more hues with black and white; (2) a generic term referring to the intensity of the component frequencies contained in any particular sound.

Tool spindle: the rapidly spinning shaft of a machine tool. Includes anything attached to the spindle; e.g., a chuck used to hold cutters and/or bits.

Tooth: a term used to describe the surface texture of a paper.

Top hat: an accessory for a Fresnel spotlight that creates a defined circular pattern of light; also called a snoot or funnel.

Tormentor: the vertical flats that form the side elements of the false proscenium.

Torque: rotational force.

Toxic: poisonous.

Trace: a line drawn by a recording instrument such as an oscilloscope.

Tracing paper: translucent paper used for drafting.

Traditional-style flats: wooden-framed, soft- or hard-covered flats.

Transduce: convert one form of energy into another.

Transducer: a device that converts one form of energy into another.

Transformer: a device that changes voltage in an electrical system.

Transparent: (in sound) without being apparent; unnoticed.

Travel: to move horizontally relative to the stage floor, as with a drape that opens in the middle and is pulled to the sides.

Traveler: any drapery that moves or opens horizontally; generally, travelers are composed of two sections of stage drapes covering the full width of the proscenium; the sections split in the middle, and each section retracts in an offstage direction.

Tread: the horizontal surface of a stair unit — the part on which you walk.

Trick line: *see* monofilament line.

Tri-amplified: a speaker system with three built-in amplifiers; one driving the woofer; one driving the mid-range speaker/driver; one driving the tweeter.

Tri square: a small, rigid, hand square with a steel blade and steel, composition, or wooden handle; used as a guide for marking 90-degree angles across narrow (under 6 inches) materials.

Trompe l'oeil: literally "to trick the eye." An illusion of three-dimensionality created with paint.

Truss: an engineered beam in which a downward force at any point on its top will be distributed over its full width by a series of interlocking triangles that channel and redirect the downward force into a horizontal force.

"Tubed" building adhesive: an adhesive product, such as Liquid Nails, packaged in a caulking tube and designed to be dispensed with a caulking gun.

Tubing cutter: a tool used for making clean right-angle cuts on steel and nonferrous metal tubing ½ inch and smaller.

Tumbler: a narrow (¾ inch thick by 1 inch wide, or 1 × 3) piece of stock used as a spacer when three or more flats are going to be booked.

Turntable: *see* revolve.

Tutu: the short, stiff skirt frequently worn by ballerinas.

Tweed: a rough-surfaced woolen fabric in plain, twill, or herringbone weave of two or more shades of the same color; used for men's and women's suits and trousers.

Tweening: the process of filling in the "in-between" images between two keyframes to give the appearance that the first image smoothly transitions into the second image. Accomplished with software programs in computer animation.

Tweeter: a high-frequency speaker generally designed reproduce wavelengths from approximately 1,000 to 20,000 Hz.

Twill: a weaving pattern that results in parallel diagonal lines or ribs; a flat surfaced, durable, heavy cotton fabric used for making dresses, men's suits, and work clothes.

Twist-drill bits: drill bits made of mild steel, filed to a point, with spiral indentations in the shaft to carry away material being removed from the hole; used for drilling holes of approximately to ½ inch in diameter in wood, plastic, mild to medium steel, and nonferrous metals.

Two-fer: an electrical Y that has female receptacles at the top of the Y and a male plug at the bottom leg of the Y; used to connect two instruments to the same circuit.

Two-handed welding: a technique in which the torch or welding handle is held in one hand and the filler rod in the other.

Typical stage load: fifty pounds per square foot is the load-carrying standard to which stage platforming is normally built. Depending on the platform's use, the required load rating may be higher or lower.

USB flash drive: a removable, rewritable flash memory data storage device with an integrated universal serial bus (USB) interface.

Unbalanced line: a sound cable in which a single insulated conductor is wrapped in a braided or foil shield.

Unbleached muslin: a cotton fabric commonly used to cover flats; available in a variety of widths from 72 inches to 33 feet; for scenic-construction purposes, it should have a thread count of 128 or 140 threads per inch.

Undercut: an indentation in a form that leaves an overhang or concave profile, such as the nostrils on a mask of a face.

Underhung: hung beneath. Lighting instruments are typically suspended underneath a pipe. A clamp is attached to the pipe and the body of the fixture hangs from a yoke suspended below the clamp.

Underscoring: using music or sound to reinforce the emotional content of a scene or moment.

Unified aniline dye: a coal-tar-derivative dye formulated to work on both animal- and plant-derivative fibers.

Unit set: a single set in which all of the play's locations are always visible and the audience's attention is usually shifted by alternately lighting various parts of the set.

Unsaturated polyester: a liquid plastic generally used as a casting resin and as the bonding agent to create the multipurpose material known by the trade name Fiberglas.

Upson board: a sheet stock composed of a paper pulp and binder compressed into 4-by-8-foot sheets.

Urethane: a class of plastics that have a variety of formulations: flexible foam, rigid foam, and liquid casting resin. Because of toxic fumes emitted when working with urethane foams, their use is not recommended.

Utility knife: a metal handle with a usually retractable replaceable blade; used for a variety of jobs including cutting cardboard and trimming fabric from the edges of flats; also called a matte knife.

Vacuforming: the process of shaping heated plastic, usually high-impact polystyrene, around a mold through the use of vacuum pressure.

Vacuum clamping: using vacuum pressure to exert force.

Valance: a horizontal element at the top of a drapery arrangement that covers the curtain rod.

Valence shell: the outermost plane of orbiting electrons in the structure of an atom.

Value: the relative lightness or darkness of an object.

Vanishing point: the point on the horizon to which a set of parallel lines recedes.

Variable-frequency drive: a solid-state device used to change the frequency of electrical power.

Varnish: a transparent coating made of synthetic or natural resinous materials suspended in an oil (oil varnish), alcohol (spirit varnish), or synthetic (polyurethane, vinyl acrylic) vehicle.

Vector files: the lines, shapes, and colors of an image stored as mathematical formulae.

Vehicle: the liquid medium — water, oil, lacquer, and the like—in which pigments, fillers, and binders are suspended to create a paint mixture; after the paint is applied, the vehicle evaporates.

Velour: a thick, heavy material with a deep pile; generally made of cotton or cotton/nylon blends; heavier weights are used for upholstery and draperies; lighter weights can be used in costuming.

Velum: an awning covering the cavea (auditorium) of a Roman theatre; also known as a velarium.

Velvet: a rich, lustrous material with a soft, thick pile; frequently made of rayon with a cotton or cotton-blend backing; used in dresses, coats, upholstery, and draperies.

Velveteen: fabric possessing the same general characteristics as velour but much lighter (6 to 8 ounces); used in upholstery and costumes.

Ventilate: a method of tying hair to the net foundation of a wig, mustache, or beard. The technique is similar to that used in hooking rugs.

Vinyl acrylic concentrates: highly saturated pigments with a vinyl acrylic binder.

Vinyl acrylic paint: paint made with a vinyl acrylic binder; in scene painting, thinned vinyl acrylic concentrates (two parts water to one part concentrate) are mixed with an opaque white base to create tints and are mixed with a transparent base for fully saturated hues; after curing for 24 hours, the paint is highly water-resistant; can be thinned with up to ten parts of water depending on particular application.

Void: an unfilled, empty space.

Volatility: in computers, loss of electronic data when a computer loses its power supply.

Volt: the unit of measurement of electrical potential.

Wafer board: a sheet stock composed of large chips of wood mixed with a binder and compressed into 4-by-8-foot sheets; stronger and cheaper than plywood; can be used for the same purposes as plywood.

Wagon: a rigid platform supported with casters; used to move set pieces on the stage.

Wale: visible, usually narrow, ridges in the surface of a fabric caused by a variation in the weaving pattern.

Walk the cues: to move about the stage as the light cues are being run so the light will be falling on a person rather than on a bare stage.

Wall pocket: a connecting box similar to a floor pocket but mounted so that its face is flush with a wall.

Wane: missing wood, and/or untrimmed bark on the edge or end of the piece of lumber.

Wardrobe crew or staff: those crew members such as dressers and wardrobe-repair personnel who work during the dress rehearsals and performances.

Warp: the vertical threads in a fabric.

Wash: the covering of a large area with a smooth layer of paint. A smooth wash consists of only one color; a blended wash is created by smoothly segueing from one color to another.

Watch tackle: a block and tackle system that provides a 3:1 mechanical advantage.

Web browser: a software program that enables you to preview and access sites on the World Wide Web.

Weft: the horizontal threads in a fabric.

Welding: the process of making a high-strength bond in metal by heating the parts to be joined to their melting points and allowing the parts to become fused together.

Welding rod: a rod, usually coated with flux, that serves as the positive electrode in arc welding.

Wheat paste: a mixture of unrefined wheat flour and water; used for attaching dutchmen and for similar low-strength gluing.

White glue: commonly known by the trade name Elmer's Glue-All, white glue is a casein or milk-based glue used extensively in scenic and property construction.

White model: *see* functional model.

Whiting: a white powder extender, basically low-grade chalk, used to increase the covering power of dry pigment and binder paint.

Wig cap: a skull cap of thin, tight-fitting mesh material. Used to cover and compress the wig-wearer's hair.

Wigmaker: one who makes, styles, and arranges wigs.

Winch: a machine having a drum around which one end of a cable is wound and the other end attached to the load; used for hoisting or hauling.

Winch-driven system: a system that uses a motorized or hand-powered winch to move a cable; frequently used to move wagons or skids across the stage or to turn small revolves.

Wings: (1) tall cloth-covered frames or narrow unframed drops that are placed on either side of the stage, parallel with the proscenium arch, to prevent the audience from seeing backstage. In the Restoration theatre, wings were usually painted to match the scene on the up-stage drop. (2) The off-stage space adjacent to the stage in a proscenium arch theatre.

Winglights: lights hung on either side of the stage, usually concealed by wings (vertical masking pieces). In this context the winglights were striplights — long, narrow, troughlike fixtures usually containing eight to twelve individual lamps.

Wire-crimping tool: specialty pliers whose jaws are designed to pressure-clamp solderless connectors to electrical wire.

Wire frame: lines used to define the shape of an object.

Wireless microphone: a microphone system that uses a short-range FM radio transmitter and receiver instead of a cable to send the signal from the microphone to the mixer.

Wire nails: small finish or box nails with very slender shafts; used for attaching delicate decorative moldings or panels to larger scenic elements.

Wire strippers: specialty pliers used for removing insulation from electrical wires.

Wood bits: paddle-shaped bits primarily for use in drilling wood, although they can be used in some plastics; must be used in a power drill; also known as spade bits.

Wood chisel: a steel blade sharpened at a 30-degree angle; used for gouging, paring, or smoothing wood.

Wood file: a file with medium-sized teeth; can be flat on both faces, flat on one face and curved on the other, or round; used for smoothing wood and plastic.

Wood rasp: an extremely coarse-toothed file; usually has one flat and one rounded face; used for rough shaping of wood.

Woofer: a low-frequency speaker with a frequency range from approximately 20 to 150–250 Hz.

Work: the object on which work is being performed.

Workable fixative: a spray that seals colors in place. "Workable" indicates that paint can effectively be applied on top of the fixative.

Working sectional: a drawing showing the sectional angle for a lighting instrument; used to determine its trim height; not to be confused with a lighting sectional.

Work light: a lighting fixture, frequently a scoop, PAR, or other wide-field-angle instrument, hung over the stage to facilitate work.

Worsted: a tightly woven, smooth-surfaced fabric of wool or wool blend; used for men's or women's suits and trousers.

Wrecking bars: generic name for the class of metal tools used to pry wood apart and remove nails.

Writable CD: a CD on which data can be recorded, and read, by the user.

X-ray: *see* striplight.

Zoom ellipse: an ellipsoidal reflector spotlight with movable lenses that allow the focal length and beam-edge sharpness to be varied.

Index

Murdock, William, 47
Music, 510–511
Muslin, 471
Musser, Tharon, 337
Mustaches, 506–509, 508–509*f*
My Fair Lady, 484
Mylar film, 210

N

Nail pullers, 186, 186*f*
Nailers, 258
Nails, 211–213, 212*f*, 213*f*
National Electrical Code (NEC), 383, 418
National Geographic, 26
Natural fibers, 467
Natural sponges, 284
Naturalism, 75
Nature of sound, 511–515
Nerve cells, retina, 91
Net, 471
Network control protocols, 432
Neutral wire, 383
Neutralization, 99
Neutrons, 374
New York professional theatre, 8
Newel posts, 260
Newsprint, 544
Nicholas Nickleby, 30*f*, 34*f*
Nicopress tool, 219, 219*f*
Noise, digital projector, 431
Non-dim, 406
Nonfabric materials, 471–473, 472*f*, 473*f*
Nose putty, 500–501, 500*f*
Nucleus, 374
Nut driver, 186, 186*f*
Nuts, 216–217, 217*f*
Nylon, 468

O

Objective information provided by clothes, 444–447, 445*f*
  age, 446
  climate and season, 446–447
  gender, 446
  historical period, 445
  occupation, 446
  socioeconomic status, 446
Oblique drawing, 132, 132*f*
Occupation of characters, costume design and, 446
Occupational Safety and Health Administration (OSHA), 188, 209

Ohm's Law, 377–378, 380
Oil coat, 206
Oil pastels, 542, 543, 553
On center, 249
Onboard preamps, 519
Online research, 26. *See also* Research in design process
Onstage effects speakers, 530
Onstage loudspeakers, 530
Opaque drops, 247
Open doweled joint, 323, 324*f*
Open-end wrench, 184, 185*f*
Opening, running of stage props, 321
Optical theory, 385–386
Orchestra
  Greek theatre, 36
  Roman theatre, 38–39
Orchestra pit, 53–54, 53*f*
Orchestral monitors, 532
Organic LED (OLED), 439
Organizational paperwork, 450–455, 451*f*, 452*f*, 453*f*, 454*f*
  character-actor dressing list, 453–454, 453*f*, 454*f*
  costume bible, 450–451
  costume calendar, 454–455
  costume chart, 451–452, 451*f*
  costume list, 452–453, 452*f*
Oriented strand board (OSB), 204, 204*f*
Orthographic projection, 131–132, 131*f*
Outboard devices, 519
Output voltage, 380, 381
Overdubs, 527
Overlay, 450
Overloaded circuit, 379
Oxidation, 234–235
Oxyacetylene welding/welder, 193–194, 194*f*, 230–232, 231*f*

P

Pageant wagons, 40, 41*f*
Paint, 276–282
  acrylic, 208–209, 467–468, 542
  aniline dye, 279–280, 294–295
  brushes, 282, 283–284, 542
  casein, 277, 290
  color mixing in, 96–97, 97*f*
  designer's gouache, 541–542
  drawing and rendering, 541–542
  dry pigment and binder, 277
  enamel, 282
  latex, 277–279, 290
  pigment dyes, 280

  polyester resin, 281–282, 334, 335
  prime coat, 245, 289
  shellac, 280–281
  varnish, 280
  vinyl acrylic, 279, 280, 285, 286, 289, 290, 295, 304
  watercolor, 541, 541*f*, 553, 553*f*
Paint cart, 286
Paint chip, 89
Paint rollers, 284
Painted steel, 205
Painters' elevations, 175, 175*f*
Palette, color, 290–292, 291*f*
Pan, 404
Panel adhesives, 274
Panel saw, 189, 189*f*
Paper
  cold-press finish, 544
  hot-press finish, 544
  rough-finish, 544
  watercolor, 544, 548
Paper clad sheets, 203
Paperclay, 329
Papier-mâché, 329
PAR can, 401–402, 402*f*
Parallel circuit, electrical, 382, 382*f*
Paraskenia, 36
Paris Opera, 48
Particle board, 204, 204*f*
Pastels
  materials, 542, 542*f*
  technique, 543, 553–554, 554*f*
Patch points, 535
Patching, 18
Pattern-drafting software, 476
Patterns and draping
Pellon, 471
Pencils
  materials, 540–541
  techniques, 554
Perceived veracity, 530
Perception, light and, 337–339
Periaktoi, 38, 39
Personal protective equipment (PPE), 225
Personality of characters, scenic design, 158
Perspective drawing, 134–152
  creating, 137–139, 137*f*, 138–139*f*
  exercises, 142–152
  principles of, 134–141
  review, 140, 141*f*
  vertical plane and, 136, 136*f*, 137